THE DINNER TABLE

Also in the anthology series

THE ART OF THE GLIMPSE
100 Irish Short Stories
Chosen by Sinéad Gleeson

**THE BIG BOOK OF CHRISTMAS
MYSTERIES**
100 of the Very Best Yuletide Whodunnits
Chosen by Otto Penzler

DEADLIER
*100 of the Best Crime Stories
Written by Women*
Chosen by Sophie Hannah

DESIRE
100 of Literature's Sexiest Stories
Chosen by Mariella Frostrup
and the *Erotic Review*

FOUND IN TRANSLATION
*100 of the Finest Short Stories
Ever Translated*
Chosen by Frank Wynne

FUNNY HA, HA
80 of the Funniest Stories Ever Written
Chosen by Paul Merton

GHOST
100 Stories to Read With the Lights On
Chosen by Louise Welsh

HOUSE OF SNOW
*An Anthology of the Greatest Writing
About Nepal*
Chosen by Ed Douglas

JACK THE RIPPER
*The Ultimate Compendium of
the Legacy and Legend of History's
Most Notorious Killer*
Chosen by Otto Penzler

LIFE SUPPORT
100 Poems to Reach for on Dark Nights
Chosen by Julia Copus

OF GODS AND MEN
100 Stories from Ancient Greece and Rome
Chosen by Daisy Dunn

QUEER
*A Collection of LGBTQ Writing
from Ancient Times to Yesterday*
Chosen by Frank Wynne

SHERLOCK
*Over 80 Stories Featuring
the Greatest Detective of all Time*
Chosen by Otto Penzler

THAT GLIMPSE OF TRUTH
100 of the Finest Short Stories Ever Written
Chosen by David Miller

THE TIME TRAVELLER'S ALMANAC
100 Stories Brought to You From the Future
Chosen by Jeff and Ann VanderMeer

THE STORY
100 Great Short Stories Written by Women
Chosen by Victoria Hislop

WE, ROBOTS
Artificial Intelligence in 100 Stories
Chosen by Simon Ings

THE WILD ISLES
*An Anthology of the Best of British
and Irish Nature Writing*
Chosen by Patrick Barkham

WILD WOMEN
*A Collection of First-hand Accounts
from Female Explorers*
Edited by Mariella Frostrup

THE DINNER TABLE

OVER 100 WRITERS ON FOOD

SELECTED BY

ELLA RISBRIDGER
& KATE YOUNG

HEAD
of
ZEUS

An Apollo Book

To our mums, Deb Paton and Nikki Risbridger, for their shared and constant commitment to the family dinner table.

(Turns out it's our favourite place to be.)

CONTENTS

INTRODUCTION

Consider this an invitation to dinner.

Not just dinner, though: a dinner party, and ideally – if we've done this right – the best dinner party of your life.

You know those evenings where it all just works? Where the food is great, and the candles never go out, and the music is neither too soft nor too loud, and the talking goes on late into the night, and nobody wants it to end? The kind of night with both beloved old friends, and their sparkling new friends, and maybe those friends will soon be your friends too? The kind of night where you want to join every conversation you overhear? And there's always another course of exquisite little bits, timed just right so you're never too full to nibble on another corner of something plump and salty and sweet and spicy and delicious, and every bite seems to suggest another perfect bite to follow?

The kind of night where the wine is just the right temperature, and never harsh, and nobody's ever drunk, just maybe a little contentedly tipsy, and there's a basket of breads that seems to endlessly replenish itself with soft white rolls and sticky-sweet rye and plump little pitta and crisp fluffy focaccia, and there's butter and brown butter and garlic butter and extra-virgin olive oil and balsamic vinegar and maybe other things to dip too? Soft labneh or swirly tahini or some kind of vivid green salsa verde? And none of it should go, but all of it somehow *does* go, this joyful clash and mishmash of cuisines and cultures and ideas and people and sauces and spices and flavours and friends? And it all somehow works? And there's maybe fairy lights, or stars, and the big gold moon, and the sound of the sea? A warm breeze through the fig trees? The crackle of the fire; the scent of coffee; the promise of breakfast to follow: the sun on the terrace (or the lawn or the balcony or the fire escape), and something perfect under a shining silver cloche, or wrapped in a white linen napkin, or eaten, with your fingers, at the top of the mountain?

No, us neither, but that's what we're hoping for. Ideally.

This book is the dinner party we'd throw, if we could invite everyone whose words about food we've ever loved. Or, at least, around one hundred of those people. Call it a selection box, if we're not already too deep in the first metaphor: a grab-bag of favourites, friends and surprising new additions spanning five continents and two thousand years. We'll meet a Japanese princess, eight hundred years ago, elegantly expressing her taste for 'iced plums'; a literary 1920s New Zealander with aspirations; the recipes and memories of a free Black woman in 1850s America; and a tribe in Tanzania who teach us how they still hunt for golden honey. A rockstar makes kimchi and grieves in middle America, and a South American poet writes a recipe for solving sorrow on 'afternoons of fine, persistent rain'. A hapless cook turns her soup blue with string-tied leeks; two women who have loved the same man become a family side by side at the sink; a single man remembers his lover while he cooks an egg for breakfast. Samuel Pepys buries his Parmesan cheese to save it from the Great Fire of London. There's a marmalade festival, and markets heaving with peaches, and a garden halfway up a mountain laden with peas practically just bursting from their perfect green pods, and Sylvia Plath living – not dying – by her recipe cards and her *Joy of Cooking* ('blessed Rombauer') and her tomato soup cake.

There is borsch that tastes like home, and crosses borders. There is Jack Kerouac, crossing state borders himself, and eating ice cream. There is a young Henry James. Virginia Woolf is here, and – somehow – also *there*, splitting herself across opposite sides of the table. There are broken hearts, and perfect solitude, and marriages. There is washing up, and the morning after.

Some of these people and pieces you will know already. Amy March and her limes are here, of course, their stinging sourness vivid 150 years on. You'll perhaps recognise Nigella Lawson on mayonnaise and literature; her perfect metaphor about confidence and surety and things that are 'meant to be difficult' finds its way into our bowl whenever we thicken egg yolks with oil. If you can't recall (as though you were there in the kitchen yourself) what Mrs Cratchit puts on the table on Christmas morning – if you don't remember the stuffing issuing forth from the goose, the gravy 'ready beforehand in a little saucepan', the round perfection of the pudding – we're confident you'll at least know the warmth of the scene as presented in *The Muppet Christmas Carol*. If you love food writing as we do, then we know you'll be able to picture Laurie Colwin, alone in her kitchen with her eggplant.

Some of them, we hope, will be new to you: a collection of 1980s readers, for instance, who wrote in to *The Sun Magazine* with their thoughts about washing up. Some of them may be familiar, but in new guises: Maya Angelou, not in memoir mode, but in the kitchen, baking with her young son. You'll find poets you're familiar with, and ones you probably aren't. You'll find excerpts from novels that sit on your shelves with well-cracked spines, and novels you'll head out in pursuit of as soon as you've had a taste.

We planned this book as if we were putting together the seating plan for the world's most extravagant dinner party. The individual pieces have something to say to their neighbours on either side: you'll find that old friends will introduce you to new friends. This means you can dip in and dip out, read one piece or twenty, start where you like and end where you like (but we hope you won't be able to put it down). It's how we put much of the book together, in satisfying little runs of ideas: Sei Shōnagon's *Refined and elegant things*, her 'pretty child eating strawberries', sent Ella off to Genevieve Taggard and to Christina Rossetti. Rosetti's 'Goblin Market' sent Kate back into the kitchen, to reach for the Mrs Beeton on the highest shelf, to find her 'Pretty Dish of Oranges'. And then of course there were oranges: oranges in *The Groundnut Cookbook*, John McPhee's orange juice in Penn Station, Olivia Potts' musings on capturing seasonal citrus in jars. And once there were jars it was impossible not to turn to Shirley Jackson and the preserves in Constance's kitchen, to the pickle factory in *Midnight's Children*, to Amy March and her limes, to making kimchi for the market in *Pachinko*, and so on and so on and so on.

The Dinner Table is a glorious celebration; a wedding without a couple to steal focus; a table constructed with a single noble purpose: the most delicious meal we could imagine offering you. We sat at the dining room table with tiny sticky slips of paper, each labelled with a key player we knew we wanted at the table, and we shuffled and moved them around until we felt everyone was perfectly placed. We couldn't imagine the party without Diana Henry, Madhur Jaffrey, Jane Austen, Jimi Famurewa. But who sits where? Who might like who? Should we pair a writer with a stranger or a friend? What placement should be avoided – unless we're really all in for a pistols-at-dawn duel?

As at any dinner party, chemistry is key; the ingredients have to be just right, the whole thing a delicate balancing act. Here, that meant that we wanted non-fiction writing to follow fiction, classic literature to bump up against contemporary memoir, poetry and journalism to sit side by side.

We wanted the aching sincerity of one piece to be cut with lightness and fun in the next. We wanted to know that a wide spectrum of feelings about food were encapsulated. Food is deeply prosaic, so sewn into the fabric of our days that it risks becoming inconsequential. Most writers end up writing about food at some point; even the absence of food is a way of writing about food. But we wanted the food here to feel tangible, to come right off the page and onto the centre of the table as it does in our lives: at once intimate and expansive, both undeniably personal and something we love to share.

The two of us talk about food for at least two hours a day, and think about it for at least another eight: What did you eat? How did they do it? How did they do *that*?

This book, then, is also the product of a half-decade of collaborative thinking about eating. Most of the time, we are on the phone when we cook. We are always propping the phone up against the toaster while one of us runs to grab another cookbook from the shelf, to check something, to argue with somebody, to figure out just what is the best way to XYZ or ABC. Our text thread is peppered with links, screenshots and confident assurances that the attached is something the recipient will love, that will change the way we see an ingredient or think about a cuisine or cook dinner that night. We are always talking and reading and cooking and thinking about and eating food, and that means we are always talking and reading and cooking and thinking about and eating food writers.

We hope you enjoy eavesdropping on the writers we've collected together, on our beloved favourites. We haven't forgotten to save you a place. Fill your plate with everything you fancy eating, pour yourself a glass of something you love and pull up a chair.

Ella and Kate
2023

I CAPTURE THE CASTLE

Dodie Smith

Born in Lancashire, **Dorothy Gladys 'Dodie' Smith** wrote her first play at the age of ten, and spent her teenage years in small stage roles with the Manchester Athenaeum Dramatic Society. After a successful career in London, writing for the stage, Smith moved to the US with her husband during the Second World War. Homesick for England, she wrote her first novel, *I Capture the Castle*, in 1948; Smith's other most famous novel features a very large number of Dalmatians. She died, back home in England, at the age of ninety-four.

We had real butter for tea because Mr. Stebbins gave Stephen some when he went over to fix about working (he started at the farm this morning); and Mrs. Stebbins had sent a comb of honey. Stephen put them down in my place so I felt like a hostess. I shouldn't think even millionaires could eat anything nicer than new bread and real butter and honey for tea.

HADZA HONEY *FROM* EATING TO EXTINCTION

Dan Saladino

Dan Saladino is a journalist, presenter and producer. His decade and a half of work on BBC's *The Food Programme* introduced him to many communities and individuals who work with rare and endangered foods. *Eating to Extinction: The World's Rarest Foods and Why We Need to Save Them*, his first book, is a rallying cry for us to consider our future food security and the impact of food homogenisation. It won multiple food book prizes, as well as the 2022 Wainwright Prize.

Lake Eyasi, Tanzania

It was April, the rainy season. Short downpours had brought pockets of colour to the greens and browns of the East African savannah as small delicate flowers bloomed. Nectar was becoming abundant and, with it, honey. I was with a group of Hadza hunters, a scattered population of just over one thousand people. The tribe has lived in the dry bush of northern Tanzania, near the shore of Lake Eyasi, for tens of thousands of years, perhaps hundreds of thousands of years. Now, fewer than two hundred Hadza live fully as hunter-gatherers, making them the last people in Africa to practise no form of agriculture. The group I was with had walked far away from the camp and deep into the bush, led by a young man named Sigwazi. As he walked, he whistled.

This wasn't a melodious tune, more a series of angular ups and downs on a musical scale, each passage finished with a high-pitched twirl. To my ears there was no obvious musical pattern to follow but something in the bush was paying close attention to this whistle. Noticing movement above the trees, Sigwazi broke into a sprint, weaving through the scrub and around baobab trees as he continued the whistle. A wordless conversation was under way, an exchange between a human and a bird. Sigwazi looked towards the flutter of activity in the canopy, and there perched on a branch was an olive-grey bird the size of a starling.

Barring a few flashes of white on its tail, the bird looked plain and unassuming, but after a few more whistles from the hunter, it revealed itself to be exceptional. 'Ach-ech-ech-ech' came its reply to Sigwazi's whistle, signalling that a deal was on. The bird had agreed to lead the hunter to honey hidden among the branches of the giant baobabs. These trees are as wide as they are tall, living for up to a thousand years, fed by a root system so deep that they can access water in periods of extreme drought. Finding a bees' nest concealed among the baobab's tall branches can take a hunter-gatherer several hours as they need to inspect tree after tree; with the assistance of a honeyguide, it takes a fraction of that time. The bird's scientific name captures the talent perfectly: *Indicator indicator*.

Somehow, over hundreds of thousands of years, the two species, humans and honeyguides, found a way of sharing their different skills. The bird can find the bees' nests but can't get to the wax it wants to eat without being stung to death. Humans, meanwhile, struggle to find the nests, but armed with smoke can pacify the bees. Theirs is the most complex and productive of any partnership between humans and wild animals.

To reach the most isolated Hadza camps from Dar es Salaam, Tanzania's largest city, involves an eighteen-hour drive by jeep. Their home is set among a patchwork of shrubs, rocks, trees and dust, a landscape occupied by humans for at least 3.5 million years. Looking out across the horizon of Hadza country, it's possible to see human history in microcosm. Just a few miles north is Laetoli, the site where a group of our distant ancestors walked through wet volcanic ash and left behind the earliest known human footprints. Even closer is the Olduvai Gorge, the place where some of the oldest stone tools and hand axes have been discovered. Within walking distance is the saltwater expanse of Lake Eyasi, where human skeletons, 130,000 years old, have been excavated.

The Hadza are no proxy for our Stone Age relatives; they are thoroughly modern humans. But their foraging way of life is the closest we have to that of early *Homo sapiens*, and the Hadza diet offers the best insight into the foods that fuelled our evolution. I watched the Hadza follow trails that were impossible for me to see, and read the earth as if it was a much-loved book, knowing exactly where golden Congolobe berries were ripest and Panjuako tubers were at their thickest, where long-snouted bush pigs were likely to feed and when the squirrel-like hyrax might gather. They picked up on sounds I didn't notice and paused to feel changes in the gentlest of breezes so they could approach animals undetected. It was still a month until the dry season, when the large game congregate around water, making them easier to find. For now, the easiest way of finding meat was to dig it out from underground, which is why earlier Sigwazi had lured a porcupine from its den beneath a baobab tree. The offal (the heart, liver and kidney) were eaten on the spot, cooked for moments on a makeshift fire, but the carcass was carried back to camp, and shared among the rest of the group. Meat, however, isn't the Hadza's favourite food. Honey is, which is why the conversation with the honeyguide is so valuable.

The collaboration between human and bird was chronicled by Portuguese missionaries in the 1500s, but it took until 2016 for outsiders to understand the conversation more fully. When a team of scientists walked through the savannah playing loops of different recorded sounds, they discovered that the attention of the honeyguide wasn't caught by just any human sound – the birds were listening out for specific phrases. In the case of the Yao people of Mozambique, this was 'brr-hm …', whereas in northern Tanzania the birds responded to the twists and twirls of the Hadza's whistles. These calls are passed down from one generation of hunter to another and, in each case, the researchers found, repeating the traditional phrases not only doubled the chance of being guided by a bird, but also tripled the chance of finding a bees' nest and honey.

What makes this even more remarkable is that the honeyguide is a brood parasite; it lays its eggs in other birds' nests. More brutal than the cuckoo, the chicks use their sharp-hooked bills to dispatch their rivals as they hatch. How the bird learns the skill of conversing with the Hadza we still don't know. One theory is that, just like the hunters, they are social learners; they watch and listen to their more experienced peers. It's possible this inter-species conversation predates the arrival of *Homo sapiens* and reaches back a million years or more to our ancestors' first use of fire and smoke. This idea is part of a compelling argument that it was honey and bee larvae, as much as meat, that made the human brain larger and helped us to outcompete all other species. Meat eating gets all the glory, the argument goes, because stone tools used in hunting turn up in the archaeological record, while evidence of eating honey does not. But there are plenty of other clues. Our closest relatives in the animal kingdom – chimpanzees, bonobos, gorillas and orangutans – all eagerly gorge on honey and bee larvae, nature's most energy-dense food. And in the earliest rock art discovered, inside caves in Spain, India, Australia and South Africa, there are depictions of honey collecting dating back at least 40,000 years.

But perhaps the most persuasive evidence of honey's importance to human evolution is the diets of the world's few remaining hunter-gatherers, including that of the Hadza. One-fifth of all of their calories across a year comes from honey, around half of which is the result of help from the honeyguide bird. The other half the Hadza can find themselves, as it comes from various species of bee that nest closer to the ground. Some are tiny, gnat-like and stingless, and produce a type of honey that is highly perfumed and delicately tangy. The Hadza find these nests by inspecting trees for the tiny needle-sized tubes used by the bees to get inside the trunk. This type of honey, called *kanowa* or *mulangeko* in Hadzabe (the Hadza's language), comes in modest, snack-like portions, and is gathered by chopping into the colonised section of tree. But on this occasion Sigwazi and the honeyguide wanted more. Together they were going to find the honey and wax of the larger (and more aggressive) *Apis mellifer*, the African honeybee.

Sigwazi watched as the bird he had attracted with his whistle hovered above one of the baobabs. This signalled there was honey; now it was time for Sigwazi to start climbing. He was short (five feet tall at most), wiry and slim. I figured his physique was the reason he was the member of the group chosen to climb the tree, but I came to realise it was more a question of bravery. Sigwazi was the one least concerned about disturbing a bees' nest, being stung or, worse still, falling thirty feet to the ground. He handed his bow and arrow to a fellow hunter, stripped off his ripped T-shirt and frayed shorts and removed the string of red and yellow beads from around his neck. By now almost naked, he started to chop up fallen branches with an axe and sharpen them into thin sticks. Baobabs are so soft and sponge-like that hunters can drive these pegs into their trunks with ease to create a makeshift ladder up towards the canopy. Swinging back and forth, Sigwazi made his way up the baobab, forcing a new peg in above his head as he climbed, clinging on, balancing and hammering all at once. As he neared the top of the tree another hunter climbed up behind and handed him a bunch of smouldering leaves. With these, Sigwazi closed in on the nest and immediately launched into a mid-air dance punctuated with high-pitched yelps. Bees were swarming around the honey thief and stinging as he scooped his hand into the nest and pulled out chunks of honeycomb. These rained down on the other Hadza hunters as Sigwazi tossed them below. They cupped their hands to their mouths and started to feast, spitting out pieces of wax as they ate, leaving behind warm melting liquid that tasted both sweet and sour, bright and acidic like citrus. As I joined them I could feel writhing larvae inside my mouth and the crunch of dead bees. The honeyguide bird perched silently nearby, waiting for its share of the raid once the crowd of hunters had gone.

When the rest of the honey was taken back to the camp, women gathered armfuls of baobab pods, each one the size of two cupped hands. With bare feet, they brought their heels down to open the pods with a crunch. Inside were clusters of kidney-shaped seeds coated in a white powdery pulp which tasted like effervescent vitamin C tablets. The seeds, pulp, water and a little honey were placed into a bucket and stirred into a whirlpool with a stick. When everything settled, it looked like a thick creamy soup. Each sip fizzed in the mouth. This, I was told, is a food Hadza babies are weaned on.

*

Someone who had watched this exact scene long before me, as a 23-year-old Cambridge student, was James Woodburn. In 1957, to complete his PhD, he travelled to Tanzania in search of Africa's last hunter-gatherers. He followed two Italian ivory hunters tracking an elephant herd. Near Lake Eyasi, after the animals were killed and the tusks removed, Woodburn watched as Hadza hunters appeared out of the scrubland and into the clearing to take away the mountain of meat (elephants are the only big game that Hadza don't hunt – they say their poison is not strong enough to kill them). Woodburn followed the hunters back to their camp and spent the next two years living alongside them. To survive Hadza country without Hadza skills, he brought in supplies of rice and lentils to add to the small amounts of wild food he managed to forage for himself.

Woodburn learned to speak Hadzade (his language skills had been honed as a military interpreter), and gained new insights that brought the Hadza to wider attention in the 1960s. This included work carried out with paediatricians, which showed how exceptionally well nourished Hadza children were compared with their contemporaries in nearby farming communities. During the six decades that have followed, Woodburn has returned to Hadza country on a regular basis, staying with the tribe, studying their way of life and recording how it has changed over time. Luckily for me, my visit to Hadza country coincided with one of his.

'They have stayed as hunter-gatherers because it is a life that makes sense to them,' Woodburn said as we sat by a campfire, the last of Sigwazi's porcupine crackling as it cooked, 'they regard it as a wonderful life.' It's a way of life that's endured, he believes, largely because of the autonomy it brings; no Hadza has control over another, a fact made possible because of the abundance of wild food around them. Apart from the very young and the very old, everyone in the camp is self-sufficient, each skilled enough to feed themselves, even children as young as six. 'Once this way of life stops making sense to them,' Woodburn said, 'it finally comes to an end.'

When Woodburn first met the Hadza, the outside world had stood at a distance. The foragers still didn't know which country they lived in and their knowledge of what lay beyond Hadza country came largely from encounters with neighbouring tribes – the Iraqw, the Datoga and the Isanzu. With these pastoralists and farmers, the Hadza traded meat, skins and honey for millet, maize, marijuana and metal (to make axes and arrowheads). Other things they knew about the outside world had been passed down the generations, including stories of abductions of their forebears. Tanzania was at the centre of the East African slave trade until the middle of the nineteenth century, which was why the Hadza, until recently, always ran from strangers who appeared in the bush. But in the mid-1960s, there was no avoiding the world outside. Following independence from Britain, the Tanzanian government, encouraged by American missionaries, attempted to settle the Hadza in villages by force. Hunter-gatherers from remote bush camps were taken away in trucks to purpose-built villages, escorted by armed guards. Many became ill from infections and died. Within two years, most of those who had survived returned to their camps and to foraging. Efforts to settle and convert the Hadza, not only to Christianity but also to agriculture, have continued. And yet, against the odds, their hunter-gatherer way of life – the life that makes sense to them – has persisted. Now, though, a new set of forces is bearing down on the Hadza. Agriculture is spilling over into their land and products made by the global food industry have reached the camps. Woodburn said he hadn't forseen the scale of these pressures on the Hadza. No one had.

*

One-third of the Earth's land surface is now dedicated to food production – a quarter of this for crops, three-quarters for grazing animals – and farming's expansion into the wild is continuing (nearly 4 million hectares of tropical rainforest are lost each year). Agriculture is reaching into parts of the world once thought impossible to be farmed. Among them, Hadza country. At the beginning of the twenty-first century, tens of thousands of hectares of land used by the Hadza was converted by outsiders into pasture for livestock or to grow crops each year. Along with it went some of the Hadza's access to wild foods, including giant baobab trees that take hundreds of years to grow. Supplies of nutritious baobab pods were depleted, and so were sources of honey. In 2012, after years of campaigning, the Hadza were awarded rights of occupancy over 150,000 hectares of land, but this still didn't stop the problem. Neighbouring tribes faced with water shortages caused by irrigation and climate change moved cattle closer to the Hadza's camps and waterholes. The cattle ate the vegetation that brought in game and disrupted migration routes which meant there was less for the Hadza to hunt. Across the whole of Africa, two-thirds of the continent's productive land is now at risk of becoming degraded, half of this severe enough to lead to desertification. The biggest cause is overgrazing of livestock.

The Hadza are ill-equipped to stop this encroachment; they have no possessions, no money and no leaders. They're skilled hunters but they avoid conflict. Instead of confronting tribes arriving on their land, they moved deeper into the bush. But even here, farmers edge ever closer, expanding pasture and planting sorghum and corn, though there's barely enough water to irritate crops. The Hadza have to contend with the effects of climate change too; they see its impact in the lack of water, disappearance of edible plants and decline in nectar and therefore quantity of honey they find. To survive, many rely on food from NGOs and missionaries. The last hunter-gatherers in Africa are being pinched from all sides.

*

A thirty-minute drive from Sigwazi's honey hunting, we reached a crossing point where different tribes gather to take water from a newly installed pump. Here, they also visit a small mudbrick hut lit by a single light bulb that hangs from the corrugated roof. Inside, from floor to ceiling, are shelves stacked with cans of sugary sodas and packets of biscuits. We were hours from the nearest city, an enormous wilderness lay between us and the nearest road, and yet some of the biggest food and drink brands in the world had made it this far.

In the place where our ancestors first evolved, sugar in plastic bottles is replacing the sweetness of the food that helped to make us human, honey. Scientists who monitor birdlife in the savannah describe melancholy scenes of birds swooping down, calling 'ach-ech-ech-ech' in the hope of a reply, as their interaction with humans becomes rarer. The conversation between the two species, thousands, possibly millions of years in the making, may soon fall silent.

Encircling the mudbrick hut were newly planted fields of corn. I felt I could have been watching a film in which hundreds of thousands of years of human history was being played on fast-forward, from wild to farmed and from foraged to processed, bottled and branded.

MEMOIRS OF AN ARABIAN PRINCESS FROM ZANZIBAR

Salamah bint Saïd

There is no better reminder that things are very, very complicated than **Sayyida Salamah bint Saïd** – or, as she was later known, **Emily Ruete**. (This biography is long, but you tell us which bit we could have cut.) Born in 1844 in modern-day Tanzania, her father was the Sultan of Oman, and her Circassian mother Jilfidan one of his many concubines. Circassia, a still-disputed region on the Black Sea, is now part of Georgia, Russia and the partially recognised state of Abkhazia; throughout the nineteenth century, it was the site of the Russian Empire's mass-murder and ethnic cleansing of up to 97 per cent of the local people. 'Their only crime', wrote one British diplomat, 'was not being Russian.' Jilfidan, then, had been brought to the Sultan's court aged about seven, either as a rescued refugee or a kidnapped and enslaved child. Jilfidan was brought up and educated alongside the Sultan's daughters, and was later the mother of two more daughters (bringing the total number of siblings to thirty-six). One of those daughters was Sayyida. Sayyida was brought up speaking Swahili and Arabic, living with her mother and brother in a palace on the sea. She taught herself to read, against her parents' wishes, and was taught by her brother (in the tradition of one of her father's wilder wives, and later battlefield nemesis) to fight, fence and shoot. Upon her father's death, when she was twelve, her thirty-six siblings divided into violent factions to claim his Sultanates and Empires. Sayyida, the youngest of them all, was something of an onlooker, and upon the death of her mother just three years later, she was given her inheritance and declared to be of age. She met a German merchant, fell pregnant, smuggled herself out of Tanzania on a British frigate, converted (reluctantly and without conviction) to Christianity, took the name of Emily and married him in secret. They moved to Germany, had three more children in as many years, and then – when the youngest child, Rosalie, was just three months old – the merchant 'jumped from a tram, and was killed'.

It is hard to parse, according to our modern sensibilities, the memoirs of a mostly-white-passing, Swahili-speaking, 'true Mahometan, undeserving Christian, half a German' Arabic widow in 1870s Hamburg. As the daughter of a Circassian slave, she looks down on the daughters of Ethiopian slaves; as the daughter of an Arabian slave-trading sultan, she reports that the British abolition of slavery is seen as nothing more than an arrogant English attempt to weaken Arab and African global positions. Her language is not always particularly palatable; her ideas sometimes jarring (and actively racist and sexist!); but her life – and the way she lived as a child at the Sultan's court – is utterly fascinating, often beautiful, and totally new to us as readers. The elaborate meals they serve and eat, in various complex permutations of people and favours, remind us that food is never just food: it's ritual, it's story, it's manners and status and grace and time and place. These extracts from her memoirs, first privately published in Germany in the 1880s, have been edited and condensed.

The translation is by **Lionel Strachey**, the man who 'brought Conan Doyle, Kipling and Chesterton to America'. The son of the Secretary to the British Embassy at Vienna, and the grandson of the man who coined the phrase 'it was a dark and stormy night', Strachey was a literary agent, translator and critic in New York. He was, according to his obituary, killed by a locomotive while out for his evening stroll by the river.

Nine years ago I conceived the idea of writing down some facts for the information of my children, who at that time knew nothing about my origin except that I was Arabian and had come from Zanzibar. Exhausted in body and in mind, I did not then expect to live until they were grown up, did not think I should ever relate to them verbally the happenings of my youth and the course of my fate. Hence I determined to record my story on paper. My memoirs were not at first intended for the general public, but for my children, to whom I wished to bequeath them as a heritage of faithful motherly love. Finally, however, upon urgent persuasion, I consented to have them published.

I finished these pages some years ago, and only the last chapter forms a recent addition, made because of a voyage I undertook to my old home, Zanzibar, with my children. May my book go out into the world, and may it meet with as many friends as was my happy lot to find.

Berlin, May, 1886.
EMILY RUETE
née SALAMAH BINT SAÏD,
PRINCESS of OMAN and ZANZIBAR.

*

It was at Bet il Mtoni, our oldest palace in the island of Zanzibar, that I first saw the light of day, and I remained there until I reached my seventh year. Bet il Mtoni is charmingly situated on the seashore, at a distance of about five miles from the town of Zanzibar, in a grove of magnificent cocoanut palms, mango trees, and other tropical giants. My birthplace takes its name from the little stream Mtoni, which, running down a short way from the interior, forks out into several branches as it flows through the palace grounds, in whose immediate rear it empties into the beautiful sparkling sheet of water dividing Zanzibar from the continent of Africa.

A single, spacious courtyard is allotted to the whole body of buildings that compose the palace, and in consequence of the variety of these structures, probably put up by degrees as necessity demanded, the general effect was repellent rather than attractive. Most perplexing to the uninitiated were the innumerable passages and corridors. Countless, too, were the apartments of the palace; their exact disposition has escaped my memory, though I have a very distinct recollection of the bathing arrangements at Bet il Mtoni. A dozen basins lay all in a row at the extreme end of the courtyard, so that when it rained you could visit this favourite place of recuperation only with the help of an umbrella.

The so-called 'Persian' bath stood apart from the rest; it was really a Turkish bath, and there was no other in Zanzibar. Each bath-house contained two basins of about four yards by three, the water reaching to the breast of a grownup person. This resort was highly popular with the residents of the palace, most of whom were in the habit of spending several hours a day there, saying their prayers, doing their work, reading, sleeping, or even eating and drinking. From four o'clock in the morning until twelve at night there was constant movement; the stream of people coming and leaving never ceased.

Orange trees, as tall as the biggest cherry trees here in Germany, bloomed in profusion all along the front of the bath-houses, and in their hospitable branches we frightened children found refuge many a time from our horribly strict school-mistress!

Human beings and animals occupied the vast courtyard together quite amicably, without disturbing each other in the very least; gazelles, peacocks, flamingoes, guinea fowl, ducks, and geese strayed about at their pleasure, and were fed and petted by old and young. A great delight for us little ones was to gather up the eggs lying on the ground, especially the enormous ostrich eggs, and to convey them to the head-cook, who would reward us for our pains with choice sweetmeats.

*

My father, Seyyid Saïd, bore the double appellation of Sultan of Zanzibar and Imam of Muscat, that of Imam being a religious title and one originally borne by my great-grandfather Ahmed, a hereditary title, moreover, which every member of our family has a right to append to his signature.

*

My mother was a Circassian by birth. She, together with a brother and a sister, led a peaceful existence on my father's farm. Of a sudden, war broke out, the country was overrun by lawless hordes, and our little family took refuge 'in a place that was under the ground' – as my mother put it, probably meaning a cellar, a thing unknown in Zanzibar. But the desperate ruffians found them out; they murdered both of my mother's parents, and carried away the three children on horseback. No tidings ever reached my mother as to the fate of either brother, or sister. She must have come into my father's possession at a tender age, as she lost her first tooth at his home, and was brought up with two of my sisters of her own years as companions. Like them she learned to read, an accomplishment which distinguished her above the other women in her position, who usually came when they were at least sixteen or eighteen, and by that time of course had no ambition to sit with little tots on a hard schoolroom mat.

*

The pleasantest spot at Bet il Mtoni was the benjile – close to the sea, in front of the main building – a huge, circular, open structure where a ball could have been given, had such a custom been in vogue with our people. This benjile somewhat resembled a merry-go-round, since the roof, too, was circular; the tent-shaped roof, the flooring, the balustrades, all were of painted wood. Here my dear father was wont to pace up and down by the hour with bent brow, sunk in deep reflection. He limped slightly; during a battle a ball had struck his thigh, where it was now permanently lodged, hindering his gait, and occasionally giving him pains. A great many cane chairs – several dozen, I am sure – stood about the benjile, but besides these, and an enormous telescope for general use, it contained nothing else. The view from our circular look-out was splendid. The Sultan was in the habit of taking coffee here two or three times a day with Azze bint Sef and all of his adult offspring. Whoever wanted to speak to my father in private would be apt to find him alone in this place at certain hours. Opposite the benjile the warship Il Ramahni lay at anchor the year round, her purpose being to wake us up early by a discharge of cannon during the month of fasting, and to man the rowboats we so often employed. A tall mast was planted before the benjile, intended for the hoisting of the signal flags which ordered the desired boats and sailors ashore. As for our culinary department, Arabian cooking, and Persian and Turkish as well, prevailed at Bet il Mtoni.

*

In a corner of the yard cattle were slaughtered, skinned, and cleaned in quantities, all for the sole use of the house, which, like every house in Zanzibar, must provide its own meat. Nearby nurses sunned themselves and their little charges, whom they were regaling with fairy tales and stories. The kitchen, too, was in the open, and the smoke ascended freely to heaven as it might fancy, for chimneys do not exist. Strife and confusion were the rule among the host of culinary sprites, the head cooks dealing out boxes on the ears in liberal style to the quarrelsome or dilatory scullions of either sex. In the kitchen the animals were cooked whole, and I have seen a fish arrive carried by two sturdy [men]; small fish were not taken in excepting by the basket load, nor fowl but by the dozen. Flour, rice, and sugar were reckoned wholesale by bags, while the butter, imported from the north, especially from the island of Socotra, came in jars of a hundredweight each. Only spices were measured by the pound. Still more astonishing was the quantity of fruit consumed. Every day thirty or forty, or even fifty, men brought loads of fruit on their backs, apart from the consignments delivered by the little rowboats which supplied the plantations along the shore. I am probably making no extravagant estimate if I put [the] daily consumption of fruit as high as the capacity of a railway van; but some days, for instance, during the mango harvest, the demand would be still larger. The slaves intrusted with all this fruit were extremely careless; they would plump the heavy baskets from their heads violently to the ground, so that half the contents would be bruised or squashed.

*

Between half past nine and ten my elder brothers left their apartments to take breakfast with my father, in which repast not a single secondary wife, however great a favourite with the Sultan, was allowed to share. Besides his children and grandchildren – those who had passed infancy, that is to say – the only persons admitted to his table were the principal wife Azze bint Sef and his sister Assha. Social distinctions in the East are never observed more rigorously than at meals; one is extremely cordial and affable toward one's guests, just as people of high station are here in Europe, or perhaps even more so, though at meals one excludes them from one's company. The custom is so ancient that no one takes offence.

*

A painter would have found rich material for his brush on the veranda. To begin with, there were quite eight or nine different facial hues to be taken account of, and the many colours and shades of the garments worn would have offered the most vivid contrasts. No less lively was the bustle and stir. Children of all ages tore about, squabbled, and fought; shouting and clapping of hands – taking the place of the Western bell-ringing – for servants, resounded incessantly; the enormous, thick, wooden sandals of the women, sometimes inlaid with silver or gold, made a distressing clatter. We children enjoyed the confusion of tongues immensely. Arabic was supposed to be the only language spoken, and in the Sultan's presence the rule was invariably obeyed; but no sooner was his back turned than a sort of Babel would break loose, Persian, Turkish, Circassian, Suahili, Nubian, Abyssinian, to say nothing of dialects. However, no one took exception to mere tumult but now and then an invalid, and our dear father was quite used to it, and never objected in the least. Here, then, on the veranda, my sisters were assembled. They were festally clad in celebration of our Sunday and of Seyyid Saïd's coming; the mothers walked up and down or stood in groups, talking and laughing and joking so vivaciously that one not knowing the country would never have taken them for the wives of the same man. From the stairs sounded the clinking of arms worn by my brothers, who had also come to see their father, in fact, to spend the whole day with him.

*

Over and over again I have been asked: 'How on earth do the people manage to exist in your country, without anything to do?' And the question is justifiable enough from the point of view of the Northerner, who simply cannot imagine life without work, and who is convinced the Oriental never stirs her little finger, but dreams away most of her time in the seclusion of the harem. Of course, natural conditions vary throughout the world, and it is they that govern our ideas, our habits, and our customs. In the North one is compelled to exert oneself in order to live at all, and very hard too, if one wishes to enjoy life, but the Southern races are greatly favoured. Nature herself has ordained that the Southerner can work, while the Northerner must. The Northern nations seem to be very conceited, and look down with pride and contempt upon the people of the tropics – not a laudable state of mind. At the same time they are blind to the fact, in Europe, that their activity is absolutely compulsory to prevent them from perishing by the hundred thousand. The European is obliged to work – that is all; hence he has no right to make such a great virtue of sheer necessity.

*

The Mahometan's day is regulated – if that is not saying too much – by his religious devotions. Five times a day does he bend the knee to God, and if he properly performs all the contingent ablutions and changes of raiment in accordance with scriptural ruling, fully three hours will be consumed. The rich are awakened between four and half-past five for the first prayer, after which they return to bed, but the common people begin the day's work with their first prayer. In our establishment, where hundreds of inmates tried to follow their individual tastes, it was hard to maintain fixed rules, although the two general repasts and the devotions compelled a measure of systematic order. Most of us, then, slept on again until eight o'clock, when the women and children were roused by a gentle and agreeable kneading process, at the hands of a female servant. A bath of fresh spring water was ready, and likewise our wearing apparel, strewn the night before with jessamine or orange blossoms, and now scented with amber and musk. Nowhere in the world is the cold bath used and appreciated more than in the East. After dressing, which usually took up an hour, we all went to see our father, to wish him 'good morning,' and then to partake of the first meal. To this we were summoned by a drum, but as the table was completely set beforehand, much less time was occupied in eating than the European method demands. It was then that the day's real activities opened. The gentlemen prepared for the audience chamber, while the ladies – who were not obliged to work – took seats at their windows, to watch the passing in the street below, and to catch such private glances as might occasionally be thrown up at them. This provided great amusement; only sometimes a cautious mother or aunt would contrive to coax one away from the coign of vantage. Two or three hours thus sped quickly by. Visits were meanwhile being exchanged among the gentlemen, the ladies sending out servants with verbal appointments for the evening. Sedately minded persons, however, went to their airy apartments, where, either alone, or in small groups, they did needlework, stitching their veils, shirts, or trousers with gold braid, or a husband's, son's, or brother's shirt with red or white silk, which needed particular skill. The remainder would read stories, visit sick or well friends in their rooms, or attend to other private affairs. By this time it was one o'clock. Servants came to remind us of the second prayer. The sun was at its height then, so that everyone was glad to open the early part of the afternoon reposing, in a thin, cool garment, on a soft, prettily woven mat with sacred inscriptions worked upon it. Between dozing, chatting, and nibbling at fruit or cake, the time passed very pleasantly until four o'clock, when we prayed for the third time; a more elaborate toilette followed, and we repaired again to the presence of the Sultan, to wish him 'good afternoon.' The grown-up children were allowed to call him 'father,' but the little ones and their mothers had to address him as 'Sir.'

Now came the second and last meal of the day, at which the family would assemble. Upon its termination, the eunuchs would carry

European chairs out upon the broad veranda, but only for the adults; the small people stood up as a mark of respect for age, which is held in greater reverence there than anywhere else. The family gathered about the Sultan, while a row of smart, well-armed eunuchs lined the background. Coffee was passed round, as well as beverages prepared from the essence of French fruits. The conversation was accompanied by a stupendous barrel organ, the biggest I ever saw; by way of change one of the large music boxes would be set going, or a blind Arabian girl named Amra, who was gifted with a lovely voice, would be ordered to sing. In about an hour and a half the family separated, each following his or her own devices. Chewing betel was a favourite pastime. It is a Suahili habit, so that the Arabs of Arabia Proper find no pleasure therein; but those of us born on the east coast of Africa, and brought up among Negroes and mulattoes, took to the habit quite readily, in spite of derision from our Asiatic relatives. We chewed betel surreptitiously, however, while absent from the Sultan, who had forbidden the practice.

With the aid of miscellaneous diversions the brief space slipped by till sundown, announced by musketry fire and drumming on the part of the Indian guard. This also constituted a signal for prayer. But the fourth observance was the most hurried of the day, since everybody not intending to pay visits would be expecting guests at home – sisters, stepmothers, stepchildren, secondary wives. For entertainment there was coffee and lemonade, cakes and fruit, jesting and laughing, reading aloud, playing cards (but not for money or any other stake), singing, listening to the sese being played upon by a Negro, sewing, stitching, lace-making – just as one felt inclined. So it is altogether wrong to suppose that the rich Oriental woman has nothing to do. True, she neither paints, plays the piano, nor dances (as understood here). But those are not the only existing methods of passing the time. Down there we are all contented; to us the feverish, everlasting chase after new pleasures and enjoyments is quite foreign. From the European point of view, therefore, the Oriental might no doubt be looked upon as a Philistine.

Upon retiring for the night we dismissed the male servants, who joined their families, living in separate dwellings apart from the house. The oil lamps were usually left burning, the candles only being extinguished. The custom of sending children over two years to bed at a certain hour had died out; they chose their own time, and often their own place, for going to sleep, so that occasionally they would have to be picked up tenderly by slaves, and transported with the least possible noise to their own little cots. Whoever had neither gone out, nor had received visitors, generally retired at ten o'clock, though some preferred to enjoy the air on the flat, well-swept roof until midnight. At about half-past seven the fifth and last prayer was supposed to be offered up. But just then one is likely to have company, or be otherwise engaged; hence a rule permitting postponement of the final devotions till bedtime. Women of wealth go to sleep by the assistance of two female slaves; one repeats the kneading operation, the other manipulates a fan. To wash the feet first in eau de Cologne is most refreshing. I may have mentioned that women keep all their clothes on, including their jewellery. Returning to the culinary department, I must give some details about the eating arrangements in my father's palace at Zanzibar. We had no special dining room, but took our meals on the veranda. There the eunuchs spread a long sefra with all the food for the whole repast. A sefra somewhat resembles a billiard table in shape; it is only a few inches high, however, and around the top runs a wide ledge.

Although we possessed a lot of European furniture – lounges, tables, chairs, and even a few wardrobes – we nevertheless sat down to eat in true Oriental fashion, upon carpets or mats next to the floor. Precedence by rank was strictly observed, the Sultan taking the head; near him were the senior children, the little ones (those over seven) coming at the end. We had numerous dishes, often as many as fifteen. Rice formed a staple at each meal, and various preparations of it were in vogue. In the way of meat, mutton and chicken were preferred. We also ate fish, oriental breads and sundry pastry and sweetmeats. Contrary to the German system, all the food was placed on the table before anybody sat down. This obviated the need of service, and the eunuchs would step back, lining up at a little distance, ready to answer commands. Frequently the Sultan would send one of them, with a particularly savoury morsel, to a child not old enough to eat at the table, or perhaps to an invalid.

I remember the special corner at Bet il Mtoni where I used to receive the platefuls he consigned to me. We mites got the same food as the grown-up people, but of course it was a privilege to have it selected by our father, who himself derived great pleasure from this. Upon sitting down, everyone said grace in a low but distinct tone: 'In the name of Allah the all merciful.' After eating the formula was: 'Thanks be to the Lord of the Universe.'

Our father was always first to take his seat, and first to rise. One plate to each individual was not the custom, all the dishes (except the rice) being served in a number of little plates standing symmetrically along the sefra, so that a couple would eat from the same plate. There was no drinking simultaneous with the eating, but afterward sherbet or sugared water was obtainable. Nor was conversation usual, excepting when the Sultan spoke to someone; the rest of the time silence prevailed – a good thing, too. Fruit or flowers were never to be seen on the sefra. A few minutes before and after the meal slaves offered basins and towels, in order that one might wash one's hands. We chiefly used our fingers when we ate solids, which came upon the table cut up into small pieces. For spoons we had employment, but knives and forks were not brought out unless to honour European guests. Persons of refinement scented their hands, besides washing them, to drive away the odour of food. Half an hour after the repast eunuchs handed round genuine Mocha in tiny cups resting on gold or silver saucers. In the East the coffee is thick and syrupy, but filtered clear; invariably drunk without milk or sugar, it is taken without any sort of eatables, though sometimes delicate slices of areca nut are provided. The coffee is poured out immediately prior to consumption, which task requires such skill that only few servants are fitted for it. The coffee-bearer carries the handsome pot, made of tin adorned with brass, in his left hand, while in his right he holds only a single small cup and saucer. Behind or next to him an assistant carries a tray with empty cups and a large reserve pot of coffee. If the company has dispersed, these men have to follow the various members, and insure their partaking of the delicious beverage. How highly coffee is esteemed by the Orientals, everybody knows. The greatest care being bestowed upon its preparation, it is specially roasted, ground, and boiled whenever wanted, and therefore is always taken perfectly fresh. Roasted beans are never kept, nor boiled coffee, either, when in the least degree stale, being then thrown away or given to the lower servants. Our second and last general meal was at four in the afternoon, and since it corresponded exactly to the first I shall not describe it. We indulged in nothing else but light refreshments, such as pastry, fruit, or lemonade.

*

When I penned the preceding [passages], a few years back, I had almost entirely given up the realisation of a wish that filled all my thought and being. The eventful times since I had left my Southern home had been a period of well-nigh incredible stress and storm. I had gone through the strangest experiences, including some that one would not even desire for an enemy. By means of a strong constitution I managed to endure the severe Northern climate a long time, but at last, yielding to my inclination for a change, two years ago I conceived the idea of revisiting Zanzibar with my three children.

*

At setting foot on shore here, among the palm trees and the minarets, a warm sensation of homelikeness flooded over me, which can only be understood by such as have been long absentees under similar circumstances. The real South I had not laid eyes on for nineteen years; during this whole time I had sat by the stove in Germany, winter after winter. Even if I had become a Northern resident, with the multifarious duties of a German housewife falling to my lot, my thoughts were usually far, far away. I knew of no entertainment, no distraction that I preferred to poring over a book describing the South. No wonder if at the aspect of Alexandria I nearly went out of my senses, and stood watching the bustle of the harbour as if in a dream.

*

[And yet] coming upon the place where I had first beheld the light of day, I sustained a severe shock.

Instead of a house an utter ruin; not a sound to rouse me from the depressing sensation caused by the unexpected sight. It took me some time to recover. One staircase was completely gone, the other overgrown and shaky enough to be dangerous. More than half the house was in ruins, left just as it had fallen; the roofs had vanished from the bathhouses, some of which were represented by piles of rubbish; the parts still standing were likewise floorless or roofless. Dilapidation and decay at every hand! In the courtyard all manner of weeds flourished.

Nothing was left to remind the spectator of the former splendours of that palace.

My friends wrote a farewell letter to me in Arabic, and sent it to me in Germany:

'They went hence without telling me they were going
That tore my heart, and filled my soul with a consuming fire
Oh, that I had clung hard to their necks when they left us
For they might have sat on my head and walked on my eyes!
They dwell in my heart…'

THE DIARY OF SAMUEL PEPYS

Samuel Pepys

Samuel Pepys, born 1633 in Fleet Street, is one of those people who makes the past seem alive. Regarded by many as the greatest English diarist, Pepys wrote more than a million words – always in shorthand and often (especially when sexual) in code – about his life and times. He saw as a schoolboy the execution of Charles I, declared himself a Cromwellian, changed his mind, became a very successful Chief Secretary of the Admiralty despite having no naval experience, and lived through both the Great Plague and the Great Fire of London. Despite these interesting times, however, it's impossible to escape the sense that Sam Pepys is one of us. He checks his watch too much ('Lord! To see how much childishness hangs on me that I cannot forbear carrying my watch in my hand... and checking what o'clock it is one hundred times'), would like his cat to stop waking him at three in the morning, and cannot keep his New Year's resolution to quit drinking. He loves wine, he loves women, he loves music, and he loves writing his diary. Also, he loves food. He loves eating, and – as in this extract – counts his Parmazan cheese among his most precious possessions. There is no circumstance in which Sam Pepys cannot manage a good and delicious dinner, and certainly no circumstance in which he doesn't think it worth recording.

Wednesday 13 June 1666

Up, and by coach to St. James's, and there did our business before the Duke as usual, having, before the Duke come out of his bed, walked in an ante-chamber with Sir H. Cholmly, who tells me there are great jarrs between the Duke of Yorke and the Duke of Albemarle, about the later's turning out one or two of the commanders put in by the Duke of Yorke.

Among others, Captain Du Tell, a Frenchman, put in by the Duke of Yorke, and mightily defended by him; and is therein led by Monsieur Blancford, that it seems hath the same command over the Duke of Yorke as Sir W. Coventry hath; which raises ill blood between them. And I do in several little things observe that Sir W. Coventry hath of late, by the by, reflected on the Duke of Albemarle and his captains, particularly in that of old Teddiman, who did deserve to be turned out this fight, and was so; but I heard Sir W. Coventry say that the Duke of Albemarle put in one as bad as he is in his room, and one that did as little.

After we had done with the Duke of Yorke, I with others to White Hall, there to attend again a Committee of Tangier, but there was none, which vexed me to the heart, and makes me mighty doubtfull that when we have one, it will be prejudiced against poor Yeabsly and to my great disadvantage thereby, my Lord Peterborough making it his business, I perceive (whether in spite to me, whom he cannot but smell to be a friend to it, or to my Lord Ashly, I know not), to obstruct it, and seems to take delight in disappointing of us; but I shall be revenged of him.

Here I staid a very great while, almost till noon, and then meeting Balty I took him with me, and to Westminster to the Exchequer about breaking of two tallys of 2000*l.* each into smaller tallys, which I have been endeavouring a good while, but to my trouble it will not, I fear, be done, though there be no reason against it, but only a little trouble to the clerks; but it is nothing to me of real profit at all.

Thence with Balty to Hales's by coach, it being the seventh day from my making my late oathes, and by them I am at liberty to dispense with any of my oathes every seventh day after I had for the six days before going performed all my vowes.

Here I find my father's picture begun, and so much to my content, that it joys my very heart to thinke that I should have his picture so well done; who, besides that he is my father, and a man that loves me, and hath ever done so, is also, at this day, one of the most carefull and innocent men, in the world.

Thence with mighty content homeward, and in my way at the Stockes did buy a couple of lobsters, and so home to dinner.

Where I find my wife and father had dined, and were going out to Hales's to sit there, so Balty and I alone to dinner, and in the middle of my grace, praying for a blessing upon (these his good creatures), my mind fell upon my lobsters: upon which I cried, Odd zooks! and Balty looked upon me like a man at a losse what I meant, thinking at first that I meant only that I had said the grace after meat instead of that before meat. But then I cried, what is become of my lobsters? Whereupon he run out of doors to overtake the coach, but could not, so came back again, and mighty merry at dinner to thinke of my surprize. After dinner to the Excise Office by appointment, and there find my Lord Bellasses and the Commissioners, and by and by the whole company come to dispute the business of our running so far behindhand there, and did come to a good issue in it, that is to say, to resolve upon having the debt due to us, and the Household and the Guards from the Excise stated, and so we shall come to know the worst of our condition and endeavour for some helpe from my Lord Treasurer.

Thence home, and put off Balty, and so, being invited, to Sir Christopher Mings's funeral, but find them gone to church. However I into the church (which is a fair, large church, and a great chappell) and there heard the service, and staid till they buried him, and then out. And there met with Sir W. Coventry (who was there out of great generosity, and no person of quality there but he) and went with him into his coach, and being in it with him there happened this extraordinary case, one of the most romantique that ever I heard of in my life, and could not have believed, but that I did see it; which was this:

About a dozen able, lusty, proper men come to the coach-side with tears in their eyes, and one of them that spoke for the rest begun and says to Sir W. Coventry, 'We are here a dozen of us that have long known and loved, and served our dead commander, Sir Christopher Mings, and have now done the last office of laying him in the ground. We would be glad we had any other to offer after him, and in revenge of him. All we have is our lives; if you will please to get His Royal Highness to give us a fireship among us all, here is a dozen of us, out of all which choose you one to be commander, and the rest of us, whoever he is, will serve him; and, if possible, do that that shall show our memory of our dead commander, and our revenge.' Sir W. Coventry was herewith much moved (as well as I, who could hardly abstain from weeping), and took their names, and so parted; telling me that he would move His Royal Highness as in a thing very extraordinary, which was done. Thereon see the next day in this book. So we parted.

The truth is, Sir Christopher Mings was a very stout man, and a man of great parts, and most excellent tongue among ordinary men; and as Sir W. Coventry says, could have been the most useful man at such a pinch of time as this. He was come into great renowne here at home, and more abroad in the West Indys. He had brought his family into a way of being great; but dying at this time, his memory and name (his father being always and at this day a shoemaker, and his mother a Hoyman's daughter; of which he was used frequently to boast) will be quite forgot in a few months as if he had never been, nor any of his name be the better by it; he having not had time to will any estate, but is dead poor rather than rich.

So we left the church and crowd, and I home (being set down on Tower Hill), and there did a little business and then in the evening went down by water to Deptford, it being very late, and there I staid out as much time as I could, and then took boat again homeward, but the officers being gone in, returned and walked to Mrs. Bagwell's house, and there (it being by this time pretty dark and past ten o'clock) went into her house and did what I would. But I was not a little fearfull of what she told me but now, which is, that her servant was dead of the plague, that her coming to me yesterday was the first day of her coming forth, and that she had new whitened the house all below stairs, but that above stairs they are not so fit for me to go up to, they being not so. So I parted thence, with a very good will, but very civil, and away to the waterside, and sent for a pint of sacke and so home, drank what I would and gave the waterman the rest; and so adieu. Home about twelve at night, and so to bed, finding most of my people gone to bed.

In my way home I called on a fisherman and bought three eeles, which cost me three shillings.

Tuesday 10 July 1666

Up, and to the office, where busy all the morning, sitting, and there presented Sir W. Coventry with my little book made up of Lovett's varnished paper, which he and the whole board liked very well. At noon home to dinner and then to the office; the yarde being very full of women (I believe above three hundred) coming to get money for their husbands and friends that are prisoners in Holland; and they lay clamouring and swearing and cursing us, that my wife and I were afeard to send a venison-pasty that we have for supper to-night to the cook's to be baked, for fear of their offering violence to it: but it went, and no hurt done. Then I took an opportunity, when they were all gone into the foreyarde, and slipt into the office and there busy all the afternoon, but by and by the women got into the garden, and come all to my closett window, and there tormented me, and I confess their cries were so sad for money, and laying down the condition of their families and their husbands, and what they have done and suffered for the King, and how ill they are used by us, and how well the Dutch are used here by the allowance of their masters, and what their husbands are offered to serve the Dutch abroad, that I do most heartily pity them, and was ready to cry to hear them, but cannot helpe them. However, when the rest were gone, I did call one to me that I heard complaine only and pity her husband and did give her some money, and she blessed me and went away.

Anon my business at the office being done I to the Tower to speak with Sir John Robinson about business, principally the bad condition of the pressed men for want of clothes, so it is represented from the fleete, and so to provide them shirts and stockings and drawers. Having done with him about that, I home and there find my wife and the two Mrs. Bateliers walking in the garden. I with them till almost 9 at night, and then they and we and Mrs. Mercer, the mother, and her daughter Anne, and our Mercer, to supper to a good venison-pasty and other good things, and had a good supper, and very merry, Mistresses Bateliers being both very good-humoured. We sang and talked, and then led them home, and there they made us drink; and, among other things, did show us, in cages, some birds brought from about Bourdeaux, that are all fat, and, examining one of them, they are so, almost all fat. Their name is [Ortolans], which are brought over to the King for him to eat, and indeed are excellent things.

We parted from them and so home to bed, it being very late, and to bed.

Tuesday 4 September 1666

Up by break of day to get away the remainder of my things; which I did by a lighter at the Iron gate and my hands so few, that it was the afternoon before we could get them all away.

Sir W. Pen and I to Tower-streete, and there met the fire burning three or four doors beyond Mr. Howell's, whose goods, poor man, his trayes, and dishes, shovells, &c., were flung all along Tower-street in the kennels, and people working therewith from one end to the other; the fire coming on in that narrow streete, on both sides, with infinite fury. Sir W. Batten not knowing how to remove his wine, did dig a pit in the garden, and laid it in there; and I took the opportunity of laying all the papers of my office that I could not otherwise dispose of. And in the evening Sir W. Pen and I did dig another, and put our wine in it; and I my Parmazan cheese, as well as my wine and some other things.

The Duke of Yorke was at the office this day, at Sir W. Pen's; but I happened not to be within. This afternoon, sitting melancholy with Sir W. Pen in our garden, and thinking of the certain burning of this office, without extraordinary means, I did propose for the sending up of all our workmen from Woolwich and Deptford yards (none whereof yet appeared), and to write to Sir W. Coventry to have the Duke of Yorke's permission to pull down houses, rather than lose this office, which would, much hinder, the King's business. So Sir W. Pen he went down this night, in order to the sending them up to-morrow morning; and I wrote to Sir W. Coventry about the business, but received no answer.

This night Mrs. Turner (who, poor woman, was removing her goods all this day, good goods into the garden, and knows not how to dispose of them), and her husband supped with my wife and I at night, in the office; upon a shoulder of mutton from the cook's, without any napkin or any thing, in a sad manner, but were merry. Only now and then walking into the garden, and saw how horridly the sky looks, all on a fire in the night, was enough to put us out of our wits; and, indeed, it was extremely dreadful, for it looks just as if it was at us; and the whole heaven on fire. I after supper walked in the darke down to Tower-streete, and there saw it all on fire, at the Trinity House on that side, and the Dolphin Taverne on this side, which was very near us; and the fire with extraordinary vehemence. Now begins the practice of blowing up of houses in Tower-streete, those next the Tower, which at first did frighten people more than anything, but it stopped the fire where it was done, it bringing down the houses to the ground in the same places they stood, and then it was easy to quench what little fire was in it, though it kindled nothing almost. W. Hewer this day went to see how his mother did, and comes late home, telling us how he hath been forced to remove her to Islington, her house in Pye-corner being burned; so that the fire is got so far that way, and all the Old Bayly, and was running down to Fleete-streete; and Paul's is burned, and all Cheapside. I wrote to my father this night, but the post-house being burned, the letter could not go.

ALL YOU HAVE EATEN: ON KEEPING A PERFECT RECORD

Rachel Khong

Rachel Khong is an American writer and editor, and the former executive editor of *Lucky Peach*. She edited a cookbook, *All About Eggs*, which delivers deliciously on its premise. Her writing has been published in *The New York Times*, *Guernica*, *Joyland*, *American Short Fiction*, the *San Francisco Chronicle*, *The Believer* and *California Sunday*. Her first novel, *Goodbye, Vitamin*, was published to great acclaim in 2017, winning the California Book Award for First Fiction, and will be followed by *Real Americans* in 2024. She is based in San Francisco.

O ver the course of his or her lifetime, the average person will eat 60,000 pounds of food, the weight of six elephants.

The average American will drink over 3,000 gallons of soda. He will eat about 28 pigs, 2,000 chickens, 5,070 apples, and 2,340 pounds of lettuce. How much of that will he remember, and for how long, and how well?

You might be able to tell me, with some certainty, what your breakfast was, but that confidence most likely diminishes when I ask about two, three, four breakfasts ago—never mind this day last year.

The human memory is famously faulty; the brain remains mostly a mystery. We know that comfort foods make the pleasure centers in our brains light up the way drugs do. We know, because of a study conducted by Northwestern University and published in the *Journal of Neuroscience*, that by recalling a moment, you're altering it slightly, like a mental game of Telephone—the more you conjure a memory, the less accurate it will be down the line. Scientists have implanted false memories in mice and grown memories in pieces of brain in test tubes. But we haven't made many noteworthy strides in the thing that seems most relevant: how *not* to forget.

Unless committed to memory or written down, what we eat vanishes as soon as it's consumed. That's the point, after all. But because the famous diarist Samuel Pepys wrote, in his first entry, "Dined at home in the garret, where my wife dressed the remains of a turkey, and in the doing of it she burned her hand," we know that Samuel Pepys, in the 1600s, ate turkey. We know that, hundreds of years ago, Samuel Pepys's wife burned her hand. We know, because she wrote it in her diary, that Anne Frank at one point ate fried potatoes for breakfast. She once ate porridge and "a hash made from kale that came out of the barrel."

*

For breakfast on January 2, 2008, I ate oatmeal with pumpkin seeds and brown sugar and drank a cup of green tea.

I know because it's the first entry in a food log I still keep today. I began it as an experiment in food as a mnemonic device. The idea was this: I'd write something objective every day that would cue my memories into the future—they'd serve as compasses by which to remember moments.

Andy Warhol kept what he called a "smell collection," switching perfumes every three months so he could reminisce more lucidly on those months whenever he smelled that period's particular scent. Food, I figured, took this even further. It involves multiple senses, and that's why memories that surround food can come on so strong.

What I'd like to have is a perfect record of every day. I've long been obsessed with this impossibility, that every day be perfectly productive and perfectly remembered. What I remember from January 2, 2008 is that after eating the oatmeal I went to the post office, where an old woman was arguing with a postal worker about postage—she thought what she'd affixed to her envelope was enough and he didn't.

I'm terrified of forgetting. My grandmother has battled Alzheimer's for years now, and to watch someone battle Alzheimer's—we say "battle," as though there's some way of winning—is terrifying. If I'm always thinking about dementia, my unscientific logic goes, it can't happen to me (the way an earthquake comes when you don't expect it, and so the best course of action is always to expect it). "Really, one might almost live one's life over, if only one could make a sufficient effort of recollection" is a sentence I once underlined in John Banville's *The Sea* (a book that I can't remember much else about). But effort alone is not enough and isn't particularly reasonable, anyway. A man named Robert Shields kept the world's longest diary: he chronicled every five minutes of his life until a stroke in 2006 rendered him unable to. He wrote about microwaving foods, washing dishes, bathroom visits, writing itself. When he died in 2007, he left 37.5 million words behind—ninety-one boxes of paper. Reading his obituary, I wondered if Robert Shields ever managed to watch a movie straight through.

*

Last spring, as part of a NASA-funded study, a crew of three men and three women with "astronaut-like" characteristics spent four months in a geodesic dome in an abandoned quarry on the northern slope of Hawaii's Mauna Loa volcano.

For those four months, they lived and ate as though they were on Mars, only venturing outside to the surrounding Mars-like, volcanic terrain, in simulated space suits.[1] Hawaii Space Exploration Analog and Simulation (HI-SEAS) is a four-year project: a series of missions meant to simulate and study the challenges of long-term space travel, in anticipation of mankind's eventual trip to Mars. This first mission's focus was food.

---

[1] At first they wore government-surplus hazmat suits—those would constrict movement and essentially do the job, was NASA's budget-minded thinking—but the crew members expressed disappointment that they weren't realer-looking space suits, and mid-way through the mission, Apollo-like suits were donated to them by the University of Maryland.

Getting to Mars will take roughly six to nine months each way, depending on trajectory; the mission itself will likely span years. So the question becomes: How do you feed astronauts for so long? On "Mars," the HI-SEAS crew alternated between two days of pre-prepared meals and two days of dome-cooked meals of shelf-stable ingredients. Researchers were interested in the answers to a number of behavioral issues: among them, the well-documented phenomenon of menu fatigue (when International Space Station astronauts grow weary of their packeted meals, they tend to lose weight). They wanted to see what patterns would evolve over time if a crew's members were allowed dietary autonomy, and given the opportunity to cook for themselves ("an alternative approach to feeding crews of long term planetary outposts," read the open call).

Everything was hyper-documented. Everything eaten was logged in painstaking detail: weighed, filmed, and evaluated. The crew filled in surveys before and after meals: queries into how hungry they were, their first impressions, their moods, how the food smelled, what its texture was, how it tasted. They documented their time spent cooking; their water usage; the quantity of leftovers, if any. The goal was to measure the effect of what they ate on their health and morale, along with other basic questions concerning resource use. How much water will it take to cook on Mars? How much water will it take to wash dishes? How much time is required; how much energy? How will everybody feel about it all? I followed news of the mission devoutly.

*

It was afternoon in Belgium and early morning for me in California when Angelo Vermeulen, the crew's commander, and I spoke over Skype.

He started with a disclaimer: he wasn't the crew's best cook. He's happiest eating bread and cheese (bread and chocolate sprinkles if it's breakfast); he cooks potatoes in his microwave. He told me that earlier in the day he'd had some *grobos*: rolled-up pickled herring and onion, held together by a toothpick, and "drowned in mayonnaise"—"it's *so* good," he said, looking worked up about it.

"Angelo used so much mayonnaise!" was what Kate Greene, a fellow crewmember, said when the two of us met a week later in San Francisco. But Angelo does not look like a person who eats "so much mayonnaise."

"Far superior genetics. We ran out of mayonnaise early," Kate said. "But it wasn't just him, it was all of us."

Their crew of six was selected from a pool of 700 candidates. Kate is a science writer, open-water swimmer, and volleyball player. When I asked her what "astronaut-like" meant and why she was picked she said it was some "combination of education, experience, and attitude": a science background, leadership experience, an adventurous attitude. An interest in cooking was not among the requirements. The cooking duties were divided from the get-go; in the kitchen, crew members worked in pairs. On non-creative days they'd eat just-add-water, camping-type meals: pre-prepared lasagna, which surprised Kate by being not terrible; a thing called "kung fu chicken" that Angelo described as "slimy" and less tolerable; a raspberry crumble dessert that's a favorite among backpackers ("That was really delicious," Kate said, "but still you felt weird about thinking it was *too* delicious"). The crew didn't eat much real astronaut food—astronaut ice cream, for example—because real astronaut food is expensive.

On creative cooking days, meals were left up to the cooks. "On the crew there were three people who had visions for food and three people who were like, 'It's my turn to cook? What do I do?'" said Kate. "Angelo, Simon [Engler], and I were the people who were like, Okay, I'll figure something out. Sian [Proctor], Yajaira [Sierra-Sastre], and Oleg [Abramov] were the people who really had it going on. Oleg would make all these traditional Russian dishes, Yajaira would make tapas and flatbread pizzas, Sian could make a soup out of anything. I do not cook well. One time in grad school I was like, 'I'm having vanilla Slimfast and oatmeal. This is the greatest meal a human being can eat!'"

The choices were of course limited on Mars, but the HI-SEAS pantry was impressively ample: grains, nuts, shelf-stable bacon, Nutella, freeze-dried and dehydrated vegetables, fruit, and meat. There was powdered milk and powdered butter ("Which you'd think would be disgusting,"

Kate said, "but we were slathering it on bread"). Angelo and Kate, separately and without any prompting, got very animated talking about "egg crystals" that look like "yellow sugar" and, when rehydrated, are just like beaten eggs. "Historically, powdered eggs have been gnarly," Kate said, "but egg crystals made *delicious* eggs." It costs $10,000 to put a pound of food in space, which makes freeze-dried and dehydrated foods especially valuable. In the absence of fresh vegetables the freeze-dried versions were, for the crew members, "almost indistinguishable from fresh stuff," Angelo said. You add water, and there's "a little bit of a sizzle when it absorbs the water."

"Freeze-dried broccoli—we all loved it a lot. We would just dump it on our plate," Kate corroborated. "Freeze-dried things were mostly better. Freeze-dried broccoli came in chunks and it was chewy. It was really good. But dehydrated broccoli was kind of mushy once you rehydrated it."

But the vegetables never varied in size ("The carrots were always the same size, the broccoli was always the same size, and after a while the flavor didn't matter," Kate said). The crew craved salt and fat, too. "One of the issues was the meat that was freeze-dried didn't have a lot of fat in it. And so we were all really starved for fat. We used a lot of oil; we just couldn't get enough. Spam was really good because it was super salty and super fatty. I had never eaten Spam but we had Spam musubi and Spam fried rice—oh my God, it was delicious."

The main food study had a big odor identification component to it: the crew took scratch-n-sniff tests, which Kate said she felt confident about at the mission's start, and less certain about near the end. "The second-to-last test," she said, "I would smell grass and feel really wistful." Their noses were mapped with sonogram because, in space, the shape of your nose changes. And there were, on top of this, studies unrelated to food. They exercised in anti-microbial shirts (laundry doesn't happen in space), evaluated their experiences hanging out with robot pets, and documented their sleep habits.

At the end of every day, after the innumerable surveys, each crew member filled out a questionnaire about how he or she felt about everyone else: rating interactions with the five other crew members and with the twenty members of Mission Support on a scale of -7 to 7. "That's always the question: did you guys get along? Yeah, of course, but you can't *always* get along. One of the crew members said it was like being married to five other people," Kate said, "and it was."

When I asked Angelo if he thought his mood was affected predominantly by the food he ate, he seemed skeptical. "Things that were impacting mood were crew dynamics, communication with mission support, communication with your significant other. We didn't have real-time communication—no Skyping or calling—but you could be writing to each other, and a combination of all that contributed to your mood."

"We all had relationships outside that we were trying to maintain in some way," Kate said. "Some were kind of new, some were tenuous, some were old and established, but they were all very difficult to maintain. A few things that could come off wrong in an e-mail could really bum you out for a long time."

She told me about another crew member whose boyfriend didn't email her at his usual time. This was roughly halfway through the mission. She started to get obsessed with the idea that maybe he got into a car accident. "Like seriously obsessed," Kate said. "I was like, 'I think your brain is telling you things that aren't actually happening. Let's just be calm about this,' and she was like, 'Okay, okay.' But she couldn't sleep that night. In the end he was just like, 'Hey, what's up?' I knew he would be fine, but I could see how she could think something serious had happened."

"My wife sent me poems every day but for a couple days she didn't," Kate said. "Something was missing from those days, and I don't think she could have realized how important they were. It was weird. Everything was bigger inside your head because you were living inside your head."

I asked Kate who the mission was harder on and she says it was harder on her wife. "When a soldier is deployed, there's a narrative that goes along with that. When an astronaut goes to space, there's a freaking narrative that goes with that. When someone leaves to pretend to go to space, there's no narrative that goes along with that. You're making it up. You're like, 'Why is this important again? Why is this something that needs to be done?' In some ways it doesn't. It's not the hero sort of role of a soldier or an astronaut. From many points of view, it's kind of ridiculous."

The mission generated a huge amount of data, which is all still being analyzed. Both Angelo and Kate were hesitant to draw any conclusions ("I'm not involved in the analysis. I just did my job," Angelo said). At some point, the results will be published in papers, and we'll have some answers about menu fatigue, about how time's passing feels in isolation, about the changing shapes of astronauts' noses.

"My personal conclusions are a little predictable, I'm afraid," Angelo told me. "Cooking is highly advantageous, for many different reasons." There were always two people in the kitchen, which was good for "crew cohesion." And he talked about cooking as being a craved-for creative outlet. It was especially gratifying for the cooks—Angelo recalled with endearing pride his *enchilagna*, a combination enchilada and lasagna he'd devised.

When I asked him about the role food played in his remembrances he sounded skeptical again: "I'm not sure how much of the event you remember because of the food," he said. "I think it works the other way around. We had monthly celebrations and the food wasn't particularly fantastic. To me it doesn't feel I remember specific instances because of the food, I remember specific instances and then the food goes along with that in my memory."

Kate: "One night Yajaira and I made tapas and it was more interesting than usual. We found some YouTube flamenco. It was pretty goofy. It had an ambience to it."

Angelo: "Certain foods got particular focus, through Sian's outreach program"—during the mission, Sian recorded a cooking show; the episodes are still available online—"so of course I remember salmon patties. I was in front of the camera and the video is on YouTube."

Angelo doesn't normally keep a journal, but kept a daily journal in "the Hab" that was submitted to a study at the mission's end. Kate opted out of that particular study but kept a personal journal for herself. She doesn't typically maintain a journal, either: "The only one I ever kept, from when I first realized I was gay, I put it in a box of books I sent media mail to Nashville and it got lost, never to be found again. So the only journal I ever kept in my life, just the one journal from when I was sixteen—it's gone forever, and thank God. Because it's horrible! It's the worst. When I was on Mars I wrote every day about how I was feeling. I was looking back on that, and it's odd how not helpful it was."

Kate recalled the day she remotely drove a rover in Canada as one of the most exciting experiences of the mission ("I kind of got it stuck on a rock"). When she asked Jean Hunter, the head of the mission, for the record of the meal she'd eaten that morning, she was surprised at how unextraordinary it was: granola and milk and tea.

Breakfast on July 9 for subject XXXX:

Body mass: **133.4 lb.**
Satiety rating before breakfast: **-2**
Satiety rating after breakfast: **1**

Foods and ratings:
ANCIENT GRAINS
Appearance: 8 Aroma: 8
Interest: 8 Acceptability: **9**
Finished: **Y** Additional servings: **N**
EARL GREY TEA
Appearance: 8 Aroma: 8
Interest: 8 Acceptability: **not rated**
Finished: **not rated**
Additional servings: **not rated**
No condiments No comments
Granola: **84.6 g** Milk **120.6 g**

*

When I look back on my meals from the past year, the food log does the job I intended more or less effectively.

I can remember, with some clarity, the particulars of given days: who I was with, how I was feeling, the subjects discussed. There was the night in October I stress-scarfed a head of romaine and peanut butter packed onto old, hard bread; the somehow not-sobering bratwurst and fries I ate on day two of a two-day hangover, while trying to keep things light with somebody to whom, the two nights before, I had aired more than I meant to. There was the night in January I cooked "rice, chicken stirfry with bell pepper and mushrooms, tomato-y Chinese broccoli, 1 bottle IPA" with my oldest, best friend, and we ate the stirfry and drank our beers slowly while commiserating about the most recent conversations we'd had with our mothers.

But reading the entries from 2008, that first year, does something else to me: it suffuses me with the same mortification as if I'd written down my most private thoughts (that reaction is what keeps me from maintaining a more conventional journal). There's nothing especially incriminating about my diet, except maybe that I ate tortilla chips with unusual frequency, but the fact that it's just food doesn't spare me from the horror and head-shaking that comes with reading old diaries. Mentions of certain meals conjure specific memories, but mostly what I'm left with are the general feelings from that year. They weren't happy ones. I was living in San Francisco at the time. A relationship was dissolving.

It seems to me that the success of a relationship depends on a shared trove of memories. Or not shared, necessarily, but not *incompatible*. That's the trouble, I think, with parents and children: parents retain memories of their children that the children themselves don't share. My father's favorite meal is breakfast and his favorite breakfast restaurant is McDonald's, and I remember—having just read Michael Pollan or watched *Super Size Me*—self-righteously not ordering my regular egg McMuffin one morning, and how that actually hurt him.

When a relationship goes south, it's hard to pinpoint just where or how—especially after a prolonged period of it heading that direction. I was at a loss with this one. Going forward, I didn't want *not* to be able to account for myself. If I could remember everything, I thought, I'd be better equipped; I'd be better able to make proper, comprehensive assessments—informed decisions. But my memory had proved itself unreliable, and I needed something better. Writing down food was a way to turn my life into facts: if I had all the facts, I could keep them straight. So the next time this happened I'd know exactly why—I'd have all the data at hand.

In the wake of that breakup there were stretches of days and weeks of identical breakfasts and identical dinners. Those days and weeks blend into one another, become indistinguishable, and who knows whether I was too sad to be imaginative or all the unimaginative food made me sadder.

*

When I asked Kate why she chose to spend four months in a dome with five strangers on pretend Mars, she said she'd always wanted to be an astronaut.

And even if she couldn't go to Mars herself, she wanted to help in whatever way she could; she wanted to help with the research that might help other people go to Mars.

"And I wanted to see if I *could*," she said. "I'm always really curious about who you are in a different context. Who am I completely removed from Earth—or pretending to be removed from Earth? When you're going further and further from this planet, with all its rules and everything you've ever known, what happens? Do you invent new rules? What matters to you when you don't have constructs? Do you take the constructs with you? On an individual level it was an exploration of who I am in a different context, and on a larger scale, going to another planet is an exploration about what humanity is in a different context."

In summer of 2008, I moved to Gainesville: a college town in the Florida panhandle, and as different for me as contexts get. It seemed unreal when I lived there, trying to write and dating people completely wrong for me in the wake of this busted-up thing. Even now, it seems unreal.

The temperature in Florida in August hovers consistently around 100 degrees. Despite the heat, I cooked constantly. A few days after moving to town, enticed by a beautiful photo of browned eggplant in the newspaper, I cooked it in my small, hot, Florida kitchen: linguine with fried eggplant, tomato, and basil and parsley. I remember, that same day, falling off my heavy, old bike. A stranger named Joe or Jon tossed the bike into the bed of his pick-up truck—as effortlessly as though it were a stuffed thing won at a state fair—and took me to his house out near the mall, far from where I lived, and cleaned my ankle with hydrogen peroxide and Q-tips, and tightened my handlebars.

That place and those years felt like make-believe—one fall in particular. There was a trip that friends and I took to Key Biscayne, an island south of Miami Beach inhabited mostly by wealthy retirees. I remember that drive, drinking 5-Hour Energy drinks and eating Klonopin with a couple new friends and the wrong-for-me person I was dating, whose grandparents' condo it was we were staying in. Recently I e-mailed them to see what they could remember. They remembered parts which, pieced together, matched what I wrote down:

Five hour energy drink; One or two klonopin (two)

D: caviar with cream cheese and toast; melon with prosciutto; Caesar salad; tomato and basil salad; shrimp and scallop angel hair pasta; so much wine; café cubano.

What I remember is early that evening, drinking sparkling wine and spreading cream cheese on slices of a soft baguette from the fancy Key Biscayne Publix, then spooning grocery-store caviar onto it ("Lumpfish caviar and Prosecco, definitely, on the balcony"). I remember cooking dinner unhurriedly ("You were comparing prices for the seafood and I was impatient")—the thinnest pasta I could find, shrimp and squid cooked in wine and lots of garlic—and eating it late ("You cooked something good, but I can't remember what") and then drinking a café Cubano even later ("It was so sweet it made our teeth hurt and then, for me at least, immediately precipitated a metabolic crisis") and how, afterward, we all went to the empty beach and got in the water which was, on that warm summer day, not even cold ("It was just so beautiful after the rain").

"And this wasn't the same trip," wrote that wrong-for-me then-boyfriend, "but remember when you and I walked all the way to that restaurant in Bill Baggs park, at the southern tip of the island, and we had that painfully sweet white sangria, and ceviche, and walked back and got tons of mosquito bites, but we didn't care, and then we were on the beach somehow and we looked at the red lights on top of all the buildings, and across the channel at Miami Beach, and went in the hot Miami ocean, and most importantly it was National Fish Day?"

And it's heartening to me that I *do* remember all that—had remembered without his prompting, or consulting the record (I have written down: "D: ceviche; awful sangria; fried plantains; shrimp paella." "It is National fish day," I wrote. "There was lightning all night!"). It's heartening that my memory isn't as unreliable as I worry it is. I remember it exactly as he describes: the too-sweet sangria at that restaurant on the water, how the two of us had giggled so hard over nothing and declared that day "National Fish Day," finding him in the kitchen at four in the morning, dipping a sausage into mustard—me taking that other half of the sausage, dipping it into mustard—the two of us deciding to drive the six hours back to Gainesville, right then.

"That is a really happy memory," he wrote to me. "That is my nicest memory from that year and from that whole period. I wish we could live it again, in some extra-dimensional parallel life."

*

Three years ago I moved back to San Francisco, which was, for me, a new-old city.

I'd lived there twice before. The first time I lived there was a cold summer in 2006, during which I met that man I'd be broken up about a couple years later. And though that summer was before I started writing down the food, and before I truly learned how to cook for myself, I can still remember flashes: a dimly lit party and drinks with limes in them and how, ill-versed in flirting, I took the limes from his drink and put them into mine. I remember a night he cooked circular ravioli he'd bought from an expensive Italian grocery store, and zucchini he'd sliced into thin coins. I remembered him splashing Colt 45—leftover from a party—into the zucchini as it was cooking, and all of that charming me: the Colt 45, the expensive ravioli, this dinner of circles.

The second time I lived in San Francisco was the time our thing fell apart. This was where my terror had originated: where I remembered the limes and the ravioli, he remembered or felt the immediacy of something else, and neither of us was right or wrong to remember what we did—all memories, of course, are valid—but still, it sucked. And now I have a record reminding me of the nights I came home drunk and sad and, with nothing else in the house, sautéed kale; blanks on the days I ran hungry to Kezar Stadium from the Lower Haight, running lap after lap after lap to turn my brain off, stopping to read short stories at the bookstore on the way home, all to turn off the inevitable thinking, and at home, of course, the inevitable thinking.

The third time in San Francisco, we met like old friends to drink gin and tonics in a dive bar not far from my new apartment (May 11, 2011: L: enchiladas; D: tom yum noodles; gin and tonics). We hadn't seen each other at all in the years that I was away—trying out life in a different context—and while we were getting along again, the way we once had, I was preemptively worrying about what might happen down the line: that I'd remember something and he'd remember something different, and that would be the end of us. A few weeks later, on the afternoon of Memorial Day, while we were sitting on a Mission stoop, sharing an It's-It (a San Francisco thing—an oatmeal-cookie ice cream sandwich covered in chocolate), I remembered—I possessed a record of—those intervening years of feeling wronged and trying alternately to forgive and not to forgive him, and not even standing a chance now, eating that half an It's-It—forgiving him.

I'm not sure what to make of this data—what conclusions, if any, to draw. What I know is that it accumulates and disappears and accumulates again. No matter how vigilantly we keep track—even if we spend four months in a geodesic dome on a remote volcano with nothing to do *but* keep track—we experience more than we have the capacity to remember; we eat more than we can retain; we feel more than we can possibly carry with us. And maybe forgetting isn't so bad. I know there is the "small green apple" from the time we went to a moving sale and he bought bricks, and it was raining lightly, and as we were gathering the bricks we noticed an apple tree at the edge of the property with its branches overhanging into the yard, and we picked two small green apples that'd been washed by the rain, and wiped them off on our shirts. They surprised us by being sweet and tart and good. We put the cores in his car's cup holders. There was the time he brought chocolate chips and two eggs and a Tupperware of milk to my apartment, and we baked cookies. There are the times he puts candy in my jacket's small pockets—usually peppermints so ancient they've melted and re-hardened inside their wrappers—which I eat anyway, and then are gone, but not gone.

WE THAT ARE YOUNG

Preti Taneja

Preti Taneja is a writer and activist, and a Professor of World Literature and Creative Writing at Newcastle University. Her three books have won awards including the Gordon Burn Prize for 'literature that is fearless in ambition and execution' for *Aftermath*, a creative nonfiction lament on terror, trauma and grief following the London Bridge attack in 2019; and the Desmond Elliott Prize for the finest literary debut novel of the year for *We That Are Young*, a reimagining of Shakespeare's *King Lear* set against a backdrop of rising fascism in contemporary India. The scene below takes place in the air, between New Delhi and Amritsar.

Up in the clouds, Radha unclips her seatbelt. The interior of the little jet is camel leather. She likes it, so soft: skin on skin. She calls the airhostess, to order their lunch. Cholay-puri and saag-meat for Bubu. He eats like a starving bachcha, using his hand to tear bits of soft puri and scoop cholay into his mouth. He picks a piece of marrowbone from the saag and sucks the inside clean.

—Equal share, family bond, he says through his food. Future proof the trust.

Radha feathers her sprout salad with her fork. She eats a pea shoot. She thinks about pav bhaji. You can't get street food in the plane. She wants a cold glass of Sancerre, and presses the button to call the hostess.

—*All in good time*, Bubu says. Your Dad's favourite pill. In ten years since I married you I have worked like a donkey for the Company. Have I ever asked for anything in return?

He does not wait for Radha to answer.

—When we get to Amritsar, make sure you take care of Ranjit.

Why he has to tell her this, she has no idea.

—We have so much work to do, to get ready for the Srinagar opening, now we are taking time for this.

Who is he actually talking to? She counts her finished olive stones. One (for sorrow), two (for joy), three (for a girl), four (for a boy), five (for a King). She scrapes her teeth over one more.

—When we get the Srinagar hotel open, you'll see what we can really do. I mean, giving our business to *Sita*? Hotel and shawls? What was your Dad thinking? All I can say is, thank God she left. The whole Northern network is dependent on that trade.

Yes, Bubu, yes it is. The little plane dips and rises. *The Kashmir Corridor*. Radha taps her nails on her knee. *A dark place, a thin place, a no place to the map*. Here come the arms and there go the drugs, liquid, solid, gas. Through hallways and in corners, through doors into rooms, light weapons, they call them, though they are heavy and hard. All wrapped in high class and soft fabric. Hush–hush – the move of things – slipping through men's hands like a beautiful shawl over skin. In a blessed communal of Allah and Shiv. A deep state. Of grace. No crack down. Consignments are increasing. Nothing so romantic. The store must be ready before winter comes, deep in the cellars of the new Company Kashmir hotel.

Bapuji has named Bubu for this business. Outright. The shawls, made from the tums of protected little chiru are a different matter. They happen, despite the wild-lifers, the media, and Gargi's legal objections. But still, all because of Bubu. He says he keeps the bribes down to workable strata right from the guys who pick the fluff off the tum of the damn hoofy goat, up to the stores on Sansad Marg. And the Kashmir Corridor stays open. In all weathers, it is open for free trade.

Bubu takes another puri and scrapes it around his bowl, chasing the last shreds of meat in the sauce.

—I cannot wait until we get the Kashmir hotel done, he says. If your sister doesn't sabotage it somehow. Why do you both have to be so senti*mental*?

Srinagar, Srinagar, late summer on the lake. Lying in a hammock in a garden in the hills, looking up through the branches of some wide, spreading tree. Her slim waist. Her long legs. The responsibility of her own beauty against violence in the streets. Fourteen mosquito-bite marks on her ankles, one for each year of life. Sita and Big Sis somewhere around. Radha had felt so aloof and lovely up there. Lonely, in the singular way of mountain flowers. Even though there was table tennis. She was the red paddle and Ranjit Uncle was the blue. And of course, there was the petting farm, with real live chickens and goats.

Now Bubu points his food covered fingers in a gun at her. He shoots at her face then licks them.

—When we get into the new hotel, Gargi Madam will know for sure that she cannot strut around pretending she's the boss.

—Gargi just wants whatever is right.

—You need to stop defending her. Radha you are 28-years-old. You need to start thinking for yourself. Stop worrying about what Big Sis will say. Don't ever forget – you're my wife. And head of Company PR.

Perfect Radha, Pretty Radha, Pukka Radha. Bubu is stuck on his favourite topic now: How Gargi Thinks She's God. Radha does not want to listen to this again. Yet she *chose* Bubu, she knows that – it wasn't as if she had been wrapped in a bow and just gifted away. Bubu's gotra was excellent, a Rajput pedigree going back in the male line right to the source. His parents were in town planning, his wider family in politics. They were new money, but it was the late 1990s, the country was opening up. Though Radha had to have it coaxed from her by Ranjit Uncle one night, she finally confessed that out of all the guys who offered for her, she was crushing on Bubu. Cosmological charts were made. Their stars matched and the family Swamiji was consulted about the date. Radha thought Gargi might disapprove, but she had only said —*Don't you think he's a bit fast?*

—I'm going to use this time in Amritsar to head up to Srinagar once or twice, Bubu says. Contractors need to know I am there. You come, be the good cop. OK? Or I'll take Jivan, not a bad idea. Yes, Jivan with the Amer-i-can accent. Do you dig his accent, Raddles? Lick-lick-like it?

Has Radha ever been glad Bubu talks so much? The little plane shudders around her. On early dates, she had thought it was sweet, that Bubu wanted her to understand him. He took her to the Habitat Centre because she liked its fortress style, and he liked the English pub there – they served these salty-spicy nuts with the drinks – he could not find them anywhere else in Delhi, he said, not even in her Daddy's hotel. She sat and listened as he told her of his childhood, Dad and Mom building the business together; going to office then coming home for lunch; taking keep-fit strolls in the evening around the colony square while Bubu learned fractional math with a tutor. Two Mercs in the driveway and ten-plus help: driver and chaukidar, cook, maid, safai wale. And so on. Happy little Bubu had been sent to St Columba's with the sons of his parents' friends; he had sat with his family over dinner each night being fed, and fed, and fed at his Mom's own direction. Uncles in the police and in the civil service, rising like English bread. Lunch on Sundays at the Lodhi restaurant, parties at the Gymkhana club, an MBA from Sloan, a year or so working for Pierce & Pierce in London. He came home, he said, after 9/11 shut down the office. Anyway the job didn't like him; and it is true, Radha thinks, he is better, in charge of his own thing. At eighteen she had been desperate to get married. Bubu was The One: she had decided when, for their fourth or fifth date, he made Bapuji laugh with his impressions of London, then got his permission to take Radha out to dinner alone. He chose biryani at Delhi O' Delhi, though she wanted shakes and burgers in the American Diner. It was too full of kids, he had said, and bad lighting (and if she thought the place was damn cool then – well she was only eighteen).

A jolt of turbulence – Bubu puts his arms out – then stretches his hands behind his head.

—For now, all conditions of our cooperation will be based on Gargi's behaviour, he says. Let's see if she can hack it at the top.

As a bride, Radha had no bargaining chips. But she would not go and live with Bubu's parents in his parents' new-build city. Even though Bubu told her that Paradise Park was *the place of the future*, even though he *promised* he would build her a mall there. So she could go from bedroom, to car, to covered shopping. Buy her favourite brands without even feeling she had left the house.

—*I don't want to*, she had said. *I like going to London; they have the best clubs, and street food you can eat until three in the morning.*

She wondered that he had never been to that road near Selfridges, near Marble Arch, so like a miniature India Gate? Such succulent shawarma they have there, and fresh-fresh juice. On her first trip to London when she was seventeen, she ate there every night after dancing at Opium: she and her school friends, allowed to go to UK together since the other girls had brothers to come too. It felt wild to go with bare legs in the street, high heels and tight dresses, sleeping on the floor all jumbled up close, fingers and hair, and hot breath, kissing cousins and what-all else in the night. Not rising each day until noon.

Bubu hadn't answered; just asked if she never felt it was unfair that she had more money than any Britisher, yet couldn't get the latest fashions unless she got on a plane. Why, he said, shouldn't India compete? He told her it was all the fault of a closed financial system based on a mirage, an endless cycle of government dreams locked up in five year plans. Till now. *You can blame the late 80s*, he had said. *And the early 90s. My uncles in Congress, your dad and Ranjit.*

No one had ever said such things to her about Bapuji before. She liked the certainty in Bubu's voice. She only had a loose idea of what he was talking about. She had footsied him under the table and said,

—*But it's the Naughties.* She expected him to laugh.

—*Right*, he had said, holding out a bite of tender lamb for her. *And what happened in the last decade? Bail out. Hello international money. Lakshmi Devi has blessed our generation with a liberalised economy; it is our duty to make the most of each rupee. It is our time, Radha, we cannot waste it; the begging bowl is going to change hands, you watch.*

He had been right. Bubu, she thought, was something of a Business Guru, just like Bapuji. Still, she refused to go and live in Paradise Park. Some of the enclaves were only half-finished; the rest were full of retired Uncles and Aunties in tower blocks, their kids in neat bungalows set around their feet. It was no country for old money to live in. She put it like this to Ranjit Uncle, of course he had agreed. He spoke to Bubu, and for ten years they have lived, instead, on the Farm with Gargi and Surendra, Bapuji and Nanu. Ranjit Uncle.

Radha turns to look out of the airplane window; all she can see are a few wispy clouds; white hairs trailing across the bald, scorched earth. She thinks about Amritsar, where Ranjit Uncle is. And Jivan.

*

MADHUR JAFFREY'S ULTIMATE CURRY BIBLE

Madhur Jaffrey

Madhur Jaffrey is an award-winning actress and bestselling cookery author, and a world-renowned authority on Indian cuisine. Born in Delhi in 1933, she moved to England in the 1950s to train as an actress at RADA, and (along with her first husband Saeed) was instrumental in introducing Ismail Merchant to James Ivory. Though she did not cook as a child in Delhi, and nearly failed cookery at school, she has since written over fifteen cookbooks and presented multiple television programmes, and her writing has shaped Indian cuisine for generations of home cooks in the UK and USA.

Just as Indians, like my mother, were once led to believe that it was not possible to have an English meal without a soup, for the British, a curry without rice and a chutney was a non-starter. The chutneys they seem to have focused on were of the sweet, sour and hot, preserve variety – rather like their own mint jellies and jams, only hot. For the British, these were the perfect foils for spicy, savoury curries and rice. Soon, a tradition of serving a vast array of condiments was established. This may be seen even today at old, colonial-style hotels such as the Raffles Hotel in Singapore. Roasted peanuts, sliced bananas, grated coconut, fried onions, pickled chillies, as well as sweet and sour chutneys were all laid out at noon with every curry-and-rice Sunday 'tiffin'.

Is any of this 'authentic'? Well, yes and no. Indians do, indeed, serve chutneys, pickles and relishes with their meals. But they are not in the least bit standardised and the taste of each item is very regional and specific to that home. For example, in our family, we always had my grandmother's black lemon pickle. An almost magical potion, it was black with both age and black pepper. Then, we had my mother's green chilli pickle. It was full of crushed mustard seeds and red chilli powder and quite sour from lime juice. Also, sometimes, we would take out my grandmother's mango and ginger sweet chutney – which was, indeed, of the preserve variety – but this was generally saved for teatime, when we used it to smother a special, savoury biscuit called a *mutthrie*.

These pickles and chutneys were permanently in the larder. What was made fresh everyday was a green chutney (usually with mint, fresh coriander and green chillies) and a salad with onions and tomatoes. According to the season, there were freshly cut cucumbers, kohlrabi, radishes, carrots and spring onions on the table as well. There was always yoghurt, either natural or made into a *raita* with roasted cumin as its main flavouring.

A Gujarati family in Bombay would have completely different pickles and chutneys and salads, seasoned with a different set of spices. So would a family in Madras or Calcutta. What the British did was just simplify and standardise what seemed like a general Indian trend.

I find it very interesting that, while yoghurt relishes are much loved throughout what was once the Indian subcontinent, they are totally absent in East and South-East Asia. It could be a lactose intolerance that is responsible for this. I have seen Malaysians put a tiny amount of yoghurt into certain meat dishes such as *kormas* in an almost symbolic gesture. They seem much more confident about the coconut milk that they pour into the same curry.

In this chapter you will find a variety of yoghurt relishes, fresh chutneys and salads, preserved chutneys and pickles and also some garnishes, such as crispy fried onions, which add an enormous amount of flavour and excitement to all Indian meals.

What do you drink with Indian meals? Indians usually drink plain water with their meals. Occasionally they might have a yoghurt *lassi*, but not much more. When I serve Indian food at dinner parties in New York, I nearly always accompany all courses with good wine. Be unafraid about this and do not be bullied into serving lager or fruity Alsatian wines. I really think they do fine Indian food an injustice. Try a good Chablis or Pinot Grigio. Amongst all the reds, try an Australian

Merlot or a reasonably priced Bordeaux. Most dry white and red wines complement Indian foods. Non-drinkers may be offered Fresh Limeade, *lassi*, or seltzer water. After dinner, serve a mildly spiced black tea or, if you like, a glorious Kashmiri saffron tea.

Papadum are the Indian wafers, generally made out of split peas, that are often served with meals. There are many parts of India where a meal without some variety of 'crunchy munchy' is quite unthinkable. It could be green plantain chips, jackfruit chips, potato, sago or rice *papadum*, crisply fried fresh or dried fish, fried vegetable fritters, anything as long as it crunches. Crispness is considered vital to the overall balance of desirable textures at a meal.

Having said that, let me add that I did not grow up with this habit. *Papadums,* we called them *papar*, were either served with drinks in our north Indian home or at wedding banquets. Sometimes when we were on a train journey and passing through the town of Hapar (which conveniently rhymed with *papar*), my mother made a special allowance and let us buy and eat its famous *papar* from hawkers at the railway platform. '*Hapar kay paper*', the hawkers with monster baskets on their heads would cry, 'the *papar* of Hapar'.

My mother used to make one variety at home out of chickpea flour. It was called *papri*, and was served only at two major religious festivals, Divali and Holi. For us, *papadums* had their time and place. It is the Indian restaurants in the West who have perpetuated the myth that all Indians eat *papadums* at all meals.

Papadums come in all sizes and flavours. Today you can even buy 'cocktail' *papadum* that are sufficient for a mouthful. When you go to your Indian grocer, he will probably have a large selection. Pick any flavour you like. There is plain, garlic flavour, green chilli, red chilli, black pepper, cumin and so on. My favourite is black pepper. The size does not matter. You can always break a *papadum* in half. What does matter is that the *papadums* be slightly flexible. If they are rock hard and brittle, they are old. Bend the packet slightly to test them.

Tahira Mazhar Ali's
Yoghurt with Jaggery (Dahi Aur Gur)   PAKISTAN

All over northern India and Pakistan, when the winter crop of sugar cane is harvested, much of it goes to make refined sugar. But not all of it. Perhaps in faithful memory of our culinary history going back to ancient times, every village saves some of the sugar cane juice to boil down and make lumps of sweet, crumbly jaggery, an unrefined sugar.

Jaggery is sold in all Indian and Pakistani markets, though it is more blessed if I comes from your own family village where its purity and freshness is guaranteed. Avoid jaggery that has turned rock hard. The softer and crumblier it is, the better.

The jaggery in Tahira Mazhar Ali's gracious home in Lahore came from her village, Wah, in north-western Pakistan, where the ground not only yields sugar cane but ancient Buddhist statuary as well, much of it to be seen at the excavations at nearby Taxila. Tahira served us lunch on her sun-drenched verandah. This simple yoghurt dish – no recipe is really required – was part of the winter meal.

serves 4–6
475 ml/16 fl oz natural yoghurt
3 tablespoons well-crumbled jaggery

Beat the yoghurt lightly with a fork until it is smooth. Put in a bowl. Scatter the jaggery over the top just before serving.

Yoghurt and Apple 'Raita'   USA

I love apple *raita*, especially if the apples are sweet and crisp. The slight sourness of the yoghurt mingled with the sweetness of the apple is very alluring. I have taken to using an apple that grows locally in New York State – Honey Crisp – but you may choose any that you like.

serves 4–6
300 ml/10 fl oz natural yoghurt
about ¼ teaspoon salt
freshly ground black pepper
⅛ teaspoon good quality pure chilli powder or cayenne pepper
About ½ an apple, peeled and cut into small dice

Put the yoghurt in a bowl. Beat lightly with a fork until smooth and creamy. Add all the remaining ingredients and mix well.

Cucumber, Mint and Tomato 'Raita'   INDIA

A simple, refreshing *raita* that may be served with all Indian meals.

serves 4–6
250 ml/8 fl oz natural yoghurt
½ teaspoon salt
freshly ground black pepper
¼ teaspoon cayenne pepper
½ teaspoon ground, roasted cumin seeds
1 medium tomato, peeled, seeded and finely chopped
1 medium cucumber, about 13-cm/5-inch in length, peeled and cut into small dice
2 tablespoons finely chopped fresh mint leaves or 1 tablespoon dried leaves, well crumbled

Put the yoghurt into a bowl and beat lightly with a fork until smooth and creamy. Add the salt, black pepper, cayenne pepper and cumin. Mix well. Add the remaining ingredients and mix again.

Parveen Haroun's
Yoghurt with Spinach and Dill (Dahi Palag)   PAKISTAN

A speciality of the Afghans who settled in the western Pakistani province of Sindh, this recipe comes from the Pakhtoon matriarch of a Karachi publishing family.

If you can get them, you may add a few tablespoons of finely chopped fresh fenugreek leaves to the spinach as well.

serves 4–6
255–285 g/9–10 oz fresh spinach, washed, drained and coarsely chopped
3 tablespoons finely chopped fresh dill
salt
300 ml/10 fl oz natural yoghurt
2 cloves garlic, peeled and crushed to a pulp
freshly ground black pepper
2 teaspoons crumbled dried mint

Put the spinach, dill, ¼ teaspoon salt and 120 ml/4 fl oz water in a medium, lidded pan. Bring to the boil, cover, reduce the heat to low, and cook for 5 minutes. Remove the lid and boil away all but 1 tablespoon or so of the water.

Put the yoghurt in a bowl. Beat lightly with a fork or whisk until smooth and creamy. Mix in ¼ teaspoon salt, the garlic, pepper and dried mint. Now put the contents of the spinach pan into the bowl with the yoghurt. Stir to mix.

Hameed and Parveen Haroon's
Yoghurt 'Kadhi' (Dahi Ki Karhi)   PAKISTAN

Kadhis, a beloved food all over the Indian subcontinent, are soupy stews generally made with chickpea flour and thinned yoghurt that are first mixed, and then cooked with a variety of additions from dumplings to vegetables. They are, for most of us, a familiar, heart-warming comfort food or soul food, call it what you may, with many regional variations.

This particular *kadhi* from the Sindh region of Pakistan is a take on the dish, not quite a true *kadhi*, but a faux one. They do without the chickpea flour altogether here.

I got this particular recipe twice, one from the son, Hameed Haroon (publisher of Pakistan's leading newspaper, *Dawn*) and again, with some subtle differences, from his mother, Parveen Haroon. The mother explained that they are Meman Muslims from Hyderabad, in Sindh (south-western Pakistan), and that the family was of Afghan descent – Afghanis who, many generations back, had settled in what was then India. This was her grandmother's recipe and originated in Afghan Manzil, as their house in Hyderabad was called. There is a fair amount of Irani blood in the family also, so those with a detective's heart should be able to ferret out a variety of influences. The Haroons like to eat this yoghurt with breads, such as the Kandahari *naan*, and with *pilafs*.

The green chillies are either left whole (the son's recipe) or cut into big pieces (the mother's way.) If you are making this dish for Westerners, I suggest you finely chop the chillies so as not to run the risk of them causing undue havoc.

serves 4–6

3 tablespoons corn or peanut oil

2 smallish onions, about 200g/7 oz, peeled and sliced into thin half-rings

2 large cloves garlic, peeled and crushed

3–4 fresh curry leaves, if available

2 medium tomatoes, coarsely chopped

2–3 fresh, hot green chillies, finely chopped

30 g/ 1 oz fresh coriander leaves and tender stems, chopped

⅛ teaspoon ground turmeric

salt

475 ml/16 fl oz natural yoghurt

Pour the oil into a medium-large frying pan and set over a medium-high heat. When the oil is hot, add the onions and stir and fry until they are golden. Put in the garlic and stir for a few seconds. Now put in the curry leaves, tomatoes, chillies, coriander, turmeric and ½ teaspoon salt. Stir and cook until the seasonings turn into a thick, dark sauce and you can see the oil at the edges of the pan. Turn off the heat.

Empty the yoghurt into a serving bowl. Beat lightly with a fork or whisk until smooth and creamy. Whisk in ½ teaspoon salt. Pour the cooked seasonings on top of the yoghurt. Stir just once in a single direction to create a swirl.

VANITY FAIR

William Makepeace Thackeray

Born in Calcutta in 1811, **William Makepeace Thackeray** was an author of satirical novels. At twenty-one, he rejected his law degree and went to Paris to pursue art and study French. After his inheritance was lost to gambling, poor investments and the collapse of two banks, he returned to England and worked as a journalist before beginning to write fiction. *Vanity Fair*, his greatest success and still his most famous work, was published as a nineteen-volume monthly serial in 1847 and 1848 before being released as a single volume with the subtitle 'A Novel without a Hero'.

A very stout, puffy man, in buckskins and Hessian boots, with several immense neckcloths that rose almost to his nose, with a red striped waistcoat and an apple green coat with steel buttons almost as large as crown pieces (it was the morning costume of a dandy or blood of those days) was reading the paper by the fire when the two girls entered, and bounced off his arm-chair, and blushed excessively, and hid his entire face almost in his neckcloths at this apparition.

"It's only your sister, Joseph," said Amelia, laughing and shaking the two fingers which he held out. "I've come home for good, you know; and this is my friend, Miss Sharp, whom you have heard me mention."

"No, never, upon my word," said the head under the neckcloth, shaking very much—"that is, yes—what abominably cold weather, Miss"—and herewith he fell to poking the fire with all his might, although it was in the middle of June.

"He's very handsome," whispered Rebecca to Amelia, rather loud.

"Do you think so?" said the latter. "I'll tell him."

"Darling! not for worlds," said Miss Sharp, starting back as timid as a fawn. She had previously made a respectful virgin-like curtsey to the gentleman, and her modest eyes gazed so perseveringly on the carpet that it was a wonder how she should have found an opportunity to see him.

"Thank you for the beautiful shawls, brother," said Amelia to the fire poker. "Are they not beautiful, Rebecca?"

"O heavenly!" said Miss Sharp, and her eyes went from the carpet straight to the chandelier.

Joseph still continued a huge clattering at the poker and tongs, puffing and blowing the while, and turning as red as his yellow face would allow him. "I can't make you such handsome presents, Joseph," continued his sister, "but while I was at school, I have embroidered for you a very beautiful pair of braces."

"Good Gad! Amelia," cried the brother, in serious alarm, "what do you mean?" and plunging with all his might at the bell-rope, that article of furniture came away in his hand, and increased the honest fellow's confusion. "For heaven's sake see if my buggy's at the door. I can't wait. I must go. D—that groom of mine. I must go."

At this minute the father of the family walked in, rattling his seals like a true British merchant. "What's the matter, Emmy?" says he.

"Joseph wants me to see if his—his buggy is at the door. What is a buggy, Papa?"

"It is a one-horse palanquin," said the old gentleman, who was a wag in his way.

Joseph at this burst out into a wild fit of laughter; in which, encountering the eye of Miss Sharp, he stopped all of a sudden, as if he had been shot.

"This young lady is your friend? Miss Sharp, I am very happy to see you. Have you and Emmy been quarrelling already with Joseph, that he wants to be off?"

"I promised Bonamy of our service, sir," said Joseph, "to dine with him."

"O fie! didn't you tell your mother you would dine here?"

"But in this dress it's impossible."

"Look at him, isn't he handsome enough to dine anywhere, Miss Sharp?"

On which, of course, Miss Sharp looked at her friend, and they both set off in a fit of laughter, highly agreeable to the old gentleman.

"Did you ever see a pair of buckskins like those at Miss Pinkerton's?" continued he, following up his advantage.

"Gracious heavens! Father," cried Joseph.

"There now, I have hurt his feelings. Mrs. Sedley, my dear, I have hurt your son's feelings. I have alluded to his buckskins. Ask Miss Sharp if I haven't? Come, Joseph, be friends with Miss Sharp, and let us all go to dinner."

"There's a pillau, Joseph, just as you like it, and Papa has brought home the best turbot in Billingsgate."

"Come, come, sir, walk downstairs with Miss Sharp, and I will follow with these two young women," said the father, and he took an arm of wife and daughter and walked merrily off.

If Miss Rebecca Sharp had determined in her heart upon making the conquest of this big beau, I don't think, ladies, we have any right to blame her; for though the task of husband-hunting is generally, and with becoming modesty, entrusted by young persons to their mammas, recollect that Miss Sharp had no kind parent to arrange these delicate matters for her, and that if she did not get a husband for herself, there was no one else in the wide world who would take the trouble off her hands. What causes young people to "come out," but the noble ambition of matrimony? What sends them trooping to watering-places? What keeps them dancing till five o'clock in the morning through a whole mortal season? What causes them to labour at pianoforte sonatas, and to learn four songs from a fashionable master at a guinea a lesson, and to play the harp if they have handsome arms and neat elbows, and to wear Lincoln Green toxophilite hats and feathers, but that they may bring down some "desirable" young man with those killing bows and arrows of theirs? What causes respectable parents to take up their carpets, set their houses topsy-turvy, and spend a fifth of their year's income in ball suppers and iced champagne? Is it sheer love of their species, and an unadulterated wish to see young people happy and dancing? Psha! they want to marry their daughters; and, as honest Mrs. Sedley has, in the depths of her kind heart, already arranged a score of little schemes for the settlement of her Amelia, so also had our beloved but unprotected Rebecca determined to do her very best to secure the husband, who was even more necessary for her than for her friend. She had a vivid imagination; she had, besides, read the Arabian Nights and Guthrie's Geography; and it is a fact that while she was dressing for dinner, and after she had asked Amelia whether her brother was very rich, she had built for herself a most magnificent castle in the air, of which she was mistress, with a husband somewhere in the background (she had not seen him as yet, and his figure would not therefore be very distinct); she had arrayed herself in an infinity of shawls, turbans, and diamond necklaces, and had mounted upon an elephant to the sound of the march in Bluebeard, in order to pay a visit of ceremony to the Grand Mogul. Charming Alnaschar visions! it is the happy privilege of youth to construct you, and many a fanciful young creature besides Rebecca Sharp has indulged in these delightful day-dreams ere now!

Joseph Sedley was twelve years older than his sister Amelia. He was in the East India Company's Civil Service, and his name appeared, at the period of which we write, in the Bengal division of the East India Register, as collector of Boggley Wollah, an honourable and lucrative post, as everybody knows: in order to know to what higher posts Joseph rose in the service, the reader is referred to the same periodical.

Boggley Wollah is situated in a fine, lonely, marshy, jungly district, famous for snipe-shooting, and where not unfrequently you may flush a tiger. Ramgunge, where there is a magistrate, is only forty miles off, and there is a cavalry station about thirty miles farther; so Joseph wrote home to his parents, when he took possession of his collectorship. He had lived for about eight years of his life, quite alone, at this charming place, scarcely seeing a Christian face except twice a year, when the detachment arrived to carry off the revenues which he had collected, to Calcutta.

Luckily, at this time he caught a liver complaint, for the cure of which he returned to Europe, and which was the source of great comfort and amusement to him in his native country. He did not live with his family while in London, but had lodgings of his own, like a gay young bachelor. Before he went to India he was too young to partake of the delightful pleasures of a man about town, and plunged into them on his return with considerable assiduity. He drove his horses in the Park; he dined at the fashionable taverns (for the Oriental Club was not as yet invented); he frequented the theatres, as the mode was in those days, or made his appearance at the opera, laboriously attired in tights and a cocked hat.

On returning to India, and ever after, he used to talk of the pleasure of this period of his existence with great enthusiasm, and give you to understand that he and Brummel were the leading bucks of the day. But he was as lonely here as in his jungle at Boggley Wollah. He scarcely knew a single soul in the metropolis: and were it not for his doctor, and the society of his blue-pill, and his liver complaint, he must have died of loneliness. He was lazy, peevish, and a bon-vivant; the appearance of a lady frightened him beyond measure; hence it was but seldom that he joined the paternal circle in Russell Square, where there was plenty of gaiety, and where the jokes of his good-natured old father frightened his amour-propre. His bulk caused Joseph much anxious thought and alarm; now and then he would make a desperate attempt to get rid of his superabundant fat; but his indolence and love of good living speedily got the better of these endeavours at reform, and he found himself again at his three meals a day. He never was well dressed; but he took the hugest pains to adorn his big person, and passed many hours daily in that occupation. His valet made a fortune out of his wardrobe: his toilet-table was covered with as many pomatums and essences as ever were employed by an old beauty: he had tried, in order to give himself a waist, every girth, stay, and waistband then invented. Like most fat men, he would have his clothes made too tight, and took care they should be of the most brilliant colours and youthful cut. When dressed at length, in the afternoon, he would issue forth to take a drive with nobody in the Park; and then would come back in order to dress again and go and dine with nobody at the Piazza Coffee-House. He was as vain as a girl; and perhaps his extreme shyness was one of the results of his extreme vanity. If Miss Rebecca can get the better of him, and at her first entrance into life, she is a young person of no ordinary cleverness.

The first move showed considerable skill. When she called Sedley a very handsome man, she knew that Amelia would tell her mother, who would probably tell Joseph, or who, at any rate, would be pleased by the compliment paid to her son. All mothers are. If you had told Sycorax that her son Caliban was as handsome as Apollo, she would have been pleased, witch as she was. Perhaps, too, Joseph Sedley would overhear the compliment—Rebecca spoke loud enough—and he did hear, and (thinking in his heart that he was a very fine man) the praise thrilled through every fibre of his big body, and made it tingle with pleasure. Then, however, came a recoil. "Is the girl making fun of me?" he thought, and straightway he bounced towards the bell, and was for retreating, as we have seen, when his father's jokes and his mother's entreaties caused him to pause and stay where he was. He conducted the young lady down to dinner in a dubious and agitated frame of mind. "Does she really think I am handsome?" thought he, "or is she only making game of me?" We have talked of Joseph Sedley being as vain as a girl. Heaven help us! the girls have only to turn the tables, and say of one of their own sex, "She is as vain as a man," and they will have perfect reason. The bearded creatures are quite as eager for praise, quite as finikin over their toilettes, quite as proud of their personal advantages, quite as conscious of their powers of fascination, as any coquette in the world.

Downstairs, then, they went, Joseph very red and blushing, Rebecca very modest, and holding her green eyes downwards. She was dressed in white, with bare shoulders as white as snow—the picture of youth, unprotected innocence, and humble virgin simplicity. "I must be very quiet," thought Rebecca, "and very much interested about India."

Now we have heard how Mrs. Sedley had prepared a fine curry for her son, just as he liked it, and in the course of dinner a portion of this dish was offered to Rebecca. "What is it?" said she, turning an appealing look to Mr. Joseph.

"Capital," said he. His mouth was full of it: his face quite red with the delightful exercise of gobbling. "Mother, it's as good as my own curries in India."

"Oh, I must try some, if it is an Indian dish," said Miss Rebecca. "I am sure everything must be good that comes from there."

"Give Miss Sharp some curry, my dear," said Mr. Sedley, laughing.

Rebecca had never tasted the dish before.

"Do you find it as good as everything else from India?" said Mr. Sedley.

"Oh, excellent!" said Rebecca, who was suffering tortures with the cayenne pepper.

"Try a chili with it, Miss Sharp," said Joseph, really interested.

"A chili," said Rebecca, gasping. "Oh yes!" She thought a chili was something cool, as its name imported, and was served with some. "How fresh and green they look," she said, and put one into her mouth. It was hotter than the curry; flesh and blood could bear it no longer. She laid down her fork. "Water, for Heaven's sake, water!" she cried. Mr. Sedley burst out laughing (he was a coarse man, from the Stock Exchange, where they love all sorts of practical jokes). "They are real Indian, I assure you," said he. "Sambo, give Miss Sharp some water."

The paternal laugh was echoed by Joseph, who thought the joke capital. The ladies only smiled a little. They thought poor Rebecca suffered too much. She would have liked to choke old Sedley, but she swallowed her mortification as well as she had the abominable curry before it, and as soon as she could speak, said, with a comical, good-humoured air, "I ought to have remembered the pepper which the Princess of Persia puts in the cream-tarts in the Arabian Nights. Do you put cayenne into your cream-tarts in India, sir?"

Old Sedley began to laugh, and thought Rebecca was a good-humoured girl. Joseph simply said, "Cream-tarts, Miss? Our cream is very bad in Bengal. We generally use goats' milk; and, 'gad, do you know, I've got to prefer it!"

"You won't like everything from India now, Miss Sharp," said the old gentleman; but when the ladies had retired after dinner, the wily old fellow said to his son, "Have a care, Joe; that girl is setting her cap at you."

"Pooh! nonsense!" said Joe, highly flattered. "I recollect, sir, there was a girl at Dumdum, a daughter of Cutler of the Artillery, and afterwards married to Lance, the surgeon, who made a dead set at me in the year '4—at me and Mulligatawney, whom I mentioned to you before dinner—a devilish good fellow Mulligatawney—he's a magistrate at Budgebudge, and sure to be in council in five years. Well, sir, the Artillery gave a ball, and Quintin, of the King's 14th, said to me, 'Sedley,' said he, 'I bet you thirteen to ten that Sophy Cutler hooks either you or Mulligatawney before the rains.' 'Done,' says I; and egad, sir—this claret's very good. Adamson's or Carbonell's?"

A slight snore was the only reply: the honest stockbroker was asleep, and so the rest of Joseph's story was lost for that day. But he was always exceedingly communicative in a man's party, and has told this delightful tale many scores of times to his apothecary, Dr. Gollop, when he came to inquire about the liver and the blue-pill.

Being an invalid, Joseph Sedley contented himself with a bottle of claret besides his Madeira at dinner, and he managed a couple of plates full of strawberries and cream, and twenty-four little rout cakes that were lying neglected in a plate near him, and certainly (for novelists have the privilege of knowing everything) he thought a great deal about the girl upstairs. "A nice, gay, merry young creature," thought he to himself. "How she looked at me when I picked up her handkerchief at dinner! She dropped it twice. Who's that singing in the drawing-room? 'Gad! shall I go up and see?"

But his modesty came rushing upon him with uncontrollable force. His father was asleep: his hat was in the hall: there was a hackney-coach standing hard by in Southampton Row. "I'll go and see the Forty Thieves," said he, "and Miss Decamp's dance"; and he slipped away gently on the pointed toes of his boots, and disappeared, without waking his worthy parent.

"There goes Joseph," said Amelia, who was looking from the open windows of the drawing-room, while Rebecca was singing at the piano.

"Miss Sharp has frightened him away," said Mrs. Sedley. "Poor Joe, why will he be so shy?"

THE COMPLETE INDIAN HOUSEKEEPER AND COOK

Flora Annie Steel and Grace Gardiner

The wives of British civil servants in India, **Flora Annie Steel** and **Grace Gardiner** published their guide to housekeeping in the British Raj in 1888. The book covers the care of domestic and farm animals, recipes, and information regarding ingredients and running a household. While considered progressive at the time (encouraging Hindi lessons for housewives with the words 'no sane Englishwoman would dream of living, say, for twenty years, in Germany, Italy, or France, without making the attempt, at any rate, to learn the language'), it is difficult to read their work today without recoiling. And yet we must read it: their work is undeniably as much a record of Britain's colonial history as military papers or legal documents. Racism begins at home, but where – for these lifelong residents of India – is home? The tension in this text – between 'home' and 'abroad', the foreign and the familiar – is part of the history of the occupation of India, and since the repercussions reverberate still, we should not and cannot look away.

Native dishes

The following native dishes have been added by request. It may be mentioned incidentally that most native recipes are inordinately greasy and sweet, and that your native cooks invariably know how to make them fairly well.

1. **Burtas.**—Burtas are macedoines of vegetables, and are useful for using up the remains. They are constantly served at breakfast. Potato

burta is mashed potato mixed with fried onions, and well seasoned. An excellent variation is cabbage and potato. Brinjal *burta* is a great favourite. The brinjals are roasted in the ashes and the skins removed. The pulp is then mashed, fried with a little butter and seasonings, including lime-juice.

2. **Chitchkee Curry.**—This is a vegetable curry. Slice some fresh onions, fry them in plenty of butter, mix the curry powder to a paste with a little gravy. Add to the butter, fry slightly, then put in an *olla podrida* of vegetables—the greater variety the better—and simmer the whole till done. Serve with rice.

3. **Dâl.**—Lentils stewed. Fry 4 onions in 1 unit butter or fat till brown, add also ¼ unit curry powder, then 5 units of washed lentils and 5 of thin stock. Stew till tender, adding more stock if required. It should be the consistency of porridge. Serve with rice kidgeree.

4. **Dâl Pooree.**—Five units of *dâl* washed. Boil till tender. Add 1 unit ground onions, ¼ of ground chillies, ¼ of ginger and turmeric mixed, a clove of garlic, and ¼ unit salt. Brown 6 onions in 2 units butter and stir to the *dâl*. Make a flour-and-water paste as for water biscuits. Take a piece of this the size of a walnut and hollow into a saucer, put into this sufficient quantity of the prepared *dâl*. Lay on another similar saucer, flute the edges, and roll out as thin as possible. When the size of a dinner plate fry in boiling *ghee*. Or the *dâl* can be made into puffs or rissoles with ordinary puff paste.

5. **Dumpoke.**—One boned chicken. Make a forcemeat with boiled rice as for pilau, and fresh herbs, and onions, and hard-boiled eggs. Stuff the chicken with this and braise it gently.

6. **Kulleah Yekhanee.**—Slice 32 units solid of lean mutton into a stewpan with enough water to cover it, add four onions, ¼ unit each of ginger and cloves, 1 unit sugar, 2 of lime juice, and ¼ unit curry powder, and salt to taste. Stew till tender.

7. **Kidgeree.**—Into 4 units of boiling *ghee* fry 4 units sliced onions, cut lengthways. Remove, add 4 units of well-washed rice, and 4 units *dâl*. Fry till the butter is absorbed. Add some slices of green ginger, peppercorns, salt, cloves, and cardamoms to taste, and a stick or two

of cinnamon. Just cover with water and simmer in a covered pan till almost quite *dry*. Care is required not to let the contents burn. They should be shaken up occasionally and stirred with a wooden spoon. Serve with the fried onions scattered over the top.

8. **Pilau.**—Slice six large onions, and two green mangoes, and fry in two units butter, and set aside. Truss a chicken as for boiling. Fry it in 2 units butter, and put into the stewpan. Cover with water and stew gently. When half done, remove and finish the cooking in a *degchi* as for a roast chicken. Wash 4 units of rice and boil in the chicken stock. When done, drain away the surplus stock, add a little butter, some raisins and almonds, cloves, &c., and let it dry. Serve round and over the chicken with the stock reduced as a gravy and a decoration of hard-boiled eggs.

Miscellaneous

1. **Batter.**—One unit flour, 2 units eggs, 6 units milk. Beat well.
2. **Breakfast Brawn.**—Take a sheep's head and trotters, both with the skin on, and stew till quite soft in lots of water garnished with herbs and a piece of fat bacon. When almost dissolved, remove the meat and bones, strain the liquor, and reduce, adding a little vinegar, black pepper, salt, onions, &c. Cut the gelatinous portions of the head in dice, also the meaty parts and the bacon, fill a round mould, decorating it with hard-boiled eggs, &c., press tight, and fill with the very much reduced liquor. It should cut quite firm when cold, and the jelly and meat should not look separate. To ensure this, fill the mould well with the meat, and keep pressed down with a weight on the top.
3. **Curry Powder, Madras.**—Coriander (*dhunnia*); turmeric (*huldi*); and cummin (*iira*), of each 8 units. Pepper (*mirch*) and dry ginger (*sonth*), of each 4 units. Fenugreek (*mêthi*); cardamoms (*ilâchii*); chillies (*lâl mirch*); and mace (*jowtri*), of each 2 units. Mustard seed (*surson*); cloves (*lông*); and poppy seed (*khus*), of each 1 unit (excellent).

4. **Curry Powder, Malay.**—Turmeric, 24 units; dry ginger, 16 units; chillies, 4 units; cardamoms, 8 units; cinnamon and cloves, 1 unit. Pound and mix. Malay curries are invariably made with cocoanut milk prepared by grating a cocoanut and steeping in boiling water. Strain after a quarter of an hour with pressure. Garlic must be used, and the cloves and cinnamon increased if a spice flavour is desired.

5. **Farce.**—Equal units of meat, panade, and butter. Add a unit or two of egg.

6. **Hunter's Beef.**—Salt in pickle for three days, then rub with mixed spices as follows: One unit each of cloves, cinnamon, cardamoms, allspice, mace, and 2 of black pepper. Continue rubbing morning and evening for eight days. Wash off the spices, lay in a flat earthen dish with suet in thin slices under and over, cover with a flour and water crust, and bake.

7. **Hams, to Boil.**—An English ham is worth a little trouble in boiling it properly. As usual, it is simply boiled, and nothing more. If fresh, it is not necessary to soak a ham more than one hour, just to remove dirt, &c. Let it be well washed and rubbed all over with vinegar and pepper, then washed again. Put one bottle country vinegar, half-bottle white wine, four carrots, six onions, some thyme, peppercorns, mace, and half-pound beef suet into enough warm water to cover the ham, boil for ten minutes, put the ham in it, and let it cool. Then boil about half-an-hour for each pound of ham, and let the whole get cold together. Hams are also excellent baked like Hunter's beef, with half-bottle wine added to the suet.

8. **Mango Chips.**—Peel any quantity of unripe mangoes, and cut them in rings after removing the stone. Thread them on strings, and hang to dry in the sun. They will keep like apple chips.

9. **Panade.**—Five units water, ½ unit butter, salt, pepper, onion-juice. Boil. Stir in 2 units flour until all is a thick smooth paste. May be made with milk.

10. **Paper Cases.**—Take an oblong sheet of paper (say half-a-sheet of notepaper), and fold exactly in three, as for an envelope. Turn the

top ply back to the outside edge, and fold exactly in two. Then the next ply to its outer edge. The paper will then consist of one broad central ply and two narrow ones. Double back, to have a division in the centre. Let the two upper narrow plies stand up in the centre, and fold in the corners of the broad ply, so as to touch the middle crease of the upper plies. The bits turned in will be exact triangles. Then fold the upper plies to match, and press quite flat. The paper will now be as it was before, but the ends will be pointed. Fold these two pointed ends in, so as to make the paper square or oblong. Then raise up the side-flaps, pinch the corners, and a neat little square box will be the result. They can be made any size, and used for anything.

11. **Vinegars.**—Vinegars are very useful for cooking, and may be made by steeping herbs, mint, &c., in vinegar for several days. The proportion is 3 units of leaves to 20 of vinegar. The following is excellent: In 30 units of vinegar steep for fourteen days 5 cloves, 2 cloves of garlick, 1 lime in slices (the thick-skinned kind), a small handful of thyme and savoury, also, if possible, tarragon, and 1 green chillie. Decant and bottle.

12. **Yeast.**—One handful hops gently stewed in 60 units water for two hours. Strain. When cool, stir in 4 units flour and 1 brown sugar. Fill bottles half full of the mixture. Cork, and tie down with string. Shake three times a day for two or three days, according to heat of weather. It should open with a pop, and foam. This has to be kept up in apostolic succession—a little of the old yeast added to the new decoction hastening fermentation. In cold weather this yeast remains good for ten days, but its goodness is easily gauged by the way it opens. One bottle of this yeast is amply sufficient for three pounds of flour, which should make a quartern loaf. It must be mixed over night in proportions of 1 unit of yeast, one of flour, 2 of lukewarm water, about ⅛ of brown sugar, and salt to taste, to a batter as thick as cream. Cover to keep out dust, and set in a warm place. Next morning it should be like a sponge. Add flour till it is too stiff to work with a spoon. Knead well, then put back to the

basin. Cover and keep warm. In about two hours it should have risen enough. Make into cottage loaves and bake.

EMPIRELAND

Sathnam Sanghera

Born in the West Midlands to Indian Punjabi parents, **Sathnam Sanghera** is an award-winning journalist and author, and columnist and features writer for *The Times*. *Empireland: How Imperialism Has Shaped Modern Britain* is his bestselling third book, an interrogation of Britain's imperial past and continuing present. Following its publication, Sanghera made *Empire State of Mind* for Channel 4, a programme which explores the impact of the British Empire on modern Britain.

I'm no fan of the British seaside. I don't need to work on my tan, I can barely swim, I grew up in the beach-free West Midlands and my heritage can be traced back in its entirety to the landlocked state of the Punjab. Frankly, the kindest thing I can bring myself to say about Brighton on this bitterly cold February afternoon is that if you close your eyes, the sea sounds a little like the M6 on a busy day – a sound which, having grown up near junction 10, I will always regard as comforting. And the only solace when I open them is that I'm not, at least, standing on the beachfront, shielding my fish and chips from marauding seagulls. Instead I'm somewhere marginally more cheerful: the graveyard at St Nicholas Church. It is located in one of the oldest parts of the city, its cornerstone dating from the Saxon period, the church being cited in the Domesday Book of 1086, though the grave I have come to lay flowers at is not as ancient, belonging to one Sake Dean Mahomed. He lived between 1759 and 1851 and is a figure so fascinating that I spent a significant chunk of time while writing this book wanting instead to turn it into a novel about him.

How was he remarkable? Well, for one thing he was, as the title of a biography by Michael Fisher conveys, 'The First Indian Author in English'. Centuries before V. S. Naipaul got cracking on *A House for*

Mr Biswas, before Salman Rushdie was put on to the English Literature Tripos at Cambridge University, Mahomed was, in the late eighteenth century at the age of thirty-four, taking out a series of adverts proposing to publish a book about his life called *Travels*, making personal visits to potential subscribers throughout southern Ireland and then publishing it from Cork. The book conveyed how Mahomed had been born into the politically turbulent city of Patna, where the English, French and Dutch each had a presence and families had to choose with whom they wanted to align themselves: the waning Mughal Emperor, their local Muslim community or one of the increasingly powerful European East India Companies. How, in 1769, while still a child, Mahomed plumped for working for the English Company's Bengal Army as a camp follower and then as a subaltern officer was taken under the wing of one Godfrey Baker, who became his patron and 'best friend'. How when he was discharged Baker persuaded him to accompany him back to Ireland, where Mahomed found himself, among other things, working for the Anglo-Irish elite as a manager – a rather nebulous position that was not quite a servant but equally not an independent gentleman.

Unfortunately, he was no Naipaul or Rushdie or Kureishi. Presented 'as a series of letters to a friend', a fashionable literary device at the time, *Travels* is not an easy read. The prose is laboured, full of allusions and rhetorical flourishes that illustrate his erudition but reveal little about what we actually want to know. So we don't learn enough about what must have been the profound emotional struggle of leaving his family to live on the other side of the world. About what exactly his intense 'friendship' with Baker involved. About how he felt when Baker was dishonourably discharged from the East India Company for embezzling funds. About what it felt like to become a sepoy at the age of just twelve. About what it felt like, as an Indian, to be employed to do the dirty work of the East India Company, coercing money from Indian villagers. About how it felt experiencing Europe, encountering poor white people for the first time in Cork, and about whether integration was difficult. Still, he got there first! As his biographer says, 'up to this point, no Indian had ever written and published a book in English, either in India or in

Britain,' and it surely counts for something that Mahomed managed to write and publish a book at a time when white supporters of slavery assumed that black people were unable to write for themselves: he was the Neil Armstrong of my field.

Another remarkable thing about the man: in 1786, more than a hundred years before the British were being cautioned against the 'sexual pollution' and racial degeneration that would come with relationships with Muslim men*, centuries before actors Joan Hooley and John White made history with one of the first interracial kisses on British television in a 1964 episode of the British soap opera *Emergency Ward 10*, even longer before I was making an almighty fuss in my memoir agonizing about defying my family's expectations to marry a good Sikh girl, Mahomed was just going ahead and doing it. In 1786, in his mid-twenties, the year his Anglo-Irish patron died, Mahomed eloped with the teenager Jane Daly. There is a high degree of uncertainty about what happened, but it seems he renounced his faith to do it, and while his biographer says that 'Jane's family does not seem to have supported the young couple – they lived in a world where a range of generally unflattering images of Indians and Muslims abounded,' the newlyweds appear to have been accepted by Cork society.

Jane was evidently an intrepid woman. In 1807, when Mahomed was approaching fifty, the pair left Ireland and moved to London with their children. They settled near fashionable Portman Square and Mahomed began work for a Scottish nobleman, Basil Cochrane. That brings us to another remarkable thing about Mahomed. In London, in 1809, he opened the first curry house in Britain. It was called the Hindostanee

---

* In *The Infidel Within: Muslims in Britain since 1800*, Humayun Ansari observes that sexual relations between Muslims and white women were taboo because they challenged notions of British racial superiority essential to maintain empire. 'Social distance was necessary to sustain the charisma of British character and its resulting prestige and authority in the minds of subjugated people, which familiarity would dissipate.' It was generally believed that Muslims lusted after white women, would lose control around them, and that white women were 'therefore in need of protection from them... At the turn of the twentieth century Indian students, who were coming to Britain in growing numbers, were described as "raw youths" who were "in no way fitted to encounter the temptations to which many of them succumb".'

Coffee House but, as Fisher explains, it didn't actually proffer coffee – it was instead an 'eating house' where Mahomed prepared 'a range of meat and vegetable dishes with Indian spices served with seasoned rice', which customers would consume while reclining on bamboo-cane sofas and chairs, under paintings of Indian landscapes. It was a unique offering in London at the time, aimed at the British who had come back from the subcontinent, and initially did so well that it expanded into a neighbouring house. Unfortunately, for ultimately unfathomable reasons, he headed into bankruptcy in 1812, but this failure gave rise to a final extraordinary chapter in this extraordinary man's life.

Not unlike certain prominent identity-shifting British Asian politicians, having spent the early years of his European residency trying to become as Western as possible, Mahomed realized his real value lay in emphasizing his Indian identity. So he moved to Brighton with his family and set up as a bathhouse keeper, flogging an Indian service dubbed 'shampooing' and which nowadays might be dubbed a kind of Turkish bath or thalassotherapy. A surprising development, perhaps, to the people who knew him best, because he had previously been dismissive about the practice in print, describing it as immoral and emasculating, but at the time Brighton was a fashionable seaside spa, with bathing machines transporting people down to the sea, and taking an 'Indian Medicated Vapour bath' seemed to fit into many people's idea of an outing. Mahomed threw himself into self-promotion, took out ads calling himself a 'Shampooing Surgeon', claimed the baths cured all ailments, 'giving full relief when everything fails; particularly Rheumatic and paralytic, gout, stiff joints, old sprains. . . aches and pains in the joints', and became a self-proclaimed expert, lying about his medical credentials, and writing a quasi-medical textbook. He had form when it came to this kind of bullshitting: he called himself everything from 'Deen' to 'Dean' to 'William Dean' and 'Sake [Sheikh] Dean Mahomed', he plagiarized a significant portion of the material in his book from other travel narratives, such as John Henry Grose's *Voyage to the East Indies*, he frequently edited his biography to suit him – claiming, for instance, that he went straight to London from India, omitting the twenty-five years he spent in Ireland, increasing his official age by up to a decade. And there were awkward mistakes, not least the member of his team who snapped a man's arm during a massage, resulting in it being amputated, and the elderly customer who died while having a shower on his premises. But at a time when George IV was building the orientally inspired Marine Pavilion as an expression of England's rapidly expanding Eastern empire, with India as its crown jewel, Mahomed's Indian baths were in tune with the zeitgeist. Both George IV and William IV partook of his vapour baths and Mahomed was awarded a Royal Warrant. He was delighted, put up pictures of royalty in his bathhouse in a gesture that would be echoed by curry-house owners of the future and was so successful that hospitals referred patients to him.

Unfortunately, Mahomed became less of a novelty over time, the death of a silent business partner created financial problems, he lost his premises to a rival and his last years were lived in relative obscurity, which maybe explains why his grave is difficult to locate in the rain and at dusk centuries later. I had imagined a sentimental scene, getting down on my knees at his grave and giving him the good news: that he had achieved more than the stiffs in the grand tombs nearby, and that his legacy is very much alive in the twenty-first century. But the gravestone is behind a locked wire fence and I end up throwing my bouquet of petrol-station flowers over it, which promptly blow back into my face, attracting the mockery of a nearby daytime drinker. Still, I manage to find a moment to reflect on Dean Mahomed's many achievements from a bench nearby. After all, this was a man who introduced curry houses to Britain (and thereby played a role in transforming our national cuisine), laid the literary ground for the likes of Naipaul and Rushdie (who in turn revolutionised English literature), helped popularize massage and the word 'shampoo', from the Hindu *champi* for 'massage', and was a pioneer in his personal life. But for me the most remarkable thing about him was simply that he was a brown man from the empire living and working in the British Isles hundreds of years ago, and he thereby demonstrates a simple and profound fact about Britain; it is a multicultural, racially diverse society because it once had a multicultural, racially diverse empire. Or as the Sri Lankan writer Ambalavaner Sivanandan once famously put it: 'we are here because you were there.'*

---

* A sentiment echoed by the historian David Olusoga who, in response to a racist remark, tweeted: 'If you don't want Nigerians in the UK all you need to do is go back to the 19th century and persuade the Victorians not to invade Nigeria.'

BRICK LANE

Monica Ali

Born in East Pakistan (now renamed Bangladesh), **Monica Ali** moved to Bolton with her family when she was three. Her debut *Brick Lane*, about a young Bangladeshi woman who moves to Tower Hamlets, is set on the eponymous street. She has since published four other novels, in addition to a number of essays and short stories. After a decade away from publishing, Ali published *Love Marriage* in 2022 to great acclaim. Ali lives in south London with her husband.

The Dr Azad question was troubling Chanu. The question was this: was it hostility or neglect that led the doctor not to return hospitality? Or it was this: was it a matter of numbers, so that one more dinner would ensure an invitation? Or possibly this: did it matter, did it make any difference at all, if the invitations continued to be one-sided? More and more frequently, it was this: what manner of snob was this Azad?

'He eats my food, he reads my books. God alone knows where else he finds any intellectual stimulation, any companion of the intellect. Shall I ask him when we will be going to his house? I can ask like this.' Chanu rubbed the back of his head, tipped his chair back and spoke with the suggestion of a yawn. 'So, Azad, what are you hiding at your house? Are we going to come around and find out?' He let his chair fall flat again.

Nazneen spooned apple into the baby's mouth. He grabbed at the spoon and sent it flying. He laughed, spraying her with gunk. She was astonished that she had made this creature, spun him out of her flesh. When she remembered that Chanu had made him too she was stunned.

'Maybe he never thinks of it,' Chanu continued. 'He just needs a little prod. Or it could be that he doesn't consider me part of his circle. A doctor is a cut above. But what is a doctor, really, when you think about it? He memorizes everything from books: broken legs, colds and viruses, eczema and asthma, rheumatism and arthritis, boils and warts. It's learning by rote. Symptom and cure. Hardly an intellectual pursuit. No. He's just a finger blown up to the size of a banana tree. Let him guard his house, and put some barbed wire around it too. I am not interested.'

Nazneen put the baby on the floor while she hunted for the spoon. Beneath the table, the files and papers had been breeding, intermarrying with balls of string, boxes of staples, rolls of labels, chains of clips. A pair of pants lay exhausted in a heap; a sock sat fossilized in dust. The spoon was nowhere to be seen. The baby crawled under the table with her and pulled her hair. His face this last month had turned from awed to quizzical. His features were not fully drawn, but they were more than sketched. When he looked at her now, he was always on the point of asking a question. Behind the question was a very big joke, and he looked as though he would let her in on it. 'Hello,' she told him, 'I'm looking for your spoon.'

'Maybe if I get the promotion,' Chanu went on, 'then he will be more inclined to extend his hospitality. That's probably the kind of man he is.'

Nazneen came up. She scooped the baby under one arm. She checked Chanu's face to see if he required any response from her. He was mulling over his words, scrunching them this way and that, into a wrinkled brow, a taut cheek. His eyes looked somewhere far off. She was not needed. She took the baby through to the kitchen and fetched another spoon. He spoke these days of 'if'. It used to be 'when'. When the promotion came through. And he never spoke about Wilkie, or his successor, Gerard, or Howard who came after him. He spoke more often of resigning.

It was Sunday morning. They would go out for a walk soon, around Brick Lane, and Chanu would push the pram and she would walk a step behind. When people stopped him in the street to admire Raqib, to give him a kiss or a tickle, Chanu would grow a couple of inches. If people did not stop him, he stopped them. 'See how alert he is. Notice the large size of his head. The bigger the head, the bigger the brain. You think I'm joking? Do you know how big dinosaurs' heads were? And do you wonder why they are extinct?' And the person would smile vaguely and walk away. At the shops, Chanu would buy vegetables. Pumpkin, gourd, spinach, okra, aubergine. Whatever was in season. He would buy spices and rice and lentils and sometimes sweetmeats: a tub of milky roshmolai, sticky brown gulabjam, golden whirls of jelabee. He would not haggle. He would not 'abase' himself, or 'act like a primitive'. He broke off bits of jelabee and fed them to Raqib, and licked his fingers where the liquid sugar spilled out.

TIPPING THE VELVET

Sarah Waters

Welsh-born **Sarah Waters** is the author of six historical novels. Her work foregrounds lesbians in parts of history where they have often been erased; she has said that there is a 'clear lesbian agenda… right there at the heart of the books'. Three of her novels have been shortlisted for the Man Booker Prize, and she has also won the Somerset Maugham Award and the *Sunday Times* Young Writer of the Year Award.

I believe I barely washed in all those weeks – and certainly I did not change my dress, for I had no other. Very early on I gave off wearing my false chignon, too, and let my hair straggle greasily about my ears. I smoked, endlessly – my fingers grew brown, from the nail to the knuckle; but I ate hardly at all. For all that I liked to watch the carcasses being towed about at Smithfield, the thought of meat upon my tongue made me nauseous, and I had stomach for none but the blandest of foods. Like a woman quickening with child I developed a curious appetite: I longed only for sweet, white bread. I gave Mary shilling after shilling, and sent her to Camden Town and Whitechapel, Limehouse and Soho, for bagels, brioches and flat Greek loaves, and buns from the Chinese bakeries. These I would eat dipped in mugs of tea, which I brewed, ferociously strong, in a pot on the hearth, and sweetened with condensed milk. It was the drink I had used to make for Kitty, in our first days together at the Canterbury Palace. The taste of it was like the taste of her; and a comfort, and a frightful torment, all at once.

THE JOY OF SNACKS

Laura Goodman

Laura Goodman ate mostly tagliatelle and yoghurt until she was seventeen. She is now a food writer with a much broader palate, as well as bylines at the *Sunday Times*, *Food52*, *Eater London*, *Lucky Peach* and *Grazia*. Her books, 2018's *Carbs* and 2022's *The Joy of Snacks* (reviewed as having 'real wisdom about how we actually eat') are celebrations of food, of fun, and of pure joy.

A schmear campaign

What are shop-bought bagels anyway? Are they a more shapely way to enjoy toast? Or are they a marketing ploy designed to sell bad bread by making us feel closer to glamorous New York City?

I grew up on real bagels from the Jewish deli – not in New York, but in suburban north-west London. Fancy London restaurants now tend to present their bagel platters as coming with a 'schmear', 'lox' and 'scallions' because they'd rather align themselves with the Big Apple and comedians and celebrity delis than with the epically grey and bollardy A41, but in Hendon, Edgware, Golders Green, you can find chewy, blistered rings that do not need to see a toaster until day three. (These are the same bakeries that supply the fancy restaurants, by the way.) And while you're there, you can pick up a babka, which you've heard about (a twisted, sweet chocolate loaf) and a bag of rugelach which you might not have (crescent-shaped chocolate pastries).

Growing up in a largely brunchless society, my family's Sunday ritual involved topping each bagel half with cream cheese and smoked salmon, or chopped liver, or egg and onion, and arranging them open-faced on big plates so everyone could take what they wanted, with a fish ball on the side.

Later, when my friends and I were very cool dudes who liked to arrive at nights out in the West End by car, my friend Joanna would drive her Ford KA to Carmelli's at 3 a.m. so we could get pre-filled, clingfilmed bagels for the road. And I've got to tell you: you cannot get close to the barefaced midnight joy of tearing at one of those be-salmoned beasts with your teeth via the supermarket baked-goods aisle.

I am thrilled to announce, though, that there is a use for your round, holey bread snacks: pizza bagels. These supermarket 'bagels' are profoundly lacking in so many ways: texture, flavour, authenticity, overall satisfaction, to name a few. But what I will say for them is this: they're bouncy. Which means they form a good base for lots of cheese and sauce (better than any pre-made pizza base I've ever tried), especially if you arrange things Sicilian-style (mozzarella *under* the sauce). Almost-instant pizza, what's not to like? It's two classic snacks in one.

You could top these further – with pepperoni, peppers, anchovies or black olives. But I think we've insulted the bagel enough.

Pizza bagels

makes 4
olive oil
2 cloves of garlic, crushed or minced
¼–½ teaspoon chilli flakes
1 x 400g tin of tomatoes
¾ teaspoon dried oregano
salt, pepper and sugar
2 bagels, halved
4 slices or about 90g mozzarella (the low-moisture stuff that comes pre-sliced)
20g pecorino, grated

1. Heat 2 tablespoons of olive oil in a wide frying pan and when it's hot, cook the garlic and chilli flakes for a minute or two
2. Add the chopped tomatoes and oregano to the pan. Stir well and

crush the tomatoes with the back of your spoon.

3. Season with salt and pepper, and add the sugar a pinch at a time if it's tasting a bit harsh.
4. Cook for about 12–14 minutes on a low heat until it's super-saucy.
5. Meanwhile, drizzle the bagel halves with olive oil and put them under a hot grill until they're lightly golden.
6. Lay one mozzarella slice across each bagel half.
7. Spoon the tomato sauce over the mozzarella.
8. Sprinkle the grated pecorino on top.
9. Grill until bubbly, brown and looking suspiciously like pizza.

THE AMAZING ADVENTURES OF KAVALIER & CLAY

Michael Chabon

Raised in Pittsburgh and Columbia on 'a hearty diet of [pop culture] crap', **Michael Chabon** is a novelist, screenwriter and columnist. Common threads and themes running through his novels include sexuality, fatherhood, home, nostalgia and Jewish identity. Pulitzer Prize-winning *The Amazing Adventures of Kavalier & Clay* tells the story of two Jewish cousins in Brooklyn who create a series of comic books in the early 1940s.

"Where is the actual flat bush?" Bacon said as they came up out of the subway. He stopped and looked across the avenue at the entrance to Prospect Park. "Do they keep it in there?"

"Actually, they move it around," said Sammy. They'd had two drinks apiece, but for some reason, Sammy didn't feel in the least intoxicated. He wondered if fear forestalled the effects of alcohol. He wondered if he were more afraid of Tracy Bacon or of showing up for dinner at Ethel's late, reeking of gin, and with the world's largest piece of trayf in tow. In the subway station, he had bought a roll of Sen-Sen and eaten four. "It's on wheels." He gave a pull on the sleeve of Bacon's blue blazer. "Come on, we're late."

"Are we?" Bacon arched an eyebrow. "You hadn't mentioned it."

"You don't even know me," said Sammy. "How can you presume to razz me?"

As he buzzed for 2-B—he had misplaced his key—he realized that he must be very, very drunk. It was the only possible explanation for what he was about to do. He wasn't sure exactly when the invitation had been extended, or at what point it became clear to Sammy that Bacon had accepted it. In the bar at the St. Regis, under the jovial gaze of Parrish's *King Cole*, their conversation had veered so quickly from Bacon's difficulties with the character of the Escapist that Sammy could not remember now what wisdom, if any, he had been able to offer on that score. Almost at once, it seemed, Bacon had launched, unprompted, into a recitation (one that, while practiced, obviously still held great interest for him) of his upbringing, education, and travels, an extravagant tale—he had lived in Texas, California, the Philippines, Puerto Rico, Hawaii, and, most recently, Seattle; his father was a brigadier general, his mother was a titled Englishwoman; he had sailed on a merchant ship; he had broken horses on Oahu; he had attended a boarding school where he played hockey and lacrosse and boxed a little—which, paradoxically, he himself claimed to view as sadly lacking in some fundamental underpinning of sense or purpose. All the while, Sammy's own upbringing and education and his travels from Pitkin Avenue to Surf Avenue, alerting him to the unmistakable smell of bullshit, had been at war with his native weakness for romance. As he sat and listened, with the ointment flavor of gin in his mouth, at once envious and unable to shake the echo of Bacon's blithe avowal—"I'm such an awful liar"—there seemed to emerge, in spite of Bacon's good looks and his actor pals and his cool gin-and-tonic of a girlfriend, and regardless of the truth or falsehood of the claims he was making, an unmistakable portrait that Sammy was surprised to find he recognized: Tracy Bacon was lonely. He lived in a hotel and ate his meals in restaurants. His actor pals took him and his tale at face value not because they were credulous, but because it was less effort to do so. And now, with an unerring instinct, he had sniffed out the loneliness in Sammy. Bacon's presence at Sammy's side now, waiting for an answer from 2-B, was testimony to this. It didn't occur to Sammy that Bacon was just drunk and twenty-one (not twenty-four) and making everything up as he went along.

"That is the most angry-sounding door buzz I've ever heard," Bacon said when it finally came.

Sammy held the lobby door for him. "That was actually the voice of my mother," he said. "There's a little wax cylinder in there."

"You're just trying to scare me," Bacon said.

They climbed the steps that had wearied Sammy's legs for so many years now. Sammy knocked. "Stand back," he said.

"Stop it now."

"Watch your fingers. Ma!"

"Look who it is."

"Don't look so excited."

"Where's your cousin?"

"They already had plans. Ma, I brought a friend. This is Mr. Tracy Bacon. He's going to be playing the Escapist. On the radio."

"Look out you don't bump your head" was the first thing Ethel said to Bacon. Then "My goodness." She smiled and held out her hand, and Sammy saw that she was impressed. Tracy Bacon made quite an impression. She stepped back to get a better look and stood there like one of the tourists Sammy waded through on his way in and out of work every day. "You're very good-looking." It just missed sounding like a wholehearted compliment; there might have been some comment intended on the deceptiveness of attractive packages.

"Thank you, Mrs. Clay," said Bacon.

Sammy winced.

"That isn't my name," Ethel said, but not unkindly. She looked at Sammy. "I never cared for that name. Well, come in, sit down, I made too much, oh well. Dinner was ready once already, and you missed the candles, I'm sorry to say, but we can't postpone sundown even for big-shot comic book writers."

"I heard they changed that rule," said Sammy.

"You smell like Sen-Sen."

"I had a little drink," he said.

"Oh, you had a drink. That's good."

"What? I can have a drink if I want."

"Of course you can have a drink. I have a bottle of slivovitz some-place. Would you like me to get it out? You can drink the whole bottle if you want."

Sammy whirled around and made a face at Bacon: What'd I tell you? They followed Ethel into the living room. The electric fan was going in the window but, in accordance with Ethel's personal theories of hygiene and thermodynamics, faced outward, so as to draw the warm air out of the room, leaving an entirely theoretical zone of coolness behind. Bubbie was already on her feet, a big confused grin on her face, her spectacles glinting. She was wearing a loose cotton dress printed with scarlet poppies.

"Mom," said Ethel, in English, "this is a friend of Sammy's. Mr. Bacon. He's an actor on the radio."

Bubbie nodded and grabbed hold of Bacon's hand. "Oh, yes, how are you?" she said in Yiddish. She seemed to recognize Tracy Bacon at once, which was odd, since she had not seemed to recognize anyone in years. It was never clear afterward who she thought Bacon was. She shook his hand vigorously with both of hers.

For some reason, the sight of Bubbie shaking Bacon's large pink hand made Ethel laugh. "Sit down, sit down," she said. "Ma, let go of him." She looked at Sammy. "Sit down." Sammy started to sit down. "What, I don't get a kiss from you anymore, Mr. Sam Clay?"

Sammy kissed his mother.

"Ma, you're hurting me! Ouch!"

She let go.

"I'd like to break your neck," she said. She seemed to be in a very good mood. "I'll get dinner on the table."

"Careful with the shovel."

"Funny."

"Is that how you talk to your mother?" said Bacon.

"Oh, I like your new friend," said Ethel. She took hold of his arm and gave his huge right biceps a pat. She looked supremely vindicated. The shock on Bacon's face appeared to be genuine. "This young man loves his mother."

"Boy, do I," said Bacon. "Can I help you in the kitchen, Mrs., uh—"

"It's Klayman. K-L-A-Y-M-A-N. Period."

"Mrs. Klayman. I have a lot of experience peeling potatoes, or whatever you might need me to do."

Now it was Ethel's turn to look shocked.

"Oh … no, it's already fixed. I'm just reheating everything again."

Sammy wanted to point out that reheating everything several times in order to remove as much flavor as possible was an integral part of Ethel's culinary technique, but he held his tongue. Bacon had embarrassed him.

"You wouldn't fit in my kitchen," Ethel said. "Sit down."

Bacon followed her into the kitchen. Sammy had yet to see his "new friend" take no for an answer. In spite of his height and his swimmer's shoulders, it was not a confidence in his own abilities that seemed to direct Tracy Bacon so much as an assuredness of being welcome wherever he went. He was golden and beautiful, and he knew how to peel a potato. To Sammy's surprise, Ethel let Bacon follow.

"I can never reach that bowl up there," he heard her say. "The one with the toucan."

"So, Bubbie," Sammy said. "How are you?"

"Fine, darling," she said. "I'm fine. How are you?"

"Come sit down." He tried to steer her into the other yellow chair. She pushed him away.

"Go. I want to stand. All day I'm sit."

From the kitchen Sammy could hear—could hardly miss—the cheerful thumping of Bacon's voice, with its lyric upper register. Like Sammy's, the constant barrage of chatter Bacon maintained seemed designed to impress and to charm, with a key difference: Bacon was impressive and charming. Ethel's burned-sugar laugh came drifting out of the kitchen. Sammy tried to hear what Bacon was saying to her.

"So what did you do today, Bubbie?" he said, flopping on the couch. "Belmont's open. Did you go out to the track?"

"Yes, yes," Bubbie said agreeably. "I went to the races."

"Did you win any money?"

"Oh, yes."

You were never sure with Bubbie whether you were really teasing her or not.

"Josef sends you a kiss," he said in Yiddish.

"I'm glad," Bubbie said in English. "And how is Samuel?"

"Samuel? Oh, he's fine," Sammy said.

"She kicked me out." Bacon emerged from the kitchen wearing a little dishwashing apron patterned with pale blue soap bubbles. "I guess I was getting in the way."

"Oh, you don't want to do that," Sammy said. "I got in the way of a dinner roll once and required nine stitches."

"Funny," said Ethel, stepping into the living room. She untied her apron and threw it at Sammy. "Come and eat."

Dinner was a fur muff, a dozen clothespins, and some old dish towels boiled up with carrots. The fact that the meal was served with a bottle of prepared horseradish enabled Sammy to conclude that it was intended to pass for braised short ribs of beef—flanken. Many of Ethel's specialties arrived thus encoded by condiments. Tracy Bacon took three helpings. He cleaned his plate with a piece of challah. His cheeks were rosy with the intensity of his pleasure in the meal. It was either that or the horseradish.

"Whew!" he said, laying down his napkin at last. "Mrs. K., I never had better in my life."

"Yes, but better what?" Sammy said.

"Did you get enough to eat?" Ethel said. She looked pleased but, it seemed to Sammy, a little taken aback.

"Did you save room for my babka?" Bubbie said.

"I *always* save room for dessert, Mrs. Kavalier," Bacon said. He turned to Sammy. "Is babka dessert?"

"An eternal question among my people," Sammy said. "There are some who argue that it's actually a kind of very small hassock."

Ethel got up to make coffee. Bacon stood up and started to clear away the dishes.

"Enough already," Sammy said, pushing him back down into his chair. "You're making me look very bad here." He gathered up the dirty plates and utensils and carried them into the tiny kitchen.

"Don't stack them," his mother said by way of thanks. "It gets the bottoms dirty."

"I'm just trying to be helpful."

"Your kind of help is worse than no help." She set the percolator on the ring and turned on the gas. "Stand back," she said, striking a match. She must have been lighting gas stoves for thirty years, but each time it was as if entering a burning building. She ran water in the sink and slid the dishes in. Steam rose from the bubbles of Lux; the dishwater must of course be antibacterially hot. "He looks just like Josef draws him," she said.

"Doesn't he, though."

"Is everything all right with your cousin?"

Sammy guessed that her feelings were hurt. "He really wanted to come, Ma," he said. "But it was short notice, you know?"

"It doesn't make any difference to me."

"I'm just saying."

"Is there news? What does the man at the agency say?"

"Hoffman says the kids are still in Portugal."

"With the nuns." As a girl, during the first war, Ethel had been sheltered briefly by Orthodox nuns. They had treated her with a kindness that she had never forgotten, and Sammy knew that she would have preferred her little nephew to remain with these Portuguese Carmelites, in the relative safety of a Lisbon orphanage, rather than to set off across a submarine-haunted ocean in a third-hand steamer with a rickety name. But the nuns were apparently under pressure from the Catholic Church in Portugal not to make harboring Jewish children from Central Europe a permanent thing.

"The boat is on its way over there now," Sammy said. "To get them. It got itself into one of these convoy things, you know, with five U.S. Navy destroyers. Thomas ought to be here in a month, Joe said."

"A month. Here." His mother handed him a dishtowel and a dish. "Dry."

"Yeah, so Joe's happy about that. He seems happy with Rosa, too. He's not working those crazy hours like he used to anymore. We're making enough money now that I was able to talk him into dropping all the books he was working on but three. I had to hire *five* guys to replace him."

"I'm glad he's settling down. He was getting wild before. Fighting. Getting hurt on purpose."

"The thing is, I think he likes it here," Sammy said. "I wouldn't be surprised if he decided to stay, even after the war's over."

"*Kayn ayn hora*," his mother said. "Let's hope he has a choice."

"That's a cheerful thought."

"I don't know this girl very well. But she seemed …" She hesitated, unwilling to go so far as to bestow actual praise on Rosa. "I got the feeling she has a good head on her shoulders." The previous month, Joe and Rosa had taken Ethel to see *Here Comes Mr. Jordan*; Ethel was partial to Robert Montgomery. "He could do much worse."

"Yeah," Sammy said. "Rosa's all right."

Then, for a minute, he just dried the dishes and forks she passed to him and set them, under his mother's scrutiny, in the rack. There was no sound but the squeak of the dishtowel, the chiming of the dishes, and the steady trickling of hot water into the sink. Bacon and Bubbie seemed, in the dining room, to have run out of things to say to each other. It was one of those prolonged silences that meant, Ethel always used to say, that somewhere an idiot had just been born.

"*I'd* like to meet someone, you know," Sammy said at last. "I mean, I've been thinking. Just recently. Meet someone nice."

His mother shut off the tap and pulled the stopper from the drain. Her hands were bright red from the scalding water.

"I'd like that, too," she said. She opened another drawer and took out the box of waxed paper. She tore off a piece, spread it on the zinc counter, and took a dish from the rack.

"So how was he?" she asked him, setting the dish upside down on the sheet of waxed paper.

"Who's that?"

She nodded toward the dining room. "That one." She folded the ends of the sheet of paper up over the dish and smoothed them down. "At the rehearsal today."

"He was all right," Sammy said. "He was good. Yeah, I think he'll do fine."

"Will he?" she said, and, lifting the wrapped dish, she looked him in the eye for the first time all evening.

Though it would recur often enough in his memory in later years, he would never know exactly what she had meant by that look.

DISOBEDIENCE

Naomi Alderman

'I went into the novel religious,' **Naomi Alderman** said, of her debut *Disobedience*, 'and by the end I wasn't.' Most famous for her bestselling fourth novel *The Power*, Alderman is a multi-talented, multi-disciplinary writer. Her work, however disparate it may seem, is threaded together with themes of faith, freedom, duty and agency: what we believe, what we know, who we are and what choice we have over all of those things. Born in London in 1974 to working-class 'unorthodox Orthodox Jews', she draws most directly on her childhood in *Disobedience*, from which the excerpt below is taken. Food is a central strand of *Disobedience*, just as (per Alderman) it binds together the North London Orthodox Jewish community. Food – the ritual around food, the religious and gendered expectations around what can (must? may?) be cooked by whom and when and for what – holds together not only those living, but those long dead. These are the things we do, and it is both privilege and prison to be the person granted permission to do them, and to be the person who has to do them. And Alderman holds all this so lightly that the food also seems delicious.

And it was evening, and it was morning, the sixth day. And when the sun set, it was Sabbath. I almost missed it completely. Dovid had to come round to my father's house to find me. I was in a happy frenzy of black rubbish bags and orderly piles slowly progressing across the room. Despite Hinda Rochel's reminder, I had forgotten, as the hours went past, the significance of sunset.

At the door, Dovid tapped his watch, smiled, pointed at the sun low on the horizon.

'It's time,' he said, and I found I knew what he meant, and I didn't resent it in the least. He looked different, somehow. I was reminded of that game we used to play as children, where he would pretend that different people were also different colours. I almost had the urge to ask him what colour I was. As we walked home, he told me what he'd done and I found I didn't resent that either. In fact, it barely surprised me. It seemed like something that had been waiting to be done. Something to do with rusted locks and wax-sealed caskets. Home again, home again, jiggety-jog, and here were the Hartogs, just waiting to be startled. I relaxed into the sensation again; this was the person I could be here, the glamorous, unexpected guest, a bewildering presence.

I considered the Hartogs as I changed my clothes for Shabbat. I'd never liked them, even when I was quite small – he smelled funny and she wore real fur coats that made me sneeze. As I grew up, and saw what influence they had in the community, that dislike mellowed into full-grown loathing. They're wealthy. That's not a crime, of course. But in the hot-house of humanity that is the north-west London Orthodox Jewish world, money can mean power. It can mean deciding the curriculum of a school, or choosing the Rabbi of a congregation, supporting one grocery shop by allowing it to undercut another, which goes broke. It can mean giving money only to education programmes which, though they don't say so in the glossy brochures, do not allow women to study Gemarah. It can mean funding people, like that guy on the street in New York, who hand out leaflets and persuade. All this, and more, Hartog had done.

For Mrs Hartog – Fruma – I had a particular loathing, not so much institutional as personal. There was a period of my life when I used to spend every Sunday at their house. My father would be judging cases at the Beth Din until the evening, the housekeeper had her day off and I would go to their house, to sit amid their opulence and do my homework. Fruma gave me lunch. She did not make good lunches, that wasn't her thing: dry bread from the fridge and slices of cheese were about her limit. She wore clickety-click high heels all round the house, even when she was preparing food, and she was always telling me whether or not I looked pretty. Mostly not.

What I hated most of all, though, was the way she'd talk about my mother. As, for example: 'Ronit, your mother wouldn't have liked you to eat like that' or 'Ronit, your mother wouldn't have wanted you to shout so loudly.' Even then, I didn't believe what she said, and even then I didn't feel guilty about it.

So, dinner with the Hartogs as an uninvited, unexpected guest. I chose a tight blue skirt with a long slit up one side and felt positively gleeful.

Sabbath, at Esti and Dovid's house, came in a welter of tiny, forgotten details, and sudden dashes to make sure that the hob was turned off, or the oven turned on, the urn plugged in, the hotplate properly ordered. I didn't participate; Esti and Dovid made it happen around me, reminding me strangely of children playing at being adults while their parents are away. I was oddly charmed by the experience; it had been so long since I'd last seen anyone participate in this peculiar form of obsessive-compulsive disorder. Everything, everything must be ready before the Sabbath, nothing must be left undone. Esti had set up a pair of candles for me to light, next to her own. She offered me the matchbox shyly, looking down as she did so, and I thought, what the hell, and lit them. I thought of my mother's silver candlesticks, of the leaves and branches of them and the shining reflective surfaces. And I did feel it, a little bit. That feeling from long ago: Sabbath peace.

*

We walked to Hartog's house. I remembered which one it was perfectly: large, set well back from the pavement behind a screen of trees, on a street of large houses. Everything about it was a little too big: the doors much taller than could be needed to accommodate anyone, the plant urns at each side of the doors oversized, the lion's-head door knocker twice the size of a fist.

I wondered what Hartog was trying to compensate for, which meant that I still had a smirk on my face when he came to the door, smiling, bustling, because she was still in the kitchen. He was wearing a dark suit with waistcoat, expensively tailored to hide the bulge over his waistband, a dark kippa, not quite concealing the increasing bald spot that was creeping out from under it. He smelled of a little too much very good-quality aftershave.

Amazingly, he didn't seem to recognize me at first. He looked me hard in the face for a moment, as though he knew he ought to know me. Or perhaps to confirm his first, awful, impression, that I was indeed a woman, and not some distinguished Rabbi. He said, 'Good Shabbes, Dovid, Rebbetzin Kuperman.'

Dr Feingold would probably say it was denial; shielding his mind from unpleasant truths.

So, I stuck out my hand and said, 'Dr Hartog. Maybe you don't remember me. I'm Ronit, the Rav's daughter?'

As though we'd met at a cocktail party once. My God. I think if I'd gone through it all, the whole of the last thirty-two years, just to experience that moment, it would have been worth it. The man jumped. He literally jumped, as though a charge had passed from my hand to his. I could almost hear a fizzing and popping in the air, could almost smell singed hair. His face turned a strange kind of yellow. He opened and closed his mouth a couple of times, his shaggy eyebrows moving as if they were trying to crawl off his forehead.

He said, 'Ron ah, Ron ah, Miss ah, Miss Krushka. I don't, I don't, I didn't, I mean I wasn't, I mean, Dovid didn't, I mean ...'

And he stopped. He looked at me, he looked at Dovid. And I swear, I swear, there was no sound from the kitchen, but he suddenly said, 'Coming, dear!'

And left us standing on the doorstep.

There was a very quiet moment. The three of us wandered into the vast arched space of the entrance hall and stood, our coats still on. We could hear some muffled conversation coming from the kitchen.

Dovid was looking guilty as hell.

Esti whispered, 'Do you think we should go?'

And I said, 'I think we're just getting started, don't you?'

And we were all smiling: these great, wide, shining smiles. We took off our coats, leaving them on one of the velvet-covered benches next to a green marble side table, walked across the hall towards the main lounge, sat down and waited. The place was just as I remembered it. The room was red: the carpet burgundy, the wallpaper scarlet with a repeated pattern in gold, the curtains dark crimson. I hadn't remembered the opulence, though, on the grandest, least tasteful scale. The huge mirrors on either side of a marble fireplace, decorated with gold curlicues, the vast crystal urns on the mantelpiece and the window sills, the Versailles-style oil paintings, covering almost every spare inch of wall space – all of fruit and flowers of course rather than naked women, but nonetheless the style implied that Mrs Hartog rather fancied herself a Marie Antoinette.

I sat back in one of the patterned-velvet armchairs, put my feet up on the coffee table and waited.

Eventually, Hartog and Fruma emerged from the kitchen to join us. Evidently they hadn't run screaming into the night, then. Hartog was smiling his what-big-teeth-I've-got smile, and Fruma had on a smaller, tighter-lipped version.

She said, 'Ronit, how wonderful to see you again. We thought we never would.'

Hoped you never would, I thought. I raised an eyebrow.

Hartog chimed in, 'Yes, it's a real mechaya to see you, Ronit. And a surprise.'

They started a duet, each finishing the other's sentence.

'Dovid never mentioned you were back in London ...'

'No, you never said, Dovid. We haven't heard anything from you ... '

'And it's been so long, although of course we understand ... '

'At a time like this you'd want to be home. With family ... '

'And old friends. Which is good.'

'Yes, it's wonderful, only we didn't know.'

'Although of course we wouldn't have minded if we had known.'

'But you see, we've got some people coming.'

'We invited them before we knew ... '

'We thought Dovid might like to see them.'

'Seeing as they knew your father so well.'

'Dayan and Rebbetzin Goldfarb.'

Fruma stopped, at that, but Hartog's voice was left, lonely and small. I almost felt sorry for the man. He said, 'And there won't be any trouble, will there?'

I said, 'Trouble, Hartog, what on earth do you mean?'

There was a long pause, before Fruma smiled nervously and offered us drinks. Far away, I thought I could scent blood on the air. Or perhaps it was that rusty-iron smell of a key turning in an old lock.

The anxious waiting was positively delicious. Hartog lapsed into an uncharacteristic silence, while Fruma became ever more twittery and indecisive, roaming restlessly between hall, kitchen and reception room. When the sound of knocking at the door finally came, they both leapt to answer it. We heard a whispered conversation in the hall, a protest from Hartog, a strangled yelp from Fruma.

I muttered to Dovid, 'Do you see what's going on here?'

He frowned and shook his head.

'Succession, Dovid. Succession.'

Esti and Dovid exchanged a glance.

Dovid said, 'We don't think so. We talked about it this morning. I'm not eminent enough.'

I rolled my eyes. 'Look at what's happening here. Do you think it's a coincidence you were invited with the Goldfarbs?'

Dovid looked blank.

'Dayan Goldfarb was a good friend of your father. He supported the shul.'

I sighed.

'Dovid, Dayan Goldfarb is one of the most influential Rabbis in Britain and that's the reason he's here tonight. If Hartog wants you to become Rav, Dayan Goldfarb would be a perfect person to support you. With him behind you, the transfer of power would be smooth; no one would argue with the Dayan's backing. Just you wait and see. By the end of the evening Hartog will have impressed on him what a learned young man you are, how you've been too modest to step forward until now, what trust the community puts in you.'

Dovid blinked. The door swung open and the Goldfarbs entered the room.

*

I was right. Naturally. Over dinner, Hartog attempted on several occasions to swing the conversation round to Dovid's achievements and merits. But, of course, Dayan and Rebbetzin Goldfarb were far more interested in hearing about what *I'd* been up to for the past few years. It wasn't anyone's fault really. It was only to be expected: the Goldfarbs hadn't seen me for seven or eight years, weren't the kind of people to listen to malicious gossip, really were genuinely interested to find out about me, to listen to my little stories of New York life.

Fruma served her five courses with increasing irritation. They'd evidently had someone in to cook for them, the food was much too good for Fruma's mean-spirited catering. The gefilte fish arrived, each creamy disc crowned with a circle of carrot, as Dayan Goldfarb asked my opinion of Stern College, where I'd taken my undergraduate degree. The gefilte fish plates departed and the golden chicken soup arrived. We spoke about work prospects in the city; the Goldfarbs had a nephew working in the financial district. The soup bowls were gathered and two roast chickens were presented, dripping clear fat on to the roast potatoes beneath, accompanied by their vegetable entourage. Rebbetzin Goldfarb named and assessed her eight children and thirty-seven grandchildren, now living in London, Manchester, Leeds, Gateshead, New York, Chicago, Toronto, Jerusalem, Bnei Brak, Antwerp, Strasbourg and two, she gasped, in Melbourne. Imagine. The plates were cleared and the desserts placed in the centre: orange cake with oranges in thick, alcoholic syrup in the centre, circular meringues topped with strawberries. Hartog tried in vain to talk about Dovid's future; the Goldfarbs asked about my career prospects. We ate the cake. Rebbetzin Goldfarb took tiny bites and made appreciative noises. She said, 'This is *wonderful*, Fruma. *Wonderful*. You must give me the recipe.'

Fruma's mouth drooped.

'Yes,' she said. 'Yes, but not on Shabbes of course.'

She was sallow. I smirked. I wanted to lean over and whisper, 'You didn't make this at all, did you, Fruma?' but Rebbetzin Goldfarb was already posing another question, so sweetly it felt impossible not to respond.

She said, 'So, Ronit, any young men in your life?'

She asked with that tender smile on her face, the one that older people always use when they want to let you know it's time to get married.

Now here's a thing. I wanted to tell her what she wanted to hear. I really did. At that moment, after such a pleasant evening's conversation, I wanted to be able to say, oh yes, a doctor. Is he Jewish? Why, certainly. We're getting married next year. We'll live in Manhattan. I could see how delightfully the conversation would proceed from that point, how we'd talk about wedding plans and about the future. I found myself longing for that conversation with all my heart.

I wanted to say that, and I saw myself wanting it and I hated the part of myself that wanted that to be true. I heard a screaming creak from far away and I found myself thinking of a lock and an old rusted key resting heavy in my palm. This is all the explanation I can offer because, honestly, which of us really understands why we do the things we do?

I said, 'Actually, Rebbetzin Goldfarb, I'm a lesbian. I live with my partner in New York. Her name is Miriam. She's an architect.'

It's not true. It's never been true. There was a Miriam, a long time ago, but we never lived together. And the architect was another woman entirely. And, let's face it, currently I'm sleeping with a married man, so I could have said *that* and shocked them just as much. Or maybe not.

I looked at Fruma. Her skin had a greyish cast. She was staring, not at me but at the Goldfarbs, unblinking and terrified. Onwards, I thought. Onwards and through is the only way.

'Yes, we're having a commitment ceremony next year. And then we're talking about kids, maybe a sperm bank but a gay couple we know say they might want to be fathers, but you know how it is.' I leaned forward, conspiratorial. I noticed that no one else leaned with me. 'They say they want children, but they still want to be out every night. Still, four incomes are better than two and it'd save a lot of paperwork.' I smiled, as though I were telling an amusing anecdote at a friend's party. 'After all, the turkey baster only gets used at Thanksgiving anyway, right?'

I folded my hands in my lap and sat back to survey the damage. The Hartogs were the best. Very satisfying to observe. Her mouth was hanging open and she was looking from Dayan Goldfarb to the

Rebbetzin and back, glassily fish-eyed. He was staring down at the table, fingers at his temples, shaking his head slowly from side to side.

Dovid was smiling. He was looking up at the ceiling, with his hand half covering his mouth, silently smirking. Sitting next to me, Esti looked as though she might start crying, which made me want to shout at her, because for God's sake did she expect me *not* to say what she already knew? Or did she expect to have been the only one for me, that I should have been as paralysed as she's obviously been all these years?

And the Goldfarbs. I should have known. I could have known, but I didn't think of how they'd feel. Or maybe I did but I didn't care. Just a moment before I did care very much indeed. Dayan Goldfarb was looking at his hands, quiet, impassive. His lips were moving, but there was no sound. And the Rebbetzin. She wasn't looking away, or trying to gauge someone else's reaction. She was just looking at me, full of sadness.

I thought I had come to all sorts of decisions about what I believe. That it is better for things to be said than remain unsaid. That I have nothing to be ashamed about. That those who live narrow lives have only themselves to blame when they find themselves shocked. As it turns out, I don't seem to have got what Scott would call 'total buy-in' from all levels of my brain on those principles. I thought I should phone Dr Feingold, just to let her know that nothing had been resolved even after all this time.

Because I did feel it. Shame. They're not bad people. None of them are. Well, maybe the Hartogs. But the Goldfarbs aren't bad people. They're not cruel or unpleasant or malicious. They didn't deserve to have their peaceful Friday night dinner overturned. They didn't deserve me smashing my life straight into theirs. It can't have been right that I did. And if I hadn't? Yeah, that wouldn't have been right either.

THE BOOK OF JEWISH FOOD

Claudia Roden

Egypt-born British cookery writer **Claudia Roden** is often credited (by Melissa Clark, and Yotam Ottolenghi) with introducing the food of Egypt and the Middle East to Britain and the US. In addition to publishing books across seven decades, she has hosted cooking programmes for the BBC and is the President of the Oxford Symposium on Food and Cookery. *The Book of Jewish Food*, her internationally acclaimed sixteen-years-in-the-making classic, includes 800 recipes and explores the diversity of Jewish food throughout the world.

Every cuisine tells a story. Jewish food tells the story of an uprooted, migrating people and their vanished worlds. It lives in people's minds and has been kept alive because of what it evokes and represents. My own world disappeared forty years ago, but it has remained powerful in my imagination. When you are cut off from your past, that past takes a stronger hold on your emotions. I was born in Zamalek, a district of Cairo with palm trees, pretty villas and gardens with bougainvillaea, scented jasmine and brilliant red flowers we called 'flamboyants'. On the map it looks like a cocoon clinging to the banks of the Nile. For the first fifteen years of my life, it was the cocoon from which I never ventured unaccompanied. I lived in an apartment building with my parents; two brothers, Ellis and Zaki; and our Yugoslav-Italian nanny, Maria Karon. Awad, the cook, who came from Lower Egypt, lived on the roof terrace, where servants had rooms. From the windows we could see the Nile and feluccas (sailing boats) gliding by. The sounds were the muezzin's call and the shouts of street vendors. It was a world full of people. It ended in 1956, after Suez, as a result of Egypt's war with Israel.

My father died in 1993 at the age of ninety-four, a few months after my mother. They had spent the last years holding hands, switching from one radio station to another listening to the latest world events, and talking passionately about their life in Egypt. They lived near me in London, and I was the audience for their constant dramatized re-enactments of the stories of all the people they had known. These stories were capable of endless change as new interpretations were explored. At 16 Woodstock Road, it seemed that we had never left Cairo.

The smell of sizzling garlic and crushed coriander seeds in the kitchen, or of rose water in a pudding, and my mother's daily meals, reinforced the feeling.

When I look through the old notes and recipes given by relatives and friends soon after they left Egypt, it rekindles memories of our old life in a vivid way. They are written in French and interspersed with remarks about who gave the recipe long ago in Egypt, how much the dishes were appreciated by a certain person, and the occasion on which they were served. Each recipe has a name. There is 'kobeba Latifa', 'fromage blanc Adèle', 'hamud Sophie', 'pasteles Iris', 'blehat Rahel', and so on. Most of the people are dead now. They were my parents' generation. But their recipes keep their memory very much alive, at least for me.

Our Cairo had been two cities that turned their backs on each other. One looked like Paris, because Khedive Ismail, who ruled in the middle of the nineteenth century, had wanted to pull Egypt into Europe and had brought in European architects to build it. The other had narrow meandering streets, mausoleums, and public baths; fountains with curvy iron grilles and windows screened by wooden lattices; Coptic churches and mosques with minarets rising into the sky like delicately embroidered candles. But our cooking was also from other cities. We made Istanbul pies, Aleppo cracked wheat salads, Castilian almond and orange cakes, egg flans from Fez.

The Egypt I knew was a French-speaking, cosmopolitan Mediterranean country in which life for the better-off was a sort of continuation of the Belle Époque in an annexe of Europe, with colonial-style clubs, opera and ballet and entertaining on a grand scale. Egypt had been part of the Ottoman Empire and a British protectorate. It was led by a foreign (Albanian) dynasty, a court made up of exiles from the Turkish aristocracy, and a royal council that spoke limited Arabic. The Jewish community had a happy and important place in the mosaic of minorities – which included Copts, Armenians, Syrian Christians, Maltese, Greeks and Italians, as well as British and French expatriates – living among the Muslim majority.

Established mainly in Cairo and Alexandria but also in a number of small towns and villages, the Jewish community was itself a mosaic of people of different origins. The original community, which was as old as antiquity, had been joined by several waves of immigrants, and these had all kept up their different cultures and identities into the twentieth century. We gave ourselves the fictional name of 'Basramite' to characterize our mixed backgrounds (no one knows where it came from). There were the Arabized inhabitants of the Haret el Yahoud – the Jewish quarter of Cairo, which we called the *hara* or simply *le quartier*, and which was built as early as 389 – and of the equally ancient Souk el Samak (fish market) in Alexandria. Descendants of Jews from the Iberian Peninsula came in the sixteenth century and then again in the nineteenth from Salonika, Smyrna, Istanbul, the Balkans, and North Africa. They were called Espagnoli and Kekeres, the latter because of the way they asked 'Qué quieres?' ('What do you want?'). Immigrants from Yemen and North Africa started coming in the Middle Ages. There were a few Ashkenazim. They were called Schlecht, meaning 'bad' in Yiddish. They claimed this was the local deformation of the word 'select', but nineteenth-century accounts reveal that they were so labelled because when they first arrived as escapees from pogroms in Russia and Eastern Europe they exclaimed in horror upon seeing the *hara*: 'Schlecht! Schlecht!' There were Italians who followed the old 'Italki' rites, and Italians from Livorno, who followed Spanish rites, and people from Iraq and Syria. My own family was from Syria and from Turkey.

The community was polyglot. Our main language was French. We spoke it with an unorthodox grammar and special intonations, infected by all the jargons of the Levant and reinforced by gesticulations and facial expressions. We used many Italian words, such as *falso* and *avvocato*. We called our grandparents *nono* and *nona*, rag and bones was *roba vecchia* (old things), *taglio bianco* (white cut) was veal. We were great talkers, switching from one language to another. Every gathering was a fight to be heard. People shouted across the room and across conversations. Strangers thought we were quarrelling. It was a closely knit community, and it felt as though we were all related. Our families were large and extended – almost tribal clans.

My two grandfathers, Elie Douek and Isaac Sassoon, had come from Aleppo at the end of the nineteenth century. My great-grandfather Haham Abraham ha Cohen Douek was the chief rabbi of that city when it was part of the Ottoman Empire. His portrait in turban and kaftan wearing medals given to him – 'personally', my father said – by the Sultan Abdul Hamid II, still hangs in the synagogue in Aleppo. The same photograph looks down at me from my study wall, as it does from the walls of many of my relatives around the world. My family in Egypt always kept the key of the synagogue. When my great-uncle Jacques went to Aleppo on his honeymoon in the 1930s, he was able to open the door with it. His widow, Régine, who now lives near the Champs-Élysées, had thought Aleppo a bit of a disappointment after his build-up. She managed to get for Jacques a place in the Jewish cemetery of Versailles – a rare privilege, because it is full – and a red-carpet funeral treatment, by telling the Paris rabbis that he was the son of Haham Abraham.

Both my grandfathers left when Aleppo ceased to be the centre of the camel-caravan trade because of the opening of the Suez Canal, and when the canal and the development of the cotton trade had turned Egypt into an 'El Dorado of the Nile Valley'. Both went to live in a newly built quarter of Cairo called Sakakini, in the Daher, where everyone was Jewish (my father insisted that I must distinguish it from the *hara*, where only the very poor were left by the time his family arrived). It was built on drained marshland by Sakakini Pasha. The streets converged like the spokes of a wheel towards a baroque rococo palace with turrets and carved angels where the Sakakini family lived. There were several synagogues, Jewish schools, ritual baths and kosher butchers. When I asked my father what their everyday life had been like, he said, 'We spent our time on the balcony talking to passers-by. The men went to work, the women prepared the meals.'

Their cooking was Aleppan. It was considered the pearl of the Arab kitchen – refined and delicate. It was labour-intensive, with a lot of pounding, hollowing, stuffing, wrapping and rolling into tiny balls and fingers. The women prided themselves on their skills and – so my father said – were happy to spend hours in the kitchen. They cooked in company, and that was part of the fun. They filled chickens with meat and pine nuts, stuffed lamb with rice, rolled vine leaves and filled pastries with mashed dates. Their crowning glory was kibbeh, which was a world in itself, with dozens of varieties. Basically, it had an outer shell of pounded wheat and meat and a spicy meat and onion filling. The apartment resounded constantly with the ringing of the metal pestle and mortar with which they pounded the meat and wheat. It smelled of mint and spices and sizzling lamb, of tamarind and orange blossom.

My grandmother Sarah Hara did not read or write, although everyone from her large extended family sought her advice on every matter. She said the rabbis in Aleppo had forbidden her to learn because she was a girl. It had something to do with girls becoming free and able to send notes to lovers. She had married a man much older than herself and was left a widow with many daughters to marry off. She wore a long brown dress called a *habara*. With a little envy, she mocked the new generation's Frenchified ways.

My maternal grandmother, Eugénie Alphandary, was from Istanbul. She was a grande dame who spoke French like a Parisian, quoted Voltaire and Victor Hugo and was fired by the ideals of 'Liberté, Égalité, Fraternité'. The private language she spoke with my mother when they did not want us children to understand was Judea-Spanish. She called it Castilian to differentiate it from the Judea-Spanish that she described as a 'degraded Spanish mix' which some other people spoke. Hers was below French in her esteem, but to us it represented a mysterious lost paradise, a world of romance and courage and glorious chivalry which enmeshed us all in invisible threads of deep longing with its songs about lovers in Seville and proverbs about meat stews and almond cakes. That world was embodied by the little pies, sharp egg and lemon sauces, and meatballs incorporating vegetables that we ate at my grandparents' home. Her cold vegetable dishes had a faint sweetness about them, the pastries an orange flavour. When we bit into a pie, we found mashed aubergine or spinach. Everything had a Spanish name, and many things had an affectionate ending, like 'pasteliko' and 'borekita,' which denoted that they were small.

The friends and relatives my grandmother entertained had names like Sol, Grazia and Elvira, and family names like Pérez y Calderón, Santos, Abravanel, Rodrigues and Toledano. But she had called her children Yvette, Marcelle, Nelly, Germaine, Giselle and Joseph. Her father was a teacher at the Alliance Israélite Universelle in Istanbul. The Alliance was one of hundreds of Jewish schools, a charitable institution with headquarters in Paris, which brought French to all the Jewish communities of the Middle East. She had won a scholarship to their *école normale* (teachers' training school) in Paris and was sent to Egypt to teach at the Alliance school there.

A few years ago, I found a book about the Jews of Egypt in the nineteenth century which contains letters by her father. He had been sent from Istanbul as a young man to assess the possibility of opening Alliance schools in Egypt and wrote back that the children spoke six languages but could not read or write and he doubted that they could ever be made to sit down. More than one school opened. My grandmother married as soon as she arrived. My grandfather Isaac, whose first wife had just died in childbirth, fell for her milky white skin and golden red hair.

Until the end of the nineteenth century, the indigenous Jews and those from other Arab countries had spoken Arabic and worn Arab clothes (they were Arab but different) – the women the *habara*, the men galabias and kaftans with turbans, skull caps and tarbooshes (fezzes). The Europeanization and 'emancipation' of the Jews began with the building of the Suez Canal and the modernization of the economy. A Jewish middle-class bourgeoisie, educated first in Jewish schools, then by Christian and secular missions, grew out of the developing cotton trade and the capitalist explosion of the country. Jewish men went into cotton, banking, the stock exchange and industries like textiles, oil pressing and sugar refining. Many stayed behind in the small trades and handicrafts. All my relatives were merchants in general commerce. They called themselves 'import-export' but they were really 'import-import', dealing with everything from towels and underwear to china, sugar, coffee, and tea. They were *khawaggat*, Europeanized men who wore suits and tarbooshes. Some toured the villages by train. Their offices and warehouses were in the bazaar area of the Hamzaoui.

My parents used to tell us how they pitied those of our relatives whose wives did not bother to give them proper breakfasts so they had to buy ful medammes (Egyptian brown beans), taamia (the Cairo name for falafel), and lentil soup from vendors at the bazaar. Later I heard from my relatives how they pitied my father because my mother did not let him eat out. It was a question of pride, not of religious orthodoxy. An account of a European Jewish traveller in Aleppo 100 years before expresses the shock he felt at seeing Jews eating food prepared by non-Jews at the bazaar. Our community in Egypt on the whole was even more lax in its religious practice, but the synagogue was an important part of our lives. It was a joyous place to meet and socialize.

Every Friday evening and on high holidays, the Grand Temple was packed with people who came to hear Rabbi Nahum's famous speeches in French. By tradition, the prime minister of Egypt always came for the Kol Nidre prayer. We also attended a small synagogue on top of a garage in the garden of a private house in Zamalek. It was packed with men swaying from side to side (not backwards and forwards, as Eastern Europeans do). They sang plaintive nasal chants in Spanish modulations and tunes from Morocco, Syria and Iraq, as well as some copied from the recitations of the Koran and the Egyptian national anthem. Every man started from the beginning of the prayer book, no matter when he arrived, so the result was a cacophony. The room glittered with chandeliers and velvet drapes embroidered with gold and silver thread. The women sat outside in the garden on golden chairs under a pergola. Dressed in coloured silks, perfumed and bejewelled, they exchanged the latest gossip about matches, dowries, and infidelities and visits to saintly tombs. Every so often, a face would appear at the window and shout 'Taisez-vous les dames!' ('Shut up, ladies!') and they would stop for a while and intone 'Amen!'

Jewish holidays were important occasions. They went on for days. Every member of the family was visited, the oldest first. There were always hundreds of people to kiss. The older relatives smelled of the rose water with which they washed. Depending on the time of day, sweetmeats and pastries or mezze (little salads and appetizers) were passed around. For the high-holiday dinners, tables were connected with planks. Huge quantities of food were prepared. Cooking went on for days. Housewives joined forces and brought their cooks. Itinerant cooks who specialized in certain dishes were also engaged.

Every family had its own special dishes for festive occasions. Although in my day the community had become relatively homogenized and many delicacies had become obligatory on every party table, those dishes which reflected the origins of families were also there, and you could trace the family's ancestry by looking at the spread on the table.

Part of the appeal for me of working on this book is that there is more to Jewish food than cooking and eating. Behind every recipe is a story of local traditions and daily life in far-off towns and villages. It is a romantic and nostalgic subject which has to do with recalling a world that has vanished. It is about ancestral memories and looking back and holding on to old cultures, and it is about identity. It has been like that since Biblical times. The Bible recalls in Exodus the wistful longings of the Jews for the foods they had left behind in Egypt.

At a gastronomic conference I attended in Jerusalem in September 1992 entitled 'Gefilte Fish or Couscous?' I was down in the basement kitchen with cooks from Poland, Georgia, Morocco, Iraq, Kurdistan and many other countries. We were preparing tastings and demonstrations of Jewish festive dishes from each of our communities while a black-bearded *mashgiah* (inspector) with a long black coat, black hat and forelocks looked over our shoulders to make sure that we did not infringe the dietary laws. I was making kobeba hamda, a Syrian Passover dish of ground rice and meat dumplings in a lemony soup, and a Persian lamb stew with quince, and I watched others prepare Sabbath, Purim, Hanukah and Rosh Hashanah specialities. The evening before, there had been a street festival with music and dancing, and the inhabitants of the street – Moroccans, Georgians and others – had brought out unending trays of food for tasting. Following all these amazing displays of dishes, the first subject for discussion at the conference was 'Is there such a thing as Jewish food?'

I am always asked that question. When I was taken out to dinner by a cousin recently and told him I was still researching Jewish food, he said emphatically, 'There is no such thing!' A few friends keep telling me that. I have just put my hand on a paper I gave at the Oxford Symposium on Food and Cookery in 1981 entitled 'Cooking in Israel: A Changing Mosaic', in which I said, 'There is really no such thing as Jewish food. What is familiar here as Jewish food is totally unknown to the Jews of Egypt, Morocco and India. Local regional food becomes Jewish when it travels with Jews to new homelands.' Thirty years ago, when all that was known in the West of Jewish food was the cooking of the Ashkenazi Jews, whose ancestors came from Eastern Europe and Russia, no one wondered if there was such a thing. Since Jews began to pour out of the Middle East and exotic places like India and Georgia from the mid 1950s, such a bewildering range of 'Jewish' dishes has come on the scene that the notion of a Jewish food culture has become questionable.

But because a culture is complex this does not mean it does not exist. The French historian Fernand Braudel, in his book *The Mediterranean*, wrote that there was undoubtedly a Jewish civilization, but that it was so individual that it was not always recognized as one. He described it as a scattering of countless islands in foreign waters, its matter dispersed like tiny drops of oil over the deep waters of other civilizations, never truly blending with them yet always dependent on them. The Jews, he said, adapted and adopted but never lost their cultural identity.

After years of researching the subject, I can say that each region or country has its own particular Jewish dishes and these are sometimes quite different from the local cuisine. Jews have adopted the foods of the countries they lived in, but in every country their cooking has had a special touch and taste and characteristic features and some entirely original dishes which have made it distinctive and recognizable. And in some countries their food was very different from that of the general population.

One reason for the differences was the adaptation of dishes to comply with the Jewish dietary laws. Because of the prohibition of combining meat and dairy foods, Jews used different cooking fats. In the Middle East, you could tell a Jewish home by the smell of oil, which was used instead of clarified butter. The substitution for forbidden foods like pork and seafood created such specialities as goose salami in Italy and Alsace and whitefish soup in Livorno in Italy.

In Jewish families, cooking has always centred around the Sabbath and religious festivals. All celebrations, whether they commemorate a religious holiday, an episode of Jewish history, or a moment in the cycle of life – a birth, a circumcision, a first tooth, a coming of age, a marriage, the inauguration of a new home, pregnancy, death – were once, and in some cases still are, ruled by tradition, and special foods were part of these traditions. The dishes chosen to celebrate these occasions became part of festive rituals and acquired embellishments as they acquired symbolic significance. They were glamorized to glorify the occasions, and that meant colouring with saffron or turmeric, sprinkling with raisins and chopped nuts, stuffing, enclosing in pie crust and pressing into a mould.

Some dishes changed because of the special dietary requirements of particular holidays. At Passover, for instance, when any leavening agents and indirectly flour and wheat are forbidden, ground almonds, potato flour, matzo meal and matzos are used to make all kinds of cakes, pies, dumplings, pancakes and fritters. The laws of the Sabbath, which prohibit any work, including lighting fires and cooking, from sunset on Friday to Saturday evening, have given rise to a very wide range of meals-in-a-pot to be prepared on Friday afternoon and left to cook overnight for Saturday lunch. These complex dishes comprise a variety of foods to be served as different courses, from the soup-and-meat course to side dishes and sometimes puddings, all in the same pot. There is also an extraordinary variety of original dishes that are to be eaten cold on Saturday. Another feature of Jewish cooking is the many substantial dairy and vegetable dishes which constitute meatless meals.

Apart from these differences, there was always, even centuries ago, a touch of otherness in Jewish cooking, a cosmopolitanism which broke even through ghetto walls. Jewish culinary interests were always wider than those of their immediate environment. Before the days of mass communication, Jews had their own network of communication. The vehicles of gastronomic knowledge were merchants and pedlars, travelling rabbis, preachers and teachers, students and cantors, professional letter carriers, beggars (who were legion) and pilgrims on their way to and from the Holy Land. They brought descriptions of exotic dishes in far-off lands, and sometimes even the exotic ingredients themselves, to the communities they stopped with, so that Jews, even in isolated places, became familiar with the foods of their foreign coreligionists.

For centuries Jews had been international merchants, for a time the only merchants in Europe and the Middle East. As early as the seventh century they were the major channel of intercourse between East and West. As importers, middlemen and wholesalers, they played a great part in the Byzantine commerce, which brought Eastern goods to Europe. The camel-caravan trade was concentrated in their hands. Jewish ships sailed the Mediterranean, and Jewish traders were said to be waiting at every port. As converted New Christians, they were among the earliest arrivals in South America with the Conquistadors, and they dealt with the New World produce. Foodstuffs were always a major part of their trade, and that had an impact on their cooking.

But the main influence on the development and shaping of their cuisine was their mobility – their propensity to move from one place to another. Jews moved to escape persecution or economic hardship, or for trade. Their history is one of migration and exile, of the disintegration and dispersion of communities and of the establishment of new ones. In their Diaspora, or dispersion, which began with the destruction of the Second Temple in the first century AD, Jews brought dishes from past homelands to new ones. The way these dishes changed and adopted new forms in a new environment created hybrids that were particular to them. It is the cooking of a nation within a nation, of a culture within a culture, the result of the interweaving of two or more cultures. The almost complete dispersion of the old communities has radiated their styles of cooking to different parts of the world. Jewish history spans more than three millennia and has touched most parts of the globe, but each dish represents a unique historical experience in a particular geographic location.

Dishes are important because they are a link with the past, a celebration of roots, a symbol of continuity. They are that part of an immigrant culture which survives the longest, kept up even when clothing, music, language and religious observance have been abandoned. Although cooking is fragile because it lives in human activity, it isn't easily destroyed. It is transmitted in every family like genes, and it has the capacity for change and for passing on new experience from one generation to another. It is possible, by examining family dishes, to define the identity and geographical origin of a family line.

The anthropologist Joelle Bahloul writes in her study of the Algerian Jewish table, *Le Culte de la table dressée: rites et traditions de la table juive algérienne*, that every family has its own culinary code, which gives it its bearings vis-à-vis its regional origin, its personal identity and its position and prestige in the old country. The code attributes a menu, a dish, a flavour and a ritual, with different table manners and different forms of conviviality, for every occasion, be it festive or ordinary and everyday. Every feast has its own rites and its own dishes and can be remembered by its tastes and its smells. In the selection of dishes – rejected or adopted, appreciated or depreciated and given mythical, ethical or historical rationalization – there is a logic that combines mythological, historic and moral significance to create a symbol.

This book was conceived as a grand comprehensive project. To finance visits to what was left of Jewish communities in various countries around the world, I took on other work and finished other books. But the more I researched and the more I discovered and the more I was fascinated, the more the project seemed impossible. I realized it could take me a life time and would fill several volumes. Scattered as the Jews have been over virtually the whole surface of the earth, residing in lands not their own for 2,000 years, part of different cultures and traditions, it was impossible to attempt to cover all their cooking, from Babylon to New York.

Not only have there been Jews in every country, but the communities themselves were complex and subdivided into groups from different origins. When I visited the old Jewish Ghetto of Venice and met the ladies who cooked for the old people's home and for the holiday meals for tourists and Venetian returnees, they explained that Venice did not have one style of Jewish cooking but four. They pointed to the three synagogues standing in the piazza, which had followed different rites – Spanish, Levantine and German – for hundreds of years. The cooking, they said, reflected those styles, and there was also an Italian cuisine, which was mainly southern Italian.

In Tunisia, there are two communities – the 'Livornese', who came from Livorno in Italy, and the local 'Tun', of Berber and Arab origins – which have separate synagogues, schools and cemeteries. They do not intermarry, and there are differences in their cooking. Indian Jewry is the most complex, with at least three different communities that have always kept apart and whose histories and cooking are different. In many countries, including Italy, Morocco, Tunisia, Turkey and Greece, Jewish cooking varied from one city to another. The cooking of Jews who originated in Eastern Europe and Russia is relatively standard, but it has changed according to whether emigrants settled in America, Canada, Britain, South Africa or France.

Jewish cooking is in some ways archaic – some of the dishes have long been lost in the countries where they were adopted – but far from being fossilized; it is very much alive and full of movement. There are so many versions of a dish, so many regional variations, so many changes occurring when it was transported to different homelands, that collecting recipes is like looking through a kaleidoscope with bits moving all the time, or trying to hit a moving target, or, as a friend suggested, walking on quicksand. It is the extraordinary diversity and richness that so attracted me to the subject sixteen years ago, and it is its enormity and complexity that made me abandon it many times.

When I decided (as I did several times) to give up, my editor, Judith Jones, convinced me that the only way to deal with the subject was to make the book a 'personal odyssey' and to forget about trying to be comprehensive. This was a very appealing idea, but I found that selecting is even more difficult than collecting. First there was the problem of what countries to represent. Could I leave out the West Indies or Mexico or Ethiopia? I started off intent on finding dishes from every possible community, from China, Libya and Afghanistan to old Provence and Ferrara. I wanted to include many dishes from the lesser-known 'exotic' communities, which have in the past been removed from the mainstream of Jewish life. In the end, I decided to concentrate more on those communities that have been in important Jewish centres and whose cooking is most widespread, and most particularly on those whose cooking is prestigious. Some of their cuisines are legendary, like those of the Moroccan and Syrian Jews, but many were a surprise to me, like the cooking of the Indian communities. The others are there too.

Another problem was to decide what dishes were representative of Jewish cooking. You cannot call everything that Jews have eaten Jewish. It is difficult to separate what is Jewish from the foods eaten by the general population, for many dishes are variations on a theme. Conversely, one of the difficulties is that people who came from Orthodox communities often assumed that they ate like everybody else, whereas many of their dishes were quite distinctive. They were not in a position to know, because they could eat only in Jewish homes. I did find a surprisingly large number of dishes that belong exclusively to various Jewish communities. Most are festive dishes. Nearly all the fish and chicken dishes in the book have been Friday night specials somewhere, and most cold things were Saturday foods. But such a collection could still be unbalanced and unrepresentative, containing too many heavy bean and chickpea (Saturday) stews and too many biscuits and almond pastries. So I have included the everyday foods and some of the grand party dishes that Jews were most fond of, and which they brought to new homelands and passed on to their children.

In the wide repertoire to choose from, there are many similar dishes varying in flavourings or methods. There are hundreds of meatballs and fish balls, hundreds of stuffed vegetables, hundreds of cheese pies (why did they like all that rolling and stuffing and wrapping?), milk puddings, fritters in syrup, to name only a few. How did I decide? I would select a dish from France, for instance, in preference to similar ones in Britain or America, because the French make it better. It was not always easy to choose even when looking at one country, however. When I asked an Algerian for a Jewish couscous, the reply was: 'From which town?' In every town it was different. In Morocco, there are Jewish specialities from Fez, Tangier, Tétouan, Marrakesh, Ouezzane, Debdou and Essaouira, and several Berber mountain villages have their own Jewish dishes.

There is also the question of authenticity. When communities emigrate, they start using what is available locally and what makes life easier – different cheeses, different rice, substitutes such as gelatine instead of calf's foot, yogurt instead of sour cream. In France, some North African *pieds noirs* use veal instead of mutton now, because under French influence they have been made to feel that mutton 'is heavy and smells too strong'. I had to decide if I should go back to the source in the country of origin or go for the modern, lighter, more elegant version which most people have switched to; how much I should substitute oil for butter or chicken fat, and baking for frying. My decisions were, of course, influenced by a concern with health and with our modern taste for lighter foods, but not if that sacrificed the authenticity of a recipe. Luckily, there are still those who know how things were done in the old homelands and how to adapt them to our world; it is from them for the most part that I took my cue. Usually I offer the alternatives. Even when a community has not moved, recipes depend on the situation of the individuals who have given them. If they are poor, they can use only what they can afford. The communities that became impoverished use more bread or potatoes, for instance, to make their dishes go further. As an example, a Passover walnut cake in a privately published book, *Sefarad Yemekleri*, to raise money for a Jewish old people's home in Istanbul, calls for a large proportion of matzo meal, whereas the same cake, when it arrived in Cairo from Istanbul in the early nineteenth century, used only walnuts. It is not always easy to decide at what point in time and on what soil dishes were at their best.

There are dozens of Jewish recipes for head, feet, spleen, stuffed intestines, heart, lungs, testicles, even penis. Most of them are delicious, but who will be brave enough to cook them these days? Anyway, most offal is not available in Anglo-Saxon countries now, because of lack of demand and health risks (in Britain, because of 'mad cow' disease).

I have been asked if I was going to offer dishes that people haven't cooked for 100 years. The answer is that I may give them a mention, but the recipes I have included are all much alive in some corner of the world, although it may be in Sydney, Australia, instead of Bombay, India; and Afoula, Israel, instead of Djerba, Tunisia.

When I was in Israel, a woman whose family came from Iraq – an anthropologist who was also a brilliant cook – invited me to her home with a woman from India so that I could ask them both for recipes. I spent the afternoon taking detailed notes, and at the end the lovely anthropologist said, 'Now, what we want from you is to go and get many other recipes for these same dishes and to find the very best version. That is what we want from you – to find the best.' That night she brought me kichree, a dish of rice and red lentils, to taste, and it was wonderful. But I did get a better one from my friend Sarni Zubaida in London, and I know I don't have to feel guilty about featuring it. After I had tried hundreds (perhaps thousands!) of recipes and many in their different versions, the selection made itself on gastronomic merits. Of course it reflects my tastes and my background, my travels, the people I have met who gave me recipes, and also the degree of enthusiasm of the friends who came to dinner and tasted my trials.

It may seem to you, on looking at the book, that I have chosen a disproportionately large number of Sephardi recipes. But the Sephardi section includes many very different cultures and regional styles, from Italian to Indian, and they all needed representation. I started off thinking I would pick only a few recipes from each community, but as I tried one after the other and found them enchanting – like discovering raw diamonds – I had to include many.

Though I grew up in a Sephardi family and that tradition has always remained a part of my life, I have lived in the Ashkenazi world since the age of fifteen – first as a schoolgirl in Paris, then having married into a

Russian Jewish family in England – so I have long been familiar with Eastern European Jewish food. But it was only when researching this book, and striving to find the best versions of dishes, that I realized just how many gems there were.

The criterion of selection throughout was to include only the most delicious.

The 'testing' meals went on for years. There were tête-à-têtes when I made small quantities for two or three, and there were great noisy banquets for up to fifteen people – seated around my oval hunting table while a dozen different dishes were passed around. The merits of the dishes and possibilities for improvement were discussed. I noted at the head of each recipe in my computer who had eaten the dish and how much they liked it. I dropped the dishes that did not meet with approval. Many of the friends who came to eat are cooks and chefs and food writers, and all are discriminating food-lovers, so it is reassuring for me to remember how much they enjoyed the dishes and how rapturously they received so many of them. Most of all, it is my family – my son, Simon, and his wife, Ros; my daughter Anna and her husband, Clive; and my daughter Nadia when she was over from New York – who went through the repertoire every week and made their comments.

History is important in the shaping of cooking traditions, and never more so than with Jewish food, which has no geographical base, no *terroir*, as the French call the native soil to which a gastronomy obeys stable and unvarying imperatives. Working on this book has been for me a voyage of discovery. To make sense of their dishes, I had to gain an insight into the culture and history of the Jews. It has been so fascinating that I have resisted recommendations that I should not burden readers with big chunks of history and have passed on what I found. It is good to be able to place a dish. The more delectable it is, the more I want to know something about it.

SALT & TIME

Alissa Timoshkina

Food writer and historian **Alissa Timoshkina** specialises in Eastern European food culture. Now based in the UK, Timoshkina grew up in Serbia and has Ukrainian-Jewish lineage. Following the Russian invasion of Ukraine in early 2022, Timoshkina launched #CookforUkraine alongside her friend Olia Hercules; it has since raised more than two million pounds for various charities. *Salt & Time: Recipes from a Russian Kitchen* was her debut cookbook.

We often need distance and time both to see things better and to feel closer to them. This is certainly true of the food of my home country, Russia – or Siberia, to be exact. When I think of that place, I can immediately hear the sound of fresh snow crunching beneath my feet. Having lived in the UK half my life, this is what I miss the most about Russia: the clarity and stillness of the fresh fallen snow. It's a bit like a blank page on which a new day can be drawn. Today, whenever I crush sea salt flakes between my fingers as I cook in my London kitchen, I think of that sound.

For many, Russian food remains a mystery, tinted with the stereotypes of the Cold War and obscured by the complexities of contemporary Russian politics. I often find that Russian cuisine is trapped somewhere between two very opposing ideas: the romanticized notion of Russians eating blinis with caviar every morning, or a stark image of the Soviets gazing at bare market shelves to the soundtrack of their rumbling stomachs. So I feel it is finally time to paint a more authentic portrait. In this book, I would like to invite you to sit next to me at my Russian table, to share my memories of growing up in Siberia and to accompany me on a journey across the vast country as well as into its fascinating history.

Born in the early 1980s in the industrial city of Omsk (famed for hosting Fyodor Dostoevsky during his exile), like many Siberians I come from a mixed heritage. Mine includes Jewish Ukrainian roots on my mum's side, my father's family comes from the Russian Far East, and we all share that unique experience of living under the Soviet regime. I never took much interest in my country until I moved away to the UK aged 15 to receive the much-sought-after British education. The initial mist of home-longing was replaced by a more critical interest in Russia's history, culture and politics. The more I delved into the academic world, the more acutely aware I became of the intricacies of my country's past, as well as of the dangerous trajectory of its current regime. While I have always loved Russian literature, classical music and cinema, the political actualities of recent decades left me feeling alienated. But, of course, it is from family that a sense of belonging really stems.

Thinking of the variety of journeys that my family has made to settle in Siberia inspired a realization in me that there have been millions of other families travelling to the region from all over the former Soviet Union and beyond, bringing their ethnic, cultural and culinary heritage along the way. And voilà – this is where my passion and interest in my home country was reignited.

Historically, Siberia was a place of exile from the mid-17th century until the 1950s. A vast region, it spans from the Ural Mountains eastwards to China, bordering Kazakhstan, Mongolia and the Arctic Ocean. The sheer size of the place, and of Russia in general, is sometimes mind-boggling and sadly often used to stir up a false sense of patriotism and nationalistic pride. However, when seen through a culinary lens, the country's vastness can be perceived as an asset and something to feel inspired by. Due to its complex history of exile and other forms of resettlement, Siberia has become a melting pot of culinary traditions from Ukraine and the Caucasus to Central Asia, Mongolia and Korea.

The intense climate, with temperatures ranging from minus to plus 40°C, doesn't make Siberia a land of plenty, and sadly I cannot recall growing up connected to the land and its produce – yet I can always remember the opulence of the markets in the summer, where the polyphony of the traders' accents was matched by the diversity of foods on offer. There were Georgian spices and herbs next to a stall of Korean pickles, nudging up against dried fruits and spice mixes from Central Asia, not to mention freshly baked Armenian lavash breads and Ukrainian unrefined sunflower oil. While summers meant cooking and eating alfresco, the almost paralysing cold of winter brought a profound indoor cosiness and an entirely new set of food rituals. Vodka and pickles were brought out as soon as the first snow hit the ground, the scarcity of daylight outside was met with the warm glow of a dinner table lamp and the need for sustenance was satisfied by giant bowls of steaming *pelmeni* dumplings and hearty soups with lots of bread and butter.

*

Syrniki Doughnuts

I firmly believe that there exists a secret *babushka* guidebook that states: 'Thou shalt overfeed thy grandchildren with *syrrniki*'. It seems that Russian grannies have an endless supply of these cottage cheese fritters and an understanding that their grandchild has a bottomless stomach that enables them to consume *all* the syrniki on offer. And while I thought as a child, 'I will never lay my eyes on another syrniki ever again,' my love of this traditional Russian breakfast-cum-dessert has never faltered. Traditionally, syrniki are formed into crumpet-like shapes and fried in a pan. However, at some point back in the early 1990s when our family acquired a deep-fat fryer, a new type of syrniki was born – a deep-fried doughnut dusted with sugar. Yes please!

When it comes to accompaniments for these doughnuts, the world is your oyster. Choose anything from natural yoghurt with fruit, to berry jams and compotes, or even dulce de leche.

makes 10-12
200g tvorog (make sure you get the right stuff from an Eastern European shop) or ricotta
2 eggs
1 tablespoon caster sugar, plus extra for dusting

½ teaspoon baking powder

pinch of salt

4 tablespoons plain flour, plus extra for dusting

2 tablespoons raisins (presoaked in rum or whisky to add that extra je ne sais quoi)

finely grated zest of 1 lemon

flavourless sunflower oil, for deep-frying

Using an electric hand whisk, whisk all the ingredients together, except the oil for deep-frying, in a mixing bowl until well incorporated and fluffy. The dough will be very runny, so use a well floured work surface and 2 tablespoons to shape it into medium-sized doughnuts. For each doughnut, scoop out a full tablespoon of the dough and roll it around in the flour until it stops sticking to the spoons and the work surface.

Heat up the oil for deep-frying in a large pan, keeping it over a medium heat to ensure the oil doesn't start to smoke. Test the temperature of the oil by dropping a little of the dough into it – it should start to sizzle but not turn dark brown immediately. Once you are happy with the oil temperature, drop the dough balls in one at a time, making sure they don't stick together. Swirl them around occasionally and remove with a slotted spoon after 1–2 minutes. They should be golden brown and crisp. Lay them out on kitchen paper and sprinkle with extra sugar.

Serve on a sharing plate with an array of accompaniments for a real feast of a breakfast, or plate them up individually with your accompaniment of choice for a moreish dessert.

ASPIC
FROM AETHERIAL WORLDS

Tatyana Tolstaya

Born in Leningrad into a family of writers, **Tatyana Nikitchna Tolstaya** is a writer, television host, publicist, essayist and novelist. Her short story collection, *Aetherial Worlds*, was awarded the Ivan Belkin Literary Award and translated into English. Tolstaya has written for the *New Yorker* and *New York Review of Books*, and co-hosted a Russian talk show, *The School for Scandal*, which discussed politics and culture.

Anya Migdal is a writer, translator, musician and actor whose translations have been published in the *New Yorker*, *Granta* and *Tin House Magazine*. She was born in Russia and moved to the US as a child; she now lives in Brooklyn.

Truth be told, I've always been afraid of it, since childhood. It's prepared not casually, or whenever the fancy strikes you, but most often for New Year's Eve, in the heart of winter, in the shortest and most brutal days of December.

Darkness comes early. There is a damp frost; you can see spiky halos around the streetlamps. You have to breathe through your mittens. Your forehead aches from the cold, and your cheeks are numb. But, wouldn't you know it, you still have to boil and chill the aspic – the name of the dish itself makes the temperature of your soul drop, and no thick grey goat-hair shawl will save you. It's a special kind of religion, making the aspic. It's a yearly sacrifice, though we don't know to whom or for what. And what would happen if you didn't make it is also a question mark.

But, for some reason, it must be done.

You must walk in the cold to the market – it's always dim there, never warm there. Past the tubs with pickled things; past the cream and the crème fraîche, redolent of girlish innocence; past the artillery depot of potatoes, radishes and cabbages; past the hills of fruit; past the signal lights of clementines – to the furthest corner. That's where the chopping block is; that's where the blood and the axe are. 'Call Russia to the Axe'. To this one right here, digging its blade into a wooden stump. Russia is here, Russia is picking out a piece of meat.

'Igor, chop up the legs for the lady.' Igor lifts his axe: *hack!* Lays out the white cow knees, cleaves the shanks. Some buy pieces of the muzzle: lips and nostrils. And those who like pork broth – they get little pig feet, with baby hooves. Holding one of those, touching its yellow skin, is creepy – what if it suddenly shook your hand in return?

None of them are really dead: that's the conundrum. There is no death. They are hacked apart, mutilated; they won't be walking anywhere, or even crawling; they've been killed but they are not dead. They know that you've come for them.

Next it's time to buy something dry and clean: onions, garlic, roots and herbs. And back home through the snow you go: *crunch, crunch*. The frosty building entryway. The lightbulb has been stolen again. You fumble in the dark for the elevator button; its red eye lights up. First the intestines appear in the elevator's wrought-iron cage, then the cabin itself. Our ancient Saint Petersburg elevators are slow; they click as they pass each floor, testing our patience. The chopped-up legs in the shopping bag are pulling your arm down, and it seems as if at the very last moment they'll refuse to get into the elevator. They'll twitch, break free, and run away, clacking across the ceramic tiles: *clippity-clop, clippity-clop, clippity-clop*. Maybe that would be for the best? No. It's too late.

At home, you wash them and throw them into the pot. You set the burner on high. Now it's boiling, raging. Now the surface is coated with grey, dirty ripples: all that's bad, all that's weighty, all that's fearful, all that suffered, darted, and tried to break loose, oinked and mooed, couldn't understand, resisted, and gasped for breath – all of it turns to muck. All the pain and all the death are gone, congealed into repugnant fluffy felt. *Finito*. Placidity, forgiveness.

Then it's time to dump this death water, to thoroughly rinse the sedated pieces under a running faucet, and to put them back into a clean pot filled with fresh water. It's simply meat, simply food; all that was fearsome is gone. A calm blue flower of propane, just a little bit of heat. Let it simmer quietly; this is a five- to six-hour undertaking.

While it cooks, you can take your time preparing the herbs and the onions. You'll be adding them to the pot in two batches. First, two hours before the broth is done cooking, and then, again, an hour later. Don't forget to stir in plenty of salt. And your labour is done. By the end of the cooking cycle, there will have been a complete transfiguration of flesh: the pot will be a lake of gold with fragrant meat, and nothing, nothing will remind us of Igor.

The kids are here; unafraid, they are looking at the pot. It's safe to show them this soup – they won't ask any tough questions.

Strain the broth, pull the meat apart, slice it with a sharp knife, as they did in the olden days, in the age of the tsar, and the other tsar, and the third tsar, before the advent of the meat grinder, before Vasily the Blind, and Ivan Kalita, and the Cumans, and Rurik, and Sineus and Truvor, who, as it turns out, never even existed.

Set up the bowls and the plates and place some fresh-pressed garlic in each one. Add the chopped-up meat. Use the ladle to pour over it some thick, golden, gelatinous broth. And that's that. Your job is done; the rest is up to the frost. Carefully take the bowls and plates out to the balcony, cover the coffins with lids, stretch some plastic wrap over them, and wait.

Might as well stay out on the balcony, bundled up in your shawl. Smoke a cigarette and look up at the winter stars, unable to identify a single one. Think about tomorrow's guests, remind yourself that you need to iron the tablecloth, to add sour cream to the horseradish, to warm the wine and chill the vodka, to grate some cold butter, to place the sauerkraut in a dish, to slice some bread. To wash your hair, to dress up, to do your makeup – foundation, mascara, lipstick.

And if you feel like senselessly crying, do it now, while nobody can see you. Do it violently, about nothing and for no reason, sobbing, wiping away your tears with your sleeve, stubbing out your cigarette against the railing of the balcony, not finding it there, and burning your fingers. Because how to reach this *there* and where this *there* is – no one knows.

RECIPES FOR SAD WOMEN

Héctor Abad Faciolince

Colombian writer **Héctor Abad Faciolince** is a novelist, essayist, journalist, translator and editor. After spending years in Italy, first to study, then again following the assassination of his father, Abad Faciolince returned to Colombia in 1993. He is currently a columnist and editorial advisor at *El Espectador* newspaper, and has written a number of award-winning novels and short story collections.

Anne McLean is a Yorkshire-based Canadian translator who learnt Spanish while travelling in Central America in her late twenties. She took a Masters degree in literary translation, and now translates the work of Spanish and Latin American authors. McLean has twice won the Independent Foreign Fiction Prize: with Javier Cercas in 2004 for her translation of *Soldiers of Salamis*, and again in 2009 with Evelio Rosero for *The Armies*.

Experience your sadness, touch it, pull its petals off, soak it in tears, wrap it up in screams and silences, copy it into notebooks, jot it down on your body, note it in the pores of your skin. For only if you don't defend yourself will it flee, at times, somewhere else that is not the centre of your private pain.

And to taste your sadness I must also recommend a melancholy dish—cauliflower in the mist. Take this sad, white, solid flower and steam it. Slowly, with that same aroma that comes from a mouth spouting laments, it softens as it cooks. And shrouded in mist, in its steaming vapour, add olive oil and garlic and a little bit of pepper; salt it with your own tears. And savour it slowly, biting it off the fork, and cry some more and more still, so that in the end this flower will gradually soak up your melancholy without leaving you dry, without leaving you tranquil, without robbing you of the only thing that's yours at this moment, the only thing that no one can now take from you, your sadness, but with the feeling of having shared with this flower unable to wilt, with this absurd, prehistoric flower that brides never request from florists, with this flower no one puts in vases, with this anomaly, this sadness in bloom, this flowered melancholy, your own cauliflower sadness.

*

On afternoons of fine, persistent rain, if your loved one is far away and the invisible weight of his absence overwhelming, cut twenty-eight fresh leaves of lemon balm from your garden and put them in a litre of water on a high heat to make an infusion. As soon as the water boils let the steam moisten your fingertips and stir it three times with a wooden spoon. Take it off the heat and let stand for two minutes. Do not add sugar, drink it sip by sip from a white cup with your back to the window. If halfway through the litre you don't notice a certain relief behind the breastbone, heat it up again and add two spoonfuls of grated sugarloaf. If the afternoon ends and the feeling persists, you can be sure he won't be coming back. Or he'll come back some other afternoon and be much changed.

*

If one day you become sick of words, as happens to us all, and you grow tired of hearing them, of saying them; if whichever you choose seems worn out, dull, disabled; if you feel nauseated when you hear "horrible" or "divine" for some everyday occurrence—you'll not be cured, obviously, by alphabet soup.

You must do the following: cook a plate of al dente spaghetti dressed with the simplest seasoning—garlic, oil and chilli. Over the pasta tossed in this mixture, grate a layer of Parmesan cheese. To the right of the deep plate full of the spaghetti thus prepared, place an open book. To the left, place an open book. In front of it a full glass of dry red wine.

Any other company is not recommended. Turn the pages of each book at random, but they must both be poetry. Only good poets cure us of an overindulgence in words. Only simple essential food cures us of gluttony.

*

May you not be seized by the miserable custom of sobbing. Cure yourself with portions of white rice. One cup will be enough. Rinse it three times until the milky water turns faint and soft like a nursemaid's breast. Add twice as much water and a pinch of salt. When the water comes to a boil stir it once. Cover the pot and turn down the heat. Ten minutes later turn off the heat without removing the lid. Wait for a quarter of an hour with the rice covered. Then you can eat it.

If you have a very fresh yolk of a duck's or chicken's egg, you can mix it into your plate of rice. The colour of the yolk in the rice will dispel your sobs and suppress your weeping. At most, somewhat later, you'll be left with the intermittent, almost jocular, involuntary embers of hiccups.

*

Few know and fewer recognise the effectiveness of the cure I'm about to explain. But it is, perhaps, the only recipe that will never disappoint. I wanted to call it the *face cure*, because there is no one who does not have in their memory a rather small group of faces, the sight of which produce joy.

The rite of tranquillity is the following. Two chairs and a table, liver pâté, toast made from fresh wholegrain bread, a chilled bottle of Sauternes, and across from you the face of a friend, a visage you know, one of those you just need to see to have your peace of mind restored.

The pâté reminds friends that they are flesh. The bread won't let them forget that all is born of the earth and all returns to her. The spirit of the Sauternes wine revives what makes us most lively—the possibility of uniting two minds.

MRS DALLOWAY

Virginia Woolf

Prolific letter-writer, diarist, novelist and essayist **Virginia Woolf** was, alongside her husband Leonard, a central member of London's artistic and literary Bloomsbury Group. In the 1920s, she was courted by aristocratic Vita Sackville-West; their relationship influenced her novels and continued until Woolf's death. A number of her distinctive Modernist novels are written as a 'stream of consciousness', inviting her readers into the interior lives of her characters, including *Mrs Dalloway*, which was first published in 1925. In a letter to her brother-in-law written seven years before the publication of her first book, she wrote of her desire to 're-form the novel and capture multitudes of things at present fugitive, enclose the whole, and shape infinite strange shapes'.

Lucy came running full tilt downstairs, having just nipped in to the drawing-room to smooth a cover, to straighten a chair, to pause a moment and feel whoever came in must think how clean, how bright, how beautifully cared for, when they saw the beautiful silver, the brass fire-irons, the new chair-covers, and the curtains of yellow chintz: she appraised each; heard a roar of voices; people already coming up from dinner; she must fly!

The Prime Minister was coming, Agnes said: so she had heard them say in the dining-room, she said, coming in with a tray of glasses. Did it matter, did it matter in the least, one Prime Minister more or less? It made no difference at this hour of the night to Mrs. Walker among the plates, saucepans, cullenders, frying-pans, chicken in aspic, ice-cream freezers, pared crusts of bread, lemons, soup tureens, and pudding basins which, however hard they washed up in the scullery seemed to be all on top of her, on the kitchen table, on chairs, while the fire blared and roared, the electric lights glared, and still supper had to be laid. All she felt was, one Prime Minister more or less made not a scrap of difference to Mrs. Walker.

The ladies were going upstairs already, said Lucy; the ladies were going up, one by one, Mrs. Dalloway walking last and almost always sending back some message to the kitchen, "My love to Mrs. Walker," that was it one night. Next morning they would go over the dishes—the soup, the salmon; the salmon, Mrs. Walker knew, as usual underdone, for she always got nervous about the pudding and left it to Jenny; so it happened, the salmon was always underdone. But some lady with fair hair and silver ornaments had said, Lucy said, about the entrée, was it really made at home? But it was the salmon that bothered Mrs. Walker, as she spun the plates round and round, and pulled in dampers and pulled out dampers; and there came a burst of laughter from the dining-room; a voice speaking; then another burst of laughter—the gentlemen enjoying themselves when the ladies had gone. The tokay, said Lucy running in. Mr. Dalloway had sent for the tokay, from the Emperor's cellars, the Imperial Tokay.

It was borne through the kitchen. Over her shoulder Lucy reported how Miss Elizabeth looked quite lovely; she couldn't take her eyes off her; in her pink dress, wearing the necklace Mr. Dalloway had given her. Jenny must remember the dog, Miss Elizabeth's fox-terrier, which, since it bit, had to be shut up and might, Elizabeth thought, want something. Jenny must remember the dog. But Jenny was not going upstairs with all those people about. There was a motor at the door already! There was a ring at the bell—and the gentlemen still in the dining-room, drinking tokay!

ELIZABETH DAVID: ENGLISH BREAD AND YEAST COOKERY

Angela Carter

Angela Carter's writing career began in Bristol when she was in her early twenties, where she and her husband were part of the folk scene. She used the proceeds of the Somerset Maugham Award she was awarded in 1969 to relocate to Tokyo without her husband, and 'learnt what it is to be a woman and became radicalised'. A novelist, poet, short story writer and journalist, her deeply feminist writing draws on a wide range of influences: gothic fantasy, fairy tales, Shakespeare, music hall and Surrealism.

My corner shop sells wrapped, sliced white loaves that, at a pinch, could poultice a wound. It also, sometimes, stocks twisted, unsliced bread with sesame seeds on top emanating from a Cypriot concern on the other side of London which can fool the unwary into thinking it is somehow a more authentic product than the Mother's Pride stuff, though authentic in *what* way I can't say. The corner shop also sells plastic bags of pitta, which is fine, though it looks a bit odd filled with butter and marmalade at breakfast. (Kebabs *a l'anglaise*.)

Five minutes walk away is one of those hot-bread outlets that sell poultices fresh from the oven. Seven minutes' walk away, virtually side by side, two shops stocking different varieties of those wholemeal breads that look hand-thrown, like studio pottery, and are fine if you have all your teeth. But, if not; then not. Perhaps the rise and rise of the poultice or factory-made loaf, which may easily be mumbled to a pap between gums, reflects the sorry state of the nation's dental health.

It is usually interpreted, however, as the result of a lack of moral fibre, as if moral fibre is somehow related to roughage in the diet. The British, the real bread lobby implies, are rapidly going, if they have not already gone, all soft, bland: and flabby, just like their staple food. The iron grip of the multinationals has squeezed all the goodness out of British bread, via the machinations of the giant miller-bakers, Allied Bakeries, Rank Hovis McDougall *et al.*, and the only way to fight back is to lob a home-made stone-ground wholemeal cob at them. (Which, in some cases, would indeed be a lethal missile.)

The real bread lobby has, of course, right, virtue, and healthy bowel movements on its side. On the whole, it is free from that paranoid nostalgia that afflicted Anthony Burgess, when he – I think it was he – laid squarely at the feet of the Welfare State the blame for the fact that Heinz baked beans no longer taste as tangy as they did when he was a boy.

The Welfare State it is, according to the formula of reactionary food fetishism, that has made us all soft and bland and flabby and that is why we dig into Mother's Pride and Wonderloaf and Sunblest with such enthusiasm. Behind this, is an ill-concealed and ugly plot – not so much to swell the coffers of the hippy wholefood entrepreneurs who concoct those loaves that either go straight through you or else stay with you, heavily on the chest, for days, nay, weeks, as to get women back where they belong. Up to their elbows in bread dough, engaged in that most arduous and everlasting of domestic chores, giving the family good, hearty, home-baked bread.

Oddly enough, in all of Europe, the British housewife is, historically, the only one of all who found herself burdened with this back-breaking and infinitely boring task, for watching bread dough rise is the next best thing to watching paint dry, activity reminiscent of some of those recorded in early Warhol movies. The average black-clad Italian, French, or Greek mama, if asked to make bread, has always tossed her head with a haughty sneer. What else are baker's for? For herself, she's got better things to do – the meat sauce, the *coq au vin*, the dolmas, and so on. Of course, it's always been more difficult, given British cuisine, for our housewives to get away with that excuse. Since we've got to have something to shine at, it turned out to be baked goods, didn't it?

And, oh God, in my misspent youth as a housewife, I, too, used to bake bread, in those hectic and desolating days just prior to the woman's movement, when middle-class women were supposed to be wonderful wives and mothers, gracious hostesses à la Miriam Stoppard, and do it all *beautifully*. I used to feel so womanly when I was baking my filthy bread. A positive ecstasy of false consciousness. I probably dealt the death blow to some local baker with a wood-fired brick-oven when I took away my custom, for in those days, there were old-fashioned bakers aplenty, no doubt then closing down on all sides under the twin onslaughts of the newly fashionable anorexia nervosa and all that compulsive home breadmaking.

However, even here, twenty years later in south London, there are a couple of perfectly decent old-fashioned bakers within easy walking distance (both stocking that indescribable speciality, bread pudding). Even if southern England *is* heavily saturated with chain bakeries, good bakers are thick on the ground from Lincolnshire on to the north and Scottish bakers are wonderful. Obviously, lots of people just pick up a Wonderloaf at the corner shop or supermarket, perhaps even habitually: but I wonder whether they don't make a distinction between bread for sandwiches and bread for, as it were, eating. Certainly, sliced white comes into its own for the former use – basically, a wrapping for a sweet or savoury filling, akin to edible greaseproof paper.

Along with the notion that British factory-made bread is bad bread comes the one that all artisan-made bread is *good* bread. Although the recipe books of Tuscany are suspiciously full of handy hints for dealing with large quantities of stale bread, it is still impossible to resist a sigh of satisfaction when the waiter weighs down the paper tablecloth with the basket of rough-hewn bread chunks in the somnolent, shadowless heat of some Florentine lunch time . . . though, since the saltless, fatless bread of the region will, by then, have been out of the oven for some hours, it is now only good for carving into putti. Or dipping into the squat tumbler you have just filled with red wine from a straw-wrapped (or possibly, plastic-coated) bottle. And that's it! Pow! It hits you. The atavistic glamour of the continental holiday; the timeless, mythic resonance of the bread and the wine . . . for what good is a continental holiday unless it is jam-packed with resonances?

It always puzzles me that Christianity got off the ground, even to the limited extent that it did, in those parts of the globe where its central metaphor – the bread and the wine – were incomprehensible. A sacramental meal of shared rice and saké, the nearest Chinese equivalents to the Mediterranean staples, suggests a very anaemic Christ indeed.

Wheat bread, in fact, is not only a specifically European staff of life, but even a specifically Mediterranean one. Northern Europe tends towards black, rye bread and wheat bread took a long time to penetrate to the northernmost parts of even our own island, where all bakers still stock the traditional crisp, flat, unleavened oat cake in large quantities. (When the Scots first clapped eyes on grain, they knew immediately what to do with it; they distilled it. No wonder the Scots proved averse to the doctrine of transubstantiation. A deity with flesh of oat cakes and blood composed of volatile spirit makes the mind reel.)

Nevertheless, part of the fuss we make when we think our bread – our BREAD – has been tampered with must, surely, relate to the sacramental quality inherent in bread in our culture. Our bread, our daily bread, has been profaned with noxious additives. Although that bread is certainly no longer our 'daily bread' within the strict meaning of the prayer. In the sixteenth century, 'bread' meant 'food' just as 'rice' (*gohan*) in Japanese still means dinner. For most of us, in those days, food *was* bread – bread with, perhaps, a condiment of cheese, onion, or bacon grease to go with it, and maybe a chickweed salad on high days and holidays.

The menus of the Lambeth poor researched before the First World War by Maud Pember Reeves for her book, *Round About a Pound a Week*, feature bread heavily at all three daily meals. Two of those meals, breakfast and supper, are composed exclusively of bread plus a smear of margarine, jam, or sweetened condensed milk. The stunted, sickly, patently under-nourished, and often dying children described by Pember Reeves do not appear to have thrived particularly well on such a diet.

One should not, of course, ascribe to magic doses of Wonderloaf and Mother's Pride the almost intolerable health, strength, and vitality of the children of Lambeth at this present time. How these kids keep it up on salt 'n' vinegar flavoured crisps, orange crush and fish fingers indeed perplexes me. One can only conclude that a varied diet of junk food is, in the final analysis, considerably more nutritious than a diet of not very much food at all and most of it starch.

In a culinary sense, though not, I suspect, in an emotional one, bread has been secularised in postwar Britain. It has become a food, like any other, no longer to be taken in large quantities. There are other things to eat, even other carbohydrate foods – rice, pasta. Yams. One of the things Pember Reeves' housewives liked about bread was its portability – a child did not have to sit down to eat a hunch of bread and marge and that was convenient if you did not have sufficient chairs, or even a table, on or at which to sit. Most families, nowadays, do manage occasional communal sit-down meals. Most homes, today, boast knives and forks. We no longer live by bread alone.

When one does not live by bread alone on a varied and interesting diet, bread changes its function while retaining its symbolism. Ceasing to be the staff of life but ever redolent with its odour of sanctity – an odour the hot bread-poultice shops have exploited commercially to the hilt – bread turns into a mere accessory, the decorative margin to a meal, or else into the material for a small but inessential meal, that very 'afternoon tea' beloved of the English upper classes, with which they used to stuff their faces in that desert of oral gratification between their vast lunches and their gargantuan dinners.

It is no surprise, therefore, to find that Elizabeth David's vast and highly lauded tome, *English Bread and Yeast Cookery*, is jammed full of tea-time recipes – buns, tea cakes, fruit breads, and so on. For David, the high priestess of postwar English cookery, she who single-handed put an olive-wood chopping block into every aspiring home, to turn her attention to currant buns means that something is up.

English Bread and Yeast Cookery is a vademecum to the art of home baking. And I use the word, 'art', rather than 'craft', advisedly, since her recipes are intended for the artist baker in her studio kitchen rather than the artisan in the common workshop.

David, ever apt with the up-market quotation, certainly knows how to add that final touch of arty glamour to the business! She whisks away the last surviving touch of dirndl skirt and Fabian Society from the concept of the home-baked loaf when she quotes a description of Virginia Woolf kneading away like nobody's business.

Virginia Woolf? Yes. Although otherwise an indifferent cook, Virginia could certainly knock you up a lovely cottage loaf. You bet. This strikes me as just the sort of pretentiously frivolous and dilettantish thing a Bloomsbury *would* be good at – knowing how to do one, just one, fatuously complicated kitchen thing and doing that one thing well enough to put the cook's nose out of joint. 'I will come into the kitchen, Louie,' she said to this young employee of hers, 'and show you how to do it.'

This attitude of the dedicated hobbyist reveals the essential marginality of the activity. David manages to turn the honourable craft of the baker into a nice accomplishment for refined ladies. Bread is put in its place; it is a special kind of art-object.

Here is, furthermore, the bitter-sweet bread of nostalgia, summoning up a bygone golden age of golden loaves, before Garfield Weston, of Allied Bakeries, the demon king in the real-bread scenario started buying up British bakeries in the Fifties and smirching with his filthy profane Canadian hands the grand old English loaf.

Although her book is full of quotations – Thomas Traherne, Keats, Chaucer – she does, however, let the heavy freight of symbolic significance borne by bread in our culture severely alone except, oddly enough, for a seventeenth-century French recipe for consecrated bread. This, she claims, sounds like brioche, which suggests it might have been used for a rather Firbankian mass. What *can* they have put in the chalice?

It is appropriate she leaves religion alone since *English Bread and Yeast Cookery* is already proving to be something like the holy book of the cult of the True Loaf, in which the metaphoric halo surrounding bread is turned back on itself, the loaf becomes not foodstuff nor symbol but fetish.

(1987)

YOUR PERFECTED HOSTESS

Elizabeth David

In among the austerity and rationing of post-war Britain, **Elizabeth David** returned from the Mediterranean to England and began writing a cookery column in *Harper's Bazaar*. *A Book of Mediterranean Food*, the first of her nine books, was published in 1950. The inclusion of once scarcely available ingredients in her recipes – such as garlic, basil, aubergines, olive oil and figs – had a lasting impact; her biographer Artemis Cooper wrote that she 'transformed the eating habits of middle-class England'.

Not so long ago it was *quiche Lorraine*. You could hardly go out to a cocktail party without somebody tipping you off about the delicious *quiche* they made in the penthouse restaurant of the new block at the far end of the Finchley Road. At the dinner-table grave discussions would arise as to the proper ingredients of a *quiche* and the desirability or otherwise of putting cheese in the filling.

No doubt it was the recipes put out by the public relations departments of our big food firms and taken up by magazines as editorial backing for advertising which in the end put the *quiche* out of business as a talking point.

By the time our aspiring cooks had absorbed instructions to make this French regional dish with a prefabricated pie-shell, a couple of triangles of processed cheese and a tin of evaporated milk, nothing much of the original remained. The Lorraine part had got away from the *quiche*, and with it its charm and glamour.

A similar fate had already overtaken the Italian *pizza* and the *salad niçoise*, which by the time they'd all finished with it turned out to be nothing more than the time-honoured English mixture of lettuce, tomato, beetroot and hard-boiled eggs. And now it's the turn of a cold soup called *crème vichyssoise*.

This recipe, as evolved some forty years ago by Louis Diat, the French-born chef of the New-York Ritz-Carlton, is, basically, every French housewife's potato and leek soup, puréed, chilled, enriched with fresh cream and sprinkled with chives. One of our troubles about reproducing this dish here in England is that leeks go out of season about the beginning, if any, of the summer, and don't normally come into the shops again until the end of it. Which means that if you must have vichyssoise during the heat-wave period then it has to come out of a tin. Those people, however, who won't stoop to tinned soups but still want to be in the swim with their vichyssoise, have taken to using cucumber instead of leeks, and watercress or mint instead of chives – which are hard to come by unless you grow them yourself. The mixture is still thick and rich and cold – and what's, after all, in a name?

All this seems to be typical of the uneasy phase which English cooking is going through. As soon as any dish with a vaguely romantic-sounding name (you may well ask why anyone should associate Vichy with romance) becomes known you find it's got befogged by the solemn mystique which can elevate a routine leek and potato soup into what the heroine of a recent upper-class-larks novel refers to as 'my perfected Vichyssoise.' Then a semi-glamour monthly publishes a recipe in which the original few pence-worth of kitchen garden vegetables are omitted entirely and their place taken by cream of chicken soup and French cream cheese. With astounding rapidity the food processors move in, and launch some even further debased version which in a wink is turning up at banquets and parties and on the menus of provincial hotels.

'INGREDIENTS Skim Milk Powder, Edible Fat, Flour, Gelatine, Super-Glycerinated Fats, Whole Dried Egg, Cayenne Pepper, Lemon, Oil, Edible Colour. Immerse unopened bag in boiling water and simmer for ten minutes.' So runs the legend on a packet of boil-in-the-bag hollandaise (cut along dotted line and squeeze into sauceboat) garnered from the deep-freeze in a self-service store in the King's Road, Chelsea.

What I'm waiting for is the day when it's going to be clever to serve some relaxed English dish like cauliflower cheese. It'll be fun to watch it going up in the world, and getting into the glossies (pin a gigantic starched linen napkin round the platter) and the sub-Mitford novels (Jean-Pierre's got a hangover and won't touch a thing except Fortnum's tinned cauliflower cheese), thence into the women's weeklies (Maureen was piping her own very special cheese dip round the cauliflower. The candles were lit...), and eventually through all the inevitable transformations and degradations until, dehydrated, double-quick deep-frozen, reboiled and debagged, it finally reaches the tables of our residential hotels and the trays of forty-guinea-a-week nursing homes.

HELLO, ROBERTO

Helen Rosner

A staff writer at the *New Yorker*, **Helen Rosner** grew up in Chicago and now lives in Brooklyn. She was the executive editor of *Eater*, the executive digital editor of *Saveur* and has written for various publications on political activism, travel, books, fashion and design. Rosner is one of the world's foremost authorities on chicken tenders.

This is long, for some definitions of long, but there is a truly excellent recipe for soup at the end of it, so your investment will pay off handsomely. Actually, if you must know, I promised myself I was going to use this space to write about literally anything except for food. I had a whole joke I was planning to do where if I mentioned anything about food I'd instead write "[redacted]" or figure out the HTML to make just a big black bar, and it would become a running gag about how I'm not contractually allowed to write about food unless it's for my day job, and the implication would be that there were lawyers censoring my email newsletter to protect the intellectual property of my employer. Whoops.

My day job does actually involve writing about food. In fact, for many years, I ran the website of a print food magazine, a fancy one that you've probably both heard of and mispronounced the name of. My position involved many things, including spending a lot of time with recipes. Not just cooking them — really, not cooking them very much at all — but a whole lot of thinking about them. As data, as content, as (forgive me) software designed to run on the hardware of the human brain and body.

As written objects, recipes are extraordinarily interesting. Somewhat uniquely among verbal instructions encountered regularly by non-specialists, recipes have evolved a very specific technical structure and vernacular. They don't read like normal writing, because the success of a recipe isn't measured in how fun it is to read, but how effectively it guides its reader to the promised real-life outcome. They follow a pretty standard structure, too: first the headnote, then a list of ingredients, then the steps. They speak in a brisk, often article-free imperative voice. *Skin and debone fillets; place in single layer in greased pan.* There's an assumption that the processor core — sorry, I mean the home cook — can handle a vast vocabulary of specialty verbs, adjectives, and nouns.

In my time at that job, I became a firm believer in this idea of recipe-as-software. I railed against the conversational recipe styles of Elizabeth David, and the stir-until-heartbreak-subsides style of cooking confessional that populated a certain type of blog. I would rage at recipes that called for "pre-heating" ovens, or didn't differentiate between "ginger, minced" and "minced ginger." I wanted no blood in my recipes, not a single drop.

For the last ten years, including the years I spent at that magazine, I've been in a relationship with a man named Jim, who is kind and handsome and extremely intelligent. Those details about his character aren't terribly relevant to the matter at hand, but I want to take a moment to brag about him, because he's one of those people who's so great that he makes me glow in his light, and it's a really fantastic flattering light that smooths my skin and fluffs my hair and generally makes me look like the sort of person who deserves to end up with such a top-notch human like Jim. This glow is a very nice externality of his greatness, and even though it's only Monday it's already been a long week, so this bit of preening is something I'm not embarrassed to indulge in right now. Jim is also really funny, and he has a nice singing voice.

He isn't perfect, thank the good lord. One of his most charming shortcomings is that as a cook, he's more enthusiastic than he is experienced. The tight, military-precise recipes that I zealously believed in do him absolutely no good. In fact, I've realized, they don't do much good for most people. Not only that, but my magazine's endless push for ever more concise recipes hadn't actually been the holy quest for crystalline perfection I'd told myself it was; it was just a morphemic belt-tightening intended to keep the recipes-per-issue number shored up against ever-shrinking page counts. (The situation was dire: In one issue, we used the word "doughnut" so many times that an official downgrade to "donut" bought enough space for a whole extra story.)

Back to Jim: When he wants to cook something, which is often but not too often, I'll sometimes take whatever recipe he plans to make, and rewrite it for him in extremely detailed language, anticipating what his questions might be and trying to include descriptions that will help him understand not just what needs to be done, but why it's done that way. The flour added to the mixer gradually so it doesn't poof out all over the counter; the salt in the pasta water to deepen the flavor; the chicken cooked skin-side down first so the fat will render out, and then you can cook the skin-up side in the chicken fat!

It turns out that this is a great way to write a recipe. It forces you to really think about what you're asking someone to do, to put your eyes behind their eyes and your hands on top of their hands, and to make sure you're taking care of them. That's the real point of a recipe, anyway: you want it to serve the person making it, not serve some maximally efficient, minimal-expressive-character Platonic ideal of a chicken piccata.

Enter Roberto. It's a lot like other sausage and bean and kale soups. But it's different from them in one key way, which is that it's better. I couldn't tell you why — maybe it's the tomato, which adds some zingy acidity to the backbone — but I suspect the name might have a lot to do with it. I first made it probably five or six years ago, a hacked-together recipe based on a vague desire for something really hearty and savory and warming and, okay, plausibly low-carb. It turned out to be so perfect and so wonderful that we started having it for dinner three or four times a week. After maybe the fifteenth or sixteenth batch we realized it needed a name — not just "sausage and bean and kale soup" but a proper name. So Jim (who, have I mentioned, is a genius) looked down at his bowl of sausage and bean and kale soup and said "Roberto. Your name is Roberto."

Here's the recipe for Roberto, thus dubbed, as I wrote it for Jim. The ingredients are just the ingredients; all the stuff you need to do to them (chop the onion, kind of thing) is in the instructions. There are lots of alternatives built in, because this recipe is very forgiving, and also because I don't want to deal with Jim texting me asking if it's okay to use turkey sausage instead of chicken sausage, which yes it obviously is, but for Jim—and maybe for a lot of cooks who are just stretching their wings—it may not be. Yet.

What you need

Olive oil
1 baseball-size onion, if you have one (if you don't have one, it's okay)
2-4 cloves garlic (enough garlic to make up approximately the volume of your thumb)
Salt
1 pound hot italian sausage (chicken or turkey if you can find it — pork sausage is fatty, which makes for good sausage but not the best soup) (do not use breakfast sausage)
1 28oz can tomatoes, diced or crushed or whole and then you can crush them yourself later in the recipe
1 14oz can of beans of any type (kidney, great northern, garbanzo, etc.)
4 cups of broth (chicken, beef, veggie, or honestly just a mix of water and wine is great)
1 bunch of kale, doesn't matter what kind but I prefer curly
Pepper
Hard, salty cheese like Parmesan or pecorino
A lemon

What you have to do

1. Get things ready for the first round of stuff-doing. Find the olive oil. Get out a soup pot and a wooden spoon. Make sure the sausage is removed from its casing, so it's like a paste of ground meat with seasonings in it, which is mostly all that sausage is. Peel and chop your onion and peel and chop your garlic.

2. Do the first things: Put the olive oil and onions in the soup pot over

medium heat, throw a pinch of salt in with it (a pinch is about a quarter teaspoon) and stir them all together. Slowly cook them all until the onions are soft and translucent, about 4 minutes, but sometimes as many as 7. Add the garlic and wooden-spoon it around in the onion until you get hit with that nostalgic garlic-and-onion smell, about 1 minute. Raise the heat to medium-high and add the sausage. Stir it into the onion and garlic, breaking it up in the pot into small pieces that could comfortably fit on a spoon. It's better to overcook than undercook the sausage: For the best flavor, you want the pieces to start to brown on the outside. It should look speckled with dark spots, like a leopard or a cute dog. This will take as many as 10 minutes. Be patient.

3. While the sausage is cooking, get ready for the second round of stuff-doing. Open your can of tomatoes. Open and drain your can of beans. Get your broth ready, or if you're using water with wine, get that ready. (I like a ratio of 3 cups of water to one cup of wine, and it's better with white wine but red is totally fine.) De-stem the kale and chop it into smaller-than-spoon-size pieces.

4. When the sausage is starting to brown and looks and smells delicious, dump in the tomatoes (including all the liquid), the beans (it's okay if there's a little liquid left in the can, add that too), and 4 cups of the broth/whatever and bring the whole thing to a simmer. If you'd used canned whole tomatoes, use your wooden spoon to break them up by violently crushing them against the side of the pot. You cannot over-crush the tomatoes.

5. Once it's at a simmer, add the kale. The pot will probably look extremely full—don't worry about that, because the kale will collapse like an empty wedding gown as soon as you start stirring it in. Get the greens in there and put the lid on and turn the heat down back to medium and let the whole thing simmer for about 5 minutes more, or even longer if you want to. Use these five minutes to grate some of the cheese into a bowl, which you can reuse later to eat one of the servings of soup out of. Not a lot of cheese, maybe a quarter cup. Taste the soup (use the wooden spoon, you're less likely to burn your

mouth) and decide how much salt and black pepper you think it needs. Then add half as much salt as you want to, and twice as much pepper. Add a little more pepper. Dump in the shredded cheese and stir it all in. The cheese has salt in it, is the secret.

6. Serve the soup, which is very hot, in bowls. Buy some time for it to cool down by cutting a lemon into wedges and squeezing a wedge of juice into each bowl. Watch out for seeds. Don't drop the wedge in like it's a glass of iced tea, just throw it away. If you have parsley and want to chop up some parsley and put it on top, you can, and it'll be good, but it's also pretty great without it.

This was first published in October, 2016, in the e-mail newsletter Helen: A Handbasket

WHAT MRS. FISHER KNOWS ABOUT OLD SOUTHERN COOKING

Abby Fisher

Abby Fisher was a formerly enslaved woman from South Carolina. After moving across the country to California, Fisher earned a living as a pickle manufacturer and published *What Mrs. Fisher Knows About Old Southern Cooking* in 1881. Unable to read or write, she dictated the cookbook to friends. The book was lost following the San Francisco earthquake and fire of 1906, but re-emerged at a 1984 Sotheby's auction in New York City. It was reprinted in 1985.

39 Ox-Tail Soup.

Take two quarts of bouillon to two ox-tails; boil down to three pints. You can put in either ochra or vermicelli. Season with salt and pepper. Skim all grease off while boiling. Have the butcher unjoint the ox-tail.

40 Calf's Head Soup.

Let the butcher open the head wide. Take the brains from it and lay into clean water with a little salt. Leave the tongue in the head when put on to boil; when the tongue is tenderly boiled or done, take it out of the pot and let it get cold for making tongue salad. Two gallons of water to a calf's head; boil to one gallon; strain it off clear for soup to one dozen guests. Take two quarts of this liquid and put to boil; two tablespoonfuls of flour and brown it; one tablespoonful of butter; rub into the brown flour till it comes to a cream, then add to the soup gradually, and stir well while adding. Season with salt and pepper, and a little red pepper.

While cooking, boil a small piece of thyme and the half of an ordinary sized onion tied tight in a clean linen rag, and to be taken out of soup when done. One teaspoonful of mustard mixed with one tablespoon-ful of wine, to be put into the tureen before pouring in the soup hot, also one glass of sherry wine. Pick all skin from brains; beat two eggs light and add to the brains, then beat the eggs and brains together to a batter; take one-quarter tea cup of powdered cracker, one tablespoonful of flour added to the brains and egg batter well beaten together. Then make this brain batter in cake the size of a hickory nut, and fry them brown in hot fat just before taking up soup, and send to table on separate dish. Serve them with the soup, two cakes to a plate of soup.

P. S. Chop parsley very fine, and boil it into the soup. You will find the calf's head soup the most delicious soup in the cookery. Study the recipe and remember it well.

41 Mock Turtle Soup.

Follow the same directions given for calf's head soup. Prepare your calf's head in the same way exactly. Use for flavor half of a lemon sliced, and put in tureen and pour hot soup on. Instead of brain-balls or cakes, make a forced meat of boiled ham chopped very fine with the yelk of a hard boiled egg; season with black pepper. Make balls the size of a hickory nut and fry in hot butter. Send to table in separate dish, serving one ball to a plate of soup. Use beef in place of ham if liked best.

42 Green Turtle Soup.

To two pounds of turtle add two quarts of water, put to boil on a slow fire and cook down to three pints. Season while boiling with pepper and salt to taste. Take three hard boiled eggs, slice very thin and lay in tureen; slice one-fourth of a lemon and put in tureen also. Then pour in tureen one gill of sherry wine. Then pour on hot soup and send to table. The above quantity will make soup for one dozen guests. If there are more to serve, increase the quantity.

43 Oyster Gumbo Soup.

Take an old chicken, cut into small pieces, salt and black pepper. Dip it well in flour, and put it on to fry, over a slow fire, till brown; don't let it burn. Cut half of a small onion very fine and sprinkle on chicken while frying. Then place chicken in soup pot, add two quarts water and let it boil to three pints. Have one quart of fresh oysters with all the liquor that belongs to them, and before dishing up soup, add oysters and let come to a boil the second time, then stir into soup one tablespoonful of gumbo quickly. Dish up and send to table. Have parsley chopped very fine and put in tureen on dishing up soup. Have dry boiled rice to go to table with gumbo in separate dish. Serve one tablespoonful of rice to a plate of gumbo.

44 Ochra Gumbo.

Get a beef shank, have it cracked and put to boil in one gallon of water. Boil to half a gallon, then strain and put back on fire. Cut ochra in small pieces and put in soup; don't put in any ends of ochra. Season with salt and pepper while cooking. Stir it occasionally and keep it from burning. To be sent to table with dry boiled rice. Never stir rice while boiling. Season rice always with salt when it is first put on to cook, and do not have too much water in rice while boiling.

45 Old Fashioned Turnip Soup.

Take two pounds veal bones to half a gallon of water, and boil to one quart. Put turnips and bones on to boil together, then strain the liquor off and send to table hot. Season while cooking with pepper and salt.

46 Chicken Soup for the Sick.

Take an old chicken and put on with one gallon of water; boil down to half a gallon. Take the yelks of two eggs, tie them up in a clean cloth with a little thyme and put in the soup after you have strained the meat from it, and put back to boil till down to three pints. Dish up and send to table hot. Season with salt and pepper to taste.

47 Corn and Tomato Soup.

Take a fresh beef bone, put on to boil with one gallon of water, and when boiling skim the grease off. Cut corn from cob and scald tomatoes with boiling water. Skin them and put both vegetables into soup, the corn ten minutes before dinner. Cut tomatoes in small pieces and let them boil in soup at least one hour.

LONGTHROAT MEMOIRS: SOUPS, SEX AND NIGERIAN TASTE BUDS

Yẹmisí Aríbisálà

Food writer, essayist, painter and food memorist **Yẹmisí Aríbisálà**'s award-winning first book is a collection of essays exploring Nigerian cuisine. Aríbisálà has written for various publications, including the *New Yorker*, *Vogue*, *Chimurenga*, *Popula*, *Google Arts & Culture*, the *Johannesburg Review of Books*, *Critical Muslim 26: Gastronomy*, *Sandwich Magazine*, the *Guardian*, *Aké Review* and *Olongo Africa*. Her food writing involves 'noting the influence of food on life and life on food and attempting to weave an accurate cultural landscape'.

Okro Soup, Gorgeous Mucilage

Siddhartha Mitter's essay 'Free Okra: Rescuing a vegetable from a slimy stereotype' was all the justification I needed in the world to unreservedly allow myself my first aesthetic bowl of okro soup. You would think I needed no permission to do this, but I live in Calabar and there is no cultural point of reference here for eulogising okro soup or being sentimental about food. Okro is much-loved but handled as perfunctorily and efficiently as an official file. Most Nigerians I know, myself included, are not naturally sentimental people. I imagine that prettifying food feels a lot like being soft when dealing with a child, stroking a dog, crying on Oprah, acting the wimp. I don't know any Nigerian – and this is no generalisation – who allows themselves the luxury of feeling so much, except in Pentecostal church services. Perhaps it's for the simple reason that you would not survive the bombardment of a weekday as a Nigerian if you did.

Siddhartha Mitter is Indian, his family originating from Calcutta and Boston. He paints a picture of the cooking okro in the very first paragraph, which I read over and over because it presents itself like a religious experience:

> *Indians often call okra 'lady's fingers', and the preparations that came off the charcoal fire that the village-raised cook preferred to the kitchen stove were everything that the name connotes: smooth, delicate and perfumed. Mustard oil infused the okra slices and deepened their flavor. Cumin, turmeric, or chilies added zest. This was okra unabashed and uncut, the perfect offset to a classic Bengali meal of pungent river fish and simple steamed rice. The pods were rich, pillowy, and moist. I became hooked on okra for life.*[1]

I have willingly taken a cue from Mitter's defensive reverence, joining him in acknowledging that there is an agenda and language of the enemy; gastronomical bullying anchored in words like 'slime' and 'goo'. I cannot write it better than he does: 'the dishes the coloniser rudely rejected turn into sources of shame.'[2]

My glossy Heritage Publishing *South African Cookbook* describes okro as 'a mucilaginous pod which becomes slimy when cooked and as such is not liked by all.'[3] The cookbook is, of course, being cordial.

Shape magazine is less diplomatic. It has listed 'okra' as number twenty-four of twenty-seven 'Ugly Foods You Should Be Eating'. They are described as '[c]one-shaped' with 'weird seeds inside' and are said to 'help your digestion and colon due to lubricating mucilage.'[4]

1 Siddhartha Mitter, 'Free Okra: Rescuing a vegetable from a slimy stereotype', *Oxford American*, 49, 2005.

2 Mitter, 'Free Okra'.

3 A Comprehensive Guide to Vegetables' in *South African Cookbook* (Heritage Publishing, 2006), 186.

4 Ysolt Usigan, 'Ugly Foods You Should Be Eating', *Shape*. Accessed 13 January 2016. http://www.shape.com/healthy-eating/diet-tips/ugly-foods-you-should-be-eating

I am grateful to Mitter for pointing out that these conclusions made by such 'authorities' exclude but in no way negate the opinion of huge tracts of the gumbo, okro, okra and quimgumbo eating world, such as Haiti, Egypt, Turkey, India and the Ivory Coast. From the US he lists New Orleans; Charleston Checotah, Oklahoma; and Cleveland, Mississippi, even though he qualifies North American enthusiasm by noting that '[m]eandering across the South on a series of okra pilgrimages, I found that okra's marginalization runs deep.'[5]

There are millions of global okro-loving citizens for whom mucilage – the 'draw' – is a fundamental craving, a deeply invested love affair, a genetic imprint. Call it what you like; it's proof that there is no such phenomenon as okro becoming less popular. South Asians show culture-confidence in cooking their 'bhindi' in curries with garam masala, cumin, turmeric and lemon juice. In her cookbook, *The Real Taste of Jamaica*, Jamaican cuisine doyenne Enid Donaldson suggests that 'ochroes' are washed and drained, while one egg is separated, the yolk beaten first, the white added after. The whole ochroes are dropped in the beaten egg, and then into a mixture of cornmeal, flour and salt. They are fried in oil in a heavy skillet until browned lightly, then drained and served hot with salt. The crispy outside texture is balanced by the soft inside texture.[6]

Japanese health researcher, Junji Takano, exhorts us to eat okro raw with mayonnaise or vinegar and pepper.[7] The suggestion should only be taken on board if one fancies the idea of a mucilaginous cucumber with exploding white seeds or perhaps if one believes this was the bona fide beauty secret of Yang Guifei, the exquisite Chinese consort of the Tang Dynasty.

It goes without saying that Nigerians are avid okro eaters, mucilage eaters, although the cooking of okro sometimes merits the use of bad words. The cooking I can describe is nothing like Mitter's poetic imagery

5 Mitter, 'Free Okra'.

6 Enid Donaldson, *The Real Taste of Jamaica* (Kingston: Ian Randle Publishers, 1996).

7 Junji Takano, 'Health Benefits of Okra'. Accessed 20 March 2016. http://www.pyroenergen.com/articles07/okra-health-benefits.htm

of Calcutta. There is the big-knife-and-wooden-board approach that you can hear from three houses away. The okro fingers are cut into small pieces, then chopped, then jounce-chopped to within an inch of life. The seeds are pounded with the knife until the personality of the vegetable is extracted from every pristine seed to create green and white surrender. The okro is then cooked in oil and stock with fish, meat and smoked crayfish until you have a pot of goo. It is cooked for close to twenty minutes until it flatlines. It is what it is. It's goo.

In more internal regions of Cross River State, okro is pounded with a mortar and pestle (otong soup) because the goal is to create the highest degree of draw. An in-law from Gboko in Benue State explained that to cook okro soup well, it is necessary to let it 'draw well-well'. The draw must be tight enough to require the snapping of wrist and upper arm to cut up the soup when lifting it to the mouth.

It's called arm-choreography: first a piece of the mound of pounded yam, gari or fufu is pulled off and rolled into a ball. It is depressed with the thumb to form a spoon, and then the spoon is used to scoop the soup. The soup is reluctant or asleep and an effective scoop involves invading the soup with the morsel of pounded yam and pulling away with a brisk tug of the arm. This is no ordinary tug; it is skilfully done so that the soup breaks away neatly without drawing messy patterns all over the utensils and the table.

Our neighbours in south-eastern Nigeria (who, technically speaking, are not our neighbours because when you are in the border towns of Manfe, Ekok, Mfum or Ekang there is no difference between Cameroon and Nigeria, or Cameroonians and Nigerians), hold in high esteem a soup called nkui. On a scale of one to ten of draw soups it is ten and a half, which means it sometimes needs to be cut with 'a something' or separated by holding it and putting pressure on it – just slightly less pressure than squeezing a tube of toothpaste. An attempt to nonchalantly pick it up like normal draw soup, would, in the first instance, require some level of grip on it. It's dangerous to attempt to put it in one's mouth without cutting it into small portions because it can snake down the throat of the eater, gagging them.

The otong soup, in the words of an Efik food purist, is another formal okra soup that is an overstatement of draw. Some people want their ogbono soup cooked with okro to make it more mucilaginous. Each to his own, but ogbono soup cooked like this holds zero appeal for me.

I was brought up cooking okro like an aside in the conversation. You got out the grater, and used the middle section that didn't grate too small. You brushed the okro against the chosen side until you had a pile of grated vegetable similar to but coarser than the one chopped with board and knife, although at least the seeds were intact. You boiled a small pan of water, dropped the fresh okro into it, stirred it to spread it out, added a small piece of potash and a pinch of Maggi, and in eight minutes it was ready. You didn't think too much about it because you were focused on the stew and the mound of ebà or àmàlà and the pieces of meat. At best it had the relevance of a cucumber raita; at worst it only functioned as lubricant to move the ebà along. It was possibly a stimulating island of green refereeing the coarse beige of ebà and the red of stew, but only for those people who think too much. It was never, ever the focus of the meal.

I married into the heavy-handed interpretation of okro soup, with the blanket-like smell of smoked crayfish, and the extended cooking until the face of the soup becomes grey. It was as if the green was an offence; an indication of undesirable rawness.

In 2008, in Lagos, I ordered a takeaway okro soup from The Yellow Chilli restaurant in Victoria Island. It was green and fresh, seeds whole and texturally intact, cooked with just a touch of palm oil for no longer than a few minutes. My first impression of the unprepossessing yellow plastic takeaway container was redeemed by the fat spirit that floated out when it was opened: a big, gamey umami aroma of he-goat meat sliding off the bone. The okro was not chopped fine, blended or grated; it was cut into even tapering Pennette Lisce-like pieces by some unpatriotic unNigerian machine. The marrow in the goat bones was like peppery butter. This was a beautiful, clever, faithful interpretation of a customarily odorous home-cooked meal, executed with respect and love and sentiment. I, the eater, was moved.

It was a one-off. I never met the person who cooked that meal but it was apparent that they were having an emotive day. I wondered if they'd had their wrist slapped for it. I returned again and again but never got that same calibre of food, with the same artistic investment. As if to confirm that the food, the day, my approach, my enthusiasm – the whole package – was a complete aberration, the person who I reluctantly offered a share of my takeaway meal to looked into the container, folded his face like an unironed napkin and said, 'It is too fresh!'

In the competition between my growing-up version and ila alásèpo, the Cross Riverian one I married into, the latter was the self-righteous winner. It wins because someone has put effort and meat into it. The Yorùbá are gastronomic lightweights who lost because they cook okro in the nonchalant way that produces a characterless green nonentity that cannot legitimately call itself a soup.

My father still eats okro with everything: boiled plantains, boiled yam, steamed rice, àmàlà, ebà – everything and anything. He certainly has no regard for the international snubbing of okro, nor have I ever heard him voice a preference for degrees of mucilaginousness, and my father is a notoriously finicky eater. I therefore gained an obsession with okro as a congenital condition, eating it all the time, some nights as comfort food before slouching off to bed. If I'm feeling ill or gloomy, ebà and okro is the surefire remedy.

Unlike my father, I am particular about how mucilaginous my okro is. The draw must be light. The okro must be cut in big chunks, the seeds intact, retaining their bursting texture between the teeth. The okro chunks must be boiled for barely five minutes in more water than is required. It is not stirred, but allowed to adjust itself. A few slivers of onion, one hot pepper, a grudging spoon of palm oil and salt is all that it needs. No meat should tarnish this meal, but lightly smoked catfish is welcome. The gari for the ebà must be well-fermented Ijebu gari that makes your teeth jump. At the end of cooking, the okro must be green, not muggy.

My congenital okro condition has not only resulted in the eating of okro but in a long-running experiment to see whether okro soup will ever become rave-reviewed fine-dining fare while retaining its integrity: cut up, mucilaginous, yet innovatively conceived, pretty enough to tempt anyone to try it at least once. The obsession is a niggling matter of wasted potential. In Lagos, one will find food designed for the fine diner from every corner of the world, and Nigerians mechanically paying good money for caricatures of these cuisines. But a well-executed bowl of okro soup not cooked with a buka mindset may be a once-in-a-lifetime occurrence, like my Yellow Chilli version, unless perhaps one travels to New Orleans.

Pierre Thiam, the Senegalese-born visionary who owns a restaurant in Brooklyn has taken food from the heart of Senegal and translated it into fine-dining feasts in New York. He sent me his version of okro soup cooked in the restaurant Yolele:

> with seafood reminiscent of its New Orleans cousin (gumbo) adding mussels, shrimp, crabmeat and lots of okra and of course palm oil. I would keep the mussels fresh in the shell and add them last to the stew until they open up (5–7 minutes). It presents quite well this way and I serve with rice or fonio (a grain that is considered as the oldest cultivated African grain). Okra is not for everyone but who cares, it's my favorite.

The Nigerian beautification proves most difficult. It was easy to find glowing testimonials in the newspapers about okro soup's two-way lubricating qualities – helping the gari down the oesophagus, and sending it out of the large intestine; a most commendable quality since alternative medical practitioners believe all disease begins in the colon. More glowing testimonials laud okro's protection of the human body from diabetes, high cholesterol, colon cancer, atherosclerosis, lung inflammation, cataracts and depression. It is loaded with vitamin A, and the contentious draw is due to calcium. It contains folic acid, iron, potassium, protein, and vitamin C. My favourite okro soup morale was in Femi Kúsá's column in *The Nation*: 'Natural Remedies for Sound Body and Mind'. It stated that 'the chlorophyll, blood of the [okro], converts to human blood, leaving behind lots of magnesium to power and calm the muscles, particularly the heart.'[8]

The mechanics of okro turning to human blood has a compelling 'Africa Magic' sound to it. But after reading widely on the proficiency of okro in keeping the body healthy, I still had to conclude that it is like the case of the fear of God not successfully making men good. No matter how therapeutic okro is, I wouldn't eat the village version or expect anyone who has no prior relationship with okro to do so, because in the first instance it is too sure of itself in its unventilated mucilaginousness. *Monkey no fine but im mama like am* cannot be the pay-off line for getting anyone to eat a bowl of Nigerian okro soup in a restaurant. Even more so than most vegetables, because of its textural peculiarity and single-minded global naysayers, okro is going to have to loosen its tie and work hard to become fine-dining fare.

My friend Reme Obaseki, a brilliant Nigerian chef, gave me his mother Shirley's okro soup recipe as a possible compromise:

> *crabs and lobster are cooked in the stock. Chopped onions are added to the stock towards the end of cooking it. The crabmeat and lobster meat are removed from their shells and put in a bowl. Blended Scotch bonnet peppers, ketchup, tabasco and Worcestershire sauce are added to the meat. The okro is cut up and plainly steamed. The shellfish sauce and cooked okro are accompanied with steamed rice, pasta Aglio e Olio or a Greek salad*

Like Mitter's Bengali description, the wording is beautiful. It appeals to the mind (the determined and vigilant centre of hostility toward the okro vegetable) but the average Nigerian would see it, admire it, and conclude it very hoity-toity for a bowl of Nigerian okro. Not real; just some kind of pretension or make-believe okro soup.

If I was going to attempt restaurant-quality okro soup, every detail would need particular attention. I would need organically grown okro.

8 Femi Kúsá, 'Natural Remedies for Sound Body and Mind', *The Nation*, 14 January 2010.

The soil matters as the very first incontrovertible requirement. The okro must not travel far from the farm to the market. It should be no bigger than an inch in length, with cactus-like needles and petite linear leaves at the base. You shouldn't be able to handle the okro without getting needles in your fingers. They must be so fresh that you feel the crack under the weight of the knife when you cut them.

That fresh feeling also translates into the quickness of cutting through each okro. In Nigeria, cutting fresh food into large pieces is done against the hand as opposed to using a chopping board and there is some sense of pride invested in this style of cutting. If you were going to chop okro into the masticated food pieces that produce the heavy-draw version of okro that I described earlier, you would start by cutting each okro against your hand. Even if one cannot comfortably handle the fresh okro, one would persevere because only wimps cut okro against boards!

The emphasis on freshness is because I believe that no one who is given fresh okro to eat can resist them. The crispness of plump pearl-coloured seeds and contrasting clover-green flesh cannot possibly offend anyone. Best of all is if the okro have fuchsia stalks.

Okro Soup

450g small, fresh, prickly okro, each cut into 6–8 large pieces

200g bawa peppers or sweet green peppers. (Bawa are large red peppers between sweet and Tatase)

50g leeks

1 or 2 very hot Scotch bonnets, if you like

300g fresh prawns (weighed in their shells)

1½ cups palm oil

Lightly smoked catfish

A few pieces of smoked fish ground in a dry mill to accentuate the flavour of the soup

A handful of dawadawa

Ground Cameroonian pepper and good sea salt

1 cup water

The palm oil is poured into an unglazed earthenware pot and heated very slightly. The heat under the pot is kept low at all times. The peppers and leeks are ground in a blender with a few drops of water and poured into the palm oil. The dawadawa and ground smoked fish are added to the ground peppers and oil. The pot is covered and the blend allowed to cook. Water is added to rehydrate the soup, especially because unglazed earthenware pots absorb moisture. The cooking of the peppers and leeks should take about 20 minutes. The smoked catfish is placed carefully in the soup when the flavours of peppers and oil are well fused and cooked. Stirring is kept to a minimum to retain the integrity of the fish. The okro goes in with a sprinkling of ground Cameroonian pepper. The heat is turned down completely and the soup covered, so that the okro steams and retains its greenness and some crunch. Once the okro is cooked (about 8 minutes if the hob fire is kept low), the prawns are added and allowed to cook for a further 5 minutes. The seasoning is adjusted. Another sparing sprinkling of Cameroonian peppers will make the face of the soup very attractive.

White bowls are warmed to serve the okro with a small hill of gari or steamed ripe plantains.

There remains the possibility that the average Nigerian will look into my pot, fold his face like an unironed napkin and proclaim it 'too fresh', but the combined aroma of palm oil, smoked fish and cooking peppers will uphold the integrity of the soup. The ground smoked fish will give quick and powerful umami and depth of flavour. The blended peppers will embellish the mucilaginousness, making it multidimensional, enjoyable for the palate yet retaining its binding quality. The draw will be elegant: light enough for the uninitiated, mucilaginous enough for the lover of mucilage. It will be green enough for the colonic irrigator, pretty enough for the fine diner.

At the very least, it will be an authentic conversational piece at the global dining table.

MAKING MENUDO WITH MY ABUELA

Jené Gutierrez

Jené Gutierrez is a writer and therapist living in Austin, Texas.

I have no memory of the first time I ate my abuela's menudo. As far back as I can recall, the dish has always been a staple and centerpiece of communion with my Mexican family. Walking into my grandparents' home, one of the first questions that greets you is "¿Tienes hambre?" and I always answer in the affirmative when it comes to menudo. Around the table, we relish the nourishment we get from this flavorful dish, slurping and sharing my abuela's transcendent soup, none of us able to deny its power to call us to the table.

I cherish the ritual of menudo for this power, how it brings all of us together in our mutual enjoyment of this familial sacrament, but also because it connects me to a culture I have never felt fully able to claim as my own, largely due to my biraciality. I straddle the boundary between two cultures, one far more imposing than the other. I felt this disconnect all the more keenly during my recent holiday trip to my grandparents' home in Corpus Christi, Texas, where I was determined to finally learn the secrets of my abuela's menudo preparation. When you're in a room among people who share a language in which you lack proficiency, you are an outsider, even when blood binds you together. No matter how hard you try to translate each word and turn of phrase, you will never feel fully present in the conversation. For me, a person who greatly values language and conversation, this proves especially frustrating.

Since I was not immersed in the language as a child, all the Spanish I've learned has been acquired in classes or self-taught. Once I enrolled in a graduate-level Spanish course only to drop out before the professor arrived on the first day, intimidated by the fluency and intimacy with which my classmates already spoke their native language. I sometimes give my father a hard time for not teaching me Spanish when I was growing up, but I understand why he didn't. For him and his sisters, children of immigrants who only spoke Spanish when they first arrived in the States, it was crucial to learn English, which they primarily did by watching TV and attending school. They were often criticized for speaking Spanish. Passing along their native language to their children did not necessarily occur to them, since they had no choice but to speak English while their native language was marginalized.

I can't ignore the deep shame I feel in never mastering Spanish. My responsibility to language compels me to focus so much on vocabulary, grammar, and saying or hearing the right thing that I can't relax and learn. I am buried under the weight of perfectionism: too many variables, too many choices, too much to analyze. I do like the way Spanish words feel in my mouth, the way they tumble out like they *almost* belong. But I have never felt they *do* belong, because there is nothing that anchors the words—they leave my mouth and nothing deep inside me resonates. Speaking Spanish is like speaking in some impersonal code, one I'm simply trying to execute to convey meaning. I don't feel comfortable or confident speaking the Spanish I do know in front of my family—I end up feeling like I disrespect them and our ancestors by butchering their language in front of them.

*

If food is like a language in how it conveys purpose, communion, and meaning, then menudo is its own dialect in my family. Menudo is special: Unlike other Mexican dishes (tacos, enchiladas, or tamales) that have been popularized by American culture, menudo has been largely ignored. Although time-consuming, the dish is relatively easy to prepare.

Made from beef tripe, specifically the cow's stomach lining, menudo is not a dish you'll hear many Americans raving about. As Pat Perini notes in a 1974 *Texas Monthly* article that rings true forty years later, "[T]ripe

. . . like most organ meats, suffers wide disdain among Anglos." Freshly butchered tripe is a white sheet with a honeycomb pattern, a pattern that induces fear and anxiety in some (one Redditor actually claims menudo as the root of their trypophobia). When my abuela instructed me to cut the manteca (fat) from the meat, I could not easily discern the white fat from the strange white meat while making cuts, and we needed sharp knives to slice through the rubbery texture.

The tripa does not, on its surface, appeal to me. But the flavor of the broth comes from this meat, a flavor I was born loving. The fact that this organ meat turns some people off somehow endears the dish to me even more. In fact, I've ordered the soup at restaurants (never as tasty as mi abuela's) only to test the reaction of some of my friends. The difficult meat is like a difficult phrase, maybe akin to an idiom—an expression that can only be appreciated in the context of its origins and culture. Menudo, then, is not for the faint of heart (or stomach). I'm with Victor Balta, though, when he writes, "[I]f a preschooler can handle it, so can you."

Widely believed to have peasant roots—haciendo owners would take the best cuts of beef for themselves and give their farmers the less desirable portions—menudo means "minute, small" and the word is also used as a metonym for the beef tripe itself. Essentially, menudo exists because of the ingenuity of peasant families, trying to create the most food out of what was on hand and to make it flavorful. Commonly served during holidays and celebrations, menudo also has the distinction of being a cure for el crudo, a hangover.

Most of the work involved in cooking menudo lies in the time spent cutting the tripe and boiling it with copious amounts of oregano for around four hours to soften it. I hadn't realized until my recent trip that the aroma I associate with menudo is oregano, an herb known for its own healing properties. After the tripe is cooked, you can add other cuts of beef—my abuela likes to boil patas (beef feet) separately with garlic and oregano, then add them to the broth, along with cubes of chuck. The chile paste—made with a red pepper like the ancho and ground up with seasoning using a molcajuete—comes next, creating a rich red color for the menudo that infuses the broth with more flavor and spice.

Last, but certainly not least, plenty of hominy is poured into the soup. Once served, we add lemon or lime and onions before diving in.

*

Each family has its own method. I had always assumed that a dish this delicious would involve a more complicated preparation. Participating in this tradition with my dad and my abuela allowed me a more intimate relationship with this beloved family food. As we prepared it together, I could imagine my ancestors gathering its few ingredients, taking the time to create a healing broth that could feed many people at once (and always enough for seconds). And I can understand and admire the determination and skill that allowed them to take an "unwanted" cut of meat and transform it into this treasure of a dish, the alchemy of waste into wealth.

*

Interpreting a foreign language is its own alchemy, but one that doesn't always yield the treasure I hope to find, the essence of meaning, an evasive thing that is often lost when I try to comprehend and translate it. This loss frustrates me, so I turn my attention to something I can understand fully, with only the knowledge of translation a body can bring. Nothing is lost in menudo, a dish created out of loss and therefore impervious to losing.

Menudo's meaning lies in its roots, ritual, and consumption, and its curative power helps restore me to a past that belongs to my Mexican family and their ancestors, a special bond that deepens my relationship to a culture that has always found creative ways to transcend oppression. Through this custom, I connect to something larger than myself, something more substantial, a thread that can be ephemerally traced back to a heritage and a lifestyle I know little about but now experience as a sharing of flavor and nourishment with my family. Receiving this act of comestible grace, I am momentarily transported without language and without analysis to a place that requires only the lifting of a spoon to my mouth to connect me with my ancestors, each bite affirming the faith I have in the miracle of their hands—how they managed to survive with the gumption and dexterity to create their own reality; to sow seeds of rubbish and create a ritual of abundance.

At home with my family, amidst a language I cannot fully comprehend and a culture that sometimes feels distant and nearly lost to me, I take my place at the table and begin the journey I have always known. I vow to always take that which has been discarded and lost and to try to redeem it, to recognize the power in what others choose to ignore and cast aside with no regard for its potential, knowing that within me is a secret inherited from my forebears that enables me to receive even these poor rations and transform them into a salve for the heart, mind, and body, a magic antidote for everything lost.

LOVE, LOSS AND KIMCHI

Michelle Zauner

Korean–American **Michelle Zauner** is an author and lead vocalist of the band Japanese Breakfast. *Crying at H Mart,* her memoir, was on *The New York Times*' hardcover bestseller list for more than a year in 2021 and 2022. The book explores Zauner's experience of growing up as the only Asian–American kid in her school in Oregon, Korean food, and her mother's death from cancer. It is currently being adapted into a film, for which Zauner will provide the music. The contest-winning essay that follows was first published in American magazine *Glamour* in 2016.

I'm so tired of white guys on TV telling me what to eat. I'm tired of Anthony Bourdain testing the waters of Korean cuisine to report back that, not only will our food not kill you, it actually *tastes* good. I don't care how many times you've traveled to Thailand, I won't listen to you—just like the white kids wouldn't listen to me, the half-Korean girl, defending the red squid tentacles in my lunch box. The same kids who teased me relentlessly back then are the ones who now celebrate our cuisine as the Next Big Thing.

I grew up in the Pacific Northwest, in a small college town that was about 90 percent white. In my adolescence I hated being half Korean; I wanted people to stop asking, "Where are you *really* from?" I could barely speak the language and didn't have any Asian friends. There was nothing about me that felt Korean—except when it came to food.

At home my mom always prepared a Korean dinner for herself and an American dinner for my dad. Despite the years he'd lived in Seoul, selling cars to the military and courting my mom at the Naija Hotel where she worked, my dad is still a white boy from Philadelphia. He's an adventurous eater (ask him about steamed dog meat), but his comfort foods are meat and potatoes.

So each night my mom prepared two meals. She'd steam broccoli and grill Dad's salmon, while boiling jjigae and plating little side dishes known as banchan. When our rice cooker announced in its familiar robotic voice, "Your delicious white rice will be ready soon!" the three of us would sit down to a wondrous mash-up of East and West. I'd create true fusion one mouthful at a time, using chopsticks to eat strips of T-bone and codfish eggs drenched in sesame oil, all in one bite. I liked my baked potatoes with fermented chili paste, my dried cuttlefish with mayonnaise.

There's a lot to love about Korean food, but what I love most is its extremes. If a dish is supposed to be served hot, it's scalding. If it's meant to be served fresh, it's still moving. Stews are served in heavy stone pots that hold the heat; crack an egg on top, and it will poach before your eyes. Cold noodle soups are served in bowls made of actual ice.

By my late teens my craving for Korean staples started to eclipse my desire for American ones. My stomach ached for al tang and kalguksu. On long family vacations, with no Korean restaurant in sight, my mom and I passed up hotel buffets in favor of microwaveable rice and roasted seaweed in our hotel room.

And when I lost my mother to a very sudden, brief, and painful fight with cancer two years ago, Korean food was my comfort food. She was diagnosed in 2014. That May she'd gone to the doctor for a stomachache only to learn she had a rare squamous cell carcinoma, stage four, and that it had spread. Our family was blindsided.

I moved back to Oregon to help my mother through chemotherapy; over the next four months, I watched her slowly disappear. The treatment took everything—her hair, her spirit, her appetite. It burned sores on her tongue. Our table, once beautiful and unique, became a battleground of protein powders and tasteless porridge. I crushed Vicodin into ice cream.

Dinnertime was a calculation of calories, an argument to get anything down. The intensity of Korean flavors and spices became too much for her to stomach. She couldn't even eat kimchi.

I began to shrink along with my mom, becoming so consumed with her health that I had no desire to eat. Over the course of her illness, I lost 15 pounds. After two rounds of chemo, she decided to discontinue treatment, and she died two months later.

As I struggled to make sense of the loss, my memories often turned to food. When I came home from college, my mom used to make galbi ssam, Korean short rib with lettuce wraps. She'd have marinated the meat two days before I'd even gotten on the plane, and she'd buy my favorite radish kimchi a week ahead to make sure it was perfectly fermented.

Then there were the childhood summers when she brought me to Seoul. Jet-lagged and sleepless, we'd snack on homemade banchan in the blue dark of Grandma's humid kitchen while my relatives slept. My mom would whisper, "This is how I know you're a true Korean."

But my mom never taught me how to make Korean food. When I would call to ask how much water to use for rice, she'd always say, "Fill until it reaches the back of your hand." When I'd beg for her galbi recipe, she gave me a haphazard ingredient list and approximate measurements and told me to just keep tasting it until it "tastes like Mom's."

After my mom died, I was so haunted by the trauma of her illness I worried I'd never remember her as the woman she had been: stylish and headstrong, always speaking her mind. When she appeared in my dreams, she was always sick.

Then I started cooking. When I first searched for Korean recipes, I found few resources, and I wasn't about to trust Bobby Flay's Korean taco monstrosity or his clumsy kimchi slaw. Then, among videos of oriental chicken salads, I found the Korean YouTube personality Maangchi. There she was, peeling the skin off an Asian pear just like my mom: in one long strip, index finger steadied on the back of the knife. She cut galbi with my mom's ambidextrous precision: positioning the chopsticks in her right hand while snipping bite-size pieces with her left. A Korean woman uses kitchen scissors the way a warrior brandishes a weapon.

I'd been looking for a recipe for jatjuk, a porridge made from pine nuts and soaked rice. It's a dish for the sick or elderly, and it was the first food I craved when my feelings of shock and loss finally made way for hunger.

I followed Maangchi's instructions carefully: soaking the rice, breaking off the tips of the pine nuts. Memories of my mother emerged as I worked—the way she stood in front of her little red cutting board, the funny intonations of her speech.

For many, Julia Child is the hero who brought boeuf bourguignon into the era of the TV dinner. She showed home cooks how to scale the culinary mountain. Maangchi did this for me after my mom died. My kitchen filled with jars containing cabbage, cucumbers, and radishes in various stages of fermentation. I could hear my mom's voice: "Never fall in love with anyone who doesn't like kimchi; they'll always smell it coming out of your pores."

I've spent over a year cooking with Maangchi. Sometimes I pause and rewind to get the steps exactly right. Other times I'll let my hands and taste buds take over from memory. My dishes are never exactly like my mom's, but that's OK—they're still a delicious tribute. The more I learn, the closer I feel to her.

One night not long ago, I had a dream: I was watching my mother as she stuffed giant heads of Napa cabbage into earthenware jars.

She looked healthy and beautiful.

THE JOY LUCK CLUB

Amy Tan

Born in California to Chinese immigrants, **Amy Tan** is an American novelist. She was fifteen when her father and brother both died from brain tumours, and her mother took Tan and her younger brother to Europe. After an early career writing for telecommunications companies and working as a language development specialist, she began writing fiction in 1985. Her debut, *The Joy Luck Club*, was published in 1989, and was on *The New York Times*' bestseller list, where each of her subsequent novels has also spent time. Her work has been translated into thirty-five languages.

Five months ago, after a crab dinner celebrating Chinese New Year, my mother gave me my "life's importance," a jade pendant on a gold chain. The pendant was not a piece of jewelry I would have chosen for myself. It was almost the size of my little finger, a mottled green and white color, intricately carved. To me, the whole effect looked wrong: too large, too green, too garishly ornate. I stuffed the necklace in my lacquer box and forgot about it.

But these days, I think about my life's importance. I wonder what it means, because my mother died three months ago, six days before my thirty-sixth birthday. And she's the only person I could have asked, to tell me about life's importance, to help me understand my grief.

I now wear that pendant every day. I think the carvings mean something, because shapes and details, which I never seem to notice until after they're pointed out to me, always mean something to Chinese people. I know I could ask Auntie Lindo, Auntie An-mei, or other Chinese friends, but I also know they would tell me a meaning that is different from what my mother intended. What if they tell me this curving line branching into three oval shapes is a pomegranate and that my mother was wishing me fertility and posterity? What if my mother really meant the carvings were a branch of pears to give me purity and honesty? Or ten-thousand-year droplets from the magic mountain, giving me my life's direction and a thousand years of fame and immortality?

And because I think about this all the time, I always notice other people wearing these same jade pendants—not the flat rectangular medallions or the round white ones with holes in the middle but ones like mine, a two-inch oblong of bright apple green. It's as though we were all sworn to the same secret covenant, so secret we don't even know what we belong to. Last weekend, for example, I saw a bartender wearing one. As I fingered mine, I asked him, "Where'd you get yours?"

"My mother gave it to me," he said.

I asked him why, which is a nosy question that only one Chinese person can ask another; in a crowd of Caucasians, two Chinese people are already like family.

"She gave it to me after I got divorced. I guess my mother's telling me I'm still worth something."

And I knew by the wonder in his voice that he had no idea what the pendant really meant.

At last year's Chinese New Year dinner, my mother had cooked eleven crabs, one crab for each person, plus an extra. She and I had bought them on Stockton Street in Chinatown. We had walked down the steep hill from my parents' flat, which was actually the first floor of a six-unit building they owned on Leavenworth near California. Their place was only six blocks from where I worked as a copywriter for a small ad agency, so two or three times a week I would drop by after work. My mother always had enough food to insist that I stay for dinner.

That year, Chinese New Year fell on a Thursday, so I got off work early to help my mother shop. My mother was seventy-one, but she still walked briskly along, her small body straight and purposeful, carrying a colorful flowery plastic bag. I dragged the metal shopping cart behind.

Every time I went with her to Chinatown, she pointed out other Chinese women her age. "Hong Kong ladies," she said, eyeing two finely dressed women in long, dark mink coats and perfect black hairdos.

"Cantonese, village people," she whispered as we passed women in knitted caps, bent over in layers of padded tops and men's vests. And my mother—wearing light-blue polyester pants, a red sweater, and a child's green down jacket—she didn't look like anybody else. She had come here in 1949, at the end of a long journey that started in Kweilin in 1944; she had gone north to Chungking, where she met my father, and then they went southeast to Shanghai and fled farther south to Hong Kong, where the boat departed for San Francisco. My mother came from many different directions.

And now she was huffing complaints in rhythm to her walk downhill. "Even you don't want them, you stuck," she said. She was fuming again about the tenants who lived on the second floor. Two years ago, she had tried to evict them on the pretext that relatives from China were coming to live there. But the couple saw through her ruse to get around rent control. They said they wouldn't budge until she produced the relatives. And after that I had to listen to her recount every new injustice this couple inflicted on her.

My mother said the gray-haired man put too many bags in the garbage cans: "Cost me extra."

And the woman, a very elegant artist type with blond hair, had supposedly painted the apartment in terrible red and green colors. "Awful," moaned my mother. "And they take bath, two three times every day. Running the water, running, running, running, never stop!"

"Last week," she said, growing angrier at each step, "the *waigoren* accuse me." She referred to all Caucasians as *waigoren*, foreigners. "They say I put poison in a fish, kill that cat."

"What cat?" I asked, even though I knew exactly which one she was talking about. I had seen that cat many times. It was a big one-eared tom with gray stripes who had learned to jump on the outside sill of my mother's kitchen window. My mother would stand on her tiptoes and bang the kitchen window to scare the cat away. And the cat would stand his ground, hissing back in response to her shouts.

"That cat always raising his tail to put a stink on my door," complained my mother.

I once saw her chase him from her stairwell with a pot of boiling water. I was tempted to ask if she really had put poison in a fish, but I had learned never to take sides against my mother.

"So what happened to that cat?" I asked.

"That cat gone! Disappear!" She threw her hands in the air and smiled, looking pleased for a moment before the scowl came back. "And that man, he raise his hand like this, show me his ugly fist and call me worst Fukien landlady. I not from Fukien. Hunh! He know nothing!" she said, satisfied she had put him in his place.

On Stockton Street, we wandered from one fish store to another, looking for the liveliest crabs.

"Don't get a dead one," warned my mother in Chinese. "Even a beggar won't eat a dead one."

I poked the crabs with a pencil to see how feisty they were. If a crab grabbed on, I lifted it out and into a plastic sack. I lifted one crab this way, only to find one of its legs had been clamped onto by another crab. In the brief tug-of-war, my crab lost a limb.

"Put it back," whispered my mother. "A missing leg is a bad sign on Chinese New Year."

But a man in a white smock came up to us. He started talking loudly to my mother in Cantonese, and my mother, who spoke Cantonese so poorly it sounded just like her Mandarin, was talking loudly back, pointing to the crab and its missing leg. And after more sharp words, that crab and its leg were put into our sack.

"Doesn't matter," said my mother. "This number eleven, extra one."

Back home, my mother unwrapped the crabs from their newspaper liners and then dumped them into a sinkful of cold water. She brought out her old wooden board and cleaver, then chopped the ginger and scallions, and poured soy sauce and sesame oil into a shallow dish. The kitchen smelled of wet newspapers and Chinese fragrances.

Then, one by one, she grabbed the crabs by their back, hoisted them out of the sink and shook them dry and awake. The crabs flexed their legs in midair between sink and stove. She stacked the crabs in a multileveled steamer that sat over two burners on the stove, put a lid on top, and lit the burners. I couldn't bear to watch so I went into the dining room.

When I was eight, I had played with a crab my mother had brought home for my birthday dinner. I had poked it, and jumped back every time its claws reached out. And I determined that the crab and I had come to a great understanding when it finally heaved itself up and walked clear across the counter. But before I could even decide what to name my new pet, my mother had dropped it into a pot of cold water and placed it on the tall stove. I had watched with growing dread, as the water heated up and the pot began to clatter with this crab trying to tap his way out of his own hot soup. To this day, I remember that crab screaming as he thrust one bright red claw out over the side of the bubbling pot. It must have been my own voice, because now I know, of course, that crabs have no vocal cords. And I also try to convince myself that they don't have enough brains to know the difference between a hot bath and a slow death.

For our New Year celebration, my mother had invited her longtime friends Lindo and Tin Jong. Without even asking, my mother knew that meant including the Jongs' children: their son Vincent, who was thirty-eight years old and still living at home, and their daughter, Waverly, who was around my age. Vincent called to see if he could also bring his girlfriend, Lisa Lum. Waverly said she would bring her new fiancé, Rich Schields, who, like Waverly, was a tax attorney at Price Waterhouse. And she added that Shoshana, her four-year-old daughter from a previous marriage, wanted to know if my parents had a VCR so she could watch *Pinocchio*, just in case she got bored. My mother also reminded me to invite Mr. Chong, my old piano teacher, who still lived three blocks away at our old apartment.

Including my mother, father and me, that made eleven people. But my mother had counted only ten, because to her way of thinking Shoshana was just a chid and didn't count, at least not as far as crabs were concerned. She hadn't considered that Waverly might not think the same way.

When the first plate of steaming crabs was passed around, Waverly was first and she picked the best crab, the brightest, the plumpest, and put it on her daughter's plate. And then she picked the next best for Rich and another good one for herself. And because she had learned this skill, of choosing the best, from her mother, it was only natural that her mother knew how to pick the next-best ones for her husband, her son, his girlfriend, and herself. And my mother, of course, considered the four remaining crabs and gave the one that looked after the best to Old Chong, because he was nearly ninety and deserved that kind of respect, and then she picked another good one for my father. That left two on the platter: a large crab with a faded orange color, and number eleven, which had the torn-off leg.

My mother shook the platter in front of me. "Take it, already cold," said my mother.

I was not too fond of crab, since I saw my birthday crab boiled alive, but I knew I could not refuse. That's the way Chinese mothers show they love their children, not through hugs and kisses but with stern offerings of steamed dumplings, duck's gizzards, and crab.

I thought I was doing the right thing, taking the crab with the missing leg. But my mother cried, "No! No! Big one, you eat it. I cannot finish."

I remember the hungry sounds everybody else was making—cracking the shells, sucking the crab meat out, scraping out tidbits with the ends of chopsticks—and my mother's quiet plate. I was the only one who noticed her prying open the shell, sniffing the crab's body and then getting up to go to the kitchen, plate in hand. She returned, without the crab, but with more bowls of soy sauce, ginger, and scallions.

And then as stomachs filled, everybody started talking at once.

"Suyuan!" called Auntie Lindo to my mother. "Why you wear that color?" Auntie Lindo gestured with a crab leg to my mother's red sweater.

"How can you wear this color anymore? Too young!" she scolded.

My mother acted as though this were a compliment. "Emporium Capwell," she said. "Nineteen dollar. Cheaper than knit it myself."

Auntie Lindo nodded her head, as if the color were worth this price. And then she pointed her crab leg toward her future son-in-law, Rich, and said, "See how this one doesn't know how to eat Chinese food."

"Crab isn't Chinese," said Waverly in her complaining voice. It was amazing how Waverly still sounded the way she did twenty-five years ago, when we were ten and she had announced to me in that same voice, "You aren't a genius like me."

Auntie Lindo looked at her daughter with exasperation. "How do you know what is Chinese, what is not Chinese?" And then she turned to Rich and said with much authority, "Why you are not eating the best part?"

And I saw Rich smiling back, with amusement, and not humility, showing in his face. He had the same coloring as the crab on his plate: reddish hair, pale cream skin, and large dots of orange freckles. While he smirked, Auntie Lindo demonstrated the proper technique, poking her chopstick into the orange spongy part: "You have to dig in here, get this out. The brain is most tastiest, you try."

Waverly and Rich grimaced at each other, united in disgust. I heard Vincent and Lisa whisper to each other, "Gross," and then they snickered too.

Uncle Tin started laughing to himself, to let us know he also had a private joke. Judging by his preamble of snorts and leg slaps, I figured he must have practiced this joke many times: "I tell my daughter, Hey, why be poor? Marry rich!" He laughed loudly and then nudged Lisa, who was sitting next to him, "Hey, don't you get it? Look what happen. She gonna marry this guy here. Rich. 'Cause I tell her to, *marry* Rich."

"When *are* you guys getting married?" asked Vincent.

"I should ask you the same thing," said Waverly. Lisa looked embarrassed when Vincent ignored the question.

"Mom, I don't like crab!" whined Shoshana.

"Nice haircut," Waverly said to me from across the table.

"Thanks, David always does a great job."

"You mean you still go to that guy on Howard Street?" Waverly asked, arching one eyebrow. "Aren't you afraid?"

I could sense the danger, but I said it anyway: "What do you mean, afraid? He's always very good."

"I mean, he *is* gay," Waverly said. "He could have AIDS. And he is cutting your hair, which is like cutting a living tissue. Maybe I'm being paranoid, being a mother, but you just can't be too safe these days…"

And I sat there feeling as if my hair were coated with disease.

"You should go see my guy," said Waverly. "Mr. Rory. He does fabulous work, although he probably charges more than you're used to."

I felt like screaming. She could be so sneaky with her insults. Every time I asked her the simplest of tax questions, for example, she could turn the conversation around and make it seem as if I were too cheap to pay for her legal advice.

She'd say things like, "I really don't like to talk about important tax matters except in my office. I mean, what if you say something casual over lunch and I give you some casual advice. And then you follow it, and it's wrong because you didn't give me the full information. I'd feel terrible. And you would too, wouldn't you?"

At that crab dinner, I was so mad about what she said about my hair that I wanted to embarrass her, to reveal in front of everybody how petty she was. So I decided to confront her about the free-lance work I'd done for her firm, eight pages of brochure copy on its tax services. The firm was now more than thirty days late in paying my invoice.

"Maybe I could afford Mr. Rory's prices if someone's firm paid me on time," I said with a teasing grin. And I was pleased to see Waverly's reaction. She was genuinely flustered, speechless.

I couldn't resist rubbing it in: "I think it's pretty ironic that a big accounting firm can't even pay its own bills on time. I mean, really, Waverly, what kind of place are you working for?"

Her face was dark and quiet.

"Hey, hey, you girls, no more fighting!" said my father, as if Waverly and I were still children arguing over tricycles and crayon colors.

"That's right, we don't want to talk about this now," said Waverly quietly.

"So how do you think the Giants are going to do?" said Vincent, trying to be funny. Nobody laughed.

I wasn't about to let her slip away this time. "Well, every time I call you on the phone, you can't talk about it then either," I said.

Waverly looked at Rich, who shrugged his shoulders. She turned back to me and sighed.

"Listen, June, I don't know how to tell you this. That stuff you wrote, well, the firm decided it was unacceptable."

"You're lying. You said it was great."

Waverly sighed again. "I know I did. I didn't want to hurt your feelings. I was trying to see if we could fix it somehow. But it won't work."

And just like that, I was starting to flail, tossed without warning into deep water, drowning and desperate. "Most copy needs fine-tuning," I said. "It's...normal not to be perfect the first time. I should have explained the process better."

"June, I really don't think..."

"Rewrites are free. I'm just as concerned about making it perfect as you are."

Waverly acted as if she didn't even hear me. "I'm trying to convince them to at least pay you for some of your time. I know you put a lot of work into it...I owe you at least that for even suggesting you do it."

"Just tell me what they want changed. I'll call you next week so we can go over it, line by line."

"June—I can't," Waverly said with cool finality. "It's just not... sophisticated. I'm sure what you write for your other clients is *wonderful*. But we're a big firm. We need somebody who understands that...our style." She said this touching her hand to her chest, as if she were referring to *her* style.

Then she laughed in a lighthearted way. "I mean, really, June. " And then she started speaking in a deep television-announcer voice: "*Three* benefits, *three* needs, *three* reasons to buy...Satisfaction *guaranteed*... for today's and tomorrow's tax needs..."

She said this in such a funny way that everybody thought it was a good joke and laughed. And then, to make matters worse, I heard my mother saying to Waverly: "True, cannot teach style. June not sophisticate like you. Must be born this way."

I was surprised at myself, how humiliated I felt. I had been outsmarted by Waverly once again, and now betrayed by my own mother. I was smiling so hard my lower lip was twitching from the strain. I tried to find something else to concentrate on, and I remember picking up my plate, and then Mr. Chong's, as if I were clearing the table, and seeing so sharply through my tears the chips on the edges of these old plates, wondering why my mother didn't use the new set I had bought her five years ago.

The table was littered with crab carcasses. Waverly and Rich lit cigarettes and put a crab shell between them for an ashtray. Shoshana had wandered over to the piano and was banging notes out with a crab claw in each hand. Mr. Chong, who had grown totally deaf over the years, watched Shoshana and applauded: "Bravo! Bravo!" And except for his strange shouts, nobody said a word. My mother went to the kitchen and returned with a plate of oranges sliced into wedges. My father poked at the remnants of his crab. Vincent cleared his throat, twice, and then patted Lisa's hand.

It was Auntie Lindo who finally spoke: "Waverly, you let her try again. You make her do too fast first time. Of course she cannot get it right."

I could hear my mother eating an orange slice. She was the only person I knew who crunched oranges, making it sound as if she were eating crisp apples instead. The sound of it was worse than gnashing teeth.

"Good one take time," continued Auntie Lindo, nodding her head in agreement with herself.

"Put in lotta action," advised Uncle Tin. "Lotta action, boy, that's what I like. Hey, that's all you need, make it right."

"Probably not," I said, and smiled before carrying the plates to the sink.

That was the night, in the kitchen, that I realized I was no better than who I was. I was a copywriter. I worked for a small ad agency. I promised every new client, "We can provide the sizzle for the meat." The sizzle always boiled down to "Three Benefits, Three Needs, Three Reasons to Buy." The meat was always coaxial cable, T-1 multiplexers, protocol converters, and the like. I was very good at what I did, succeeding at something small like that.

I turned on the water to wash the dishes. And I no longer felt angry at Waverly. I felt tired and foolish, as if I had been running to escape someone chasing me, only to look behind and discover there was no one there.

I picked up my mother's plate, the one she had carried into the kitchen at the start of the dinner. The crab was untouched. I lifted the shell and smelled the crab. Maybe it was because I didn't like crab in the first place. I couldn't tell what was wrong with it.

After everybody left, my mother joined me in the kitchen. I was putting dishes away. She put water on for more tea and sat down at the small kitchen table. I waited for her to chastise me.

"Good dinner, Ma," I said politely.

"Not so good," she said, jabbing at her mouth with a toothpick.

"What happened to your crab? Why'd you throw it away?"

"Not so good," she said again. "That crab die. Even a beggar don't want it."

"How could you tell? I didn't smell anything wrong."

"Can tell even before cook!" She was standing now, looking out the kitchen window into the night. "I shake that crab before cook. His legs—droopy. His mouth—wide open, already like a dead person."

"Why'd you cook it if you knew it was already dead?"

"I thought…maybe only just die. Maybe taste not too bad. But I can smell, dead taste, not firm."

"What if someone else had picked that crab?"

My mother looked at me and smiled. "Only *you* pick that crab. Nobody else take it. I already know this. Everybody else want best quality. You thinking different."

She said it in a way as if this were proof-proof of something good. She always said things that didn't make any sense, that sounded both good and bad at the same time.

I was putting away the last of the chipped plates and then I remembered something else. 'Ma, why don't you ever use those new dishes I bought you? If you didn't like them, you should have told me. I could have changed the pattern.'

"Of course, I like," she said, irritated. "Sometime I think something is so good, I want to save it. Then I forget I save it."

And then, as if she had just now remembered, she unhooked the clasp of her gold necklace and took it off, wadding the chain and the jade pendant in her palm. She grabbed my hand and put the necklace in my palm, then shut my fingers around it.

"No, Ma," I protested. "I can't take this."

"*Nala, nala*"—Take it, take it—she said, as if she were scolding me. And then she continued in Chinese. "For a long time, I wanted to give you this necklace. See, I wore this on my skin, so when you put it on your skin, then you know my meaning. This is your life's importance. "

I looked at the necklace, the pendant with the light green jade. I wanted to give it back. I didn't want to accept it. And yet I also felt as if I had already swallowed it.

"You're giving this to me only because of what happened tonight," I finally said.

"What happen?"

"What Waverly said. What everybody said."

"Tss! Why you listen to her? Why you want to follow behind her, chasing her words? She is like this crab." My mother poked a shell in the garbage can. "Always walking sideways, moving crooked. You can make your legs go the other way."

I put the necklace on. It felt cool.

"Not so good, this jade," she said matter-of-factly, touching the pendant, and then she added in Chinese: "This is young jade. It is a very light color now, but if you wear it every day it will become more green."

My father hasn't eaten well since my mother died. So I am here, in the kitchen, to cook him dinner. I'm slicing tofu. I've decided to make him a spicy bean-curd dish. My mother used to tell me how hot things restore the spirit and health. But I'm making this mostly because I know my father loves this dish and I know how to cook it. I like the smell of it: ginger, scallions, and a red chili sauce that tickles my nose the minute I open the jar.

Above me, I hear the old pipes shake into action with a *thunk!* and then the water running in my sink dwindles to a trickle. One of the tenants upstairs must be taking a shower. I remember my mother complaining: "Even you don't want them, you stuck." And now I know what she meant.

As I rinse the tofu in the sink, I am startled by a dark mass that appears suddenly at the window. It's the one-eared tomcat from upstairs. He's balancing on the sill, rubbing his flank against the window.

My mother didn't kill that damn cat after all, and I'm relieved. And then I see this cat rubbing more vigorously on the window and he starts to raise his tail.

"Get away from there!" I shout, and slap my hand on the window three times. But the cat just narrows his eyes, flattens his one ear, and hisses back at me.

BUILDING COMMUNITY

Memuna Konteh

> **Memuna Konteh** is a writer with a particular interest in identity, politics and culture. She has bylines at *AZ*, *Gal-dem*, *Glamour*, *Vittles*, *Digital Spy*, *Raconteur*, and more. Mahungeh Konteh (her mother) is available to cater African food on request in North Yorkshire.

Unlike her UberEats-addicted daughter, cooking is my mum's second nature. In Sierra Leone, she earned a bachelor's degree in home economics and had established an events catering service with friends by her early twenties. Their specialities were traditional Sierra Leonean dishes like pepper soup, ebeh and binch (a palm-oil stew made with black-eyed beans, served over plantains, boiled cassava or rice), but they also cooked Middle Eastern foods like kibbeh and shawarma, inspired by the country's growing Lebanese community. In 2002, our family moved to Manchester for my father's PhD scholarship. Like many skilled immigrants with qualifications from their home countries, my mum's home economics degree wasn't recognised by British institutions so she eventually began working in care and braiding hair to help support the family.

Even when she was extremely busy, my mum would always find time and occasion to cook in grand ways. The spread at my fifth birthday party was worthy of kings (even if I was more excited about the Chupa Chups tower than anything else): several rice dishes, vermicelli noodle stir-fry, coconut wan-pot with fish and (African-style) beef biryani. Everyone left with full stomachs and enough takeaway boxes to feed their families for a week. In Manchester, my mum was never short of functions to cook for and the sizeable Sierra Leonean community there meant there were enough West African grocers, butchers and fishmongers (shout-out

New Smithfield Wholesale Market) to source the vital ingredients of our cuisine that you can't find anywhere else: potato and cassava leaves, crain crain, and ogiri.

When we moved across county borders to York in 2006, we were confronted for the first time with the cultural isolation and racism that's specific to the WASPiest 'safest' place in the UK. In primary school I became afraid to take foods like lafidi (plain buttered rice with sardines) in my packed lunch and by secondary school I had convinced my mum to let me eat the underwhelming canteen food to save myself the hassle. Having to put up with the abuse our senile next-door neighbour hurled at my mum for barbecuing fish in our own back garden and more grotesque acts of anti-Blackness (like the mystery dog walker who would invite their pup to shit exclusively in our drive) only compounded our frustrations. The result for me and my siblings was a hypervigilance and a misplaced resentment for the food we were raised on. At one point my younger sister point-blank refused to eat any Sierra Leonean food, though she was happy to try dishes like nettle soup in her friends' homes.

For mum, however, it only fortified her conviction to carry on our food traditions and unify York's small but burgeoning Black community through food. So we put on more barbecues, hosted dinners and threw parties, and even invited a few friendly white neighbours, who were pleasantly surprised by the fresh, 'exotic' flavours and free booze (BYOB being an insult in West African cultures). Slowly my parents built the connections they'd felt starved of with the growing populations of other Africans through my mum's braiding business, her church and my dad's mosque.

Today, York's Black community is composed mostly of Nigerians, Ghanaians, Kenyans, Zimbabweans and Zambians. My mum says this is because of York Hospital's recruitment drive for doctors and nurses from those countries, but there is also a growing number of African and Caribbean students attending university in York. Having parents at the centre of this unique mix of nationalities exposed me to other African food cultures. I discovered the many differences and similarities that exist between the wide array of culinary traditions that exist on the continent. All of this gave me a new found affinity for my Africanness and an appreciation of the lengths my mum and her friends go to, to sustain their (and their children's) relationship with African foods.

There isn't an African food supplier in York, so once a month my mum or one of her friends travels out of town to buy meat and produce to then distribute among the community. Their go-to shop is Bantuway in Manchester, part of a wider chain of African food stores across the country. It stocks everything from oxtail, tripe, yam and cassava to palm oil (the base of most Sierra Leonean stews), garri and fufu powder. Throughout the month, stock bought in Bantuway is supplemented by ingredients purchased in the local South Asian stores, like Freshways which opened in 2009 and the more recent addition, Zam Zam Supermarket & Halal Butchers in Rochdale.

Some of our staples are so specific that they're difficult to find even in Manchester, so whenever my mum visits Sierra Leone, she returns with home-grown foodstuffs like our native short-grain red rough rice (similar to the broken jasmine rice used in Senegalese/Ivorian jollof), organic village honey and kanya – a fragrant mix of ground cassava (or rice flour), peanuts and sugar which can be enjoyed on its own or made into various desserts. She usually leaves for these trips with an empty suitcase just to transport food as there are always requests to bring things back for other households.

When my mum isn't shopping for others, she's cooking for church events, engagement parties and weddings, christenings, graduation parties and birthdays. Her eagerness to help means that there's never a shortage of people knocking on our door with food for the family whenever she's away or otherwise unable to cook. Sierra Leone is a relatively small player in the world of African cuisine, so mum looks at the events that she caters as an opportunity to introduce others to our food and grow her skills in other cuisines. Of course, her most frequently-asked-for dishes are the obvious ones – jollof rice, fried rice, couscous and chicken – but she particularly enjoys making small plates and hors d'oeuvres including fish and meat pies (which look more like miniature pasties than the pies of the West), roast meat skewers known in Nigeria as suya, gizzard, fish balls and my personal favourite, akara, a sweet fritter made from overripe bananas and rice flour.

When I moved to London and saw the convenience of sourcing African food in such a multicultural city, I realised the true extent of the hard work and planning my mum puts into providing traditional meals for us on a daily basis. My attachment to her cooking grew stronger and has meant I eat more African food when in York than in London, despite the fantastic assortment of African restaurants near me in south west. (I literally live around the corner from the iconic Asafo Ghanaian restaurant, a stone's throw from Nigerian venue Enish, and up the road from Adam's Ethiopian.) While all of these places are amazing in their own right and I'm grateful for the options, I've grown to associate African food with either my home or the hall party. For me, the formality of restaurant dining doesn't marry well with a food culture that favours eating with hands, buffets and takeaway boxes.

The annexation of York's small African community has made cooking and eating our food an even more sentimental, communal and experimental experience, opening me up to incredible cross-cultural combinations like the sadza my Zimbabwean friend Clinton made for me over Christmas, which I paired with an egusi soup made by my sister and her Nigerian boyfriend. Such mixtures are much rarer in London because there's simply too much choice. The sheer scale and diversity of these communities and the easy access to nation-specific foods creates firm boundaries and an insularity amongst Londoners. Even within a single nationality, the need to venture outside of one's ethnic cuisine is almost non-existent because of the availability of ethnically distinct restaurants and eateries (for example the Krio Kanteen which is specifically marketed towards ethnically Krio Sierra Leoneans).

I still feel for Africans in York and surrounding parts of North Yorkshire who can't readily travel to larger cities and don't have the connections that my mum and her friends have. I spoke to the owners of Bantuway about the possibility of them opening a store closer to York and they said it's unlikely for now as demand is insufficient and commercial rent in York is amongst the highest in the region. They direct me towards their online store, which is gaining traction but the stock is limited. Even in the post-Covid economy, internet-shopping for African food may seem alien to people used to gauging quality through direct use of the senses.

I hope as the African community in York grows even more, the demand will become apparent and someone will come along to plug the gap with African restaurants and grocers. Until then, the scarcity of African food in North Yorkshire can be looked upon as an opportunity for Africans to build and sustain relationships with one another, across nationalities and across borders.

THE PRICE OF RICE

Su Hwang

Born in Seoul, **Su Hwang** was raised in New York City, moved to the Bay Area, and eventually settled in Minneapolis, Minnesota. She describes herself as a poet, activist, and stargazer, is a teaching artist with the Minnesota Prison Writing Workshop, and co-founder of Poetry Asylum. Hwang's poetry collection *Bodega* received the 2020 Minnesota Book Award in poetry and was a finalist for the 2021 Kate Tufts Discovery Award.

Grain to water ratio must be precise or the result
will be *catastrophe*. I let my mother speak

in hyperbole—concessions you allow someone who
survived civil war, someone whose father was taken

by silhouetted men in the dagger of night, someone
who's toiled since the age of ten, someone

who still eats last at the dinner table. Too much
liquid, she tells me, you get porridge: jook—which

sounds eerily similar to *gook*. The ways we must survive
mortal, moral combat. When I'd come down

with a cold, she'd prepare my favorite remedy: congee,
dashes of soy sauce and sesame oil, garnished

with finely chopped scallions. Simple, filling. An entire
meal that fed a mother and her mother fleeing

with three daughters and the eldest son, now
estranged—how a fistful of rice boiled down

with extra water satisfied rumbling bellies amid
rubble mountains, ghost artillery—the peninsula

cut in half by outsiders then left to spar for eternity:
one blind, one cursed; existential, consequential.

My mother wistfully recalls what remains, memory
broken by age and a willing, as I drown my iPhone

in a satchel of abundance. How I used to play, spreading
its stickiness on loose-leaf paper as glue, constructing

hats to pretend I was a nurse mending wounds or
a famous chef summoning feasts. When I first asked

how to prepare the perfect heap of cooked rice, she
casually filled the pot, placed her hand on top as if she

were performing sacrament or taking my temperature,
letting the water crawl between knuckles and wrist.

Eyeballing it. But I wanted exactitude—a basic
math. She used to tease when I had a kernel stuck

on my cheek or held hostage by my hair: *Saving it
for later?* I've never saved anything in my life

when that's all she's ever known, using her body
to carry and shield, cushioning me from every

possible blow—taking it, taking it—so I'd never
have to be intimately acquainted with the same

country of hunger: polishing each granule clean
with spit for a bit of salvation—a pearl.

EPIPHANY IN THE BEANS *FROM* BRAIDING SWEETGRASS

Robin Wall Kimmerer

Author, scientist and professor **Robin Wall Kimmerer** is an enrolled member of the Citizen Potawatomi Nation. Before the publication of her first book, Kimmerer was a university teacher, publishing scientific articles on restoration ecology and mosses, and brought up her two daughters. Her work is centred on ecological knowledge, outreach to Indigenous communities, and creative writing. In addition to her two acclaimed non-fiction works, she has written a short book for Penguin about language and nature, and has edited an anthology of writing about trees. *Braiding Sweetgrass*, from which we have taken the extract below, became a *New York Times* bestseller seven years after publication.

It came to me while picking beans, the secret of happiness.

I was hunting among the spiraling vines that envelop my teepees of pole beans, lifting the dark-green leaves to find handfuls of pods, long and green, firm and furred with tender fuzz. I snapped them off where they hung in slender twosomes, bit into one, and tasted nothing but August, distilled into pure, crisp beaniness. This summer abundance is destined for the freezer, to emerge again in deep midwinter when the air tastes only of snow. By the time I finished searching through just one trellis, my basket was full.

To go and empty it in the kitchen, I stepped between heavy squash vines and around tomato plants fallen under the weight of their fruit. They sprawled at the feet of the sunflowers, whose heads bowed with the weight of maturing seeds. Lifting my basket over the row of potatoes,

I noticed an open furrow revealing a nest of red skins where the girls left off harvesting that morning. I kicked some soil over them so the sun wouldn't green them up.

They complain about garden chores, as kids are supposed to do, but once they start they get caught up in the softness of the dirt and the smell of the day and it is hours later when they come back into the house. Seeds for this basket of beans were poked into the ground by their fingers back in May. Seeing them plant and harvest makes me feel like a good mother, teaching them how to provide for themselves.

The seeds, though, we did not provide for ourselves. When Skywoman buried her beloved daughter in the earth, the plants that are special gifts to the people sprang from her body. Tobacco grew from her head. From her hair, sweetgrass. Her heart gave us the strawberry. From her breasts grew corn, from her belly the squash, and we see in her hands the long-fingered clusters of beans.

How do I show my girls I love them on a morning in June? I pick them wild strawberries. On a February afternoon we build snowmen and then sit by the fire. In March we make maple syrup. We pick violets in May and go swimming in July. On an August night we lay out blankets and watch meteor showers. In November, that great teacher the woodpile comes into our lives. That's just the beginning. How do we show our children our love? Each in our own way by a shower of gifts and a heavy rain of lessons.

Maybe it was the smell of ripe tomatoes, or the oriole singing, or that certain slant of light on a yellow afternoon and the beans hanging thick around me. It just came to me in a wash of happiness that made me laugh out loud, startling the chickadees who were picking at the sunflowers, raining black and white hulls on the ground. I knew it with a certainty as warm and clear as the September sunshine. The land loves us back. She loves us with beans and tomatoes, with roasting ears and blackberries and birdsongs. By a shower of gifts and a heavy rain of lessons. She provides for us and teaches us to provide for ourselves. That's what good mothers do.

I looked around at the garden and could feel her delight in giving us these beautiful raspberries, squash, basil, potatoes, asparagus, lettuce, kale and beets, broccoli, peppers, brussels sprouts, carrots, dill, onions, leeks, spinach. It reminded me of my little girls' answer to "How much do I love you?" "Thiiiiiiiis much," with arms stretched wide, they replied. This is really why I made my daughters learn to garden—so they would always have a mother to love them, long after I am gone.

The epiphany in the beans. I spend a lot of time thinking about our relationships with land, how we are given so much and what we might give back. I try to work through the equations of reciprocity and responsibility, the whys and wherefores of building sustainable relationships with ecosystems. All in my head. But suddenly there was no intellectualizing, no rationalizing, just the pure sensation of baskets full of mother love. The ultimate reciprocity, loving and being loved in return.

Now, the plant scientist who sits at my desk and wears my clothes and sometimes borrows my car—she might cringe to hear me assert that a garden is a way that the land says, "I love you." Isn't it supposed to be just a matter of increasing net primary productivity of the artificially selected domesticated genotypes, manipulating environmental conditions through input of labor and materials to enhance yield? Adaptive cultural behaviors that produce a nutritious diet and increase individual fitness are selected for. What's love got to do with it? If a garden thrives, it loves you? If a garden fails, do you attribute potato blight to a withdrawal of affection? Do unripe peppers signal a rift in the relationship?

I have to explain things to her sometimes. Gardens are simultaneously a material and a spiritual undertaking. That's hard for scientists, so fully brainwashed by Cartesian dualism, to grasp. "Well, how would you know it's love and not just good soil?" she asks. "Where's the evidence? What are the key elements for detecting loving behavior?"

That's easy. No one would doubt that I love my children, and even a quantitative social psychologist would find no fault with my list of loving behaviors:

- nurturing health and well-being
- protection from harm
- encouraging individual growth and development
- desire to be together
- generous sharing of resources
- working together for a common goal
- celebration of shared values
- interdependence
- sacrifice by one for the other
- creation of beauty

If we observed these behaviors between humans, we would say, "She loves that person." You might also observe these actions between a person and a bit of carefully tended ground and say, "She loves that garden." Why then, seeing this list, would you not make the leap to say that the garden loves her back?

The exchange between plants and people has shaped the evolutionary history of both. Farms, orchards, and vineyards are stocked with species we have domesticated. Our appetite for their fruits leads us to till, prune, irrigate, fertilize, and weed on their behalf. Perhaps they have domesticated us. Wild plants have changed to stand in well-behaved rows and wild humans have changed to settle alongside the fields and care for the plants—a kind of mutual taming.

We are linked in a co-evolutionary circle. The sweeter the peach, the more frequently we disperse its seeds, nurture its young, and protect them from harm. Food plants and people act as selective forces on each other's evolution—the thriving of one in the best interest of the other. This, to me, sounds a bit like love.

I sat once in a graduate writing workshop on relationships to the land. The students all demonstrated a deep respect and affection for nature. They said that nature was the place where they experienced the greatest sense of belonging and well-being. They professed without reservation that they loved the earth. And then I asked them, "Do you think that the earth loves you back?" No one was willing to answer that.

It was as if I had brought a two-headed porcupine into the classroom. Unexpected. Prickly. They backed slowly away. Here was a room full of writers, passionately wallowing in unrequited love of nature.

So I made it hypothetical and asked, "What do you suppose would happen *if* people believed this crazy notion that the earth loved them back?" The floodgates opened. They all wanted to talk at once. We were suddenly off the deep end, heading for world peace and perfect harmony.

One student summed it up: "You wouldn't harm what gives you love."

Knowing that you love the earth changes you, activates you to defend and protect and celebrate. But when you feel that the earth loves you in return, that feeling transforms the relationship from a one-way street into a sacred bond.

My daughter Linden grows one of my favorite gardens in the world. She brings up all kinds of good things to eat from her thin mountain soil, things I can only dream of, like tomatillos and chile. She makes compost and flowers, but the best part isn't the plants. It's that she phones me to chat while she weeds. We water and weed and harvest, visiting happily as we did when she was a girl despite the three thousand miles between us. Linden is immensely busy, and so I ask her why she gardens, given how much time it takes.

She does it for the food and the satisfaction of hard work yielding something so prolific, she says. And it makes her feel at home in a place, to have her hands in the earth. I ask her, "Do you love your garden?" even though I already know the answer. But then I ask, tentatively, "Do you feel that your garden loves you back?" She's quiet for a minute; she's never glib about such things. "I'm certain of it," she says. "My garden takes care of me like my own mama." I can die happy.

I once knew and loved a man who lived most of his life in the city, but when he was dragged off to the ocean or the woods he seemed to enjoy it well enough—as long as he could find an Internet connection. He had lived in a lot of places, so I asked him where he found his greatest sense of place. He didn't understand the expression. I explained that I wanted to know where he felt most nurtured and supported. What is the place that you understand best? That you know best and knows you in return?

He didn't take long to answer. "My car," he said. "In my car. It provides me with everything I need, in just the way I like it. My favorite music. Seat position fully adjustable. Automatic mirrors. Two cup holders. I'm safe. And it always takes me where I want to go." Years later, he tried to kill himself. In his car.

He never grew a relationship with the land, choosing instead the splendid isolation of technology. He was like one of those little withered seeds you find in the bottom of the seed packet, the one who never touched the earth.

I wonder if much that ails our society stems from the fact that we have allowed ourselves to be cut off from that love of, and from, the land. It is medicine for broken land and empty hearts.

Larkin used to complain mightily about weeding. But now when she comes home, she asks if she can go dig potatoes. I see her on her knees, unearthing red skins and Yukon Golds and singing to herself. Larkin is in graduate school now, studying food systems and working with urban gardeners, growing vegetables for the food pantry on land reclaimed from empty lots. At-risk youth do the planting and hoeing and harvesting. The kids are surprised that the food they harvest is free. They've had to pay for everything they've ever gotten before. They greet fresh carrots, straight from the ground, with suspicion at first, until they eat one. She is passing on the gift, and the transformation is profound.

Of course, much of what fills our mouths is taken forcibly from the earth. That form of taking does no honor to the farmer, to the plants, or to the disappearing soil. It's hard to recognize food that is mummified in plastic, bought and sold, as a gift anymore. Everybody knows you can't buy love.

In a garden, food arises from partnership. If I don't pick rocks and pull weeds, I'm not fulfilling my end of the bargain. I can do these things with my handy opposable thumb and capacity to use tools, to shovel manure. But I can no more create a tomato or embroider a trellis in beans than I can turn lead into gold. That is the plants' responsibility and their gift: animating the inanimate. Now *there* is a gift.

People often ask me what one thing I would recommend to restore relationship between land and people. My answer is almost always,

"Plant a garden." It's good for the health of the earth and it's good for the health of people. A garden is a nursery for nurturing connection, the soil for cultivation of practical reverence. And its power goes far beyond the garden gate—once you develop a relationship with a little patch of earth, it becomes a seed itself.

Something essential happens in a vegetable garden. It's a place where if you can't say "I love you" out loud, you can say it in seeds. And the land will reciprocate, in beans.

HALLELUJAH! THE WELCOME TABLE

Maya Angelou

Perhaps it might be surprising to find the great memoirist, poet and civil rights activist in a collection of food writing, but **Maya Angelou**'s 'kitchen is the stuff of legend', wrote her biographer Marcia Gillespie. Somehow finding time in her wide-ranging work (lesser-known highlights include as a brothel madam, opera singer, nightclub dancer, newspaper editor, film director and possessor of more than fifty honorary degrees) and extraordinary life ('sister' to Martin Luther King Jr., confidant to Oprah Winfrey, mother), Angelou also wrote two cookbooks. And they are great, too.

My mother, Vivian Baxter, was a great believer in self-reliance. Each tub should sit on its own bottom and each shoulder should be pressed to its own wheel.

My six-year-old son, Guy, and I were between addresses. That was how we described our condition when we lost one apartment and before we found another. In the meantime, of course, we went across town to my mother's house.

When I was seventeen and Guy was two months old, we lived with my mother in her fourteen-room house on Post Street in San Francisco. Then one morning I announced my plans to move. I told her that I had found a job and two rentals with cooking privileges and that the landlady would babysit my child. She controlled her surprise and said, "All right, but when you cross over my doorsill, remember you have been raised. Throughout life you will have to make many adjustments and even some compromises, but don't let anybody raise you. You know the difference between right and wrong. Do right. You've been raised.

"And remember this," she added. "You can always come home."

Whenever the world was too much with me late and soon, I returned to Vivian Baxter's house. I didn't savor not sitting on my own bottom and not putting my own shoulder to my own wheel, but I was never made uncomfortable returning to her.

She treated each return as a welcome opportunity to teach me something she had overlooked or that I had not understood. She relished one incident, which she said could only have taken place in her kitchen.

Guy sat at the kitchen table, watching her cook. He kept up a running chatter about school, his playmates, and his teachers, and he filled his conversation with his requests that his grandmother make a dessert for me.

He told her how hard I worked, how at this very moment I was probably seeing about an apartment, and how I deserved a dessert. A good dessert made for me by my mother.

Mother had had just about enough of that. "If she needs a dessert why don't you make it for her?"

"Oh, Grandma, I'm only six years old."

Mother said, "If you are old enough to try to bully me into making something for your mother, then you are old enough to make it yourself. Do you want to try?"

He laughed and said, "Sure."

She said she would show him how to make a bread pudding, after he washed his hands. "Cleanliness is next to godliness" was my mother's mantra. Mother set him on a kitchen stool so he could reach the sink.

"A good cook washes his hands ten times an hour; a great cook, twenty times."

Each time he touched a piece of food he climbed up onto the stool and washed his hands.

She let him butter stale bread, which was then placed in the oven to toast, and she showed him how to break eggs without dropping shells into the mixing bowl.

He whisked milk and then sugar into the eggs. He put raisins in warm water so they could plump.

There was an undeniable air of secret happenings when I entered the house that night. I looked at Mother, and her smile was like a promising but sealed envelope, and Guy was about to explode. I had to give them their due.

"What's going on? What have you people been doing?" Mother said, "Ask your son."

"Well, Guy? What's the news?"

"Mom, well ... I can't tell you until after dinner. Are you ready to eat right now? We can sit down and have dinner. Then we can have dessert. Oooo-weee." He spoke so fast he hardly had time to breathe.

He could not sit still at the dinner table.

Mother finally told him the dessert was cool enough and he could bring it out.

The baked bread pudding was puffed up and toasty brown, but I only had eyes for Guy. He strutted and preened. Pride and self-congratulations were his shoulder pads, and he nearly had to put both hands over his mouth to keep from blurting out his achievement.

When Mother placed the bread pudding in front of her to serve it, he could hold off no longer.

"I cooked this for her, Grandmother. My mother should serve it." Vivian Baxter agreed and slid the dessert over to me. Guy asked, "Is it good, is it good? I made it myself."

I had not tasted one bite, but I answered, "My son, this is the best bread pudding in the world."

It was true then, and even as you read about it today it is still the best bread pudding in the world.

JUBILEE: RECIPES FROM TWO CENTURIES OF AFRICAN AMERICAN COOKING

Toni Tipton-Martin

> **Toni Tipton-Martin** is the first Black person to edit the food section of a major US newspaper; the recipient of a Julia Child Award, and not one but two James Beard Awards; an acclaimed television presenter, historian, consultant, journalist, and mother of four. Her work makes visible the often-ignored world of Black cooks through time, bringing their skills, wisdom and artistry into public vision, sometimes for the first time. She lives in Baltimore.

"All I want to know is who is bringing the chocolate cake," Aunt M. quietly demanded in a way that let everyone know she wasn't pleased.

Aunt M. (for Meredieth) was wonderful and warm most of the time. Just don't forget to write back, and don't mess with her family reunion. But on a blistering hot weekend in July 1994, we were guilty of at least one of those crimes—we just didn't know it yet.

Although my husband, Bruce, and I roared through several northeastern Ohio counties on US 422 toward the Pennsylvania border, we were going to be late for the annual Martin homecoming. The family had gathered in Warren or Youngstown, Ohio, or Sharon, Pennsylvania, on the fourth Sunday of July every year for the past sixty-five or so—a way for the family to celebrate the birth of new babies, congratulate graduates, or welcome brides and grooms to the clan. The gathering is also about great food and eating. Especially dessert. No amount of hectic living or working overtime was going to destroy the tradition.

Aunt M. was frantically pacing about, mumbling "Oh, this is just terrible," at every turn around the long cloth-covered table. Already well past 1 p.m. and aware of the delay, family members arrived steadily, hurriedly situating favorite dishes in place—some still warm from the oven. It was a wonderful spread: three versions of macaroni and cheese, scalloped potatoes, baked beans, green beans, fresh beets, crusty fried chicken, potato and macaroni salads, homemade cloverleaf rolls.

But there was no chocolate cake.

In the same way that Mrs. Hemingway seemed baffled in Africa, several busy generations of our family were stunned by Aunt M.'s exasperation. We forgot that homemade treats are like a birthright, essential to special-occasion traditions, an expression of appreciation, conviviality, love. Our African ancestors made puddings from fruits and nuts; sweet potato, rice or coconut breads spiced with ginger; cassava pone; and fruit salads so heavenly they earned the name "ambrosia" in America. In plantation kitchens, pastry cooks earned formidable reputations for temperamental desserts like "omelette soufflé," and free black pastry cooks and confectioners fashioned business enterprises from their knowledge and experience in baking, forming a key segment of the black economy.

But to Aunt M., we had caved to the lure of store-bought goodies. The long table displayed plastic tubs filled with miniature brownies and sugar cookies studded with M&M's candies, pies with machine-formed crusts in see-through clamshell boxes, and bubble trays of cupcakes topped with brightly colored neon frosting and confetti sprinkles. No chocolate cake—none that was made from scratch in a home, anyway.

We copped to our misdeed, acknowledged our need to atone for indifference to homemade chocolate cake, and decided a family griot (a West African term for a storyteller who uses the arts to preserve oral tradition) could hand down revelations of the perseverance, resistance, self-reliance, and power of baking throughout African American history—and be someone to remind us that baking is just plain *fun*.

That someone turned out to be me. For help, I looked to the culinary historian David S. Shields, author of *The Culinarian: Lives and Careers from the First Age of American Fine Dining* and *Southern Provisions: The Creation and Revival of a Cuisine*. Shields's stunning research chronicles ignored and forgotten cooks and restaurateurs, primarily from the nineteenth-century Carolina Lowcountry, including some of the influential black confectioners and pastry shop owners I celebrate in this chapter. I encountered pastry cooks in historical probes exploring the lives of free people of color, African American women, and black entrepreneurs as well.

These portraits of accomplishment stand in stark contrast to African American stereotypes and literary characters dutifully baking cakes in wash tubs and tomato cans for the mistress, industriously creating sweets of scarcity—vinegar and mock fruit pies, cakes baked with leftover bread crumbs leavened with corncob soda, and molasses candies. The ancestors did make those things, and their ingenuity is to be honored; they *also* left a legacy of recipes for elaborate cakes baked at Christmastime and for secret special occasions and tremendous skill they used both in enslavement and servitude, and to empower themselves and their communities.

"Of slaves, among the most valuable, rating next to skilled carpenters, were pastry cooks," Shields affirmed in *Southern Provisions*. In advertisements announcing slave sales, pastry cooks were "always distinguished from mere 'cooks,'" Shields added, and "the usual descriptor for a kitchen artists of the highest accomplishment was a 'complete pastry cook.'" (The tradition of baking is especially rich in South Carolina, Georgia, and North Florida, in part because the availability of sugarcane, sorghum, citrus, and spices, but also because of a seemingly unlimited supply of enslaved Dominican workers who helped pastry and confection businesses thrive.)

And while the pain of enslavement reverberates for centuries, and through the centuries, too, black bakers have used their skills and savvy to create wealth, self-sufficiency, and generations of protégés to carry on their legacy and to build their own economic power.

Names and stories from history came alive for me as I researched further. Sally Seymour, "the founding matriarch of the greatest of South

Carolina's African American dynasties," as Dr. Shields described her, was trained by one of Charleston's professional pastry chefs during the early 1970s. Once set free, she taught free and enslaved pastry cooks in the ship she established on Charleston's Tradd Street. Her network of business-savvy apprentices, including her daughter Eliza Seymour Lee, Camila Johnson, Eliza Dwight, Martha Gilchrist, Hannah Hetty, Elizabeth Holton, Mary Holton, and Cato McCloud.

In the Colonial North, Jean Baptiste and Catherine Point DuSable of Santo Domingo, Hispaniola (today in the Dominican Republic), established a trading post at the mouth of the Chicago River on the site of modern-day Chicago, which included a bake-house along with a five-room house, horse mill, dairy, smokehouse, poultry house, workshop, stable, and barn. Samuel Fraunces, tavern owner and presidential chef and steward, created a wide variety of the highest quality desserts, such as cakes, tarts, jellies, syllabubs, blancmange, and sweetmeats at his New York establishment, the Queen's Head Tavern. Once-enslaved Phillis Wheatley, who became one of the most famous American poets of the late 1700s, was married to John Peters, who operated a bakery and grocery in Boston. Tunis G. Campbell started a bakery in New York City after publishing *Hotel Keepers, Head Waiters, and Housekeepers' Guide* in 1848.

I asked myself: How could we not be inspired by Elizabeth Hewlett Marshall? She survived widowhood by working as a domestic, then opened a bakery in the basement of her home in what became New York's Central Park to support herself and her four children, her granddaughter Maritcha Lyons recalled in *We Are Your Sisters: Black Women in the Nineteenth Century*. Shouldn't we be proud of Harriet Owens Bynum, one of the important "race women" honored in *The Negro Trail Blazers of California*, a compilation of pioneering accomplishments? Bynum owned a bakeshop and a dairy in segregated Los Angeles, then became a realtor to ensure that the "poor class of colored laborers were given a square deal in the purchase of homes," she said with humility in 1915.

Activists Mary McLeod Bethune and Dr. Dorothy Height also boosted my baking enthusiasm. Bethune was an educator, human rights advocate, daughter of formerly enslaved parents, and founder of the National Council of Negro Women. Dr. Height, her protégé, became President and CEO of the NCNW. A woman of political influence, Bethune advised presidents and conferred a philosophical attitude of living to serve, which she said she left to "my people," and to those who shared her vision of world peace. In 1904, she founded the Daytona Educational and Industrial Training School, which is known today as Bethune-Cookman University, to cultivate the values of faith, courage, brotherhood, dignity, ambition, and responsibility as tools to enact equality.

Among other work and life lessons taught at the school, Bethune turned a spotlight on the connection between domestic science, baking, and self-reliance. Money earned by baking and selling sweet potato pies kept the school's doors open. Culinary students lived by her affirmation: "Cease to be a drudge, seek to be an artist."

Bethune's traditions flourished under Dr. Height's tireless leadership of the NCNW—a legacy of strong African American family values, cultural price, and respect for diversity. Under her watch, the NCNW also published *The Black Family Reunion Cookbook*, a classic; in the introduction, Dr. Height spoke of the "power of breaking bread in the building of communities."

Dr. Height and Bethune's hopeful aspirations encourage me. And I believe that remembering them can lead us to appreciate and embrace one another as extended family, celebrating what makes us unique and finding life-giving spirit in family traditions that create long-lasting memories. With their uplifting words and the ancestral wisdom of black pastry cooks, I can confidently spur my family's next generation to pick up some flour, sugar, chocolate, and a few eggs and bake a cake for Aunt M.

THE HOURS

Michael Cunningham

'I have this fantasy I'll find I have written some kind of vast epic novel that would include the Crimean war and interstellar space travel,' the novelist **Michael Cunningham** glumly told the *Guardian* in 2011, in an interview to celebrate the publication of his then-new novel. Happily for the many readers who love him, that book (like most of Cunningham's work) is a minutely observed slim volume about the inner lives of exquisite people. It somehow manages to be both funny and heartbreaking, simultaneously lyrical and clean. The extract below is taken from *The Hours*, his Pulitzer Prize-winning 1998 reimagining of Woolf's *Mrs Dalloway*, which is set across a single day in three timelines: Virginia Woolf herself, 1980s New York socialite Clarissa Dalloway and Laura Brown, a 1950s frustrated housewife living a life too small for itself, struggling to bond with her little son and longing to return to her book (*Mrs Dalloway*, naturally).

Mrs. Brown

—*life, London, this moment of June.*

She begins sifting flour into a blue bowl. Outside the window is the brief interlude of grass that separates this house from the neighbors'; the shadow of a bird streaks across the blinding white stucco of the neighbors' garage. Laura is briefly, deeply pleased by the shadow of the bird, the bands of brilliant white and green. The bowl on the counter before her is a pale, chalky, slightly faded blue with a thin band of white leaves at the rim. The leaves are identical, stylized, slightly cartoonish, canted at rakish angles, and it seems perfect and inevitable that one of them has suffered a small, precisely triangular nick in its side. A fine white rain of flour falls into the bowl.

"There we are," she says to Richie. "Do you want to see?"

"Yes," he answers.

She kneels to show him the sifted flour. "Now. We have to measure out four cups. Oh, my. Do you know how many four is?"

He holds up four fingers. "Good," she says. "Very good."

At this moment she could devour him, not ravenously but adoringly, infinitely gently, the way she used to take the Host into her mouth before she married and converted (her mother will never forgive her, never). She is full of a love so strong, so unambiguous, it resembles appetite.

"You're such a good, smart boy," she says.

Richie grins; he looks ardently into her face. She looks back at him. They pause, motionless, watching each other, and for a moment she is precisely what she appears to be: a pregnant woman kneeling in a kitchen with her three-year-old son, who knows the number four. She is herself and she is the perfect picture of herself; there is no difference. She is going to produce a birthday cake—only a cake—but in her mind at this moment the cake is glossy and resplendent as any photograph in any magazine; it is better, even, than the photographs of cakes in magazines. She imagines making, out of the humblest materials, a cake with all the balance and authority of an urn or a house. The cake will speak of bounty and delight the way a good house speaks of comfort and safety. This, she thinks, is how artists or architects must feel (it's an awfully grand comparison, she knows, maybe even a little foolish, but still), faced with canvas, with stone, with oil or wet cement. Wasn't a book like *Mrs. Dalloway* once just empty paper and a pot of ink? It's only a cake, she tells herself. But still. There are cakes and then there are cakes. At this moment, holding a bowl full of sifted flour in an orderly house under the California sky, she hopes to be as satisfied and as filled with anticipation as a writer putting down the first sentence, a builder beginning to draw the plans.

"Okeydoke," she says to Richie. "You do the first one."

She hands him a bright aluminum cup measure. It is the first time he's been entrusted with a job like this. Laura sets a second bowl, empty, on the floor for him. He holds the measuring cup in both hands.

"Here goes," she says.

Guiding Richie's hands with her own, she helps him dip the cup into the flour. The cup goes in easily, and through its thin wall he can feel the silkiness and slight grit of the sifted flour. A tiny cloud rises in the cup's wake. Mother and son bring it up again, heaped with flour. Flour cascades down the silver sides. Laura tells the boy to hold the cup steady, which he nervously manages to do, and with one quick gesture she dismisses the grainy little heap on top and creates a flawless white surface exactly level with the lip of the cup. He continues holding the cup with both hands.

"Good," she says. "Now we put it in the other bowl. Do you think you can do that by yourself?"

"Yes," he says, though he is not at all certain. He believes this cup of flour to be singular and irreplaceable. It is one thing to be asked to carry a cabbage across the street, quite another to be asked to carry the recently unearthed head of Rilke's Apollo.

"Here we go, then," she says.

He cautiously moves the cup to the other bowl and holds it there, paralyzed, over the bowl's gleaming white concavity (it is the next smaller in a series of nesting bowls, pale green, with the same band of white leaves at its rim). He understands that he's expected to dump the flour into the bowl but it seems possible that he's misunderstood the directions, and will ruin everything; it seems possible that by spilling out the flour he will cause some larger catastrophe, upset some precarious balance. He wants to look at his mother's face but can't take his eyes off the cup.

"Turn it over," she says.

He turns it over in one hurried, frightened motion. The flour hesitates for a fraction of a second, then spills out. The flour falls solidly, in a mound that loosely echoes the shape of the measuring cup. A bigger cloud rises, almost touches his face, then vanishes. He stares down at what he's made: a white hill, slightly granular, speckled with pinpoint shadows, standing up from the glossy, creamier white of the bowl's interior.

"Oopsie," his mother says.

He looks at her in terror. His eyes fill with tears.

Laura sighs. Why is he so delicate, so prone to fits of inexplicable remorse? Why does she have to be so careful with him? For a moment—a moment—Richie's shape subtly changes. He becomes larger, brighter. His head expands. A dead-white glow seems, briefly, to surround him. For a moment she wants only to leave—not to harm him, she'd never do that—but to be free, blameless, unaccountable.

"No, no," Laura says. "It's good. Very good. That's just exactly right."

He smiles tearfully, suddenly proud of himself, almost insanely relieved. All right, then; nothing was needed but a few kind words, a bit of reassurance. She sighs. She gently touches his hair.

"Now, then," she says. "Are you ready to do another one?"

He nods with such guileless, unguarded enthusiasm that her throat constricts in a spasm of love. It seems suddenly easy to bake a cake, to raise a child. She loves her son purely, as mothers do—she does not resent him, does not wish to leave. She loves her husband, and is glad to be married. It seems possible (it does not seem impossible) that she's slipped across an invisible line, the line that has always separated her from what she would prefer to feel, who she would prefer to be. It does not seem impossible that she has undergone a subtle but profound transformation, here in this kitchen, at this most ordinary of moments: She has caught up with herself. She has worked so long, so hard, in such good faith, and now she's gotten the knack of living happily, as herself, the way a child learns at a particular moment to balance on a two-wheel bicycle. It seems she will be fine. She will not lose hope. She will not mourn her lost possibilities, her unexplored talents (what if she has no talents, after all?). She will remain devoted to her son, her husband, her home and duties, all her gifts. She will want this second child.

A PAIR OF SILK STOCKINGS

Kate Chopin

Missouri-born **Kate Chopin** moved to Louisiana with her husband in the late-nineteenth century. During her career she wrote around one hundred short stories or novels, the majority between 1889 and 1904. Her most famous work, *The Awakening*, was labelled 'a masterpiece' in *The New York Times* in 1972, in an article by Linda Wolfe which also noted that 'her work was so shocking for its time that it was buried'. Following this piece, Chopin's writing experienced a resurgence, and her stories of women, of marriage and of sexuality made their way back into bookshops.

Little Mrs. Sommers one day found herself the unexpected possessor of fifteen dollars. It seemed to her a very large amount of money, and the way in which it stuffed and bulged her worn old porte-monnaie gave her a feeling of importance such as she had not enjoyed for years.

The question of investment was one that occupied her greatly. For a day or two she walked about apparently in a dreamy state, but really absorbed in speculation and calculation. She did not wish to act hastily, to do anything she might afterward regret. But it was during the still hours of the night when she lay awake revolving plans in her mind that she seemed to see her way clearly toward a proper and judicious use of the money.

A dollar or two should be added to the price usually paid for Janie's shoes, which would insure their lasting an appreciable time longer than they usually did. She would buy so and so many yards of percale for new shirt waists for the boys and Janie and Mag. She had intended to make the old ones do by skilful patching. Mag should have another gown.

She had seen some beautiful patterns, veritable bargains in the shop windows. And still there would be left enough for new stockings—two pairs apiece—and what darning that would save for a while! She would get caps for the boys and sailor-hats for the girls. The vision of her little brood looking fresh and dainty and new for once in their lives excited her and made her restless and wakeful with anticipation.

The neighbors sometimes talked of certain "better days" that little Mrs. Sommers had known before she had ever thought of being Mrs. Sommers. She herself indulged in no such morbid retrospection. She had no time—no second of time to devote to the past. The needs of the present absorbed her every faculty. A vision of the future like some dim, gaunt monster sometimes appalled her, but luckily to-morrow never comes.

Mrs. Sommers was one who knew the value of bargains; who could stand for hours making her way inch by inch toward the desired object that was selling below cost. She could elbow her way if need be; she had learned to clutch a piece of goods and hold it and stick to it with persistence and determination till her turn came to be served, no matter when it came.

But that day she was a little faint and tired. She had swallowed a light luncheon—no! when she came to think of it, between getting the children fed and the place righted, and preparing herself for the shopping bout, she had actually forgotten to eat any luncheon at all!

She sat herself upon a revolving stool before a counter that was comparatively deserted, trying to gather strength and courage to charge through an eager multitude that was besieging breastworks of shirting and figured lawn. An all-gone limp feeling had come over her and she rested her hand aimlessly upon the counter. She wore no gloves. By degrees she grew aware that her hand had encountered something very soothing, very pleasant to touch. She looked down to see that her hand lay upon a pile of silk stockings. A placard nearby announced that they had been reduced in price from two dollars and fifty cents to one dollar and ninety-eight cents; and a young girl who stood behind the counter asked her if she wished to examine their line of silk hosiery. She smiled, just as if she had been asked to inspect a tiara of diamonds with the ultimate view of purchasing it. But she went on feeling the soft, sheeny luxurious things—with both hands now, holding them up to see them glisten, and to feel them glide serpent-like through her fingers.

Two hectic blotches came suddenly into her pale cheeks. She looked up at the girl.

"Do you think there are any eights-and-a-half among these?"

There were any number of eights-and-a-half. In fact, there were more of that size than any other. Here was a light-blue pair; there were some lavender, some all-black and various shades of tan and gray. Mrs. Sommers selected a black pair and looked at them very long and closely. She pretended to be examining their texture, which the clerk assured her was excellent.

"A dollar and ninety-eight cents," she mused aloud. "Well, I'll take this pair." She handed the girl a five-dollar bill and waited for her change and for her parcel. What a very small parcel it was! It seemed lost in the depths of her shabby old shopping-bag.

Mrs. Sommers after that did not move in the direction of the bargain counter. She took the elevator, which carried her to an upper floor into the region of the ladies' waiting-rooms. Here, in a retired corner, she exchanged her cotton stockings for the new silk ones which she had just bought. She was not going through any acute mental process or reasoning with herself, nor was she striving to explain to her satisfaction the motive of her action. She was not thinking at all. She seemed for the time to be taking a rest from that laborious and fatiguing function and to have abandoned herself to some mechanical impulse that directed her actions and freed her of responsibility.

How good was the touch of the raw silk to her flesh! She felt like lying back in the cushioned chair and reveling for a while in the luxury of it. She did for a little while. Then she replaced her shoes, rolled the cotton stockings together and thrust them into her bag. After doing this she crossed straight over to the shoe department and took her seat to be fitted.

She was fastidious. The clerk could not make her out; he could not reconcile her shoes with her stockings, and she was not too easily pleased.

She held back her skirts and turned her feet one way and her head another way as she glanced down at the polished, pointed-tipped boots. Her foot and ankle looked very pretty. She could not realize that they belonged to her and were a part of herself. She wanted an excellent and stylish fit, she told the young fellow who served her, and she did not mind the difference of a dollar or two more in the price so long as she got what she desired.

It was a long time since Mrs. Sommers had been fitted with gloves. On rare occasions when she had bought a pair they were always "bargains," so cheap that it would have been preposterous and unreasonable to have expected them to be fitted to the hand.

Now she rested her elbow on the cushion of the glove counter, and a pretty, pleasant young creature, delicate and deft of touch, drew a long-wristed "kid" over Mrs. Sommers's hand. She smoothed it down over the wrist and buttoned it neatly, and both lost themselves for a second or two in admiring contemplation of the little symmetrical gloved hand. But there were other places where money might be spent.

There were books and magazines piled up in the window of a stall a few paces down the street. Mrs. Sommers bought two high-priced magazines such as she had been accustomed to read in the days when she had been accustomed to other pleasant things. She carried them without wrapping. As well as she could she lifted her skirts at the crossings. Her stockings and boots and well-fitting gloves had worked marvels in her bearing—had given her a feeling of assurance, a sense of belonging to the well-dressed multitude.

She was very hungry. Another time she would have stilled the cravings for food until reaching her own home, where she would have brewed herself a cup of tea and taken a snack of anything that was available. But the impulse that was guiding her would not suffer her to entertain any such thought.

There was a restaurant at the corner. She had never entered its doors; from the outside she had sometimes caught glimpses of spotless damask and shining crystal, and soft-stepping waiters serving people of fashion.

When she entered her appearance created no surprise, no consternation, as she had half feared it might. She seated herself at a small table alone, and an attentive waiter at once approached to take her order. She did not want a profusion; she craved a nice and tasty bite—a half dozen blue-points, a plump chop with cress, a something sweet—a crème-frappée, for instance; a glass of Rhine wine, and after all a small cup of black coffee.

While waiting to be served she removed her gloves very leisurely and laid them beside her. Then she picked up a magazine and glanced through it, cutting the pages with a blunt edge of her knife. It was all very agreeable. The damask was even more spotless than it had seemed through the window, and the crystal more sparkling. There were quiet ladies and gentlemen, who did not notice her, lunching at the small tables like her own. A soft, pleasing strain of music could be heard, and a gentle breeze was blowing through the window. She tasted a bite, and she read a word or two, and she sipped the amber wine and wiggled her toes in the silk stockings. The price of it made no difference. She counted the money out to the waiter and left an extra coin on his tray, whereupon he bowed before her as before a princess of royal blood.

There was still money in her purse, and her next temptation presented itself in the shape of a matinee poster.

It was a little later when she entered the theatre, the play had begun and the house seemed to her to be packed. But there were vacant seats here and there, and into one of them she was ushered, between brilliantly dressed women who had gone there to kill time and eat candy and display their gaudy attire. There were many others who were there solely for the play and acting. It is safe to say there was no one present who bore quite the attitude which Mrs. Sommers did to her surroundings. She gathered in the whole—stage and players and people in one wide impression, and absorbed it and enjoyed it. She laughed at the comedy and wept—she and the gaudy woman next to her wept over the tragedy. And they talked a little together over it. And the gaudy woman wiped her eyes and sniffled on a tiny square of filmy, perfumed lace and passed little Mrs. Sommers her box of candy.

The play was over, the music ceased, the crowd filed out. It was like a dream ended. People scattered in all directions. Mrs. Sommers went to the corner and waited for the cable car.

A man with keen eyes, who sat opposite to her, seemed to like the study of her small, pale face. It puzzled him to decipher what he saw there. In truth, he saw nothing—unless he were wizard enough to detect a poignant wish, a powerful longing that the cable car would never stop anywhere, but go on and on with her forever.

REFINED AND ELEGANT THINGS *FROM* THE PILLOW BOOK

Sei Shōnagon

Though her true name remains a topic of debate among scholars, **Sei Shōnagon** was the pen name of a diarist, poet and author who was writing in around 1000, during the middle Heian Period in Japan. *The Pillow Book* is a collection of essays, observations, poetry and lists written during her years serving Empress Teishi, or Sadako, as a court lady.

Meredith McKinney is an award-winning translator of classical and modern Japanese literature. She lived and taught in Japan for twenty years, and is now Honorary Associate Professor at the Japan Centre, Australian National University in Canberra. She was born in Queensland in 1950, to the Indigenous Australian land rights activist and poet Judith Wright and her husband Jack, a soldier, farmer and philosopher. It is possible to see both the poet and the philosopher present in McKinney's clear, beautiful, direct translation of *The Pillow Book*.

[39] *Refined and elegant things* – A girl's over-robe of white on white over pale violet-grey. The eggs of the spot-billed duck. Shaved ice with a sweet syrup, served in a shiny new metal bowl. A crystal rosary. Wisteria flowers. Snow on plum blossoms. An adorable little child eating strawberries.

MILLIONS OF STRAWBERRIES

Genevieve Taggard

Born in 1894, **Genevieve Taggard** was the daughter of school-teacher missionaries, and grew up to become a radical socialist, Guggenheim Fellow and poet. She taught at several of the so-called 'Seven Sisters' colleges – prestigious women-only institutions created and funded to rival and match the all-male 'Ivy League'. While she is lesser-known today, in her lifetime her radical and charming work was very popular. She died in 1948, leaving behind her husband and daughter.

Marcia and I went over the curve,
Eating our way down
Jewels of strawberries we didn't deserve,
Eating our way down
Till our hands were sticky, and our lips painted.
And over us the hot day fainted,
And we saw snakes,
And got scratched,
And a lust overcame us for the red unmatched
Small buds of berries,
Till we lay down—
Eating our way down—
And rolled in the berries like two little dogs,
Rolled
In the late gold.
And gnats hummed,

And it was cold,
And home we went, home without a berry,
Painted red and brown,
Eating our way down.

GOBLIN MARKET

Christina Rossetti

Regarded by her family of poets as *the* poet, the great **Christina Rossetti** was born in 1830. Her father was a political exile from Italy, her mother a governess, and they brought their four children up to value above all things high art and higher intellect. All four became writers: Maria, the eldest, was a Dante scholar; and the boys – Dante Gabriel and William – founded and led the Pre-Raphaelite movement. They expected that Christina, her first poems nationally and professionally published at just 17, would join them. Caught, however, between Victorian notions of the angel in the house, and the radical artistic anarcho-sexual freedom that would later shape the life of her sisters-in-law, sisters-out-law, nieces and great-nieces, Christina opted out. She had had a wild temper as a child (she and Gabriel were the 'two storms' of the family) and to the distress of her family, spent her adult life in a constant struggle to be seen only as 'calm and sedate'. And yet she wrote, and her poems (though she refused to allow them to be read aloud) could hardly be called sedate at all. The gorgeous, sexy depth and flavour of *Goblin Market* undercuts the supposed 'message' of the poem, to be better behaved in future: nobody who reads *Goblin Market* is so deluded as to believe they might resist the song of the goblins, and their baskets full of temptation. This is a hungry woman, a hungry poet; and when you read her work, *you're hungry too*.

Morning and evening
Maids heard the goblins cry:
"Come buy our orchard fruits,
Come buy, come buy:
Apples and quinces,
Lemons and oranges,
Plump unpeck'd cherries,

Melons and raspberries,
Bloom-down-cheek'd peaches,
Swart-headed mulberries,
Wild free-born cranberries,
Crab-apples, dewberries,
Pine-apples, blackberries,
Apricots, strawberries;—
All ripe together
In summer weather,—
Morns that pass by,
Fair eves that fly;
Come buy, come buy:
Our grapes fresh from the vine,
Pomegranates full and fine,
Dates and sharp bullaces,
Rare pears and greengages,
Damsons and bilberries,
Taste them and try:
Currants and gooseberries,
Bright-fire-like barberries,
Figs to fill your mouth,
Citrons from the South,
Sweet to tongue and sound to eye;
Come buy, come buy."

Evening by evening
Among the brookside rushes,
Laura bow'd her head to hear,
Lizzie veil'd her blushes:
Crouching close together
In the cooling weather,
With clasping arms and cautioning lips,
With tingling cheeks and finger tips.
"Lie close," Laura said,

Pricking up her golden head:
"We must not look at goblin men,
We must not buy their fruits:
Who knows upon what soil they fed
Their hungry thirsty roots?"
"Come buy," call the goblins
Hobbling down the glen.

"Oh," cried Lizzie, "Laura, Laura,
You should not peep at goblin men."
Lizzie cover'd up her eyes,
Cover'd close lest they should look;
Laura rear'd her glossy head,
And whisper'd like the restless brook:
"Look, Lizzie, look, Lizzie,
Down the glen tramp little men.
One hauls a basket,
One bears a plate,
One lugs a golden dish
Of many pounds weight.
How fair the vine must grow
Whose grapes are so luscious;
How warm the wind must blow
Through those fruit bushes."
"No," said Lizzie, "No, no, no;
Their offers should not charm us,
Their evil gifts would harm us."
She thrust a dimpled finger
In each ear, shut eyes and ran:
Curious Laura chose to linger
Wondering at each merchant man.
One had a cat's face,
One whisk'd a tail,
One tramp'd at a rat's pace,

One crawl'd like a snail,
One like a wombat prowl'd obtuse and furry,
One like a ratel tumbled hurry skurry.
She heard a voice like voice of doves
Cooing all together:
They sounded kind and full of loves
In the pleasant weather.

Laura stretch'd her gleaming neck
Like a rush-imbedded swan,
Like a lily from the beck,
Like a moonlit poplar branch,
Like a vessel at the launch
When its last restraint is gone.

Backwards up the mossy glen
Turn'd and troop'd the goblin men,
With their shrill repeated cry,
"Come buy, come buy."
When they reach'd where Laura was
They stood stock still upon the moss,
Leering at each other,
Brother with queer brother;
Signalling each other,
Brother with sly brother.
One set his basket down,
One rear'd his plate;
One began to weave a crown
Of tendrils, leaves, and rough nuts brown
(Men sell not such in any town);
One heav'd the golden weight
Of dish and fruit to offer her:
"Come buy, come buy," was still their cry.
Laura stared but did not stir,

Long'd but had no money:
The whisk-tail'd merchant bade her taste
In tones as smooth as honey,
The cat-faced purr'd,
The rat-faced spoke a word
Of welcome, and the snail-paced even was heard;
One parrot-voiced and jolly
Cried "Pretty Goblin" still for "Pretty Polly;"—
One whistled like a bird.

But sweet-tooth Laura spoke in haste:
"Good folk, I have no coin;
To take were to purloin:
I have no copper in my purse,
I have no silver either,
And all my gold is on the furze
That shakes in windy weather
Above the rusty heather."
"You have much gold upon your head,"
They answer'd all together:
"Buy from us with a golden curl."
She clipp'd a precious golden lock,
She dropp'd a tear more rare than pearl,
Then suck'd their fruit globes fair or red:
Sweeter than honey from the rock,
Stronger than man-rejoicing wine,
Clearer than water flow'd that juice;
She never tasted such before,
How should it cloy with length of use?
She suck'd and suck'd and suck'd the more
Fruits which that unknown orchard bore;
She suck'd until her lips were sore;
Then flung the emptied rinds away
But gather'd up one kernel stone,

And knew not was it night or day
As she turn'd home alone.

Lizzie met her at the gate
Full of wise upbraidings:
"Dear, you should not stay so late,
Twilight is not good for maidens;
Should not loiter in the glen
In the haunts of goblin men.
Do you not remember Jeanie,
How she met them in the moonlight,
Took their gifts both choice and many,
Ate their fruits and wore their flowers
Pluck'd from bowers
Where summer ripens at all hours?
But ever in the noonlight
She pined and pined away;
Sought them by night and day,
Found them no more, but dwindled and grew grey;
Then fell with the first snow,
While to this day no grass will grow
Where she lies low:
I planted daisies there a year ago
That never blow.
You should not loiter so."
"Nay, hush," said Laura:
"Nay, hush, my sister:
I ate and ate my fill,
Yet my mouth waters still;
To-morrow night I will
Buy more;" and kiss'd her:
"Have done with sorrow;
I'll bring you plums to-morrow
Fresh on their mother twigs,

Cherries worth getting;
You cannot think what figs
My teeth have met in,
What melons icy-cold
Piled on a dish of gold
Too huge for me to hold,
What peaches with a velvet nap,
Pellucid grapes without one seed:
Odorous indeed must be the mead
Whereon they grow, and pure the wave they drink
With lilies at the brink,
And sugar-sweet their sap."

Golden head by golden head,
Like two pigeons in one nest
Folded in each other's wings,
They lay down in their curtain'd bed:
Like two blossoms on one stem,
Like two flakes of new-fall'n snow,
Like two wands of ivory
Tipp'd with gold for awful kings.
Moon and stars gaz'd in at them,
Wind sang to them lullaby,
Lumbering owls forbore to fly,
Not a bat flapp'd to and fro
Round their rest:
Cheek to cheek and breast to breast
Lock'd together in one nest.

Early in the morning
When the first cock crow'd his warning,
Neat like bees, as sweet and busy,
Laura rose with Lizzie:
Fetch'd in honey, milk'd the cows,

Air'd and set to rights the house,
Kneaded cakes of whitest wheat,
Cakes for dainty mouths to eat,
Next churn'd butter, whipp'd up cream,
Fed their poultry, sat and sew'd;
Talk'd as modest maidens should:
Lizzie with an open heart,
Laura in an absent dream,
One content, one sick in part;
One warbling for the mere bright day's delight,
One longing for the night.

At length slow evening came:
They went with pitchers to the reedy brook;
Lizzie most placid in her look,
Laura most like a leaping flame.
They drew the gurgling water from its deep;
Lizzie pluck'd purple and rich golden flags,
Then turning homeward said: "The sunset flushes
Those furthest loftiest crags;
Come, Laura, not another maiden lags.
No wilful squirrel wags,
The beasts and birds are fast asleep."
But Laura loiter'd still among the rushes
And said the bank was steep.

And said the hour was early still
The dew not fall'n, the wind not chill;
Listening ever, but not catching
The customary cry,
"Come buy, come buy,"
With its iterated jingle
Of sugar-baited words:
Not for all her watching

Once discerning even one goblin
Racing, whisking, tumbling, hobbling;
Let alone the herds
That used to tramp along the glen,
In groups or single,
Of brisk fruit-merchant men.

Till Lizzie urged, "O Laura, come;
I hear the fruit-call but I dare not look:
You should not loiter longer at this brook:
Come with me home.
The stars rise, the moon bends her arc,
Each glowworm winks her spark,
Let us get home before the night grows dark:
For clouds may gather
Though this is summer weather,
Put out the lights and drench us through;
Then if we lost our way what should we do?"

Laura turn'd cold as stone
To find her sister heard that cry alone,
That goblin cry,
"Come buy our fruits, come buy."
Must she then buy no more such dainty fruit?
Must she no more such succous pasture find,
Gone deaf and blind?
Her tree of life droop'd from the root:
She said not one word in her heart's sore ache;
But peering thro' the dimness, nought discerning,
Trudg'd home, her pitcher dripping all the way;
So crept to bed, and lay
Silent till Lizzie slept;
Then sat up in a passionate yearning,
And gnash'd her teeth for baulk'd desire, and wept

As if her heart would break.

Day after day, night after night,
Laura kept watch in vain
In sullen silence of exceeding pain.
She never caught again the goblin cry:
"Come buy, come buy;"—
She never spied the goblin men
Hawking their fruits along the glen:
But when the noon wax'd bright
Her hair grew thin and grey;
She dwindled, as the fair full moon doth turn
To swift decay and burn
Her fire away.

One day remembering her kernel-stone
She set it by a wall that faced the south;
Dew'd it with tears, hoped for a root,
Watch'd for a waxing shoot,
But there came none;
It never saw the sun,
It never felt the trickling moisture run:
While with sunk eyes and faded mouth
She dream'd of melons, as a traveller sees
False waves in desert drouth
With shade of leaf-crown'd trees,
And burns the thirstier in the sandful breeze.

She no more swept the house,
Tended the fowls or cows,
Fetch'd honey, kneaded cakes of wheat,
Brought water from the brook:
But sat down listless in the chimney-nook
And would not eat.

Tender Lizzie could not bear
To watch her sister's cankerous care
Yet not to share.
She night and morning
Caught the goblins' cry:
"Come buy our orchard fruits,
Come buy, come buy;"—
Beside the brook, along the glen,
She heard the tramp of goblin men,
The yoke and stir
Poor Laura could not hear;
Long'd to buy fruit to comfort her,
But fear'd to pay too dear.
She thought of Jeanie in her grave,
Who should have been a bride;
But who for joys brides hope to have
Fell sick and died
In her gay prime,
In earliest winter time
With the first glazing rime,
With the first snow-fall of crisp winter time.

Till Laura dwindling
Seem'd knocking at Death's door:
Then Lizzie weigh'd no more
Better and worse;
But put a silver penny in her purse,
Kiss'd Laura, cross'd the heath with clumps of furze
At twilight, halted by the brook:
And for the first time in her life
Began to listen and look.

Laugh'd every goblin
When they spied her peeping:

Came towards her hobbling,
Flying, running, leaping,
Puffing and blowing,
Chuckling, clapping, crowing,
Clucking and gobbling,
Mopping and mowing,
Full of airs and graces,
Pulling wry faces,
Demure grimaces,
Cat-like and rat-like,
Ratel- and wombat-like,
Snail-paced in a hurry,
Parrot-voiced and whistler,
Helter skelter, hurry skurry,
Chattering like magpies,
Fluttering like pigeons,
Gliding like fishes,—
Hugg'd her and kiss'd her:
Squeez'd and caress'd her:
Stretch'd up their dishes,
Panniers, and plates:
"Look at our apples
Russet and dun,
Bob at our cherries,
Bite at our peaches,
Citrons and dates,
Grapes for the asking,
Pears red with basking
Out in the sun,
Plums on their twigs;
Pluck them and suck them,
Pomegranates, figs."—

"Good folk," said Lizzie,
Mindful of Jeanie:
"Give me much and many: —
Held out her apron,
Toss'd them her penny.
"Nay, take a seat with us,
Honour and eat with us,"
They answer'd grinning:
"Our feast is but beginning.
Night yet is early,
Warm and dew-pearly,
Wakeful and starry:
Such fruits as these
No man can carry:
Half their bloom would fly,
Half their dew would dry,
Half their flavour would pass by.
Sit down and feast with us,
Be welcome guest with us,
Cheer you and rest with us."—
"Thank you," said Lizzie: "But one waits
At home alone for me:
So without further parleying,
If you will not sell me any
Of your fruits though much and many,
Give me back my silver penny
I toss'd you for a fee."—
They began to scratch their pates,
No longer wagging, purring,
But visibly demurring,
Grunting and snarling.
One call'd her proud,
Cross-grain'd, uncivil;
Their tones wax'd loud,

Their looks were evil.
Lashing their tails
They trod and hustled her,
Elbow'd and jostled her,
Claw'd with their nails,
Barking, mewing, hissing, mocking,
Tore her gown and soil'd her stocking,
Twitch'd her hair out by the roots,
Stamp'd upon her tender feet,
Held her hands and squeez'd their fruits
Against her mouth to make her eat.

White and golden Lizzie stood,
Like a lily in a flood,—
Like a rock of blue-vein'd stone
Lash'd by tides obstreperously,—
Like a beacon left alone
In a hoary roaring sea,
Sending up a golden fire,—
Like a fruit-crown'd orange-tree
White with blossoms honey-sweet
Sore beset by wasp and bee,—
Like a royal virgin town
Topp'd with gilded dome and spire
Close beleaguer'd by a fleet
Mad to tug her standard down.

One may lead a horse to water,
Twenty cannot make him drink.
Though the goblins cuff'd and caught her,
Coax'd and fought her,
Bullied and besought her,
Scratch'd her, pinch'd her black as ink,
Kick'd and knock'd her,

Maul'd and mock'd her,
Lizzie utter'd not a word;
Would not open lip from lip
Lest they should cram a mouthful in:
But laugh'd in heart to feel the drip
Of juice that syrupp'd all her face,
And lodg'd in dimples of her chin,
And streak'd her neck which quaked like curd.
At last the evil people,
Worn out by her resistance,
Flung back her penny, kick'd their fruit
Along whichever road they took,
Not leaving root or stone or shoot;
Some writh'd into the ground,
Some div'd into the brook
With ring and ripple,
Some scudded on the gale without a sound,
Some vanish'd in the distance.

In a smart, ache, tingle,
Lizzie went her way;
Knew not was it night or day;
Sprang up the bank, tore thro' the furze,
Threaded copse and dingle,
And heard her penny jingle
Bouncing in her purse,—
Its bounce was music to her ear.
She ran and ran
As if she fear'd some goblin man
Dogg'd her with gibe or curse
Or something worse:
But not one goblin scurried after,
Nor was she prick'd by fear;
The kind heart made her windy-paced

That urged her home quite out of breath with haste
And inward laughter.

She cried, "Laura," up the garden,
"Did you miss me?
Come and kiss me.
Never mind my bruises,
Hug me, kiss me, suck my juices
Squeez'd from goblin fruits for you,
Goblin pulp and goblin dew.
Eat me, drink me, love me;
Laura, make much of me;
For your sake I have braved the glen
And had to do with goblin merchant men."

Laura started from her chair,
Flung her arms up in the air,
Clutch'd her hair:
"Lizzie, Lizzie, have you tasted
For my sake the fruit forbidden?
Must your light like mine be hidden,
Your young life like mine be wasted,
Undone in mine undoing,
And ruin'd in my ruin,
Thirsty, canker'd, goblin-ridden?"—
She clung about her sister,
Kiss'd and kiss'd and kiss'd her:
Tears once again
Refresh'd her shrunken eyes,
Dropping like rain
After long sultry drouth;
Shaking with aguish fear, and pain,
She kiss'd and kiss'd her with a hungry mouth.

Her lips began to scorch,
That juice was wormwood to her tongue,
She loath'd the feast:
Writhing as one possess'd she leap'd and sung,
Rent all her robe, and wrung
Her hands in lamentable haste,
And beat her breast.
Her locks stream'd like the torch
Borne by a racer at full speed,
Or like the mane of horses in their flight,
Or like an eagle when she stems the light
Straight toward the sun,
Or like a caged thing freed,
Or like a flying flag when armies run.

Swift fire spread through her veins, knock'd at her heart,
Met the fire smouldering there
And overbore its lesser flame;
She gorged on bitterness without a name:
Ah! fool, to choose such part
Of soul-consuming care!
Sense fail'd in the mortal strife:
Like the watch-tower of a town
Which an earthquake shatters down,
Like a lightning-stricken mast,
Like a wind-uprooted tree
Spun about,
Like a foam-topp'd waterspout
Cast down headlong in the sea,
She fell at last;
Pleasure past and anguish past,
Is it death or is it life?

Life out of death.
That night long Lizzie watch'd by her,
Counted her pulse's flagging stir,
Felt for her breath,
Held water to her lips, and cool'd her face
With tears and fanning leaves:
But when the first birds chirp'd about their eaves,
And early reapers plodded to the place
Of golden sheaves,
And dew-wet grass
Bow'd in the morning winds so brisk to pass,
And new buds with new day
Open'd of cup-like lilies on the stream,
Laura awoke as from a dream,
Laugh'd in the innocent old way,
Hugg'd Lizzie but not twice or thrice;
Her gleaming locks show'd not one thread of grey,
Her breath was sweet as May
And light danced in her eyes.

Days, weeks, months, years
Afterwards, when both were wives
With children of their own;
Their mother-hearts beset with fears,
Their lives bound up in tender lives;
Laura would call the little ones
And tell them of her early prime,
Those pleasant days long gone
Of not-returning time:
Would talk about the haunted glen,
The wicked, quaint fruit-merchant men,
Their fruits like honey to the throat
But poison in the blood;
(Men sell not such in any town):

Would tell them how her sister stood
In deadly peril to do her good,
And win the fiery antidote:
Then joining hands to little hands
Would bid them cling together,
"For there is no friend like a sister
In calm or stormy weather;
To cheer one on the tedious way,
To fetch one if one goes astray,
To lift one if one totters down,
To strengthen whilst one stands."

BEETON'S BOOK OF HOUSEHOLD MANAGEMENT

Mrs Beeton

'I must frankly own, that if I had known, beforehand, that this book would have cost me the labour which it has, I should never have been courageous enough to commence it,' wrote **Isabella Mary Beeton**, exhausted, and speaking for cookbook writers everywhere. It seems fitting that Mrs Beeton, the grandmother of English cookery writing, should so exactly mirror the feelings of anyone just coming to the end of an enormous project. And what a project it is: *Mrs Beeton's Book Of Household Management* runs to forty-four chapters (later, and posthumously, this number rose to seventy-four) on every aspect of cooking, provisioning and generally managing a household. It was an immediate bestseller and has never been out of print. Although the recipes were taken from all sources, including readers of Beeton's husband's magazines, 'no recipe went into the book without a successful trial,' as her half-sister remembered. 'And the home at Pinner was the scene of many experiments and some failures. I remember Isabella coming out of the kitchen one day, "This won't do at all," she said, and gave me the cake that had turned out like a biscuit. I thought it very good. It had currants in it.' (This may also feel hauntingly familiar to any cookbook writer who has tried to test a recipe on loving friends and family.) Beeton was working on the proofs of her next book until the day before her death, in 1865, from a post-partum infection. She was just twenty-eight years old.

Orange cream.

1463

Iingredients

1 oz. of isinglass
6 large oranges
1 lemon
Sugar, to taste
Water
½ pint of good cream

Mode

Squeeze the juice from the oranges and lemon; strain it, and put it into a saucepan with the isinglass, and sufficient water to make in all 1 ½ pints.

Rub the sugar on the orange and lemon-rind, add it to the other ingredients, and boil all together for about 10 minutes.

Strain through a muslin bag, and, when cold, beat up with it ½ pint of thick cream.

Wet a mould, or soak it in cold water; pour in the cream, and put it in a cool place to set.

If the weather is very cold, 1 oz. of isinglass will be found sufficient for the above proportion of ingredients.

Time:
10 minutes to boil the juice and water.

Average cost:
With the best isinglass: 3s.
Sufficient to fill a quart mould.
Seasonable from November to May.

Orange creams.

1464

Ingredients
1 Seville orange
1 tablespoonful of brandy
¼ lb. of loaf sugar
The yolks of 4 eggs
1 pint of cream

Mode

Boil the rind of the Seville orange until tender, and beat it in a mortar to a pulp; add to it the brandy, the strained juice of the orange, and the sugar, and beat all together for about 10 minutes, adding the well-beaten yolks of eggs.

Bring the cream to the boiling point, and pour it very gradually to the other ingredients, and beat the mixture till nearly cold; put it into custard-cups, place the cups in a deep dish of boiling water, where let them remain till quite cold.

Take the cups out of the water, wipe them, and garnish the tops of the creams with candied orange-peel or preserved chips.

Time:
Altogether, ¾ hour.

Average cost:
With cream at 1s. per pint: 1s. 7d.
Sufficient to make 7 or 8 creams.
Seasonable from November to May.

Note: To render this dish more economical, substitute milk for the cream, but add a small pinch of isinglass to make the creams firm.

SEVILLE ORANGE (Citrus vulgaris) – This variety, called also bitter orange, is of the same species as the sweet orange, and grows in great abundance on the banks of the Guadalquiver, in Andalusia, whence this fruit is chiefly obtained. In that part of Spain there are very extensive orchards of these oranges, which form the chief wealth of the monasteries.

The pulp of the bitter orange is not eaten raw. In the yellow rind, separated from the white spongy substance immediately below it, is contained an essential oil, which is an agreeable warm aromatic, much superior for many purposes to that of the common orange. The best marmalade and the richest wine are made from this orange; and from its flowers the best orange-flower water is distilled. Seville oranges are also preserved whole as a sweetmeat.

Orange fritters

1465

Ingredients
For the batter
½ lb. of flour
½ oz. of butter
½ saltspoonful of salt
2 eggs
Milk
Oranges
Hot lard or clarified dripping

Mode

Make a nice light batter with the above proportion of flour, butter, salt, eggs, and sufficient milk to make it the proper consistency; peel the oranges, remove as much of the white skin as possible, and divide each orange into eight pieces, without breaking the thin skin, unless it be to remove the pips; dip each piece of orange in the batter.

Have ready a pan of boiling lard or clarified dripping; drop in the oranges and fry them a delicate brown from 8 to 10 minutes.

When done, lay them on a piece of blotting-paper before the fire, to drain away the greasy moisture, and dish them on a white d'oyley; sprinkle over them plenty of pounded sugar, and serve quickly.

Time:
8 to 10 minutes to fry the fritters; 5 minutes to drain them.

Average cost:
9d.
Sufficient for 4 or 5 persons.
Seasonable from November to May.

A pretty dish of oranges

1466

Ingredients
6 large oranges
½ lb. of loaf sugar
¼ pint of water
½ pint of cream
2 tablespoonfuls of any kind of liqueur
Sugar to taste

Mode

Put the sugar and water into a saucepan, and boil them until the sugar becomes brittle, which may be ascertained by taking up a small quantity in a spoon, and dipping it in cold water; if the sugar is sufficiently boiled, it will easily snap.

Peel the oranges, remove as much of the white pith as possible, and divide them into nice-sized slices, without breaking the thin white skin which surrounds the juicy pulp.

Place the pieces of orange on small skewers, dip them into the hot sugar, and arrange them in layers round a plain mould, which should be well oiled with the purest salad-oil. The sides of the mould only should be lined with the oranges, and the centre left open for the cream.

Let the sugar become firm by cooling; turn the oranges carefully out on a dish, and fill the centre with whipped cream, flavoured with any kind of liqueur, and sweetened with pounded sugar.

This is an exceedingly ornamental and nice dish for the supper-table.

Time:
10 minutes to boil the sugar.

Average cost:
1s. 8d.
Sufficient for 1 mould.
Seasonable from November to May.

THE GROUNDNUT COOKBOOK

Duval Timothy, Folayemi Brown and Jacob Todd

After years of hosting pop-up dinners and workshops, London-based friends **Duval Timothy, Folayemi Brown** and **Jacob Fodio Todd** published *The Groundnut Cookbook* in 2015. Their food project The Groundnut was a space to explore their identities; their adaptation of sub-Saharan food reflects their heritage, from England, Ghana, Nigeria, Sierra Leone and South Sudan.

Across West Africa, oranges are skilfully peeled on the street. They're sold to people who drink the juice from a hole at the top of the fruit, and the orange functions as both the cup and the drink. Peeling the fruit makes the skin more malleable and easier to squeeze without it splitting. Each roadside vendor will often have a modest set-up selling just oranges.

Through repetition, they have mastered the technique of elegantly spiralling around the entire surface of each orange with a sharp knife in a matter of seconds. The often beautifully arranged pyramids of oranges and the fresh aroma of citrus from the ongoing peeling draws attention to these humble stalls. The yellow, orange and reddish colours of citrus fruits supposedly develop during cool winters. In tropical regions, cool winters don't exist in the same way, so you might commonly drink from a green orange.

This orange juice is as fresh as it gets and a lot of fun to drink. Most types of orange will work, but try to choose firm oranges with a bit of give. In general the heavier the orange is, the juicier it will be.

Orange juice

serves 4
(one orange per person)
Time: 4 minutes per orange
4 oranges

Peel the orange, starting from the top, using a small sharp knife or vegetable peeler to remove all the skin, leaving the white pith intact. When peeling, try to remove an equal amount of skin around the entire orange. *Any deep cuts will cause the orange to fracture and juice might squirt out of the wrong part when you drink.*

Cut a 2cm-wide hole at the top of the orange and remove the core at the top of the fruit. With a small knife, pierce the flesh of the orange in a few places through the hole at the top, making sure not to pierce the skin anywhere. *Doing this means that when you squeeze the orange, the juice will push out through the middle of the orange and up to the drinking hole rather than potentially splitting the skin.*

To drink, put your mouth to the hole in the orange and suck the juice while gently squeezing the fruit. Squeeze the fruit evenly around its surface as you continue to drink until no more juice is released. Once you have squeezed the juice, you can rip the fruit apart and enjoy the flesh.

ORANGES

John McPhee

A staff writer at the *New Yorker* since 1965, all of **John McPhee**'s thirty books have their roots in pieces he wrote for the magazine. In 1999 he was awarded a Pulitzer Prize for *Annals of the Former World*, a geological history of North America he wrote over the course of two decades. He has turned his literary reportage to subjects as diverse as a profile of Senator Bill Bradley's Princeton basketball days, a journey on a merchant ship along the coast of South America, and 'Soviet culture at the brink of the Union's collapse'. *Oranges* was inspired by the glass of juice he bought daily on his morning commute through Penn Station. He has taught non-fiction writing at Princeton University, where he is the Ferris Professor of Journalism, since 1974.

The custom of drinking orange juice with breakfast is not very widespread, taking the world as a whole, and it is thought by many peoples to be a distinctly American habit. But many Danes drink it regularly with breakfast, and so do Hondurans, Filipinos, Jamaicans, and the wealthier citizens of Trinidad and Tobago. The day is started with orange juice in the Colombian Andes, and, to some extent, in Kuwait. Bolivians don't touch it at breakfast time, but they drink it steadily for the rest of the day. The 'play lunch', or morning tea, that Australian children carry with them to school is usually an orange, peeled spirally halfway down, with the peel replaced around the fruit. The child unwinds the peel and holds the orange as if it were an ice-cream cone. People in Nepal almost never peel oranges, preferring to eat them in cut quarters, the way American athletes do. The sour oranges of Afghanistan customarily appear as seasoning agents on Afghan dinner tables. Squeezed over Afghan food, they cut the grease. The Shamouti Orange, of Israel, is seedless and sweet, has a thick skin, and grows in Hadera, Gaza, Tiberias, Jericho, the Jordan Valley, and Jaffa; it is exported from Jaffa, and for that reason is known universally beyond Israel as the Jaffa Orange. The Jaffa Orange is the variety that British people consider superior to all others, possibly because Richard the Lionhearted spent the winter of 1191–92 in the citrus groves of Jaffa. Citrus trees are spread across the North African coast from Alexandria to Tangier, the city whose name was given to tangerines. Oranges tend to become less tart the closer they are grown to the equator, and in Brazil there is one kind of orange that has virtually no acid in it at all. In the principal towns of Trinidad and Tobago, oranges are sold on street corners. The vender cuts them in half and sprinkles salt on them. In Jamaica, people halve oranges, get down on their hands and knees, and clean floors with one half in each hand. Jamaican mechanics use oranges to clear away grease and oil. The blood orange of Spain, its flesh streaked with red, is prized throughout Europe. Blood oranges grow well in Florida, but they frighten American women. Spain has about thirty-five million orange trees, grows six billion oranges a year, and exports more oranges than any other country, including the United States. In the Campania region of Italy, land is scarce; on a typical small patch, set on a steep slope, orange trees are interspersed with olive and walnut trees, grapes are trained to cover trellises overhead, and as many as five different vegetables are grown on the ground below. The overall effect is that a greengrocer's shop is springing out of the hillside. Italy produces more than four billion oranges a year, but most of its citrus industry is scattered in gardens of one or two acres. A Frenchman sits at the dinner table, and, as the finishing flourish of the meal, slowly and gently disrobes an orange. In France, peeling the fruit is not yet considered an inconvenience. French preferences run to the blood oranges and the Thomson Navels of Spain, and to the thick-skinned, bland Maltaises, which the French import not from Malta but from Tunisia. France itself only grows about four hundred thousand oranges each year, almost wholly in the Department of the Alpes Maritimes. Sometimes, Europeans eat oranges with knives and forks. On occasion, they serve a dessert orange that has previously been peeled with such extraordinary care that strips of the peel arc outward like the petals of a flower from the separated and reassembled segments in the centre. The Swiss sometimes serve oranges under a smothering of sugar and whipped cream; on a hot day in a Swiss garden, orange juice with ice is a luxurious drink. Norwegian children like to remove the top of an orange, make a little hole, push a lump of sugar into it, and then suck out the juice. English children make orange-peel teeth and wedge them over their gums on Halloween. Irish children take oranges to the movies, where they eat them while they watch the show, tossing the peels at each other and at the people on the screen. In Reykjavik, Iceland, in greenhouses that are heated by volcanic springs, orange trees yearly bear fruit. In the New York Botanical Garden, six mature orange trees are growing in the soil of the Bronx. Their trunks are six inches in diameter, and they bear well every year. The oranges are for viewing and are not supposed to be picked. When people walk past them, however, they sometimes find them irresistible.

The first known reference to oranges occurs in the second book of the *Five Classics*, which appeared in China around 500 BC and is generally regarded as having been edited by Confucius. The main course of the migration of the fruit – from its origins near the South China Sea, down into the Malay Archipelago, then on four thousand miles of ocean current to the east coast of Africa, across the desert by caravan and into the Mediterranean basin, then over the Atlantic to the American continents – closely and sometimes exactly kept pace with the major journeys of civilisation. There were no oranges in the Western Hemisphere before Columbus himself introduced them. It was Pizarro who took them to Peru. The seeds the Spaniards carried came from trees that had entered Spain as a result of the rise of Islam. The development of orange botany owes something to Vasco da Gama and even more to Alexander the Great; oranges had symbolic importance in the paintings of Renaissance masters; in other times, at least two overwhelming invasions of the Italian peninsula were inspired by the visions of paradise that oranges engendered in northern minds. Oranges were once the fruit of the gods, to whom they were the golden apples of the Hesperides, which were stolen by Hercules. Then, in successive declensions, oranges became the fruit of emperors and kings, of the upper prelacy, of the aristocracy, and, by the eighteenth century, of the rich bourgeoisie. Another hundred years went by before they came within reach of the middle classes, and not until early in this century did they at last become a fruit of the community.

Just after the Second World War, three scientists working in central Florida surprised themselves with a simple idea that resulted in the development of commercial orange-juice concentrate. A couple of dozen enormous factories sprang out of the hammocks, and Florida, which can be counted on in most seasons to produce about a quarter of all the oranges grown in the world, was soon putting most of them through the process that results in small, trim cans, about two inches in diameter and four inches high, containing orange juice that has been boiled to high viscosity in a vacuum, separated into several component parts, reassembled, flavoured, and then frozen solid. People in the United States used to consume more fresh oranges than all other fresh fruits combined, but in less than twenty years the per-capita consumption has gone down seventy-five per cent, as appearances of actual oranges in most of the United States have become steadily less frequent. Fresh, whole, round, orange oranges are hardly extinct, of course, but they have seen better days since they left the garden of the Hesperides.

Fresh oranges have become, in a way, old-fashioned. The frozen product made from them is pure and sweet, with a laboratory-controlled balance between its acids and its sugars; its colour and its flavour components are as uniform as science can make them, and a consumer opening the six-ounce can is confident that the drink he is about to reconstitute will taste almost exactly like the juice that he took out of the last can he bought. Fresh orange juice, on the other hand, is probably less consistent in flavour than any other natural or fermented drink, with the possible exception of wine.

The taste and aroma of oranges differ by type, season, county, state, and country, and even as a result of the position of the individual orange in the framework of the tree on which it grew. Ground fruit – the orange that one can reach and pick from the ground – is not as sweet as fruit that grows high on the tree. Outside fruit is sweeter than inside fruit. Oranges grown on the south side of a tree are sweeter than oranges grown on the east or west sides, and oranges grown on the north side are the least sweet of the lot. The quantity of juice in an orange, and even the amount of Vitamin C it contains, will follow the same pattern of variation. Beyond this, there are differentiations of quality inside a single orange. Individual segments vary from one another in their content of acid and sugar. But that is cutting it pretty fine. Orange men, the ones who actually work in the groves, don't discriminate to that extent. When they eat an orange, they snap out the long, thin blades of their fruit knives and peel it down, halfway, from the blossom end, which is always sweeter and juicier than the stem end. They eat the blossom half and throw the rest of the orange away.

An orange grown in Florida usually has a thin and tightly fitting skin, and it is also heavy with juice. Californians say that if you want to eat a Florida orange you have to get into a bathtub first. California oranges are light in weight and have thick skins that break easily and come off in hunks. The flesh inside is marvellously sweet, and the segments almost separate themselves. In Florida, it is said that you can run over a California orange with a ten-ton truck and not even wet the pavement. The differences from which these hyperboles arise will prevail in the two states even if the type of orange is the same. In arid climates, like California's, oranges develop a thick albedo, which is the white part of the skin. Florida is one of the two or three most rained-upon states in the United States. California uses the Colorado River and similarly impressive sources to irrigate its oranges, but of course irrigation can only do so much. The annual difference in rainfall between the Florida and California orange-growing areas is one million one hundred and forty thousand gallons per acre. For years, California was the leading orange state, but Florida surpassed California in 1942, and grows three times as many oranges now. California oranges, for their part, can safely be called three times as beautiful.

The colour of an orange has no absolute correlation with the maturity of the flesh and juice inside. An orange can be as sweet and ripe as it will ever be and still glisten like an emerald in the tree. Cold – coolness, rather – is what makes an orange orange. In some parts of the world, the weather never gets cold enough to change the colour; in Thailand, for example, an orange is a green fruit, and travelling Thais often blink with wonder at the sight of oranges the colour of flame. The ideal night-time temperature in an orange grove is forty degrees. Some of the most beautiful oranges in the world are grown in Bermuda, where the temperature, night after night, falls consistently to that level. Andrew Marvell's poem wherein the 'remote Bermudas ride in the ocean's bosom unespied' was written in the sixteen-fifties, and contains a description, from hearsay, of Bermuda's remarkable oranges, set against their dark foliage like 'golden lamps in a green night'. Cool air comes down every night into the San Joaquin Valley in California, which is formed by the Coast Range to the west and the Sierra Nevadas to the east. The tops of the Sierras are usually covered with snow, and before dawn the temperature in the valley edges down to the frost point. In such cosmetic surroundings, it is no wonder that growers have heavily implanted the San Joaquin Valley with the Washington Navel Orange, which is the most beautiful orange grown in any quantity in the United States, and is certainly as attractive to the eye as any orange grown in the world. Its colour will go to a deep, flaring cadmium orange, and its surface has a suggestion of coarseness, which complements its perfect ellipsoid shape.

Among orange groups, the navel orange is an old one. In his *Hesperides, or Four Books on the Culture and Use of the Golden Apples*, Giovanni Battista Ferrari, a Sienese Jesuit priest of the seventeenth century, described it, saying: 'This orange imitates to some extent the fertility of the tree which bears it, in that it struggles, though unsuccessfully, to reproduce the fruit upon itself.' It is thus a kind of monster. Just beneath the navel-like opening in the blossom end of each navel orange, there is a small and, more or less, foetal orange, usually having five or six pithy segments. The navel strain that we know now originated in Bahia, Brazil, probably as a bud sport, or mutation, of the Brazilian Selecta Orange. In 1870, an American Presbyterian missionary in Bahia was impressed by the seedlessness and rich flavour of this unusual orange with an umbilicus at its blossom end, and sent twelve nursery-size trees to the United States Department of Agriculture in Washington. The department propagated the trees and sent the progeny to anyone who cared to give them a try. In 1873, Mrs Luther C. Tibbets, of Riverside, California, wrote for a pair of trees, got them, and planted them in her yard. Mrs Tibbets' trees caught the attention of her neighbours and, eventually, of the world. From them have descended virtually every navel orange grown anywhere on earth today, including the Carter, the Golden Nugget, the Surprise, the Golden Buckeye, the Robertson, and the Thomson. The patriarchal one should by rights be called the Bahia, but merely because of its brief residence in the District of Columbia it has been known for ninety-six years as the Washington Navel Orange.

In the United States, in a typical year, around twenty-five billion oranges are grown. These include, among others, Maltese Ovals, Pope Summers, Nonpareils, Rubys, Sanford Bloods, Early Oblongs, Magnum Bonums, St Michaels, Mediterranean Sweets, Lamb Summers, Lue Gim Gongs, Drake Stars, Whites, Whittakers, Weldons, Starks, Osceolas, Majorcas, Homosassas, Enterprises, Arcadias, Circassians, Centennials, Fosters, Dillars, Bessies, and Boones, but not – in all of these cases – in any appreciable quantity. Actually, one variety alone constitutes fully half of the total crop. Originally known in California as the Rivers Late Orange and in Florida as the Hart's Tardiff, it was imported into the United States early in the eighteen-seventies in unlabelled packages from the Thomas Rivers Nursery, of Sawbridgeworth, Hertfordshire. The easygoing Mr Rivers had not only left off the name of the orange trees; he also failed to note where he had found them. They grew to be big, vigorous trees that bore remarkable quantities of almost seedless fruit containing lots of juice, which had a racy tartness in delicious proportion to its ample sugars. As supposedly different varieties, the trees were already beginning to prosper when an orange grower from Spain, travelling in California, felt suddenly at home in a grove of the so-called Rivers Lates. 'That,' said the Spanish grower, clearing up all mysteries with one unequivocal remark, 'is the Late Orange of Valencia.'

Out of the bewildering catalogue of orange varieties and strains, the

Valencia has emerged in this century as something close to a universal orange. It is more widely and extensively planted than any other. From Florida and California and Central and South America to South Africa and Australia, Valencias grow in abundance in nearly all the orange centres of the world except Valencia. Having given the world the most remunerative orange yet known, Spain now specialises in its celebrated strains of bloods and navels. Only two per cent of the Spanish crop are Valencias, and perhaps only half of that comes from the groves of Valencia itself; much of the remainder grows in old, untended groves near Seville, where cattle wander through and munch oranges on the trees, on either bank of the Guadalquivir.

The Valencia is a spring and summer orange, and the Washington Navel ripens in the fall and winter. The two varieties overlap twice with perfect timing in California – where, together, they are almost all of the total crop – and the orange industry there never stops. In Florida, the Valencia harvest begins in late March and ends in June, and for about four months there is no picking. Florida grows few navel oranges, somewhat to the state's embarrassment. Florida growers tried hard enough, some seventy or eighty years ago, but the Washington Navel, in the language of pomology, proved to be too shy a bearer there. Instead, to meet the fall and winter markets, Florida growers have a number of locally developed early varieties to choose from, and in the main they seem to prefer three: the Pineapple Orange, the Parson Brown, and the Hamlin.

The Pineapple developed in the eighteen-seventies and was so named because its full, heavy aroma gave packinghouse employees the feeling that they were working in Hawaii rather than in Florida. The Pineapple is fairly seedy, usually containing about a dozen seeds, but it is rich in flavour, loaded with juice, and pretty to look at, with its smooth-textured, bright-orange skin and its slightly elongated shape. The skin is weak, though, and highly subject to decay. Most oranges, with appropriate care, will live about a month after they are picked. Pineapple Oranges don't have anything like that kind of stamina. (The Temple Orange and the Murcott Honey Orange, which are not actually oranges, ripen at the same time that Pineapples do. They are natural hybrids, almost certainly tangors – half orange, half tangerine – and they are so sweet that people on diets sometimes eat them before dinner in order to throttle their appetites. Oranges float, but these have so much sugar in them that if you drop one into a bucket of water it will go straight to the bottom. Murcotts were named for Charles Murcott Smith, one of the first men to propagate them. Advertisements have, from time to time, claimed that Temple Oranges were native to the Orient and sacred to a little-known sect of the Buddhist faith, and the seeds from which Florida's trees eventually sprang were stolen from a temple against the resistance of guardian priests. Temple Oranges are in fact named for William Chase Temple, who, long ago, was general manager of the Florida Citrus Exchange.)

Parson Nathan L. Brown was a Florida clergyman who grew oranges to supplement his income; the seedy, pebble-skinned orange that now carries his name was discovered in his grove about a hundred years ago. It tends to have pale-yellow flesh and pale-yellow juice, for, in general, the colour of orange juice is light among early-season oranges, deeper in mid-season varieties, and deeper still in late ones.

The seedless, smooth-skinned Hamlin, also named for a Florida grove owner, ripens in October, ordinarily about two weeks ahead of the Parson Brown.

Both Hamlins and Parson Browns, when they are harvested, are usually as green as grass. They have to be ripe, because an orange will not continue to ripen after it has been picked. Many other fruits – apples and pears, for example – go on ripening for weeks after they leave the tree. Their flesh contains a great deal of starch, and as they go on breathing (all fruit breathes until it dies, and should be eaten before it is dead), they gradually convert the starch to sugar. When oranges breathe, there is no starch within them to be converted. Whatever sugars, acids, and flavour essences they have were necessarily acquired on the tree. Hence, an advertisement for 'tree-ripened' oranges is essentially a canard. There is no other way to ripen oranges. It is against the law to market oranges that are not tree-ripened – that is to say, oranges that are not ripe. Women see a patch or even a hint of green on an orange in a store and they seem to feel that they are making a knowledgeable decision when they avoid it. Some take home a can of concentrated orange juice instead. A good part, if not all, of the juice inside the can may have come from perfectly ripe, bright-green oranges.

Some oranges that become orange while they are still unripe may turn green again as they ripen. When cool nights finally come to Florida, around the first of the year, the Valencia crop is fully developed in size and shape, but it is still three months away from ripeness. Sliced through the middle at that time, a Valencia looks something like a partitioned cupful of rice, and its taste is overpoweringly acid. But in the winter coolness, the exterior surface turns to bright orange, and the Valencia appears to be perfect for picking. Warm nights return, however, during the time of the Valencia harvest. On the trees in late spring, the Valencias turn green again, growing sweeter each day and greener each night.

MARMALADE: A VERY BRITISH OBSESSION

Olivia Potts

Olivia Potts read English at Cambridge and trained and practised as a barrister before leaving the bar to train in pâtisserie at Le Cordon Bleu. Her award-winning memoir, *A Half Baked Idea*, about the sudden death of her mother and her subsequent pastry-based career change, was published in 2019. Her first cookbook, *Butter: A Celebration*, was published to acclaim in 2022, and was described by Nigella Lawson as 'quite frankly, my dream book'. Though he was late for one of their early dates because his marmalade hadn't reached setting point (more on this below), Potts and her husband now live in Manchester with their son.

The dark wood-panelled dining room is quiet, heavy with concentration. Around the room, six pairs of judges sit at tables crowded with glass jars. As the light catches the jars they glow amber, saffron, primrose. The only real sounds are the murmurs as the pairs of judges consult, and the regular *pop!* of sterilized jars as they open. Occasionally, there is the tap of a pen against glass, signifying that a gold medal has been awarded, followed by quiet applause or cheers depending on how sugar-drunk the judges are.

This is the judging room of the World's Original Marmalade Awards, an annual event in Penrith, England, in the English Lake District. I'm here because I'm obsessed with marmalade. Not with making or eating it – although I enjoy both – but the enigma it represents. I suppose I'm obsessed with those obsessed with it: what is the appeal? Marmalade is made from a sour, bitter fruit that doesn't grow in the UK; a fruit that requires days of preparation to render remotely edible. And yet, marmalade holds a central role in British life and British culture. It appears in the diaries of Samuel Pepys; James Bond and Paddington Bear eat it. Officers that served in British wars received jars of marmalade to remind them of their home country. Captain Scott took jars to the Antarctic with him, and Edmund Hillary took one up Everest. Marmalade is part of our national myth. I want to know why.

*

Marmalade in Britain is overwhelmingly made from *citrus aurantium*, the bitter orange grown in the Spanish city of Seville. This city produces over 4 million kilos of the orange a year, almost entirely for export to Britain for the marmalade market. How on earth did that happen?

Some would have you believe that marmalade was born in a vacuum. That, like Post-it notes or penicillin, it was invented all of a sudden, brought about by a confluence of unlikely factors. The story goes like this: it was a dark and stormy night. The rain fell in torrents, and a Spanish cargo ship was forced to take an unscheduled dock in Dundee, though it could as well have been anywhere; any port in a storm. Its cargo: oranges. A Dundee grocer, James Keiller, rashly buys up the whole load of them. He quickly discovers these oranges aren't sweet and fleshy, but face-puckering sour and bitter, more pip than fruit. His mother, Janet, in an attempt to produce *something*, boils them up with tons of sugar. And so, marmalade was born.

The truth, I'm afraid, is rather more prosaic. We know that Seville orange marmalade in Britain predates this charming tale: there are British recipes for conserves of Seville oranges as far back as the 1587 *A Book of Cookrye*, and a marmalade very much like the one we eat today appears in a recipe book by Eliza Cholmondeley published around 1677. The Keiller family probably were the first to produce Seville orange marmalade on a commercial scale, but the Spanish ship story was and is just good PR. It is likely, according to C. Anne Wilson's *The Book of Marmalade*, that the cargo ship would only have been carrying large quantities of Seville oranges because there was a ready market for them in Scotland, and that Janet Keiller would not have needed to invent a recipe for the orange marmalade, as many were in circulation by that point in England and Scotland. The expansion of the railways came at just the right time for the Keillers, and when Queen Victoria took a shine to the stuff, it quickly became fashionable in London. Once commercial production was underway, marmalade became a celebrated British export, perfect for overseas trade, able to travel long distances preserved by its sugar content, and capable of withstanding extremes of temperature.

In any event, marmalade was also made with other things long before it was made with the Seville orange. Early marmalades were often made from quince, and closely resembled what we now call membrillo: a thick paste that could be moulded and would hold its shape. A recipe from 1587 reads "stir it till it be thick or stiff that your stick will stand upright of itself." Like membrillo, this marmalade was eaten after dinner, alongside sweetmeats, and as a digestion aid (one thing the Scottish did do in the nineteenth century was move marmalade from dinner to the breakfast table). It was a luxury item, sometimes flavored with prized ambergris, rose, and musk. It was given as gifts as a show of generosity and riches: Henry VIII received "one box of marmalade" from Hull of Exeter in 1524.

Quinces also gave marmalade its name: the word comes from the Portuguese name for the fruit, *marmelo*. Indeed, early port records tell us that marmalade first arrived in the UK from Portugal, though our appetite for the stuff meant it was soon coming from Spain and Italy too. It didn't take long for English travellers to discover the recipe – a happy occurrence, since quinces grow very well on our temperate isle. We were, for a short time at least, an independent marmalade-making nation, until we got a taste for the foreign bitter orange.

Only in English does marmalade connote a citrus-based preserve containing peel. In Greek (*marmelada*), French (*marmalade*), and Italian (*marmellata*), the word just means "jam," with the fruit added afterward to distinguish. Thus *marmellata di arance* is orange jam: sweet, pulpy. Only *marmellata di arance amare* is what the English think of as marmalade. And it's not just Romance languages: *marmelad* in Swedish, *Marmelade* in German, and *marmelade* in Danish, all generic terms for any fruit cooked in sugar. The British clearly think of marmalade differently from the rest of the world.

*

There are many ways to make marmalade. Some boil the fruit whole; others prefer to cut the peel first. The merits of pressure cooking are fiercely debated. But broadly speaking, marmalade is made by separating the citrus fruit into its different components – pips, peel, pith, juice – and boiling, before adding sugar and boiling again. Generally, the pith, pips, and flesh are tied up in a muslin bag. The peel is sliced into equal-sized strips or chips. The muslin bag and peel are left to soak overnight in the water. The following day, the peel is cooked until tender. Sugar is added, along with any reserved juice, and heated gently until it dissolves, before the heat is ratcheted up to bring the mixture to a rolling boil. In 10–15 minutes, the mixture should have reached 105°C/220°F – jam temperature – meaning that it will set once cool. If you make it with Seville oranges, it's something of a nose-to-tail preserve: the pips and the pith contain enough natural pectin, a gelling agent, to set the marmalade without additional ingredients. Nothing is wasted. In theory, it's a straightforward process; in practice it is riddled with possible unforced errors. You can overboil it, underboil it, add too much acid, add too little acid; you can burn the syrup in the same batch you undercook the peel. You can pot too hot, you can pot too cool. Over the years, my husband, Sam, has encountered every one of them.

It was Sam who properly brought marmalade into my life. He was late for one of our early dates because he was waiting for his marmalade to set. He arrived, clutching a sticky, still-warm jar of Seville orange marmalade, in lieu of flowers. Back then, I didn't even really eat marmalade. I certainly would never have countenanced making my own. Why would anyone bother? Was he aware that you can buy it in the supermarket? I was a criminal barrister, and the point in my life where I would ditch criminal law in favour of retraining in pâtisserie was still years in the future.

But Sam came from a long line of marmalade lovers and marmalade makers. In marmalade season – in the UK, Seville oranges are only available for a few brief weeks from the end of December to mid-February – it's all his family talks about, with long WhatsApp threads devoted to techniques, yields, sets. Sam was a good cook, but not an especially enthusiastic one: he cooked simple, functional meals. But marmalade was different. Marmalade-making was, for him, non-negotiable. Even if we had shelves packed full of the previous years' labours, when January rolled around, more must be made.

(It's not just Sam and his family who are fanatics. So devoted are the marmalade makers of the UK that it's possible to buy canned, prepared Seville orange peel and pulp, "Ma Made," the marmalade equivalent of a cake mix box – just in case you get that marmalade-making hankering outside of season.)

For the first few years of our relationship, this was something I simply endured. Love the man, love his marmalade. As I got into cooking, I tried to make my own a few times, with varying success, but never quite caught the bug. (Besides which, we had an awful lot to get through. Even a small batch is a lot of marmalade for two people.) It all seemed so *unpredictable*; some years, whole batches had to be reboiled as Sam muttered darkly about it being a "low-pectin year."

Once you're hooked, of course, this is all part of the appeal. Lucy Deedes is a veteran of both the homemade and artisan classes of the World's Original Marmalade Awards, scoring three gold medals in the artisan. "You have to get things right at the right time. I've never made jam because it's not much of a challenge. Marmalade only has three ingredients, but every batch is different, and sometimes it just doesn't turn out."

In other words: the tricky, maddening nature of marmalade is precisely why people love making it. It's a bit like sourdough: if you're going to get into it, you have to *really* get into it. Even then, failure lurks around every corner – but so does the possibility of improvement. That's irresistible to a certain sort of person; marmalade attracts the obsessive. Helena Atlee, author of *The Land Where Lemons Grow*, puts it more bluntly. "Marmalade attracts bigots. They believe in one true product made from the sour oranges the British call Sevilles, and coming most probably from a steamy Scottish kitchen in Dundee."

I want to meet some of these obsessives, and understand the hold that marmalade has over so many. And I think I know where to find them: the World's Original Marmalade Awards.

*

I arrived at Dalemain, where the awards are held, against the odds, having battled Storm Ciara to make it to the flooded and snowbound Lake District. At that point, I was fairly sure that extreme weather conditions would be the biggest challenge the awards would face this year. How much February Olivia had to learn. I first spoke to Jane Hasell-McCosh, who is the founder of the awards, over the phone, asking if I could interview her and perhaps a couple of the judges for this piece. '"We can do one better than that," she told me. "Would you like to help us judge?"

I agreed on the spot, but afterward, I began to worry that I didn't know enough about marmalade for the gig. Thanks to Sam, I eat it far more than I used to, and would tend to choose it over jam. But is that enough? Well, it was too late for that. On my way up to the judging, I braced myself for the marmalade obsessives of which Helena Atlee writes – if not bigots, then at least fundamentalists. I was ready to be told there is only one true way to make and enjoy marmalade, and that any deviation from it is an aberration and, possibly, a perversion.

Dalemain is astonishing. The main frontage is Georgian, built in 1744, with the old hall dating far further back to the 12th century. It has been in the family for over 300 years. Although from the outside the house looks like a National Trust property, when you step inside you immediately realize it is a family home. Laundry hangs in the huge stone kitchen, dogs weave between legs, and back copies of *Vogue* spill out from under a table in the hallway. On the walls, portraits of distant ancestors mingle with recent family photos. In one of the guest rooms, a bed gifted by Queen Anne still resides. (The mattress, I am told, has been changed.)

The awards began as a one-off. Fifteen years ago, rural Britain was still struggling after being decimated four years earlier by the outbreak of foot-and-mouth disease, a highly infectious disease which affects cows and other cloven-footed animals, and generally requires widespread culling of livestock. Jane wanted to do something to bring her local community together, something cheering. There was never any plan for it to become a regular event.

The fact that it did is perhaps down to Jane's formidable organizational nous, though I believe her when she tells me how much the growth and success of the event took her by surprise. That first year, around 60 jars were received, almost exclusively from local competitors. This year, there are more than 3,000 entrants from 40 countries around the world, plus spin-off festivals in Japan and Australia. During the time I spent at Dalemain, two separate production companies were filming.

After 15 years, judging has been honed to a fine art. The way it works is this: the marmalades are tasted on plastic spoons (never double-dipped), without the interference of bread, oatcakes or any other vehicle. Bath Oliver biscuits (a savoury cracker) are on the table as a palate cleanser. Each entry has a scorecard and is judged on its appearance, texture and flavour, with points available for lack of smudges on the jar, colour, brightness, peel distribution, jar filled to the top, balance of jelly to peel, set, size of peel, texture of peel, balance of flavours, balance of acidity, length of finish, and "overall harmony." The marmalades can receive a commended, a bronze, a silver, a gold, or nothing at all. Those which have scored top marks are then re-judged: there is a Best in Show awarded to the top homemade marmalade, and a "Double Gold" award given to a handful of the very best across the categories. The winner of the best homemade marmalade is sold in the luxury London department store, Fortnum & Mason.

After a short briefing, and armed with our spoons, we were ready to start judging.

There are more categories than you could shake a stick at: in the homemade category, as well as the standard Seville orange (which have two sub-categories), dark and chunky marmalade and "other citrus," there are categories for children, first-timers, men, gardeners (where the predominant ingredient beyond the citrus was grown by the competitor), octogenarians, and campanologists (bell-ringers). Special categories of former years have included everything from peers, political and clergy, to hairdressers.

The range is mind-boggling: a sweet potato and coffee marmalade from Taiwan sat alongside a lime glitter marmalade, which looked like something a teenage girl would daub on her eyelids. A coconut and chocolate marmalade elicited groans when it was plucked from a crate, followed by raised eyebrows and "not bad!"s once actually tasted. I tasted fruits I've never even heard of, let alone tried: daidai (the Japanese equivalent of the Seville orange, bitter, pocked, and pithy), tachibana (a wild mandarin found in Southern Taiwan and Japan), kawachi bankan (a Japanese pomelo), and tangelo (a sweet tangy orange that tastes, to me at least, like jelly beans).

It is no coincidence that some of the most striking and delicious citrus fruits previously unknown to me come from Japan, and that the Japanese tend to enjoy particular success at the awards. Marmalade is big news in Japan, despite the absence of Seville oranges. Two years ago, Seiko and Yoriko Ninomiya, Japanese marmalade-makers, received a double-gold award for their marmalade, a yuzu and ginger and, suspended in the jelly, tiny yuzu peel stars. They came to marmalade as a hobby after they retired from careers in the airline industry. They have been involved in the inaugural Japanese Marmalade Awards, which are held at Yawatahama, where the citrus groves tumble down the hills to the ocean. This year, they have come to the Lake District to help judge the World Awards.

I was told by more seasoned judges that when I tasted a full-mark, gold marmalade, I would know immediately. And they were right. I was the first person to try one of the marmalades that ultimately won the Double Gold International Marmalade award in the artisan category, and it was stop-you-in-your-tracks good. It too was a Japanese marmalade, made from the endangered tachibana fruit, which tastes like a Seville orange crossed with a mandarin – but it's not just the flavour that set it apart. This was a reduced sugar marmalade, which often results in a loose, syrupy set, but here was a set so perfect that many full-sugar marmalades fail to achieve; crystal clear, wibbly jelly; identical, perfectly cooked peel was suspended throughout the jar. How could a marmalade be so *clever*? I wanted to ring everyone I know and tell them about this stuff.

*

It's hard to comprehend when you're sitting in the stone kitchen of Dalemain, but marmalade's appeal is not what it once was. Thane Prince, a British cookery writer, preserves specialist and judge of *The Big Allotment Challenge*, tells me that British tastes and customs have moved on. "It's old-fashioned. I think the appeal was that it was exotic. A luxury product, and these things always have caché. But now it's just old-fashioned. And people don't have breakfast in the same way." During the height of marmalade's popularity, a cooked "Full English" breakfast, accompanied by toast and marmalade was standard. But Britain's marmalade consumption has been in decline since the 1960s. Perhaps establishing marmalade as a breakfast food was actually sealing its fate. We have less time for breakfast now; we pick something up on the go, from a coffee shop. More and more of us avoid sugar, or carbs in general. None of this bodes well for marmalade's future.

Its bitterness probably doesn't help, either. We are programmed to dislike bitterness, as Jennifer McLagan explains in her book *Bitter: A Taste of the World's Most Dangerous Flavor*. In nature, bitterness often suggests something poisonous, which is why babies screw up their faces at bitter tastes. As we age, we lose taste buds, and learn to like bitter things: coffee, cigarettes, Campari, dark chocolate. But each is a struggle. And with marmalade, many of us seemingly never get off the ground, plumping instead for jam, or peanut butter. It is certainly true that peanut butter and chocolate spread are gaining ground in the share of the spreads market, where marmalade resides. Marmalade sales were in steady decline from 2013.

Even in decline, though, marmalade has sway in the supermarkets because of its status as a basket item: one that shoppers use to judge where to shop. As such, it is a common loss leader, meaning retailers sell it at a rock-bottom price to get people through their doors. At the time of writing, a one-pound jar of marmalade can be had for as little as 27p (34¢), an impossible price on which to make a profit.

But, the tide may be turning. The 2017 release of *Paddington 2* – which involved a set piece showing Paddington making marmalade in prison – increased marmalade sales by 3 per cent in the UK after a steady four-year decline, according to supermarket data collected by research firm Kantar. It's fitting, perhaps, that Britain's distinctly un-British national preserve might be saved by a bear from darkest Peru.

*

I didn't get the conclusion I expected to when I began researching marmalade. I thought my marmalade journey would end with the festival that accompanies the World's Original Marmalade Awards: a festival festooned in orange and oranges which celebrates this absurd tradition, as well as the people who perpetuate it. In a normal year, there are classes and presentations, tastings and exhibitions, a church service, all devoted to marmalade. Even the sheep go orange: 50 were dyed in readiness for this year's festival (it was supposed to be fewer but Jane tells me they "got carried away.") At the judging in Dalemain in February, the excitement for the festival was palpable. But of course, it was not to be: COVID-19 swept in far more comprehensively and destructively than Storm Ciara. A festival that attracts hundreds of international visitors and involves repeated tastings was off the table long before we went into lockdown.

Even as a peripheral player in the awards, it was deflating. But then I came home and made marmalade.

*

I am standing in my kitchen in London in front of a large pan full of orange jelly, trying to put all the advice and tips that I was given over my four days in Dalemain into practice. I need to make sure the peel is fully cooked before adding the sugar. I need to avoid squeezing the muslin bag so the jelly doesn't become cloudy. Despite my best efforts, I turn my back for one second (OK, two minutes) to wash out my jars for sterilizing, and turn back to find that the marmalade has whooshed up and spilled all over my hobs in a big sticky puddle. I soldier on, undeterred. Fifteen sticky minutes later, my marmalade is approaching the magic 105°C. I deploy the wrinkle test – twice, just to be sure – which involves cooling a spoonful of the mixture on a frozen plate, to see if it forms a skin which wrinkles. I leave the marmalade a few minutes before potting, determined not to make the classic "potting too hot" error (which introduces tiny air bubbles into the finished product). And, although no one but me or Sam will ever see this batch, I make sure each jar is filled *right* to the top.

I stand back and admire my five-and-a-half jars and… I get it. Of course I do. How could I not? My jelly isn't quite crystal clear, but it is basketball orange, bright and glowing. I dropped saffron strands into a couple of the jars, stirring last minute, and they hang, suspended in the jelly, perfect threads. It may not be award-winning, but it is the best I have ever made. It really does feel like I've potted sunshine, a moment in time.

British food writer Diana Henry describes preserving as "holding onto a season, a particular mood" – she calls it "one of the most poetic branches of cooking." I love this idea. Simone de Beauvoir felt similarly. "The housewife has caught duration in the snare of sugar, she has enclosed life in jars." There are few fruits for which this is more true than the Seville orange, which you can find in the shops for a handful of weeks; the ability to pot and revisit that season six months down the line is its own breed of kitchen magic. Each jar tells the story of both the season and the maker. When I spoke to fellow judge Will Torrent about the nature of the marmalade awards, he found that this emotional quality seeped into the judging as well as making of the marmalade.

"There will be a story that has led to that marmalade maker entering at that point. Food awards can sometimes become very serious. It becomes very technical, and yes there is a technical element to this, but at the same time – and I think this is the way I judge – it's, 'How does it make me feel?' And it brings such joy, and it rubs off on everyone else."

But right now, since global lockdown, it's more than that. There is something inherently optimistic about preservation, about putting something away for your future. You are saying, "I will be here in a year's time, and so will this marmalade." Making marmalade is a lot of effort, and by that token, it is a commitment. Marmalade is a tether to your own future, it's a savings account. It is shoring yourself up against the instability and uncertainty of life. You do not make marmalade without a small optimism, a hope of orange-coloured happiness in your future.

Marmalade is something stable in an uncertain world. It has survived plagues and wars, fires and uprisings. I know that the marmalade I make today will still be there tomorrow. It doesn't actually need a festival – it doesn't even need supermarket sales. Marmalade has staying power. *That* is surely why the British love marmalade so much: because tomorrow everything will be different, but marmalade will be the same.

WE HAVE ALWAYS LIVED IN THE CASTLE

Shirley Jackson

Shirley Jackson is best known for her novels and short stories, which reviews have called 'sinister', 'chilling', 'terrifying', 'subtle' and 'perfect'. In her biography *A Rather Haunted Life*, Ruth Franklin identifies Jackson's roots in the American Gothic, as well as her 'unique contribution to the genre': her focus on the internal lives of women. *We Have Always Lived in the Castle*, a Gothic novel described in the *New Yorker* as Jackson's 'masterpiece' and one of *Time* Magazine's Ten Best Books in 1962, was her final novel for adults.

A change was coming, and nobody knew it but me. Constance suspected, perhaps; I noticed that she stood occasionally in her garden and looked not down at the plants she was tending, and not back at our house, but outward, toward the trees which hid the fence, and sometimes she looked long and curiously down the length of the driveway, as though wondering how it would feel to walk along it to the gates. I watched her. On Saturday morning, after Helen Clarke had come to tea, Constance looked at the driveway three times. Uncle Julian was not well on Saturday morning, after tiring himself at tea, and stayed in his bed in his warm room next to the kitchen, looking out of the window beside his pillow, calling now and then to make Constance notice him. Even Jonas was fretful—he was running up a storm, our mother used to say—and could not sleep quietly; all during those days when the change was coming Jonas stayed restless. From a deep sleep he would start suddenly, lifting his head as though listening, and then, on his feet and moving in one quick ripple, he ran up the stairs and across the beds and around through the doors in and out and then down the stairs and across the hall and over the chair in the dining room and around the table and through the kitchen and out into the garden where he would slow, sauntering, and then pause to lick a paw and flick an ear and take a look at the day. At night we could hear him running, feel him cross our feet as we lay in bed, running up a storm.

All the omens spoke of change. I woke up on Saturday morning and thought I heard them calling me; they want me to get up, I thought before I came fully awake and remembered that they were dead; Constance never called me to wake up. When I dressed and came downstairs that morning she was waiting to make my breakfast, and I told her, "I thought I heard them calling me this morning."

"Hurry with your breakfast," she said. "It's another lovely day."

After breakfast on the good mornings when I did not have to go into the village I had my work to do. Always on Wednesday mornings I went around the fence. It was necessary for me to check constantly to be sure that the wires were not broken and the gates were securely locked. I could make the repairs myself, winding the wire back together where it had torn, tightening loose strands, and it was a pleasure to know, every Wednesday morning, that we were safe for another week.

On Sunday mornings I examined my safeguards, the box of silver dollars I had buried by the creek, and the doll buried in the long field, and the book nailed to the tree in the pine woods; so long as they were where I had put them nothing could get in to harm us. I had always buried things, even when I was small; I remember that once I quartered the long field and buried something in each quarter to make the grass grow higher as I grew taller, so I would always be able to hide there. I once buried six blue marbles in the creek bed to make the river beyond run dry. "Here is treasure for you to bury," Constance used to say to me when I was small, giving me a penny, or a bright ribbon; I had buried all my baby teeth as they came out one by one and perhaps someday they would grow as dragons. All our land was enriched with my treasures buried in it, thickly inhabited just below the surface with my marbles and my teeth and my colored stones, all perhaps turned to jewels by now, held together under the ground in a powerful taut web which never loosened, but held fast to guard us.

On Tuesdays and Fridays I went into the village, and on Thursday, which was my most powerful day, I went into the big attic and dressed in their clothes.

Mondays we neatened the house, Constance and I, going into every room with mops and dustcloths, carefully setting the little things back after we had dusted, never altering the perfect line of our mother's tortoise-shell comb. Every spring we washed and polished the house for another year, but on Mondays we neatened; very little dust fell in their rooms, but even that little could not be permitted to stay. Sometimes Constance tried to neaten Uncle Julian's room, but Uncle Julian disliked being disturbed and kept his things in their own places, and Constance had to be content with washing his medicine glasses and changing his bed. I was not allowed in Uncle Julian's room.

On Saturday mornings I helped Constance. I was not allowed to handle knives, but when she worked in the garden I cared for her tools, keeping them bright and clean, and I carried great baskets of flowers, sometimes, or vegetables which Constance picked to make into food. The entire cellar of our house was filled with food. All the Blackwood women had made food and had taken pride in adding to the great supply of food in our cellar. There were jars of jam made by great-grandmothers, with labels in thin pale writing, almost unreadable by now, and pickles made by great-aunts and vegetables put up by our grandmother, and even our mother had left behind her six jars of apple jelly. Constance had worked all her life at adding to the food in the cellar, and her rows and rows of jars were easily the handsomest, and shone among the others. "You bury food the way I bury treasure," I told her sometimes, and she answered me once: "The food comes from the ground and can't be permitted to stay there and rot; *some*thing has to be done with it." All the Blackwood women had taken the food that came from the ground and preserved it, and the deeply colored rows of jellies and pickles and bottled vegetables and fruit, maroon and amber and dark rich green, stood side by side in our cellar and would stand there forever, a poem by the Blackwood women. Each year Constance and Uncle Julian and I had jam or preserve or pickle that Constance had made, but we never touched what belonged to the others; Constance said it would kill us if we ate it.

This Saturday morning I had apricot jam on my toast, and I thought of Constance making it and putting it away carefully for me to eat on some bright morning, never dreaming that a change would be coming before the jar was finished.

"Lazy Merricat," Constance said to me, "stop dreaming over your toast; I want you in the garden on this lovely day."

She was arranging Uncle Julian's tray, putting his hot milk into a jug painted with yellow daisies, and trimming his toast so it would be tiny and hot and square; if anything looked large, or difficult to eat, Uncle Julian would leave it on the plate. Constance always took Uncle Julian's tray in to him in the morning because he slept painfully and sometimes lay awake in the darkness waiting for the first light and the comfort of Constance with his tray. Some nights, when his heart hurt him badly, he might take one more pill than usual, and then lie all morning drowsy and dull, unwilling to sip from his hot milk, but wanting to know that Constance was busy in the kitchen next door to his bedroom, or in the garden where he could see her from his pillow. On his very good mornings she brought him into the kitchen for his breakfast, and he would sit at his old desk in the corner, spilling crumbs among his notes, studying his papers while he ate. "If I am spared," he always said to Constance, "I will write the book myself. If not, see that my notes are entrusted to some worthy cynic who will not be too concerned with the truth."

I wanted to be kinder to Uncle Julian, so this morning I hoped he would enjoy his breakfast and later come out into the garden in his wheel chair and sit in the sun. "Maybe there will be a tulip open today," I said, looking out through the open kitchen door into the bright sunlight.

"Not until tomorrow, I think," said Constance, who always knew. "Wear your boots if you wander today; it will still be quite wet in the woods."

"There's a change coming," I said.

"It's spring, silly," she said, and took up Uncle Julian's tray. "Don't run off while I'm gone; there's work to be done."

She opened Uncle Julian's door and I heard her say good morning to him. When he said good morning back his voice was old and I knew that he was not well. Constance would have to stay near him all day.

"Is your father home yet, child?" he asked her.

"No, not today," Constance said. "Let me get your other pillow. It's a lovely day."

"He's a busy man," Uncle Julian said. "Bring me a pencil, my dear; I want to make a note of that. He's a very busy man."

"Take some hot milk; it will make you warm."

"You're not Dorothy. You're my niece Constance."

"Drink."

"Good morning, Constance."

"Good morning, Uncle Julian."

I decided that I would choose three powerful words, words of strong protection, and so long as these great words were never spoken aloud no change would come. I wrote the first word—*melody*—in the apricot jam on my toast with the handle of a spoon and then put the toast in my mouth and ate it very quickly. I was one-third safe. Constance came out of Uncle Julian's room carrying the tray.

"He's not well this morning," she said. "He left most of his breakfast and he's very tired."

"If I had a winged horse I could fly him to the moon; he would be more comfortable there."

"Later I'll take him out into the sunshine, and perhaps make him a little eggnog."

"Everything's safe on the moon."

She looked at me distantly. "Dandelion greens," she said. "And radishes. I thought of working in the vegetable garden this morning, but I don't want to leave Uncle Julian. I hope that the carrots . . ." She tapped her fingers on the table, thinking. "Rhubarb," she said.

I carried my breakfast dishes over to the sink and set them down; I was deciding on my second magic word, which I thought might very well be *Gloucester*. It was strong, and I thought it would do, although Uncle Julian might take it into his head to say almost anything and no word was truly safe when Uncle Julian was talking.

"Why not make a pie for Uncle Julian?"

Constance smiled. "You mean, why not make a pie for Merricat? Shall I make a rhubarb pie?"

"Jonas and I dislike rhubarb."

"But it has the prettiest colors of all; nothing is so pretty on the shelves as rhubarb jam."

"Make it for the shelves, then. Make me a dandelion pie."

"Silly Merricat," Constance said. She was wearing her blue dress, the sunlight was patterned on the kitchen floor, and color was beginning to show in the garden outside. Jonas sat on the step, washing, and Constance began to sing as she turned to wash the dishes. I was two-thirds safe, with only one magic word to find.

Later Uncle Julian still slept and Constance thought to take five minutes and run down to the vegetable garden to gather what she could; I sat at the kitchen table listening for Uncle Julian so I could call Constance if he awakened, but when she came back he was still quiet. I ate tiny sweet raw carrots while Constance washed the vegetables and put them away. "We will have a spring salad," she said.

"We eat the year away. We eat the spring and the summer and the fall. We wait for something to grow and then we eat it."

"Silly Merricat," Constance said.

At twenty minutes after eleven by the kitchen clock she took off her apron, glanced in at Uncle Julian, and went, as she always did, upstairs to her room to wait until I called her. I went to the front door and unlocked it and opened it just as the doctor's car turned into the drive. He was in a hurry, always, and he stopped his car quickly and ran up the steps; "Good morning, Miss Blackwood," he said, going past me and down the hall, and by the time he had reached the kitchen he had his coat off and was ready to put it over the back of one of the kitchen chairs. He went directly to Uncle Julian's room without a glance at me or at the kitchen, and then when he opened Uncle Julian's door he was suddenly still, and gentle. "Good morning, Mr. Blackwood," he said, his voice easy, "how are things today?"

"Where's the old fool?" Uncle Julian said, as he always did. "Why didn't Jack Mason come?"

Dr. Mason was the one Constance called the night they all died.

"Dr. Mason couldn't make it today," the doctor said, as he always did. "I'm Dr. Levy. I've come to see you instead."

"Rather have Jack Mason."

"I'll do the best I can."

"Always said I'd outlive the old fool." Uncle Julian laughed thinly. "Why are you pretending with me? Jack Mason died three years ago."

"Mr. Blackwood," the doctor said, "it is a pleasure to have you as a patient." He closed the door very quietly. I thought of using *digitalis* as my third magic word, but it was too easy for someone to say, and at last I decided on *Pegasus*. I took a glass from the cabinet, and said the word very distinctly into the glass, then filled it with water and drank. Uncle Julian's door opened, and the doctor stood in the doorway for a minute.

"Remember, now," he said. "And I'll see you next Saturday."

"Quack," Uncle Julian said.

The doctor turned, smiling, and then the smile disappeared and he began to hurry again. He took up his coat and went off down the hall. I followed him and by the time I came to the front door he was already going down the steps. "Goodbye, Miss Blackwood," he said, not looking around, and got into his car and started at once, going faster and faster until he reached the gates and turned onto the highway. I locked the front door and went to the foot of the stairs. "Constance?" I called.

"Coming," she said from upstairs. "Coming, Merricat."

Uncle Julian was better later in the day, and sat out in the warm afternoon sun, hands folded in his lap, half-dreaming. I lay near him on the marble bench our mother had liked to sit on, and Constance knelt in the dirt, both hands buried as though she were growing, kneading the dirt and turning it, touching the plants on their roots.

"It was a fine morning," Uncle Julian said, his voice going on and on, "a fine bright morning, and none of them knew it was their last. She was downstairs first, my niece Constance. I woke up and heard her moving in the kitchen—I slept upstairs then, I could still go upstairs, and I slept with my wife in our room—and I thought, this is a fine morning, never dreaming then that it was their last. Then I heard my nephew—no, it was my brother; my brother came downstairs first after Constance. I heard him whistling. Constance?"

"Yes?"

"What was the tune my brother used to whistle, and always off-key?"

Constance thought, her hands in the ground, and hummed softly, and I shivered.

"Of course. I never had a head for music; I could remember what people looked like and what they said and what they did but I could never remember what they sang. It was my brother who came downstairs after Constance, never caring of course if he woke people with his noise and his whistling, never thinking that perhaps I might still be asleep, although as it happened I was already awake." Uncle Julian sighed, and lifted his head to look curiously, once, around the garden. "He never knew it was his last morning on earth. He might have been quieter, I think, if he did know. I heard him in the kitchen with Constance and I said to my wife—she was awake, too; his noise had awakened her—I said to my wife, you had better get dressed; we live here with my brother and his wife, after all, and we must remember to show them that we are friendly and eager to help out wherever we can; dress and go down to Constance in the kitchen. She did as she was told; our wives always did as they were told, although my sister-in-law lay in bed late that morning; perhaps *she* had a premonition and wanted to take her earthly rest while she could. I heard them all. I heard the boy go downstairs. I thought of dressing; Constance?"

"Yes, Uncle Julian?"

"I could still dress myself in those days, you know, although that *was* the last day. I could still walk around by myself, and dress myself, and feed myself, and I had no pain. I slept well in those days as a strong man should. I was not young, but I was strong and I slept well and I could still dress myself."

"Would you like a rug over your knees?"

"No, my dear, I thank you. You have been a good niece to me, although there are some grounds for supposing you an undutiful daughter.

My sister-in-law came downstairs before I did. We had pancakes for breakfast, tiny thin hot pancakes, and my brother had two fried eggs and my wife—although I did not encourage her to eat heavily, since we were living with my brother—took largely of sausage. Homemade sausage, made by Constance. Constance?"

"Yes, Uncle Julian?"

"I think if I had known it was her last breakfast I would have permitted her more sausage. I am surprised, now I think of it, that no one suspected it was their last morning; they might not have grudged my wife more sausage *then*. My brother sometimes remarked upon what we ate, my wife and I; he was a just man, and never stinted his food, so long as we did not take too much. He watched my wife take sausage that morning, Constance. I saw him watching her. We took little enough from him, Constance. He had pancakes and fried eggs and sausage but I felt that he was going to speak to my wife; the boy ate hugely. I am pleased that the breakfast was particularly good that day."

"I could make you sausage next week, Uncle Julian; I think homemade sausage would not disagree with you if you had very little."

"My brother never grudged our food if we did not take too much. My wife helped to wash the dishes."

"I was very grateful to her."

"She might have done more, I think now. She entertained my sister-in-law, and she saw to our clothes, and she helped with the dishes in the mornings, but I believe that my brother thought that she might have done more. He went off after breakfast to see a man on business."

"He wanted an arbor built; it was his plan to start a grape arbor."

"I am sorry about that; we might now be eating jam from our own grapes. I was always better able to chat after he was gone; I recall that I entertained the ladies that morning, and we sat here in the garden. We talked about music; my wife was quite musical although she had never learned to play. My sister-in-law had a delicate touch; it was always said of her that she had a delicate touch, and she played in the evenings usually. Not that evening, of course. She was not able to play that evening. In the morning we thought she would play in the evening as usual. Do you recall that I was very entertaining in the garden that morning, Constance?"

"I was weeding the vegetables," Constance said. "I could hear you all laughing."

"I was quite entertaining; I am happy for that now." He was quiet for a minute, folding and refolding his hands. I wanted to be kinder to him, but I could not fold his hands for him, and there was nothing I could bring him, so I lay still and listened to him talk. Constance frowned, staring at a leaf, and the shadows moved softly across the lawn.

"The boy was off somewhere," Uncle Julian said at last in his sad old voice. "The boy had gone off somewhere—was he fishing, Constance?"

"He was climbing the chestnut tree."

"I remember. Of course. I remember all of it very clearly, my dear, and I have it all down in my notes. It was the last morning of all and I would not like to forget. He was climbing the chestnut tree, shouting down to us from very high in the tree, and dropping twigs until my sister-in-law spoke sharply to him. She disliked the twigs falling into her hair, and my wife disliked it too, although she would never have been the first to speak. I think my wife was civil to your mother, Constance. I would hate to think not; we lived in my brother's house and ate his food. I know my brother was home for lunch."

"We had a rarebit," Constance said. "I had been working with the vegetables all morning and I had to make something quickly for lunch."

"It was a rarebit we had. I have often wondered why the arsenic was never put into the rarebit. It is an interesting point, and one I shall bring out forcefully in my book. Why was the arsenic not put into the rarebit? They would have lost some hours of life on that last day, but it would all have been over with that much sooner. Constance, if there is one dish you prepare which I strongly dislike, it is a rarebit. I have never cared for rarebit."

"I know, Uncle Julian. I never serve it to you."

"It would have been most suitable for the arsenic. I had a salad instead, I recall. There was an apple pudding for dessert, left over from the night before."

"The sun is going down." Constance rose and brushed the dirt from her hands. "You'll be chilly unless I take you indoors."

"It would have been far more suitable in the rarebit, Constance. Odd that the point was never brought out at the time. Arsenic is tasteless, you know, although I swear a rarebit is not. Where am I going?"

"You are going indoors. You will rest in your room for an hour until your dinner, and after dinner I will play for you, if you like."

"I cannot afford the time, my dear. I have a thousand details to remember and note down, and not a minute to waste. I would hate to lose any small thing from their last day; my book must be complete. I think, on the whole, it was a pleasant day for all of them, and of course it is much better that they never supposed it was to be their last. I think I am chilly, Constance."

"You will be tucked away in your room in a minute."

I came slowly behind them, unwilling to leave the darkening garden; Jonas came after me, moving toward the light in the house. When Jonas and I came inside Constance was just closing the door to Uncle Julian's room, and she smiled at me. "He's practically asleep already," she said softly.

"When I'm as old as Uncle Julian will you take care of me?" I asked her.

"If I'm still around," she said, and I was chilled. I sat in my corner holding Jonas and watched her move quickly and silently around our bright kitchen. In a few minutes she would ask me to set the table for the three of us in the dining room, and then after dinner it would be night and we would sit warmly together in the kitchen where we were guarded by the house and no one from outside could see so much as a light.

MIDNIGHT'S CHILDREN

Salman Rushdie

Raised in Bombay, **Salman Rushdie** moved to England to attend Rugby School and Cambridge University. The multi-prize-winning author of fifteen novels, he holds honorary doctorates and fellowships at six European and six American universities, and is currently Distinguished Writer in Residence at New York University. His books have been translated into over forty languages. *Midnight's Children*, selected by public vote as the Best of the Booker in 2008 (the best of the award's first forty winners), is a postcolonial, postmodern novel about 1,001 children born at the exact moment of India's independence and partition.

My special blends: I've been saving them up. Symbolic value of the pickling process: all the six hundred million eggs which gave birth to the population of India could fit inside a single, standard-sized pickle-jar; six hundred million spermatozoa could be lifted on a single spoon. Every pickle-jar (you will forgive me if I become florid for a moment) contains, therefore, the most exalted of possibilities: the feasibility of the chutnification of history; the grand hope of the pickling of time! I, however, have pickled chapters. Tonight, by screwing the lid firmly on to a jar bearing the legend *Special Formula No. 30: 'Abracadabra'*, I reach the end of my long-winded autobiography; in words and pickles, I have immortalized my memories, although distortions are inevitable in both methods. We must live, I'm afraid, with the shadows of imperfection.

These days, I manage the factory for Mary. Alice – 'Mrs Fernandes' – controls the finances; my responsibility is for the creative aspects of our work. (Of course I have forgiven Mary her crime; I need mothers as well as fathers, and a mother is beyond blame.) Amid the wholly-female workforce of Braganza Pickles, beneath the saffron-and-green winking of neon Mumbadevi, I choose mangoes tomatoes limes from the women who come at dawn with baskets on their heads. Mary, with her ancient hatred of 'the mens', admits no males except myself into her new, comfortable universe . . . myself, and of course my son. Alice, I suspect, still has her little liaisons; and Padma fell for me from the first, seeing in me an outlet for her vast reservoir of pent-up solicitude; I cannot answer for the rest of them, but the formidable competence of the Narlikar females is reflected, on this factory floor, in the strong-armed dedication of the vat-stirrers.

What is required for chutnification? Raw materials, obviously – fruit, vegetables, fish, vinegar, spices. Daily visits from Koli women with their saris hitched up between their legs. Cucumbers aubergines mint. But also: eyes, blue as ice, which are undeceived by the superficial blandishments of fruit – which can see corruption beneath citrus-skin; fingers which, with featheriest touch, can probe the secret inconstant hearts of green tomatoes: and above all a nose capable of discerning the hidden languages of what-must-be-pickled, its humours and messages and emotions . . . at Braganza Pickles, I supervise the production of Mary's legendary recipes; but there are also my special blends, in which, thanks to the powers of my drained nasal passages, I am able to include memories, dreams, ideas, so that once they enter mass-production all who consume them will know what pepper-pots achieved in Pakistan, or how it felt to be in the Sundarbans . . . believe don't believe but it's true. Thirty jars stand upon a shelf, waiting to be unleashed upon the amnesiac nation.

(And beside them, one jar stands empty.)

The process of revision should be constant and endless; don't think I'm satisfied with what I've done! Among my unhappinesses: an overly-harsh taste from those jars containing memories of my father; a certain ambiguity in the love-flavour of 'Jamila Singer' (Special Formula No. 22), which might lead the unperceptive to conclude that I've invented the whole story of the baby-swap to justify an incestuous love; vague implausibilities in the jar labelled 'Accident in a washing-chest' – the pickle raises questions which are not fully answered, such as: Why did Saleem need an accident to acquire his powers? Most of the other children didn't . . . Or again, in 'All-India radio' and others, a discordant note in the orchestrated flavours: would Mary's confession have come as a shock to a true telepath? Sometimes, in the pickles' version of history, Saleem appears to have known too little; at other times, too much . . . yes, I should revise and revise, improve and improve; but there is neither the time nor the energy. I am obliged to offer no more than this stubborn sentence: It happened that way because that's how it happened.

There is also the matter of the spice bases. The intricacies of turmeric and cumin, the subtlety of fenugreek, when to use large (and when small) cardamoms; the myriad possible effects of garlic, garam masala, stick cinnamon, coriander, ginger . . . not to mention the flavourful contributions of the occasional speck of dirt. (Saleem is no longer obsessed with purity.) In the spice bases, I reconcile myself to the inevitable distortions of the pickling process. To pickle is to give immortality, after all: fish, vegetables, fruit hang embalmed in spice-and-vinegar; a certain alteration, a slight intensification of taste, is a small matter, surely? The art is to change the flavour in degree, but not in kind; and above all (in my thirty jars and a jar) to give it shape and form – that is to say, meaning. (I have mentioned my fear of absurdity.)

One day, perhaps, the world may taste the pickles of history. They may be too strong for some palates, their smell may be overpowering, tears may rise to eyes; I hope nevertheless that it will be possible to say of them that they possess the authentic taste of truth . . . that they are, despite everything, acts of love.

*

One empty jar . . . how to end? Happily, with Mary in her teak rocking-chair and a son who has begun to speak? Amid recipes, and thirty jars with chapter-headings for names? In melancholy, drowning in memories of Jamila and Parvati and even of Evie Burns? Or with the magic children . . . but then, should I be glad that some escaped, or end in the tragedy of the disintegrating effects of drainage? (Because in drainage lie the origins of the cracks: my hapless, pulverized body, drained above and below, began to crack because it was dried out. Parched, it yielded at last to the effects of a lifetime's battering. And now there is rip tear crunch, and a stench issuing through the fissures, which must be the smell of death. Control: I must retain control as long as possible.)

Or with questions: now that I can, I swear, see the cracks on the backs of my hands, cracks along my hairline and between my toes, why do I not bleed? Am I already so emptied desiccated pickled? Am I already the mummy of myself?

Or dreams: because last night the ghost of Reverend Mother appeared to me, staring down through the hole in a perforated cloud, waiting for my death so that she could weep a monsoon for forty days . . . and I, floating outside my body, looked down on the foreshortened image of myself, and saw a grey-haired dwarf who once, in a mirror, looked relieved.

*

No, that won't do, I shall have to write the future as I have written the past, to set it down with the absolute certainty of a prophet. But the future cannot be preserved in a jar; one jar must remain empty . . . What cannot be pickled, because it has not taken place, is that I shall reach my birthday, thirty-one today, and no doubt a marriage will take place, and Padma will have henna-tracery on her palms and soles, and also a new name, perhaps Naseem in honour of Reverend Mother's watching ghost, and outside the window there will be fireworks and crowds, because it will be Independence Day and the many-headed multitudes will be in the streets, and Kashmir will be waiting. I will have train-tickets in my pocket, there will be a taxi-cab driven by a country boy who once dreamed, at the Pioneer Café, of film-stardom, we will drive south south south into the heart of the tumultuous crowds, who will be throwing balloons of paint at each other, at the wound-up windows of the cab, as if it were the day of the paint-festival of Holi; and along Hornby Vellard, where a dog was left to die, the crowd, the dense crowd, the crowd without boundaries, growing until it fills the world, will make progress impossible, we will abandon our taxi-cab and the dreams of its driver, on our feet in the thronging crowd, and yes, I will be separated from Padma, my dung-lotus extending an arm towards me across the turbulent sea, until she drowns in the crowd and I am alone in the vastness of the numbers, the numbers marching one two three, I am being buffeted right and left while rip tear crunch reaches its climax, and my body is screaming, it cannot take this kind of treatment any more, but now I see familiar faces in the crowd, they are all here, my grandfather Aadam and his wife Naseem, and Alia and Mustapha and Hanif and Emerald, and Amina who was Mumtaz, and Nadir who became Qasim, and Pia and Zafar who wet his bed and also General Zulfikar, they throng around me pushing shoving crushing, and the cracks are widening, pieces of my body are falling off, there is Jamila who has left her nunnery to be present on this last day, night is falling has fallen, there is a countdown ticktocking to midnight, fireworks and stars, the cardboard cut-outs of wrestlers, and I see that I shall never reach Kashmir, like Jehangir the Mughal Emperor I shall die with Kashmir on my lips, unable to see the valley of delights to which men go to enjoy life or to end it, or both; because now I see other figures in the crowd, the terrifying figure of a war hero with lethal knees, who has found out how I cheated him of his birthright, he is pushing towards me through the crowd which is now wholly composed of familiar faces, there is Rashid the rickshaw boy arm-in-arm with the Rani of Cooch Naheen, and Ayooba Shaheed Farooq with Mutasim the Handsome, and from another direction, the direction of Haji Ali's island tomb, I see a mythological apparition approaching, the Black Angel, except that as it nears me its face is green its eyes are black, a centre-parting in its hair, on the left green and on the right black, its eyes the eyes of Widows; Shiva and the Angel are closing closing, I hear lies being spoken in the night, anything you want to be you kin be, the greatest lie of all, cracking now, fission of Saleem, I am the bomb in Bombay, watch me explode, bones splitting breaking beneath the awful pressure of the crowd, bag of bones falling down down down, just as once at Jallianwala, but Dyer seems not to be present today, no Mercurochrome, only a broken creature spilling pieces of itself into the street, because I have been so-many too-many persons, life unlike syntax allows one more than three, and at last somewhere the striking of a clock, twelve chimes, release.

Yes, they will trample me underfoot, the numbers marching one two three, four hundred million five hundred six, reducing me to specks of voiceless dust, just as, all in good time, they will trample my son who is not my son, and his son who will not be his, and his who will not be his, until the thousand and first generation, until a thousand and one midnights have bestowed their terrible gifts and a thousand and one children have died, because it is the privilege and the curse of midnight's children to be both masters and victims of their times, to forsake privacy and be sucked into the annihilating whirlpool of the multitudes, and to be unable to live or die in peace.

LITTLE WOMEN

Louisa May Alcott

Louisa May Alcott, or Lou, was not entirely sure about writing a book about girls. 'Never liked girls or knew many,' Alcott wrote privately, 'except my sisters.' That 'book about girls' has, of course, come to define Alcott's life and work. *Little Women* has never been out of print, and the March sisters live in fifty translations and countless adaptations for film, TV and radio. There is even an anime and an opera. The original text (funnier, stranger and slyer than many of the adaptations) tells the story of four girls, earnest-but-vain Meg; boy-adjacent author-avatar Jo; poor, doomed Beth; and spiky, charming Amy. Their father is away fighting in the Civil War, their saintly Marmee spends her time urging them to be better people, and the rich neighbour boy Laurie is trying desperately to become the secret fifth sister. There is a great deal of food in *Little Women* (and its many and increasingly weird sequels), but in the extract below food is not just food: it becomes social currency, shame, secrets, guilt, joy, desire, and despair. Amy hates to be so poor she can't afford pickled limes, and who can blame her? The pickled limes in this passage are, we think, somewhere between a modern preserved lemon and a Haribo Tangfastic. (If you have a reliable recipe, please contact the editors.)

"That boy is a perfect cyclops, isn't he?" said Amy one day, as Laurie clattered by on horseback, with a flourish of his whip as he passed.

"How dare you say so, when he's got both his eyes? And very handsome ones they are, too," cried Jo, who resented any slighting remarks about her friend.

"I didn't say anything about his eyes, and I don't see why you need fire up when I admire his riding."

"Oh, my goodness! That little goose means a centaur, and she called him a Cyclops," exclaimed Jo, with a burst of laughter.

"You needn't be so rude, it's only a 'lapse of lingy', as Mr. Davis says," retorted Amy, finishing Jo with her Latin. "I just wish I had a little of the money Laurie spends on that horse," she added, as if to herself, yet hoping her sisters would hear.

"Why?" asked Meg kindly, for Jo had gone off in another laugh at Amy's second blunder.

"I need it so much. I'm dreadfully in debt, and it won't be my turn to have the rag money for a month."

"In debt, Amy? What do you mean?" And Meg looked sober.

"Why, I owe at least a dozen pickled limes, and I can't pay them, you know, till I have money, for Marmee forbade my having anything charged at the shop."

"Tell me all about it. Are limes the fashion now? It used to be pricking bits of rubber to make balls." And Meg tried to keep her countenance, Amy looked so grave and important.

"Why, you see, the girls are always buying them, and unless you want to be thought mean, you must do it too. It's nothing but limes now, for everyone is sucking them in their desks in schooltime, and trading them off for pencils, bead rings, paper dolls, or something else, at recess. If one girl likes another, she gives her a lime. If she's mad with her, she eats one before her face, and doesn't offer even a suck. They treat by turns, and I've had ever so many but haven't returned them, and I ought for they are debts of honor, you know."

"How much will pay them off and restore your credit?" asked Meg, taking out her purse.

"A quarter would more than do it, and leave a few cents over for a treat for you. Don't you like limes?"

"Not much. You may have my share. Here's the money. Make it last as long as you can, for it isn't very plenty, you know."

"Oh, thank you! It must be so nice to have pocket money! I'll have a grand feast, for I haven't tasted a lime this week. I felt delicate about taking any, as I couldn't return them, and I'm actually suffering for one."

Next day Amy was rather late at school, but could not resist the temptation of displaying, with pardonable pride, a moist brown-paper parcel, before she consigned it to the inmost recesses of her desk. During the next few minutes the rumor that Amy March had got twenty-four delicious limes (she ate one on the way) and was going to treat circulated through her 'set', and the attentions of her friends became quite overwhelming. Katy Brown invited her to her next party on the spot. Mary Kingsley insisted on lending her her watch till recess, and Jenny Snow, a satirical young lady, who had basely twitted Amy upon her limeless state, promptly buried the hatchet and offered to furnish answers to certain appalling sums. But Amy had not forgotten Miss Snow's cutting remarks about 'some persons whose noses were not too flat to smell other people's limes, and stuck-up people who were not too proud to ask for them', and she instantly crushed 'that Snow girl's' hopes by the withering telegram, "You needn't be so polite all of a sudden, for you won't get any."

A distinguished personage happened to visit the school that morning, and Amy's beautifully drawn maps received praise, which honor to her foe rankled in the soul of Miss Snow, and caused Miss March to assume the airs of a studious young peacock. But, alas, alas! Pride goes before a fall, and the revengeful Snow turned the tables with disastrous success. No sooner had the guest paid the usual stale compliments and bowed himself out, than Jenny, under pretense of asking an important question, informed Mr. Davis, the teacher, that Amy March had pickled limes in her desk.

Now Mr. Davis had declared limes a contraband article, and solemnly vowed to publicly ferrule the first person who was found breaking the law. This much-enduring man had succeeded in banishing chewing gum after a long and stormy war, had made a bonfire of the confiscated novels and newspapers, had suppressed a private post office, had forbidden distortions of the face, nicknames, and caricatures, and done all that one man could do to keep half a hundred rebellious girls in order. Boys are trying enough to human patience, goodness knows, but girls are infinitely more so, especially to nervous gentlemen with tyrannical tempers and no more talent for teaching than Dr. Blimber. Mr. Davis knew any quantity of Greek, Latin, algebra, and ologies of all sorts so he was called a fine teacher, and manners, morals, feelings, and examples were not considered of any particular importance. It was a most unfortunate moment for denouncing Amy, and Jenny knew it. Mr. Davis had evidently taken his coffee too strong that morning, there was an east wind, which always affected his neuralgia, and his pupils had not done him the credit which he felt he deserved. Therefore, to use the expressive, if not elegant, language of a schoolgirl, "He was as nervous as a witch and as cross as a bear". The word 'limes' was like fire to powder, his yellow face flushed, and he rapped on his desk with an energy which made Jenny skip to her seat with unusual rapidity.

"Young ladies, attention, if you please!"

At the stern order the buzz ceased, and fifty pairs of blue, black, gray, and brown eyes were obediently fixed upon his awful countenance.

"Miss March, come to the desk."

Amy rose to comply with outward composure, but a secret fear oppressed her, for the limes weighed upon her conscience.

"Bring with you the limes you have in your desk," was the unexpected command which arrested her before she got out of her seat.

"Don't take all." whispered her neighbor, a young lady of great presence of mind.

Amy hastily shook out half a dozen and laid the rest down before Mr. Davis, feeling that any man possessing a human heart would relent when that delicious perfume met his nose. Unfortunately, Mr. Davis particularly detested the odor of the fashionable pickle, and disgust added to his wrath.

"Is that all?"

"Not quite," stammered Amy.

"Bring the rest immediately."

With a despairing glance at her set, she obeyed.

"You are sure there are no more?"

"I never lie, sir."

"So I see. Now take these disgusting things two by two, and throw them out of the window."

There was a simultaneous sigh, which created quite a little gust, as the last hope fled, and the treat was ravished from their longing lips.

Scarlet with shame and anger, Amy went to and fro six dreadful times, and as each doomed couple, looking oh, so plump and juicy, fell from her reluctant hands, a shout from the street completed the anguish of the girls, for it told them that their feast was being exulted over by the little Irish children, who were their sworn foes. This—this was too much. All flashed indignant or appealing glances at the inexorable Davis, and one passionate lime lover burst into tears.

As Amy returned from her last trip, Mr. Davis gave a portentous "Hem!" and said, in his most impressive manner...

"Young ladies, you remember what I said to you a week ago. I am sorry this has happened, but I never allow my rules to be infringed, and I never break my word. Miss March, hold out your hand."

Amy started, and put both hands behind her, turning on him an imploring look which pleaded for her better than the words she could not utter. She was rather a favorite with 'old Davis', as, of course, he was called, and it's my private belief that he would have broken his word if the indignation of one irrepressible young lady had not found vent in a hiss. That hiss, faint as it was, irritated the irascible gentleman, and sealed the culprit's fate.

"Your hand, Miss March!" was the only answer her mute appeal received, and too proud to cry or beseech, Amy set her teeth, threw back her head defiantly, and bore without flinching several tingling blows on her little palm. They were neither many nor heavy, but that made no difference to her. For the first time in her life she had been struck, and the disgrace, in her eyes, was as deep as if he had knocked her down.

"You will now stand on the platform till recess," said Mr. Davis, resolved to do the thing thoroughly, since he had begun.

That was dreadful. It would have been bad enough to go to her seat, and see the pitying faces of her friends, or the satisfied ones of her few enemies, but to face the whole school, with that shame fresh upon her, seemed impossible, and for a second she felt as if she could only drop down where she stood, and break her heart with crying. A bitter sense of wrong and the thought of Jenny Snow helped her to bear it, and, taking the ignominious place, she fixed her eyes on the stove funnel above what now seemed a sea of faces, and stood there, so motionless and white that the girls found it hard to study with that pathetic figure before them.

During the fifteen minutes that followed, the proud and sensitive little girl suffered a shame and pain which she never forgot. To others it might seem a ludicrous or trivial affair, but to her it was a hard experience, for during the twelve years of her life she had been governed by love alone, and a blow of that sort had never touched her before. The smart of her hand and the ache of her heart were forgotten in the sting of the thought, "I shall have to tell at home, and they will be so disappointed in me!"

The fifteen minutes seemed an hour, but they came to an end at last, and the word 'Recess!' had never seemed so welcome to her before.

"You can go, Miss March," said Mr. Davis, looking, as he felt, uncomfortable.

He did not soon forget the reproachful glance Amy gave him, as she went, without a word to anyone, straight into the anteroom, snatched her things, and left the place "forever," as she passionately declared to herself. She was in a sad state when she got home, and when the older girls arrived, some time later, an indignation meeting was held at once. Mrs. March did not say much but looked disturbed, and comforted her afflicted little daughter in her tenderest manner. Meg bathed the insulted hand with glycerine and tears, Beth felt that even her beloved kittens would fail as a balm for griefs like this, Jo wrathfully proposed that Mr. Davis be arrested without delay, and Hannah shook her fist at the 'villain' and pounded potatoes for dinner as if she had him under her pestle.

No notice was taken of Amy's flight, except by her mates, but the sharp-eyed demoiselles discovered that Mr. Davis was quite benignant in the afternoon, also unusually nervous. Just before school closed, Jo appeared, wearing a grim expression as she stalked up to the desk, and delivered a letter from her mother, then collected Amy's property, and departed, carefully scraping the mud from her boots on the door mat, as if she shook the dust of the place off her feet.

"Yes, you can have a vacation from school, but I want you to study a little every day with Beth," said Mrs. March that evening. "I don't approve of corporal punishment, especially for girls. I dislike Mr. Davis's manner of teaching and don't think the girls you associate with are doing you any good, so I shall ask your father's advice before I send you anywhere else."

"That's good! I wish all the girls would leave, and spoil his old school. It's perfectly maddening to think of those lovely limes," sighed Amy, with the air of a martyr.

"I am not sorry you lost them, for you broke the rules, and deserved some punishment for disobedience," was the severe reply, which rather disappointed the young lady, who expected nothing but sympathy.

"Do you mean you are glad I was disgraced before the whole school?" cried Amy.

"I should not have chosen that way of mending a fault," replied her mother, "but I'm not sure that it won't do you more good than a bolder method. You are getting to be rather conceited, my dear, and it is quite time you set about correcting it. You have a good many little gifts and virtues, but there is no need of parading them, for conceit spoils the finest genius. There is not much danger that real talent or goodness will be overlooked long, even if it is, the consciousness of possessing and using it well should satisfy one, and the great charm of all power is modesty."

"So it is!" cried Laurie, who was playing chess in a corner with Jo. "I knew a girl once, who had a really remarkable talent for music, and she didn't know it, never guessed what sweet little things she composed when she was alone, and wouldn't have believed it if anyone had told her."

"I wish I'd known that nice girl. Maybe she would have helped me, I'm so stupid," said Beth, who stood beside him, listening eagerly.

"You do know her, and she helps you better than anyone else could," answered Laurie, looking at her with such mischievous meaning in his merry black eyes that Beth suddenly turned very red, and hid her face in the sofa cushion, quite overcome by such an unexpected discovery.

Jo let Laurie win the game to pay for that praise of her Beth, who could not be prevailed upon to play for them after her compliment. So Laurie did his best, and sang delightfully, being in a particularly lively humor, for to the Marches he seldom showed the moody side of his character. When he was gone, Amy, who had been pensive all evening, said suddenly, as if busy over some new idea, "Is Laurie an accomplished boy?"

"Yes, he has had an excellent education, and has much talent. He will make a fine man, if not spoiled by petting," replied her mother.

"And he isn't conceited, is he?" asked Amy.

"Not in the least. That is why he is so charming and we all like him so much."

"I see. It's nice to have accomplishments and be elegant, but not to show off or get perked up," said Amy thoughtfully.

"These things are always seen and felt in a person's manner and conversations, if modestly used, but it is not necessary to display them," said Mrs. March.

"Any more than it's proper to wear all your bonnets and gowns and ribbons at once, that folks may know you've got them," added Jo, and the lecture ended in a laugh.

WHAT MRS. FISHER KNOWS ABOUT OLD SOUTHERN COOKING

Abby Fisher

Abby Fisher was a formerly enslaved woman from South Carolina. After moving across the country to California, Fisher earned a living as a pickle manufacturer and published *What Mrs. Fisher Knows About Old Southern Cooking* in 1881. Unable to read or write, she dictated the cookbook to friends. The book was lost following the San Francisco earthquake and fire of 1906, but reemerged at a 1984 Sotheby's auction in New York City. It was reprinted in 1985.

86 Sweet Watermelon Hind Pickle.

Take the melon rind and scrape all the meat from the inside, and then carefully slice all the outside of rind from the white part of the rind, then lay or cover the white part over with salt. It will have to remain under salt one week before pickling; the rind will keep in salt from year to year. When you want to pickle it, take it from the salt and put into clear water, change the water three times a day – must be changed say every four hours – then take the rind from water and dry it with a clean cloth. Have your vinegar boiling, and put the rind into it and let it scald four minutes, then take it off the fire and let it lay in vinegar four days; then take it from the vinegar, drain, and sprinkle sugar thickly over it and let it remain so one day.

To make syrup, take the syrup from the rind and add eight pounds more sugar to it, and put to boil; boil till a thick and clear syrup. Weigh ten pounds of rind to twelve pounds of sugar; cover the rind with four pounds of it and make the syrup with the remaining eight pounds. While the syrup is cooking add one teacupful of white ginger root and the peel of three lemons. When the syrup is cooked, then put the rind into the boiling syrup, and let it cook till you can pass a fork through it with ease, then it is done. When cooled put in jar or bottles with one pint of vinegar to one quart of syrup, thus the pickle is made. See that they be well covered with vinegar and syrup as directed.

87 Onion Pickles.

Take as many small onions as you desire to pickle and peel them, then put them in a keg or barrel. Lay down one layer of onions about three inches thick, cover them all over with salt freely; then another layer of onions in the same way and cover with salt, and repeat in this manner until all the onions are covered with salt. Let them remain one or two days, then take the onions out of the salt and put them in clear water, letting them remain in the water long enough to be seasoned with salt to your taste. If very salty, you had better change the first water after three or four hours. Put the onions in a large cullender or wire sieve and let the water all drain from them, then put them into a keg, cover them with vinegar, and let them remain in the vinegar twenty-four hours. Take the vinegar from them and put it on to boil, seasoning it with the following spices: Two gallons of vinegar will take one teacupful of allspice, two tablespoonfuls of cloves, one-half teacupful of black pepper (wash and pick all gravel from the pepper before putting in vinegar), one-fourth pound of white ginger, one-fourth pound of Chile peppers. This seasoning must be boiled in the vinegar, and when boiled twenty minutes, strain vinegar from the spices through a cullender on to the pickles, and always prepare enough in this way to have your pickles well covered with vinegar.

88 Plain Pickles.

Any vegetable you want to pickle under this head, say small or large cucumbers, cabbage or green tomatoes, have them fresh and put them into a barrel, one layer of cucumbers, or other vegetable, about three inches deep, covering thickly with salt, and repeating layers and salt until you have under brine all you desire to pickle. Let them remain under the brine, if you want to pickle right away, for twenty-four hours, which is long enough, but they will keep a long time by always having them well pressed down with a heavy rock. If you are going to pickle vegetables twenty-four hours after putting them in salt, let them lay in fresh water for two hours, so as to get the smell of the old brine off them. Take them out of the water and put to drain on a sieve made for that purpose of galvanized iron, square, three by four feet, or larger, if needed. Let them drain two or three days, then put in a clean keg or barrel and cover thoroughly with vinegar. Sprinkle over a keg of pickles two ounces of powdered alum while under the vinegar. Let them so remain twelve or twenty-four hours, then pour off the vinegar from the pickles into a large kettle and put to boil. Season while boiling, to five gallons of vinegar, one teacupful of allspice, one-fourth pound of ginger root, two ounces of cloves, one-half teacupful of black pepper, two tablespoonfuls of cayenne pepper. If you do not like pickles very hot, use one-half the quantity of peppers. When it boils with the seasonings twenty minutes, pour the boiling vinegar over the pickles.

Make enough vinegar from these directions to cover well your pickles. They will keep a long time if under vinegar. Sprinkle over a five-gallon keg, when you put the vinegar on the pickles, two or three ounces of powdered alum, if you like pickles brittle.

89 Brandy Peaches.

Always have the cling peach, free from decay. Peel the peaches and put down in a jar; one layer of peaches about four peaches deep, covering thickly with granulated sugar; then another layer of peaches covered with sugar, and continue in this manner until you get all the peaches in the jar you wish to brandy. Let them remain under sugar twenty-four hours; then take the same juice that comes from the peaches while under sugar, boil it and pour over the peaches boiling hot. Let them remain in this boiling syrup until it cools. Take this same syrup and put on to boil, adding more sugar so as to make it thick. When it is thoroughly cooked or all sugar is dissolved, put up the peaches in glass jars, and to one teacupful of syrup add one teacupful of brandy and pour over the peaches, continuing the same proportions of syrup and brandy until the peaches are completely covered with the mixture. Cork the jars and put in closet. You need not seal the jars unless you wish.

90 Brandy Peaches No. 2.

Have the cling peach, free from decay. Peel as in preceding recipe. Weigh the peaches after peeling, or measure them in a gallon measure, so as to allow one pound of sugar to one gallon of peaches in making the syrup. Then put the sugar on the fire to make the syrup, adding enough clear water to keep the sugar from burning while melting. Let the syrup boil until it gets as thick as honey. Put your peeled peaches in a stone jar one that is air-tight. Set the jar, with the peaches in it, in a kettle on the fire and fill the kettle (not the jar) with cold water. Then take one teacupful of syrup to one teacupful of brandy and pour it on the peaches until they are covered thoroughly with the brandy and syrup. Let the water in the kettle around the jar of peaches boil for three hours, and no longer. Close the jar up tight, so as to keep the heat in it while boiling. After three hours of actual boiling, lift the kettle with jar in it from the fire, and set aside to cool where a draught of air will not strike it.

When thoroughly cool, pack the peaches in glass jars, and fill with brandy and syrup as directed where peaches are boiled. If not enough, use equal proportions of brandy and syrup till the peaches are covered. These brandy peaches are great appetizers, especially for invalids.

91 Quince Preserves.

Never use decayed fruit. Put quinces in a kettle of boiling water on the fire, well covered with water, and let boil until they are soft enough to stick a fork into them easily. Then take them off the fire and peel them, cutting them into four pieces and taking all the core out nicely. Put a layer of sugar, then a layer of quinces about six inches deep, then cover thickly with sugar. You must have an equal quantity of sugar and quinces, say pound to pound. Let them remain in sugar a day and night, then put the sugar the quinces were in on to boil, and when it comes to a boil, put the quinces into the syrup. Let them remain in boiling syrup on the fire ten minutes, then take them out and put others in the same syrup, to remain boiling ten minutes. Then put the others back into the syrup again some length of time, and keep repeating the change in this manner for the whole day, as quinces take a whole day to preserve. When they get the color of gold coin they are preserved. Then put them in jars when cold, and put the same syrup on them. If there is not enough syrup to cover them fully, make more syrup. Use granulated sugar with all preserves, and a porcelain kettle for all preserves and pickles.

92 Syrups for Preserves.

To ten pounds of sugar add three pints of clear water, hot or cold. When it commences to boil skim the froth from it with a spoon, and let it boil until the froth ceases to collect, then the syrup is made.

93 Preserved Peaches.

Have cling peaches, peel them, cut them in half and take the kernels out. Put peaches in sugar, a layer of peaches, then a layer of sugar. Weigh peaches and sugar equally. Each layer of peaches should be about six inches deep; then cover with sugar. Keep repeating sugar and peaches in this manner until you get them all under sugar. Let them remain so one day and night. Next day take sugar and juice from the peaches and put on to boil, and when it comes to a boil, put the peaches in the syrup and let them boil ten minutes. Then take them out and put others in, and when the first lot gets cold put them back into syrup again, and keep repeating in this manner, letting them boil for ten minutes at a time, until preserved. When the peaches look the color of gold coin they are preserved. When they are cold put them in jars, cover with syrup, seal or cork, and set away in a dark closet. Use the syrup they were preserved in; if you have not enough, make more. In preserving any kind of fruit, while cooking always keep the froth well skimmed off top of syrup, and don't neglect it.

94 Pear Preserves.

Are to be prepared the same way that peaches are prepared, except in case you want to preserve them whole, then do not cut them into pieces, but only peel them and lay them under sugar in the same manner as the peaches are done, also take one-quarter pound of white ginger root to ten pounds of pears, crack or bruise it, and sprinkle it over each layer of pears, under the sugar; let them remain a day and night, and take the juice and sugar from the pears next day and put to boil for the syrup with the ginger in it; let them boil for ten minutes at a time, and repeat till done; skim the froth off the top of the syrup whenever it appears. When the pears are cold put in jars or bottles and place in a dark closet; they are preserved when they get to the color of gold coin.

If you cannot bruise the ginger root slice it in pieces with a knife and put on pears as directed.

95 Currant Jelly.

Be sure and have fresh currants that are not running the juice off. Put the currants in a cloth or bag and squeeze the juice thoroughly from the fruit, then strain the juice through a thin cloth. Measure the juice of the currants; then measure an equal quantity of sugar and place the sugar in a baking pan and put on the stove to heat through thoroughly—it must neither brown nor burn—then put the currant juice and sugar on in a porcelain kettle to boil; it must boil slowly, and whenever the froth or foam gathers on the top of the jelly, skim it all off, so as to let the jelly boil clear. Let the currant juice commence boiling before you put the sugar in, then boil both together for thirty minutes; then dip up some of the jelly and pour it in a saucer and seat in the air: if it congeals in five minutes it is made, if not, let it cook on, and about every ten minutes try it again as before, until it congeals. Have boiling water, and as soon as your jelly is cooked dip your glasses in the boiling water and then turn them upside down long enough for the water to drain out of them. Pour the jelly into the glasses while they are hot, and then seat them in the air to cool with the jelly in them. To paper them after they get cold, have good brandy; cut some thin paper for the inside of the glass and wet it in the brandy, then lay it on the jelly inside of the glass; after covering them put away in a dark place. Use granulated sugar.

96 Cranberry Jelly.

Follow the same directions as given in Recipe No. 95 for making currant jelly. Use granulated sugar.

97 Strawberry Jam.

Must have fresh berries that are not running. Squeeze the juice from the berries through a clean linen cloth; then add one-half pint of sugar to every pint of juice and put on to boil in a porcelain kettle, and when it boils as thick as honey add the berries that you squeezed the juice from to the syrup and let it continue to boil until it gets as thick as mush, when it will be cooked enough. You can put it up in glasses or jars; put paper on the top wet with brandy, and then cover and put in a dark place. Use granulated sugar.

98 Raspberry and Currant Jam combined.

Take an equal quantity of both kinds of fruit and squeeze the juice from them; measure the juice and put one pint of it to one-half pint of sugar; then put on to boil, letting it boil till thick as honey; then add the berries and currants that you squeezed the juice from, and let all boil together till thick as mush, when it will be cooked. Put up in bowls, jars or glasses, covering inside with paper wet in brandy, and then put away in a dark place. Use granulated sugar.

99 Marmalade Peach.

Peel the peaches and take the seeds away. Use the freestone peach, taking one-half pound of sugar to one pound of peaches. Sprinkle the sugar thickly over the peaches and let them lay in the sugar one night; next morning mash the peaches and sugar thoroughly, and put to cook, and let it cook slowly. Do not put any water to it. It requires five hours cooking. Use porcelain kettle and keep from burning. Use granulated sugar. Can be put up in glasses, jars or bowls.

100 Crab Apple Jelly.

Put the apples to boil; one quart of water to one quart of apples and let them boil till soft; then mash the apples and put the apples and the water they were boiled in in a linen rag, and let all the juice drip into a vessel; measure the juice and take one quart of the dripped juice to one quart of sugar, and put on to boil for jelly. Boil thirty minutes and then dip some into a saucer and set in the air to cool; if it is congealed when cool, it is done. Put up in glasses, first dipping the glasses into boiling hot water and letting them drain; put the jelly into the glasses hot, and then set to cool.

PACHINKO

Min Jin Lee

Born in Seoul, **Min Jin Lee** moved with her family to Queens when she was seven. After pursuing an undergraduate degree at Yale, then law school at Georgetown University, she worked as a corporate lawyer in New York City. Chronic liver disease and extreme working hours led her to focus instead on her writing. She has written two novels: 2007's *Free Food for Millionaires* and 2017's *Pachinko*, which is an epic historical novel set across the twentieth century, about four generations of a Korean family who emigrate to Japan. The book was reviewed as 'vivid', 'immersive' and 'brilliantly drawn' and was adapted for television in 2022.

For Sunja, Isak's arrest had forced her to consider what would happen if the unthinkable occurred. Would Yoseb ask her and her children to leave? Where would she go, and how would she get there? How would she take care of her children? Kyunghee would not ask her to leave, but even so—she was only a wife. Sunja had to have a plan and money in case she had to return home to her mother with her sons.

So Sunja had to find work. She would become a peddler. It was one thing for a woman like her mother to take in boarders and to work alongside her husband to earn money, but something altogether different for a young woman to stand in an open market and sell food to strangers, shouting until she was hoarse. Yoseb tried to forbid her from getting a job, but she could not listen to him. With tears streaming down her face, she told her brother-in-law that Isak would want her to earn money for the boys' schooling. To this, Yoseb yielded. Nevertheless, he prohibited Kyunghee from working outdoors, and his wife obeyed. Kyunghee was allowed to put up the pickles with Sunja, but she couldn't sell them. Yoseb couldn't protest too much, because the household was desperate for cash. In a way, the two women tried to obey Yoseb in their disobedience—they did not want to hurt Yoseb by defying him, but the financial burdens had become impossible for one man to bear alone.

Her first day of selling took place one week after Isak was jailed. After Sunja dropped off Isak's food at the jail, she wheeled a wooden cart holding a large clay jar of kimchi to the market. The open-air market in Ikaino was a patchwork of modest retail shops selling housewares, cloth, tatami mats, and electric goods, and it hosted a collection of hawkers like her who peddled homemade scallion pancakes, rolled sushi, and soybean paste.

Kyunghee watched Mozasu at home. Nearby the peddlers selling *gochujang* and *doenjang*, Sunja noticed two young Korean women selling fried wheat crackers. Sunja pushed her cart toward them, hoping to wedge herself between the cracker stall and the soybean-paste lady.

"You can't stink up our area," the older of the two cracker sellers said. "Go to the other side." She pointed to the fish section.

When Sunja moved closer to the women selling dried anchovies and seaweed, the older Korean women there were even less welcoming.

"If you don't move your shitty-looking cart, I'll have my sons piss in your pot. Do you understand, country girl?" said a tall woman wearing a white kerchief on her head.

Sunja couldn't come up with a reply, because she was so surprised. None of them were even selling kimchi, and *doenjang* could smell just as pungently.

She kept walking until she couldn't see any more *ajumma*s and ended up near the train station entrance where the live chickens were sold. The intense funk of animal carcasses over-whelmed her. There was a space big enough for her cart between the pig butcher and the chickens.

Wielding an enormous knife, a Japanese butcher was cutting up a hog the size of a child. A large bucket filled with its blood rested by his feet. Two hogs' heads lay on the front table. The butcher was an older gentleman with ropy, muscular arms and thick veins. He was sweating profusely, and he smiled at her.

Sunja parked her cart in the empty lot by his stall. Whenever a train stopped, she could feel its deceleration beneath her sandals. Passengers would disembark, and many of them came into the market from the entrance nearby, but none stopped in front of her cart. Sunja tried not to cry. Her breasts were heavy with milk, and she missed being at home with Kyunghee and Mozasu. She wiped her face with her sleeves, trying to remember what the best market *ajumma*s would do back home.

"Kimchi! Delicious kimchi! Try this delicious kimchi, and never make it at home again!" she shouted. Passersby turned to look at her, and Sunja, mortified, looked away from them. No one bought anything. After the butcher finished with his hog, he washed his hands and gave her twenty-five sen, and Sunja filled a container for him. He didn't seem to mind that she didn't speak Japanese. He put down the kimchi container by the hogs' heads, then reached behind his stall to take out his bento. The butcher placed a piece of kimchi neatly on top of his white rice with his chopsticks and ate a bite of rice and kimchi in front of her.

"*Oishi*! *Oishi nee*! *Honto oishi*," he said, smiling.

She bowed to him.

At lunchtime, Kyunghee brought Mozasu for her to nurse, and Sunja remembered that she had no choice but to recoup the cost of the cabbage, radish, and spices. At the end of the day, she had to show more money than they had spent.

Kyunghee watched the cart while Sunja nursed the baby with her body turned toward the wall.

"I'd be afraid," Kyunghee said. "You know how I'd said that I wanted to be a kimchi *ajumma*? I don't think I realized what it would feel like to stand here. You're so brave."

"What choice do we have?" Sunja said, looking down at her beautiful baby.

"Do you want me to stay here? And wait with you?"

"You'll get in trouble," Sunja said. "You should be home when Noa gets back from school, and you have to make dinner. I'm sorry I can't help you, Sister."

"What I have to do is easy," Kyunghee said.

It was almost two o'clock in the afternoon, and the air felt cooler as the sun turned away from them.

"I'm not going to come home until I sell the whole jar."

"Really?"

Sunja nodded. Her baby, Mozasu, resembled Isak. He looked nothing like Noa, who was olive-skinned with thick, glossy hair. Noa's bright eyes noticed everything. Except for his mouth, Noa looked almost identical to a young Hansu. At school, Noa sat still during lessons, waited for his turn, and he was praised as an excellent student. Noa had been an easy baby, and Mozasu was a happy baby, too, delighted to be put into a stranger's arms. When she thought about how much she loved her boys, she recalled her parents. Sunja felt so far away from her mother and father. Now she was standing outside a rumbling train station, trying to sell kimchi. There was no shame in her work, but it couldn't be what they'd wanted for her. Nevertheless, she felt her parents would have wanted her to make money, especially now.

When Sunja finished nursing, Kyunghee put down two sugared rolls and a bottle filled with reconstituted powdered milk on the cart.

"You have to eat, Sunja. You're nursing, and that's not easy, right? You have to drink lots of water and milk."

Kyunghee turned around so Sunja could tuck Mozasu into the sling on Kyunghee's back. Kyunghee secured the baby tightly around her torso.

"I'll go home and wait for Noa and make dinner. You come home soon, okay? We're a good team."

Mozasu's small head rested between Kyunghee's thin shoulder blades, and Sunja watched them walk away. When they were out of earshot, Sunja cried out, "Kimchi! Delicious Kimchi! Kimchi! Delicious kimchi! *Oishi desu! Oishi* kimchi!"

This sound, the sound of her own voice, felt familiar, not because it was her own voice but because it reminded her of all the times she'd gone to the market as a girl—first with her father, later by herself as a young woman, then as a lover yearning for the gaze of her beloved. The chorus of women hawking had always been with her, and now she'd joined them. "Kimchi! Kimchi! Homemade kimchi! The most delicious kimchi in Ikaino! More tasty than your grandmother's! *Oishi desu, oishi!*" She tried to sound cheerful, because back home, she had always frequented the nicest *ajumma*s. When the passersby glanced in her direction, she bowed and smiled at them. "*Oishi*! *Oishi*!"

The pig butcher looked up from his counter and smiled at her proudly.

That evening, Sunja did not go home until she could see the bottom of the kimchi jar.

Sunja could sell whatever kimchi she and Kyunghee were able to make now, and this ability to sell had given her a kind of strength. If they could've made more kimchi, she felt sure that she could've sold that, too, but fermenting took time, and it wasn't always possible to find the right ingredients. Even when they made a decent profit, the price of cabbages could spike the following week, or worse, they might not be available at all. When there were no cabbages at the market, the women pickled radishes, cucumbers, garlic, or chives, and sometimes Kyunghee pickled carrots or eggplant without garlic or chili paste, because the Japanese preferred those kinds of pickles. Sunja thought about land all the time. The little kitchen garden her mother had kept behind the house had nourished them even when the boardinghouse guests ate double what they paid. The price of fresh food kept rising, and working people couldn't afford the most basic things. Recently, some customers would ask to buy a cup of kimchi because they couldn't afford a jar of it.

If Sunja had no kimchi or pickles to sell, she sold other things. Sunja roasted sweet potatoes and chestnuts; she boiled ears of corn. She had two carts now, and she hooked them together like the cars of a train—one cart with a makeshift coal stove and another just for pickles. The carts took up the better part of the kitchen because they had to keep them inside the house for fear of getting them stolen. She split the profits equally with Kyunghee, and Sunja put aside every sen she could for the boys' schooling and for their passage back home in case they had to leave.

When Mozasu turned five months old, Sunja also started selling candy at the market. Produce had been getting increasingly scarce, and by chance, Kyunghee had obtained two wholesale bags of black sugar from a Korean grocer whose Japanese brother-in-law worked in the military.

At her usual spot by the pork butcher's stall, Sunja stoked the fire beneath the metal bowl used to melt sugar. The steel box that functioned as a stove had been giving her trouble; as soon as she could afford it, Sunja planned on having a proper stove made up for her cart. She rolled up her sleeves and moved the live coals around to circulate the air and raise the heat.

"*Agasshi*, do you have kimchi today?"

It was a man's voice, and Sunja looked up. About Isak's age, he dressed like her brother-in-law—tidy without drawing much attention to himself. His face was cleanly shaven, and his fingernails were neat. The lenses of his eyeglasses were very thick and the heavy frames detracted from his good features.

"No, sir. No kimchi today. Just candy. It's not ready, though."

"Oh. When will you have kimchi again?"

"Hard to say. There isn't much cabbage to buy, and the last batch of kimchi we put up isn't ready yet," Sunja said, and returned to the coals.

"A day or two? A week?"

Sunja looked up again, surprised by his insistence.

"The kimchi might be ready in three days or so. If the weather continues to get warmer, then it might be two, sir. But I don't think that soon," Sunja said flatly, hoping he would let her start with the candy making. Sometimes, she sold a few bags to the young women getting off the train at about this time.

"How much kimchi will you have when it's ready?"

"I'll have plenty to sell you. Do you know how much you want? Most of my customers like to bring their own containers. How much do you think you need?" Her customers were Korean women who worked in factories and didn't have time to make their own *banchan*. When she sold sweets, her customers were children and young women. "Just stop by in three days, and if you bring your own container—"

The young man laughed.

"Well, I was thinking that maybe you can sell me everything you make."

He adjusted his eyeglasses.

"You can't eat that much kimchi! And how would you keep the rest of it fresh?" Sunja replied, shaking her head at his foolishness. "It's going to be summer in a couple of months, and it's hot here already."

"I'm sorry. I should have explained. My name is Kim Changho, and I manage the *yakiniku* restaurant right by Tsuruhashi Station. News of your excellent kimchi has spread far."

Sunja wiped her hands on the apron that she wore over her padded cotton vest, keeping a close eye on the hot coals.

"It's my sister-in-law who knows what she's doing in the kitchen. I just sell it and help her make it."

"Yes, yes, I'd heard that, too. Well, I'm looking for some women to make all the kimchi and *banchan* for the restaurant. I can get you cabbage and—"

"Where, sir? Where do you get cabbage? We looked everywhere. My sister-in-law goes to the market early in the morning and still—"

"I can get it," he said, smiling.

Sunja didn't know what to say. The candy-making metal bowl was hot already, and it was time to put in the sugar and water, but she didn't want to start now. If this person was serious, then it was important to hear him out. She heard the train arrive. She had missed her first batch of customers already.

"Where's your restaurant again?"

"It's the big restaurant on the side street behind the train station. On the same street as the pharmacy—you know, the one owned by the skinny Japanese pharmacist, Okada-san? He wears black glasses like mine?" He pushed his glasses up on his nose again and smiled like a boy.

"Oh, I know where the pharmacy is."

This was the shop where all the Koreans went when they were really sick and were willing to pay for good medicine. Okada was not a friendly man, but he was honest; he was reputed to be able to cure many ailments.

The young man didn't seem like anyone who was trying to take advantage of her, but she couldn't be sure. In the few short months working as a vendor, she'd given credit to a few customers and had not been repaid. People were willing to lie about small things and to disregard your interests.

Kim Changho gave her a business card. "Here's the address. Can you bring your kimchi when it's done? Bring all of it. I'll pay you in cash, and I'll get you more cabbage."

Sunja nodded, not saying anything. If she had only one customer for the kimchi, then she'd have more time to make other things to sell. The hardest part had been procuring the cabbage, so if this man could do that, then the work would be much easier. Kyunghee had been scouring the market with Mozasu on her back to track down these scarce ingredients and often returned home with a light market basket. Sunja promised to bring him what she had.

The restaurant was the largest storefront on the short side street parallel to the train station. Unlike the other businesses nearby, its sign was lettered handsomely by a professional sign maker. The two women admired the large black letters carved and painted into a vast wooden plaque. They wondered what the words meant. It was obviously a Korean *galbi* house—the scent of grilled meat could be detected from two blocks away— but the sign had difficult Japanese lettering that neither of them could read. Sunja grasped the handlebar of the carts loaded with all the kimchi they'd put up in the past few weeks and took a deep breath. If the kimchi sales to the restaurant were steady, they'd have a regular income. She could buy eggs more often for Isak's and Noa's meals and get heavy wool cloth for Kyunghee, who wanted to sew new coats for Yoseb and Noa.

Yoseb had been staying away from home, complaining of the sight and smell of all the kimchi ingredients spilling out from the kitchen. He didn't want to live in a kimchi factory. His dissatisfaction was the primary reason why the women preferred to sell candy, but sugar was far more difficult to find than cabbage or sweet potatoes. Although Noa didn't complain of it, the kimchi odor affected him the most. Like all the other Korean children at the local school, Noa was taunted and pushed around, but now that his clean-looking clothes smelled immutably of onions, chili, garlic, and shrimp paste, the teacher himself made Noa sit in the back of the classroom next to the group of Korean children whose mothers raised pigs in their homes. Everyone at school called the children who lived with pigs *buta*. Noa, whose *tsumei* was Nobuo, sat with the *buta* children and was called garlic turd.

At home, Noa asked his aunt for snacks and meals that didn't contain garlic, hoping this would keep the children from saying bad things to him. When she asked him why, Noa told his aunt the truth. Even though it cost more, Kyunghee bought Noa large milk rolls from the bakery for his breakfast and made him potato *korokke* or *yakisoba* for his school bento.

The children were merciless, but Noa didn't fight them; rather, he worked harder on his studies, and to the surprise of his teachers, he was the first or second in academic rank in his second grade class. At school, Noa didn't have any friends, and when the Korean children played in the streets, he didn't join them. The only person he looked forward to seeing was his uncle, but these days, when Yoseb was home, he was not himself.

In the street, Kyunghee and Sunja stood quietly in front of the restaurant, unable to enter. The door was ajar, but it was not open for business. Despite Kyunghee's initial excitement at the prospect of selling more kimchi, she'd been reasonably skeptical of the offer and had refused to let Sunja go to an unknown place by herself. She'd insisted on coming along, toting Mozasu on her back. They didn't tell Yoseb about coming here, but they planned on telling him everything after the first meeting.

"I'll stay out here with the cart and wait," Kyunghee said, patting Mozasu rhythmically with her right hand. The baby was resting calmly in the sling on Kyunghee's back.

"Shouldn't I bring the kimchi in?" Sunja said.

"Why don't you ask him to come outside?

"We can both go in."

"I'll wait outside. But if you don't come outside soon, then I'll come in, all right?"

"But how will you push the cart and—"

"I can push the cart. Mozasu is fine." The baby was now laying his head drowsily on her back, and she kept up a reliable rocking motion.

"Go on inside, and I'll wait. Just ask Kim Changho to come out here. Don't keep talking to him inside, all right?"

"But I thought we'd talk to him together."

Sunja stared at her sister-in-law, not knowing what she should do, and then it occurred to her that her sister-in-law was afraid of going into the restaurant. If her husband asked her what had happened, she could say honestly that she was outside the whole time.

CRAZY RICH ASIANS

Kevin Kwan

Born in Singapore as the youngest of three boys, **Kevin Kwan** grew up in a well-connected Chinese Singaporean family. His novels explore worlds he is intimately familiar with; he has said he is 'an observer', 'not a creative person', and that 'everything's actually drawn from observation and reality'; that he doesn't 'have the imagination to dream up plastic surgery for fish'. His bestselling *Crazy Rich Asians*, a celebration and skewering of the Singaporean ultrawealthy, has been translated into more than thirty languages. The film adaptation was Hollywood's highest-grossing romantic comedy in a decade, and the two sequels are in development.

"What a treat! I don't think I've been welcomed at the airport like this since I was a little kid," Nick said, recalling the times in his childhood when a large group of family members would gather at the airport. A visit to the airport back then was a thrilling event, since it also meant that his father would take him for a hot fudge sundae at the Swensen's Ice Cream Parlor in the old terminal. People seemed to go away on longer trips back then, and there were always tears from the women saying goodbye to relatives heading overseas or welcoming home children who had spent the school year abroad. He once even overheard his older cousin Alex whisper to his father just before Harry Leong was about to board a plane, "Be sure to pick me up the latest *Penthouse* on your layover in Los Angeles."

Colin settled behind the wheel and began adjusting the mirrors to fit his sightlines. "Where to? Straight to the hotel, or *makan*?"[1]

"I can definitely eat," Nick said. He turned around to look at Rachel, knowing she probably wanted to go straight to the hotel and collapse into bed. "Feeling okay, Rachel?"

---

[1] Malay for "eat."

"I'm great," Rachel replied. "Actually, I'm kinda hungry too."

"It's breakfast time back in New York, that's why," Colin noted.

"Did you have a good flight? Did you watch a lot of movies?" Araminta asked.

"Rachel went on a Colin Firth binge," Nick announced.

Araminta squealed. "OMG—I *love* him! He'll always be the one and only Mr. Darcy for me!"

"Okay, I think we can be friends now," Rachel declared. She looked out the window, amazed by the swaying palm trees and profusion of bougainvillea that lined the sides of the brightly lit highway. It was almost ten o'clock at night, but everything about this city seemed unnaturally bright—effervescent, almost.

"Nicky, where should we take Rachel for her first local meal?" Colin asked.

"Hmm . . . should we welcome Rachel with a feast of Hainanese chicken rice at Chatterbox? Or should we head straight for chili crab at East Coast?" Nick asked, feeling excited and torn at the same time— there were about a hundred different eating places he wanted Rachel to experience *right now*.

"How about some satay?" Rachel suggested. "Nick is always going on and on about how you've never tasted decent satay until you've had it in Singapore."

"That settles it—we're going to Lau Pa Sat," Colin announced. "Rachel, you'll get to experience your first true hawker center. And they have the best satay."

"You think so? I like that place in Sembawang better," Araminta said.

"NOOOO! What are you talking about, *lah*? The fellow from the original Satay Club is still at Lau Pa Sat," Colin said insistently.

"You're wrong," Araminta replied firmly. "That original Satay Club guy moved to Sembawang."

"Lies! That was his cousin. An imposter!" Colin was adamant.

"Personally, I've always liked the satay at Newton," Nick cut in.

"*Newton?* You've lost your mind, Nicky. Newton is only for expats and tourists—there aren't any good satay stalls left," Colin said.

"Welcome to Singapore, Rachel—where arguing about food is the national pastime," Araminta declared. "This is probably the only country in the world where *grown men* can get into fistfights over which specific food stall in some godforsaken shopping center has the best rendition of some obscure fried noodle dish. It's like a pissing contest!"

Rachel giggled. Araminta and Colin were so funny and down-to-earth, she liked them both instantly.

Soon they were on Robinson Road, in the heart of the down-town financial district. Nestled in the shadows of massive towers was Lau Pa Sat—or "old market" in the Hokkien dialect—an octagonal open-air pavilion that housed a bustling hive of food stalls. Walking from the car park across the street, Rachel could already smell the delicious spice-filled aromas wafting through the balmy air. As they were about to enter the great food hall, Nick turned to Rachel and said, "You're going to go nuts for this place—it's the oldest Victorian structure in all of Southeast Asia."

Rachel stared up at the soaring cast-iron filigree arches that radiated out across the vaulted ceilings. "Looks like the inside of a cathedral," she said.

"Where the masses come to worship food," Nick quipped.

Sure enough, even though it was past ten, the place teemed with hundreds of fervent diners. Rows and rows of brightly lit food stalls offered up a greater array of dishes than Rachel had ever witnessed under one roof. As they walked around, peering at the various stalls where men and women were frenziedly cooking their delicacies, Rachel shook her head in awe. "There's just so much to take in, I don't know where to start."

"Just point to whatever looks interesting and I'll order it," Colin offered. "The beauty of the hawker center is that each vendor basically sells just one dish, so whether it's fried pork dumplings or fish-ball soup, they've spent a lifetime perfecting it."

"More than one lifetime. A lot of these people are second- and third-generation hawkers, cooking old family recipes," Nick chimed in.

A few minutes later, the four of them were seated just outside the main hall under a huge tree strung with yellow lights, every inch of their table covered with colorful plastic plates piled high with the greatest hits of Singaporean street cuisine. There was the famous *char kuay teow*, a fried omelet with oysters called *orh luak*, Malay *rojak* salad bursting with chunks of pineapple and cucumber, Hokkien-style noodles in a thick garlicky gravy, a fish cake smoked in coconut leaves called *otah otah*, and a hundred sticks of chicken and beef satay.

Rachel had never seen anything like this feast. "This is insane! Every dish looks like it came from a different part of Asia."

"That's Singapore for you—the true originators of fusion cuisine," Nick boasted. "You know, because of all the ships passing through from Europe, the Middle East, and India in the nineteenth century, all these amazing flavors and textures could intermingle."

As Rachel tasted the *char kuay teow*, her eyes widened in delight at the rice noodles flash-fried with seafood, egg, and bean sprouts in a dark soy sauce. "Why doesn't it ever taste like this at home?"

"Gotta love that burned-wok flavor," Nick remarked.

"I bet you'll love this," Araminta said, handing Rachel a plate of *roti paratha*. Rachel tore off some of the doughy golden pastry and dipped it into the rich curry sauce.

"Mmmm . . . heaven!"

Then it was time for the satay. Rachel bit into the succulent grilled chicken, savoring its smoky sweetness carefully. The rest of them watched her intently. "Okay Nick, you were right. I've never had decent satay until now."

"To think you doubted me," Nick tut-tutted with a smile.

"I can't believe we're pigging out at this hour!" Rachel giggled, reaching for another stick of satay.

"Get used to it. I know you probably want to go straight to bed, but we have to keep you up for a few more hours so that you'll adjust better to the time change," Colin said.

"Aiyah, Colin just wants to monopolize Nick for as long as possible," Araminta declared. "These two are inseparable whenever Nick's in town."

"Hey, I have to make the most out of this time, especially since mommie dearest is away," Colin said in his own defense. "Rachel—you're in luck, not having to deal with Nicky's mum the minute you arrive."

"Colin, don't you start scaring her," Nick chided.

"Oh Nick, I almost forgot—I ran into your mum the other day at Churchill Club," Araminta began. "She grabbed me by the arm and said, Aramintaaaaa! Aiyoh, you're too dark! You better stop going into the sun so much, otherwise on your wedding day you will be so black people will think you are Malay!'"

Everyone roared with laughter, except Rachel. "She *was* kidding, I hope?"

"Of course not. Nick's mum doesn't kid," Araminta said, continuing to laugh.

"Rachel, you'll understand once you meet Nicky's mum. I love her like my own mother, but she's one of a kind," Colin explained, trying to put her at ease. "Anyway, it's perfect that your parents are gone, Nick, because *this* weekend your presence is required at my bachelor party."

"Rachel, you'll have to come to *my* bachelorette party," Araminta declared. "Let's show the boys how it's *really* done!"

"You bet," Rachel said, clinking her beer with Araminta's.

Nick gazed at his girlfriend, thrilled that she had so effortlessly charmed his friends. He could still hardly believe that she was actually here with him, and that they had the whole summer ahead of them. "Welcome to Singapore, Rachel," he joyously declared, lifting up his bottle of Tiger beer in a toast. Rachel gazed into Nick's sparkling eyes. She had never seen him as happy as he was tonight, and she wondered how she could possibly have been worried about coming on this trip.

"How does it feel to be here?" Colin asked.

"Well," Rachel mused, "an hour ago we landed in the most beautiful, modern airport I've ever seen, and now we're sitting under these huge tropical trees by a nineteenth-century food hall, having the most glorious feast. I don't ever want to leave!"

Nick grinned broadly, not noticing the look Araminta had just given Colin.

MARKET *FROM* SETTLERS: JOURNEYS THROUGH THE FOOD, FAITH AND CULTURE OF BLACK AFRICAN LONDON

Jimi Famurewa

Born in England to Nigerian immigrant parents, **Jimi Famurewa** grew up in London. A journalist and food critic, his writing has been published in the *Guardian*, *Wired*, *GQ*, *Empire* and *Time Out*, and he is a regular guest judge on BBC's *MasterChef*. Famurewa won the 2020 and 2021 Restaurant Writing Awards from the Guild of Food Writers for his column in *ES Magazine*. His first book, *Settlers: Journeys Through the Food, Faith and Culture of Black African London*, is 'a blend of memoir, social history and reportage' (the *Guardian*) and asks what it is to be Black, African, and British. Famurewa lives in south-east London with his family.

London's markets can be a portal. I have slalomed past haggling Lewisham aunties on my way to the gym and, with a jolt, suddenly been a child again, traipsing after my mum on a Saturday morning, stepping over squelched tomatoes at Woolwich market and looking on at gnarled tubers of yam going into thin plastic bags. I have stumbled, a little tipsy, past Peckham salon windows where entire families loiter late into the night and a hair stylist sews in weave with a slumbering baby trussed to her back, and felt a tug of recognition, as oblivious

White friends have wandered on. I have spied bundles of multicoloured scouring nets hung at the door of a Walworth Road Sierra Leonean supermarket and been reminded, with a shudder, of the adolescent bucket baths we endured when all we craved was the boundless luxury of a working shower. They are slippages really; moments when those of us who grew up immersed in Black African London, but now perhaps spend much less time in it, spot the seams between those worlds.

But if you have known these sites of Black African and Afro-Caribbean social interaction, commerce and cultural connection – if you have bought a phone card to make international calls, lingered by the tiny storefront that sells Ghanaian Kumawood DVDs or complained to a shopkeeper that the plantains are priced at more than the industry-standard three for £1 – then you will know that few places have the same transportive, polyphonic power of Dalston's Ridley Road. Officially ratified in 1926, but founded long before then in the late nineteenth century, this living, breathing strip of London history was not specifically established as a Black market. In fact, to the contrary, it has ebbed and flowed with the varying tides of British immigration, offering tailored goods, an entrepreneurial foothold and a meeting point to East End communities that have included White working class, Irish, Jewish, Turkish, East Asian, South Asian and more, as well as Black African and Afro-Caribbean.

Though, of course, if you have visited the market in the last 20 years or so, then you will know that there is a specifically West African tenor to much of its long, unruly stretch of stalls, shops and pitches. Because here, after the Kurdish butchers thudding their cleavers down, the tablefuls of bagged gold jewellery, and the stall that appears to sell nothing but net curtains, are the distinctive blue plastic drums of a cargo shipping company. Here are dried bales of Norwegian stockfish, spongey folds of honeycomb tripe, massed pyramids of hacked-off cow foot, and baskets of handle-less palm-frond brooms. Here, as any child who has ever been to Ridley Road will tell you, agog, are giant, live African land snails, writhing on top of each other in a cardboard box, and yours for £5 each amid an accompanying soundtrack of tinny Afrobeats, shouted Yoruba and stallholders crying out, 'Don't pass me by, my brother!' On more than one occasion, I have come to Ridley Road and felt, even if for a flickering moment, I could be back in Lagos's labyrinthine Alade market, walking its tight pathways and hearing the sing-song, hawker's refrain of 'Come-and-check, come-and-check'.

The temptation to exoticize should be resisted (land snails and goats' heads are, in their own way, just as ordinary and redolent of East London as jellied eels and salt beef). But that Black African-run businesses in places like Ridley Road can imprint a certain character on the London landscape, and serve, in some way, as conscious analogues of establishments in African cities, is significant. And you only need to spend some time in any of these places, among the jokes and arguments and constant phone calls, to know that they are about more than just purchases.

They, along with the neighbouring businesses of other immigrant diasporas, are spaces of political importance, as well as cultural and social significance. Or, rather, their presence often represents creativity and an indomitable, against-the-odds success. In 2013, the exploratory 'Ordinary Streets' project found that the practice of mutualism – namely subdividing commercial buildings on Rye Lane in Peckham into micro-premises able to house cupboard-sized phone shops, money transfer services and salons – meant that when it came to both number of businesses and people employed, Peckham town centre outstripped even the recently built Westfield Stratford shopping centre (2,100 and 13,400 respectively, compared with Westfield's 300 retail units and 8,500 jobs). Add the fact that many of these subdivided Rye Lane premises are rented on cheap, flexible, pop-up style leases, thereby circumventing the initial outlay that is another barrier to entry for immigrant heritage business owners, and they feel all the more nimble and ingenious.

However, to look at these African small businesses as merely representative of multicultural triumph would, again, be overly simplistic. True, the visibility of Black African and Afro-Caribbean-oriented shops and market stalls speaks to how well established London's Black community has become. What's more, the ready availability of ingredients and goods that previous generations of Black African settlers could only dream of accessing in the UK signals a hard-won collapsing of the distance between indigenous life and life in diaspora. And yet the complexities and challenges of this world can always be discerned.

High street remittance businesses – places, for the uninitiated, where you can send money back home – offer a daily reminder that a large portion of London's African immigrant population are constantly battling to send funds to those with even less. Subdivided businesses – hastily built structures where different entrepreneurs operate cheek-by-jowl – indicate the struggle to find space, in community markets that are increasingly under threat of effectively being gentrified out of existence. Black African entrepreneurialism, for all its supposed prominence in places like Brixton and Peckham and Dalston, is fraught with difficulty and impermanence; a harsh reality borne out by the fact that, as per figures released in 2021, just 11.2 per cent of Britain's Black worker population are self-employed, the lowest number by ethnicity, compared with 23.2 per cent of workers from the combined Pakistani and Bangladeshi ethnic group. In these figures, we can glimpse something of the long-running, ongoing battle to assume ownership of the businesses that serve the Black community.

So, it is true. African and Afro-Caribbean traders lining streets like Ridley Road are a vivid, evocative sign of Black fortitude, adaptability and connection to home. But they are also symbols of continued struggle; sacred, emotionally resonant and fundamentally egalitarian spaces mortally threatened by the ravages of urban regeneration and a social landscape redrawn by the pandemic. Yes, Black African presence in London's markets can be a portal to many things. And you only need to look back to see why these are portals worth preserving.

I am pretty sure that the first time I ever tried genuine West African suya, the thin-cut, fearsomely spiced Northern Nigerian barbecued beef sold all across the world, it had been smuggled into the country by a relative. Bought on a Lagos roadside, frozen pre-flight and stashed in an odour-blocking tin within their hand luggage, it had nonetheless lost nothing in transit; brown, peppery strips of meat, almost transformed into a bovine crumb, and crash-landing on the palate as an intoxicating rush of salt, Cameroonian pepper heat and groundnut sweetness. It was the catalyst for a long-standing addiction that has involved eating it at Peckham hole-in-the-walls, on Nigerian beaches and at more than one funeral. But what I didn't realize at the time of that first, contraband delivery was that I was actually playing my part in a long-standing tradition of indigenous foodstuffs being muled from Africa to the UK. Because the available historic record is pretty clear on this: before there were African restaurants, specialist African supermarkets or even Afro-Caribbean fruits and vegetables readily available on London's streets, there were ingredients either posted or surreptitiously stashed in suitcases.

'I write my mother that I was in White country, and I miss ... our African food,' that was how Opeolu Solanke-Ogunbiyi, matron of the pioneering West African Students' Union (WASU) hostel and author of a 2009 memoir, described the yearning she felt while in London during 1933. She and her husband, WASU founder and barrister Ladipo Solanke, were there establishing their headquarters and a vibrant social hub for the interwar period's growing community of Black African overseas students. Later in her memoir, Solanke-Ogunbiyi goes on to describe the consignments of specific ingredients her mother dries and ships to Tilbury ('Dried fish, dried ewedu, dried okra, dried bitterleaf [spinach-like greens used in West African soups] ...') not just to sate her own cravings but also to help fuel the small restaurant within WASU. The sense is that these deliveries were legal. But, food writer Yẹmisí Aríbisálà, in her book *Longthroat Memoirs*, encapsulates the situation that those in the nascent Nigerian diaspora would have experienced during much of the early to mid-twentieth century and beyond. 'If Nigerian restaurants were so easily replaced by others,' she writes, 'we would not need entire Nigerian food sections in London's Brixton Market, or customs officers at the airport collecting bribes to turn a blind eye to dried afang wrapped in old newspapers and hidden in underwear bags.' It's a vivid description of the lengths Africans in London would, anecdotally, routinely go to (and, as evidenced by that smuggled suya, will still go to) in order to scratch a particular culinary itch. But, more than that, it tells you something of the importance that specific ingredients and tastes held for Black African and Afro-Caribbean communities in London, particularly during the interwar and post-war periods; how they tried to combat the unfamiliarity of life in the cold, perplexing and demanding metropole with some form of familiarity on their plates.

And in this, the fake-it-until-you-can-make-it era, Africans and Caribbeans would have to get especially creative to make versions of their food with what was available in Britain. Solanke-Ogunbiyi describes using ground rice instead of gari – the fermented cassava flour whipped into a smooth accompaniment for stews – in dishes during the 1930s. Bernice Green, a participant in the British Library's oral history project examining Caribbean foodways in Britain, explains how in 1960s London her family grated carrot into a dish to impart the orange tinge of pumpkin stew in lieu of any actual pumpkins.

In the end, though pioneering food stalls in places like Brixton and Shepherd's Bush began stocking products to appeal to an increasingly West Indian clientele, salvation came in the form of other immigrant communities. Specifically, it was butchers and grocers serving London's Jewish diaspora who recognized shared tastes – for oxtails, old layer chickens, tongues and trotters – among their traditional customer base and both Afro-Caribbean and Black African locals. Green, again, talks about Ridley Road being one of the first places where predominantly Jewish traders began, in the late 1950s and early 1960s, to source produce specifically geared towards the Black diaspora. 'There was a Jewish man on the corner, Regent Groceries,' she says. 'And when I explained to him the rice I wanted, he used to get things to suit me . . . It was lots of stalls with Jewish people. There was not a Caribbean person selling in the market there. All Jewish. And they would ask you what you want, what you're missing, and they would make enquiries about getting them for you. And that is how Ridley Road spread to being such a market for Black people.'

This status that Ridley Road, and other markets like it, held as a rare place where an atomized and often harassed Black population could freely congregate is key. Procuring non-native ingredients became something of a sacred weekly act; particularly vital because of the possibility it afforded to connect to both your roots and other Black Africans and Afro-Caribbeans making their bewildered way through the capital. As the African American writer Henry Louis Gates Jr put it in *Black London*, his 1976 dispatch from the capital's unlicensed 'blues parties', African churches and 'the ritual of the gut' that occurred in places like Ridley Road and Brixton: 'Market Day means keeping one's stomach in tune with the Islands, at the expense of salted fish and chips or steak and kidney pie.'

There was a power in the availability of Black produce, then. But the hands that this power was concentrated in came to be an issue. 'We used to go to a shop called Charlie's in Kilburn,' explains Nky Iweka, a British-Nigerian chef, cookbook author and restaurateur who grew up in 1980s London. 'Charlie was a White, Irish guy, and I remember that he'd have the red onions and would be like, "Oh, they're from Nigeria." And they would be so expensive. God, he made a fortune, that man.' This point about the inflated sums African Londoners would willingly pay for specialist imported goods is delivered with a smile. But it conceals an important truth. The sense of gratitude and migrant fellowship that shoppers like Bernice Green felt in the post-*Windrush* era began to dwindle; White traders profiting off London's Black community became a point of contention and, you imagine, the subject of much disgruntled teeth-kissing in the queue. And by the time the 1980s and 1990s rolled around, when shops predominantly run by the South Asian community had effectively cornered the market on cassava, plantain, palm oil and any number of other Black household essentials, it had become a widely acknowledged sticking point. Why, came the repeated question, were Black Africans and Afro-Caribbeans lining the pockets of shop owners and stall holders with no connection to the community or affinity with the products they were selling their Black customers?

In the field of Black hair and beauty products – a billion-pound industry in the UK alone – this frustration has, at times, felt especially pronounced. With Black women spending six times as much as their White counterparts on hair products, the historic lack of genuinely Black-owned cosmetics businesses on London high streets has come to carry a deeper significance within the community. You could say that this issue is about purchasing power, ownership, cultural pride and an intangible sense that, beyond the cold, hard transactional process of money changing hands for goods, you should only offer your eager patronage to someone who understands and appreciates your need.

As the writer Yomi Adegoke noted, in a 2016 story on the issue, 'Many of the existing male vendors [in South Asian-owned hair shops] simply don't know enough about Black female hair because, well, they don't have it. And unlike e-cigs and electronics, there's no shorthand guide on how it all works.'

It is worth treading carefully here, with full awareness that tensions between London's Black and South Asian diasporas have traditionally been rooted in misplaced intra-ethnic bigotry and suspicion. But the idea that the Black community could move to the other side of the counter, and seize control of the businesses that were increasingly central to their lives in London, was clearly a hugely meaningful one. That was the broader context, anyway. For Eugene Takwa, a Cameroon-born shopkeeper who opened Woolwich's African Cash and Carry, initially alongside his brother, in 1987, establishing a Black-owned retail business was a simple matter of recognizing what was missing from the landscape.

'At that time, you had to go to Dalston, Brixton or Lewisham, and most of them were Asian shops,' says Takwa, from behind his counter, lean and stern in jeans and woollen black hat, in an accent that still carries more than a hint of his homeland. 'Very few Africans had shops. And it was more that there were certain things that Asian [shopkeepers] wouldn't know to import. Things like African vegetables. Yam and cassava was already coming from South America. But certain things like African spices, and ewedu and bitterleaf. Those were really out of the question, and you couldn't get them unless you travelled.'

Over in West London, a few years later, Nigerian-born Monsurat 'Iyabo' Obisesan was having a similar epiphany about another relatively untapped part of town. 'My aunt used to live in Chiswick, and she told me there were no African shops in Shepherd's Bush,' she explains. 'Just an Asian one. But because they don't eat our food, they wouldn't have all those fresh vegetables. That was what pushed me and encouraged me.'

Obisesan is small and bustling, with a strikingly beautiful face beneath her tight-wrapped headscarf and the fast, easy intimacy of someone who runs a public-facing business. By 1996, she had opened her first stall in Shepherd's Bush market. And this era of the late 1980s and early-to-mid 1990s can be viewed as a specific boom time for African-owned and specifically African-oriented businesses, encompassing Takwa's and Obisesan's, plus John & Biola's Foods in Camberwell, and Bims African Food Store, a neighbourhood institution on Peckham's Rye Lane, run by the politician and community fixture, the late Bola Amole.

You could say that this surge of business ownership was merely a reflection of the stage Black African settlers – and, primarily, West African settlers – had reached; an inevitable marker of the social progression of the generation that arrived here in the 1980s. Yet the speed at which many of these ventures were established – the ambition and desire that is embodied in each bakery, remittance desk or burgeoning import/export empire – speaks, to me, of an acute, deeper yearning among Black Africans to be their own bosses. Nigerians especially are, in my experience, entrepreneurial to an almost pathological degree. In addition to their day jobs, my older relatives have, at various points, run franchised pick-and-mix kiosks, hired out crockery for events and offered computer training classes on the side.

After receiving a voluntary redundancy payout from her administrative job at the Commonwealth, my mother opened an internet café that, though it ultimately became a costly and burdensome enterprise, still ranks to her as the realization of a lifelong dream. I cannot picture myself at a family party without also hearing a bellowing chorus of uncles, talking all at once about their hypothetical business ideas.

Obviously, this kind of industriousness is a universal hallmark of the immigrant experience; a means to combat the foreign newcomer's unfavourable odds. But active side hustles – driving taxis, catering parties, working evening cleaning jobs – have long cut across class borders and been part of the accepted reality of what it is to be Black African in diaspora. It is a proactiveness shaped by both natural, burning ambition and the understanding that, within the disorienting machine of traditional Western employment, opportunities will not necessarily be meted out fairly. 'I used to work in a bank in Nigeria,' says Obisesan, who also spent some time selling jewellery in Italy and Switzerland. 'And I was thinking that I wanted to do that in this country. But, you know, at that time it wasn't easy for a Black person to get work in a bank.' She laughs. 'And most of the time that I tried to work for other people, I would just get fed up with it and something would make me leave the job.' In this light, London's African-owned businesses are really just the most obvious, visible expressions of a deeper, intangible longing. Namely, a desire for agency, for autonomy, and for the kind of cash-in-hand, person-to-person businesses that could prosper away from the restraints of White society.

Interviewed for Gates Jr's *Black London*, the Jamaican-born photographer Armet Francis lands on the idea that, for the older generation of *Windrush*-era migrants, the Caribbean way of life was something to be actively sustained and sought out in specific Black spaces; that it was 'an alive thing . . . in the form of a memory they nurture through dances and through the marketplace, and especially through the church'. The same, you'd venture, can be said of the more Afrocentric Black businesses that have proliferated in the last 30 years.

Yes, they are significant in terms of the customer and the relative ease with which Africans can now access ingredients and products that would once have had to be smuggled into suitcases, privately shipped here in dried form, or inventively synthesized from what could be found in a British post-war larder. But London's Black African shops were and are just as significant for the person on the other side of the counter. Not just because there was a good deal of collective self-esteem bound up in seizing control of the businesses that most actively served the community, but also because they offered an alternative route to employment, social advancement and the promised land of self-sufficiency in the metropole; a space and localized, diaspora-specific economy where the Africanness that made the world of mainstream work harder to access could be repurposed as a huge financial and professional benefit.

It is notable that, in contrast to the South Asian and East Asian communities that gained a generational foothold in the UK through establishing mass-appeal businesses in the fields of retail, restaurants and takeaway food, African British entrepreneurialism has historically been centred on specifically African (and, by extension, Black) need.

Or, as a woman called Maria, the squat, beanie-hatted proprietor of Victory Convenience Store, a crammed cornucopia of African goods on Ridley Road, put it to me on a blustery winter morning: 'It's not so easy to get a job out there these days.' She gestured with her head beyond the open doors of her shop; out towards the frustrating, unfair Western world that lay beyond the dented tins of Milo instant chocolate drink, the bags of dried crayfish and the Sellotape-wrapped bales of stockfish that marked this little, raggedly cultivated patch of African familiarity. Ultimately, Black African-owned high street businesses offer a chance for customer and trader alike to do things as they would in their respective mother countries. To find, as Gates Jr had it, 'a city block full of Black folk who speak the same tongues'. What the shops in African London's market spaces offer, really, is the chance to conduct yourself as you would back home. But that, as these traders would learn the hard way, is a proposition racked with its own unique difficulties and complications.

Even on a quiet weekday morning, TM African Foods is a scene; a whirl of colour and dazzling brightness and the kind of brusque, warm interaction that feels definably African. In this space, set hard against Goldhawk Road in West London and beyond an unremarkable blue-on-yellow sign, are bottles of luridly orange African Fanta, heaped sacks of Tilda rice, display baskets of smoked mackerel and gilded packets of dried spices all flashing beneath the clinically white strip-lighting. Here, despite the teetering roll call of familiar labels on the shelves – Ovaltine malted chocolate, Exeter corned beef, Robb muscular ointment – is atypical order and cleanliness; a scent that holds freshness and a back note of ginger, rather than the mothballed dankness that generally accompanies imported African goods and leaps unbidden from the suitcases of just-arrived relatives from the motherland. And here, conducting it all as customers file in and out seeking pale garden eggs and okra and squishy loaves of sweetened bread, is Obisesan, a fixture of this neighbourhood for more than 25 years and the diminutive force who maintains some sort of order.

'Mr Chas,' she calls out to the tall, only sporadically seen man who appears to be her sole employee. He skulks into view near the back of the shop, beside the clear bags of raw shea butter. 'Please. Bring two boxes of chicken Indomie up from downstairs,' she says, referring to the Indonesian instant noodle brand that is wildly popular among Nigerians. Then she is pricing up a sheaf of foil takeaway containers for a woman making moin-moin (the pale orange Nigerian bean curd cake) for an event, confirming to a passing man that, yes, the plantain is still three for £1 and beckoning in a pensionable shopper in a drooping face mask. 'Your chair is there, sister,' she says gently, as the older woman takes a seat at the back, amid some boxes. Later on, Obisesan will talk about the unusually close, reciprocal and almost familial relationship she has with her customers 'They were the ones that really encouraged and supported me to start,' she says. On the rare occasions she has returned to Nigeria on holiday, she has received multiple panicked messages from regulars who fear she has closed down forever.

The same is true south of the river, in Takwa's shop, where the bundles of potato leaf often come with a side order of philosophy, a revealing nugget of information about the local community's buying habits (West African palm-frond brooms are, apparently, increasingly popular among South-East London's Chinese population) and some jockeying over price. And so, to stand among the happily chaotic thrum of these places is to seal it: Black African and Afro-Caribbean shops are about much, much more than the act of merely buying goods or services. They are that rare place where the impersonal, clenched world of London recedes and is replaced with something warmer, louder and more familiar. To put it simply, you cannot sit down and hang out for a while in the middle of Tesco; you cannot, as Obisesan's customers do, call ahead on the phone to ask for some jollof rice seasoning or premium Ghana gari to be put aside for you.

'Sometimes when you're in these places and observing what's going on, there's not even a money exchange,' says the Jamaican-born historian Aleema Gray. 'People just go in there for a chat. Or because they're building a house back home and want advice. These places are central to how people in a community thrive and survive.' Gray would know this more than most. Quite some distance from the stereotypical idea of a museum worker – the island lilt of her voice and her thickly bundled dreadlocks act as clues that she was raised as a practising Rastafarian by her Jamaican parents – she was nonetheless the driving force and curator behind Feeding Black, an exhibition that ran at the Museum of London Docklands between 2021 and 2022, and sought to explore the significance and impact of four Black-owned, South-London-based food businesses. Through recorded oral histories, photography, and artefacts plucked from the shelves of the businesses, Feeding Black underlined the acute closeness of the customer-shopkeeper relationship within London's Black African and Afro-Caribbean communities. 'Brother Junior [the Jamaican-born owner of long-standing Woolwich-based greengrocers Junior's Caribbean Stall] described his job as being like a social worker,' says Gray with a smile.

But even that might be selling it short. Black shopkeepers, and by extension their shops, act as a mirror for the ebb and flow of their communities as they evolve over the years. Obisesan, who has had to keep pace with demand shaped by a growing Congolese and Sierra Leonean clientele, notes that most of her products are 'things people have asked for'. In the 1990s, Takwa's product knowledge had to adapt to a sudden influx of Ugandans displaced by Idi Amin's regime. And, as Gray explains with a laugh, even Brother Junior affects a fake West African accent when he is serving Nigerian customers. These businesses, as borne out by their money transfer capabilities and the often bewildering array of items crammed into a small space, are crucial points of crossover and interchange for linked but distinct Black cultures. It is not especially surprising, for instance, to learn that the Ordinary Streets project discovered that 61 per cent of Peckham Rye's largely foreign-born business owners speak two to three different languages.

Takwa is in no doubt about the importance of his role in the community as sage, interpreter and human hard drive for a quarter of a century of mostly ignored Black British history. In fact, he sees his intimate, hyper-specific knowledge of the largely Black African clientele that he serves as the most valuable remaining weapon in his arsenal, amid rising competition and brutal pricing wars. 'In the last ten years, there have been more than twenty other Asian-owned shops that have opened in the area,' he says. 'I can't compete with them when it comes to price. But [I'm] still hanging on because of the product knowledge. Because I know what different countries go for, and if someone picks the wrong thing, I will tell them. One of the things that most customers know is that I won't lie to them. You can go to some African shops and they'll tell you anything in order to make a sale. But I won't. My goal in life has never been to be rich.'

However, one of the more crucial functions of these businesses brings us back to the lady taking a load off in TM African Foods. Simply put, Black African small businesses in particular, and local Black businesses in general, are spaces that are consciously set apart from the strictures of the White Western world. The behaviours that are implicitly permissible within a Black-owned shop – unhurried lingering, haggling on price, speaking at volume in thick-accented patois or pidgin or, perhaps, not even in English at all – signal a rare and treasured atmosphere of Black freedom, forged in these ostensible sites of commerce. Gray describes Brother Junior's stall as a place that, in contrast to her working life as a historian, 'makes me feel real'. Set against a historic backdrop of a Black London subject to colour bars, prejudice and overzealous policing, they are points of unobserved congregation; urban oases where you can unclench, exhale and be the unmodified version of yourself that wider British society implicitly asks you to muffle. I have felt it myself, pushing through the door at my barbers and entering an exclusively Black, male world of cranked dance-hall music, arguments, free-flowing Wray & Nephew rum, and, on some days, very, very few people actually getting their hair cut.

But what of the traders and business owners who find themselves conscripted into maintaining these precious (but, at times, quite challenging) spaces? The ones tasked with balancing the needs of their livelihood and a disinhibited clientele that, occasionally, expect bent rules, credit and abundant discounts? Well, for some, it is a tacit social contract that they understand and are (just about) happy to honour. 'Some people will come in, skip the queue, put any coin down and just say, "Take," before they walk out,' explains Obisesan, with a shake of her head. 'I don't take that from them any more. But sometimes, I will take some money off [the price of an item], just to keep the customer and make them happy.'

Takwa, who first came to London in 1986 to study marketing, takes a more hardline approach. And it is one that I see first-hand, when a bustling young Nigerian woman attempts – after much grousing about the unfairness of Takwa's prices – to pay one pound less for the three drooping bundles of potato leaf she has put on the counter. 'That's not my price,' says Takwa, calmly but firmly. 'That's your price.' After much clucking and complaint ('Don't be letting our things be too expensive, *oga*') she grudgingly pays, gathers her plastic bag and hustles out into the roar of Woolwich. To Takwa, stand-offs like this indicate both the tricky balance he has to strike as a Black shopkeeper and, in his view, the changing demographic make-up of his particular patch of African London.

'There has been an influx of people from African countries since the year 2000, and a lot of them behave like they are back home,' he says, citing 'aggressiveness' and customers that have attempted to get a refund on previously bought, perfectly fine vegetables he has sold. 'It's not even a question of class,' he adds. 'You see people who are hustlers; people who have crossed the Mediterranean or come through the desert and have that animal, survival instinct. [It's] something that you didn't have in the 1970s, 1980s or 1990s. But they have brought it here.' Though Takwa has a better vantage point on the community than most, it seems an extreme stance on what is, at its mildest, the theatre of haggling and a friction between buyers and sellers that has probably existed as long as markets have. But, for him, it isn't just about this perceived sensibility change among Britain's Black African diaspora. No, for Takwa it is also that the behaviour of some of his customers – the feeling, in his words, that 'they are doing me a favour by shopping here' – points to a deeper tension between Africa and Britain; between the old ways and the new.

'The thing with some Africans is that they want to be African when it suits them and European or English when *that* suits them,' he says, with a mischievous chuckle. 'Some people will come here and say, "The customer is always right." And then, these same people will say, "This is an African shop, you shouldn't do this. Your prices don't change. You're too stiff." To which I say, "Well, we either do it the European way, where the customer is always right and you don't argue about the price. Or you don't ask for a discount. Because you don't ask for a discount when you go into an English shop. You take the price and you pay it."'

Again, it is worth acknowledging that Takwa's stance on this is probably heavily flavoured by his 25 years of service behind the counter. For all the shared history and friendship he clearly has within the neighbourhood – for all the Woolwich locals who, like Gray, have known him since they were children – his is a world of shoplifters and counterfeit notes and customers seemingly always looking for confrontation with him. However, his portrait of the demands of his clientele helps to illustrate just how freighted with emotion and cultural importance Black African businesses can be. They are places where people go to be themselves. Places where they expect an unwritten, amorphous set of traditional expectations and needs to be met. They are, really, a locus for both the longing for home and the tussling contradictions of what it is to be simultaneously of both Africa and Britain. 'For some people', as Takwa observes, 'the body is here, but the mind is back home.'

By this logic, Black African-run shops and market stalls are environments where both body and mind can briefly be in concert. But serving this function for the community is clearly difficult to begin with: a study by the British Business Bank found that, in 2019, the average annual revenue for Black business owners was £10,000 less than that for White entrepreneurs – and especially draining to sustain. 'It's very stressful,' admits Obisesan, as she buzzes around her shop, calling out occasionally for the elusive Mr Chas. 'The customers, the deliveries, getting staff – those things are very challenging.' She pauses. 'But I have a passion for it. A lot of people open shops without that passion, and in the next six months it will close.'

Here we see the fragility of the ecosystem of Black shops and businesses in places like Shepherd's Bush, Woolwich, Dalston, Peckham and beyond; that, for all their cultural significance, they are really just one overworked person, trying to appease a community while swinging from one bill to the next. So what happens to these businesses when you throw in the transformative force of gentrification? Or a post-war Black African diaspora that is ageing, evolving and, in some cases, moving away from cities like London? How about if you add a generation-shifting pandemic, and all its unanticipated difficulties, consequences and social reconfigurations, into the mix? These businesses may embody bedraggled, purposefully laid-back sanctuaries of tradition to many, but – as evidenced by the complex, contradictory demands of the British Africans in Takwa's cash and carry – at some point the realities of the world outside tend to encroach. The march of time, especially in a city like London, cannot be outrun. And if the market is the beating heart of African London, then, in recent years, its fading pulse has been a little concerning.

Ridley Road Market's history has always been as much about conflict and politics as produce and community. In the early 1900s, when it was a ragged collection of traders controlled by the police force rather than the council, morning disputes over who got the best pitch would be settled with fist fights. In 1962, the British aristocrat and former MP Sir Oswald Mosley's British Union of Fascists, who had taken to staging neo-Nazi rallies on the street, were forcibly beaten back by a local consortium of Jews, anti-fascists and stallholders in an incident that made national news.

And so it holds that, on a bright, blue-skied late summer day in the second year of the coronavirus pandemic, the first thing I see at Ridley Road is a protestor, standing on a bench opposite Dalston Kingsland Station and addressing an ambivalent lunchtime crowd from his improvised pulpit. 'Leave our children alone,' he says into a raised megaphone, as other protestors circulate with pamphlets. 'No vaccine for our children!' Covid vaccine hesitancy in multicultural communities like this one is not exactly what has brought me here today; that, specifically, is a meeting with a local activist called Kieran Kirkwood. Yet this scene feels like a fitting metaphor for both the unpredictable crackle and energy of the market and what has been an especially fractious, challenging and emotional last few years for spaces like this. Not to mention the people who cherish them.

'When I think of the London that I love and that I'm a bit nostalgic for, it is the market that I think of,' says Kirkwood, once we have made contact, laughed a little at the scene around the protestors, and then made our way to a nearby café. 'Now I'm seeing it change every day and watching people getting displaced from these areas. And places where they can gather socially or get affordable food and drink slowly ebbing away.' Kirkwood, who prefers gender-neutral pronouns, is young and compact, of both Black Jamaican and White English heritage, and with hair combed into a striking blowout Afro. They grew up nearby in Stoke Newington and had history working with the (ultimately successful) campaign to save Tottenham's Latin Village from redevelopment. But, by their own admission, it was an incident in 2018 that finally prompted action closer to home and gave other members of the local community – which had been gentrifying at a frightening rate for at least the past 20 years – 'a catalyst and a clear point of resistance'. Specifically, the spark came in October of that year, when all the businesses within Ridley Shopping Village (a market-adjacent, indoor space made up of lots of Black African and Afro-Caribbean small businesses, plus affordable local artists' studios) were informed they would need to vacate the premises in two weeks as it was being turned into a mixed-use office, retail and housing block.

'We thought it must be illegal,' says Kirkwood of the eviction order. 'But it turned out their contracts did say [they were subject to only] 14 working days' notice. Which is fucked up, considering these are people's livelihoods we're talking about.' At that time, by Kirkwood's admission, the Shopping Village needed 'paint, new toilets, proper investment'. But this, in their view, is an example of 'managed decline'. The proposed new development would have featured five luxury flats and just 10 per cent of its workspaces designated as affordable.

It would not stand. And so, organizing under the umbrella of a newly formed group called Save Ridley Road, Kirkwood and other local activists protested against the move, organized a rally for the following week on 27 October 2018 (attended by more than 200 people) and, alongside the London Renters Union, marched on the West Hampstead offices of Rainbow Properties, the managing company representing the landlord of the building. This resulted in Rainbow withdrawing its eviction notice, a symbolic retreat that Kirkwood theorizes has had huge ramifications for all of Ridley Road Market, beyond the specific short-term future of the Shopping Village. 'If people from the community hadn't stepped in, the Shopping Village wouldn't be there, it would have been turned into some bullshit, and that would have been a big nail in the coffin for Ridley Road Market because it would have meant loads of disruption.'

When we meet, edging into late 2021, Save Ridley Road are celebrating another victory of sorts. Rainbow Properties has agreed to enter into a period of consultation with the campaign and Hackney Council, to discuss the future of redevelopment plans it had updated. Kirkwood, though wary of the ensuing consultation becoming 'a one-way thing from them', points to this recent success – the fruit of almost three years of campaigning – as an example of what it takes to prosper against those riding roughshod over a city's history. 'It feels like the fight to save Black London, basically,' says Kirkwood. 'Because where our communities live is in those social spaces, in markets, and in affordable housing and retail. The story of Ridley Road recently, and of this campaign, is something I use to talk to people who feel they haven't got much to believe in. The traders are still there. The market is still alive and kicking. If it wasn't for the campaign, I don't know what this place would look like, to be honest.'

That the complicated issue of urban regeneration affects all manner of communities, not just Black ones, is worth stressing. What's also notable, amid all this, is that it has taken activists like Kirkwood to fight on behalf of the traders and artists in Ridley Road Shopping Village. For the traders, the people these changes would most directly affect, the threat seemed intractable and hard to fully comprehend. And, again, this brings us into contact with the way Black businesses – and especially those adjacent to markets – often exist at a conscious remove from mainstream society. 'There was a lot of defeatism from the [Black] traders I spoke to,' adds Kirkwood. 'Some wanted to fight, but lots of them were talking about feeling this pressure of, not even the developer, but just society in general. When they say, "This is too big for us," they're talking about the whole system. There was a lot of mistrust as well. And mistrust of "activists" even coming and talking to people.'

This feeling of scepticism and wariness towards any form of authority – no doubt heightened by the legal grey area that trade around markets has traditionally occupied – is important. It is something I definitely felt as I roamed the market in the months after meeting Kirkwood, asking traders about the redevelopment plans, only to be met with either stony silence or the sort of noncommittal, one-word answers you'd imagine are reserved for particularly blatant undercover policemen. Maria, at Victory Convenience Store, when she wasn't ducking basic questions about how long she'd lived in London ('That's my privacy. You're going too far into my privacy'), only seemed dimly aware of the battle over Ridley Shopping Village in the sense it was something that might affect local parking. And this wariness towards, or lack of engagement with, the forces shaping their livelihoods, was a stance that Gray also discovered, throughout the interview process of Feeding Black.

'There's definitely an ambivalent relationship that Black-owned businesses have with the state,' she says. 'And there's an ambivalence within the community. It's like people saying, "You know, we're not sure about this vaccine thing. We're going to just be using our ointments and drinking our herbs."' With that, we are back to the anti-vaccine protestor with the megaphone standing at the mouth of Ridley Road, and the relevant issue of what effect Covid had on the Black African and Afro-Caribbean entrepreneurs in this already threatened ecosystem. The truth, as is often the case, is more complex than it first appears.

Naturally, months of lockdown, government-mandated closure, tricky-to-access financial support and staff and proprietors either falling ill or being forced to isolate represented an extinction-level event for plenty of Black high street businesses. A British Business Bank survey in 2020 found that 61 per cent of Asian and other minority-owned business enterprises had either paused or stopped permanently because of Covid. I saw my own universe of regular Black stop-offs shrink a little (either through a barber who never returned to his shop post-lockdown or Nigerian bakery Angel's keeping the shutters down on its Peckham branch for an indefinite period). And it seemed, thanks to both the crowded public spaces that are especially important to those of African and Caribbean heritage and the fact that those communities were in the high-risk category for the virus, that Covid carried an acutely high toll for the Black marketplace. 'People were already being isolated because of social cleansing,' suggests Kirkwood, 'and so the pandemic meant they were even more isolated because of social distancing.'

However, the contrasting view to all of this is that markets and shops became all the more crucial in this period. Especially during those fearful, early months of the pandemic. At a time when Britain's large supermarkets were characterized by long queues, jittery, ill-tempered shoppers, and shelves ransacked by people panic-buying flour, yeast and toilet roll London's local cash and carries became comparative nirvanas: dizzyingly well-stocked lands of plenty that were cheap and quick and offered a lifeline in terms of both specialized produce and human interaction. When I think of late spring in 2020, I think of myself roaming the aisles of a Turkish-run African supermarket in Catford, heaping a basket with the yams, Scotch bonnet peppers and bottles of palm oil I would regularly deliver to my mother as she spent the first throes of lockdown alone in her house.

What's more, money transfer businesses became even more of a lifeline throughout this period of global difficulty. Particularly for those Black African diasporas for whom remittance is especially crucial. 'Sending money home, whether you're Ghanaian or Somali, is a huge aspect of the economies of diaspora,' says Ismail Einashe, a British-Somali writer who wrote a 2020 article for the BBC about the strain felt in the money transfer pipeline during Covid. 'But Somalis transfer more than a billion pounds every year to Somalia – which is more than the country receives in aid. They are really important payments.' This was doubly true at a time when people on both continents were falling ill, losing work or, in many cases, having to find ways to help fund the family funerals that they would only be able to attend via Zoom. It's a reminder of just how vital the connection offered through businesses like Obisesan and Takwa's is. Not just to African London's well-being but also to its sense of self.

And what is striking is that the personal difficulties felt by London-based Somalis (and others in the community) during the pandemic – loss of work, the need to isolate or shield – did not impact the flow of money as drastically as many expected. 'At the beginning, in spring 2020, the World Bank and the IMF were thinking a lot of these crucial payments were going to end,' explains Einashe. 'But actually it didn't happen. The drop in the amount of money sent wasn't as bad as had been predicted. [The payments] didn't stop, because people in the diaspora made huge sacrifices.'

Of course, one of the other ways the pandemic affected business at African shops in particular was through the embrace of the herbal and natural remedies Gray references. Obisesan did a brisk trade in oruwo, the dried-bark anti-malarial that she keeps in plastic bottles behind her counter (next to the Agbo jedi root that's supposedly a remedy for piles). And Takwa lights up when I ask if he saw an uptick in demand for goods linked to health. 'Oh, the things we were selling,' he says with a gleeful whistle, before detailing the immunity-boosting kola nuts and tubs of the anti-inflammatory muscle rub Aboniki balm that were flying off his shelves. In the months before there was a readily available vaccine against Covid, these purported herbal solutions – covering everything from turmeric and ginger to plants with proven, if mild, anti-malarial properties – were heartily embraced by the Black community around the world. And then, in the months that followed November 2020, after the Oxford/AstraZeneca vaccine had been approved, fondness for these non-pharmaceutical protections – and misinformation about Covid disseminated on WhatsApp – was blamed by official bodies for the high rate of vaccine hesitancy among Britain's Black population. (By April 2021, 64 per cent of Black over-50s had been vaccinated, compared with 93 per cent of White people in the same age category). If you spent any time with Black Africans or Afro-Caribbeans throughout that first phase of the pandemic, you will know the pronounced, unwavering scepticism the emergence of the vaccine seemed to rouse in many of them. At this time, Black businesses offered a solution and a balm (often literal) to those worries.

If you are, as I am, a British-Nigerian with faith in both science and the vaccine – and you have been socialized and educated to implicitly trust institutions – it is tricky terrain to navigate. There is, of course, historic justification for Black communities displaying healthy suspicion when faced with medical remedies pushed by governments and big business. In 1994, for instance, a Pfizer anti-meningitis drug was responsible for 11 deaths in the Nigerian state of Kano. Further afield in the US, the notorious Tuskegee trials – which, starting in 1932, misled Black men in order to observe the effects of untreated syphilis – led to a 40-year scandal and dozens of preventable deaths. It is no surprise that these stories had particular weight in the midst of a global health crisis. But it is hard to shake the sense that, alongside the social disadvantages and employment patterns that made Britain's Black population especially susceptible to the virus, unfounded rumours about a perfectly safe vaccine were just another way for disadvantaged communities to bear the brunt of Covid's ravages.

Specifically, this applied to transmission-prone, multi-generational households that were the long-term consequence of prejudice within post-war housing. Elsewhere, it was unconscious ethnic bias within the NHS (in 2021, a Race and Health Observatory report found that 'ethnic inequalities in health outcomes are evident at every stage throughout the life course, from birth to death') fostering ill health and a justified sense of apprehension. As the historian David Olusoga noted in a 2021 *Guardian* column on the issue: 'The pandemic has acted like a vast searchlight, sweeping across society, illuminating unpleasant truths that were lurking in the darkness.' Decades of building inequality within society, so entrenched that successive British governments had struggled to identify it let alone meaningfully address it, were clarified by Covid. It was a tragic perfect storm, with Black life at its centre.

The altered landscape of lockdown and the drift towards those natural Covid remedies (however contentious they were) gave small, market-adjacent Black businesses an undoubted boost. But if we are to take anything from London's shifting landscape – and, specifically, the succession of campaigns launched to try to preserve these markets and cherished immigrant-run businesses – then it can look as though these spaces are fighting a losing battle. The tide of history might be against them. Partly this is generational. As is often the case with immigrants who establish small retail businesses so their children may have better opportunities, there is a question of succession. 'My children are not interested in taking over,' says Obisesan, with a tinge of regret. 'Before they went to uni they used to really help me, but now they are really not interested. This is the problem. Sometimes I sit down and think, "Let's say tomorrow I retire. Is there a young person to take over the shop? Or even anybody my age?" It's a lot of challenges and it's hard. My brother, it is not easy.'

Gray, for her part, tends to agree that the people currently running these businesses in the Black community – and those frequenting them – may represent the last of a dying breed. 'I'm quite pessimistic because, really, these places are only appealing to the older generation,' she says. 'I don't want to generalize. I'm young. But we care more about pictures, what we can put on the 'Gram and that whole performance. I think we're making a move towards things that have that online appeal.' This is a theory borne out by the emergence, in recent years, of Black African and Afro-Caribbean services like the app Oja and the online grocery delivery operation Trap Fruits: slick, digitally savvy companies that carry some of the spirit of the Black businesses that are their forbears without replicating their dusty, defiantly analogue personal touch.

And then, of course, there is the unstoppable, oat milk tsunami of gentrification. Early 2022 brought the welcome news that, thanks to the Save Ridley Road campaign, Hackney Council agreed to take over management of the ShoppingVillage, listed it as an Asset of Community Value and vowed to sensitively update facilities, offer stability to current tenants and preserve it as an indoor market for the next generation. But, just to further highlight the game of redevelopment Whac-A-Mole that tends to dog immigrant-run businesses in London, Takwa has learned that the days of his cash and carry are numbered. In late 2021, long-brewing plans to transform the area around Woolwich Arsenal Station, a vital connecting point for the delayed, £18.7 billion Crossrail project, were approved by the council. Subject to the signing of a compulsory purchase order (as detailed on a crumpled letter that is pushed my way over the counter), Takwa's place, and many of the other phone shops, butchers and takeaway businesses that have stood near it for years, will in the coming months be moved on, replaced by a £400 million development comprising accommodation, a restaurant and a cinema. More than 25 years of local immigrant history is about to be razed or relocated. But Takwa is typically sanguine and unemotional about his disappearing business and legacy – and whether there would be any value in mounting a Ridley Road-style objection.

'Whether you fight it or not, it's not going to change anything,' he says. 'The council has approved the plan, and it will be a maximum of two more years. I still want to retire. I'm sixty-five and I'll be sixty-six this year.' Add in the fact that the pandemic has led to Black Africans and Afro-Caribbeans of all generations leaving the country ('I really think the pandemic has made people question this idea of home,' says Gray. 'Lots of people [my age] are going to Nigeria, they're going to Jamaica') and it makes the Black marketplace that has grown so impressively in recent years look all the more endangered.

However, I am not so sure. Yes, in contrast to the boom years of the 1980s and 1990s, it seems to be getting increasingly difficult to sustain these businesses. The odds remain firmly stacked against Black entrepreneurs trying to build an empire from nothing more than a market stall and a bulk order of imported goods. And, true enough, there is clearly a generational drift from the tradition of aunties proudly wheeling a granny bag to places like Peckham or Brixton or Ridley Road. But the embrace of herbal Covid remedies during the pandemic, for all its attendant issues, showed the enduring power and importance of these spaces, and that, amid the grief, chaos and restrictive isolation of the pandemic, Black Africans and Afro-Caribbeans clung to the traditional and the familiar – found solace in solutions steeped in a precolonial past and ancestral knowledge. If something is already old, and proven, then it never goes out of fashion. It's relevant that, more often than not, African supermarkets are places to get traditional brooms, the chewing sticks, or *pako Ijebu*, that West Africans use as an oral hygiene aid, and calabash bowls made from hollowed-out gourds. And so as long as there are Black African Brits craving connection, a portal, and that intangible sense of home, there will be these businesses and people running them.

Because, really, if these places are anything, then they are purveyors of cultural continuity; spaces that uphold the important idea that, even in a world of Dyson vacuum cleaners, electric toothbrushes and expensive ceramics, there is a value, grace and power in the old and supposedly outmoded way of doing things.

INTRODUCTION
FROM NOSE TO TAIL EATING

Anthony Bourdain

In the *New Yorker*, Helen Rosner wrote of **Anthony Bourdain** that he is 'a television megastar, a fluid and conversational writer, a social-media gadfly, a pointed cultural commentator, and seemingly everyone's best friend'. His *New Yorker* essay 'Don't Eat Before Reading This', a warts-and-all (actually, a tough-steak-old-fish-cigarettes-and-all) piece about his time in New York City restaurants, became the basis for his bestseller *Kitchen Confidential: Adventures in the Culinary Underbelly*. He was a chef and critic who felt at home among 'short ribs, oxtail, beef shoulder, cabbage, turnips, carrots, and potatoes'; his ecstatic introduction for Fergus Henderson's *Nose to Tail Eating* seems entirely in keeping with this.

The book you hold in your hand has been considered, for too many years, to be a cult masterpiece, an obscure project of desire for chefs, food writers, cookbook collectors and international foodies, yearned for, sought out, searched for by those who didn't own a copy, cherished and protected by those lucky few who did. Published in 1999, copies quickly began to disappear. A few lucky chefs would return from their pilgrimages to The Restaurant, glassy-eyed, like new converts, smiling serenely. They wouldn't brag about their find. (They might then be asked to lend their copies.) They didn't show them around – The Book might become damaged or smudged. Once in a great while, when a fellow chef, or intensely curious gourmet would raise the subject, some might let slip with quiet understatement, 'Oh yeah. I have a copy. I bought it at The Restaurant.' This would usually be followed by a long moment of pained silence as others less fortunate ground their teeth and clenched their fists with envy.

Fergus Henderson's magnificent, legendary *Nose to Tail Eating*, now re-issued is an historic document which flew in the face of accepted culinary doctrine, both as proud proclamation of the true glories of pork, offal and the neglected bits of animals we love to eat, and as a refutation of the once deeply held belief that the English couldn't, and never could, cook. The Restaurant, St. John, when it first opened in London's then-off-the-beaten-path Smithfield district, had an electrifying effect on chefs who ate there – and this Book helped spread the word. You could make a good argument that Fergus Henderson's early and unpredictable success in a plain whitewashed room on St. John Street in London made it permissible for all of us – chefs as far away as New York, San Francisco and Portland – to reconsider dishes and menu items which were once the very foundations of French, Italian and yes, even American cuisine. Every time you see pork belly or bone marrow, kidneys or trotters (increasingly 'hot' offerings) on an American menu, you might well owe a debt of thanks to Fergus who showed so many of us the way – who allowed chefs who might otherwise have feared to do so to go against the tide. Anytime you see cheeks, tripes or marrow on a New York City menu, you can feel the ripples of his influence – and the special place he holds in the affections of his fellow chefs.

After eating the Roast Bone Marrow and Parsley Salad at St. John, I declared it my always and forever choice for 'Death Row Meal', the last meal I'd choose to put in my mouth before they turned up the juice. Every subsequent experience at The Restaurant hit me like a percussion grenade: an eye-opening, inspiring, thoroughly pleasurable yet stripped down adventure in dining, a nonsense-free exaltation of what's good – and has always been good – about food and cooking at its best. Like many of St. John's customers, I immediately became annoyingly evangelical on the subject, attributing to Fergus all kinds of revolutionary/reactionary socio-political motives. My enthusiastic rant in my book *A Cook's Tour* made him sound like George Washington, Ho Chi Minh, Lord Nelson, Orson

Welles, Pablo Picasso and Abbie Hoffman all rolled into one. I saw his simple, honest, traditional English country fare as a thumb in the eye to the establishment, an outrageously timed head butt to the growing hordes of politically correct, the PETA people, the European Union, practitioners of an arch, ironic Fusion Cuisine and all those chefs who were fussing about with tall, overly sculpted entrées of little substance and less soul.

I'm sure I embarrassed him. Because, of course, Fergus Henderson is no bomb-throwing ideologue. I doubt very much if the words 'cutting edge' ever occurred to him. I'm quite sure, now that I've come to know him, that he in no way saw the lovely, unassuming and unpretentious food in this book to be an insult or an affront to anyone, much less a statement of any kind. It is instead, I think, a reminder – and a respectful one at that – of what is good about food – about the essential, nearly forgotten elements of a great meal, a homage, an honouring of the foodstuffs we eat, a refutation of nothing more than waste and disregard. If *Nose to Tail* makes a statement, it's that nearly every part of nearly everything we eat can be delicious in the hands of a patient and talented cook – something most good cooks and most French and Italian mothers have known for centuries. It honours the past at least as much as it points the way to a brave new future. This is fundamentally, though, a book about simple, good things.

Ask any chef of any three-star Michelin restaurant what their favourite single dish to eat is and you will often get an answer like 'confit of duck' or 'my mother's pied cochon' or 'a well braised shank of lamb or veal'. These were the dishes that first taught many of us to cook, the absolute foundation of haute cuisine. Nearly anyone – after a few tries – can grill a filet mignon or a sirloin steak. A trained chimp can steam a lobster. But it takes love, and time and respect for one's ingredients to deal with a pig's ear or a kidney properly. And the rewards are enormous. The Crispy Pigs' Tails at St. John are some of the most delicious things you will ever put in your mouth. And while it's easy to associate St. John and Fergus with unrestrained carnivorousness, he brings the same appreciation for every part of the ingredient to seafood: his Soft Roes on Toast, an elementary presentation of a particular issue of herring, is destined to be – one day – the next big thing on New York menus, a 'where have you been my whole life?' appetizer.

St. John has quickly become a must-try in the international travelling chef circuit. Chefs, foodies, food writers and cooks on sabbatical, travelling perhaps through the great multi-starred restaurants of London, France and Spain often stop there for a taste of the real, to find out what all the buzz is about. Who IS this Fergus Henderson? WHY do people who visit his restaurant and eat his food return with glazed, blissful, and strangely knowing looks on their faces? I remember with pleasure, a few years ago, walking into a hot restaurant on New York's Lower East Side and seeing Fergus's Roast Bone Marrow and Parsley Salad reproduced, note for note, on the menu – and the comforting sense of recognition that I had a soulmate in their kitchen. That the chef, whoever she was, was 'one of us', somebody who'd 'been', someone hip to the restaurant that so many of us would love to run but for various reasons, just can't.

Scared? Intimidated? Grossed out? Put off by memories of Mom, or some long ago lunch lady, coming at you with a slab of ineptly and indifferently fried liver, or by some comedian's jokes about haggis? Does the phrase 'Eat IT! It's good for you!' still strike fear in your heart? Consider the following incident, at a recent special meal held at Portland's Heathman Restaurant. The menu, in my honour, consisted entirely of offal and nasty bits: kidneys, livers, cockscombs, brawn and sweetbreads. The entering crowd bore expressions ranging from apprehensive to hopeful. It was the older customers who looked the most optimistic. They remembered the early days of American menus, when ox heart and tripe bore no mysteries, and they recalled those things with pleasure. Southerners, who had never forgotten chitterlings and pigs' feet and hog maws, seemed almost misty-eyed. And culinary novices – young cooks, heavily pierced and tattooed metalheads, thin, well dressed adventuresses, practitioners of 'extreme' eating who saw the night's fare, perhaps, as an extension of 'extreme' sports – all came looking excited but uncertain. To see the expression on their faces after a few bites of rabbit kidney or sweetbread was a beautiful thing. A moment of recognition, a calming, reassuring wave of satisfaction, the dawning knowledge that yes, this can be good. I like it. I love it. I want it again.

Of course, it's not all hooves and snouts and guts. Lamb and Barley Stew, Roast Woodcock, Mutton and Beans, Jugged Hare, Kedgeree and Boiled Ham and Parsley Sauce are about as unthreatening as you can get: simple, nourishing, beautiful to gaze upon; country cooking at its very finest. Skate, Capers and Bread and Devilled Crab should not frighten – only delight – even the most conservative eater and will hopefully lure them into deeper waters. Warm Pig's Head should make a convert of anyone who thought they'd never eat a dish with 'head' in its name. It is a dish so wonderful, so goddamn amazing that it borders on religious epiphany.

Fergus Henderson is a quiet, modest man, prone to dry statements – as when contemplating a roast suckling pig: 'This was a noble animal. A happy pig.' But he inspires hyperbole in others. First-time visitors to St. John frequently come away transformed and raving about the experience. A trip to the bare, abattoir-like space becomes a voyage of discovery – or, more accurately, of re-discovery; of long forgotten childhoods, or childhoods we never had but somehow had always yearned for. It is my favourite restaurant in the world, and I suspect a lot of people share my devotion. Hopefully, these pages will be the start of your own voyage. Welcome to the club.

Anthony Bourdain
2004

NOSE TO TAIL EATING

Fergus Henderson

The king of 'nose to tail eating', **Fergus Henderson** OBE has no formal culinary training and a Michelin star. Fergus and his wife Margot share not only three children, but also a culinary empire that has redefined British cooking. Half the chefs in London have learnt from the Hendersons' St John/Rochelle Canteen restaurant empire, where there is famously no music, no art, no flowers and no colour except the extraordinary food on the plates. Their cooking popularised the now universally recognised importance of local, seasonal, thoughtful food, and has also been described as '400 years out of date'.

Four Things I Should Mention

When having lunch at Sweetings, you sit at a bar behind which a waiter is trapped, you order your smoked eel, they yell to a runner who delivers your eel over your shoulder to the waiter, who then places it under the counter and then in front of you as if they had it all along. Not an entirely practical way of getting your food, but a splendid eating ritual, and a wonderful lunch.

'Nose to Tail Eating' means it would be disingenuous to the animal not to make the most of the whole beast; there is a set of delights, textural and flavoursome, which lie beyond the fillet.

This is a book about cooking and eating at home with friends and relations, not replicating restaurant plates of food.

Do not be afraid of cooking, as your ingredients will know, and misbehave. Enjoy your cooking and the food will behave; moreover it will pass your pleasure on to those who eat it.

HOMECOMING: VOICES OF THE WINDRUSH GENERATION

Colin Grant

Colin Grant is a British writer and historian of Jamaican origin. He is the author of six books, a Fellow of the Royal Society of Literature, a teacher of creative non-fiction writing, and has written for the *Guardian, Observer, New Statesman, TLS, London Review of Books, Granta* and *New York Review of Books*. His most recent book, *Homecoming: Voices of the Windrush Generation*, draws on over a hundred first-hand interviews, and is an oral history of Caribbean British lives in postwar Britain. He and his family live in Brighton.

Bert Williams

Oh man, it was just eat, because you don't taste; when I first came here to England we used to buy the English mustard just to let the food have a bit of taste. We used to get pepper sauce from home.

We couldn't even get rice; we used to get that Carolina rice, which is a split rice which the English use for rice pudding.

Shirley Williams

And Indian pickles, mum used to bottle it up in plastic bottles and send it from Guiana, because dad used to get free plastic bottles from his job as a pharmacist, and she'd secure it with reels of tape so it didn't leak, and pack them in the boxes for me.

Bert Williams

One good thing. When we first came here, the butcher wouldn't charge you for trotters and pig's tail at that time, and pig's head. The ears and things. That was a nice part, because we used to use a pig's tail in the soup, so you'd boil the peas with the pigtail in and then you'd put your rice in. That's beautiful.

But if we wanted proper rice we had to either go to Brixton to get it or send word, so people from London would come down visiting and they'd bring it. My brother and sister would come down and bring yam and cassava and coco; that sort of thing, you couldn't get that in Brighton at all. They would bring plantain, sorrel, a lot of Jamaican product. But they might only come every two months – like you see in the prisoner of war films. But what we did, we bought the ordinary food, the beef and the chicken, and we just do what we'd do in the Caribbean with it, if you do fried chickens or curries or anything like that.

Agnes DeAbreu

I missed the kind of food you could get back home. It wasn't just the food, though, is how we cook it. It was funny how some things were more primitive than back home. Even though back in St Vincent we didn't have a stove, we had a wood fire. Our kitchen was separate, not in the house. We used to cook what we grew on the land. Unfortunately there was not many places to get Caribbean food but there was a shop owned by an English lady and she used to try and get yam. I don't know where from but she could get it.

Ethlyn Adams

It was just Mrs Henry selling West Indian food in Luton, in the market. Bageye [my husband] used to cuss some bad words, say she charge too much. No one else was selling so you had to go to her. You'd go for a pound of yam, long so, and the end bit would be rotten. But don't bother ask Mrs Henry to chop off the rotten part. She would tell you, 'Is so me buy it; it so it must sell.'

Don Letts

My parents, hardcore Jamaicans: chicken, rice and peas, ackee, salt fish, plantain, dumpling, sweet potato, yam, callaloo, the works.

Every Saturday we went to the market, you didn't have a choice. Rain, cold and fucking freezing wearing short trousers, not wanting to go. You'd have to go with your mum and dad to Brixton market and it was very much an Afro-Caribbean thing back then – not this trendy thing it is now – totally Jamaican food. The main bit was Granville Arcade, which is now the food village or whatever, but that was just packed with every representative from every Caribbean island.

Bert Williams

Going to Brixton was like going back home really, I was very comfortable there, just being amongst black people; especially when you live in Brighton and you feel you're the only one here, there was others, but you felt you were the only one. So going to Brixton was like going back home. There's black people there, and you didn't just go for the food, you go to feel good about yourself. You do go to eat though and the first thing you do, before you do your shopping, is go and have some food, because they had West Indian restaurants; and the only place you could get music as well, West Indian music, was in Brixton.

Not only that, you were picking up new words as well, new things, that was the idea of buying the records, listening to the music. That time it was the Trojan label really selling; you've got to remember that in the sixties, reggae music, it gave you messages, new words were coming out and the conditions in Jamaica. It gives you a reminder of what Jamaica was like, I loved it.

Don Letts

The market, I'm thinking with hindsight, was a really buzzing hive of cultural activity but, coming from a ten-year-old's perspective on a Saturday morning, it was a pain in the arse and you couldn't wait to get home to watch TV.

At the market they'd be getting their ground provisions; maybe not ackee, that was expensive, it was a luxury. It was a little slice of back home. It was like you'd picked up a bit of Kingston, Jamaica and plonked it in the middle of London and then took away the sunshine and dropped the temperature SEVERAL degrees.

It wasn't just the food; you had the barbershops, which were key central bases where the men would come and talk shit – politics and whatever else. I went to a guy who was a barber in Jamaica and he opened up in his basement. You'd have your record shops that would spring up and cater to the community so it was this kind of oasis of sub-culture.

Bert Williams

It was a home from home, you walk around Brixton and you walk from shop to shop. There was English guys selling stuff as well, it wasn't all Jamaicans, but you'd target where the black guys are selling stuff. You talk to them, 'Wha'appen?' 'Wha'gwan?' You know. You could come out with the lingo and stuff like that. When I first came to England nobody understood me ... nobody, when I talk everybody says, 'Pardon?' And I hated the word pardon. Every time they say, 'Pardon? I beg your pardon?' Because they didn't understand you. So going to Brixton was like, you could come out with all your verbals.

LARK RISE TO CANDLEFORD

Flora Thompson

Flora Thompson was a post-office clerk, a housewife, and one of the great chroniclers of the nineteenth century. Largely self-educated, and beginning work at fourteen, she crafted three extraordinary books about her childhood, later published in one volume as *Lark Rise to Candleford*. Excerpted below, these three volumes detail a vanished world almost impossible to imagine today: an agrarian England, suffused with both poverty and wealth entirely alien to us, where everyone ate what they grew, and kept a pig, and worked, and suffered, and loved. In Thompson's work, though, these years are still alive and so vivid you can taste them: rosemary and lard, bacon and communal bread, the smell of earth and the puff of pipe smoke and the first tomato, love-apples, ever seen by anyone in the village.

The family pig was everybody's pride and everybody's business. Mother spent hours boiling up the 'little taturs' to mash and mix with the pot-liquor, in which food had been cooked, to feed to the pig for its evening meal and help out the expensive barley meal. The children, on their way home from school, would fill their arms with sow thistle, dandelion, and choice long grass, or roam along the hedgerows on wet evenings collecting snails in a pail for the pig's supper. These piggy crunched up with great relish. 'Feyther', over and above farming out the sty, bedding down, doctoring, and so on, would even go without his nightly half-pint when, towards the end, the barley-meal bill mounted until 'it fair frightened anybody'.

Sometimes, when the weekly income would not run to a sufficient quantity of fattening food, an arrangement would be made with the baker or miller that he should give credit now, and when the pig was killed receive a portion of the meat in payment. More often than not one-half the pig-meat would be mortgaged in this way, and it was no uncommon thing to hear a woman say, 'Us be going to kill half a pig, please God, come Friday,' leaving the uninitiated to conclude that the other half would still run about in the sty.

Some of the families killed two separate half pigs a year; others one, or even two, whole ones, and the meat provided them with bacon for the winter or longer. Fresh meat was a luxury only seen in a few of the cottages on Sunday, when six-pennyworth of pieces would be bought to make a meat pudding. If a small joint came their way as a Saturday night bargain, those without oven grates would roast it by suspending it on a string before the fire, with one of the children in attendance as turnspit. Or a 'Pot-roast' would be made by placing the meat with a little lard or other fat in an iron saucepan and keeping it well shaken over the fire. But, after all, as they said, there was nothing to beat a 'toad'. For this the meat was enclosed whole in a suet crust and well boiled, a method which preserved all the delicious juices of the meat and provided a good pudding into the bargain. When some superior person tried to give them a hint, the women used to say, 'You tell us how to get the victuals; we can cook it all right when we've got it'; and they could.

When the pig was fattened—and the fatter the better—the date of execution had to be decided upon. It had to take place some time during the first two quarters of the moon; for, if the pig was killed when the moon was waning the bacon would shrink in cooking, and they wanted it to 'plimp up'. The next thing was to engage the travelling pork butcher, or pig-sticker, and, as he was a thatcher by day, he always had to kill after dark, the scene being lighted with lanterns and the fire of burning straw which at a later stage of the proceedings was to singe the bristles off the victim.

The killing was a noisy, bloody business, in the course of which the animal was hoisted to a rough bench that it might bleed thoroughly and so preserve the quality of the meat. The job was often bungled, the pig sometimes getting away and having to be chased; but country people of that day had little sympathy for the sufferings of animals, and men, women, and children would gather round to see the sight.

After the carcass had been singed, the pig-sticker would pull off the detachable, gristly, outer coverings of the toes, known locally as 'the shoes', and fling them among the children, who scrambled for, then sucked and gnawed them, straight from the filth of the sty and blackened by fire as they were.

The whole scene, with its mud and blood, flaring lights and dark shadows, was as savage as anything to be seen in an African jungle. The children at the end house would steal out of bed to the window. 'Look! Look! It's hell, and those are the devils,' Edmund would whisper, pointing to the men tossing the burning straw with their pitchforks; but Laura felt sick and would creep back into bed and cry: she was sorry for the pig.

But, hidden from the children, there was another aspect of the pig-killing. Months of hard work and self-denial were brought on that night to a successful conclusion. It was a time to rejoice, and rejoice they did, with beer flowing freely and the first delicious dish of pig's fry sizzling in the frying-pan.

The next day, when the carcass had been cut up, joints of pork were distributed to those neighbours who had sent similar ones at their own pig-killing. Small plates of fry and other oddments were sent to others as a pure compliment, and no one who happened to be ill or down on his luck at these occasions was ever forgotten.

Then the housewife 'got down to it', as she said. Hams and sides of bacon were salted, to be taken out of the brine later and hung on the wall near the fireplace to dry. Lard was dried out, hogs' puddings were made, and the chitterlings were cleaned and turned three days in succession under running water, according to ancient ritual. It was a busy time, but a happy one, with the larder full and something over to give away, and all the pride and importance of owning such riches.

On the following Sunday came the official 'pig feast', when fathers and mothers, sisters and brothers, married children and grandchildren who lived within walking distance arrived to dinner.

If the house had no oven, permission was obtained from an old couple in one of the thatched cottages to heat up the big bread-baking oven in their wash-house. This was like a large cupboard with an iron door, lined with brick and going far back into the wall. Faggots of wood were lighted inside and the door was closed upon them until the oven was well heated. Then the ashes were swept out and baking-tins with joints of pork, potatoes, batter puddings, pork pies, and sometimes a cake or two, were popped inside and left to bake without further attention.

Meanwhile, at home, three or four different kinds of vegetables would be cooked, and always a meat pudding, made in a basin. No feast and few Sunday dinners were considered complete without that item, which was eaten alone, without vegetables, when a joint was to follow. On ordinary days the pudding would be a roly-poly containing fruit, currants, or jam; but it still appeared as a first course, the idea being that it took the edge off the appetite. At the pig feast there would be no sweet pudding, for that could be had any day, and who wanted sweet things when there was plenty of meat to be had!

But this glorious plenty only came once or at most twice a year, and there were all the other days to provide for. How was it done on ten shillings a week? Well, for one thing, food was much cheaper than it is to-day. Then, in addition to the bacon, all vegetables, including potatoes, were home-grown and grown in abundance. The men took great pride in their gardens and allotments and there was always competition amongst them as to who should have the earliest and choicest of each kind. Fat green peas, broad beans as big as a halfpenny, cauliflowers a child could make an armchair of, runner beans and cabbage and kale, all in their seasons went into the pot with the roly-poly and slip of bacon.

Then they ate plenty of green food, all home-grown and freshly pulled; lettuce and radishes and young onions with pearly heads and leaves like fine grass. A few slices of bread and home-made lard, flavoured with rosemary, and plenty of green food 'went down good' as they used to say.

Bread had to be bought, and that was a heavy item, with so many growing children to be fed; but flour for the daily pudding and an occasional plain cake could be laid in for the winter without any cash outlay. After the harvest had been carried from the fields, the women and children swarmed over the stubble picking up the ears of wheat the horse-rake had missed. Gleaning, or 'leazing', as it was called locally.

Up and down and over and over the stubble they hurried, backs bent, eyes on the ground, one hand outstretched to pick up the ears, the other resting on the small of the back with the 'handful'. When this had been completed, it was bound round with a wisp of straw and erected with others in a double rank, like the harvesters erected their sheaves in shocks, beside the leazer's water-can and dinner-basket. It was hard work, from as soon as possible after daybreak until nightfall, with only two short breaks for refreshment; but the single ears mounted, and a woman with four or five strong, well-disciplined children would carry a good load home on her head every night. And they enjoyed doing it, for it was pleasant in the fields under the pale blue August sky, with the clover springing green in the stubble and the hedges bright with hips and haws and feathery with traveller's joy. When the rest-hour came, the children would wander off down the hedgerows gathering crab-apples or sloes, or searching for mushrooms, while the mothers reclined and suckled their babes and drank their cold tea and gossiped or dozed until it was time to be at it again.

At the end of the fortnight or three weeks that the leazing lasted, the corn would be thrashed out at home and sent to the miller, who paid himself for grinding by taking toll of the flour. Great was the excitement in a good year when the flour came home—one bushel, two bushels, or even more in large, industrious families. The mealy-white sack with its contents was often kept for a time on show on a chair in the living-room and it was a common thing for a passer-by to be invited to 'step inside an' see our little bit o' leazings'. They liked to have the product of their labour before their own eyes and to let others admire it, just as the artist likes to show his picture and the composer to hear his opus played. 'Them's better'n any o' yer oil-paintin's,' a man would say, pointing to the flitches on his wall, and the women felt the same about the leazings.

Here, then, were the three chief ingredients of the one hot meal a day, bacon from the flitch, vegetables from the garden, and flour for the roly-poly. This meal, called 'tea', was taken in the evening, when the men were home from the fields and the children from school, for neither could get home at midday.

About four o'clock, smoke would go up from the chimneys, as the fire was made up and the big iron boiler, or the three-legged pot, was slung on the hook of the chimney-chain. Everything was cooked in the one utensil; the square of bacon, amounting to little more than a taste each; cabbage, or other green vegetables in one net, potatoes in another, and the roly-poly swathed in a cloth. It sounds a haphazard method in these days of gas and electric cookers; but it answered its purpose, for, by carefully timing the putting in of each item and keeping the simmering of the pot well regulated, each item was kept intact and an appetising meal was produced. The water in which the food had been cooked, the potato parings, and other vegetable trimmings were the pig's share.

When the men came home from work they would find the table spread with a clean whitey-brown cloth, upon which would be knives and two-pronged steel forks with buckhorn handles. The vegetables would then be turned out into big round yellow crockery dishes and the bacon cut into dice, with much the largest cube upon Feyther's plate, and the whole family would sit down to the chief meal of the day. True, it was seldom that all could find places at the central table; but some of the smaller children could sit upon stools with the seat of a chair for a table, or on the doorstep with their plates on their laps.

Good manners prevailed. The children were given their share of the food, there was no picking and choosing, and they were expected to eat it in silence. 'Please' and 'Thank you' were permitted, but nothing more. Father and Mother might talk if they wanted to; but usually they were content to concentrate upon their enjoyment of the meal. Father might shovel green peas into his mouth with his knife, Mother might drink her tea from her saucer, and some of the children might lick their plates when the food was devoured; but who could eat peas with a two-pronged fork, or wait for tea to cool after the heat and flurry of cooking, and licking the plates passed as a graceful compliment to Mother's good dinner. 'Thank God for my good dinner. Thank Father and Mother. Amen' was the grace used in one family, and it certainly had the merit of giving credit where credit was due.

For other meals they depended largely on bread and butter, or, more often, bread and lard, eaten with any relish that happened to be at hand. Fresh butter was too costly for general use, but a pound was sometimes purchased in the summer, when it cost tenpence. Margarine, then called 'butterine', was already on the market, but was little used there, as most people preferred lard, especially when it was their own home-made lard flavoured with rosemary leaves. In summer there was always plenty of green food from the garden and home-made jam as long as it lasted, and sometimes an egg or two, where fowls were kept, or when eggs were plentiful and sold at twenty a shilling.

When bread and lard appeared alone, the men would spread mustard on their slices and the children would be given a scraping of black treacle or a sprinkling of brown sugar. Some children, who preferred it, would have 'sop'—bread steeped in boiling water, then strained and sugar added.

Milk was a rare luxury, as it had to be fetched a mile and a half from the farmhouse. The cost was not great: a penny a jug or can, irrespective of size. It was, of course, skimmed milk, but hand-skimmed, not separated, and so still had some small proportion of cream left. A few families fetched it daily; but many did not bother about it. The women said they preferred their tea neat, and it did not seem to occur to them that the children needed milk. Many of them never tasted it from the time they were weaned until they went out in the world. Yet they were stout-limbed and rosy-cheeked and full of life and mischief.

The skimmed milk was supposed by the farmer to be sold at a penny a pint, that remaining unsold going to feed his own calves and pigs. But the dairymaid did not trouble to measure it; she just filled the proffered vessel and let it go as 'a pen'orth'. Of course, the jugs and cans got larger and larger. One old woman increased the size of her vessels by degrees until she had the impudence to take a small, new, tin cooking boiler which was filled without question. The children at the end house wondered what she could do with so much milk, as she had only her husband and herself at home. 'That'll make you a nice big rice pudding, Queenie', one of them said tentatively.

'Pudden! Lor' bless 'ee!' was Queenie's reply. 'I don't ever make no rice puddens. That milk's for my pig's supper, an', my! ain't 'ee just about thrivin' on it. Can't hardly see out of his eyes, bless him!'

'Poverty's no disgrace, but 'tis a great inconvenience' was a common saying among the Lark Rise people; but that put the case too mildly, for their poverty was no less than a hampering drag upon them. Everybody had enough to eat and a shelter which, though it fell far short of modern requirements, satisfied them. Coal at a shilling a hundredweight and a pint of paraffin for lighting had to be squeezed out of the weekly wage; but for boots, clothes, illness, holidays, amusements, and household renewals there was no provision whatever. How did they manage?

Boots were often bought with the extra money the men earned in the harvest field. When that was paid, those lucky families which were not in arrears with their rent would have a new pair all round, from the father's hobnailed dreadnoughts to little pink kid slippers for the baby. Then some careful housewives paid a few pence every week into the boot club run by a shopkeeper in the market town. This helped; but it was not sufficient, and how to get a pair of new boots for 'our young Ern or Alf' was a problem which kept many a mother awake at night.

Girls needed boots, too, and good, stout, nailed ones for those rough and muddy roads; but they were not particular, any boots would do. At a confirmation class which Laura attended, the clergyman's daughter, after weeks of careful preparation, asked her catechumens: 'Now, are you sure you are all of you thoroughly prepared for to-morrow. Is there anything you would like to ask me?'

'Yes, miss,' piped up a voice in a corner, 'me mother says have you got a pair of your old boots you could give me, for I haven't got any fit to go in.'

Alice got her boots on that occasion; but there was not a confirmation every day. Still, boots were obtained somehow; nobody went barefoot, even though some of the toes might sometimes stick out beyond the toe of the boot.

To obtain clothes was an even more difficult matter. Mothers of families sometimes said in despair that they supposed they would have to black their own backsides and go naked. They never quite came to that; but it was difficult to keep decently covered, and that was a pity because they did dearly love what they called 'anything a bit dressy'. This taste was not encouraged by the garments made by the girls in school from material given by the Rectory people—roomy chemises and wide-legged drawers made of unbleached calico, beautifully sewn, but without an inch of trimming; harsh, but strong flannel petticoats and worsted stockings that would almost stand up with no legs in them— although these were gratefully received and had their merits, for they wore for years and the calico improved with washing.

For outer garments they had to depend upon daughters, sisters, and aunts away in service, who all sent parcels, not only of their own clothes, but also of those they could beg from their mistresses. These were worn and altered and dyed and turned and ultimately patched and darned as long as the shreds hung together.

But, in spite of their poverty and the worry and anxiety attending it, they were not unhappy, and, though poor, there was nothing sordid about their lives. 'The nearer the bone the sweeter the meat', they used to say, and they were getting very near the bone from which their country ancestors had fed. Their children and children's children would have to depend wholly upon whatever was carved for them from the communal joint, and for their pleasure upon the mass enjoyments of a new era. But for that generation there was still a small picking left to supplement the weekly wage. They had their home-cured bacon, their 'bit o' leazings', their small wheat or barley patch on the allotment; their knowledge of herbs for their homely simples, and the wild fruits and berries of the countryside for jam, jellies, and wine, and round about them as part of their lives were the last relics of country customs and the last echoes of country songs, ballads, and game rhymes. This last picking, though meagre, was sweet.

ULYSSES

James Joyce

If you ignore everything you know about **James Joyce**, you will have a much better time. When someone is as respected, feared and famed as the Great Irish Novelist, it's almost impossible to come to their work on your own terms – as something absorbing, funny, bitter, tactile and alive. Better, then, just to say that Joyce was born in 1882 in Dublin, Ireland; he was a resident of Pula, Croatia; Trieste, Italy; Zurich, Switzerland; and Paris, France; he married Nora Barnacle in London in 1931, and they had two children, Giorgio (1905) and Lucia (1907). His books changed literature forever, and if you let them, they will change you too.

Mr Leopold Bloom ate with relish the inner organs of beasts and fowls. He liked thick giblet soup, nutty gizzards, a stuffed roast heart, liver slices fried with crustcrumbs, fried hencod's roes. Most of all he liked grilled mutton kidneys which gave to his palate a fine tang of faintly scented urine.

Kidneys were in his mind as he moved about the kitchen softly, righting her breakfast things on the humpy tray. Gelid light and air were in the kitchen but out of doors gentle summer morning everywhere. Made him feel a bit peckish.

The coals were reddening.

Another slice of bread and butter: three, four: right. She didn't like her plate full. Right. He turned from the tray, lifted the kettle off the hob and set it sideways on the fire. It sat there, dull and squat, its spout stuck out. Cup of tea soon. Good. Mouth dry. The cat walked stiffly round a leg of the table with tail on high.

—Mkgnao!

—O, there you are, Mr Bloom said, turning from the fire.

The cat mewed in answer and stalked again stiffly round a leg of the table, mewing. Just how she stalks over my writingtable. Prr. Scratch my head. Prr.

Mr Bloom watched curiously, kindly, the lithe black form. Clean to see: the gloss of her sleek hide, the white button under the butt of her tail, the green flashing eyes. He bent down to her, his hands on his knees.

—Milk for the pussens, he said.

—Mrkgnao! the cat cried.

They call them stupid. They understand what we say better than we understand them. She understands all she wants to. Vindictive too. Wonder what I look like to her. Height of a tower? No, she can jump me.

—Afraid of the chickens she is, he said mockingly. Afraid of the chookchooks. I never saw such a stupid pussens as the pussens.

Cruel. Her nature. Curious mice never squeal. Seem to like it.

—Mrkrgnao! the cat said loudly.

She blinked up out of her avid shameclosing eyes, mewing plaintively and long, showing him her milk-white teeth. He watched the dark eyeslits narrowing with greed till her eyes were green stones. Then he went to the dresser, took the jug Hanlon's milkman had just filled for him, poured warmbubbled milk on a saucer and set it slowly on the floor.

—Gurrhr! she cried, running to lap.

He watched the bristles shining wirily in the weak light as she tipped three times and licked lightly. Wonder is it true if you clip them they can't mouse after. Why? They shine in the dark, perhaps, the tips. Or kind of feelers in the dark, perhaps.

He listened to her licking lap. Ham and eggs, no. No good eggs with this drouth. Want pure fresh water. Thursday: not a good day either for a mutton kidney at Buckley's. Fried with butter, a shake of pepper. Better a pork kidney at Dlugacz's. While the kettle is boiling. She lapped slower, then licking the saucer clean. Why are their tongues so rough? To lap better, all porous holes. Nothing she can eat? He glanced round him. No.

On quietly creaky boots he went up the staircase to the hall, paused by the bedroom door. She might like something tasty. Thin bread and butter she likes in the morning. Still perhaps: once in a way.

He said softly in the bare hall:

—I am going round the corner. Be back in a minute.

And when he had heard his voice say it he added:

—You don't want anything for breakfast?

A sleepy soft grunt answered:

—Mn.

No. She did not want anything. He heard then a warm heavy sigh, softer, as she turned over and the loose brass quoits of the bedstead jingled. Must get those settled really. Pity. All the way from Gibraltar. Forgotten any little Spanish she knew. Wonder what her father gave for it. Old style. Ah yes, of course. Bought it at the governor's auction. Got a short knock. Hard as nails at a bargain, old Tweedy. Yes, sir. At Plevna that was. I rose from the ranks, sir, and I'm proud of it. Still he had brains enough to make that corner in stamps. Now that was farseeing.

His hand took his hat from the peg over his initialled heavy overcoat, and his lost property office secondhand waterproof. Stamps: stickyback pictures. Daresay lots of officers are in the swim too. Course they do. The sweated legend in the crown of his hat told him mutely: Plasto's high grade ha. He peeped quickly inside the leather headband. White slip of paper. Quite safe.

On the doorstep he felt in his hip pocket for the latchkey. Not there. In the trousers I left off. Must get it. Potato I have. Creaky wardrobe. No use disturbing her. She turned over sleepily that time. He pulled the halldoor to after him very quietly, more, till the footleaf dropped gently over the threshold, a limp lid. Looked shut. All right till I come back anyhow.

He crossed to the bright side, avoiding the loose cellarflap of number seventyfive. The sun was nearing the steeple of George's church. Be a warm day I fancy. Specially in these black clothes feel it more. Black conducts, reflects (refracts is it?), the heat. But I couldn't go in that light suit. Make a picnic of it. His eyelids sank quietly often as he walked in happy warmth. Boland's breadvan delivering with trays our daily but she prefers yesterday's loaves turnovers crisp crowns hot. Makes you feel young. Somewhere in the east: early morning: set off at dawn, travel round in front of the sun, steal a day's march on him. Keep it up for ever never grow a day older technically. Walk along a strand, strange land, come to a city gate, sentry there, old ranker too, old Tweedy's big moustaches leaning on a long kind of a spear. Wander through awned streets. Turbaned faces going by. Dark caves of carpet shops, big man, Turko the terrible, seated crosslegged smoking a coiled pipe. Cries of sellers in the streets. Drink water scented with fennel, sherbet. Wander along all day. Might meet a robber or two. Well, meet him. Getting on to sundown. The shadows of the mosques along the pillars: priest with a scroll rolled up. A shiver of the trees, signal, the evening wind. I pass on. Fading gold sky. A mother watches from her doorway. She calls her children home in their dark language. High wall: beyond strings twanged. Night sky moon, violet, colour of Molly's new garters. Strings. Listen. A girl playing one of these instruments what do you call them: dulcimers. I pass.

Probably not a bit like it really. Kind of stuff you read: in the track of the sun. Sunburst on the titlepage. He smiled, pleasing himself. What Arthur Griffith said about the headpiece over the *Freeman* leader: a homerule sun rising up in the northwest from the laneway behind the bank of Ireland. He prolonged his pleased smile. Ikey touch that: homerule sun rising up in the north-west.

He approached Larry O'Rourke's. From the cellar grating floated up the flabby gush of porter. Through the open doorway the bar squirted out whiffs of ginger, teadust, biscuitmush. Good house, however: just the end of the city traffic. For instance M'Auley's down there: n. g. as position. Of course if they ran a tramline along the North Circular from the cattle market to the quays value would go up like a shot.

Bald head over the blind. Cute old codger. No use canvassing him for an ad. Still he knows his own business best. There he is, sure enough, my bold Larry, leaning against the sugarbin in his shirtsleeves watching the aproned curate swab up with mop and bucket. Simon Dedalus takes him off to a tee with his eyes screwed up. Do you know what I'm going to tell you? What's that, Mr O'Rourke? Do you know what? The Russians, they'd only be an eight o'clock breakfast for the Japanese.

Stop and say a word: about the funeral perhaps. Sad thing about poor Dignam, Mr O'Rourke.

Turning into Dorset street he said freshly in greeting through the doorway:

—Good day, Mr O'Rourke.

—Good day to you.

—Lovely weather, sir.

—'Tis all that.

Where do they get the money? Coming up redheaded curates from the county Leitrim, rinsing empties and old man in the cellar. Then, lo and behold, they blossom out as Adam Findlaters or Dan Tallons. Then think of the competition. General thirst. Good puzzle would be cross Dublin without passing a pub. Save it they can't. Off the drunks perhaps. Put down three and carry five. What is that? A bob here and there, dribs and drabs. On the wholesale orders perhaps. Doing a double shuffle with the town travellers. Square it with the boss and we'll split the job, see?

How much would that tot to off the porter in the month? Say ten barrels of stuff. Say he got ten per cent off. O more. Ten. Fifteen. He passed Saint Joseph's, National school. Brats' clamour. Windows open. Fresh air helps memory. Or a lilt. Ahbeesee defeegee kelomen opeecue rustyouvee double you. Boys are they? Yes. Inishturk. Inishark. Inishboffin. At their joggerfry. Mine. Slieve Bloom.

He halted before Dlugacz's window, staring at the hanks of sausages, polonies, black and white. Fifty multiplied by. The figures whitened in his mind unsolved: displeased, he let them fade. The shiny links packed with forcemeat fed his gaze and he breathed in tranquilly the lukewarm breath of cooked spicy pig's blood.

A kidney oozed bloodgouts on the willowpatterned dish: the last. He stood by the nextdoor girl at the counter. Would she buy it too, calling the items from a slip in her hand. Chapped: washing soda. And a pound and a half of Denny's sausages. His eyes rested on her vigorous hips. Woods his name is. Wonder what he does. Wife is oldish. New blood. No followers allowed. Strong pair of arms. Whacking a carpet on the clothesline. She does whack it, by George. The way her crooked skirt swings at each whack.

The ferreteyed porkbutcher folded the sausages he had snipped off with blotchy fingers, sausagepink. Sound meat there like a stallfed heifer.

He took up a page from the pile of cut sheets. The model farm at Kinnereth on the lakeshore of Tiberias. Can become ideal winter sanatorium. Moses Montefiore. I thought he was. Farmhouse, wall round it, blurred cattle cropping. He held the page from him: interesting: read it nearer, the blurred cropping cattle, the page rustling. A young white heifer. Those mornings in the cattlemarket the beasts lowing in their pens, branded sheep, flop and fall of dung, the breeders in hobnailed boots trudging through the litter, slapping a palm on a ripemeated hindquarter, there's a prime one, unpeeled switches in their hands. He held the page aslant patiently, bending his senses and his will, his soft subject gaze at rest. The crooked skirt swinging whack by whack by whack.

The porkbutcher snapped two sheets from the pile, wrapped up her prime sausages and made a red grimace.

—Now, my miss, he said.

She tendered a coin, smiling boldly, holding her thick wrist out.

—Thank you, my miss. And one shilling threepence change. For you, please?

Mr Bloom pointed quickly. To catch up and walk behind her if she went slowly, behind her moving hams. Pleasant to see first thing in the morning. Hurry up, damn it. Make hay while the sun shines. She stood outside the shop in sunlight and sauntered lazily to the right. He sighed down his nose: they never understand. Sodachapped hands. Crusted toenails too. Brown scapulars in tatters, defending her both ways. The sting of disregard glowed to weak pleasure within his breast. For another: a constable off duty cuddled her in Eccles Lane. They like them sizeable. Prime sausage. O please, Mr Policeman, I'm lost in the wood.

—Threepence, please.

His hand accepted the moist tender gland and slid it into a sidepocket. Then it fetched up three coins from his trousers' pocket and laid them on the rubber prickles. They lay, were read quickly and quickly slid, disc by disc, into the till.

—Thank you, sir. Another time.

A speck of eager fire from foxeyes thanked him. He withdrew his gaze after an instant. No: better not: another time.

—Good morning, he said, moving away.

—Good morning, sir.

No sign. Gone. What matter?

He walked back along Dorset street, reading gravely. Agendath Netaim: planter's company. To purchase vast sandy tracts from Turkish government and plant with eucalyptus trees. Excellent for shade, fuel and construction. Orangegroves and immense melonfields north of Jaffa. You pay eight marks and they plant a dunam of land for you with olives, oranges, almonds or citrons. Olives cheaper: oranges need artificial irrigation. Every year you get a sending of the crop. Your name entered for life as owner in the book of the union. Can pay ten down and the balance in yearly instalments. Bleibtreustrasse 34, Berlin, W. 15.

Nothing doing. Still an idea behind it.

He looked at the cattle, blurred in silver heat. Silvered powdered olivetrees. Quiet long days: pruning ripening. Olives are packed in jars, eh? I have a few left from Andrews. Molly spitting them out. Knows the taste of them now. Oranges in tissue paper packed in crates. Citrons too. Wonder is poor Citron still alive in Saint Kevin's parade. And Mastiansky with the old cither. Pleasant evenings we had then. Molly in Citron's basketchair. Nice to hold, cool waxen fruit, hold in the hand, lift it to the nostrils and smell the perfume. Like that, heavy, sweet, wild perfume. Always the same, year after year. They fetched high prices too Moisel told me. Arbutus place: Pleasants street: pleasant old times. Must be without a flaw, he said. Coming all that way: Spain, Gibraltar, Mediterranean, the Levant. Crates lined up on the quayside at Jaffa, chap ticking them off in a book, navvies handling them in soiled dungarees. There's whatdoyoucallhim out of. How do you? Doesn't see. Chap you know just to salute bit of a bore. His back is like that Norwegian captain's. Wonder if I'll meet him today. Watering cart. To provoke the rain. On earth as it is in heaven.

A cloud began to cover the sun wholly slowly wholly. Grey. Far.

No, not like that. A barren land, bare waste. Vulcanic lake, the dead sea: no fish, weedless, sunk deep in the earth. No wind would lift those waves, grey metal, poisonous foggy waters. Brimstone they called it raining down: the cities of the plain: Sodom, Gomorrah, Edom. All dead names. A dead sea in a dead land, grey and old. Old now. It bore the oldest, the first race. A bent hag crossed from Cassidy's clutching a noggin bottle by the neck. The oldest people. Wandered far away over all the earth, captivity to captivity, multiplying, dying, being born everywhere. It lay there now. Now it could bear no more. Dead: an old woman's: the grey sunken cunt of the world.

Desolation.

Grey horror seared his flesh. Folding the page into his pocket he turned into Eccles Street, hurrying homeward. Cold oils slid along his veins, chilling his blood: age crusting him with a salt cloak. Well, I am here now. Morning mouth bad images. Got up wrong side of the bed. Must begin again those Sandow's exercises. On the hands down. Blotchy brown brick houses. Number eighty still unlet. Why is that? Valuation is only twenty-eight. Towers, Battersby, North, MacArthur: parlour windows plastered with bills. Plasters on a sore eye. To smell the gentle smoke of tea, fume of the pan, sizzling butter. Be near her ample bedwarmed flesh. Yes, yes.

Quick warm sunlight came running from Berkeley Road, swiftly, in slim sandals, along the brightening footpath. Runs, she runs to meet me, a girl with gold hair on the wind.

Two letters and a card lay on the hallfloor. He stopped and gathered them. Mrs Marion Bloom. His quick heart slowed at once. Bold hand. Mrs Marion.

—Poldy!

Entering the bedroom he halfclosed his eyes and walked through warm yellow twilight towards her tousled head.

—Who are the letters for?

He looked at them. Mullingar. Milly.

—A letter for me from Milly, he said carefully, and a card to you. And a letter for you.

He laid her card and letter on the twill bedspread near the curve of her knees.

—Do you want the blind up?

Letting the blind up by gentle tugs halfway his backward eye saw her glance at the letter and tuck it under her pillow.

—That do? he asked, turning.

She was reading the card, propped on her elbow.

—She got the things, she said.

He waited till she had laid the card aside and curled herself back slowly with a snug sigh.

—Hurry up with that tea, she said. I'm parched.

—The kettle is boiling, he said.

But he delayed to clear the chair: her striped petticoat, tossed soiled linen: and lifted all in an armful on to the foot of the bed.

As he went down the kitchen stairs she called:

—Poldy!

—What?

—Scald the teapot.

On the boil sure enough: a plume of steam from the spout. He scalded and rinsed out the teapot and put in four full spoons of tea, tilting the kettle then to let water flow in. Having set it to draw, he took off the kettle and crushed the pan flat on the live coals and watched the lump of butter slide and melt. While he unwrapped the kidney the cat mewed hungrily against him. Give her too much meat she won't mouse. Say they won't eat pork. Kosher. Here. He let the bloodsmeared paper fall to her and dropped the kidney amid the sizzling butter sauce. Pepper. He sprinkled it through his fingers, ringwise, from the chipped eggcup.

Then he slit open his letter, glancing down the page and over. Thanks: new tam: Mr Coghlan: lough Owel picnic: young student: Blazes Boylan's seaside girls.

The tea was drawn. He filled his own moustachecup, sham crown Derby, smiling. Silly Milly's birthday gift. Only five she was then. No wait: four. I gave her the amberoid necklace she broke. Putting pieces of folded brown paper in the letterbox for her. He smiled, pouring.

O, Milly Bloom, you are my darling.

You are my looking glass from night to morning.
I'd rather have you without a farthing
Than Katey Keogh with her ass and garden.

Poor old professor Goodwin. Dreadful old case. Still he was a courteous old chap. Oldfashioned way he used to bow Molly off the platform. And the little mirror in his silk hat. The night Milly brought it into the parlour. O, look what I found in professor Goodwin's hat! All we laughed. Sex breaking out even then. Pert little piece she was.

He prodded a fork into the kidney and slapped it over: then fitted the teapot on the tray. Its hump bumped as he took it up. Everything on it? Bread and butter, four, sugar, spoon, her cream. Yes. He carried it upstairs, his thumb hooked in the teapot handle.

Nudging the door open with his knee he carried the tray in and set it on the chair by the bedhead.

—What a time you were, she said.

She set the brasses jingling as she raised herself briskly, an elbow on the pillow. He looked calmly down on her bulk and between her large soft bubs, sloping within her nightdress like a shegoat's udder. The warmth of her couched body rose on the air, mingling with the fragrance of the tea she poured.

A strip of torn envelope peeped from under the dimpled pillow. In the act of going he stayed to straighten the bedspread.

—Who was the letter from? he asked.

Bold hand. Marion.

—O, Boylan, she said. He's bringing the programme.

—What are you singing?

—*La ci darem* with J. C. Doyle, she said, and *Love's Old Sweet Song.*

Her full lips, drinking, smiled. Rather stale smell that incense leaves next day. Like foul flowerwater.

—Would you like the window open a little?

She doubled a slice of bread into her mouth, asking:

—What time is the funeral?

—Eleven, I think, he answered. I didn't see the paper.

Following the pointing of her finger he took up a leg of her soiled drawers from the bed. No? Then, a twisted grey garter looped round a stocking: rumpled, shiny sole.

—No: that book.

Other stocking. Her petticoat.

—It must have fell down, she said.

He felt here and there. *Voglio e non vorrei*. Wonder if she pronounces that right: *voglio*. Not in the bed. Must have slid down. He stooped and lifted the valance. The book, fallen, sprawled against the bulge of the orange-keyed chamberpot.

—Show here, she said. I put a mark in it. There's a word I wanted to ask you.

She swallowed a draught of tea from her cup held by nothandle and, having wiped her fingertips smartly on the blanket, began to search the text with the hairpin till she reached the word.

—Met him what? he asked.

—Here, she said. What does that mean?

He leaned downwards and read near her polished thumbnail.

—Metempsychosis?

—Yes. Who's he when he's at home?

—Metempsychosis, he said, frowning. It's Greek: from the Greek. That means the transmigration of souls.

—O, rocks! she said. Tell us in plain words.

He smiled, glancing askance at her mocking eye. The same young eyes. The first night after the charades. Dolphin's Barn. He turned over the smudged pages. *Ruby: the Pride of the Ring*. Hello. Illustration. Fierce Italian with carriagewhip. Must be Ruby pride of the on the floor naked. Sheet kindly lent. *The monster Maffei desisted and flung his victim from him with an oath*. Cruelty behind it all. Doped animals. Trapeze at Hengler's. Had to look the other way. Mob gaping. Break your neck and we'll break our sides. Families of them. Bone them young so they metempsychosis. That we live after death. Our souls. That a man's soul after he dies. Dignam's soul . . .

—Did you finish it? he asked.

—Yes, she said. There's nothing smutty in it. Is she in love with the first fellow all the time?

—Never read it. Do you want another?

—Yes. Get another of Paul de Kock's. Nice name he has.

She poured more tea into her cup, watching its flow sideways.

Must get that Capel street library book renewed or they'll write to Kearney, my guarantor. Reincarnation: that's the word.

—Some people believe, he said, that we go on living in another body after death, that we lived before. They call it reincarnation. That we all lived before on the earth thousands of years ago or some other planet. They say we have forgotten it. Some say they remember their past lives.

The sluggish cream wound curdling spirals through her tea. Better remind her of the word: metempsychosis. An example would be better. An example.

The *Bath of the Nymph* over the bed. Given away with the Easter number of *Photo Bits*: Splendid master-piece in art colours. Tea before you put milk in. Not unlike her with her hair down: slimmer. Three and six I gave for the frame. She said it would look nice over the bed. Naked nymphs: Greece: and for instance all the people that lived then.

He turned the pages back.

—Metempsychosis, he said, is what the ancient Greeks called it. They used to believe you could be changed into an animal or a tree, for instance. What they called nymphs, for example.

Her spoon ceased to stir up the sugar. She gazed straight before her, inhaling through her arched nostrils.

—There's a smell of burn, she said. Did you leave anything on the fire?

—The kidney! he cried suddenly.

He fitted the book roughly into his inner pocket and, stubbing his toes against the broken commode, hurried out towards the smell, stepping hastily down the stairs with a flurried stork's legs. Pungent smoke shot up in an angry jet from a side of the pan. By prodding a prong of the fork under the kidney he detached it and turned it turtle on its back. Only a little burned. He tossed it off the pan on to a plate and let the scanty brown gravy trickle over it.

Cup of tea now. He sat down, cut and buttered a slice of the loaf. He shore away the burnt flesh and flung it to the cat. Then he put a forkful into his mouth, chewing with discernment the toothsome pliant meat. Done to a turn. A mouthful of tea. Then he cut away dies of bread, sopped one in the gravy and put it in his mouth. What was that about some young student and a picnic? He creased out the letter at his side, reading it slowly as he chewed, sopping another die of bread in the gravy and raising it to his mouth.

Dearest Papli,

Thanks ever so much for the lovely birthday present. It suits me splendid. Everyone says I'm quite the belle in my new tam. I got mummy's lovely box of creams and am writing. They are lovely. I am getting on swimming in the photo business now. Mr Coghlan took one of me and Mrs will send when developed. We did great biz yesterday. Fair day and all the beef to the heels were in. We are going to lough Owel on Monday with a few friends to make a scrap picnic. Give my love to mummy and to yourself a big kiss and thanks. I hear them at the piano downstairs. There is to be a concert in the Greville Arms on Saturday. There is a young student comes here some evenings named Bannon his cousins or something are big swells he sings Boylan's (I was on the pop of writing Blazes Boylan's) song about those seaside girls. Tell him silly Milly sends my best respects. Must now close with fondest love.

Your fond daughter,   MILLY.

P.S. Excuse bad writing, am in a hurry. Byby.   M.

Fifteen yesterday. Curious, fifteenth of the month too. Her first birthday away from home. Separation. Remember the summer morning she was born, running to knock up Mrs Thornton in Denzille street. Jolly old woman. Lots of babies she must have helped into the world. She knew from the first poor little Rudy wouldn't live. Well, God is good, sir. She knew at once. He would be eleven now if he had lived.

His vacant face stared pitying at the postscript. Excuse bad writing. Hurry. Piano downstairs. Coming out of her shell. Row with her in the XL Café about the bracelet. Wouldn't eat her cakes or speak or look. Sauce-box. He sopped other dies of bread in the gravy and ate piece after piece of kidney. Twelve and six a week. Not much. Still, she might do worse. Music hall stage. Young student. He drank a draught of cooler tea to wash down his meal. Then he read the letter again: twice.

O well: she knows how to mind herself. But if not? No, nothing has happened. Of course it might. Wait in any case till it does. A wild piece of goods. Her slim legs running up the staircase. Destiny. Ripening now. Vain: very.

He smiled with troubled affection at the kitchen window. Day I caught her in the street pinching her cheeks to make them red. Anæmic a little. Was given milk too long. On the *Erin's King* that day round the Kish. Damned old tub pitching about. Not a bit funky. Her pale blue scarf loose in the wind with her hair.

> *All dimpled cheeks and curls,*
> *Your head it simply swirls.*

Seaside girls. Torn envelope. Hands stuck in his trousers' pockets, jarvey off for the day, singing. Friend of the family. Swurls, he says. Pier with lamps, summer evening, band,

> *Those girls, those girls,*
> *Those lovely seaside girls*

Milly too. Young kisses: the first. Far away now past. Mrs Marion. Reading lying back now, counting the strands of her hair, smiling, braiding.

A soft qualm regret, flowed down his backbone, increasing. Will happen, yes. Prevent. Useless: can't move. Girl's sweet light lips. Will happen too. He felt the flowing qualm spread over him. Useless to move now. Lips kissed, kissing kissed. Full gluey woman's lips.

Better where she is down there: away. Occupy her. Wanted a dog to pass the time. Might take a trip down there. August bank holiday, only two and six return. Six weeks off however. Might work a press pass. Or through M'Coy.

The cat, having cleaned all her fur, returned to the meatstained paper, nosed at it and stalked to the door. She looked back at him, mewing. Wants to go out. Wait before a door sometime it will open. Let her wait. Has the fidgets. Electric. Thunder in the air. Was washing at her ear with her back to the fire too.

He felt heavy, full: then a gentle loosening of his bowels. He stood up, undoing the waistband of his trousers. The cat mewed to him.

—Miaow! he said in answer. Wait till I'm ready.

EMBROIDERIES

Marjane Satrapi

Marjane Satrapi's bestselling, critically acclaimed autobiographical comic books describe the lives of girls and women in Iran. Concerned for her safety following the Iranian Revolution, Satrapi's parents organised for her to attend school in Vienna, where she was precariously housed with friends, relatives, and even on the street. After obtaining a master's degree in Tehran, she moved to France to study, and was eventually told by her family that Iran was no longer safe for her. *Embroideries*, from which the below is excerpted, is a conversation around a samovar; the men have retired to take a nap, and the women remain to drink tea, and to talk sex. First published in English in 2005, it was reviewed in the *Guardian* as 'a paean to taking pleasure seriously'. Satrapi lives in Paris with her Swedish husband. As a result of her peripatetic life, she speaks six languages fluently.

It was really delicious! Thank you.

It's the Missus who should be thanked. A true gourmet.

Satrapi flatters me.

My grandmother called my grandfather Satrapi, never by his first name. She said one must respect one's husband.

After lunch, the men left as usual to take a nap, and the rest of us, the women, started to clean up.

Marji, my child, take care of the samovar.

Yes, Grandma.

The samovar was my responsibility. I took care of it morning, noon and night. It must be said that the morning samovar didn't play exactly the same role as at other times of the day.

The morning samovar

My grandma was an opium addict. The doctor had told her to take it to lessen her pain (in any case, that's what she said). And so, on waking up and finding herself in a state of withdrawal, she was often in a very very bad mood, but it never lasted for long. She had only to dissolve a small bit of burnt opium* in her tea to regain her sense of humor and her natural kindness. It was just a matter of waiting.

* what is left at the bottom of an opium pipe after it's been smoked.

My
grandma
before:
→

My
grandma
after:
→

"Opium has many virtues," my grandmother would say.
"It's not just good for reducing pain."

Look at me, I have always had wide open eyes like you...

... So when I was younger, I took a little taste before going to parties. It made my eyelids heavy. It gave me a languorous look.

By the way, you should learn to close your eyes a little.

You really think that I look vibrant and intelligent like this?

No, but you'll find lovers more easily.

Thanks to her half-closed eyes, my grandma got married three times. My grandfather was her last husband.

~ The noon and night samovar ~

The tea that we prepared at these times had a completely different function.

Everyone gathered around this drink in order to devote themselves to their favorite activity : DISCUSSION.

This discussion had its own purpose:

To speak behind others' backs is the ventilator of the heart.

You must allow around three quarters of an hour for the tea to cook and reach its proper strength in a Samovar. (It really is about cooking and not steeping.)

When I finally arrived in the living room with my tray, the others had just finished the dishes.

What timing!

Ah, finally!

Bravo, my granddaughter! Bravo!

Bravo, Marji!

May God keep you!

Happiness!   Oh!   Ah!

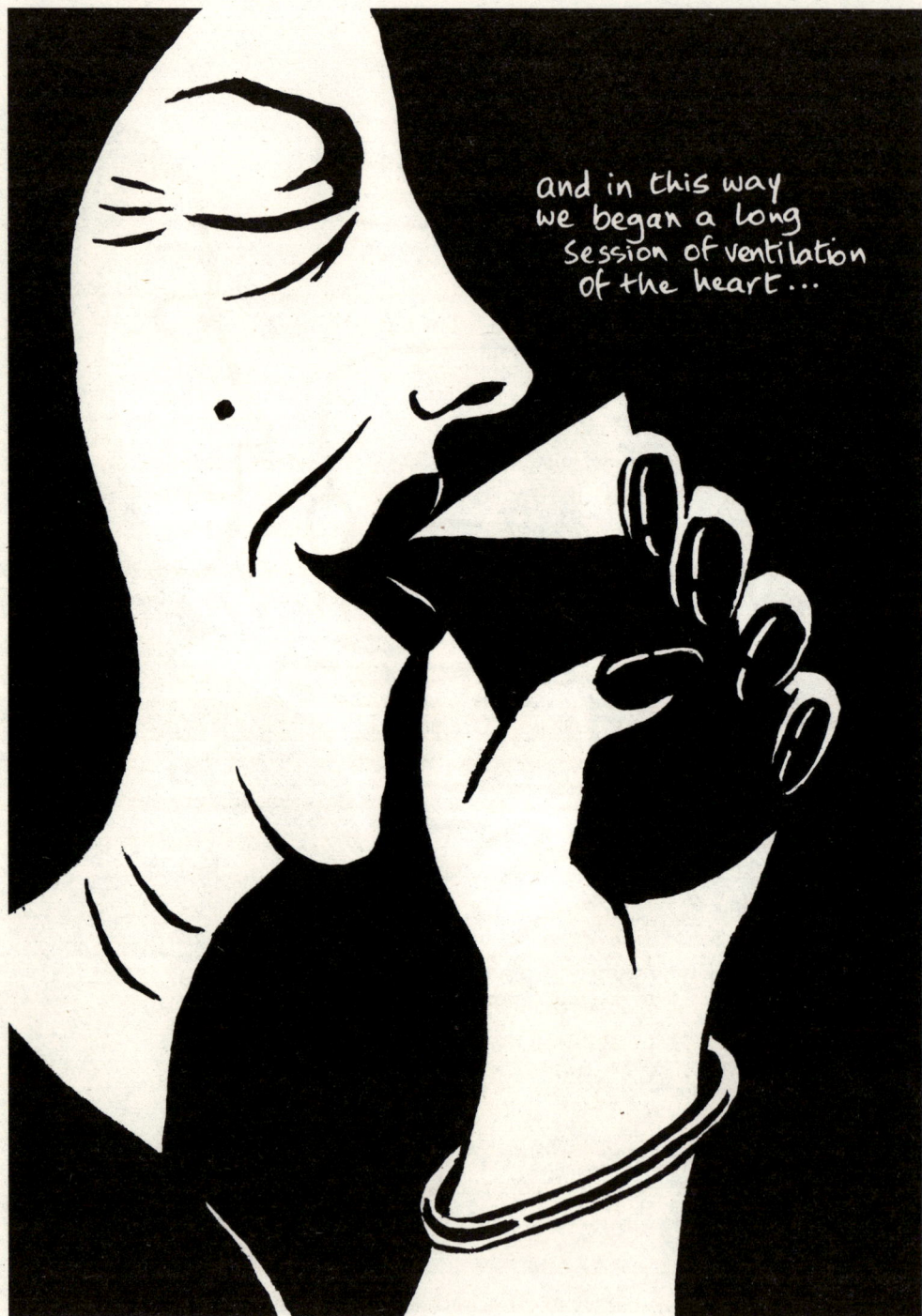

SEA OF POPPIES

Amitav Ghosh

The Indian novelist **Amitav Ghosh** is an artist of 'connections and cross-connections'. Although in this quote he was speaking specifically about the connections between the regions with which his books are most concerned – The Bay of Bengal, the Arabian Sea and the Indian Ocean – it applies, we think, more broadly to his work as a whole. His novels (and non-fiction books) seek to interrogate the ways the world is knitted together, revealing and sometimes unpicking each seam to show what darkness has been hidden beneath. Born in 1956, Ghosh is the recipient of four honorary doctorates and two lifetime achievement awards, a fellow of the Royal Society of Literature, shortlisted for the Booker International for his entire body of work, and the 2018 holder of India's oldest and highest literary honour. He is also completely, compulsively readable. The *Ibis* trilogy, the 1,600-page, three-book epic (named for the opium ship that binds the three volumes together) is of course meticulously researched, politically important and historically revelatory. But it is also funny, beautiful, violent, sexy, smart, learnéd, and *hungry*. This is a novel, of course, of connections and cross-connections and cross-cross-cross connections; where the petals of the opium-poppies are pressed into roti-like wrappers for packaging the opium that connects Britain to Bihar to China, while a woman makes real rotis and sees while swimming a vision of a great ship, and knows she must sketch out the ship from her dream onto a poppy-paper packet to keep it safe... This extract is the opening to the first book in the trilogy, *Sea of Poppies*, and we hope it makes you eat rotis and read more.

The vision of a tall-masted ship, at sail on the ocean, came to Deeti on an otherwise ordinary day, but she knew instantly that the apparition was a sign of destiny for she had never seen such a vessel before, not even in a dream: how could she have, living as she did in northern Bihar, four hundred miles from the coast? Her village was so far inland that the sea seemed as distant as the netherworld: it was the chasm of darkness where the holy Ganga disappeared into the Kala-Pani, 'the Black Water'.

It happened at the end of winter, in a year when the poppies were strangely slow to shed their petals: for mile after mile, from Benares onwards, the Ganga seemed to be flowing between twin glaciers, both its banks being blanketed by thick drifts of white-petalled flowers. It was as if the snows of the high Himalayas had descended on the plains to await the arrival of Holi and its springtime profusion of colour.

The village in which Deeti lived was on the outskirts of the town of Ghazipur, some fifty miles east of Benares. Like all her neighbours, Deeti was preoccupied with the lateness of her poppy crop: that day, she rose early and went through the motions of her daily routine, laying out a freshly washed dhoti and kameez for Hukam Singh, her husband, and preparing the rotis and achar he would eat at midday. Once his meal had been wrapped and packed, she broke off to pay a quick visit to her shrine room: later, after she'd bathed and changed, Deeti would do a proper puja, with flowers and offerings; now, being clothed still in her night-time sari, she merely stopped at the door, to join her hands in a brief genuflection.

Soon a squeaking wheel announced the arrival of the ox-cart that would take Hukam Singh to the factory where he worked, in Ghazipur, three miles away. Although not far, the distance was too great for Hukam Singh to cover on foot, for he had been wounded in the leg while serving as a sepoy in a British regiment. The disability was not so severe as to require crutches, however, and Hukam Singh was able to make his way to the cart without assistance. Deeti followed a step behind, carrying his food and water, handing the cloth-wrapped package to him after he had climbed in.

Kalua, the driver of the ox-cart, was a giant of a man, but he made no move to help his passenger and was careful to keep his face hidden from him: he was of the leather-workers' caste and Hukam Singh, as a high-caste Rajput, believed that the sight of his face would bode ill for the day ahead. Now, on climbing into the back of the cart, the former sepoy sat facing to the rear, with his bundle balanced on his lap, to prevent its coming into direct contact with any of the driver's belongings. Thus they would sit, driver and passenger, as the cart creaked along the road to Ghazipur – conversing amicably enough, but never exchanging glances.

Deeti, too, was careful to keep her face covered in the driver's presence: it was only when she went back inside, to wake Kabutri, her six-year-old daughter, that she allowed the ghungta of her sari to slip off her head. Kabutri was lying curled on her mat and Deeti knew, because of her quickly changing pouts and smiles, that she was deep in a dream: she was about to rouse her when she stopped her hand and stepped back. In her daughter's sleeping face, she could see the lineaments of her own likeness – the same full lips, rounded nose and upturned chin – except that in the child the lines were still clean and sharply drawn, whereas in herself they had grown smudged and indistinct. After seven years of marriage, Deeti was not much more than a child herself, but a few tendrils of white had already appeared in her thick black hair. The skin of her face, parched and darkened by the sun, had begun to flake and crack around the corners of her mouth and her eyes. Yet, despite the careworn commonplaceness of her appearance, there was one respect in which she stood out from the ordinary: she had light grey eyes, a feature that was unusual in that part of the country. Such was the colour – or perhaps colourlessness – of her eyes that they made her seem at once blind and all-seeing. This had the effect of unnerving the young, and of reinforcing their prejudices and superstitions to the point where they would sometimes shout taunts at her – *chudaliya, dainiya* – as if she were a witch: but Deeti had only to turn her eyes on them to make them scatter and run off. Although not above taking a little pleasure in her powers of discomfiture, Deeti was glad, for her daughter's sake, that this was one aspect of her appearance that she had not passed on – she delighted in Kabutri's dark eyes, which were as black as her shiny hair. Now, looking down on her daughter's dreaming face, Deeti smiled and decided that she wouldn't wake her after all: in three or four years the girl would be married and gone; there would be enough time for her to work when she was received into her husband's house; in her few remaining years at home she might as well rest.

With scarcely a pause for a mouthful of roti, Deeti stepped outside, on to the flat threshold of beaten earth that divided the mud-walled dwelling from the poppy fields beyond. By the light of the newly risen sun, she saw, greatly to her relief, that some of her flowers had at last begun to shed their petals. On the adjacent field, her husband's younger brother, Chandan Singh, was already out with his eight-bladed nukha in hand. He was using the tool's tiny teeth to make notches on some of the bare pods – if the sap flowed freely overnight he would bring his family out tomorrow, to tap the field. The timing had to be exactly right because the priceless sap flowed only for a brief period in the plant's span of life: a day or two, this way or that, and the pods were of no more value than the blossoms of a weed.

Chandan Singh had seen her too and he was not a person who could let anyone pass by in silence. A slack-jawed youth with a brood of five children of his own, he never missed an opportunity to remind Deeti of her paucity of offspring. *Ka bhaíl?* he called out, licking a drop of fresh sap from the tip of his instrument. What's the matter? Working alone again? How long can you carry on like this? You need a son, to give you a helping hand. You're not barren, after all . . .

Being accustomed to her brother-in-law's ways, Deeti had no difficulty in ignoring his jibes: turning her back on him, she headed into her own field, carrying a wide wicker basket at her waist. Between the rows of flowers, the ground was carpeted in papery petals and she scooped them up in handfuls, dropping them into her basket. A week or two before, she would have taken care to creep sideways, so as not to disturb the flowers, but today she all but flounced as she went and was none too sorry when her swishing sari swept clusters of petals off the ripening pods. When the basket was full, she carried it back and emptied it next to the outdoor chula where she did most of her cooking. This part of the threshold was shaded by two enormous mango trees, which had just begun to sprout the dimples that would grow into the first buds of spring. Relieved to be out of the sun, Deeti squatted beside her oven and thrust an armload of firewood into last night's embers, which could still be seen glowing, deep inside the ashes.

Kabutri was awake now, and when she showed her face in the doorway, her mother was no longer in a mood to be indulgent. So late? she snapped. Where were you? *Kám-o-káj na hoi?* You think there's no work to be done?

Deeti gave her daughter the job of sweeping the poppy petals into a heap while she busied herself in stoking the fire and heating a heavy iron tawa. Once this griddle was heated through, she sprinkled a handful of petals on it and pressed them down with a bundled-up rag. Darkening as they toasted, the petals began to cling together so that in a minute or two they looked exactly like the round wheat-flour rotis Deeti had packed for her husband's midday meal. And 'roti' was indeed the name by which these poppy-petal wrappers were known although their purpose was entirely different from that of their namesake: they were to be sold to the Sudder Opium Factory, in Ghazipur, where they would be used to line the earthenware containers in which opium was packed.

Kabutri, in the meanwhile, had kneaded some atta and rolled out a few real rotis. Deeti cooked them quickly, before poking out the fire: the rotis were put aside, to be eaten later with yesterday's left-overs – a dish of stale alu-posth, potatoes cooked in poppy-seed paste. Now, her mind turned to her shrine room again: with the hour of the noontime puja drawing close, it was time to go down to the river for a bath. After massaging poppy-seed oil into Kabutri's hair and her own, Deeti draped her spare sari over her shoulder and led her daughter towards the water, across the field.

The poppies ended at a sandbank that sloped gently down to the Ganga; warmed by the sun, the sand was hot enough to sting the soles of their bare feet. The burden of motherly decorum slipped suddenly off Deeti's bowed shoulders and she began to run after her daughter, who had skipped on ahead. A pace or two from the water's edge, they shouted an invocation to the river – *Jai Ganga Mayya ki . . .* – and gulped down a draught of air, before throwing themselves in.

They were both laughing when they came up again: it was the time of year when, after the initial shock of contact, the water soon reveals itself to be refreshingly cool. Although the full heat of summer was still several weeks away, the flow of the Ganga had already begun to dwindle. Turning in the direction of Benares, in the west, Deeti hoisted her daughter aloft, to pour out a handful of water as a tribute to the holy city. Along with the offering, a leaf flowed out of the child's cupped palms. They turned to watch as the river carried it downstream towards the ghats of Ghazipur.

The walls of Ghazipur's opium factory were partially obscured by mango and jackfruit trees but the British flag that flew on top of it was just visible above the foliage, as was the steeple of the church in which the factory's overseers prayed. At the factory's ghat on the Ganga, a one-masted pateli barge could be seen, flying the pennant of the English East India Company. It had brought in a shipment of *chalán* opium, from one of the Company's outlying sub-agencies, and was being unloaded by a long line of coolies.

Ma, said Kabutri, looking up at her mother, where is that boat going?

It was Kabutri's question that triggered Deeti's vision: her eyes suddenly conjured up a picture of an immense ship with two tall masts. Suspended from the masts were great sails of a dazzling shade of white. The prow of the ship tapered into a figurehead with a long bill, like a stork or a heron. There was a man in the background, standing near the bow, and although she could not see him clearly, she had a sense of a distinctive and unfamiliar presence.

Deeti knew that the vision was not materially present in front of her – as, for example, was the barge moored near the factory. She had never seen the sea, never left the district, never spoken any language but her native Bhojpuri, yet not for a moment did she doubt that the ship existed somewhere and was heading in her direction. The knowledge of this terrified her, for she had never set eyes on anything that remotely resembled this apparition, and had no idea what it might portend.

Kabutri knew that something unusual had happened, for she waited a minute or two before asking: Ma? What are you looking at? What have you seen?

Deeti's face was a mask of fear and foreboding as she said, in a shaky voice: Beti – I saw a jahaj – a ship.

Do you mean that boat over there?

No, beti: it was a ship like I've never seen before. It was like a great bird, with sails like wings and a long beak.

Casting a glance downriver, Kabutri said: Can you draw for me what you saw?

Deeti answered with a nod and they waded ashore. They changed quickly and filled a pitcher with water from the Ganga, for the puja room. When they were back at home, Deeti lit a lamp before leading Kabutri into the shrine. The room was dark, with soot-blackened walls, and it smelled strongly of oil and incense. There was a small altar inside, with statues of Shivji and Bhagwan Ganesh, and framed prints of Ma Durga and Shri Krishna. But the room was a shrine not just to the gods but also to Deeti's personal pantheon, and it contained many tokens of her family and forebears – among them such relics as her dead father's wooden clogs, a necklace of rudraksha beads left to her by her mother, and faded imprints of her grandparents' feet, taken on their funeral pyres. The walls around the altar were devoted to pictures that Deeti had drawn herself, in outline, on papery poppy-petal discs: such were the charcoal portraits of two brothers and a sister, all of whom had died as children. A few living relatives were represented too, but only by diagrammatic images drawn on mango leaves – Deeti believed it to be bad luck to attempt overly realistic portraits of those who had yet to leave this earth. Thus her beloved older brother, Kesri Singh, was depicted by a few strokes that stood for his sepoy's rifle and his upturned moustache.

Now, on entering her puja room, Deeti picked up a green mango leaf, dipped a fingertip in a container of bright red sindoor and drew, with a few strokes, two wing-like triangles hanging suspended above a long curved shape that ended in a hooked bill. It could have been a bird in flight but Kabutri recognized it at once for what it was – an image of a two-masted vessel with unfurled sails. She was amazed that her mother had drawn the image as though she were representing a living being.

Are you going to put it in the puja room? she asked.

Yes, said Deeti.

The child could not understand why a ship should find a place in the family pantheon. But why? she said.

I don't know, said Deeti, for she too was puzzled by the sureness of her intuition: I just know that it must be there; and not just the ship, but also many of those who are in it; they too must be on the walls of our puja room.

But who are they? said the puzzled child.

I don't know yet, Deeti told her. But I will when I see them.

*

ALICE'S ADVENTURES IN WONDERLAND

Lewis Carroll

Charles Dodgson, Maths teacher, is usually better remembered as the author of *Alice's Adventures in Wonderland*. **Lewis Carroll,** born in 1832, was known in his lifetime first for his extraordinary grasp of mathematical logic; then his puzzle column in *Vanity Fair*; then his career as a photographer; and finally, his novels for children. *Alice* and its sequel were an instant success, and remain – justifiably – universally beloved across the globe for their innate understanding of child-logic and refusal to ever patronize even the youngest reader. It is generally accepted that Carroll himself preferred the company of children to adults, and around them lost the stammer he had since his schooldays, having 'next to no interest in the adult world'. The adult world, as parodied in the extract below, is full of baffling and silly rules; the conventions and conversations of grown-up people are revealed as ridiculous; and their tea-parties so shrouded in murky etiquette that nobody ever gets anything delicious to eat. *Alice* is supposed, by the framing, to be a tale told to three little girls on a riverbank: the daughters of a colleague, the middle girl of whom was Alice Pleasance Liddell. The book begins on the seventh birthday of the real Alice, 4 May, and her name appears in an acrostic poem on the last page of *Through the Looking Glass*. Carroll's complex and perhaps problematic relationship to childhood (and the real Alice) has been much debated; but he has been dead for one hundred years, and Alice herself for almost as long. The riverbank still winds through Oxford, *Alice* has never been out of print, and we will never know any more; what remains to us is only the passing of time, and Wonderland itself. In Wonderland all things are possible, and time moves differently there.

Still she haunts me, phantomwise,
Alice moving under skies
Never seen by waking eyes.

There was a table set out under a tree in front of the house, and the March Hare and the Hatter were having tea at it: a Dormouse was sitting between them, fast asleep, and the other two were using it as a cushion, resting their elbows on it, and talking over its head. "Very uncomfortable for the Dormouse," thought Alice; "only, as it's asleep, I suppose it doesn't mind."

The table was a large one, but the three were all crowded together at one corner of it: "No room! No room!" they cried out when they saw Alice coming. "There's *plenty* of room!" said Alice indignantly, and she sat down in a large arm-chair at one end of the table.

"Have some wine," the March Hare said in an encouraging tone.

Alice looked all round the table, but there was nothing on it but tea. "I don't see any wine," she remarked.

"There isn't any," said the March Hare.

"Then it wasn't very civil of you to offer it," said Alice angrily.

"It wasn't very civil of you to sit down without being invited," said the March Hare.

"I didn't know it was *your* table," said Alice; "it's laid for a great many more than three."

"Your hair wants cutting," said the Hatter. He had been looking at Alice for some time with great curiosity, and this was his first speech.

"You should learn not to make personal remarks," Alice said with some severity; "it's very rude."

The Hatter opened his eyes very wide on hearing this; but all he *said* was, "Why is a raven like a writing-desk?"

"Come, we shall have some fun now!" thought Alice. "I'm glad they've begun asking riddles.—I believe I can guess that," she added aloud.

"Do you mean that you think you can find out the answer to it?" said the March Hare.

"Exactly so," said Alice.

"Then you should say what you mean," the March Hare went on.

"I do," Alice hastily replied; "at least—at least I mean what I say— that's the same thing, you know."

"Not the same thing a bit!" said the Hatter. "You might just as well say that 'I see what I eat' is the same thing as 'I eat what I see'!"

"You might just as well say," added the March Hare, "that 'I like what I get' is the same thing as 'I get what I like'!"

"You might just as well say," added the Dormouse, who seemed to be talking in his sleep, "that 'I breathe when I sleep' is the same thing as 'I sleep when I breathe'!"

"It *is* the same thing with you," said the Hatter, and here the conversation dropped, and the party sat silent for a minute, while Alice thought over all she could remember about ravens and writing-desks, which wasn't much.

The Hatter was the first to break the silence. "What day of the month is it?" he said, turning to Alice: he had taken his watch out of his pocket, and was looking at it uneasily, shaking it every now and then, and holding it to his ear.

Alice considered a little, and then said "The fourth."

"Two days wrong!" sighed the Hatter. "I told you butter wouldn't suit the works!" he added looking angrily at the March Hare.

"It was the *best* butter," the March Hare meekly replied.

"Yes, but some crumbs must have got in as well," the Hatter grumbled: "you shouldn't have put it in with the bread-knife."

The March Hare took the watch and looked at it gloomily: then he dipped it into his cup of tea, and looked at it again: but he could think of nothing better to say than his first remark, "It was the *best* butter, you know."

Alice had been looking over his shoulder with some curiosity. "What a funny watch!" she remarked. "It tells the day of the month, and doesn't tell what o'clock it is!"

"Why should it?" muttered the Hatter. "Does *your* watch tell you what year it is?"

"Of course not," Alice replied very readily: "but that's because it stays the same year for such a long time together."

"Which is just the case with *mine*," said the Hatter.

Alice felt dreadfully puzzled. The Hatter's remark seemed to have no sort of meaning in it, and yet it was certainly English. "I don't quite understand you," she said, as politely as she could.

"The Dormouse is asleep again," said the Hatter, and he poured a little hot tea upon its nose.

The Dormouse shook its head impatiently, and said, without opening its eyes, "Of course, of course; just what I was going to remark myself."

"Have you guessed the riddle yet?" the Hatter said, turning to Alice again.

"No, I give it up," Alice replied: "what's the answer?"

"I haven't the slightest idea," said the Hatter.

"Nor I," said the March Hare.

Alice sighed wearily. "I think you might do something better with the time," she said, "than waste it in asking riddles that have no answers."

"If you knew Time as well as I do," said the Hatter, "you wouldn't talk about wasting *it*. It's *him*."

"I don't know what you mean," said Alice.

"Of course you don't!" the Hatter said, tossing his head contemptuously. "I dare say you never even spoke to Time!"

"Perhaps not," Alice cautiously replied: "but I know I have to beat time when I learn music."

"Ah! that accounts for it," said the Hatter. "He won't stand beating. Now, if you only kept on good terms with him, he'd do almost anything you liked with the clock. For instance, suppose it were nine o'clock in the morning, just time to begin lessons: you'd only have to whisper a hint to Time, and round goes the clock in a twinkling! Half-past one, time for dinner!"

("I only wish it was," the March Hare said to itself in a whisper.)

"That would be grand, certainly," said Alice thoughtfully: "but then—I shouldn't be hungry for it, you know."

"Not at first, perhaps," said the Hatter: "but you could keep it to half-past one as long as you liked."

"Is that the way *you* manage?" Alice asked.

The Hatter shook his head mournfully. "Not I!" he replied. "We quarrelled last March—just before *he* went mad, you know—" (pointing with his tea spoon at the March Hare,) "—it was at the great concert given by the Queen of Hearts, and I had to sing

'Twinkle, twinkle, little bat!

How I wonder what you're at!'

You know the song, perhaps?"

"I've heard something like it," said Alice.

"It goes on, you know," the Hatter continued, "in this way:—

'Up above the world you fly,

Like a tea-tray in the sky.

 Twinkle, twinkle—'"

Here the Dormouse shook itself, and began singing in its sleep *"Twinkle, twinkle, twinkle, twinkle*—" and went on so long that they had to pinch it to make it stop.

"Well, I'd hardly finished the first verse," said the Hatter, "when the Queen jumped up and bawled out, 'He's murdering the time! Off with his head!'"

"How dreadfully savage!" exclaimed Alice.

"And ever since that," the Hatter went on in a mournful tone, "he won't do a thing I ask! It's always six o'clock now."

A bright idea came into Alice's head. "Is that the reason so many tea-things are put out here?" she asked.

"Yes, that's it," said the Hatter with a sigh: "it's always tea-time, and we've no time to wash the things between whiles."

"Then you keep moving round, I suppose?" said Alice.

"Exactly so," said the Hatter: "as the things get used up."

"But what happens when you come to the beginning again?" Alice ventured to ask.

"Suppose we change the subject," the March Hare interrupted, yawning. "I'm getting tired of this. I vote the young lady tells us a story."

"I'm afraid I don't know one," said Alice, rather alarmed at the proposal.

"Then the Dormouse shall!" they both cried. "Wake up, Dormouse!" And they pinched it on both sides at once.

The Dormouse slowly opened his eyes. "I wasn't asleep," he said in a hoarse, feeble voice: "I heard every word you fellows were saying."

"Tell us a story!" said the March Hare.

"Yes, please do!" pleaded Alice.

"And be quick about it," added the Hatter, "or you'll be asleep again before it's done."

"Once upon a time there were three little sisters," the Dormouse began in a great hurry; "and their names were Elsie, Lacie, and Tillie; and they lived at the bottom of a well—"

"What did they live on?" said Alice, who always took a great interest in questions of eating and drinking.

"They lived on treacle," said the Dormouse, after thinking a minute or two.

"They couldn't have done that, you know," Alice gently remarked; "they'd have been ill."

"So they were," said the Dormouse; "*very* ill."

Alice tried to fancy to herself what such an extraordinary ways of living would be like, but it puzzled her too much, so she went on: "But why did they live at the bottom of a well?"

"Take some more tea," the March Hare said to Alice, very earnestly.

"I've had nothing yet," Alice replied in an offended tone, "so I can't take more."

"You mean you can't take *less*," said the Hatter: "it's very easy to take *more* than nothing."

"Nobody asked *your* opinion," said Alice.

"Who's making personal remarks now?" the Hatter asked triumphantly.

Alice did not quite know what to say to this: so she helped herself to some tea and bread-and-butter, and then turned to the Dormouse, and repeated her question. "Why did they live at the bottom of a well?"

The Dormouse again took a minute or two to think about it, and then said, "It was a treacle-well."

"There's no such thing!" Alice was beginning very angrily, but the Hatter and the March Hare went "Sh! sh!" and the Dormouse sulkily remarked, "If you can't be civil, you'd better finish the story for yourself."

"No, please go on!" Alice said very humbly; "I won't interrupt again. I dare say there may be *one*."

"One, indeed!" said the Dormouse indignantly. However, he consented to go on.

"And so these three little sisters—they were learning to draw, you know—"

"What did they draw?" said Alice, quite forgetting her promise.

"Treacle," said the Dormouse, without considering at all this time.

"I want a clean cup," interrupted the Hatter: "let's all move one place on."

He moved on as he spoke, and the Dormouse followed him: the March Hare moved into the Dormouse's place, and Alice rather unwillingly took the place of the March Hare. The Hatter was the only one who got any advantage from the change: and Alice was a good deal worse off than before, as the March Hare had just upset the milk-jug into his plate.

Alice did not wish to offend the Dormouse again, so she began very cautiously: "But I don't understand. Where did they draw the treacle from?"

"You can draw water out of a water-well," said the Hatter; "so I should think you could draw treacle out of a treacle-well—eh, stupid?"

"But they were *in* the well," Alice said to the Dormouse, not choosing to notice this last remark.

"Of course they were," said the Dormouse; "—well in."

This answer so confused poor Alice, that she let the Dormouse go on for some time without interrupting it.

"They were learning to draw," the Dormouse went on, yawning and rubbing its eyes, for it was getting very sleepy; "and they drew all manner of things—everything that begins with an M—"

"Why with an M?" said Alice.

"Why not?" said the March Hare.

Alice was silent.

The Dormouse had closed its eyes by this time, and was going off into a doze; but, on being pinched by the Hatter, it woke up again with a little shriek, and went on: "—that begins with an M, such as mouse-traps, and the moon, and memory, and muchness—you know you say things are "much of a muchness"—did you ever see such a thing as a drawing of a muchness?"

"Really, now you ask me," said Alice, very much confused, "I don't think—"

"Then you shouldn't talk," said the Hatter.

This piece of rudeness was more than Alice could bear: she got up in great disgust, and walked off; the Dormouse fell asleep instantly, and neither of the others took the least notice of her going, though she looked back once or twice, half hoping that they would call after her: the last time she saw them, they were trying to put the Dormouse into the teapot.

"At any rate I'll never go *there* again!" said Alice as she picked her way through the wood. "It's the stupidest tea-party I ever was at in all my life!"

Just as she said this, she noticed that one of the trees had a door leading right into it. "That's very curious!" she thought. "But everything's curious today. I think I may as well go in at once." And in she went.

Once more she found herself in the long hall, and close to the little glass table. "Now, I'll manage better this time," she said to herself, and began by taking the little golden key, and unlocking the door that led into the garden. Then she went to work nibbling at the mushroom (she had kept a piece of it in her pocket) till she was about a foot high: then she walked down the little passage: and *then*—she found herself at last in the beautiful garden, among the bright flower-beds and the cool fountains.

THE GARDEN PARTY

Katherine Mansfield

The only writer of whom Virginia Woolf was ever jealous, **Katherine Mansfield** was born in New Zealand in 1888. (Intriguingly, she and Woolf were introduced by Lytton Strachey, the cousin of the translator on p. 12 who was mown down by a locomotive while taking his evening stroll. Perhaps they can discuss him.) Associated with the Bloomsbury Group through sheer force of talent, despite being both colonial (!) and 'smelling like a civet cat' (Woolf at her *most* obnoxious) she is recognized and remembered as one of the most important of the modernist writers. Before her death, hideously early at the age of 34, she wrote dozens of perfect short stories. Her stories are so very real, so very funny, sad, tender and clever that it is genuinely sort of heartbreaking to remember that she has been dead for one hundred years and that there will never be any more. This is our favourite of all of them, and we hope that you will think of it whenever you sneak a bit of whipped cream before breakfast on the morning of a celebration; unpack badly labelled catering sandwiches ('egg-and-mice?'); or run away to eat a solitary wedge of bread and butter out of doors.

And after all the weather was ideal. They could not have had a more perfect day for a garden-party if they had ordered it. Windless, warm, the sky without a cloud. Only the blue was veiled with a haze of light gold, as it is sometimes in early summer. The gardener had been up since dawn, mowing the lawns and sweeping them, until the grass and the dark flat rosettes where the daisy plants had been seemed to shine. As for the roses, you could not help feeling they understood that roses are the only flowers that impress people at garden-parties; the only flowers that everybody is certain of knowing. Hundreds, yes, literally hundreds, had come out in a single night; the green bushes bowed down as though they had been visited by archangels.

Breakfast was not yet over before the men came to put up the marquee.

"Where do you want the marquee put, mother?"

"My dear child, it's no use asking me. I'm determined to leave everything to you children this year. Forget I am your mother. Treat me as an honoured guest."

But Meg could not possibly go and supervise the men. She had washed her hair before breakfast, and she sat drinking her coffee in a green turban, with a dark wet curl stamped on each cheek. Jose, the butterfly, always came down in a silk petticoat and a kimono jacket.

"You'll have to go, Laura; you're the artistic one."

Away Laura flew, still holding her piece of bread-and-butter. It's so delicious to have an excuse for eating out of doors, and besides, she loved having to arrange things; she always felt she could do it so much better than anybody else.

Four men in their shirt-sleeves stood grouped together on the garden path. They carried staves covered with rolls of canvas, and they had big tool-bags slung on their backs. They looked impressive. Laura wished now that she had not got the bread-and-butter, but there was nowhere to put it, and she couldn't possibly throw it away. She blushed and tried to look severe and even a little bit short-sighted as she came up to them.

"Good morning," she said, copying her mother's voice. But that sounded so fearfully affected that she was ashamed, and stammered like a little girl, "Oh—er—have you come—is it about the marquee?"

"That's right, miss," said the tallest of the men, a lanky, freckled fellow, and he shifted his tool-bag, knocked back his straw hat and smiled down at her. "That's about it."

His smile was so easy, so friendly that Laura recovered. What nice eyes he had, small, but such a dark blue! And now she looked at the others, they were smiling too. "Cheer up, we won't bite," their smile seemed to say. How very nice workmen were! And what a beautiful morning! She mustn't mention the morning; she must be business-like. The marquee.

"Well, what about the lily-lawn? Would that do?"

And she pointed to the lily-lawn with the hand that didn't hold the bread-and-butter. They turned, they stared in the direction. A little fat chap thrust out his under-lip, and the tall fellow frowned.

"I don't fancy it," said he. "Not conspicuous enough. You see, with a thing like a marquee," and he turned to Laura in his easy way, "you want to put it somewhere where it'll give you a bang slap in the eye, if you follow me."

Laura's upbringing made her wonder for a moment whether it was quite respectful of a workman to talk to her of bangs slap in the eye. But she did quite follow him.

"A corner of the tennis-court," she suggested. "But the band's going to be in one corner."

"H'm, going to have a band, are you?" said another of the workmen. He was pale. He had a haggard look as his dark eyes scanned the tennis-court. What was he thinking?

"Only a very small band," said Laura gently. Perhaps he wouldn't mind so much if the band was quite small. But the tall fellow interrupted.

"Look here, miss, that's the place. Against those trees. Over there. That'll do fine."

Against the karakas. Then the karaka-trees would be hidden. And they were so lovely, with their broad, gleaming leaves, and their clusters of yellow fruit. They were like trees you imagined growing on a desert island, proud, solitary, lifting their leaves and fruits to the sun in a kind of silent splendour. Must they be hidden by a marquee?

They must. Already the men had shouldered their staves and were making for the place. Only the tall fellow was left. He bent down, pinched a sprig of lavender, put his thumb and forefinger to his nose and snuffed up the smell. When Laura saw that gesture she forgot all about the karakas in her wonder at him caring for things like that—caring for the smell of lavender. How many men that she knew would have done such a thing? Oh, how extraordinarily nice workmen were, she thought. Why couldn't she have workmen for her friends rather than the silly boys she danced with and who came to Sunday night supper? She would get on much better with men like these.

It's all the fault, she decided, as the tall fellow drew something on the back of an envelope, something that was to be looped up or left to hang, of these absurd class distinctions. Well, for her part, she didn't feel them. Not a bit, not an atom.... And now there came the chock-chock of wooden hammers. Some one whistled, some one sang out, "Are you right there, matey?" "Matey!" The friendliness of it, the—the—Just to prove how happy she was, just to show the tall fellow how at home she felt, and how she despised stupid conventions, Laura took a big bite of her bread-and-butter as she stared at the little drawing. She felt just like a work-girl.

"Laura, Laura, where are you? Telephone, Laura!" a voice cried from the house.

"Coming!" Away she skimmed, over the lawn, up the path, up the steps, across the veranda, and into the porch. In the hall her father and Laurie were brushing their hats ready to go to the office.

"I say, Laura," said Laurie very fast, "you might just give a squiz at my coat before this afternoon. See if it wants pressing."

"I will," said she. Suddenly she couldn't stop herself. She ran at Laurie and gave him a small, quick squeeze. "Oh, I do love parties, don't you?" gasped Laura.

"Ra-ther," said Laurie's warm, boyish voice, and he squeezed his sister too, and gave her a gentle push. "Dash off to the telephone, old girl."

The telephone. "Yes, yes; oh yes. Kitty? Good morning, dear. Come to lunch? Do, dear. Delighted of course. It will only be a very scratch meal—just the sandwich crusts and broken meringue-shells and what's left over. Yes, isn't it a perfect morning? Your white? Oh, I certainly should. One moment—hold the line. Mother's calling." And Laura sat back. "What, mother? Can't hear."

Mrs. Sheridan's voice floated down the stairs. "Tell her to wear that sweet hat she had on last Sunday."

"Mother says you're to wear that *sweet* hat you had on last Sunday. Good. One o'clock. Bye-bye."

Laura put back the receiver, flung her arms over her head, took a deep breath, stretched and let them fall. "Huh," she sighed, and the moment after the sigh she sat up quickly. She was still, listening. All the doors in the house seemed to be open. The house was alive with soft, quick steps and running voices. The green baize door that led to the kitchen regions swung open and shut with a muffled thud. And now there came a long, chuckling absurd sound. It was the heavy piano being moved on its stiff castors. But the air! If you stopped to notice, was the air always like this? Little faint winds were playing chase, in at the tops of the windows, out at the doors. And there were two tiny spots of sun, one on the inkpot, one on a silver photograph frame, playing too. Darling little spots. Especially the one on the inkpot lid. It was quite warm. A warm little silver star. She could have kissed it.

The front door bell pealed, and there sounded the rustle of Sadie's print skirt on the stairs. A man's voice murmured; Sadie answered, careless, "I'm sure I don't know. Wait. I'll ask Mrs. Sheridan."

"What is it, Sadie?" Laura came into the hall.

"It's the florist, Miss Laura."

It was, indeed. There, just inside the door, stood a wide, shallow tray full of pots of pink lilies. No other kind. Nothing but lilies—canna lilies, big pink flowers, wide open, radiant, almost frighteningly alive on bright crimson stems.

"O-oh, Sadie!" said Laura, and the sound was like a little moan. She crouched down as if to warm herself at that blaze of lilies; she felt they were in her fingers, on her lips, growing in her breast.

"It's some mistake," she said faintly. "Nobody ever ordered so many. Sadie, go and find mother."

But at that moment Mrs. Sheridan joined them.

"It's quite right," she said calmly. "Yes, I ordered them. Aren't they lovely?" She pressed Laura's arm. "I was passing the shop yesterday, and I saw them in the window. And I suddenly thought for once in my life I shall have enough canna lilies. The garden-party will be a good excuse."

"But I thought you said you didn't mean to interfere," said Laura. Sadie had gone. The florist's man was still outside at his van. She put her arm round her mother's neck and gently, very gently, she bit her mother's ear.

"My darling child, you wouldn't like a logical mother, would you? Don't do that. Here's the man."

He carried more lilies still, another whole tray.

"Bank them up, just inside the door, on both sides of the porch, please," said Mrs. Sheridan. "Don't you agree, Laura?"

"Oh, I *do*, mother."

In the drawing-room Meg, Jose and good little Hans had at last succeeded in moving the piano.

"Now, if we put this chesterfield against the wall and move everything out of the room except the chairs, don't you think?"

"Quite."

"Hans, move these tables into the smoking-room, and bring a sweeper to take these marks off the carpet and—one moment, Hans—" Jose loved giving orders to the servants, and they loved obeying her. She always made them feel they were taking part in some drama. "Tell mother and Miss Laura to come here at once."

"Very good, Miss Jose."

She turned to Meg. "I want to hear what the piano sounds like, just in case I'm asked to sing this afternoon. Let's try over 'This life is Weary.'"

Pom! Ta-ta-ta *Tee*-ta! The piano burst out so passionately that Jose's face changed. She clasped her hands. She looked mournfully and enigmatically at her mother and Laura as they came in.

This Life is *Wee*-ary, A Tear—a Sigh.

A Love that *Chan*-ges, This Life is *Wee*-ary,

A Tear—a Sigh. A Love that *Chan*-ges,

And then. . . Good-bye!

But at the word "Good-bye," and although the piano sounded more desperate than ever, her face broke into a brilliant, dreadfully unsympathetic smile.

"Aren't I in good voice, mummy?" she beamed.

This Life is *Wee*-ary,

Hope comes to Die.

A Dream—a *Wa*-kening.

But now Sadie interrupted them. "What is it, Sadie?"

"If you please, m'm, cook says have you got the flags for the sandwiches?"

"The flags for the sandwiches, Sadie?" echoed Mrs. Sheridan dreamily. And the children knew by her face that she hadn't got them. "Let me see." And she said to Sadie firmly, "Tell cook I'll let her have them in ten minutes."

Sadie went.

"Now, Laura," said her mother quickly, "come with me into the smoking-room. I've got the names somewhere on the back of an envelope. You'll have to write them out for me. Meg, go upstairs this minute and take that wet thing off your head. Jose, run and finish dressing this instant. Do you hear me, children, or shall I have to tell your father when he comes home to-night? And—and, Jose, pacify cook if you do go into the kitchen, will you? I'm terrified of her this morning."

The envelope was found at last behind the dining-room clock, though how it had got there Mrs. Sheridan could not imagine.

"One of you children must have stolen it out of my bag, because I remember vividly—cream-cheese and lemon-curd. Have you done that?"

"Yes."

"Egg and—" Mrs. Sheridan held the envelope away from her. "It looks like mice. It can't be mice, can it?"

"Olive, pet," said Laura, looking over her shoulder.

"Yes, of course, olive. What a horrible combination it sounds. Egg and olive."

They were finished at last, and Laura took them off to the kitchen. She found Jose there pacifying the cook, who did not look at all terrifying.

"I have never seen such exquisite sandwiches," said Jose's rapturous voice. "How many kinds did you say there were, cook? Fifteen?"

"Fifteen, Miss Jose."

"Well, cook, I congratulate you."

Cook swept up crusts with the long sandwich knife, and smiled broadly.

"Godber's has come," announced Sadie, issuing out of the pantry. She had seen the man pass the window.

That meant the cream puffs had come. Godber's were famous for their cream puffs. Nobody ever thought of making them at home.

"Bring them in and put them on the table, my girl," ordered cook.

Sadie brought them in and went back to the door. Of course Laura and Jose were far too grown-up to really care about such things. All the same, they couldn't help agreeing that the puffs looked very attractive. Very. Cook began arranging them, shaking off the extra icing sugar.

"Don't they carry one back to all one's parties?" said Laura.

"I suppose they do," said practical Jose, who never liked to be carried back. "They look beautifully light and feathery, I must say."

"Have one each, my dears," said cook in her comfortable voice. "Yer ma won't know."

Oh, impossible. Fancy cream puffs so soon after breakfast. The very idea made one shudder. All the same, two minutes later Jose and Laura were licking their fingers with that absorbed inward look that only comes from whipped cream.

"Let's go into the garden, out by the back way," suggested Laura. "I want to see how the men are getting on with the marquee. They're such awfully nice men."

But the back door was blocked by cook, Sadie, Godber's man and Hans.

Something had happened.

"Tuk-tuk-tuk," clucked cook like an agitated hen. Sadie had her hand clapped to her cheek as though she had toothache. Hans's face was screwed up in the effort to understand. Only Godber's man seemed to be enjoying himself; it was his story.

"What's the matter? What's happened?"

"There's been a horrible accident," said Cook. "A man killed."

"A man killed! Where? How? When?"

But Godber's man wasn't going to have his story snatched from under his very nose.

"Know those little cottages just below here, miss?" Know them? Of course, she knew them. "Well, there's a young chap living there, name of Scott, a carter. His horse shied at a traction-engine, corner of Hawke Street this morning, and he was thrown out on the back of his head. Killed."

"Dead!" Laura stared at Godber's man.

"Dead when they picked him up," said Godber's man with relish. "They were taking the body home as I come up here." And he said to the cook, "He's left a wife and five little ones."

"Jose, come here." Laura caught hold of her sister's sleeve and dragged her through the kitchen to the other side of the green baize door. There she paused and leaned against it. "Jose!" she said, horrified, "however are we going to stop everything?"

"Stop everything, Laura!" cried Jose in astonishment. "What do you mean?"

"Stop the garden-party, of course." Why did Jose pretend?

But Jose was still more amazed. "Stop the garden-party? My dear Laura, don't be so absurd. Of course we can't do anything of the kind. Nobody expects us to. Don't be so extravagant."

"But we can't possibly have a garden-party with a man dead just outside the front gate."

That really was extravagant, for the little cottages were in a lane to themselves at the very bottom of a steep rise that led up to the house. A broad road ran between. True, they were far too near. They were the greatest possible eyesore, and they had no right to be in that neighbourhood at all. They were little mean dwellings painted a chocolate brown. In the garden patches there was nothing but cabbage stalks, sick hens and tomato cans. The very smoke coming out of their chimneys was poverty-stricken. Little rags and shreds of smoke, so unlike the great silvery plumes that uncurled from the Sheridans' chimneys. Washerwomen lived in the lane and sweeps and a cobbler, and a man whose house-front was studded all over with minute bird-cages. Children swarmed. When the Sheridans were little they were forbidden to set foot there because of the revolting language and of what they might catch. But since they were grown up, Laura and Laurie on their prowls sometimes walked through. It was disgusting and sordid. They came out with a shudder. But still one must go everywhere; one must see everything. So through they went.

"And just think of what the band would sound like to that poor woman," said Laura.

"Oh, Laura!" Jose began to be seriously annoyed. "If you're going to stop a band playing every time some one has an accident, you'll lead a very strenuous life. I'm every bit as sorry about it as you. I feel just as sympathetic." Her eyes hardened. She looked at her sister just as she used to when they were little and fighting together. "You won't bring a drunken workman back to life by being sentimental," she said softly.

"Drunk! Who said he was drunk?" Laura turned furiously on Jose. She said, just as they had used to say on those occasions, "I'm going straight up to tell mother."

"Do, dear," cooed Jose.

"Mother, can I come into your room?" Laura turned the big glass door-knob.

"Of course, child. Why, what's the matter? What's given you such a colour?" And Mrs. Sheridan turned round from her dressing-table. She was trying on a new hat.

"Mother, a man's been killed," began Laura.

"*Not* in the garden?" interrupted her mother.

"No, no!"

"Oh, what a fright you gave me!" Mrs. Sheridan sighed with relief, and took off the big hat and held it on her knees.

"But listen, mother," said Laura. Breathless, half-choking, she told the dreadful story. "Of course, we can't have our party, can we?" she pleaded. "The band and everybody arriving. They'd hear us, mother; they're nearly neighbours!"

To Laura's astonishment her mother behaved just like Jose; it was harder to bear because she seemed amused. She refused to take Laura seriously.

"But, my dear child, use your common sense. It's only by accident we've heard of it. If some one had died there normally—and I can't understand how they keep alive in those poky little holes—we should still be having our party, shouldn't we?"

Laura had to say "yes" to that, but she felt it was all wrong. She sat down on her mother's sofa and pinched the cushion frill.

"Mother, isn't it terribly heartless of us?" she asked.

"Darling!" Mrs. Sheridan got up and came over to her, carrying the hat. Before Laura could stop her she had popped it on. "My child!" said her mother, "the hat is yours. It's made for you. It's much too young for me. I have never seen you look such a picture. Look at yourself!" And she held up her hand-mirror.

"But, mother," Laura began again. She couldn't look at herself; she turned aside.

This time Mrs. Sheridan lost patience just as Jose had done.

"You are being very absurd, Laura," she said coldly. "People like that don't expect sacrifices from us. And it's not very sympathetic to spoil everybody's enjoyment as you're doing now."

"I don't understand," said Laura, and she walked quickly out of the room into her own bedroom. There, quite by chance, the first thing she saw was this charming girl in the mirror, in her black hat trimmed with gold daisies, and a long black velvet ribbon. Never had she imagined she could look like that. Is mother right? she thought. And now she hoped her mother was right. Am I being extravagant? Perhaps it was extravagant. Just for a moment she had another glimpse of that poor woman and those little children, and the body being carried into the house. But it all seemed blurred, unreal, like a picture in the newspaper. I'll remember it again after the party's over, she decided. And somehow that seemed quite the best plan....

Lunch was over by half-past one. By half-past two they were all ready for the fray. The green-coated band had arrived and was established in a corner of the tennis-court.

"My dear!" trilled Kitty Maitland, "aren't they too like frogs for words? You ought to have arranged them round the pond with the conductor in the middle on a leaf."

Laurie arrived and hailed them on his way to dress. At the sight of him Laura remembered the accident again. She wanted to tell him. If Laurie agreed with the others, then it was bound to be all right. And she followed him into the hall.

"Laurie!"

"Hallo!" He was half-way upstairs, but when he turned round and saw Laura he suddenly puffed out his cheeks and goggled his eyes at her. "My word, Laura! You do look stunning," said Laurie. "What an absolutely topping hat!"

Laura said faintly "Is it?" and smiled up at Laurie, and didn't tell him after all.

Soon after that people began coming in streams. The band struck up; the hired waiters ran from the house to the marquee. Wherever you looked there were couples strolling, bending to the flowers, greeting, moving on over the lawn. They were like bright birds that had alighted in the Sheridans' garden for this one afternoon, on their way to—where? Ah, what happiness it is to be with people who all are happy, to press hands, press cheeks, smile into eyes.

"Darling Laura, how well you look!"

"What a becoming hat, child!"

"Laura, you look quite Spanish. I've never seen you look so striking."

And Laura, glowing, answered softly, "Have you had tea? Won't you have an ice? The passion-fruit ices really are rather special." She ran to her father and begged him. "Daddy darling, can't the band have something to drink?"

And the perfect afternoon slowly ripened, slowly faded, slowly its petals closed.

"Never a more delightful garden-party...." "The greatest success...." "Quite the most...."

Laura helped her mother with the good-byes. They stood side by side in the porch till it was all over.

"All over, all over, thank heaven," said Mrs. Sheridan. "Round up the others, Laura. Let's go and have some fresh coffee. I'm exhausted. Yes, it's been very successful. But oh, these parties, these parties! Why will you children insist on giving parties!" And they all of them sat down in the deserted marquee.

"Have a sandwich, daddy dear. I wrote the flag."

"Thanks." Mr. Sheridan took a bite and the sandwich was gone. He took another. "I suppose you didn't hear of a beastly accident that happened to-day?" he said.

"My dear," said Mrs. Sheridan, holding up her hand, "we did. It nearly ruined the party. Laura insisted we should put it off."

"Oh, mother!" Laura didn't want to be teased about it.

"It was a horrible affair all the same," said Mr. Sheridan. "The chap was married too. Lived just below in the lane, and leaves a wife and half a dozen kiddies, so they say."

An awkward little silence fell. Mrs. Sheridan fidgeted with her cup. Really, it was very tactless of father....

Suddenly she looked up. There on the table were all those sandwiches, cakes, puffs, all uneaten, all going to be wasted. She had one of her brilliant ideas.

"I know," she said. "Let's make up a basket. Let's send that poor creature some of this perfectly good food. At any rate, it will be the greatest treat for the children. Don't you agree? And she's sure to have neighbours calling in and so on. What a point to have it all ready prepared. Laura!" She jumped up. "Get me the big basket out of the stairs cupboard."

"But, mother, do you really think it's a good idea?" said Laura.

Again, how curious, she seemed to be different from them all. To take scraps from their party. Would the poor woman really like that?

"Of course! What's the matter with you to-day? An hour or two ago you were insisting on us being sympathetic, and now—"

Oh well! Laura ran for the basket. It was filled, it was heaped by her mother.

"Take it yourself, darling," said she. "Run down just as you are. No, wait, take the arum lilies too. People of that class are so impressed by arum lilies."

"The stems will ruin her lace frock," said practical Jose.

So they would. Just in time. "Only the basket, then. And, Laura!"— her mother followed her out of the marquee—"don't on any account—"

"What mother?"

No, better not put such ideas into the child's head! "Nothing! Run along."

It was just growing dusky as Laura shut their garden gates. A big dog ran by like a shadow. The road gleamed white, and down below in the hollow the little cottages were in deep shade. How quiet it seemed after the afternoon. Here she was going down the hill to somewhere where a man lay dead, and she couldn't realize it. Why couldn't she?

She stopped a minute. And it seemed to her that kisses, voices, tinkling spoons, laughter, the smell of crushed grass were somehow inside her. She had no room for anything else. How strange! She looked up at the pale sky, and all she thought was, "Yes, it was the most successful party."

Now the broad road was crossed. The lane began, smoky and dark. Women in shawls and men's tweed caps hurried by. Men hung over the palings; the children played in the doorways. A low hum came from the mean little cottages. In some of them there was a flicker of light, and a shadow, crab-like, moved across the window. Laura bent her head and hurried on. She wished now she had put on a coat. How her frock shone! And the big hat with the velvet streamer—if only it was another hat! Were the people looking at her? They must be. It was a mistake to have come; she knew all along it was a mistake. Should she go back even now?

No, too late. This was the house. It must be. A dark knot of people stood outside. Beside the gate an old, old woman with a crutch sat in a chair, watching. She had her feet on a newspaper. The voices stopped as Laura drew near. The group parted. It was as though she was expected, as though they had known she was coming here.

Laura was terribly nervous. Tossing the velvet ribbon over her shoulder, she said to a woman standing by, "Is this Mrs. Scott's house?" and the woman, smiling queerly, said, "It is, my lass."

Oh, to be away from this! She actually said, "Help me, God," as she walked up the tiny path and knocked. To be away from those staring eyes, or to be covered up in anything, one of those women's shawls even. I'll just leave the basket and go, she decided. I shan't even wait for it to be emptied.

Then the door opened. A little woman in black showed in the gloom.

Laura said, "Are you Mrs. Scott?" But to her horror the woman answered, "Walk in please, miss," and she was shut in the passage.

"No," said Laura, "I don't want to come in. I only want to leave this basket. Mother sent—"

The little woman in the gloomy passage seemed not to have heard her. "Step this way, please, miss," she said in an oily voice, and Laura followed her.

She found herself in a wretched little low kitchen, lighted by a smoky lamp. There was a woman sitting before the fire.

"Em," said the little creature who had let her in. "Em! It's a young lady." She turned to Laura. She said meaningly, "I'm 'er sister, miss. You'll excuse 'er, won't you?"

"Oh, but of course!" said Laura. "Please, please don't disturb her. I—I only want to leave—"

But at that moment the woman at the fire turned round. Her face, puffed up, red, with swollen eyes and swollen lips, looked terrible. She seemed as though she couldn't understand why Laura was there. What did it mean? Why was this stranger standing in the kitchen with a basket? What was it all about? And the poor face puckered up again.

"All right, my dear," said the other. "I'll thenk the young lady."

And again she began, "You'll excuse her, miss, I'm sure," and her face, swollen too, tried an oily smile.

Laura only wanted to get out, to get away. She was back in the passage. The door opened. She walked straight through into the bedroom, where the dead man was lying.

"You'd like a look at 'im, wouldn't you?" said Em's sister, and she brushed past Laura over to the bed. "Don't be afraid, my lass,"—and now her voice sounded fond and sly, and fondly she drew down the sheet—"'e looks a picture. There's nothing to show. Come along, my dear."

Laura came.

There lay a young man, fast asleep—sleeping so soundly, so deeply, that he was far, far away from them both. Oh, so remote, so peaceful. He was dreaming. Never wake him up again. His head was sunk in the pillow, his eyes were closed; they were blind under the closed eyelids. He was given up to his dream. What did garden-parties and baskets and lace frocks matter to him? He was far from all those things. He was wonderful, beautiful. While they were laughing and while the band was playing, this marvel had come to the lane. Happy... happy.... All is well, said that sleeping face. This is just as it should be. I am content.

But all the same you had to cry, and she couldn't go out of the room without saying something to him. Laura gave a loud childish sob.

"Forgive my hat," she said.

And this time she didn't wait for Em's sister. She found her way out of the door, down the path, past all those dark people. At the corner of the lane she met Laurie.

He stepped out of the shadow. "Is that you, Laura?"

"Yes."

"Mother was getting anxious. Was it all right?"

"Yes, quite. Oh, Laurie!" She took his arm, she pressed up against him.

"I say, you're not crying, are you?" asked her brother.

Laura shook her head. She was.

Laurie put his arm round her shoulder. "Don't cry," he said in his warm, loving voice. "Was it awful?"

"No," sobbed Laura. "It was simply marvellous. But Laurie—" She stopped, she looked at her brother. "Isn't life," she stammered, "isn't life—" But what life was she couldn't explain. No matter. He quite understood.

"*Isn't* it, darling?" said Laurie.

TINY MOONS

Nina Mingya Powles

London-based poet, writer, and zinemaker **Nina Mingya Powles** grew up in New Zealand and holds an MA in Creative Writing from Victoria University of Wellington. She was the co-winner of the 2018 Women Poets' Prize, and won the 2019 Nan Shepherd Prize for Nature Writing. *Tiny Moons: A Year of Eating in Shanghai* is a collection of essays about food and belonging, a travel memoir, and a journey through eating as Powles 'attempts to find a way back towards her Chinese–Malaysian heritage'.

Boiled Dumplings

饺子

My life with dumplings began in a crowded restaurant with jade-green walls. It smelled like meat and jasmine tea. Clinking porcelain, guttural shouts, chopsticks clattering onto the tiled floor. Old women with very few teeth pushed carts piled high with bamboo steamers. I pointed at what I wanted to eat: three dumplings and a 7-Up, please. Mum had taught me the names but I was always too shy to speak Chinese. As usual I ate the outside part, the slippery skin, my favourite part of the dumpling. Then I sheepishly tipped the filling into my dad's bowl. Bored of sitting still, I slid off my seat and wound my way past the carts and tables to the front window where three big lobsters snoozed in a tank of cloudy water. We always left with a box of mooncakes wrapped in red tissue paper, and a handful of peppermints.

*

It is said that jiaozi, boiled dumplings, began as a cure for frostbite. In the middle of a harsh northern winter almost two thousand years ago, a Chinese physician named Zhang Zhongjing made little dough parcels filled with lamb, chilli, ginger and garlic, folded them in the shape of an ear, cooked them in boiling water, and fed them to those suffering from the cold. He called them 嬌耳 jiao'er – tender ears.

All over China, jiaozi are eaten for every meal and every snack in between, but ten times more than usual are consumed on the eve of the Lunar New Year. The communal act of making dumplings represents the family coming together, something that might only happen once a year, with the mass exodus of young people from rural villages to the cities. If you look into people's windows just before midnight, you'll see them shaping balls of dough into discs in the palms of their hands, laying them out on the table in a row, then filling and folding them in the traditional crescent shape. The grandma might fix up the wonky ones so they don't burst open in the boiling water. The steamed-up windows almost shut out the light of fireworks shooting across the building tops.

*

The beginning feels far away now. I remember the feeling of eating alone for the first time in Shanghai, a few days after I arrived. The idea seemed unbearable but the alternative was eating alone in my room. I could at least go outside, leave the confines of campus and join the noise and colours of the city. I forced myself to say to the cashier: 'Zheli chi, xiexie.' *I'll eat in, thank you.* Congyou banmian and a bowl of mini wontons. There was a young student slurping noodles opposite me, totally immersed in her e-book. She looked startled when I asked if she could pass me the soy sauce,

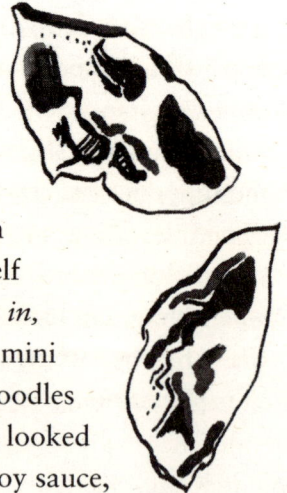

but did so with a half-smile. When I raised my arm to take the sticky bottle from her, our palms almost touched.

In *The Lonely City*, Olivia Laing writes of the importance of small, everyday exchanges she has while living alone in New York City. She begins to track and record these seemingly mundane, split-second conversations. It was the same for me, especially in the depths of that first summer in Shanghai, when the university campus emptied of other students, when I hardly spoke to anyone face-to-face except for the women who served breakfast at the canteen, or the lady who wrapped zongzi by hand and soaked them in giant rice cookers in the back of her shop. In those long months, ordering food for myself became a point of contact with the outside world. For stretches of days I never said a word aloud in English, only fragments of Mandarin. I was beginning to find a home in this language, one shared by my mother and her family but here and now, at this exact point in time, occupied only by me. The language was a lifeline, an opening, and eating alone became a silent ritual.

My last meal in Shanghai that final winter is a small plate of jiaozi filled with pork and Chinese cabbage, with a basket of chewy, flaky spring onion pancakes. As usual, I am eating by myself. It helps that in this city there are likely thousands of people or even hundreds of thousands eating their bowl of noodles or dumplings alone at any given moment. For a short while, I am one of them.

Dongbei Feng is a northern-style Chinese restaurant inside a shopping mall in Wujiaochang, the busy shopping area within walking distance from campus. Students, both local and foreign, are everywhere. In the months leading up to my departure, they've begun demolishing the buildings that contain my beloved food-court restaurants. Dongbei Feng still stands, as does the place where I go to eat my favourite spring onion noodles, but not for long. If I come back to visit in a year's time, Wujiaochang will be unrecognisable. This phenomenon is nothing new – since the late 1980s, when China opened up to the West and began its rapid race to modernisation, shiny new shopping malls and residential developments are being built all the time, squeezing out the old street vendors and small traders. "Old" malls built ten years ago are now being replaced by newer, bigger ones; the city is constantly building and re-building itself. New xiaochi food streets and food courts re-emerge all the time. In a year's time, students will simply flock elsewhere for their cheap dumpling fix.

These are the dumplings I grew up with. Seconds ago they were ladled from the pot of boiling water onto my plate, still steaming and glistening, their pearly white skins a little wonky and uneven: a reassuring sign that the dough has been rolled by hand, not machine. The pork and cabbage filling is seasoned with ginger, spring onions and soy sauce, with an egg to bind the mix together. Sometimes also a little sesame oil, five-spice or MSG powder, depending on whose secret recipe it is. Dedicated dumpling restaurants such as this one serve delicious vegetarian options too: egg and chives, egg and tomato (a particularly northern combination), mushroom and chives. On the table, there are always three condiments in porcelain jars: soy sauce, black vinegar and chilli oil.

Jiaozi remind me of helping my mother in our steam-filled kitchen at home by the sea. They remind me of the cold, dark month I spent studying in Beijing when I was nineteen, the sun permanently clouded by a thick haze of pollution, living off jiaozi every morning and evening. When I ordered them to takeaway, I received black vinegar in a little plastic bag tied shut with a rubber band. Extra chilli oil for extra cold, homesick afternoons. What does it mean to taste something and be transported to so many places at once, all of them a piece of home? To be half-elsewhere all the time, half-here and not-here. There are two sides of myself: one longing for the city, one at peace near the sea.

*

I will never be ready to say goodbye to Shanghai, so I don't. When it's time to leave, I take with me as much as I can carry. Winter in Shanghai will soon give way to summer in Wellington. This is, for me, as natural as the changing of the seasons.

I take dumplings with me wherever I go. The summer after leaving,

I visit Katrin at her home in Frankfurt and we fold jiaozi together at her small kitchen table, using a vegan filling of chopped aubergines, mushrooms, tofu, spring onions and spinach. Next I fly to San Francisco, where Jessie and Karen live – we've been friends since middle school in Shanghai. We stroll together through San Francisco's Chinatown to buy ingredients: shiitake mushrooms, fresh tofu, bok choi, ginger. I step inside a shop crammed with Chinese kitchen utensils. There are paper lanterns hanging from every bit of ceiling and strings of lights coiled around the doorways. I point to a brilliant blue cloth lantern I want to bring home with me and hang in my bedroom. It's her last one, the shopkeeper tells me, and all covered in dust, so it's only ten dollars. She smiles. The pattern of yellow and pink peonies against blue is almost identical to Maggie Cheung's cheongsam in *In the Mood for Love*, that slow-burning, blue-tinted film. The tenement buildings are painted green and pink and blue and gold. Groups of aunties and grandmas congregate on every corner chatting in Hakka and Cantonese, their shopping bags full of chives and melons and daikon. In any city anywhere, if there's a Chinatown I'll feel at home.

We fold our jiaozi on Jessie's bedroom floor in her shared apartment on Polk Street. It's muscle memory by now: I dip my fingers in a little water and dab it around the edge of the dough to make a glue, place a teaspoon of filling in the centre of the circle, fold it into a half circle and make six to eight folds along the rim, squeezing the dough between my thumb and forefinger. We fall into a familiar rhythm, the silence broken occasionally by fits of laughter. We have each been taught this skill a long time ago – by mothers, sisters, friends – and it connects us to a place both real and unreal, a home that no longer exists but is preserved in memory. I place little dishes of soy sauce and vinegar between the bowls of dumplings and we have a picnic on the floor, lilac San Francisco sunset clouds shifting in the sky beyond.

*

When I chance upon a Chinese grocer's or any Asian supermarket anywhere in the world, I fall into a trance. I sway in front of aisles packed with a hundred different brands of instant noodles. I become giddy at the sight of all the snacks my mother loves: the dried plums in bright purple packets, rice crackers, dried peas, pungent vacuum-packed salted cuttlefish. I resist the urge to stroke the green-gold papayas and mangoes. I head for the freezer section, where the dumpling skins are stacked according to national variety: for Korean mandu, for Japanese gyoza, for Tibetan momos. In London's Chinatown in the middle of winter I once bought a kumquat tree, just because they were there, and because my parents had a kumquat tree on the balcony of one of the many houses I grew up in. In her essay "Crying in H Mart", the American musician and writer Michelle Zauner, who is of Korean descent, describes her local Korean supermarket as a kind of sanctuary and magic portal. Sitting in a Korean food court in suburban Philadelphia, she wonders who else around her is missing home. What memory are they reliving? Where are they trying to reach? Who are they desperately trying not to forget? If she saw me, she might know.

Where I live now, the nearest Asian supermarket is a bus and a train ride away. This means I must teach myself to make my own dough for the jiaozi pi, dumpling skins, something I always thought was beyond me – a skill reserved only for the most experienced Chinese aunties and grandmas.

The first time I try, I'm cooking for one. There are only two ingredients: flour and water. I make a well in the flour with a spoon and add lukewarm water. Different recipes call for different temperatures: cold water makes for a stiff dough, making it better for fried dumplings; hot or just-boiled water creates a softer, more malleable texture, better for sealing the jiaozi edges tightly before boiling. The family-run website that I rely on for most Chinese recipes, The Woks of Life, calls for less water in humid climates. Fuchsia Dunlop in *Every Grain of Rice* calls for cold water. I choose blood temperature. Rain streams down the kitchen skylight.

The dough is soft and pliant. I pull the ball into two halves and then in half again. I roll them into cylinders and cut them into small gnocchi-like chunks, before shaping the chunks into balls by rolling them between my palms. I press down with the heel of my palm to flatten each ball into a disc, leaving an imprint of my palm lines.

The jiaozi pi shouldn't be perfectly flat. Unlike sheets of pasta rolled out to make ravioli or tortellini, the circle of dough for jiaozi should be thicker in the centre and thinner around the edge. This means the centre can hold the xianr, the filling, without breaking, while the edges can be tightly sealed. I use the edge of a rolling pin to flatten the edge of the circle, rotating it with my other hand. It's the kind of swift movement that I never thought I'd be capable of, but now it comes easily to me, even though I'm hopelessly uncoordinated when it comes to speed and rhythm. When cooking, my body falls into a natural rhythm I didn't know I had.

I take a small spoonful of the chopped filling (peas, tofu, mushrooms, spring onions, garlic and ginger, with a little soy sauce and oyster sauce and sesame oil). I place it in the centre of the circle, then seal it with two or three folds on each side so that the curved outer edge is moulded round my fingers. Every homemade jiaozi looks like this: formed inside a cupped hand, pressed shut by firm fingers. Each dumpling holds the shape of my skin.

*

It's summer in Wellington, and I go swimming with my friend Rose in Oriental Bay in the evening after work. The moon has already risen by late afternoon, a shy arc just visible against deepening blue. We wriggle into our swimsuits beneath the sun and the moon.

Rose, who was born in Shanghai but grew up in Whanganui, swims out to the floating platform and back again three times. I dip my body three-quarters into the water and paddle gently, wary of jellyfish and the stinging cold. We dry off clumsily, becoming aware of the gnawing feeling in our stomachs and a weakening in the backs of our knees.

I love swimming, partly because of that particular kind of post-swim hunger that can only compared to hunger after sex. The ache that tells you if you don't go eat something soon your limbs might liquefy. It must have something to do with the weight of water on our muscles, the strain of using parts of our body we never use on land.

With sand still between our toes and thighs, we sit by the window in a Chinese takeaway. We eat bowls of dumplings and noodles and chat over clouds of steam. A Taste of Home – undeniably the best name for a noodle shop – is the only place we've found in Wellington that has thick, chewy hand-pulled noodles and handmade dumplings. We sip peach juice between mouthfuls of soup and chilli oil, cheeks red and eyes watering. I balance a steaming dumpling between my chopsticks while the sea wind beats against the windows.

THE ISLAND KITCHEN

Selina Periampillai

Born in Britain to Mauritian parents, **Selina Periampillai** is a writer and self-taught chef. After putting on her first supper club in her London home and hosting multiple pop-ups, Periampillai began sharing her recipes. She is now a respected voice on Mauritian cuisine, writing recipes for numerous outlets online including Air Mauritius, JamieOliver.com, and Great British Chefs. *The Island Kitchen*, her debut book, is the first-ever cookbook of Indian Ocean recipes, and was shortlisted in 2019 for the Jane Grigson Trust Award.

Mauritius is known for its white-sand beaches fringed with coral reefs lying under turquoise seas. But it's also a gourmet paradise, with a magical mélange of flavours. The food is the story of the people who migrated to the island – which lies at the confluence of Asia, Europe and Africa's maritime routes – over the centuries. It is a cuisine that came from native Africans forced here as slaves, French colonisers who ruled in the eighteenth century, the Chinese who travelled from Guangzhou in the 1780s and Guangdong in the nineteenth century, and Indians who arrived as indentured labourers and whose descendants now make up over half of the population. Our penchant for afternoon tea lies with the British, who took over in 1810.

When the Portuguese discovered Mauritius in 1507, calling it and its neighbours Rodrigues and Réunion the 'Ilhas Mascarenhas' (the Mascarene Islands) – named after the explorer Pedro Mascarenhas who first set foot there – there were no indigenous people and therefore no native cuisine. The dodo, our endemic flightless bird, now extinct, was still thriving.

The mish mash of people who landed around the 330km of coastline meant that Creole (also known as 'Creole Morisyen', which came about as French colonisers tried to communicate with the slaves forced here from Africa) became the language of the island. The influx of cultures brought manifold types of dish together on the Mauritian table: from India came *cari* (curry); from France, *rougailles* (light stews) scented with thyme, *bouillon* (soup), *daube* and *coq au vin* – as well as fabulous pastries and tarts; from China, rice, noodles and dumplings, and the wonderful *gateau zingli*, sesame balls made from sweet potato, glutinous rice or sometimes red bean paste, deep fried until slightly chewy inside and crisp outside, then flecked with sesame seeds.

The food of Mauritius comes alive in the place locals call the Grand Bazaar, in the middle of Port Louis' Central Market. Stalls are stacked with just-picked fruit and vegetables in a kaleidoscope of colours. You'll see: huddles of yellow dwarf bananas; blushing pink lychees just plucked from the trees, their leaves still attached; deep green and red chillies of all shapes and sizes; and piles of chou chou, prickly breadfruit and baby pineapples (the sweetest I've ever tasted). Stall-holders cook over little burners and charcoal grills. Soft brown *roti* cooked on a *tawa* are smeared with butterbean curry, coriander chutney and chilli before being curled into a *papier cornet* and wrapped in pages of an old telephone directory. One bite and I'm in heaven, truly back in the land of my parents, my second home.

Introduced to Réunion by Chinese immigrants from the Canton region, 'bouchon' is now one of the island's most popular snacks. These zesty little steamed parcels are filled with seasoned minced pork or chicken and served with a soy and ginger dipping sauce. The traditional way to cook these is to use a bamboo steamer, which you can find in most Asian stores and supermarkets. I find adding a round of greaseproof paper or torn cabbage leaves in the base of the steamer can stop the dumplings sticking.

Another version of these 'bouchons' is sold on food trucks as 'pain bouchon gratiné': a French baguette stuffed with the dumplings and liberally covered with melted cheese – to die for!

Pork dumplings with soy ginger dip
Bouchons, réunion

500g minced pork

2 spring onions, finely chopped

3 kaffir lime leaves, finely chopped, or zest of 1 lime

2 tbsp light soy sauce

1 tbsp grated fresh root ginger

1 tsp chilli flakes

Plain flour, for dusting

1 pack of chilled wonton pastry wrappers (available from Asian supermarkets)

Freshly ground black pepper

For the dipping sauce:

4 tbsp light soy sauce

2 tbsp sesame oil

2 tbsp rice wine vinegar

2 tsp brown sugar

1 red chilli, finely chopped

1 tbsp finely chopped chives

Makes: approx. 24 dumplings
Prep: 25 mins
Cook: 10 mins per batch

- First, make the dipping sauce. Mix all the ingredients together well in a small bowl and leave aside to infuse while you make the dumplings.
- In a large mixing bowl, add the minced pork, spring onion, kaffir lime leaves, soy sauce, ginger, chilli and pepper to season. Mix well.
- To assemble the dumplings, dust some flour on to a work surface and fill a small glass with some cold water. Take the first wonton pastry wrapper and place in a diamond shape with a corner, not an edge, nearest to you.
- Using your finger, slightly dampen all edges of the wrapper with the

water; this will help it stick together. Take 1 scant tablespoon of the pork mixture, shape it into a ball and place in the centre of the wrapper.

- Take the corner closest to you and the opposite corner and bring those together, sealing the edge. Then bring up the other two corners into the centre, scrunching them into a little pouch. The pork filling should be well enclosed, but add a little more water to completely seal the edges if needed.

- Repeat with the remaining wonton pastry to make all your dumplings. A few extra hands help and make it fun! (Leftover wrappers will keep in a sealed container in the fridge for a week or so.)

- Put a few of the dumplings in a single layer inside a bamboo steamer lined with greaseproof paper or torn cabbage leaves, leaving some space between them so they don't stick together. Put the steamer over a pan of simmering water, cover and cook for around 10 minutes until the pork is cooked throughout. When they're done, the wrappers will appear translucent and the filling opaque. You can cut one open to check. Take them out gently with tongs, then steam the rest of the dumplings in batches. Serve immediately, bundled onto a platter with the dipping sauce.

UNEARTHED

Claire Ratinon

Part nature writing, part incitement to garden, part history, part treatise, and part memoir, **Claire Ratinon**'s extraordinary book *Unearthed* charts her first year in the countryside. After years of working in the city, Ratinon stumbled across a rooftop farm in New York and fell in love. After quitting her job in documentary production, she became obsessed with soil, roots and the ways we work with the earth to survive and sustain ourselves. Drawing on her Mauritian heritage, Ratinon's work not only sparkles with her love for the natural world, but crackles with the political and cultural tensions that underpin so much of why we do things the way we do them – and how we can, and must, change. She is now the gardening columnist for the *Guardian* and a driving force for land justice.

T he temperature is starting to tilt. Letting the chickens out in the morning is becoming an ever-chillier task, and I'm watering less and less. As I generally do when the autumnal equinox arrives, I've started to panic because I 'haven't enjoyed the good weather enough' and I want to squeeze in more walks and adventures before the season turns. As I make breakfast and Sam tries to find somewhere for us to spend the morning exploring, the voices coming out of the radio are discussing the National Trust and a report that it is soon to release. It's going to state the obvious: that the existence of some of the manor houses and other properties in its care was made possible by the slave trade and colonialism. You'd have thought the work of historical inquiry would be welcomed by those who find this country's history interesting, yet there is resistance, and the radio presenter – in a bid to provide 'balance' – feels compelled to mention it. My heart sinks.

This reluctance to acknowledge how the dominant accounts of history are incomplete feels as illogical as it does dispiriting. Excoriating 'settled' history is more than a search for what has been erased. Deepening the excavations of these ugly and complex periods of our collective history can offer us a lens through which to view the many ways in which the exploitative dynamics of imperialism and colonialism are still alive and well today. While I reflect on the colonialism in my past and the way it arises in my present, international investment companies and global agribusiness have bought up millions of hectares of farmland throughout the continent of Africa; private companies hold patents on products developed using the plant knowledge they gleaned from indigenous communities; and the destruction of ecologies and the displacement of people from their lands, to make way for the interests of those who seek to profit from it, carry on. All I hear are the fading cries of a dwindling set of the Empire's apologists and I'm determined not to give their dissent more attention than it deserves.

Although the early morning was cool, the sun has started to climb. I've never trusted the English weather as it steps from one season into the next, so I put on an extra layer, just in case, while Sam tells me about a walk in a nearby village around a set of structures with a strange origin story. An eccentric squire, a known drunkard and an MP at twenty-three years old in 1780, built a series of functionless monuments – follies, they call them – in and around the village of Brightling. Intriguing and odd, and close enough for us to fill our flasks with tea and head out for the next couple of hours.

The drive takes us steadily upwards, noodling through single-file country lanes, until we're high enough to see the landscape open outwards in all directions. From here, it is just about possible to look south and see the blue line of the sea at the horizon. The air is hazy warm and entirely absent of moisture. The sky is a soft light blue and a red kite hangs, hovering, in the middle of it. The trail doesn't appear to have a start or an end point, so we park up and head in the direction of the nearest structure. We follow the directions along a hedgerow of bramble and gorse and, on the other side, newborn calves, their mothers and a bull with a face framed by curls watch us as we pass them by. The first folly we come to is a tower – a turret really – mostly hidden from view by a circular woodland of trees surrounding it. It's an imposing structure made of stone, with barred windows, and where it stands, disembodied, it has no obvious purpose. There might have been a time when you could have climbed the circular staircase inside it, but to what end is unclear. The vantage from the ground is impressive enough; a tower here is quite pointless.

Following the dropped pins on Sam's phone, we head back over the field and into the village, past a pretty little stone cottage with a tree full of apples that are just out of reach. The next folly that we find is in the churchyard. It's a pyramid and it is this man's mausoleum. It's an odd thing, maybe twenty feet or so high, taking up far more room than the weathered headstones of its neighbours. The story goes that he organised its construction before his death and was entombed inside it, seated upright at a table with a bottle of wine. We laugh at its absurdity and ostentatiousness, and how strange it is to see a pyramid in a little village churchyard. I circumnavigate it and peer into where the door would have been, as Sam reads out more about John 'Mad Jack' Fuller.

'Mad Jack was a patron of the arts and sciences, bought Eastbourne its first lifeboat, bought Bodiam Castle to save it from destruction and was an outspoken supporter of slavery. This article describes him as a vociferous anti-abolitionist.'

I should have guessed, and I certainly could have. It's no great surprise that a man with such excessive wealth, who built these idiotic temples to nothing at all, would likely have amassed his fortune through exploitation. I feel nauseous. I've come to hate how a place, a structure or a building can appear intriguing or beautiful one moment and yet, when standing in the fullness of its history – its origin story – can become sour and grotesque. How can I not bristle at the fact that he is celebrated as a philanthropist while also being described as an enthusiastic supporter of slavery?

I walk back to the road to sit on a bench and wait for Sam. He's on a video call to his grandad and I don't want Pops to see me, yet again, feeling blue. There's no one else around, so I quietly watch the dwindling hollyhocks growing out of the pavement. There's an almost-empty noticeboard attached to the wall behind me. Just a copy of the latest parish-meeting agenda, with two items to be discussed and a laminated notice explaining how to spot the 'non-native' Asian yellow-legged hornet. Underneath these notices there is one more piece of paper, pinned to the board, and it reads:

> St Thomas a Becket Church and the Black Lives Matter Movement
> We are united in our dedication to standing up to racism and oppression, and standing in solidarity with the black community. Black lives matter to Brightling Parish Church, and they should matter to every individual.
> The PCC of Brightling acknowledge Jack Fuller's involvement and support of the slave trade during his lifetime. St Thomas a Becket Church operates an open and inclusive policy, and welcomes visitors and worshipers from all ethnic backgrounds.

> Brightling PCC, August 2020

These words are far less visible and imposing than the structures they gesture towards. These words that were written by someone on the Parish Council and approved by the other members, then typed out on a computer in someone's home and printed out and cut to size. These words that are pinned on the noticeboard for whoever walks by to read. These words that refer to these nearly 200-year-old structures, which would have been unquestionably celebrated until this summer prompted reflection on what being selective about the stories we tell might do to someone like me.

I wonder who else has seen this notice? It's possible that I'm the first Black person to have read it. This unexpected expression of solidarity tells me that the people in this little village considered the possibility that someone like me would come along one day to see this peculiar pyramid in the middle of a churchyard. And they tell me that those same people want everyone to know that, much as they are committed to preserving the structures Mad Jack commissioned, because they are part of the village's history, they are able to acknowledge the abhorrence of his views, too. They are a handful of words. A small gesture in the grand scheme of things, but, in this moment, they suggest to me that change is possible and offer me a little welcome relief.

There are people who wish for history to be tidy. They don't want to think about the ninety-three National Trust properties with links to colonialism and slavery, or how Kew Gardens is reckoning with the exploitation that is part of its legacy. They wish for the past to stay in the past, because what's done is done, and they would prefer us to believe that while there was domination, there was benevolence and benefit, too. And they want us to concede that, despite the extraction and destruction, no negative consequences persist to this day. They want us to accept that other histories – our histories – are unsubstantiated, irrelevant and non-existent, while refusing to acknowledge what was deliberately left out. It strikes me as strange to want our collective story to be this way. To be incomplete, erased and untold. And for as long as I, and those like me, exist and refuse to accept this erasure, the search for our stories will go on.

After all, what fabrications would we have to accept in order to believe that these powerful people and institutions, with their cataclysmic actions, have left no trace at all? There must be acknowledgement of these truths and restitution for what was taken, and for what continues to be taken to this day. The Chagossians must be allowed to return to their homeland and must be compensated for all they have endured. So where erasure has caused silence to fall, our voices must rise to demand a just world.

The idea of reparations is a contentious one – not that I think it ought to be. But then for me to believe in its potential for justice doesn't compel me to consider what I stand to lose. It is those who know, or at least suspect, that the material comfort of their lives – the wealth, the privilege, the great swathes of land – is disproportionate who dismiss the call for reparations outright. It would need to be a multilateral, international, cross-generational undertaking to create a system that could move incrementally towards equity. The scope is unfathomable and it would cost the privileged more than they could bear to relinquish, and that's why, I believe, the conversation never truly reaches those with the power to deliver it. And yet I also believe that one day – probably not in my lifetime – the notion of addressing historical injustices won't be shrugged off any more. Tiny gestures have been made (like those from Kew Gardens and the National Trust), of truth and reconciliation, that cause me to hope the tide will turn one day.

The word 'reparations', at its root, means to repair, and there's much repair to be done, alongside and beyond tangible restitutions. Reparations in the form of land return, debt cancellation and wealth restoration are justice. Repairing our relationship with the land is the spiritual work of our lifetimes. Because there were other thefts, alongside the stealing of bodies and lands, of plants and soils, of agency and control, of governance and rule. A robbery of spirit took place, and still does. A robbery of history and hope, of culture and tradition, of imagination and dreaming up futures on our own terms. I can barely stand to think of the brutality of those forced migrations and the volume of suffering that was borne. It was a pain so enduring that it persists to this day, in the bodies of its many descendants. All this space taken up by suffering where there might otherwise have been ingenuity and insight, visions and faith, and the chance to wonder and wander. It was a devastating realisation that even my most earnest aspirations took shape within a system that did not have my thriving in mind. The limitations on our imaginings of what is possible persist, as do the oppressive systems that create and enforce their parameters. I will never know who I might have been, outside its burdensome vision. And while I know there is plenty for me to be thankful for – an abundance of privilege and comfort, for starters – I am caught in grief over the possibilities lost because my understandings, my hopes and my thoughts are refracted through the prisms of whiteness, of the English language, of being on this land but not of this land.

And so I seek repair. A tending to the wounds inflicted as a result of realisations like these. Having the room and the grace to seek whatever truths and stories remain, to stitch my heart together with the shreds of ancestry that I can find, and to be allowed to mourn for what will always be lost. Repair looks like being able to trace the threads of the trauma that is woven through my bloodline and allowing it to lead me to the resilience, the marronage, that is also my inheritance. It is naming what was taken, disappeared and erased and daring to reclaim what remains. That is what repair looks like to me, today, as I sit at the base of the copper beech, its silvery bark against my back, and listen to a buzzard call out into the sky above me. As I claim stewardship over a parcel of soil and devote myself to its well-being and choose to see it, not as a piece of this country that troubles me, but as land where the soil is the connective tissue between my body, my labour, my tenderness and the earth.

Repair is reclamation. And to me that has been reclaiming an unbounded relationship with the natural world through growing food. Something that felt unavailable to me for most of my life, and that continues to be a site of discomfort and disconnection to so many who haven't found their way back to it yet. Because we are descended from those who were torn from or left the land of their people, the land that they knew was part of who they were. We are descended from those who were taken to where their bodies were used, dehumanised and broken into pieces, forced into a labour that worked the land from sunrise and into the night, when the moonlight was bright enough. We are descended from people for whom this labour was once a ritual of sustenance and providing – a labour that was honourable and revered, before it was used as a tool of their oppression. We are descended from those who fled that wretched place, running as fast as they could, discarding their chains and undue debt, to escape into the sanctuary of the trees.

I am descended from people who came to see this labour that positioned the work of sowing seeds and harvesting as lowly and undignified and filthy. As work to rise above, and not root into. We must reclaim the stories we tell about the task of growing food and about those who do it on our behalf. We must regard them, once again, with gratitude and reverence, as they are the upholders of life. And we must seek repair not only for ourselves, but on behalf of our ancestors – those whose bones turned into our bones. We must pursue repair for our descendants, so that they might one day know freedom from ancestral trauma while holding fast to the power of ancestral resilience. Repair is not a solo pursuit, even though our journeys are individual ones and the path can be lonely to travel. We must heal in community, at the feet of ancestral wisdom and alongside those who seek the same peace as we do.

Growing food is as sacred as it is elemental. It is one of the few actions we can point towards as the reason we humans continue to exist. With every bite, we consume the offering of an unfathomable number of beings, both human and more-than-human. We consume sunshine and water, the miracle of photosynthesis and the generosity of decomposition. All these entities and elements and processes make our being alive possible. Our aliveness is a community endeavour.

Growing food is how I repair my broken heart and weave myself back into the tapestry of a rich and defiant ancestry. An ancestry that I feel in my pulse, because I have no family records. It is how I have grounded myself into this present – my own particular present – and have grasped the possibility of wading, barefoot, into the long grass and feeling a rootedness manifest as the weight of me pushes down into the earth. It is plants that brought me here. They extended their root systems and leafy branches towards me and showed me where to go. It is with them as my guides that I see now that, although I thought I had nowhere to call home, it's to the earth that I – we – truly belong.

The trees breathe for you, the bees buzz for you, the mycelium burrows deep into the soil for you. Our ancestors knew how to live in accordance with the truth of our interdependence and we must learn to do the same. We must sink down into the structures of our cells to find what was embedded by generations of those who stood in the dignity of their rightful place as stewards of the earth. When the hush of a woodland's silence raises the hairs on our necks, or we shudder exquisitely when our hot skin hits agonisingly cool water, or we feel an expansiveness arise in our heart-space when standing on the precipice of a cliff or canyon or mountainside and breathe deep, we can touch that remembering. The salt that gathers on our skin, the tears that we shed, the breath that flows across our lips are all manifestations of how profoundly we are connected. The earth dwells in the water that steadies our cells and in the marrow that runs through our bones. Our interconnection was known to our ancestors, and it is our duty to remember this now. We must seek to become intimate with what is indiscrete and divine, for the sake of this planet, our only home.

So I am growing the food that raised me – the cucumbers, okra and tiny bitter melons – and I am doing so right here, where I am. Dancing with the seasons and waking up to birdsong, and pausing to breathe in the cool air after the rain. This is how I have pieced myself back together. This is how I have found, at long last, belonging. A sense of belonging that cannot be undermined by that which is man-made. No borders or delineations, no identifiers or manufactured belief in our separatedness from one another can convince me that I do not belong. A sense of belonging that is an action. A noun that's more of a verb. A belonging that needs to be nurtured as the soil does and so, when I feel it slipping away, or being wrestled from my grasp, I sow another seed and trust what germiates and grows to this ground where I now live. I'll care for it as it cares for me, and I'll look to it when I need reminding of what it is to know home.

My dad gave me cucumber seeds and he believed they could grow here, when I thought this place to be too grey and cold and cruel. I sowed a few more seeds in June – a little too late, by most growers' advice – to nurture in our new greenhouse. Then, in July, I took them out of their pots and into planters filled with compost and the fine-textured soil provided by the neighbourhood moles. While my attempt to grow okra came to little, the cucumber plants grew in a frenzy through August and started to flower as the month came to an end, and I've been watching them closely every day, urging them to keep limping along into September. At dusk, I close the door and the window against the night, fleece at my side to drape over them if the temperatures drop too low. And today, as autumn's presence becomes undeniable, my parents arrive to spend the day.

As always, dad's distracted by all the things in the house that need fixing, so I get my mum to nudge him into the garden and towards the greenhouse. I pull back the big leaves obscuring the cucumbers that are hanging there, clinging on to the last of the season's energy, so that he can, for the first time, witness his cucumbers growing here for himself. His furrowed brow turns into a look of disbelief, then gives way to a wide and happy smile. It's a smile I've been lucky to see so many times. The smile that is his, and that he gave to me. I hand him the secateurs and he snips one cucumber from the vine, then another. He places them in the crux of his elbow and cradles them in his arms tenderly. Then he turns to my mum, holding them up in the air and says, 'Pran enn foto! Mo bizin montre mo ser!'

THE BOOK OF DELIGHTS

Ross Gay

Ross Gay is an American poet, essayist and National Book Award finalist; the winner of a National Book Critics Circle Award and a Kingsley Tufts Poetry Award; and a professor at Indiana University. Or, as his website puts it: *Ross Gay is interested in joy.* Born in 1974 in Ohio, he is the author of four books of poetry and two books of *New York Times* bestselling essays. *The Book of Delights*, from which the extract below is taken, is the kind of book you need to keep by your bed as an antidote to the way things seem sometimes: a reminder that joy is there to be searched for, dug for, cleaned off and held up to the light.

Today I have smuggled three fig cuttings onto a flight from Philadelphia to Detroit. Truth be told, no smuggling has occurred, given as I was carrying the things open and notorious, their roots tucked into some moist compost in a plastic bag. But smuggling makes it sound more thrilling than what it *appears*—carrying a few sticks in a bag—and therefore more like what it *is*: carrying living creatures for replanting about seven hundred miles away. Which, you might have already gone there, given as I've told you already they're figs, is another way of saying I'm carrying joy around in my bag. Actually, right now it's in the overhead compartment in that plastic bag probably a little funky with my dirty clothes.

This is one of those delights that keeps piling up, as the fig tree I took these cuttings from, in Stephanie's mother's backyard in Frenchtown, New Jersey, was itself made of a cutting from a grove of figs farther down the Delaware in Langhorne, Pennsylvania, where my friend Jay's family lived and where his father grew a wonderful garden, including bitter melon, Asian pears, peaches, ong choi, and, yes, these figs. When I first asked if I could transplant some of Mr. Lau's figs (he was moving and I was heartbroken that that garden would no longer be a sanctuary to me) he said yes, if he even said that, walked me out to the grove of figs beneath his massive chestnut tree, grabbed a pickax, and started hacking.

I was kind of terrified, green green thumb that I was. (Two ancillary delights—Mr. Lau, old school, OG, actually got a turtle, drilled a hole in its shell, tied a string to a nut about the hole's size, which he then dropped into that hole, tying the other end of the string to a stick in the middle of his lettuces so that he could have a steady [if coerced] slug patrol. That's not the delight. The delight is that his son, my pal Jay, under cover of night, dislodged the nut from the shell, carried the critter on his bike [one handed, no helmet] to a nearby tributary of Neshaminy Creek, the thing's River Jordan. Ancillary delight two, with a twinge of irony: when people say they have a black thumb, meaning they can't grow anything, I say yeah, me too, then talk about the abundant garden these black thumbs are growing.) Then we stuck the cuttings in a bucket full of water, and he did in fact tell me not to let them dry out.

Yesterday, when I dug up a few of Stephanie's mother's figs, I used a shovel and hacked at the roots like Mr. Lau, though I was sending soothing mindbeams to the tree as I did so (which I'm guessing Mr. Lau was not—ref. aforementioned turtle tale). After I got a few well-rooted cuttings, I took them to the bucket near the hose, filled it up, dropped them in, showered and dressed for the funeral of a beloved twenty-year-old kid named Rachel who fell to her death a few nights ago. While Stephanie was telling me over the phone about Rachel's death she said two butterflies alighted on the butterfly bush we had just planted. When we were standing in the back corner of the funeral home during the eulogies—I moved there because I'm tall and called Stephanie over so we could listen together—Stephanie caught sight of a silver gleam on the gray carpet. When the eulogy was over, she picked it up: a single elephant earring. Elephants were Rachel's favorite animal. She adored them.

When we got home, after the pizza and guacamole (my guacamole—a delight. Another delight: here's the recipe: avocado, onion, garlic, salt. Really!), I grabbed the bucket, trimmed the cuttings into sticks, potted them in the plastic bag, and set them on the counter, where they sat like promises. Little converters. Little dreamers of coming back into bloom. And how we might carry that with us wherever we go.

MARRIAGE

Luisa Muradyan

Born in Odessa, Ukraine, **Luisa Muradyan** holds a PhD in Poetry from the University of Houston. She is the author of *American Radiance* (2018), and her poems have appeared in Poetry International and the Los Angeles Review, as well as many other poetry journals and magazines.

Marriage is a lifelong commitment
to buy groceries for another person.
Each week I buy you seven plums
because they are your morning ritual.
Every once in a while you bring home
a bag of persimmons and I slowly undress
them by the sink. We have not yet figured out
the right way to eat a pomegranate,
though the last time we were in Jerusalem
someone told me it was the forbidden fruit
and not the apple which I am ashamed
to admit I almost never wash. I am unclean
in many ways, like the ham and cheese
Lunchable I hid from my grandmother
or the turkey bacon that remarkably tastes like bacon
because maybe it is bacon. There is honesty
in the oatmeal but not the Greek yogurt
that was never eaten by the ancient Greeks, though
the wisdom of Aristotle
is printed on the side, *we are what we repeatedly do.*
You repeatedly standing in front of the milk calling.
Me repeatedly staring in the bbq aisle singing.

There are love poems everywhere but here in this breakfast pastry aisle
I hand you a box of Pop-Tarts
and say "put this in my toaster"
and you know exactly what I mean.

INVITING A FRIEND TO SUPPER

Ben Jonson

A playwright and poet, **Ben Jonson** is one of the best-known writers of English Renaissance literature. His satirical comedies are still widely performed today and he brought (as Alexander Pope noted) 'critical learning into vogue'. After attending Westminster School, he followed his stepfather into work as a bricklayer, before serving in the military, and then joined Philip Henslowe's theatre company as an actor and playwright. His poetry oeuvre includes tributes to his friends and contemporaries, including William Shakespeare, John Donne, and Francis Bacon. An ability to read from the Latin Bible allowed him to plead 'benefit of the clergy' and avoid execution when, in his late twenties, he killed a fellow actor in a duel. He had at least two children and is thought to have outlived them.

Tonight, grave sir, both my poor house, and I
    Do equally desire your company;
    Not that we think us worthy such a guest,
But that your worth will dignify our feast
With those that come, whose grace may make that seem
Something, which else could hope for no esteem.
It is the fair acceptance, sir, creates
The entertainment perfect, not the cates.
Yet shall you have, to rectify your palate,
An olive, capers, or some better salad
Ushering the mutton; with a short-legged hen,
If we can get her, full of eggs, and then
Lemons, and wine for sauce; to these a cony
Is not to be despaired of, for our money;

And, though fowl now be scarce, yet there are clerks,
The sky not falling, think we may have larks.
I'll tell you of more, and lie, so you will come:
Of partridge, pheasant, woodcock, of which some
May yet be there, and godwit, if we can;
Knat, rail, and ruff too. Howsoe'er, my man
Shall read a piece of Virgil, Tacitus,
Livy, or of some better book to us,
Of which we'll speak our minds, amidst our meat;
And I'll profess no verses to repeat.
To this, if ought appear which I not know of,
That will the pastry, not my paper, show of.
Digestive cheese and fruit there sure will be;
But that which most doth take my Muse and me,
Is a pure cup of rich Canary wine,
Which is the Mermaid's now, but shall be mine;
Of which had Horace, or Anacreon tasted,
Their lives, as so their lines, till now had lasted.
Tobacco, nectar, or the Thespian spring,
Are all but Luther's beer to this I sing.
Of this we will sup free, but moderately,
And we will have no Pooley, or Parrot by,
Nor shall our cups make any guilty men;
But, at our parting we will be as when
We innocently met. No simple word
That shall be uttered at our mirthful board,
Shall make us sad next morning or affright
The liberty that we'll enjoy tonight.

EARLY MORNING RISER

Katherine Heiny

Katherine Heiny is, apparently, the author of more than twenty YA novels under various pseudonyms, and if you know which ones they are, please tell us so we can buy them all. This is the kind of writer Katherine Heiny is: once you know about her work, you want to read everything she has ever written. The extract below is from her third book (and second novel) *Early Morning Riser*: a funny, beautiful story about people and the ways they love each other – which is, perhaps, the common thread in Heiny's work. She now lives outside Washington DC with her husband, a former spy. She has two sons, a stepson and a stepdaughter.

After the movie was over, Jane left Jimmy's house and went to Glen's to buy groceries for both of them. Buying Jimmy's food—Pop-Tarts, boxed macaroni and cheese, potato chips, peanut butter, saltines—was like shopping for someone who lived in a fallout shelter. Her own list was equally depressing: a packet of chicken breasts, six eggs, a half gallon of milk, one bag of salad, the smallest container of yogurt, the smallest bottle of syrup. A single person's groceries.

She was in the frozen foods aisle, buying a mere pint of strawberry ice cream, when a shopping cart blocked her path. She looked up in annoyance. It was Duncan.

"You were lost in thought," he said. "Anything interesting?"

"Not really," Jane said. "I haven't seen—seen you around much."

She flushed. She knew she hadn't seen him around much because he was dating a Charlevoix woman named Tabitha who worked in a bakery that, according to Freida, sold overpriced croissants. But Jane didn't want Duncan to know she still kept track of his romantic life.

"Tabitha and I broke up," Duncan said, apparently not at all deceived. "She was moving downstate, and I don't do so well with long-distance relationships."

"Oh," Jane said. "That's a shame."

"Well, I don't know about that." Duncan sounded cheerful, as he always did about breakups. "Her herb garden bothered my hay fever no end."

Jane nodded; she'd known relationships that hinged on less.

He was wearing a dark gold-colored shirt that matched the golden glints in his auburn hair. Jane noticed that he had new lines around his mouth. Just imagine: lines carved by experiences that Jane knew nothing about.

They regarded each other for a moment that was really only a regular moment but that seemed as endless as a river, as open as a mountain vista. Duncan looked at her and his amber-flecked brown eyes seemed to Jane, as they always had, to fix her in a warm spotlight.

Duncan rocked his shopping cart back and forth so it nudged hers gently. Nudge. Nudge. Finally, he said, "I see you've bleached the hair on your upper lip."

Jane sighed. "Yes, but I didn't know it was going to make me look like Colonel Sanders."

"More like a very pretty Mark Twain," Duncan said.

And just like that, they were a couple again.

Well, *almost* just like that. First, they had to pay for their groceries, and there was a little flurry of embarrassment over which checkout line to choose. The first lane was problematic because Duncan had had the cashier's grandmother's painted satinwood cabinet in his workshop for about a year now, and the cashier was likely to bring it up and be unpleasant about it. The cashier in the other lane was a woman Duncan had slept with a number of years ago after a car show in Manistee, and while she would (probably) not be unpleasant, Jane would just as soon not talk to someone Duncan had had sex with right before she herself was planning to have sex with him. But luckily, Mr. Fairmont came out from behind the customer service desk and opened a third lane, and he and Duncan had a small discussion about walleye fishing.

"Walleye are just so darned *smart*," Mr. Fairmont said.

"They're smart, but they're lazy," Duncan said. "I find if you can just get the worm in front of them—"

"That's all well and good if you're using a worm harness," Mr. Fairmont said, somewhat critically. "If not, just forget it."

Afterward, Jane loaded her groceries into her car, and Duncan loaded his groceries into his rust-spotted white van. They drove in a caravan straight to Jane's house and made love on the old leather sofa without even unpacking the groceries, and Jane's strawberry ice cream melted right down to a puddle.

Jane was asleep in Duncan's arms when the phone rang the next morning at seven thirty. She answered drowsily.

"Hello, Jane, dear," Aggie said. "Now that you and Duncan are back together, I feel I can ask—"

"Wait—how did you know about that?" Jane asked. She and Duncan had been back together for about eighteen hours.

"Well, last night I was watching the coverage of the California wildfires on CNN," Aggie said, "and Gary got upset."

"Gary cares about the wildfires?" Jane asked. Up until this point, she hadn't known Gary cared about anything but himself.

"No, no, he disapproves of CNN," Aggie said. "He says the news ticker makes him nervous. Often a little drive and a piece of pie calm him down, so we drove over to the pie shop in Petoskey, and on the way, we saw Duncan's van parked down the street from your house. I said to Gary, 'Why, I believe Duncan's taken up with Jane again. Either that, or Mary Winslow is being unfaithful to her husband.'"

"Oh," Jane said.

"Anyway," Aggie continued, "we brought Jimmy a piece of coconut cream pie, and when we dropped it off at his house, I couldn't help noticing that the porch railing is loose, and I wonder if you might ask Duncan to tighten it down."

Jane glanced over at Duncan. He was still asleep. His eyelashes made golden crescents on his cheeks. Look at that, Duncan asleep in her bed.

"I'd be happy to do that, Aggie," Jane said in a strange, upbeat voice she didn't recognize as her own. "I'll take Duncan over there with me today. Thank you *so* much for letting me know. And thank you for *all* you do for Jimmy. You really are so *very* kind."

The world was as bright and shiny as a fishing lure.

If Aggie knew Jane and Duncan were back together, then it was just a matter of days—perhaps hours or even minutes—before everyone else in Boyne City knew, too. So Jane called Freida and told her right away.

"Why, that's—wonderful," Freida said in the uncertain tone people use when setting up Wi-Fi networks. "Do you know that he still clears my driveway every single time it snows?"

"He does?" Jane didn't mind that Duncan did that; she only minded that she didn't know about it. That was how Boyne City she'd become.

"Oh, yes," Freida said. "And once, my car got stuck in the school parking lot, and he came over right away and pulled my car out with his van. He really is much nicer than most people think."

Jane even told her mother, who said, "Duncan again? I thought he was over you."

"Well, it turns out he wasn't," Jane said cheerfully. She was too happy to take offense.

Everyone seemed baffled, even if (unlike her mother) they were too polite to say so, and Jane couldn't blame them. They all knew she and Duncan had broken up the first time because he didn't want to commit, and he showed no signs of having changed his mind about that. It was Jane who'd changed. She understood now that time was too valuable to deny yourself things that gave you pleasure. There had to be more to life than teaching second grade, and taking care of Jimmy, and drinking a whole bottle of red wine while you watched *The Bachelor* (though that last part was pretty nice). She wanted Duncan—she had never stopped wanting him—and now she was willing to take him on his terms.

Jimmy's reaction was much better. Jane and Duncan told him together when they went over to drop off his groceries later the next day.

Jimmy smiled broadly—the smile that made you realize how handsome he would have been if he'd been born just a little smarter—and shook Duncan's hand over and over, saying, "Good for you, buddy! Good for you!"

Then he turned to Jane and said, "Now we can have Duncan and Aggie and Gary over for Taco Tuesday!"

Taco Tuesday was a tradition Jane had started with Jimmy. It had originally been Pizza Night, but that was before Jane discovered how often Jimmy ordered pizza on his own. So they'd switched to tacos, and now on Tuesday nights, Jane brought the ingredients and made tacos and they watched a video Jimmy had chosen. Last week, they'd watched *Ernest Scared Stupid*, and of all the prices Jane had paid for her mother's accident, she thought watching that movie might have been the highest.

Now she felt insulted, too. Wasn't her presence alone enough to make Taco Tuesday successful? Now they had to have Aggie and Gary, too? *Gary?*

But this time around, Jane was determined to do everything right. She wouldn't be jealous, not of Aggie, not of Duncan's legion of ex-girlfriends, not of the new waitress at Robert's with the long, dark eyelashes, not of the girl at the video store who carried her breasts in front of her as though they were a couple of large cupcakes. She would not be demanding, not of Duncan's time, not of his attention, not of his commitment, not of his money. (He didn't have any, so that part would be easy.) She would be all the things she had always meant to be in their relationship and somehow never managed to be: wise and cool and levelheaded and regal and hopelessly alluring, like a single ball bearing gleaming on a black velvet background, or maybe a Swedish nanny. If that meant inviting Aggie and Gary to Taco Tuesday, so be it.

She smiled. "Of course, we can include them. We can invite Freida, too."

Jane called them later that night. Freida said she would be delighted, and Aggie said that Gary had some issue with tacos—apparently he'd found a stone in a street taco in 1980 and been off them ever since—but she would bring enchiladas.

*

Aggie and Gary were already on the porch of Jimmy's house on Tuesday when Jane and Duncan arrived. Jane and Duncan had made love less than an hour before, and Jane's mind was pleasantly slowed, like her classroom's Newton's cradle when someone had set it going very slowly: *tick . . . tick . . . tick.*

Aggie was wearing a dark purple sheath dress with an apple-green cardigan, and by all that was good and holy, Jane thought, she should have looked like Barney the dinosaur, but she didn't. As always, Aggie's wide-faced, rosy-lipped, flaxen-haired prettiness took Jane by surprise.

"Oh, hello," Aggie said, ringing the doorbell. "Now, Gary, I'm sure you remember Duncan's girlfriend, Jane."

Gary peered at Jane. "You're not the one with the fondness for Grape-Nuts, are you?"

"No," Jane said, sighing. "That must've been someone else."

Jimmy answered the door wearing the chinos and yellow polo shirt that Jane knew he considered his best outfit. (Honestly, Jimmy could break your heart without half trying.) The shirt was tight across Jimmy's stomach. All that pizza, Jane supposed.

Before they could go inside, Freida's car pulled up to the curb, and Freida got out. "Hey, everyone!" she called.

"Who's that?" Gary asked.

Aggie *tsked* in an annoyed way, but Jimmy said helpfully, "That's Freida Fitzgerald."

Gary looked doubtful. "Is she new in town?"

"Gary," Duncan said patiently, "she's taught music at the high school going on twenty years now."

Freida came up the porch steps, carrying her mandolin case. She was slightly out of breath and had ringlets of brown hair pressed flat against her forehead from the heat.

"Hi, Freida!" Jimmy said. "Are you going to play the mandolin?"

"You bet I am," she answered cheerfully. She noticed Gary staring at her. "Hey, how are you, Gary?"

"She knows me," Gary said to Aggie.

"Of course I know you!" Freida exclaimed. "We've known each other for *years*. I've been to your house, you've been to my house. You handle my homeowner's insurance."

Gary frowned. "Broad form or comprehensive?"

"Maybe we should all go inside now," Duncan suggested.

"Yes, please," Aggie said. "I've been holding this dish of enchiladas so long my fingers are numb."

They all went into the kitchen to help themselves to drinks. Jane was relieved at this self-service. If they waited for Jimmy to serve drinks, they'd be here all night. Normally, Jane would stay in the kitchen to make dinner, but tonight Aggie was doing that, so Jane was free to sit in the living room with everyone else.

Jimmy seemed very excited to have guests and told a long, confusing story about how some lady was threatening Duncan with legal action if he didn't refinish her grandfather's trestle table, which he'd had for at least a year and for which he'd already accepted payment.

"People," Duncan said, shaking his head.

Freida settled herself on the couch next to Jane and took out her mandolin. Part of being friends with Freida meant getting used to her playing the mandolin all the time—softly if people were talking, louder if they weren't. If the conversation got heated, she would strum faster; if they were all tired, she would play something soothing. It was like having a constant soundtrack to your life, or maybe a mandolin-playing Greek chorus, because sometimes she sang, too—little snatches of lyrics that always seemed to fit the occasion. When Aggie called to Duncan from the kitchen to please adjust the air conditioning, Freida sang, "'You can fill my pipe and then go fetch my slippers,'" and when Gary got up to look for the bathroom, Freida sang, " 'I can't help but wonder where I'm bound.' "

"Dinner is ready!" Aggie called.

Everything Aggie ever made was delicious, and the enchiladas were no exception. After dinner, Jane cleared the table and ran water in the sink for the dishes.

Aggie came in to help her. "Now, if you'll wash the dishes, I'll clean out the fridge," Aggie said, which was annoying because Jane was *already* washing the dishes. She didn't need to be told.

Aggie began unscrewing the lids of jars from the fridge and sniffing them. "Gah!" she said each time, and threw the jar in the recycling bin. There was no *particular* reason that this should make Jane feel like swatting Aggie with her own pie server, but it did. Aggie dumped the last jar and began wiping down the inside of the refrigerator. Jane moved on to washing the glasses.

They cleaned in silence for a minute or two. Then Aggie said, "How are things with Duncan? He seems very happy."

Jane had noticed that Aggie often asked a question, then answered it herself. She supposed that was a real estate agent habit—*How do you like this place? I love that third bedroom!*—but it also might be the result of living with Gary.

"What makes you say that?" she asked.

"Oh, well, he and I were in the hardware store buying hinges for my kitchen cupboard yesterday, and I asked how you were, and he looked all sort of pleased. Normally, when I ask about some girl he's seeing, he looks, I don't know, sort of *belligerent*."

Duncan and Aggie had gone to the hardware store together? To buy hinges? Jane's mind raced like a beagle down that alley, and then she made it stop. She didn't do that anymore.

"I think you're good for Duncan," Aggie continued. "He needs someone who isn't so concerned with being glamorous all the time, someone who isn't outrageously pretty—"

Funny how this conversation was making Jane feel, well, belligerent. They finished cleaning the kitchen in that tiresome way that you clean someone else's kitchen, when you know you won't be there to enjoy the fruits of your labor. Jane rinsed out the sink and wandered into the living room where the others were gathered around the television.

"I don't understand this movie," Gary said suddenly. "Not one bit. It's almost like the baby is talking."

"The baby *is* talking," Jimmy told him. "I mean, not really, because babies can't talk. Some actor is talking. You're just supposed to think it's the baby."

"But the baby's lips aren't moving." Gary pushed his glasses up his nose and stared at Jimmy accusingly.

"Well, maybe not talking," Jimmy said patiently. "More, like, those are supposed to be the baby's thoughts."

"Then it should be called *Look Who's Thinking*," Gary said.

Jane had sometimes thought that Jimmy and Gary could be combined into a whole functioning person, but now she decided she was wrong about that. They would need a third person, maybe even a fourth.

She sat on the arm of Duncan's chair. He smiled and put his arm around her. "Hello, darlin'."

Freida strummed her mandolin and sang:

You don't have to call me darlin', darlin',
You never even called me by my name.

Jane gave her an annoyed look, and Freida immediately glanced up at the ceiling in a show of innocence.

Always, the worst part of visiting Jimmy was saying good-bye, knowing that you were abandoning him to the Lifetime Movie Network and gray bedsheets and cold pizza. (Now he didn't even have cold pizza—Aggie had thrown it all out.) But it was better than usual tonight because Jane was not alone. Jimmy walked them to the door, and they went out into a summer night as soft and deep as raven feathers.

"Oh, Jimmy, I nearly forgot," Aggie called. "I left you some enchiladas in the fridge—just cover them with foil and bake at three-fifty until they're warmed through, and add the sauce at the last minute."

"I sure will," Jimmy said, although Jane knew the chances of him doing that were less than zero, literally less than zero—negative chances.

Freida had put her mandolin in its striped cotton bag, but she sang, " 'Good night, ladies, we're going to leave you now!' " softly as she walked to her car.

"Now, Gary," Aggie said as she followed Jane and Duncan down the sidewalk, "I need to stop at Glen's on the way home for flaked coconut so I can make Swedish coffee cake tomorrow. It won't take but a minute, and you can wait in the car."

"Now, that's something I don't miss," Duncan said to Jane in a low voice.

"What is?"

"Being told to wait in the car."

That did seem to sum up what married life with Aggie must be like, but part of Jane was now longing for coffee cake with flaked coconut in it.

"Good night, everybody!" Jimmy called from the front porch. "Good night! Good night!"

The ancient porch light threw a buttery spotlight down on him, burnishing his hair and gilding his yellow shirt, and moths swarmed around him like confetti. He waved goodbye, smiling, and Jane could almost believe he was happy.

DISHWASHING

Maxine Hong Kingston

The daughter of first-generation Chinese immigrants, **Maxine Hong Kingston** was born in California in 1940. Her first literary publication, an essay entitled 'I Am an American', won her a five-dollar prize from *Girl Scout Magazine*, and the theme of this title persisted throughout her subsequent and illustrious adult career. A Professor Emerita at the University of California, her work grapples with the experiences of Chinese Americans, blending fact and fiction, myth and truth. She is the author of more than half a dozen books.

Dishwashing is not interesting, either to do or to think about. Thinking has dignified other mundane things, though. At least it will postpone the dishwashing, which stupefies. After eating, I look at the dishes in the sink and on the counters, the cat's dirty bowl and saucer underfoot, swipe at the dabs and smears recognizable from several meals ago, pick up a cup from among the many on chairs and beside beds, and think about suicide. Also about what to write in the suicide note.

The note is an act of kindness. The criminals who most upset us are the ones who refuse to give satisfying motives. "I don't want to wash the dishes one more time." A plain note, no hidden meanings.

I run water into the frying pan—its black underside just clears the faucet because of the pile-up—but the scrubber and the sponges are hidden somewhere in the bottom of the sink. Thwarted at the start. The frying pan fills; the pile shifts; greasy water splashes on me and spills. I turn off the water and get out of the kitchen. Let the pan soak itself clean. No way to wash the pot and the blender underneath it nor the dishes under that, the crystal wine glasses at the bottom. The dishpan and the drain are buried, too, so I can't let the cold, dirty water out.

When the mood to do so overcomes me, I'll take these dishes out and start all over.

Once in a while, early in the morning, my powers at their strongest, I can enjoy washing dishes. First, reorganize the pile, then fill the dishpan again with clean water. I like water running on my wrists and the way bubbles separate from the suds and float about for quite awhile. I am the one who touches each thing, each utensil and each plate and bowl; I wipe every surface. I like putting the like items together back on the shelves. Until the next time somebody eats, I open the drawers and cupboards every few minutes to look at the neatness I've wrought.

Unfortunately, such well-being comes so rarely, and the mornings are so short, they ought not be wasted on dishes. Better to do dishes in the afternoon, "the devil's time," Tennessee Williams calls it, or in the evening immediately before dinner. The same solution for bedmaking—that is, right before going to bed. I try to limit the number of items I wash to only those needed for dinner, but since I can't find them without doing those on top, the obstructing ones get washed too. I trudge, I drudge.

The one person I know who is a worse dishwasher than I am pushes the dishes from the previous meal to the middle of the table to make places for clean saucers, no plates left.

Another person pulls a dish out of the sink and uses it as is.

When my father was a young man, working in a laundry on Mott Street in New York, he and his partners raced at meals. Last one to finish eating washed the dishes. They ate fast.

Technology is not the answer. I have had electric dishwashers, and they make little difference. The electric dishwasher does not clear the table, collect the cups from upstairs and downstairs, scrape, wipe the counters and the top of the stove. One's life has to be in an orderly phase to load and arrange the dishes inside the dishwasher. Once they're gathered in one spot like that, the momentum to do the rest of the task is fired up.

Although dishwashing is lonely work, I do not welcome assistance. With somebody else in the kitchen, I hurry to get at the worst messes to spare her or him. Alone, I wash two plates, and take a break. Helpers think that dishwashing includes unloading the dishwasher, sweeping and mopping the floor, defrosting the refrigerator, and de-crusting the oven, cleaning the kitchen, and cleaning the dining room.

In *Living Poor With Style*, Ernest Callenbach says that it is unsanitary to wipe dry because the dish cloth spreads the germs evenly over everything. Air drying is better, he says, meaning letting everything sit in the drainer. (He also recommends washing the cooking implements as you finish each step of cooking. Impossible. I did that once in a temporary state of grace, which was spoiled by having to wash dishes.)

Paper plates are no solution. There are no paper pots and pans and spatulas and mixing bowls. The plates are the easiest part of dishwashing.

I prop books and magazines behind the faucet handles. Some people have television sets in their kitchens. Books with small print are best; you don't turn the pages so often and dislodge the book into the water.

I do enjoy washing other people's dishes. I like the different dishes, different sink, different view out the window. Perhaps neighbors could move over one house each night and do one another's dishes. You usually do other folks' dishes at a holiday or a party.

I like using a new sponge or dishcloth or soap or gloves, but the next time, they're not new.

In *Hawai'i Over the Rainbow*, Kazuo Miyamoto says that in the World War II relocation camps for Americans of Japanese Ancestry, the women had the holiday of their lives—no cooking, no dishwashing. They felt more at leisure than back home because of the communal dining halls and camp kitchens. I can believe it.

Compared to dishes, scrubbing the toilets is not bad, a fast job. Also you can neglect toilets one more week, and you only have one or two of them.

I typed a zen koan on an index card, which I have glued to the wall beside the sink. You may cut this out and use it if you like:

"I have just entered the monastery. Please teach me."
"Have you eaten your rice?"
"I have."
"Then you had better wash your bowl."

At that moment, the new monk found enlightenment.

This koan hasn't helped yet with the dishwashing; that is, no one in the family has picked up on it. It would probably be more enlightening to post Miyamoto or Callenbach's words. But I have a glimmering that if I solve this koan, I can solve dishwashing too. If I can solve dishwashing, I can solve life and suicide. I haven't solved it but have a few clues.

The koan does not say that the monk was enlightened after he washed the bowl. "At that moment" seems to be at the instant when he heard the advice.

I hope the koan doesn't mean that one has to pay consequences for pleasure; you eat, therefore you wash bowl. Dismal. Dismal.

It could mean something about reaching enlightenment through the quotidian, which is dishwashing.

The monk did not gain his enlightenment after washing the dishes day after day, meal after meal. Just that one bowl. Just hearing about that one bowl.

I have come up with a revolutionary meaning: Each monk in that monastery washed his own bowl. The koan suggests a system for the division of labor. Each member of the family takes his or her dishes to the sink and does them. Pots and pans negotiable. Cat dishes negotiable too.

The koan shows that dishwashing is important. A life-and-death matter, to be dealt with three times a day.

ON WASHING DISHES

The Readers of *The Sun* Magazine

The Sun magazine is an American publication that has, for the past half-century, published work that aims to 'evoke the splendour and heartache of being human'. It has a wide remit in terms of form, and publishes interviews, long-form essays and memoir writing, short fiction, poetry and photography. In 1984, *The Sun* magazine invited its readers to write in about 'washing up'; the letters that follow are the published collection.

Were Sisyphus told to stand in front of a dishwashing sink at a communal home and keep it spotless he would have been sentenced by Pluto to no less a task than his interminable rock rolling. I have lived communally thirteen years and have found few parameters more telling of the harmony in a group home than the process by which dishes are cleaned. Dishes, like molds, pop up everywhere, growing in quantity until they stick out — the scourge of the household.

However, it's time dishwashing was elevated to its proper place as one of the great celebrations of life — the kiss of love to the chef who gave birth to the sumptuous feast just consumed. In our home an unwritten rule — if you don't cook you clean up — has worked very well. What a thrill to stand before encrusted wastage and in a few moments wave the wand of spotlessness, preparing for another culinary delight. Yes, I'm talking about fighting your way to the sink to serve with verve. In this arena of dynamic exercise can come the flood of one's favorite music, a pleasant conversation, or deep meditation, capped by the crown of task completion gratification. I must confess I love to wash dishes, and I encourage its promotion from the mundane to the sublime.

Often people ask me for advice on how to visit other communities without being a drain. I think the advice holds true for any wanderer of the planet. When visiting a home, wash the dishes, play with the children, and make bread — and you'll be welcome everywhere.

Patch Adams
Arlington, Virginia

Our one-course meal was just enough, and dusk is going out with the tide. We lean together in the fine warm sand, against the huge timber that's been out to sea and back. We both think of saving the dishes for tomorrow, when the path to the creek will be easier to navigate. But that would mean hot tea postponed ten shivering minutes in the cold dawn. I'll wash them tonight. The thought of this task that awaits me is like realizing you have to pee in the middle of a splendid dream. The sooner I get up, the sooner I'll be back to the warm fire and your quiet company.

I gather up the aluminum pot, the forks and cups, and throw the last sandy potato to whatever night creature might be watching from the brush. With a lumbering effort, I'm over the log and onto the empty beach with my load. The fog has drifted in and filled the canyons; seagulls appear from the white mist and vanish again in silence. The trickling of the creek guides me to it. I squat down with my clanking pots at the edge of the water; the pebbles dig a little deeper into my bare feet. From somewhere in the mist, a gull complains of my intrusion. I scoop up a handful of wet gravel and begin to scrub. The cornbread crusted onto the pan while we were talking about islands and truths. Truth: dirt can actually clean with the help of water. After scraping and scratching for some time, I rinse the pot clear and watch bits of food dart downstream toward the great darkness that fills the horizon. Once I've put the forks and cups in the pot, I remember to hear the waves rushing. My fingers and toes are wrinkled from the wet and cold, and yet strangely, I am not in a hurry to return to our camp. In fact, I am completely happy to sit back on the cool rocks and mix the smells of sage and mint with the salty ocean mist in my lungs. Over there, an occasional spark dances up from behind the bone-white log where you wait. I will have to tell you, my love, that I almost didn't come back.

Michele Shockey
San Francisco, California

I have one bowl (wooden), one wooden spoon, and one knife. I eat mainly raw fruits, nuts, and vegetables and haven't had to use dish soap for more than 10 years. I think about how much water, dish soap, natural gas, coal, and nuclear power I haven't needed. I multiple the amount by millions of us doing away with most of our dishwashing. If THE SUN had asked its readers to write about "Not Washing Dishes," I could have said a lot more.

Dennis Nelson
Santa Cruz, California

The Yiddish word *baleboosteh*, is defined by Leo Rosten as a woman who is an excellent and praiseworthy homemaker — a woman whose house is so clean "you can eat off the floor."

I was trained to be a *baleboosteh* by my *baleboosteh* mother, who convinced me, for instance, that a woman who leaves a sinkful of dirty dishes is marching surely toward some unknown but terrible doom from which she will never be redeemed. Actually, the sink doesn't have to be *full* of dirty dishes. According to Ma's theory, a woman who leaves even one dirty glass and spoon unwashed is a disgrace to herself, her family, the community, womanhood, and the Jewish people.

I've never even considered getting an automatic dishwasher. I didn't ask, but I'm positive that the mere placing of dishes into a machine, letting them accumulate all day until there's a full load, and then washing them all at once, would not get you off the hook. There would still be dirty dishes in the house, wouldn't there, even though they've been tucked away, out of sight?

I remember the day my mother taught me to bake a cake. "Are you finished with the baking powder? Then, wash the container and put it away. Are you through with the spoon? with the bowl? with the spatula? with the vanilla extract? Wash them and put them away!" By the time I set the cake into the oven (the very clean oven), all the ingredients and utensils were back in their proper places, the counter was clean, and Ma was wiping up the floor.

All this rigorous training has brought me to my present craziness. I'm a neatness nut, who longs to be a wild and free spirit. I want to be the kind of cook who has wonderfully sticky pots and pans and overflowing casseroles bubbling onto the stove. I long to stir and mix and create amongst the lushness of unbounded disorder — chocolate dripping down the walls, an exotic amaretto sauce splashing happily onto the floor, bowls, spoons, strainers, knives, pans, all flung about with abandon.

And when I write, I want the muse to sit on my shoulder while, in a creative furor, at a desk that is rampant with artistic chaos — stacks of manuscripts, books, pencil stubs, dirty coffee cups, half-eaten, stale sandwiches, cookie crumbs — I wildly pound on the typewriter, the muse applauding my reckless genius.

But such is not the scene. Right now, I'm sitting at my orderly desk, in my spotless house. The laundry is done, supper is cooking peacefully on the shining stove, and there isn't a dirty dish anywhere. May the muse forgive me. I can't help myself.

Barbara Mitchell
Park Forest, Illinois

The house my parents live in now is not the house I grew up in so it holds few associations for me. It's a brick house in a rural subdivision and has ten rooms, including two full kitchens, one upstairs and one down. The upstairs one has a built-in dishwasher.

From the time I was four until I left home to get married at eighteen, we lived in a five-room frame house where all the dishes were washed by hand. My mother washed and I dried. She didn't like me to wash; she didn't trust me to get the dishes clean. After dinner my father sat in the living room and read the evening paper. The time during which the dishes were washed, dried and put away was the only time my mother and I talked. Occasionally my father would yell from the living room SHUT UP. It meant he couldn't concentrate on his newspaper with our voices in the background. Sometimes we whispered but more often we kept quiet. My mother said it was no use making him mad.

While drying the dishes one evening when I was ten, I asked my mother how babies were made. My friends had been discussing it at school. The current theory was that the mother and father went to the doctor and the doctor prayed for a baby and then the mother and father went home and rubbed each other "down there." When I asked my mother, she was holding a pot lid under the faucet and the steam was rising up from the rinse water in little angry puffs. Haven't you got anything better to think about than that, she said. Get your mind out of the gutter. That was the last word she spoke to me on the subject of sex until the night before my wedding when she called me into the kitchen to explain the use of condoms. Then it was my turn to be angry.

The day after the wedding my husband and I left for California. For the next couple of years, I washed the dishes each evening while he turned out one elaborate art project after another in his pursuit of a degree in advertising. Later we were divorced.

My second husband and I have a dishwasher. Most of the time I do the dishes. I never get over the pleasure of slamming the door on the sticky plates, the sugar in the bottom of the iced tea glasses, the goo between the fork tines, and letting scalding water and the detergent too strong for human hands do their work. Sometimes my husband loads the dishwasher. We have two daughters, twelve and six, who know how it works but haven't actually run it yet.

I explained where babies come from to my older daughter when she was four. I've put books into both daughter's hands that cover every aspect of growing up from *Period* to *The Wonderful Story of How You Were Born* to *The Facts of Love*. They don't connect sex with the gutter; the reference would have to be explained to them like some archaic phrase from *The Canterbury Tales*. They don't know how it is to grow up in a household where the mother stands at the sink washing dishes while the father sits in his easy chair reading the newspaper and occasionally yelling SHUT UP. They would also have a hard time understanding how modesty could make a woman stand washing dishes night after night and sometimes weeping from the pain of her bleeding hemorrhoids because she was ashamed for a doctor to examine that part of her anatomy.

Sometimes I take my daughters to visit their grandparents in the ten-room brick house. We seldom spend more than one night. My mother still insists on doing the dishes by hand rather than wasting the hot water and detergent it would take to put them through the dishwasher. My daughters have been cautioned not to mention anything of a sexual nature in front of their grandmother.

After dinner my father feels the need of a cigarette. He goes out on the terrace to sit in a lawn chair and have a leisurely smoke. My mother and I wash the dishes in silence out of habit. The old resentments stir just under the polite surface we take pains to preserve. When everything is neat we go into the living room and sit down to visit. Sometimes it's hard to think of things to say.

Carol Collier
Wendell, N.C.

I washed for 500 people my freshman year. I washed them for my apartment mates. I washed them for my neighbors. I'm going to wash them for my wife-to-be. And I'd wash them for you if you give me something to eat when I'm with you.

That is the Law of Return. Don't ever rob somebody's labor. Be considerate. If you receive from someone give to them in some way. Sir Albert Howard, the "father" of organic gardening, deduced this law in nature and it operates in human social relations as well. Don't be a good American and rip somebody off; be a good human being and give in return for what you're given. Good tradesmen know this rule. Not living by it leads to talking behind somebody's back, hard feelings, and that emptiness that accompanies all shallow living. Give and it shall be given unto you. Make some food or wash some dishes. You won't lose your reward.

Larry Pahl
Glen Ellyn, Illinois

During my days of pre-adolescent indiscriminate t.v. watching, I chanced upon a movie of the play, "Mary-Mary." Mary's husband had left her partly because Mary could never receive a compliment without a retort.

She was also a very stubborn woman. I found her character appealing, a heartening break from the bland blondes and dark-haired vamps of the 1950's. Another trend of the Fifties was viewing love as eternal, or at least masochistic, so, true to bad form, Mary's husband returns. Once more with a love-sick waver to his voice he praises her. "Mary, your skin is like porcelain." Mary replies, "You mean like the kitchen sink?" He's upset, heartbroken, furious. Women were supposed to swoon or silently smile when men noticed them favorably, my twelve-year-old mind guessed. What Mary's husband didn't understand and that I did was that this time Mary was actually embellishing his compliment. Before olive drab and stainless steel took over in the Sixties, kitchen sinks *were* beautiful.

The gleam of clean white porcelain and enamel excites me. When the last of the steamed broccoli bits, rice kernels, miscellaneous mush and unidentifiable colored liquids have swirled and settled into the sink's metal catch, I sigh with pleasure. The dishes themselves are evidently inconsequential in this process. When the utensils are examined before being placed in their drawer, there are occasional rejects that have butter and eggs or something similarly crusty and yellowish white still clinging to them, hiding their potential gleam. My dishes are only dishes. Chipped Salvation Army finds and Amway products do not mix to become mirrors. My friends do not ohh and ahh when they pick up their plates for Thanksgiving dinner. No special effect stars glisten from the rims of my china and glass. I don't care. It only matters that the sink is empty, stain-free and white.

The occasional flecks on my dishware are leftovers from childhood hostilities as well as my meals. The chores that were fun, from my tomboy perspective, were delegated to my brother. I loved yanking and yanking on the lawnmower's pull-cord as it sputtered, shook, and finally roared. The smell of a pile of juicy grass clippings made me want to roll and purr. Early in childhood, though, I suspected that something stank on the female end of the chores. With anticipatory dread, I saw my fate ready to dump on me in the form of chores my older sister so willingly performed. I was furious. Once again, in reverse anthropomorphism, I viewed myself as an ox waiting for its yoke. My sister I pictured as a slobbering idiot. Even though she never drooled, I imagined her mincing her steps and kow-towing to the unwritten law of female servitude with spittle hanging from the sides of her taut smile. The thought of my skinny little girl arms in water filled with bread crumbs, oil, floating lettuce shreds, and gristle disgusted me. Though they were small, I knew my arms were meant to throw balls, climb trees, saw wood, or even take out the garbage. Anything, as long as it was outside and active, was better than cleaning the dirty dishes of a family that often seemed alien to me, despite all the normal signs that said they were mine. I was also indignant. Perhaps it was the influence of t.v. that encouraged me to view relationships in black and white but I reasoned that if my brother didn't have to stay inside after dinner to scrape and wash then I shouldn't either.

I weaseled my way out of washing the dishes as long as possible. Finally, when I was in the eighth grade, my sister — happily sneering, "It's about time" — passed her task to me. I was right about my arms though. China plates and delicate glasses slipped out of my watery hands. Every evening, one or two plates broke as they hit the sink's white porcelain. I was silently exultant, sure that I was constitutionally incapable of this onerous task. My mother, however, was more persistent than I was. Although she would have blinked vacantly upon hearing the term "passive-aggressive," she recognized my behavior as such when she saw it. Within a week we owned a brand new set of dishes, yellow unbreakable Melmac. Their flowers and leaves hid under the remains of the meals that I continued to scrape into the black plastic hole of the garbage disposal. And, like Mary-Mary, I soon believed that a kitchen sink, no dirty dishes in sight, was indeed an object to be admired.

Connie Cronin
Albany, California

Washing dishes is always a calming activity for me. In fact, cleaning anything is a way for me to unwind — yet nothing compares to those dishes. Whether they be mine alone or a course for six, I enjoy cleaning them. I find the activity calming after the stormy effort of meals: It frees my mind to wander and provides my hands a warm occupation while the food digests.

The action of cleaning and the end result is a completion that is predictable. In life, when so many completions are unpredictable, I find peace in that.

Alan Ransenberg
Atlanta, Georgia

In many spiritual systems the act of eating has been used as a metaphor for the assimilation of experience. The Christian Eucharist is a notable example. The Eucharist is also an example of finger food — very few dirty dishes to clean up following the ceremony. Spiritual dining in a more general sense certainly has its share of dirty dishes and leftovers. Most of us eat very little of the daily bread that is allotted to our lives. The uneaten or unlived portion is left on the dish and our dirty dishes are usually left to pile up in the sink of the unconscious. I once rented a house that had previously been occupied by two bachelors. They had apparently subsisted on a diet of t.v. dinners. I could tell this because there was a six-foot-deep pile of discarded t.v. dinner containers beside the back door of the house. Sometimes I cannot help but wonder how large the pile of dirty dishes is beside the back door of my conscious mind.

Doing the dishes in a spiritual sense requires the forgiving or discarding of the uneaten or unlived portions and the cleansing with water of the workspace or dish. In this way baptism may be said to be a metaphor for doing the dishes. This purification must be more than the once in a lifetime ritual encountered in traditional religion. Ideally one should be able to step from each moment of time reborn and innocent. But in order to accomplish this an ongoing process of doing the dishes is necessary. Actually it is more of an undoing than a doing. The major block to digesting all that life offers us is guilt. By judging ourselves to be unworthy or incapable, a stifling of the spirit results. The adding of guilt and recrimination gradually over time wraps the self into a mummy-like shell. Guilt is only possible if an illusion of self is held to be more valuable than the reality of self. Forgiveness is the peeling away of the illusions, the undoing of guilt. The guiltless are able to consume all of life. They lick the platter clean.

Larry Taylor
Durham, N.C.

People think dishwashing machines know how to wash dishes by themselves. This isn't true. There is a man who goes from house to house, teaching them. His name is Alex.

It is not easy to teach machines to wash dishes. Machines don't understand the idea of dishes, since they don't eat. Machines would rather wax floors, which makes a lot of sense to them. Machines spend most of their time on the floor.

Alex teaches them to wash dishes, though they plead with him to teach them to wax floors. "Imagine a dish is a small round piece of the floor," he tells them, but they are still not very enthusiastic.

They are machines, so they must do what he tells them. And he tells them to wash dishes.

Once they start doing it, though, they like it. In that way, machines are very like people. Once they start doing something they like it.

Sparrow
New York, New York

Washing dishes, hanging clothes to dry, sweeping the floor, making the bed — daily tasks of simplicity and service, acts which connect us to humanity, acts imbued with power because they've been performed so many times by ourselves and countless others.

Once, while I was hanging clothes out on the line, time unfolded for an instant. I stood still with my arms raised to the clothesline and saw the millions of women stretching behind me in the same posture, the same act of hanging freshly washed clothing in the sun to dry. I saw my connection with them — the women with brown skin and yellow skin, wearing desert robes and pioneer aprons, slaves and freewomen — all of us united in the same act with the same intention. I felt that what I was doing was somehow holy, because it was human, because it was necessary, because it was always done, always will be done: put clothes in water, put clothes in sun, put clothes on body, put clothes in water — a circle with well-worn grooves. "As it was in the beginning, is now, and ever shall be, world without end, amen." This moment was a gift of grace to me.

We often find daily tasks tedious because they are never truly completed. The dish I wash today will have to be washed again tomorrow, and the bed I make this morning I will undo again tonight. But there is also a secret in the repetitiveness and the endless lack of completion. There is a Zen story of the village simpleton who attained enlightenment by following Buddha's instructions to repeat "broom sweeps, broom sweeps" while sweeping the town streets. Washing dishes is like this. Crouching at stream's edge, bending over a wooden tub, standing at a stainless steel sink — washing dishes, just this.

Nega Seese
Seattle, Washington

When I think of washing dishes I think of two things; one is that when I first got married I was faced with serious dish washing for the first time. I decided I would only wash dishes when I felt like it. I have never changed that decision because it works out wonderfully. I feel like washing dishes quite often actually, and so the dishes get clean and I never have to deal with the resentment of doing a job because I am "supposed to." This attitude has crept into many facets of life and I have discovered from this a rather important lesson. I have a little sign on my bulletin board that says "Delete SHOULD."

The other thing I think of is Alan Watts. Alan Watts, I am told, used to wash dishes very *very* slowly. One at a time. He would hold them up and admire them in every stage of the process. "Look how clean it is, look HOW it shines!" he would exclaim with delight. It seems he saw a life lesson in this little task also.

Renais Jeanne Hill
Seattle, Washington

HERE I AM, WASHING DISHES AGAIN

Shirley Jackson

Shirley Jackson was the author of American Gothic novels and short stories (you can find her characters, and generations worth of preserves, on pp. 272–282). She was also a woman writing in the mid-twentieth century, one of the housewives feeling the 'strange stirring, a sense of dissatisfaction', as identified in Betty Friedan's *The Feminine Mystique*. In addition to her fiction, then, Jackson wrote extensively about her own domestic life for *Women's Home Companion* and *Good Housekeeping* and *Woman's Day*; essays and articles that she later collected and fictionalised as *Let Me Tell You* and *Life Among the Savages*, a 'disrespectful memoir of [her] children'.

Here I am, washing dishes again. If I were any sort of a proper housewife at all, I'd start my dishwashing at a specific hour in the morning, duly aproned, trim and competent, instead of heaving the dishpan high while my neighbours and no doubt the rest of the world are off on some blissful pursuit – frying doughnuts, perhaps, or flying kites with their children. Three times a day, seven days a week, how on earth many weeks a year? What sort of look do I have on my face? The subway rider's, probably, sort of resigned and do-all-the-glasses-before-Times-Square.

I don't really hate these brass faucets and the complete perfect circle of the dishpan, though – I love the things, I own them, they are so essential to a part of me that I like to be near them, and when I am away from home, next to the children the thing I miss most is the sight of my own dear sink. When I wash dishes, I stare into the dishpan and at my own hands, which are the only alien things in the dishwater, the only things that don't rattle.

The green glasses from the five-and-ten love their bath; they roll luxuriously in the soapy water and seem almost to stretch. They're trying to forget their humble ten-cent origin, and they sort of hope that everyone else will forget it too. I watch them sitting on the table, holding themselves proudly; they expect that guests—they don't expect much, anymore, from members of the family—will comment on them and hold them up appreciatively. "Where did you get these lovely glasses?" someone may ask, and all along the table the glasses stiffen, not daring to glance at one another, tense until I answer, "I bought them at an auction. I expect they're quite valuable, really." Then along the table the green glasses will preen themselves, relaxing, and nod condescendingly at me. They have grown quite fond of me because of that little lie, and make a definite effort not to break when I drop them. I have noticed, too, half a dozen times, that if I forget, and confess that they did come from the five-and-ten, then inside twenty-four hours one or another of the glasses, no longer able to stand the disgrace, will plunge nobly to its death on the floor. I have only six of these glasses left, and the five-and-ten no longer carries them. My great hope is that someday I *shall* find some at an auction.

I really spend a lot more time in the kitchen than I ought, although it doesn't surprise anything in the kitchen to find me there, considering what a busybody I am, always meddling in things that are clearly none of my business. Take the forks, for instance; I'm sure I've done nothing to clear up *that* unhappy situation. I have two kitchen forks, one with four prongs and one with two prongs, and the four-pronged fork is of course my favorite because of its amiability; it is a far sweeter and more malleable character than the two-pronged fork, which was originally the fork to an inexpensive carving set, and regards this fact as an automatic entrée into the dining room.

My two forks are insanely jealous of each other, and I find that I must take a path of great caution with them, something I would not do for many of my friends. I try to keep out of their quarrels—who wouldn't be afraid of an angry fork?—but I am always fumbling the delicate balance of power that is all that keeps them from each other's throats. For instance, four-prongs is traditionally the fork for scrambling eggs, but two-prongs takes precedence in the dishwasher. Four-prongs prides himself on the fact that no two-pronged fork knows how to scramble eggs adequately. There is, however, some hair-thin line between scrambling eggs and beating eggs; past that certain line the job rightly belongs to an eggbeater. If I try to force four-prongs beyong his notions of right and fitting duty, he turns limp and useless in my hands.

Then, of course, as though my life were not enough complicated, when I finally give up on four-prongs and take out the eggbeater, *that* surly character is offended in turn, and twists himself into a rigid, disobedient confusion of metal when I try to turn the handle. I get a lot of unnecessary sarcasm from that eggbeater, too. I have let cake batter stand, half-mixed, for half an hour while the eggbeater and the fork calmed down, and at least twice I have had to set them on opposite sides of the kitchen table to keep them from tangling themselves into a snarling battle. All this, while two-prongs sits sedately watching, observing that any vulgar fork with four prongs is bound to get himself into low trouble, particularly if he consorts with eggbeaters.

Two-prongs is the kitchen carving-and-roast fork, and I shall never forget the taut moment in the kitchen when I inadvertently tried to lift a roast out of the pan with four-prongs. I was in a hurry, company was waiting, the gravy was not made, and four-prongs was the nearest fork. There was a moment of absolute resistance, then the incredulous turn of four-prongs in my hand, the sudden furious clatter of two-prongs from the stove where he had been waiting, the slippery tipping of the roasting pan; even the potholder hesitated. There was nothing I could say, of course. I was at fault, so I picked the roast up off the floor, kicked the interfering roasting pan into a corner, set four-prongs pointedly in the sink, and went to work with two-prongs, who was mollified, but sullen for several days.

I do not mean to say that I am under the thumb of my forks, any more than I am honestly afraid of the meat grinder's threats, or the bullying of the coffeepot. It is simply that one cannot live a day in the middle of so many personalities without occasionally treading on some fork's toes, or sideswiping the fundamental makeup of a dishtowel. A dishtowel is, I think, the most easily cowed of all kitchen implements, excepting only the steel wool, which hides a heart of gold under its gruff exterior. My striped dishtowels take a vulgar, unholy joy in getting into the living room to clean up spilled juice. There is one teatowel that adores my three-year-old daughter, I think because she once carried it off to her doll carriage to serve as a blanket, which is a pleasure usually beyond the reach of dishtowels. My daughter's friend is pleased to serve her now in any menial capacity, and has occasionally done service as a bib, at which it is well meaning but inefficient, as it prefers to lie back and admire her rather than catch the little bits of bacon and butter she is apt to let fall from her mouth.

When I turn my back on the sink to take up the dishtowel, the kitchen brightens and beams at me reassuringly. It rather resents being polished up, and there was quite a scene recently about the new curtains. I explained that I had made them myself, and was a little proud of them, and wanted to take the old ones down, but a great loyal voice was raised for the old curtains, and when they went into the hamper regardless, to be washed and turned into dust cloths, a vast silent resentment confronted me and my new curtains. The new curtains were edged awry, until I was persuaded I had sewn them wrong; the rods slipped down persistently. The color of the new curtains, by morning lite, was made so vivid, so glaring, by the subdued martyrdom of the rest of the kitchen, that I was almost convinced that they were a mistake. But I gave my kitchen time; it is primarily easygoing and friendly, and it will adapt to anything. I brought the old curtains back, in their new role as dust cloths, and left them on the table for a while, so that they might reassure their friends that they were happy and well treated. I gave the floor a wash—it hates washing, like a puppy, but, like a puppy, always feels better afterward—and promised the pantry new shelf paper, and things calmed down. There was only one morning, all things considered, when it was really *impossible* to serve breakfast in the kitchen.

My husband and son, who are gadget-happy, set up for me to use in my kitchen a magnetic metal bar, about four inches long, that takes, and keeps, a violent hold on any metal objects near it, so that I have had to pry my can openers away from it and occasionally, working too near, have had fear for the fillings in my teeth, or my wedding ring, or the tips of my shoelaces. When I moved the kitchen table over to the opposite wall, things were a little better, but I still felt, using my two forks or the can opener, the strong steady pull of the magnet against me, so that if I let go of the fork for a minute it would fly across the room to lodge securely against the magnet.

For a while I wondered about this, the advisability of having one spot in a kitchen to which all utensils would naturally gravitate, but now it reassures me. At least I can always be sure of finding my two warring forks there, nestling snugly in the broad magnetic arms of their common refuge, their maniac suspicions of each other lulled by the fact that it is big enough for both. Furthermore, I can feel through my wall magnet, even from the worktable across the room, the sure haunting echo of one magnet after another throughout the house: From the toy closet, my son's collection of magnets and small metal toys joins its siren voice to the master one in the kitchen. From beyond it, the magnets in all the various toys in the upstairs playroom call shrilly to my forks. From far above comes the thin sweet voice of the magnet in the new lock to the attic workshop. My forks tremble, look at me imploringly, and resign themselves to their work.

Sometimes, wandering as I do round my kitchen, I feel the magnetic pull myself, the urge to flatten myself against the wall and, until I am taken down for some practical purpose, lie there quiet, stilled, at rest.

Perhaps it's the magnet that holds me to my kitchen. Perhaps it's the fact that I keep my fountain pen and notebook on the shelf near the clock, so that I always have to go into the kitchen to sign letters, as well as to see what time it is or, as a last resort, to wash dishes.

Perhaps I'll wait and dry these tomorrow after breakfast.

EXCERPTS FROM MEMORIAL

Bryan Washington

Bryan Washington, born in 1993, won the International Dylan Thomas Prize for his debut short story collection *Lot* at the age of just twenty-seven. He is Writer and Scholar in Residence at Rice University, Texas; a National Book Foundation 5 Under 35 winner; a Lambda Literary Award winner; Forbes 30 Under 30 recipient; a finalist for more awards than we have space to list; and a columnist for the *New York Times Magazine*. He is, as all these things suggest, a phenomenal novelist and writer. The extracts below are taken from his novel *Memorial*, a remarkably beautiful, funny, tender story about loving and losing the people in your life.

3.

It's still dark when I'm up the next morning, but Mitsuko's mincing shrimp. She's hunched over the cutting board, beside eggs, flour, and honey.

Do you eat, she says.

I tell her I do.

We don't say shit while she's working. Mitsuko blitzes everything in a food processor. Drops the mixture in a skillet, dabbing everything with soy sauce, folding the batter gradually. I take my pills, watching her do all this, and she ignores me the entire time, working at her own pace.

When I sit on the sofa, Mitsuko stops rolling. I stand to set the table, and she starts rolling again.

Once she's finished, she fills a bowl with some pickled cucumbers, with a plate for the omelette, leaving another one out for me. We chew hunched over the counter, hip to hip.

So, Mitsuko says, how long have you been sleeping with my son?

Or is it casual, she says.

Not really, I say.

I don't know how it works, says Mitsuko.

I think it's the same for everyone.

It isn't, says Mitsuko.

She says, I'm sure you can tell that Michael and I are very close.

We've been together for four years, I say. More or less.

More, Mitsuko asks, or less?

A little more, I say.

But just a little, she says.

Mike's better with numbers, I say.

It occurs to me, out of nowhere, that my posture is entirely fucked up. Mitsuko's is impeccable, even at a lean. So I straighten up, and then I stoop, and Mitsuko raises an eyebrow.

She snorts, and says, My son could not be worse with numbers.

After that, we eat in silence. Scattered Spanish filters in through the window. The kids next door kick a soccer ball against the wall, until their father steps outside screaming, asking which one of them has lost their minds.

While Mitsuko's focused on her food, I really look at her. It's clear that, at one point, she was a startlingly beautiful woman.

Then she meets my eyes. I blink like something's in them.

She says, I realize that this must be strange for you, too.

No, I say, it's fine.

So you're a liar, says Mitsuko.

I'm being honest. Really.

I'm fluent in fine, says Mitsuko. Fine means fucked.

Did my son tell you how long he'd be gone, she says.

A month, I say. Maybe two. I don't know. We didn't talk too much about it.

Of course not.

But did he tell *you*?

Tell me what?

How long he'd be gone, I say. Or that he was leaving?

Mitsuko looks me in the eyes. She cracks her knuckles on the counter.

No, she says. My son neglected to give me that information. But this could be a good thing. I needed to get out of Japan for a while. No sense in rushing back to Tokyo to look at a dying man.

So, I ask, you're staying here? Until Mike gets back?

My voice cracks, just a bit. But Mitsuko spots it. She grins.

Would that be a problem, she asks.

No, I say. That's not what I meant.

Then what did you mean?

I'm sorry, I say. I really was just asking.

It's enough for Mitsuko to cross her arms. She leans on the counter, and her hair slips down her shoulders. I make a point to slow my breathing, to let my shoulders droop just a bit.

Then I think staying here is exactly what I'll do, says Mitsuko. I could use the time off. Your place is filthy, but it'll work until Michael makes it back.

And that's absolutely okay, I say. Totally perfect.

Remember, says Mitsuko, you're the one who let him leave.

You're right, I say. I'm the one who let him leave.

How generous, says Mitsuko, but then she doesn't say anything else.

Once Mitsuko's finished her bowl, she drops it in the sink. She turns on the faucet. Reaches for mine. The omelette was delicious, the sort of thing Mike would cook, because he did everything in the kitchen, and I think that this could have been the problem to begin with.

Nice chat, says Mitsuko, and I apologize, but I'm not sure why.

*

21.

Here is the root of the problem, our problem: the night before Mike left, in bed, before we fucked, he asked if I thought we were working.

What the fuck kind of question is that? I asked. Working? Are you saying we're done? Right after we bring home your fucking mother?

I'm asking a question, said Mike. That's all.

Just say it. Don't be a little bitch.

Benson, I am literally only asking what you think.

I think you should just come out and say what you're trying to say, I said. If you think we're done, just say it. I'll pack my shit tomorrow.

It's not that simple, said Mike, and then he put his face in his palms.

But it is, I said.

You are the only one that's been fucking around, I said.

This again, said Mike.

Yes, I said. Again. Again and again and again. And now you're leaving for who the fuck knows where. For who the fuck knows how long.

You're not being fair, said Mike. That isn't fair. It's my dad.

A man you couldn't give a fuck about!

That won't matter when he's dead.

We'd been whispering. We hadn't looked at each other. I felt Mike's body relax beside me.

Look, said Mike. Just because something isn't working doesn't mean it's broken. You just have to want to fix it. The want has to be there.

Tell me, I said. Do you want to fix it?

I guess that's what I'm trying to find out, said Mike.

*

4.

The next day, Mitsuko's cooking potatoes and okayu and a sliver of fish. She sets a bowl aside for me, with some scallions dashed over the porridge. Then she sips tea by the counter, and I drink water like a drowning man, and I never see her take a pill or check her blood pressure or anything else.

Once she's finished, Mitsuko slips on a jacket and shoes. I don't ask where she's going. I won't make the same mistakes twice.

*

5.

Mitsuko and I form something like an evening routine: She cooks. I set the table. We both eat at the counter. Later, I wipe it down while Mitsuko hits the dishes.

Otherwise, we mostly keep to ourselves. It's probably better that way.

But I've learned a few things. Little things.

Like how, back home, she works at a jewelry store in Shimokitazawa.

Or how she flies to LA three times a year, to meet a man, or to meet a friend, or to meet a man who is also a friend.

And she's hardly flashy, but all of her clothes are *nice*. Every sock and skirt and earring is clearly part of a larger, varied whole.

Mike, meanwhile, wears the same three things seven days a week.

He has no patience for schedules, routines, or patterns of any kind.

Before me, he saw whoever he wanted, whenever he wanted, fucking them however he wanted, and then he'd leave when he got bored.

Living with Mitsuko is, in other words, entirely unlike living with her son, whose gayness she is comfortable with, or at least not entirely uncomfortable with, or at least less disagreeable toward than my own parents, probably.

When Mitsuko asks about laundry detergent, I tell her it's in the cupboard under the sink.

When she asks where we do laundry, I point to the laundromat across the street.

When she asks where we buy groceries, I give her a few names, but she looks skeptical at all of them.

Will they have natto, she asks.

I say the H Mart just might.

You know what natto is, asks Mitsuko, frowning.

Soybeans, I say, right? Mike uses it.

And for the first time in our acquaintance, Mitsuko looks confused.

Here in Houston, she says. The city where you could hardly find daikon a few years ago?

Yeah, I say.

And *you* eat natto, she says.

I do, I say.

I don't believe you.

Because you don't think I could like it?

How the hell would I know what you like, says Mitsuko.

That night, I hear the television from the bedroom. Mitsuko's scrolling through movies. She settles on *War of the Worlds*, and I listen as Tom Cruise chases after his son. The kid's gone to join the resistance or some shit, although the viewer knows he's a goner. But Tom doesn't see that. He goes after the kid anyway.

So I'm dozing off when my phone dings. I'm thinking it's Ximena, but it's actually Mike.

He's sent a picture of his face in front of what looks like a train station. He's not quite smiling. The background is clogged with bodies.

And he's texted: HOW ARE THINGS?

I type: How the fuck do you expect.

A few minutes later, Mike sends another selfie. There's the back-drop of a neighborhood. It looks quiet, bookended by telephone poles. If you adjust the brightness and squint hard enough, you can see up his nose.

looks cool, I say.

IT IS

found him yet?

YEAH

and?

HE'S DOING FINE

HE'S NOT REALLY DOING FINE

IDREK

Mike sends another photo of some trees. And then one of some other train station. There are plenty of things we should be talking about, but here we are, talking around exactly all of them.

So I text: where can you get natto here

Y?

Your mom says she wants to make some.

And Mike's response is immediate, possibly the fastest he's ever replied to me: WHAT THE FUCK?

*

Once, I asked Mike if he wanted kids. We were at a pub in the Heights, watching two drunk whiteboys fall all over each other. One of them would stand from his barstool, and the other guy would catch him. Then the other guy would stand, and they'd repeat the performance again.

Mike had already finished his beer, but he managed to spit some up anyways.

It was around this time that we had the monogamy conversation. Mike's the one who brought it up.

I didn't refuse him outright, but I never affirmed him either.

I'm just saying we should think about opening things up, said Mike.

There's nothing to think about, I said.

I wouldn't care what you did, said Mike, as long as you came back home.

You aren't in a relationship with yourself, I said.

Just consider it, said Mike. Really. All I'm saying is that it's a big world out there.

World? I said. What the fuck? What world? We live in one place.

You know what I'm saying.

And the thing is, I did know. I knew. And I'd thought about it. But I was less worried, at the time, about what Mike would do than how

I'd handle it: If I opened the door, even just a crack, would I still have a reason to step back inside?

We didn't actually decide anything, between the two of us. But a non-decision is a choice in itself.

*

6.

The next morning, for the very first time, Mike's mother knocks on my door. She's fully dressed, while I lean on the doorway in a tank top and boxers.

Take your time, she says.

Jesus Christ, she says.

We leave five minutes later. Our Black neighbors wave from their porch. There's a question on the grandfather's face, and I wonder if he'll ask it.

But Mitsuko doesn't look away. If anything, she walks slower. Staring him down.

Mike's car is filthy with clothes: our hoodies and socks and a loose pair of shoes. The whole thing smells like him, and I know his mother smells it, too. When I toss a pair of shorts behind us, she grunts, and there's a jock strap in the back seat, and I pray to no god in particular that Mitsuko doesn't catch it.

We've pulled out of the neighborhood, and into town, when she says, You're sure they'll have what I need?

They should, I say. You and Mike make the same things.

Maybe similar, says Mitsuko. Not same.

We drive through the mix of locals beginning their day. Whole swathes of Houston look like chunks of other countries. There are potholes beside gourmet bakeries beside taquerías beside noodle bars, copied and pasted onto a graying landscape.

At a stoplight, these two smiling guys walk a toddler across the street, holding the little girl's hands on either side. One of the men is white. The other one's brown. They look like something straight out of *OutSmart*. I glance at Mitsuko, and her face doesn't tell me much.

So, she says, you're Black.

You noticed, I say.

Just barely, says Mitsuko. And how did you find my son?

Accidentally, I say.

Let me guess, it was Grindr.

It wasn't.

You found my son on the internet.

No.

We met at a get-together, I say. An acquaintance introduced us.

Sure, says Mitsuko.

Once the couple crosses the road, their daughter looks up at them, beaming. She is the happiest that a child has ever been, ever. If Mike had seen them, he'd feign some sort of choking, or he'd honk his horn, or he'd grow sober, not saying much at all.

*

My sister met him accidentally. It happened during Halloween, at a bar off Westheimer. I'd wandered away from him to take a piss, and when I made it back to the table, Lydia was stirring her Coke beside him. She wore some witchy getup, a costume with too many straps. Mike had on a toga. I'd gone as myself.

I was just talking to Mark, said Lydia.

You didn't say you had a little sister, said Mike.

They went on like that, back and forth. Lydia ordered more drinks. When I asked if she didn't have a date to get back to, she smiled and told me she'd just have to reschedule it. *This*, she said, was special. She'd never meet her baby brother's boyfriend for the first time again.

Lydia was Mike's age. A few years older than me. She wrote copy for the Buffalo Soldier Museum downtown, and if you told her you didn't know Houston had one of those, she'd say that's because it's for niggas.

But that evening, she played it cool. Laughed at our jokes. Paid for more beer.

Just before last call, Lydia gave Mike her number.

Wow, said Mike. This is a first.

Life is long, said Lydia.

Cheers, said Mike.

Later that night, Lydia texted me.

He's funny, she said.

Too funny for you, she added.

*

On Sunday mornings Mike drove us from market to market, all over the Northside. He juggled onions and guanabana and garlic and pineapples. He'd haggle with vendors in his shitty Spanish, and those evenings he'd cook three versions of the same fucking meal. I'd take a bite of one, and then a bite of the second. Then Mike would motion me toward the third. I usually went with the second.

Mike said this was practice for him. It was how he'd get better. I told him that not everyone did this, and he said there was a reason for that.

I didn't grow up with their palates, he said. They can assume a lot of shit that I can't.

So you force it on me, I said. Down my throat.

You'll miss it when it's gone, said Mike.

*

Our local H Mart is, inconceivably, closed for the day, and the next grocery store I bring Mitsuko to instead is objectively filthy—but there's natto. There's also a metal detector by the entrance. The doorway is flanked by a fried chicken vendor in scrubs. Older women and their children finger carrots on our left, and a little girl wandering the aisles wears a branch of parsley like a crown.

I drift around looking for a shopping cart. I find one with three wheels. We end up filling the whole thing, and also the basket, and also the crooks of Mitsuko's elbows.

At the register, I feel for my wallet, and I wait for Mitsuko to stop me. But she doesn't. So I pull out my card slowly, and that's when Mitsuko plucks a bill from her bag, shaking her head.

The girl behind the register laughs, tugging at a braid.

Just like a nigga, she says.

Isn't it, says Mitsuko.

*

Mitsuko's chewing vitamins when I make it back to the apartment, and I'm ducking toward the bedroom when she calls my name.

Can you cook a chicken, she says.

You mean boil it, I say.

I meant what I said.

Like, frying wings?

Absolutely not, says Mitsuko. Come here.

She's more comfortable in Mike's kitchen than I've ever been. He'd arranged everything to his liking, but Mitsuko's reorganized all of it. Everything in the drawers, all of the ladles and spatulas and sticks. The bowls were a certain way, and now they are not. Plus, all of Mike's spices. And the utensils, too. I never knew where he'd kept his chopsticks—they just materialized whenever we needed them—but now the place looks unrecognizable. She's flipped it on its head. It's entirely disorienting, but for once I can actually settle in.

Mitsuko grabs the chicken by one leg, balancing the other with a cleaver. In one fluid motion, she slices it entirely in half.

Jesus fuck, I say.

Quiet, says Mitsuko.

She proceeds to break down the carcass, bone by bone, stuffing the remains in a pot on the stove for stock. When she's finished clipping the fat, Mitsuko shakes each limb with a flick of her wrist. Her seasonings are lined up. She douses the meat in what looks like a pool of salt. But she doesn't say shit about it, and eventually she pirouettes to the side, flinging the chicken into a pan. It sizzles like a sheet of rain.

If I were at home, I would've marinated this, says Mitsuko. But I'm not at home.

Once she's finished and the meat's cooked, Mitsuko sets two bowls on the table, which is new. I sit across from her.

We eat, mostly in silence.

Did you get that, says Mitsuko.

Well, I say, bits and pieces.

She looks me over a little coolly.

That's all right, she says, but you're going to learn.

You have to, she adds.

*

Mike texts me that night. His father's doing worse.

worse? I say.

CAN'T SLEEP, WON'T EAT, BREATHING HEAVY, says Mike.

i'm sorry

YOU DIDN'T PUT IT INSIDE OF HIM

When I ask Mike what the next steps look like, he tells me they don't know yet. He tells me his father is stubborn. But the one certainty Mike has is that he's glad he flew over, or he thinks that he's glad, or he can't really imagine having not flown over.

It's too much to parse over the phone, over a screen. I tell Mike that I dismembered a chicken with his mother.

Mike writes, ???

i know, I text. i'm shocked

YOU ENJOY IT?

I survived

HA. THINK YOU'LL TRY AGAIN?

we'll see

I wait for Mike to ask about his mother. Or how we're doing in Texas. But he doesn't. The dots on my screen appear, and disappear, and reappear again, but nothing comes through.

So I ask him how *he's* doing, how he's really doing, and he sends me a selfie.

He's shaven, wincing in the photo. I can see his whole face for the first time in a year.

*

8.

When I'm up the next morning, Mitsuko's already gone. Her jacket is gone. Her shades are gone. I check for her shoes and they're gone.

I look for a note, and Mitsuko's left one on the table.

It's written entirely in kanji.

I could pull my fucking ears off.

But then I finally notice that she's taken the laundry baskets. Hers, and mine, and all of the detergent.

When Mitsuko comes back, I'm lying on the sofa. She takes one look at me, opens her mouth, and closes it again.

Then she says, My son called.

She says, He sounded horrible.

*

Mike and I once spent the night in Galveston for a long weekend. We hadn't gone on trips together, not a single one, so this was a brand-new thing. But for the first time in months, he'd taken time off from the café. My gig was closed for a holiday weekend. We had a weird energy brewing around the apartment with both of us there, just lying around. And then there were the neighbors, who'd knocked on our door the night before, warning us that they'd be hosting some sort of marathon quinceañera. They spent the entire first night outside in the yard, shouting and dancing and beating a piñata. Around two in the morning, they locked hands to sing a song about Jesus. Once their sixth chorus rolled around, I told Mike it didn't matter where we went, as long as we went somewhere else. But he was already snoring.

So the sand was a grimy pale. Our end of the beach was scarce. A high school couple argued about prom under a makeshift fort behind us. Some girls rolled around in the water in front of us while their mother tucked her head in a Ferrante novel. Every now and then, she'd look up at her girls, and then at us. When Mike finally waved, she wiggled her fingers.

We laid out a towel, took off our shirts, and glazed in the sun for the whole afternoon. For lunch, we drifted up the pier for fish tacos. The woman who sold them was missing an ear. They were delicious, and we ordered four more, and then we watched some boys do somersaults in the sand by the dock. A pair of older couples mimicked them, lounging around the corner, husbands and wives looking round and unbothered.

Eventually, we bought more tacos from the one-eared woman. She said, Buena suerte a ambos, and I asked Mike what that meant.

He told me we were lucky charms. Everything we touched turned to gold.

And we walked the food back to our tiny spot in the sand. I fell asleep with Mike's calves on my shoulders.

When I woke up, the beach had cleared out. Windows glowed from beach houses lining the pier.

I felt around for Mike. He wasn't on the towel. But his trunks were right beside me, and I felt this sort of chill.

That's when he called from the water. He stood in the coastline, far enough out to float away. He yelled my name, waving his arms, with this big-ass grin on his face, and when I started to make my way over, he yelled for me to strip.

I looked to see who else was on the coast. Mike yelled for me to stop.

He said that nobody cared.

And if they did, it didn't matter.

And, sometimes, it helps to think that I was someone who could do that. I could strip buck-naked on the beach, sprinting through the sand, because I felt that strongly about anyone.

*

13.

Mitsuko buys nine cookbooks from I don't know where. She says we're going to start with the classics. She's been brighter since she heard from her son, a little like Mike's given her a charge—and that night, Mitsuko cooks what she tells me is his favorite: potato korokke, crowded beside onions and gravy, surrounded by sliced tomatoes and lettuce. She mashes the potatoes with pork through her fingers, drizzling the mixture with salt and pepper, molding tiny patties and flipping them in flour and egg yolks and panko. I watch them crisp from the counter, and Mitsuko watches me watch them.

It is the most personal thing she's shared with me so far, and I tell her that.

She looks at me for a while, then says, Don't be stupid.

*

17.

The next morning, before I head to work, Mitsuko says she needs a ride downtown. She'd mailed herself ingredients from Japan to the FedEx building by the Marriott.

So we pull out of the neighborhood, and off I-45, dodging the never-ending construction on Elgin. As I hook a right at a stoplight under the bridge, a disheveled guy in a Rockets sweater sips from a paper bag. He's seen better days, but the sweater's brand-new. It's got the tags and everything.

He nods our way. I nod back. Then the light changes, and we both turn back to our lives.

Tell me something about my son that I don't know, says Mitsuko.

Well, I say.

But, the thing is, I've got nothing.

Mike is irritable.

Short-winded.

He does this thing with his tongue.

For the first few months, he'd trace shapes across my back in bed. Whenever I got them right, he'd chew on my shoulder.

Mike knows a little bit of Spanish, I say.

That's nice, says Mitsuko.

He has to. For his job.

Also, I say, he's really into food.

Thank you for that, says Mitsuko. Really. You're a wealth of knowledge.

But tell me, she says, when did you know you were gay?

I take my eyes off the road, nearly swerving onto the sidewalk. Some loiterers in shades hop away from the curb. They flick me off through the rearview window.

Never mind, says Mitsuko.

Sorry, I say, it wasn't you.

Of course it wasn't me, says Mitsuko.

We resettle into traffic.

If it helps, she says, I had no idea Mike was that way.

He never told me, says Mitsuko. Or his father. I had friends whose children are gay. Sons who sleep with sons. Girls who sleep with boys and girls.

But not mine, says Mitsuko. I didn't see it.

And then one day, she says, I just knew. Before he left home, it clicked. Everything finally made sense.

There was nothing to say after that, says Mitsuko. We both understood.

Cruising into the parking garage, we find a spot just across from the elevator. Once I've settled the car in park, we sit in the darkness.

What kind of guy did you think your son would end up with, I say.

Is that your real question, says Mitsuko, or are you asking something else?

Are you asking if I thought the man would be Japanese? she asks. Or if I care that you're Black?

A white dude emerges from the elevator in front of us, looking extremely distressed. He fumbles with his keys for a second. At the sound of his car alarm, his whole body relaxes.

If you put it that way, I say.

Well, says Mitsuko, I didn't think about that. That wasn't my business. Isn't. I'm his mother.

Or are you really asking what I think about *you*, she says.

Another white guy in a suit unlocks the car beside us. He peeks into my window, frowning above his tie.

I'd tell you, says Mitsuko, but you might drive us into the wall.

I trail Mitsuko as we walk past each suite, up an escalator, and over a crossway. The staff in the FedEx are mostly women, mostly Black.

They look at Mitsuko. They look at me.

A light-speed calculus blips across their eyes.

Once we've reached the front of the line, I smile as wide as I can. Mitsuko still hasn't taken off her shades. She hands one woman a card and receives an armful of envelopes. When she's asked if she needs a basket, Mitsuko declines.

That's what he's for, she says, nodding at me.

My kind of woman, says a lady behind the counter, chuckling.

On the drive back, I ask Mitsuko what her home in Tokyo's like. She raises an eyebrow.

Quiet, she says.

I've literally just parked by the apartment when my cell rings.

Ben, says Mike.

Godfuckingdammit, I say.

It's been a minute, says Mike.

I agree that it has.

One of our Black neighbors is sitting on her porch. She's rocking in her chair, watching the streetlights flicker. The block's quiet, for once, and the mosquitoes are out, and the woman swats her elbows from time to time, wiping her mouth with the crook of her arm.

Well, I say to Mike.

How are things, I ask. Are you at your father's?

I am, says Mike. Or we were. We're out now. Took a little trip.

He's not doing well, says Mike.

I'm sorry, I say.

And instead of Mike's usual You Didn't Do It, or his You Don't Have to Say That, he just says, Thank you.

That's when I understand.

But how's my mother, says Mike.

Just lovely, I say. Still adjusting to our shared proximity.

That's what she told me.

Go figure.

But it's a compliment, says Mike. Could be worse. Ma says you've been cooking.

We play house together, yes.

I can't even imagine it.

Just because the neighborhood's snoring, that doesn't mean it's asleep. There's a house party going on a few houses down. Some whitegirls stumble onto a lawn, laughing with red Solo cups. They glance back at the door they came from, and one of them covers her mouth, and her friend latches on to her shoulders, balancing them upright.

Hey, I say, when are you coming home?

Scattered voices slip through the phone, and also the sound of motion. For Mike, it's midday.

That's the question, isn't it, says Mike.

It is.

Mike asks if I want him to come back, and I don't say a word.

We're both silent. Both holding the line.

I owe him a lot, says Mike.

Not everything, he says. But I think I should see him through this, you know?

I know, I say.

So when he's gone, says Mike, I'll come back.

When he's gone, I say, you'll come back.

The whitegirls up the road stumble into the grass, laughing all over each other. The streetlights keep flickering. A chill settles in. And our neighbor, as if snapping out of a reverie, smiles and waves my way, putting her whole shoulder into it.

And you, says Mike. How are you doing?

The other day I saw a pigeon fly away with some cash, I say.

Go figure. It's probably for booze.

You think so?

Duh, says Mike. Don't overthink it.

I shut the door behind me as quietly as I can, but Mitsuko's already asleep on the sofa.

There's a bowl of rice on the counter, covered with a paper towel. It's still a little warm.

*

26.

Nearly three weeks in, it's almost astounding how little Mitsuko and I have talked about her son. When I tell her this, she shakes her head.

What is there to discuss? she says. What could *you* possibly tell me? I asked you once already and you gave me nothing.

He came out of my body, says Mitsuko. He's a homosexual. He left his mother with a stranger. I've already got everything I need to know.

She's sitting at the table, scrolling through her tablet. I'm in the kitchen, leaning over the stove.

I don't know, I say.

Exactly, says Mitsuko. You don't. So don't worry about it.

Maybe you could tell me a story, I say, and Mitsuko actually laughs.

A story is an heirloom, she says. It's a personal thing.

Okay, I say.

You don't ask for heirlooms. They're just given to you.

Okay, okay.

Check the rice, says Mitsuko.

I figure she's just cutting me off, but then I look at the stove and it's bubbling.

*

29.

I watch Mitsuko crack an egg with her palm in the kitchen. I think it's a fluke, but then she does it again.

Wait, I say. Wait!

What, says Mitsuko.

How did you do that?

Do what?

Mitsuko gives me this look like she's entirely exasperated. But then she does it again, executing the cleanest of breaks.

*

31.

I text Mike in the evening, thinking he'll just be starting his day, after Mitsuko and I finish an elaborate collaboration: udon cooked in a hot pot, beside abura-age and kamaboko and spinach and two chicken legs.

When Mitsuko cracks an egg into the pot, tasting a spoonful, she actually doesn't grimace.

It's edible, she says.

Really?

Really.

Once we've brought everything below a simmer, I take some photos. All of them are blurry. But when I send them to Mike, he responds immediately.

Nice! he says.

Mike has never, not once, used an exclamation point in our correspondence. Ever. He's not one of those people.

I ask if he's all right.

The next message he sends takes a little longer to arrive.

I'll call soon, he says.

Everything will be OK, he says.

I promise, he says, and that's what I take to sleep with me.

*

Mike's never promised me anything. Only delivered or didn't. He always said that promises were only words, and words only meant what you made them.

*

It's late when I hear the front lock jiggling.

I slip on basketball shorts, some sandals, and dip into the living room. Mitsuko's sliding into a jacket and her pair of graying sneakers. She gives me a look when I cough in the hallway.

You can come, she says, but keep your mouth shut.

We walk from the apartment to the next street over, and then a few blocks more. The air is mild for Houston. A little too crisp for February. Plodding behind Mitsuko on the sidewalk, I wonder what we look like to anyone peeking from their windows.

Eventually, we stop in front of what looks like a church. Something Methodist. I look at Mitsuko, and then at the signage, and she waves me over to the building's entrance, which is unlocked.

There's a light on by the pulpit, but otherwise the altar's empty. The aisles are cleared. The seats are clean. The church's windows are stained with various highlights from the Old Testament.

Once we've reached the head of the pulpit, Mitsuko takes to her knees.

I feel ridiculous standing behind her, so I settle into the space on her right.

We stay like that for a while. Mitsuko mutters gently, quietly, in Japanese. Her hands are clasped. Her head is bowed. At one point, I hear Mike's name, and then once again, but that's all I get.

It's been at least a decade since I've stepped in a church. I'd been baptized, as a teenager, because my mother had insisted. The pastor dunked me in the water and everything. Afterward, I came out soaking, feeling brand-new, like money, and I ate a wafer and drank some wine and never went back again.

I wonder how long Mitsuko's been doing this.

I wonder if it's even legal. If we're trespassing somehow.

But once Mitsuko's finished, she nods toward the choir bleachers at no one at all. Then she stands beside me, steadying herself on my shoulder.

Hurry up, she says. We're leaving.

Back in the apartment, I pour us both a glass of water. Mitsuko doesn't thank me, but she takes it anyway.

In case you're wondering, she says, that's what it's come to. It's absurd.

I don't think it's absurd, I say.

It's absurd, says Mitsuko.

I watch her drink her water. That's all she has to say. So I take my glass back to the bedroom, draining the rest on the way.

A SINGLE MAN

Christopher Isherwood

In rural Cheshire, at the turn of the century, **Christopher Isherwood** was born as the grandson and heir of an English country squire. For the next eighty-two years, Isherwood would travel far from Stockport: he would move to California, have many lovers (including his school friend W. H. Auden), write two dozen books, spend years as a Hindu monk, and become a pillar of the Gay Liberation movement. He was the kind of person sent down from Cambridge for writing joke answers on all of his exam papers. He saw being asked to leave not as a problem, but as the beginning of his real life: that of a proudly queer Anglo-American novelist, playwright, screenwriter and diarist. Isherwood's books largely remain in print, and his novel *Goodbye to Berlin*, based on his time in Germany at the end of the thirties, remains widely beloved as the origin of the musical *Cabaret*.

O bediently, it washes, shaves, brushes its hair; for it accepts its responsibilities to others. It is even glad that it has its place among them. It knows what is expected of it.

It knows its name. It is called George.

By the time it has gotten dressed, it has become *he*; has become already more or less George – though still not the whole George they demand and are prepared to recognise. Those who call him on the phone at this hour of the morning would be bewildered, maybe even scared, if they could realise what this three-quarters-human thing is that they are talking to. But, of course, they never could – its voice's mimicry of their George is nearly perfect. Even Charlotte is taken by it. Only two or three times has she sensed something uncanny, and asked, 'Geo – are you *all right*?'

He crosses the front room, which he calls his study, and comes down the staircase. The stairs turn a corner; they are narrow and steep. You can touch both handrails with your elbows and you have to bend your head – even if, like George, you are only five eight. This is a tightly planned little house. He often feels protected by its smallness; there is hardly room enough here to feel lonely.

Nevertheless—

Think of two people, living together day after day, year after year, in this small space, standing elbow to elbow, cooking at the same small stove, squeezing past each other on the narrow stairs, shaving in front of the same small bathroom mirror, constantly jogging, jostling, bumping against each other's bodies by mistake or on purpose, sensually, aggressively, awkwardly, impatiently, in rage or in love – think what deep though invisible tracks they must leave, everywhere, behind them! The doorway into the kitchen has been built too narrow. Two people in a hurry, with plates of food in their hands, are apt to keep colliding here. And it is here, nearly every morning, that George, having reached the bottom of the stairs, has this sensation of suddenly finding himself on an abrupt, totally broken-off, jagged edge – as though the track had disappeared down a landslide. It is here that he stops short and knows, with a sick newness, almost as though it were for the first time: Jim is dead. Is dead.

*

Today, there are more ants, winding in column across the floor, climbing up over the sink and threatening the closet where he keeps the jams and the honey. Doggedly, he destroys them with a Flit-gun and has a sudden glimpse of himself doing this; an obstinate, malevolent old thing imposing his will upon these instructive and admirable insects. Life destroying life before an audience of objects – pots and pans, knives and forks, cans and bottles – that have no part in the kingdom of evolution. Why? Why? It is some cosmic enemy, some arch-tyrant who tries to blind us to his very existence by setting us against our natural allies, the fellow-victims of his tyranny? But, alas, by the time George has thought all this, the ants are already dead and mopped up on a wet cloth and rinsed down the sink.

He fixes himself a plate of poached eggs, with bacon and toast and coffee, and sits down to eat them at the kitchen table. And meanwhile, around and around in his head, goes the nursery jingle his Nanny taught him when he was a child in England, all those years ago:

Poached eggs on toast are very nice—

(He sees her so plainly still, grey-haired with mouse-bright eyes, a plump little body carrying in the nursery breakfast-tray, short of breath from climbing all those stairs. She used to grumble at their steepness and call them 'The Wooden Mountains' – one of the magic phrases of his childhood.)

Poached eggs on toast are very nice,
If you try them once you'll want them twice!

Ah, the heartbreakingly insecure smugness of those nursery pleasures! Master George enjoying his eggs; Nanny watching him and smiling reassurance that all is safe in their dear tiny doomed world!

*

Breakfast with Jim used to be one of the best times of their day. It was then, while they were drinking their second and third cups of coffee, that they had their best talks. They talked about everything that came into their heads – including death, of course, and is there survival, and, if so, what exactly it is that survives. They even discussed the relative advantages and disadvantages of getting killed instantly and of knowing you're about to die. But now George can't for the life of him remember what Jim's views were on this. Such questions are hard to take seriously. They seem so academic.

Just suppose that the dead do revisit the living. That something approximately to be described as Jim can return to see how George is making out. Would this be at all satisfactory? Would it even be worth while? At best, surely, it would be like the brief visit of an observer from another country, who is permitted to peep in for a moment from the vast outdoors of his freedom and see, at a distance, through glass, this figure who sits solitary at the small table in the narrow room, eating his poached eggs humbly and dully, a prisoner for life?

I PROMISE WHEN I LIFT YOUR EGG

Jack Underwood

Jack Underwood is a poet, writer, critic and senior lecturer in creative writing at Goldsmiths. His debut collection *Happiness* won the Somerset Maugham Award in 2015, and his poems have been published in the *Observer*, the *TLS*, the *Poetry Review* and many others. He lives in London and has a small daughter.

from the water with my special spoon,
carry it to a cup as if it were a bald man
whistling steam to a tune he had just made up;
when I take my green handled egg-knife
to whip off the top and inside it is more
than yellow, like a laugh about to happen,
or butter pushed into light; when you dunk
gorgeously in, softly exploding the yolk
like a new idea finding one coloured term
for its articulation; when the little promise
of the egg, contained inside from the moment
it was laid, is broken by your tongue, then,
like love, it is remade, I promise.

TWO KITCHENS

Rachel Roddy

Rachel Roddy is a writer who cooks, or a cook who writes. Either way, she started off as a successful actress, living and working in London. But at the age of thirty-three and following a break-up, she sold her house, went to the airport and flew to Naples on a whim. She took a boat to Sicily and fell in love – and in some ways, never left. She now lives in Testaccio, Rome, with her Sicilian partner and their son. She has written three cookbooks, and writes a long-running weekly *Guardian* column, about the lure of everyday Italian cooking.

Ideally there are always two half-dozen cartons of eggs in the kitchen. I don't mind if one carton is already open – I feel reassured by the sight of one in progress and one in reserve, and the knowledge that if all else fails, at least we have eggs, and therefore a meal.

'Eggs are in deep trouble. Take care when buying them,' wrote Jane Grigson in 1974. They are in just as deep now, with production ever more intensive and labels often misleading, so we have to take even more care, especially those of us who live in cities and aren't lucky enough to know the hens our eggs come from. Take care, ask questions, be fussy and read boxes: there are bad and good eggs out there. We usually get eggs from our butcher, who gets them from the farm that supplies him with chickens. Occasionally, my friend Cinzia gives us eggs from her friend's chickens in her home town of Velletri, about 45 minutes north of Rome. She messages on her way back, *ho uova per te*, I have eggs for you. So I walk up the road to collect them, safely wrapped in a neat packet made from a series of clever folds. Back home, it is usually Luca who unwraps them: *careful, careful*, he whispers. I am never absolutely sure I believe him.

A smooth, perfect oval; all eggs are beautiful, even those born in circumstances that don't bear thinking about. Fresh eggs, though, from chickens that have run, flapped and pecked at grains, worms and kitchen scraps, have textures, colours and speckles that are a joy to behold. You really have to crack Cinzia's eggs to break them. A decisive tap with a knife blade is best for the shell that cracks rather than collapses. Because the eggs are so fresh, the plump white clings protectively to the yolk, which is more reddy-orange than yellow, a colour that explains why in Italian the yolk is called *il rosso*, the red. Whip these with sugar over the heat and your *zabaione* will be the colour of a desert sunrise. At my parents' house in Dorset too, where the kids collect eggs from the coop, the deeply coloured yolks are a thing of beauty. During his recent trip to Dorset, Vincenzo pricked a just-collected egg, made a pin hole in the top of it, threw back his head and drank the egg through the hole, something he used to do in Sicily as a boy. The expression about teaching your grandmother to suck eggs finally made sense. I was not tempted.

Eggs are accomplished things, multi-talented in fact. They can be the star, possibly taking you by surprise; Sicilians love to hide eggs in baked pasta or at the heart of a meat roll called *braciola*. They are just as happy to co-star, share a plate or be the supporting player without whom the whole thing might fall apart. Eggs emulsify, enrich, bind and even whip themselves into peaks. Quite simply, eggs are marvellous.

They are also the ultimate fast food, an exercise in simplicity and pure flavour. Boil, crack, beat: a four-minute boiled egg with bread, butter, salt and lots of black pepper could well be my perfect meal. Nothing else feels so complete. A three-minute fried egg, possibly with a slice of prosciutto draped over at the last moment so that the fat melts into the yolk. A 45-second omelette, maybe with herbs, rolled or folded and eaten with a glass of wine. And then there is the faithful answer to the Sunday night question: what are we going to eat?

EMMA

Jane Austen

A chronicler of the lives and loves of young women at the turn of the nineteenth century, **Jane Austen** was the author of some of the best romantic comedies in the English canon. Her books combine sharply satirical observations of her social class with love stories so richly drawn that they continue to inspire and inform writers today. The daughter of a Hampshire clergyman and his wife, Austen was born in 1775, the seventh of eight children. She shared with many of her characters a state of insecurity determined by gender and class; upon her father's death in 1805, she, her mother, and her beloved sister Cassandra were left with £160 a year, a precarious financial position. Austen's brothers helped where they could; most importantly, her brother Henry acted as publishing liaison and helped her to sell her books (anonymously), which brought the family a measure of financial freedom and Austen some modest success. Despite a proposal that would have offered financial security, and numerous suitors, Austen never married. She advised a niece seeking guidance regarding a relationship against '...accepting him unless you really do like him. Anything is to be preferred or endured rather than marrying without affection.' Her six full-length novels (two were published posthumously) have rarely been out of print in the two hundred years since her death at the age of forty-one. It was near impossible for us to pick just one extract, but we have settled on this, in which we meet Emma ('a heroine whom no one but myself will much like'), her father Mr. Woodhouse, and an egg boiled very soft.

Mr. Woodhouse was fond of society in his own way. He liked very much to have his friends come and see him; and from various united causes, from his long residence at Hartfield, and his good nature, from his fortune, his house, and his daughter, he could command the visits of his own little circle, in a great measure, as he liked. He had not much intercourse with any families beyond that circle; his horror of late hours, and large dinner-parties, made him unfit for any acquaintance but such as would visit him on his own terms. Fortunately for him, Highbury, including Randalls in the same parish, and Donwell Abbey in the parish adjoining, the seat of Mr. Knightley, comprehended many such. Not unfrequently, through Emma's persuasion, he had some of the chosen and the best to dine with him: but evening parties were what he preferred; and, unless he fancied himself at any time unequal to company, there was scarcely an evening in the week in which Emma could not make up a card-table for him.

Real, long-standing regard brought the Westons and Mr. Knightley; and by Mr. Elton, a young man living alone without liking it, the privilege of exchanging any vacant evening of his own blank solitude for the elegancies and society of Mr. Woodhouse's drawing-room, and the smiles of his lovely daughter, was in no danger of being thrown away.

After these came a second set; among the most come-at-able of whom were Mrs. and Miss Bates, and Mrs. Goddard, three ladies almost always at the service of an invitation from Hartfield, and who were fetched and carried home so often, that Mr. Woodhouse thought it no hardship for either James or the horses. Had it taken place only once a year, it would have been a grievance.

Mrs. Bates, the widow of a former vicar of Highbury, was a very old lady, almost past every thing but tea and quadrille. She lived with her single daughter in a very small way, and was considered with all the regard and respect which a harmless old lady, under such untoward circumstances, can excite. Her daughter enjoyed a most uncommon degree of popularity for a woman neither young, handsome, rich, nor married. Miss Bates stood in the very worst predicament in the world for having much of the public favour; and she had no intellectual superiority to make atonement to herself, or frighten those who might hate her into outward respect. She had never boasted either beauty or cleverness. Her youth had passed without distinction, and her middle of life was devoted to the care of a failing mother, and the endeavour to make a small income go as far as possible. And yet she was a happy woman, and a woman whom no one named without good-will. It was her own universal good-will and contented temper which worked such wonders. She loved every body, was interested in every body's happiness, quicksighted to every body's merits; thought herself a most fortunate creature, and surrounded with blessings in such an excellent mother, and so many good neighbours and friends, and a home that wanted for nothing. The simplicity and cheerfulness of her nature, her contented and grateful spirit, were a recommendation to every body, and a mine of felicity to herself. She was a great talker upon little matters, which exactly suited Mr. Woodhouse, full of trivial communications and harmless gossip.

Mrs. Goddard was the mistress of a School—not of a seminary, or an establishment, or any thing which professed, in long sentences of refined nonsense, to combine liberal acquirements with elegant morality, upon new principles and new systems—and where young ladies for enormous pay might be screwed out of health and into vanity—but a real, honest, old-fashioned Boarding-school, where a reasonable quantity of accomplishments were sold at a reasonable price, and where girls might be sent to be out of the way, and scramble themselves into a little education, without any danger of coming back prodigies. Mrs. Goddard's school was in high repute—and very deservedly; for Highbury was reckoned a particularly healthy spot: she had an ample house and garden, gave the children plenty of wholesome food, let them run about a great deal in the summer, and in winter dressed their chilblains with her own hands. It was no wonder that a train of twenty young couple now walked after her to church. She was a plain, motherly kind of woman, who had worked hard in her youth, and now thought herself entitled to the occasional holiday of a tea-visit; and having formerly owed much to Mr. Woodhouse's kindness, felt his particular claim on her to leave her neat parlour, hung round with fancy-work, whenever she could, and win or lose a few sixpences by his fireside.

These were the ladies whom Emma found herself very frequently able to collect; and happy was she, for her father's sake, in the power; though, as far as she was herself concerned, it was no remedy for the absence of Mrs. Weston. She was delighted to see her father look comfortable, and very much pleased with herself for contriving things so well; but the quiet prosings of three such women made her feel that every evening so spent was indeed one of the long evenings she had fearfully anticipated.

As she sat one morning, looking forward to exactly such a close of the present day, a note was brought from Mrs. Goddard, requesting, in most respectful terms, to be allowed to bring Miss Smith with her; a most welcome request: for Miss Smith was a girl of seventeen, whom Emma knew very well by sight, and had long felt an interest in, on account of her beauty. A very gracious invitation was returned, and the evening no longer dreaded by the fair mistress of the mansion.

Harriet Smith was the natural daughter of somebody. Somebody had placed her, several years back, at Mrs. Goddard's school, and somebody had lately raised her from the condition of scholar to that of parlour-boarder. This was all that was generally known of her history. She had no visible friends but what had been acquired at Highbury, and was now just returned from a long visit in the country to some young ladies who had been at school there with her.

She was a very pretty girl, and her beauty happened to be of a sort which Emma particularly admired. She was short, plump, and fair, with a fine bloom, blue eyes, light hair, regular features, and a look of great sweetness, and, before the end of the evening, Emma was as much pleased with her manners as her person, and quite determined to continue the acquaintance.

She was not struck by any thing remarkably clever in Miss Smith's conversation, but she found her altogether very engaging—not inconveniently shy, not unwilling to talk—and yet so far from pushing, shewing so proper and becoming a deference, seeming so pleasantly grateful for being admitted to Hartfield, and so artlessly impressed by the appearance of every thing in so superior a style to what she had been used to, that she must have good sense, and deserve encouragement. Encouragement should be given. Those soft blue eyes, and all those natural graces, should not be wasted on the inferior society of Highbury and its connexions. The acquaintance she had already formed were unworthy of her. The friends from whom she had just parted, though very good sort of people, must be doing her harm. They were a family of the name of Martin, whom Emma well knew by character, as renting a large farm of Mr. Knightley, and residing in the parish of Donwell— very creditably, she believed—she knew Mr. Knightley thought highly of them—but they must be coarse and unpolished, and very unfit to be the intimates of a girl who wanted only a little more knowledge and elegance to be quite perfect. *She* would notice her; she would improve her; she would detach her from her bad acquaintance, and introduce her into good society; she would form her opinions and her manners. It would be an interesting, and certainly a very kind undertaking; highly becoming her own situation in life, her leisure, and powers.

She was so busy in admiring those soft blue eyes, in talking and listening, and forming all these schemes in the in-betweens, that the evening flew away at a very unusual rate; and the supper-table, which always closed such parties, and for which she had been used to sit and watch the due time, was all set out and ready, and moved forwards to the fire, before she was aware. With an alacrity beyond the common impulse of a spirit which yet was never indifferent to the credit of doing every thing well and attentively, with the real good-will of a mind delighted with its own ideas, did she then do all the honours of the meal, and help and recommend the minced chicken and scalloped oysters, with an urgency which she knew would be acceptable to the early hours and civil scruples of their guests.

Upon such occasions poor Mr. Woodhouse's feelings were in sad warfare. He loved to have the cloth laid, because it had been the fashion of his youth, but his conviction of suppers being very unwholesome made him rather sorry to see any thing put on it; and while his hospitality would have welcomed his visitors to every thing, his care for their health made him grieve that they would eat.

Such another small basin of thin gruel as his own was all that he could, with thorough self-approbation, recommend; though he might constrain himself, while the ladies were comfortably clearing the nicer things, to say:

"Mrs. Bates, let me propose your venturing on one of these eggs. An egg boiled very soft is not unwholesome. Serle understands boiling an egg better than any body. I would not recommend an egg boiled by any body else; but you need not be afraid, they are very small, you see—one of our small eggs will not hurt you. Miss Bates, let Emma help you to a *little* bit of tart—a *very* little bit. Ours are all apple-tarts. You need not be afraid of unwholesome preserves here. I do not advise the custard. Mrs. Goddard, what say you to *half* a glass of wine? A *small* half-glass, put into a tumbler of water? I do not think it could disagree with you."

Emma allowed her father to talk—but supplied her visitors in a much more satisfactory style, and on the present evening had particular pleasure in sending them away happy. The happiness of Miss Smith was quite equal to her intentions. Miss Woodhouse was so great a personage in Highbury, that the prospect of the introduction had given as much panic as pleasure; but the humble, grateful little girl went off with highly gratified feelings, delighted with the affability with which Miss Woodhouse had treated her all the evening, and actually shaken hands with her at last!

P IS FOR PEAS
FROM AN ALPHABET
FOR GOURMETS

M. F. K. Fisher

If **Mary Frances Kennedy Fisher** had been born a day later, she would have laboured her life under the extraordinary name *Independencia*. As it was, she was born 3 July 1908, in Michigan, into a childhood full of food, love, chaos and helping in the kitchen. As a young newlywed she moved to France with her first husband, a place she would call home (alongside California) for the rest of her life. She wrote more than twenty books about the art and pleasure of eating, most of which remain in print. Her life was not easy, and her books are beautiful, joyful, heartbreaking and tender. Fisher died in 1992, leaving two daughters, Anna and Kennedy.

P is for peas... naturally! and for a few reasons why the best peas I ever ate in my life were, in truth, the best peas I ever ate in my life.

Every good cook, from Fanny Farmer to Escoffier, agrees on three things about these delicate messengers to our palates from the kind earth-mother: they must be very green, they must be freshly gathered, and they must be shelled at the very last second of the very last minute.

My peas, that is, the ones that reached an almost unbelievable summit of perfection, an occasion that most probably never would happen again, met these three gastronomical requirements to a point of near-ridiculous exactitude. It is possible, however, that even this technical impeccability would not have been enough without the mysterious blending, that one time, of weather, place, other hungers than my own. After all, I can compare bliss with near bliss, for I have often, blessed me, eaten superlative green peas.

Once, for instance, my grandmother ran out into her garden, filled her apron with the fattest pods, sat rocking jerkily with a kind of nervous merriment for a very few minutes as she shelled them – and before we knew it she had put down upon the white-covered table a round dish of peas in cream. We ate them with our spoons, something we never could have done at home! Perhaps that added to their fragile, poignant flavour, but not much: they were truly *good*.

And then once in Paris, in June (what a hackneyed but wonderful combination of the somewhat overrated time-and-place motif!), I lunched at Foyot's, and in the dim room where hot-house roses stood on all the tables the very month roses climbed crazily outside on every trellis, I watched the headwaiter, as skilled as a magician, dry peas over a flame in a generous pan, add what looked like an equal weight of butter, which almost visibly sent out a cloud of sweet-smelling hay and meadow air, and then swirl the whole.

At the end he did a showy trick, more to amuse himself than me, but I sat open-mouthed, and I can still see the arc of little green vegetables flow up into the air and then fall, with a satisfying shush, back into the pan some three or four feet below and at least a yard from where they took off. I gasped, the headwaiter bowed faintly but with pride, and then we went about the comparatively mundane procedure of serving, tasting, and eating.

Those petits pois au beurre were, like my grandmother's, à la crème mode d'Iowa, good – *very* good. They made me think of paraphrasing Sidney Smith's remark about strawberries and saying, 'Doubtless God could have made a better green pea, but doubtless He never did.'

That was, however, before the year I started out, on a spring date set by strict local custom, to grow peas in a steep terraced garden among the vineyards between Montreux and Lausanne, on the Lake of Geneva.

The weather seemed perfect for planting by May Day, and I had the earth ready, the dry peas ready, the poles ready to set up. But Otto and Jules, my mentors, said no so sternly that I promised to wait until 15 May, which could easily be labelled Pea-Planting Day in Swiss almanacs. They were right, of course: we had a cold snap that would have blackened any sprout about 10 May. As I remember, the moon, its rising, and a dash of hailstones came into the picture too.

And then on 15 May, a balmy sweet day if ever I saw one, my seeds went into the warm, welcoming earth, and I could agree with an old gardening manual which said understandingly, 'Perhaps no vegetable is set out in greater expectancy . . . for the early planting fever is impatient.'

A week later I put in another row, and so on for a month, and they did as they were meant to, which is one of the most satisfying things that can possibly happen to a gardener, whether greenhorn and eager or professional and weatherworn.

Then came the day with stars on it: time for what my grandmother would have called 'the first mess of peas'.

The house at Le Pâquis was still a-building, shapes of rooms but no roof, no windows, trestles everywhere on the wide terrace high above the lake, the ancient apple tree heavily laden with button-sized green fruit, plums colouring on the branches at the far end near the little meadow, set so surprisingly among the vineyards that gave Le Pâquis its name.

We put a clean cloth, red and white, over one of the carpenters' tables, and we kicked wood curls aside to make room for our feet under the chairs brought up from the apartment in Vevey. I set out tumblers, plates, silver, smooth, unironed napkins sweet from the meadow grass where they had dried.

While some of us bent over the dwarf-pea bushes and tossed the crisp pods into baskets, others built a hearth from stones and a couple of roof tiles lying about and made a lively little fire. I had a big kettle with spring water in the bottom of it, just off simmering, and salt and pepper and a pat of fine butter to hand. Then I put the bottles of Dézelay in the fountain, under the timeless spurt of icy mountain water, and ran down to be the liaison between the harvesters and my mother, who sat shelling peas from the basket on her lap into the pot between her feet, her fingers as intent and nimble as a lacemaker's.

I dashed up and down the steep terraces with the baskets, and my mother would groan and then hum happily when another one appeared, and below I could hear my father and our friends cursing just as happily at their wry backs and their aching thighs, while the peas came off their stems and into the baskets with a small sound audible in that still high air, so many hundred feet above the distant and completely silent Léman. It was suddenly almost twilight. The last sunlight on the Dents du Midi was fire-rosy, with immeasurable coldness in it.

'Time, gentlemen, time,' my mother called in an unrehearsed and astonishing imitation of a Cornish barmaid.

They came in grateful hurry up the steep paths, almost nothing now in their baskets, and looks of smug success upon their faces. We raced through the rest of the shelling, and then while we ate rolled prosciutto and drank Swiss bitters or brandy and soda or sherry, according to our various habits, I dashed like an eighteenth-century courier on a secret mission of utmost military importance, the pot cautiously braced in front of me, to the little hearth.

I stirred up the fire. When the scant half-inch of water boiled, I tossed in the peas, a good six quarts or more, and slapped on the heavy lid as if a devil might get out. The minute steam showed I shook the whole like mad. Someone brought me a curl of thin pink ham and a glass of wine cold from the fountain. Revivified, if that were any more possible, I shook the pot again.

I looked up at the terrace, a shambles of sawed beams, cement mixers, and empty sardine tins left from the workmen's lunches. There sat most of the people in the world I loved, in a thin light that was pink with Alpen glow, blue with a veil of pine smoke from the hearth. Their voices sang with a certain remoteness into the clear air, and suddenly from across the curve of the Lower Corniche a cow in Monsieur Rogivue's orchard moved her head among the meadow flowers and shook her bell in a slow, melodious rhythm, a kind of hymn. My father lifted up his face at the sweet sound and, his fists all stained with green-pea juice, said passionately, 'God, but I feel good!' I felt near to tears.

The peas were now done. After one more shake I whipped off the lid and threw in the big pat of butter, which had a bas-relief of William Tell upon it. I shook in salt, ground in pepper, and then swirled the pot over the low flames until Tell had disappeared. Then I ran like hell, up the path lined with candytuft and pinks, past the fountain where bottles shone promisingly through the crystal water, to the table.

Small brown roasted chickens lay on every plate, the best ones I have ever eaten, done for me that afternoon by Madame Doellenbach of the Vieux Vevey and not chilled since but cooled in their own intangibly delicate juices. There was a salad of mountain lettuces. There was honest bread. There was plenty of limpid wine, the kind Brillat-Savarin said was like rock-water, tempting enough to make a hydrophobic drink. Later there was cheese, an Emmenthaler and a smuggled Roblichon . . .

. . . And later still we walked dreamily away, along the Upper Corniche to a café terrace, where we sat watching fireworks far across the lake at Evian, and drinking café noir and a very fine *fine*.

But what really mattered, what piped the high unforgettable tune of perfection, were the peas, which came from their hot pot onto our thick china plates in a cloud, a kind of miasma, of everything that anyone could ever want from them, even in a dream. I recalled the three basic requisites, according to Fanny Farmer and Escoffier . . . and again I recalled Sidney Smith, who once said that his idea of Heaven (and he was a cleric!) was pâté de foie gras to the sound of trumpets. Mine, that night and this night too, is fresh green garden peas, picked and shelled by my friends, to the sound of a cowbell.

I

Conveniently, P is for pâté as well as peas, and I continue to feel near enough to Sidney Smith, my long-time ideal of a charming person, to agree with him that the former can be as heavenly as the latter, with or without the sound of trumpets!

I used to think, and perhaps still do, that I can never really have enough pâté de foie gras. I spent almost a half a year in Strasbourg once and could eat it at will, or at least whenever I could justify splurging from twenty to forty American cents for a generous slice of it, which seemed to be more often than not.

There was a 'patriotic' *brasserie*, reputedly run by the French government at a hideous financial loss in order to indoctrinate Gallic gaiety into the morbid confused basically Germanic citizens, and there we could eat delicious, well-served pâté in aspic for six francs, as I remember, which would rightly have cost three times as much in any café less bent toward propaganda.

Once in a while we went to a very pompous, small, elegant restaurant, Prussian as a slashed cheek, and ordered pâté de foie gras truffé en brioche, a culinary trick that has always fascinated me, like the Baked Alaska of my adolescence. How does the rich goose liver stay whole and fresh while the dough bakes? And how did the ice cream stay cold and firm while the magic white mound of meringue turned gold? (I prefer to remain puzzled over the former, and leave the latter to my wide-eyed children.)

I used to go, now and then in Strasbourg, to the Doyen offices and choose little or big pots, according to my purse, to be sent back to America. The eighteenth-century Doyen, the founder, is said to be the man who first put truffles into his paste of fat goose livers and spice and brandy, and he or whoever else it may have been who consummated this celestial wedding of high flavour should be tendered some special gastronomical salute, it seems to me, just as should the brave soul who first ate a tomato, and the equally hardy one who first evolved a Camembert cheese from a fermenting pudding of old cream. There is nothing much better in this Western world than a fine, unctuous, truffled pâté, and I suspect that when next I taste one, packed and shipped from Strasbourg itself, I shall be hard put to it not to shed a tear of impious nostalgic bliss upon it.

Meanwhile I look back with no great difficulty to many a pâté maison I have enjoyed, most of which had never even seen the shadow of a fat goose liver. They were delicious.

In general, from Paris to New York, the smaller the maison of which it was the pâté, the better it tasted: an inverse attempt to be important, I suppose, made the little restaurants exert themselves to produce an honourable substitute for the real thing, while the big ones simply took it for granted that anyone who could afford them would of course order nothing but genuine pâté de foie gras de Strasbourg.

Whatever the materialistic reasons for this triumph, I have eaten many unheralded pâtés that almost, if not quite, comforted me for the unavoidable realisation that they were but substitutes. I have often made them myself, not always with as good fortune as some of the professional chefs whose loaves I have cut into, but still passing well – passing damn well. I have found that it takes time to make them properly, that they improve with ageing, that they must hold only the best of whatever ingredients they call for (no cheap butter, for instance, no 'cooking' brandy), and that they must be quietly but sternly heady with the fumes of freshly ground pepper, fine smoky bacon fat, sweet butter, honest booze. If properly served, cold and smooth from their casseroles or terrines, with good crusty bread and good red wine, they need touch the lock to none.

The best of these pâtés that I have ever tasted, but not made myself, was one sent to a friend in Dijon from Brillat-Savarin's town of Belley, and kept on a ledge in the wine cellar all summer. Then, one of the first nippy days of fall, Monsieur Ollagnier lifted it down from its cobwebs. While we all leaned, noses to windward, over the table, he broke open the hard flour crust that was the seal. He lifted it off delicately, in one fine piece, mildewed on top and closed impregnably, underneath, with yellow, cold, chaste fat. He plunged his knife sharply, surely, into one end of the casserole.

Madame Ollagnier clashed the plates roughly toward him, as if afraid to lose one crumb upon the cloth, and their son stood up pontifically, for nineteen that is, and prepared to pour the Nuit-St-Georges Grands Suchots, with which we planned to drink to countless unpresent souls.

The pâté itself was truly a hunters' dish, worthy of Belley and its mighty ghost, a heady, gamy mixture, laced as tight as an 1880 belle with the best local brandy, high as a kite with spices and forest herbs, a true pâté de gibier à la mode de whoever made it, like this one of mine:

Pâté Fin (pour Fêtes)

1 hare (or equivalent bulk of quail, pheasant, duck, what you will), the best parts	1 pound good meat from hare or whatever meat is being used (scraps)
equal weight of lean bacon in thin strips	6 ounces pork
	6 ounces veal
3 or 4 thinly sliced truffles, if possible	1 pound bacon
	1 egg
1 scant cup brandy	bay, nutmeg, etc., as desired

Bone the best parts of the hare (assuming you are making a pâté de lièvre), and put them with an equal weight of bacon and the sliced truffles into a casserole. Marinate in brandy to cover.

Make a forcemeat of the clean scrapmeat, pork, veal, and bacon, and run through a fine meat grinder twice. Mix well with the egg and brandy and put through a fine sieve.

Line an oval or round terrine carefully with the marinated bacon strips, and then fill it with alternating layers of hare, forcemeat, and bacon, scattering the precious truffles judiciously. Cover with bacon. Put on bay, etc., as desired. Cover with a heavy lid, set in a pan of water, and bake in a slow (325°) oven. When the ample grease that rises to the top is quite clear, the pâté is done, and not before.

Remove from oven, cool, and then let chill at least two days before serving. If care is taken to use only the best ingredients, and to see that the top 'butter' is absolutely clear before removing from the stove, this pâté will last in a cold place for many months, and it will be worth the guarding of it.

I would, if I could, send a pot of it, in Heaven surely, to Sidney Smith himself.

THE TIME TRAVELLER'S WIFE

Audrey Niffenegger

An acclaimed visual artist, **Audrey Niffenegger**'s first novels were essentially self-produced intaglio letterpress sculptures. Her commercial debut, on the other hand, was an instant bestseller: *The Time Traveller's Wife*, published in 2003, sold several million copies and has been adapted twice for the screen. The novel is a love story with a science fiction premise: Henry suffers from a genetic condition that causes him to travel involuntarily through time, and Clare is the artist he meets over and over and over again, and eventually (but what's *eventually* to a time traveller?) marries. Niffenegger is herself married to the cartoonist Eddie Campbell.

Saturday, November 30, 1991 (Henry is 28, Clare is 20)

Henry: Clare has invited me to dinner at her apartment. Charisse, Clare's roommate, and Gomez, Charisse's boyfriend, will also be dining. At 6:59 p.m. Central Standard Time, I stand in my Sunday best in Clare's vestibule with my finger on her buzzer, fragrant yellow freesia and an Australian Cabernet in my other arm, and my heart in my mouth. I have not been to Clare's before, nor have I met any of her friends. I have no idea what to expect.

The buzzer makes a horrible sound and I open the door. "All the way up!" hollers a deep male voice. I plod up four flights of stairs. The person attached to the voice is tall and blond, sports the world's most immaculate pompadour and a cigarette and is wearing a Solidarnosc T-shirt. He seems familiar, but I can't place him. For a person named Gomez he looks very . . .Polish. I find out later that his real name is Jan Gomolinski.

"Welcome, Library Boy!" Gomez booms.

"Comrade!" I reply, and hand him the flowers and the wine. We eyeball each other, achieve *détente*, and with a flourish Gomez ushers me into the apartment.

It's one of those wonderful endless railroad apartments from the twenties—a long hallway with rooms attached almost as afterthoughts. There are two aesthetics at work here, funky and Victorian. This plays out in the spectacle of antique petit point chairs with heavy carved legs next to velvet Elvis paintings. I can hear Duke Ellington's *I Got It Bad and That Ain't Good* playing at the end of the hall, and Gomez leads me in that direction.

Clare and Charisse are in the kitchen. "My kittens, I have brought you a new toy," Gomez intones. "It answers to the name of Henry, but you can call it Library Boy." I meet Clare's eyes. She shrugs her shoulders and holds her face out to be kissed; I oblige with a chaste peck and turn to shake hands with Charisse, who is short and round in a very pleasing way, all curves and long black hair. She has such a kind face that I have an urge to confide something, anything, to her, just to see her reaction. She's a small Filipino Madonna. In a sweet, Don't Fuck With Me voice she says, "Oh, Gomez, do shut up. Hello, Henry. I'm Charisse Bonavant. Please ignore Gomez, I just keep him around to lift heavy objects."

"And sex. Don't forget the sex," Gomez reminds her. He looks at me. "Beer?"

"Sure." He delves into the fridge and hands me a Blatz. I pry off the cap and take a long pull. The kitchen looks as though a Pillsbury dough factory has exploded in it. Clare sees the direction of my gaze. I suddenly recollect that she doesn't know how to cook.

"It's a work in progress," says Clare.

"It's an installation piece," says Charisse.

"Are we going to eat it?" asks Gomez.

I look from one to the other, and we all burst out laughing. "Do any of you know how to cook?"

"No."

"Gomez can make rice."

"Only Rice-A-Roni."

"Clare knows how to order pizza."

"And Thai—I can order Thai, too."

"Charisse knows how to *eat*."

"*Shut up, Gomez*," say Charisse and Clare in unison.

"Well, uh. . .what was that going to be?" I inquire, nodding at the disaster on the counter. Clare hands me a magazine clipping. It's a recipe for Chicken and Shiitake Risotto with Winter Squash and Pine Nut Dressing. It's from *Gourmand*, and there are about twenty ingredients. "Do you have all this stuff?"

Clare nods. "The shopping part I can do. It's the assembly that perplexes."

I examine the chaos more closely. "I could make something out of this."

"You can cook?" I nod.

"It cooks! Dinner is saved! Have another beer!" Gomez exclaims. Charisse looks relieved, and smiles warmly at me. Clare, who has been hanging back almost fearfully, sidles over to me and whispers, "You're not mad?" I kiss her, just a tad longer than is really polite in front of other people. I straighten up, take off my jacket, and roll up my sleeves. "Give me an apron," I demand. "You, Gomez—open that wine. Clare, clean up all that spilled stuff, it's turning to cement. Charisse, would you set the table?"

One hour and forty-three minutes later we are sitting around the dining room table eating Chicken Risotto Stew with Puréed Squash. Everything has lots of butter in it. We are all drunk as skunks.

Clare: The whole time Henry is making dinner Gomez is standing around the kitchen making jokes and smoking and drinking beer and whenever no one is looking he makes awful faces at me. Finally Charisse catches him and draws her finger across her throat and he stops. We are talking about the most banal stuff: our jobs, and school, and where we grew up, and all the usual things that people talk about when they meet each other for the first time. Gomez tells Henry about his job being a lawyer, representing abused and neglected children who are wards of the state. Charisse regales us with tales of her exploits at Lusus Naturae, a tiny software company that is trying to make computers understand when people talk to them, and her art, which is making pictures that you look at on a computer. Henry tells stories about the Newberry Library and the odd people who come to study the books.

"Does the Newberry really have a book made out of human skin?" Charisse asks Henry.

"Yep. *The Chronicles of Nawat Wuzeer Hyderabed*. It was found in the palace of the King of Delhi in 1857. Come by some time and I'll pull it out for you."

Charisse shudders and grins. Henry is stirring the stew. When he says "Chow time," we all flock to the table. All this time Gomez and Henry have been drinking beer and Charisse and I have been sipping wine and Gomez has been topping up our glasses and we have not been eating much but I do not realize how drunk we all are until I almost miss sitting down on the chair Henry holds for me and Gomez almost sets his own hair on fire while lighting the candles.

Gomez holds up his glass. "The Revolution!"

Charisse and I raise our glasses, and Henry does, too. "The Revolution!" We begin eating, with enthusiasm. The risotto is slippery and mild, the squash is sweet, the chicken is swimming in butter. It makes me want to cry, it's so good.

Henry takes a bite, then points his fork at Gomez. "Which revolution?"

"Pardon?"

"Which revolution are we toasting?" Charisse and I look at each other in alarm, but it is too late.

Gomez smiles and my heart sinks. "The next one."

"The one where the proletariat rises up and the rich get eaten and capitalism is vanquished in favor of a classless society?"

"That very one."

Henry winks at me. "That seems rather hard on Clare. And what are you planning to do with the intelligentsia?"

"Oh," Gomez says, "we will probably eat them, too. But we'll keep you around, as a cook. This is outstanding grub."

Charisse touches Henry's arm, confidentially. "We aren't really going to eat anybody," she says. "We are just going to redistribute their assets."

"That's a relief," Henry replies. "I wasn't looking forward to cooking Clare."

Gomez says, "It's a shame, though. I'm sure Clare would be very tasty."

"I wonder what cannibal cuisine is like?" I say. "Is there a cannibal cookbook?"

"*The Cooked and The Raw*," says Charisse.

Henry objects. "That's not really a how-to. I don't think Lévi-Strauss gives any recipes."

"We could just adapt a recipe," says Gomez, taking another helping of the chicken. "You know, Clare with Porcini Mushrooms and Marinara Sauce over Linguini. Or Breast of Clare à la Orange. Or—"

"Hey," I say. "What if I don't *want* to be eaten?"

"Sorry, Clare," Gomez says gravely. "I'm afraid you have to be eaten for the greater good."

Henry catches my eye, and smiles. "Don't worry, Clare; come the Revolution I'll hide you at the Newberry. You can live in the stacks and I'll feed you Snickers and Doritos from the Staff Lunchroom. They'll never find you."

I shake my head. "What about 'First, we kill all the lawyers'?"

"No," Gomez says. "You can't do anything without lawyers. The Revolution would get all balled up in ten minutes if lawyers weren't there to keep it in line."

"But my dad's a lawyer," I tell him, "so you can't eat us after all."

"He's the wrong kind of lawyer," Gomez says. "He does estates for rich people. I, on the other hand, represent the poor oppressed children—"

"Oh, shut up, Gomez," says Charisse. "You're hurting Clare's feelings."

"I'm not! Clare wants to be eaten for the Revolution, don't you, Clare?"

"No."

"Oh."

"What about the Categorical Imperative?" asks Henry.

"Say what?"

"You know, the Golden Rule. Don't eat other people unless you are willing to be eaten."

Gomez is cleaning his nails with the tines of his fork. "Don't you think it's really Eat or Be Eaten that makes the world go round?"

"Yeah, mostly. But aren't you yourself a case in point for altruism?" Henry asks.

"Sure, but I am widely considered to be a dangerous nutcase." Gomez says this with feigned indifference, but I can see that he is puzzled by Henry. "Clare," he says, "what about dessert?"

"Ohmigod, I almost forgot," I say, standing up too fast and grabbing the table for support. "I'll get it."

"I'll help you," says Gomez, following me into the kitchen. I'm wearing heels and as I walk into the kitchen I catch the door sill and stagger forward and Gomez grabs me. For a moment we stand pressed together and I feel his hands on my waist, but he lets me go. "You're drunk, Clare," Gomez tells me.

"I know. So are you." I press the button on the coffee maker and coffee begins to drip into the pot. I lean against the counter and carefully take the cellophane off the plate of brownies. Gomez is standing close behind me, and he says very quietly, leaning so that his breath tickles my ear, "He's the same guy."

"What do you mean?"

"That guy I warned you about. Henry, he's the guy—"

Charisse walks into the kitchen and Gomez jumps away from me and opens the fridge. "Hey," she says. "Can I help?"

"Here, take the coffee cups…." We all juggle cups and saucers and plates and brownies and make it safely back to the table. Henry is waiting as though he's at the dentist, with a look of patient dread. I laugh, it's so exactly the look he used to have when I brought him food in the Meadow…but he doesn't remember, he hasn't been there yet. "Relax," I say. "It's only brownies. Even I can do brownies." Everyone laughs and sits down. The brownies turn out to be kind of undercooked. "Brownies tartare," says Charisse. "Salmonella fudge," says Gomez. Henry says, "I've always liked dough," and licks his fingers. Gomez rolls a cigarette, lights it, and takes a deep drag.

BRIDGET JONES'S DIARY

Helen Fielding

Translated into thirty-two languages, sold in forty countries, and selling more than fifteen million copies, **Helen Fielding**'s satirical Bridget Jones has been hailed as one of the characters and novels that defined the twentieth century. When asked to write a dating column for London's *Evening Standard* in the nineties, Fielding demurred: too embarrassing, too vulnerable, too exposing. Instead she offered them Bridget: a comic creation who nonetheless echoed the very real feelings of being single in the city. Over the next twenty years, Bridget's remit extended to four novels, three movies, and a lifetime of love, betrayal, grief, motherhood, friendship and more. Fielding has written two other novels, is the mother of two children, and divides her time between London and Los Angeles.

Monday 20 November

8st 12 (v.g.), cigarettes 0 (v. bad to smoke when performing culinary miracles), alcohol units 3, calories 200 (effort of going to supermarket must have burnt off more calories than purchased, let alone ate).

7 p.m. Just returned from hideous middle-class Singleton guilt experience at supermarket, standing at checkout next to functional adults with children buying beans, fish fingers, alphabetti spaghetti, etc., when had the following in my trolley:

20 heads of garlic	36 oranges
tin of goose fat	4 pints of double cream
bottle of Grand Marnier	4 vanilla pods at £1.39 each.
8 tuna steaks	

Have to start preparations tonight as working tomorrow.

8 p.m. Ugh, do not feel like cooking. Especially dealing with grotesque bag of chicken carcasses: completely disgusting.

10 p.m. Have got chicken carcasses in pan now. Trouble is, Marco says am supposed to tie flavour-enhancing leek and celery together with string but only string have got is blue. Oh well, expect it will be OK.

11 p.m. God, stock took bloody ages to do but worth it as will end up with over 2 gallons, frozen in ice-cube form and only cost £1.70. Mmm, confit of oranges will be delicious also. Now all have got to do is finely slice thirty-six oranges and grate zest. Shouldn't take too long.

1 a.m. Too tired to stay awake now but stock is supposed to cook for another two hours and oranges need another hour in oven. I know. Will leave the stock on v. low heat overnight, also oranges on lowest oven setting, so will become v. tender in manner of a stew.

Tuesday 21 November

8st 11 (nerves eat fat), alcohol units 9 (v. bad indeed), cigarettes 37 (v.v. bad), calories 3479 (and all disgusting).

9.30 a.m. Just opened pan. Hoped-for 2-gallon stock taste-explosion has turned into burnt chicken carcasses coated in jelly. Orange confit looks fantastic, though, just like in picture only darker. Must go to work. Am going to leave by four, then will think of answer to soup crisis.

5 p.m. Oh God. Entire day has turned into nightmare. Richard Finch gave me a real blowing-up at the morning meeting in front of everyone. 'Bridget, put that recipe book away for God's sake. Fireworks Burns Kids. I'm thinking maiming, I'm thinking happy family celebrations turned into nightmares. I'm thinking twenty years on. What about that kid who had his penis burnt off by bangers in his pockets back in the sixties? Where is he now? Bridget, find me the Fireworks Kid with no Penis. Find me the Sixties Guy Fawkes Bobbit.'

Ugh. I was just grumpily making my forty-eighth phone call to find out if there was a burnt-off-penis victims support group when my phone rang.

'Hello, darling, it's Mummy here.' She sounded unusually high-pitched and hysterical.

'Hi, Mum.'

'Hello, darling, just called to say 'bye before I go, and hope everything goes well.'

'Go? Go where?'

'Oh. Ahahahaha. I told you, Julio and I are popping over to Portugal for a couple of weeks, just to see the family and so on, get a bit of a suntan before Christmas.'

'You didn't tell me.'

'Oh, don't be a silly-willy, darling. Of course I told you. You must learn to listen. Anyway, do take care, won't you?'

'Yes.'

'Oh, darling, just one more thing.'

'What?'

'For some reason I've been so busy I forgot to order my travellers' cheques from the bank.'

'Oh, don't worry, you can get them at the airport.'

'But the thing is, darling, I'm just on my way to the airport now, and I've forgotten my banker's card.'

I blinked at the phone.

'Such a nuisance. I was wondering . . . You couldn't possibly lend me some cash? I mean not much, just a couple of hundred quid or something so I can get some travellers' cheques.'

The way she said it reminded me of the way winos ask for money for a cup of tea.

'I'm in the middle of work, Mum. Can't Julio lend you some money?'

She went all huffy. 'I can't believe you're being so mean, darling. After all I've done for you. I gave you the gift of *life* and you can't even loan your mother a few pounds for some travellers' cheques.'

'But how am I going to get it to you? I'll have to go out to the cashpoint and put it on a motorbike. Then it will be stolen and it'll all be ridiculous. Where are you?'

'Oooh. Well, actually, as luck would have it I'm ever so close, so if you just pop out to the NatWest opposite I'll meet you there in five minutes,' she gabbled. 'Super, darling. Byee!'

'Bridget, where the *fuck* are you off to?' yelled Richard as I tried to sneak out. 'You found the Banger Bobbit Boy yet?'

'Got a hot tip,' I said, tapping my nose, then made a dash for it.

I was waiting for my money to come, freshly baked and piping hot, out of the cashpoint, wondering how my mother was going to manage for two weeks in Portugal on two hundred pounds, when I spotted her scurrying towards me, wearing sunglasses, even though it was pissing with rain, and looking shiftily from side to side.

'Oh, there you are, darling. You are sweet. Thank you very much. Must dash, going to miss the plane. Byee!' she said, grabbing the banknotes from my hand.

'What's going on?' I said. 'What are you doing outside here when it's not on your way to the airport? How are you going to manage without your banker's card? Why can't Julio lend you the money? Why? What are you up to? What?'

For a second she looked frightened, as if she was going to cry, then, her eyes fixed on the middle distance, she adopted her wounded Princess Diana look.

'I'll be fine, darling.' She gave her special brave smile. 'Take care,' she said in a faltering voice, hugged me quickly then was off, waving the traffic to a standstill and tripping across the road.

7 p.m. Just got home. Right. Calm, calm. Inner poise. Soup will be absolutely fine. Will simply cook and puree vegetables as instructed and then – to give concentration of flavour – rinse blue jelly off chicken carcases and boil them up with cream in the soup.

8.30 p.m. All going marvellously. Guests are all in living room. Mark Darcy is being v. nice and brought champagne and a box of Belgian chocolates. Have not done main course yet apart from fondant potatoes but sure will be v. quick. Anyway, soup is first.

8.35 p.m. Oh my God. Just took lid off casserole to remove carcasses. Soup is bright blue.

9 p.m. Love the lovely friends. Were more than sporting about the blue soup, Mark Darcy and Tom even making lengthy argument for less colour prejudice in the world of food. Why, after all, as Mark said – just because one cannot readily think of a blue vegetable – should one object to blue soup? Fish fingers, after all, are not naturally orange. (Truth is, after all the effort, soup just tasted like big bowl of boiled cream which Vile Richard rather unkindly pointed out. At which point Mark Darcy asked him what he did for a living, which was v. amusing because Vile Richard was sacked last week for fiddling his expenses.) Never mind, anyway. Main course will be v. tasty. Right, will start on velouté of cherry tomatoes.

9.15 p.m. Oh dear. Think there must have been something in the blender, e.g. Fairy Liquid, as cherry tomato puree seems to be foaming and three times original volume. Also fondant potatoes were meant to be ready ten minutes ago and are hard as rock. Maybe should put in microwave. Aargh aargh. Just looked in fridge and tuna is not there. What has become of tuna? What? What?

9.30 p.m. Thank God. Jude and Mark Darcy came in kitchen and helped me make big omelette and mashed up half-done fondant potatoes and fried them in the frying pan in manner of hash browns, and put the recipe book on the table so we could all look at the pictures of what chargrilled tuna would have been like. At least orange confit will be good. Looks fantastic. Tom said not to bother with Grand Marnier Creme Anglaise but merely drink Grand Marnier.

10 p.m. V. sad. Looked expectantly round table as everyone took first mouthful of confit. There was an embarrassed silence.

'What's this, hon?' said Tom eventually. 'Is it marmalade?'

Horror-struck, took mouthful myself. It was, as he said, marmalade. Realize after all effort and expense have served my guests:

Blue soup
Omelette
Marmalade

Am disastrous failure. Michelin-star cookery? Kwik-fit, more like.

Did not think things could get any worse after the marmalade. But no sooner was the horrible meal cleared away than the phone went. Fortunately I took it in the bedroom. It was Dad.

'Are you on your own?' he said.

'No. Everyone's round here. Jude and everyone. Why?'

'I – wanted you to be with someone when . . . I'm sorry, Bridget. I'm afraid there's been some rather bad news.'

'What? What?'

'Your mother and Julio are wanted by the police.'

2 a.m. Northamptonshire in single bed in the Alconburys' spare room. Ugh. Had to sit down and get my breath back while Dad said, 'Bridget? Bridget? Bridget?' over and over again in manner of a parrot.

'What's happened?' I managed to get out eventually.

'I'm afraid they – possibly, and I pray, without your mother's knowledge – have defrauded a large number of people, including myself, and some of our very closest friends, out of a great deal of money. We don't know the scale of the fraud at the moment, but I'm afraid, from what the police are saying, it's possible that your mother may have to go to prison for a considerable period of time.'

'Oh my God. So that's why she's gone off to Portugal with my two hundred quid.'

'She may well be further afield by now.'

I saw the future unfolding before me like a horrible nightmare: Richard Finch dubbing me *Good Afternoon!*'s 'Suddenly Single's Jailbird's Daughter, and forcing me to do a live interview down the line from the Holloway visitors' room before being Suddenly Sacked on air.

'What did they do?'

'Apparently Julio, using your mother as – as it were – 'front man', has relieved Una and Geoffrey, Nigel and Elizabeth and Malcolm and Elaine' (oh my God, Mark Darcy's parents) 'of quite considerable sums of money – many, many thousands of pounds, as down payments on time-share apartments.'

'Didn't you know?'

'No. Presumably because they were unable to overcome some slight vestigial embarrassment about doing business with the greasy beperfumed wop who has cuckolded one of their oldest friends they omitted to mention the whole business to me.'

'So what happened?'

'The time-share apartments never existed. Not a penny of your mother's and my savings or pension fund remains. I also was unwise enough to leave the house in her name, and she has remortgaged it. We are ruined, destitute and homeless, Bridget, and your mother is to be branded a common criminal.'

After that he broke down. Una came to the phone, saying that she was going to give Dad some Ovaltine. I told her I'd be there in two hours but she said not to drive till I'd got over the shock, there was nothing to be done, and to leave it till the morning.

Replacing the receiver, I slumped against the wall cursing myself feebly for leaving my cigarettes in the living room. Immediately though, Jude appeared with a glass of Grand Marnier.

'What happened?' she said.

I told her the whole story, pouring the Grand Marnier straight down my throat as I did. Jude didn't say a word but immediately went and fetched Mark Darcy.

'I blame myself,' he said, running his hands through his hair. 'I should have made myself more clear at the Tarts and Vicars party. I knew there was something dodgy about Julio.'

'What do you mean?'

'I heard him talking on his portable phone by the herbaceous border. He didn't know he was being overheard. If I'd had any idea that my parents were involved I'd . . .' He shook his head. 'Now I think about it, I do remember my mother mentioning something, but I got so aerated at the mere mention of the words "time-share" that I must have terrorized her into shutting up. Where's your mother now?'

'I don't know. Portugal? Rio de Janeiro? Having her hair done?'

He started to pace around the room firing questions like a top barrister.

'What's being done to find her?' 'What are the sums involved?' 'How did the matter come to light?' 'What is the police's involvement?' 'Who knows about it?' 'Where is your father now?' 'Would you like to go to him?' 'Will you allow me to take you?' It was pretty damn sexy, I can tell you.

Jude appeared with coffee. Mark decided the best thing would be if he got his driver to take him and me up to Grafton Underwood and, for a fleeting second, I experienced the totally novel sensation of being grateful to my mother.

It was all very dramatic when we got to Una and Geoffrey's, with Enderbys and Alconburys all over the shop, everyone in tears and Mark Darcy striding around making phone calls. Found myself feeling guilty, since part of self – despite horror – was hugely enjoying the fact of normal business being suspended, everything different from usual and everyone allowed to throw entire glasses of sherry and salmon-paste sandwiches down their throats in manner of Christmas. Was exactly the same feeling as when Granny turned schizophrenic and took all her clothes off, ran off into Penny Husbands-Bosworth's orchard and had to be rounded up by the police.

SUCH A FUN AGE

Kiley Reid

Kiley Reid's debut novel *Such A Fun Age* was an immediate *New York Times* bestseller and was longlisted for the Booker Prize for Fiction. Dealing deftly with the relationship between a Black babysitter, a white child and the child's mother, Reid drew inspiration from both her own privileged childhood and six years working as a nanny in New York. She lives in Philadelphia with her husband.

Jodi was meant to sit next to her daughter Prudence, but Prudence had quickly remembered her obsession with a now very tipsy Rachel and begged her mother to switch. Peter and Catherine settled in at the head of the table, next to Walter and Payne. Next to Alix, Briar fiddled with the strap that buckled her into her booster seat. Across from Alix, Emira reached forward and touched a hideously sparkled pumpkin that read *Give Thanks!* in gold around its plastic body. "This is all so nice," she said.

"Oh. It's not . . ." Alix threw her hair behind her shoulders as she sat down. She tried to explain, but like everything else she'd said in the last hour it was more for Kelley than anyone else, which meant she couldn't find her words. Kelley took his seat next to Emira and winked at Briar in front of him. "Well, it was kind of a joke," Alix said. "But it's silly, though—"

"She's right, A." Jodi stepped in and saved her. "This is absolutely lovely. Pru?" Jodi looked to her left and squared her daughter's face. "This is a *very* special treat that you are sitting next to Miss Rachel, so you need to behave, okay?"

Prudence did the same sneaky face she always did when Jodi alluded to such a thing as consequences. Rachel high-fived Prudence and said, "Us single ladies will be fine over here, right, Cleo?"

Two-year-old Cleo shook her head. "No, thank you."

Peter looked over at Alix but said to the entire group, "Should we say grace of some kind?"

Walter raised his chin at his daughter from the other side of the table. "Pru knows a prayer, don't you, Pru?"

Jodi mumbled, "Oh, God."

"That's perfect," Alix said. "Do you wanna help us out?"

Prudence looked around the table as if she were about to execute a very rude and smelly prank. She folded her hands on the table and giggled to herself. "For food and health and happy days, receive our gratitude and praise. And when we serve others may we, repay our debt of love to thee. Amen."

The adults at the table said, "Amen," and Walter echoed, "That's fantastic, kiddo."

Tamra leaned forward. "They taught her that at preschool?"

Jodi reached for a pot of sweet potatoes. "Don't even get me started."

Alix encouraged everyone to dig in, and those wonderful jingles of dinnerware hitting plates and porcelain started to drift up toward the ceiling.

Everything *sounded* like the Thanksgiving she wanted, which made the evening even more eerie. The guests looked festive and warm under the glow of the chandelier. The snow swirled effortlessly behind the front window panes. And the front hall of her home had switched to a dining room quite easily; it smelled like a mix of berries, brown sugar, baked crusts, and burning flames. Briar pointed to every item of food that Alix put on her plate and asked, "Mama? Mama, is dis hot?" Payne stood on Walter's knee and bounced adorably with a binky in his hand. Rachel applied strawberry ChapStick to Prudence's little lips, to which Jodi prompted, "What do you say, Pru?" Tamra replied to Imani's interest in this activity by raising her eyebrows and saying, "Don't even think about it." Everything sounded so homey and sweet and domestic, but across from Alix was her beloved babysitter, Emira, with what seemed from above the table like Kelley Copeland's hand on her left knee. As Alix spooned asparagus for Briar, she tried not to look at Emira while wondering, *How much do you know?* In a lull, Peter looked over to

Emira and Kelley and asked, "So how did you two meet?"

Alix watched Kelley and Emira wait for the other one to answer, and this private language between them made her writhe in her seat. "They met on the train, honey." She said this as she cut Briar's turkey. "Isn't that right?"

"Ummm . . ." Kelley reached for his glass of wine and then, at the last second, grabbed his water. "That is . . . incorrect."

"Well." Emira looked at him. "Not entirely, though."

"Uh-ohhh," Walter boomed. "What's the real story then, Kelley? Come on, now. Let's have it."

At the other end of the table, Prudence blew bubbles into a plastic cup of milk. Jodi eyed her and whispered, "Prudence? That's one."

"I don't . . . uhh . . ." Kelley looked unbearably cute as he struggled, and Alix had to look into her lap. "I don't know if it's appropriate."

"Ohmygod," Rachel said. "They had a one-night stand." This seemed to please her greatly, and the fact that she sat next to two four-year-olds and across from a two-year-old did not interfere with her excitement. "Do not be shy, girl. We've all been there. These two met on a one-night stand" —she pointed a fork at Walter and Jodi— "and look at them now."

Around a cheekful of mashed potatoes, Jodi said, "Really, Rach?" as Walter said, "Hear, hear!"

"We didn't have a one-night stand," Kelley said. Alix swallowed her food. She watched Kelley look at Emira. Emira examined the details of her plate. Kelley stopped cutting into a turkey leg to say, "I met Emira at Market Depot, when she was being held by the police."

Alix's mouth cupped open and she quickly closed it. The table collectively took in this information as Prudence held up a marshmallow that was melted to black on one side. Prudence showed it to Imani and whispered, "This looks like a caca doo-doo."

Tamra leaned forward to see around Emira to Kelley. "You were there?"

"Yeah, I saw what was happening and I pulled out my phone."

"Wait a second, you're kidding." Peter sat back in his chair. In his left arm, Catherine started to wake up. "I remember you now."

Rachel snorted and said, "Whoops."

"Sorry, yeah," Kelley said to Peter. "I didn't expect you to remember me. You definitely had other things to worry about."

"You had your phone up," Peter remembered, "and you were recording."

"There's a video?" Tamra asked. She looked to Alix with a face that said, *I knew it.*

"Well, yes, but that's Emira's property now. Sorry." Kelley half laughed. "This isn't exactly Thanksgiving conversation. I probably should have said we met on Tinder or something. I'm sorry." This time he apologized to Emira.

Alix stared across the table at her sitter, feeling as if she'd been very publicly uninvited to a gathering that she herself had organized. The betrayal Alix felt (*Why wouldn't you just tell me where you really met? Why would you say the train?*) was quickly replaced by a new backstabbing confusion (*Why did you call Peter that night? Why wouldn't you just call me?*).

Emira adjusted her earring and picked her fork up again. "No, it's fine. We *did* meet for real on the train a few days later, though," she promised. "And then we just . . . kept seeing each other."

"Well, Jesus, Kelley. I'm glad you're here," Peter said. "And I'm glad that something good came out of that night. Emira, you're a saint for not suing that entire franchise. Which you could definitely do if there's a video."

Walter raised his glass to himself. " Abso-friggin-lutely."

"Oh, yeah no." Emira shook her head. "No, I would die if that video got out. I haven't even watched it."

"I'd be the same way," Jodi said.

"But umm . . ." Emira pivoted. "How did you guys meet, Mrs. Chamberlain? I guess I've never asked."

"You mean," Peter said, "how did Alix pursue me at the most disgusting bar I've ever been to?"

Alix forced a laugh. "*Pursue* is generous."

"Mama," Briar said, "I want to open the pie."

Alix shushed her. "Pie is for later."

Peter went on to tell a story that Alix had heard many times but never really annoyed her until now. The whole evening she found herself falling in and out of love with her husband quite abruptly, and through his account of how they met, she was both pleased that he depicted Alix as *stunning*, waving and buying him a beer from across a bar, and irked that he mentioned her being so nervous that she drank the beer herself. With Kelley sitting so close to her, Alix continued to switch from offense to defense. When Peter finished his story, she thought, *That's right, Kelley. I drink beer now. With my husband, who I've had sex with more than one time.*

Tamra looked to Alix and asked, "Is that when you were working at Hunter?"

"Yes, it was." Alix nodded. She wanted to say something about the obnoxious dollar drink specials this bar had provided, and how appreciated these specials were because she was making less than forty grand at the time, but Kelley seemingly took her tiny pause as an opportunity to ask, rather loudly, "And what do you do now, Alex? Emira said you're writing a history book. Is that right?"

Rachel said, "A *history* book?" as Peter said, "Now *that's* being generous."

Emira's eyes went small as she looked up at Alix.

Alix's face and neck turned hot against the sweater she now wished she had changed out of. She waved her head side to side and took up her glass of wine. "Bri, sit up my love," she said. "Well, it's umm"—she took a sip—"it's *my* little history." On *my*, she placed a hand to her chest, and it reminded her of hugging Emira the morning after Market Depot, and how Emira just sort of leaned in as if she'd had trouble hearing, instead of just hugging her back. "I have a book coming out with HarperCollins, and it'll have the best letters I've written and received since I started my business."

"That's really only half of it." Tamra turned to Emira as she went on. "I'm sure you've seen her Instagram and all the things she has her hands in."

"Oh, no." Emira smiled. "I don't have Instagram."

"Girl!" Tamra feigned dramatic shock. "We have got to get you caught up!"

"You don't have Instagram?" Next to Alix, Jodi's amazement was more genuine. "That's amazing. Even Prudence has one."

Emira said, "Really?"

"Well, I run it, and it's private," Jodi assured her, "but it keeps our distant family members very happy."

"So it's like a history of your business?" Kelley wouldn't let it go. Alix knew exactly what he was doing, but how could she fight him at the dinner table, in front of her friends and in front of Emira?

"Mm-hmm," she said. "Exactly."

"And when did it start?"

"Well . . . I started my business in 2009, so—"

"Oh wow, okay." Kelley smiled across the table. "That's a brief history."

"Wait, when did we all meet?" Jodi stepped in. "2011?"

"Rachel, I can't believe you were the *experienced* parent back then," Tamra said.

"Taught you bitches everything I know," Rachel said.

Imani and Cleo looked at their mother, seeking corroboration that a bad word had been said. Tamra shook her head in confirmation and put a finger to lips.

"You know what?" Peter said. "I want to make a toast."

Alix thought both *Oh Jesus* and *Thank God*. Peter was so good at making things easy and sociable but only in a way that made it seem like a TV show was ending. With all 141 pounds of her being, Alix wished she could just turn this night off.

"I know it wasn't easy for Alix to leave you ladies," Peter said. "And believe it or not, I miss you all very much too. As Alix writes her book and her business continues to grow, I've seen how much she's come to lean on you, how much you encourage her, and how much easier you make her life. And Emira, that includes you now too. I'm very happy, or should I say *thankful*, to be outnumbered by so many amazing women tonight. So here's to you."

Everyone raised their glasses and said cheers. Briar managed to get a green bean on her fork by herself. When she held it up and showed it to Walter, he said, "That's tremendous."

A CHRISTMAS CAROL

Charles Dickens

Born in Portsmouth in 1812, **Charles Dickens** was a novelist who informed vast portions of our shared vision of Victorian London. After a well-documented childhood spent working in a shoe polish factory to aid his debt-ridden family, he abandoned dreams of becoming an actor in the (doomed, sadly) hope of winning over the middle-class family of the girl he loved, and found work in a law office. To supplement his income, he began to write as a parliamentary reporter, a journalist, and then began publishing short stories. His first novel, *The Pickwick Papers*, was published in monthly instalments; by the final chapters, circulation had increased exponentially, and Dickens found he was able to make a living as a novelist. He lectured against slavery in the United States, toured France, Switzerland and Italy with Augustus Egg and Wilkie Collins, was intrigued by ghosts and the paranormal, and survived a train derailment with his mistress. *A Christmas Carol* was first published in 1843; Dickens wrote it in six weeks and was persuaded by his publishers to cover half the printing costs as they were unconvinced there was an audience for a Christmas story. It has never been out of print and has been adapted countless times for every possible performance genre. It popularized 'Merry Christmas' as a greeting, put 'scrooge' in the Oxford English Dictionary, and cemented turkey as the bird of Christmas.

"Y ou have never seen the like of me before!" exclaimed the Spirit.

"Never," Scrooge made answer to it.

"Have never walked forth with the younger members of my family; meaning (for I am very young) my elder brothers born in these later years?" pursued the Phantom.

"I don't think I have," said Scrooge. "I am afraid I have not. Have you had many brothers, Spirit?"

"More than eighteen hundred," said the Ghost.

"A tremendous family to provide for!" muttered Scrooge.

The Ghost of Christmas Present rose.

"Spirit," said Scrooge submissively, "conduct me where you will. I went forth last night on compulsion, and I learnt a lesson which is working now. To-night, if you have aught to teach me, let me profit by it."

"Touch my robe!"

Scrooge did as he was told, and held it fast.

Holly, mistletoe, red berries, ivy, turkeys, geese, game, poultry, brawn, meat, pigs, sausages, oysters, pies, puddings, fruit, and punch, all vanished instantly. So did the room, the fire, the ruddy glow, the hour of night, and they stood in the city streets on Christmas morning, where (for the weather was severe) the people made a rough, but brisk and not unpleasant kind of music, in scraping the snow from the pavement in front of their dwellings, and from the tops of their houses, whence it was mad delight to the boys to see it come plumping down into the road below, and splitting into artificial little snow-storms.

The house fronts looked black enough, and the windows blacker, contrasting with the smooth white sheet of snow upon the roofs, and with the dirtier snow upon the ground; which last deposit had been ploughed up in deep furrows by the heavy wheels of carts and waggons; furrows that crossed and re-crossed each other hundreds of times where the great streets branched off; and made intricate channels, hard to trace in the thick yellow mud and icy water. The sky was gloomy, and the shortest streets were choked up with a dingy mist, half thawed, half frozen, whose heavier particles descended in a shower of sooty atoms, as if all the chimneys in Great Britain had, by one consent, caught fire, and were blazing away to their dear hearts' content. There was nothing very cheerful in the climate or the town, and yet was there an air of cheerfulness abroad that the clearest summer air and brightest summer sun might have endeavoured to diffuse in vain.

For, the people who were shovelling away on the housetops were jovial and full of glee; calling out to one another from the parapets, and now and then exchanging a facetious snowball—better-natured missile far than many a wordy jest—laughing heartily if it went right and not less heartily if it went wrong. The poulterers' shops were still half open, and the fruiterers' were radiant in their glory. There were great, round, pot-bellied baskets of chestnuts, shaped like the waistcoats of jolly old gentlemen, lolling at the doors, and tumbling out into the street in their apoplectic opulence. There were ruddy, brown-faced, broad-girthed Spanish Onions, shining in the fatness of their growth like Spanish Friars, and winking from their shelves in wanton slyness at the girls as they went by, and glanced demurely at the hung-up mistletoe. There were pears and apples, clustered high in blooming pyramids; there were bunches of grapes, made, in the shopkeepers' benevolence to dangle from conspicuous hooks, that people's mouths might water gratis as they passed; there were piles of filberts, mossy and brown, recalling, in their fragrance, ancient walks among the woods, and pleasant shufflings ankle deep through withered leaves; there were Norfolk Biffins, squat and swarthy, setting off the yellow of the oranges and lemons, and, in the great compactness of their juicy persons, urgently entreating and beseeching to be carried home in paper bags and eaten after dinner. The very gold and silver fish, set forth among these choice fruits in a bowl, though members of a dull and stagnant-blooded race, appeared to know that there was something going on; and, to a fish, went gasping round and round their little world in slow and passionless excitement.

The Grocers'! oh, the Grocers'! nearly closed, with perhaps two shutters down, or one; but through those gaps such glimpses! It was not alone that the scales descending on the counter made a merry sound, or that the twine and roller parted company so briskly, or that the canisters were rattled up and down like juggling tricks, or even that the blended scents of tea and coffee were so grateful to the nose, or even that the raisins were so plentiful and rare, the almonds so extremely white, the sticks of cinnamon so long and straight, the other spices so delicious, the candied fruits so caked and spotted with molten sugar as to make the coldest lookers-on feel faint and subsequently bilious. Nor was it that the figs were moist and pulpy, or that the French plums blushed in modest tartness from their highly-decorated boxes, or that everything was good to eat and in its Christmas dress; but the customers were all so hurried and so eager in the hopeful promise of the day, that they tumbled up against each other at the door, crashing their wicker baskets wildly, and left their purchases upon the counter, and came running back to fetch them, and committed hundreds of the like mistakes, in the best humour possible; while the Grocer and his people were so frank and fresh that the polished hearts with which they fastened their aprons behind might have been their own, worn outside for general inspection, and for Christmas daws to peck at if they chose.

But soon the steeples called good people all, to church and chapel, and away they came, flocking through the streets in their best clothes, and with their gayest faces. And at the same time there emerged from scores of bye-streets, lanes, and nameless turnings, innumerable people, carrying their dinners to the bakers' shops. The sight of these poor revellers appeared to interest the Spirit very much, for he stood with Scrooge beside him in a baker's doorway, and taking off the covers as their bearers passed, sprinkled incense on their dinners from his torch. And it was a very uncommon kind of torch, for once or twice when there were angry words between some dinner-carriers who had jostled each other, he shed a few drops of water on them from it, and their good humour was restored directly. For they said, it was a shame to quarrel upon Christmas Day. And so it was! God love it, so it was!

In time the bells ceased, and the bakers were shut up; and yet there was a genial shadowing forth of all these dinners and the progress of their cooking, in the thawed blotch of wet above each baker's oven; where the pavement smoked as if its stones were cooking too.

"Is there a peculiar flavour in what you sprinkle from your torch?" asked Scrooge.

"There is. My own."

"Would it apply to any kind of dinner on this day?" asked Scrooge.

"To any kindly given. To a poor one most."

"Why to a poor one most?" asked Scrooge.

"Because it needs it most."

"Spirit," said Scrooge, after a moment's thought, "I wonder you, of all the beings in the many worlds about us, should desire to cramp these people's opportunities of innocent enjoyment."

"I!" cried the Spirit.

"You would deprive them of their means of dining every seventh day, often the only day on which they can be said to dine at all," said Scrooge. "Wouldn't you?"

"I!" cried the Spirit.

"You seek to close these places on the Seventh Day?" said Scrooge. "And it comes to the same thing."

"*I* seek!" exclaimed the Spirit.

"Forgive me if I am wrong. It has been done in your name, or at least in that of your family," said Scrooge.

"There are some upon this earth of yours," returned the Spirit, "who lay claim to know us, and who do their deeds of passion, pride, ill-will, hatred, envy, bigotry, and selfishness in our name, who are as strange to us and all our kith and kin, as if they had never lived. Remember that, and charge their doings on themselves, not us."

Scrooge promised that he would; and they went on, invisible, as they had been before, into the suburbs of the town. It was a remarkable quality of the Ghost (which Scrooge had observed at the baker's), that notwithstanding his gigantic size, he could accommodate himself to any place with ease; and that he stood beneath a low roof quite as gracefully and like a supernatural creature, as it was possible he could have done in any lofty hall.

And perhaps it was the pleasure the good Spirit had in showing off this power of his, or else it was his own kind, generous, hearty nature, and his sympathy with all poor men, that led him straight to Scrooge's clerk's; for there he went, and took Scrooge with him, holding to his robe; and on the threshold of the door the Spirit smiled, and stopped to bless Bob Cratchit's dwelling with the sprinkling of his torch. Think of that! Bob had but fifteen "Bob" a-week himself; he pocketed on Saturdays but fifteen copies of his Christian name; and yet the Ghost of Christmas Present blessed his four-roomed house!

Then up rose Mrs. Cratchit, Cratchit's wife, dressed out but poorly in a twice-turned gown, but brave in ribbons, which are cheap and make a goodly show for sixpence; and she laid the cloth, assisted by Belinda

Cratchit, second of her daughters, also brave in ribbons; while Master Peter Cratchit plunged a fork into the saucepan of potatoes, and getting the corners of his monstrous shirt collar (Bob's private property, conferred upon his son and heir in honour of the day) into his mouth, rejoiced to find himself so gallantly attired, and yearned to show his linen in the fashionable Parks. And now two smaller Cratchits, boy and girl, came tearing in, screaming that outside the baker's they had smelt the goose, and known it for their own; and basking in luxurious thoughts of sage and onion, these young Cratchits danced about the table, and exalted Master Peter Cratchit to the skies, while he (not proud, although his collars nearly choked him) blew the fire, until the slow potatoes bubbling up, knocked loudly at the saucepan-lid to be let out and peeled.

"What has ever got your precious father then?" said Mrs. Cratchit. "And your brother, Tiny Tim! And Martha warn't as late last Christmas Day by half-an-hour?"

"Here's Martha, mother!" said a girl, appearing as she spoke.

"Here's Martha, mother!" cried the two young Cratchits. "Hurrah! There's *such* a goose, Martha!"

"Why, bless your heart alive, my dear, how late you are!" said Mrs. Cratchit, kissing her a dozen times, and taking off her shawl and bonnet for her with officious zeal.

"We'd a deal of work to finish up last night," replied the girl, "and had to clear away this morning, mother!"

"Well! Never mind so long as you are come," said Mrs. Cratchit. "Sit ye down before the fire, my dear, and have a warm, Lord bless ye!"

"No, no! There's father coming," cried the two young Cratchits, who were everywhere at once. "Hide, Martha, hide!"

So Martha hid herself, and in came little Bob, the father, with at least three feet of comforter exclusive of the fringe, hanging down before him; and his threadbare clothes darned up and brushed, to look seasonable; and Tiny Tim upon his shoulder. Alas for Tiny Tim, he bore a little crutch, and had his limbs supported by an iron frame!

"Why, where's our Martha?" cried Bob Cratchit, looking round.

"Not coming," said Mrs. Cratchit.

"Not coming!" said Bob, with a sudden declension in his high spirits; for he had been Tim's blood horse all the way from church, and had come home rampant. "Not coming upon Christmas Day!"

Martha didn't like to see him disappointed, if it were only in joke; so she came out prematurely from behind the closet door, and ran into his arms, while the two young Cratchits hustled Tiny Tim, and bore him off into the wash-house, that he might hear the pudding singing in the copper.

"And how did little Tim behave?" asked Mrs. Cratchit, when she had rallied Bob on his credulity, and Bob had hugged his daughter to his heart's content.

"As good as gold," said Bob, "and better. Somehow he gets thoughtful, sitting by himself so much, and thinks the strangest things you ever heard. He told me, coming home, that he hoped the people saw him in the church, because he was a cripple, and it might be pleasant to them to remember upon Christmas Day, who made lame beggars walk, and blind men see."

Bob's voice was tremulous when he told them this, and trembled more when he said that Tiny Tim was growing strong and hearty.

His active little crutch was heard upon the floor, and back came Tiny Tim before another word was spoken, escorted by his brother and sister to his stool before the fire; and while Bob, turning up his cuffs—as if, poor fellow, they were capable of being made more shabby—compounded some hot mixture in a jug with gin and lemons, and stirred it round and round and put it on the hob to simmer; Master Peter, and the two ubiquitous young Cratchits went to fetch the goose, with which they soon returned in high procession.

Such a bustle ensued that you might have thought a goose the rarest of all birds; a feathered phenomenon, to which a black swan was a matter of course—and in truth it was something very like it in that house. Mrs. Cratchit made the gravy (ready beforehand in a little saucepan) hissing hot; Master Peter mashed the potatoes with incredible vigour; Miss Belinda sweetened up the apple-sauce; Martha dusted the hot plates; Bob took Tiny Tim beside him in a tiny corner at the table; the two young Cratchits set chairs for everybody, not forgetting themselves, and mounting guard upon their posts, crammed spoons into their mouths, lest they should shriek for goose before their turn came to be helped. At last the dishes were set on, and grace was said. It was succeeded by a breathless pause, as Mrs. Cratchit, looking slowly all along the carving-knife, prepared to plunge it in the breast; but when she did, and when the long expected gush of stuffing issued forth, one murmur of delight arose all round the board, and even Tiny Tim, excited by the two young Cratchits, beat on the table with the handle of his knife, and feebly cried Hurrah!

There never was such a goose. Bob said he didn't believe there ever was such a goose cooked. Its tenderness and flavour, size and cheapness, were the themes of universal admiration. Eked out by apple-sauce and mashed potatoes, it was a sufficient dinner for the whole family; indeed, as Mrs. Cratchit said with great delight (surveying one small atom of a bone upon the dish), they hadn't ate it all at last! Yet every one had had enough, and the youngest Cratchits in particular, were steeped in sage and onion to the eyebrows! But now, the plates being changed by Miss Belinda, Mrs. Cratchit left the room alone—too nervous to bear witnesses—to take the pudding up and bring it in.

Suppose it should not be done enough! Suppose it should break in turning out! Suppose somebody should have got over the wall of the back-yard, and stolen it, while they were merry with the goose—a supposition at which the two young Cratchits became livid! All sorts of horrors were supposed.

Hallo! A great deal of steam! The pudding was out of the copper. A smell like a washing-day! That was the cloth. A smell like an eating-house and a pastrycook's next door to each other, with a laundress's next door to that! That was the pudding! In half a minute Mrs. Cratchit entered—flushed, but smiling proudly—with the pudding, like a speckled cannon-ball, so hard and firm, blazing in half of half-a-quartern of ignited brandy, and bedight with Christmas holly stuck into the top.

Oh, a wonderful pudding! Bob Cratchit said, and calmly too, that he regarded it as the greatest success achieved by Mrs. Cratchit since their marriage. Mrs. Cratchit said that now the weight was off her mind, she would confess she had had her doubts about the quantity of flour. Everybody had something to say about it, but nobody said or thought it was at all a small pudding for a large family. It would have been flat heresy to do so. Any Cratchit would have blushed to hint at such a thing.

At last the dinner was all done, the cloth was cleared, the hearth swept, and the fire made up. The compound in the jug being tasted, and considered perfect, apples and oranges were put upon the table, and a shovel-full of chestnuts on the fire. Then all the Cratchit family drew round the hearth, in what Bob Cratchit called a circle, meaning half a one; and at Bob Cratchit's elbow stood the family display of glass. Two tumblers, and a custard-cup without a handle.

These held the hot stuff from the jug, however, as well as golden goblets would have done; and Bob served it out with beaming looks, while the chestnuts on the fire sputtered and cracked noisily. Then Bob proposed:

"A Merry Christmas to us all, my dears. God bless us!"

Which all the family re-echoed.

"God bless us every one!" said Tiny Tim, the last of all.

He sat very close to his father's side upon his little stool. Bob held his withered little hand in his, as if he loved the child, and wished to keep him by his side, and dreaded that he might be taken from him.

"Spirit," said Scrooge, with an interest he had never felt before, "tell me if Tiny Tim will live."

"I see a vacant seat," replied the Ghost, "in the poor chimney-corner, and a crutch without an owner, carefully preserved. If these shadows remain unaltered by the Future, the child will die."

"No, no," said Scrooge. "Oh, no, kind Spirit! say he will be spared."

"If these shadows remain unaltered by the Future, none other of my race," returned the Ghost, "will find him here. What then? If he be like to die, he had better do it, and decrease the surplus population."

Scrooge hung his head to hear his own words quoted by the Spirit, and was overcome with penitence and grief.

"Man," said the Ghost, "if man you be in heart, not adamant, forbear that wicked cant until you have discovered What the surplus is, and

Where it is. Will you decide what men shall live, what men shall die? It may be, that in the sight of Heaven, you are more worthless and less fit to live than millions like this poor man's child. Oh God! to hear the Insect on the leaf pronouncing on the too much life among his hungry brothers in the dust!"

Scrooge bent before the Ghost's rebuke, and trembling cast his eyes upon the ground. But he raised them speedily, on hearing his own name.

"Mr. Scrooge!" said Bob; "I'll give you Mr. Scrooge, the Founder of the Feast!"

"The Founder of the Feast indeed!" cried Mrs. Cratchit, reddening. "I wish I had him here. I'd give him a piece of my mind to feast upon, and I hope he'd have a good appetite for it."

"My dear," said Bob, "the children! Christmas Day."

"It should be Christmas Day, I am sure," said she, "on which one drinks the health of such an odious, stingy, hard, unfeeling man as Mr. Scrooge. You know he is, Robert! Nobody knows it better than you do, poor fellow!"

"My dear," was Bob's mild answer, "Christmas Day."

"I'll drink his health for your sake and the Day's," said Mrs. Cratchit, "not for his. Long life to him! A merry Christmas and a happy new year! He'll be very merry and very happy, I have no doubt!"

The children drank the toast after her. It was the first of their proceedings which had no heartiness. Tiny Tim drank it last of all, but he didn't care twopence for it. Scrooge was the Ogre of the family. The mention of his name cast a dark shadow on the party, which was not dispelled for full five minutes.

After it had passed away, they were ten times merrier than before, from the mere relief of Scrooge the Baleful being done with. Bob Cratchit told them how he had a situation in his eye for Master Peter, which would bring in, if obtained, full five-and-sixpence weekly. The two young Cratchits laughed tremendously at the idea of Peter's being a man of business; and Peter himself looked thoughtfully at the fire from between his collars, as if he were deliberating what particular investments he should favour when he came into the receipt of that bewildering income.

Martha, who was a poor apprentice at a milliner's, then told them what kind of work she had to do, and how many hours she worked at a stretch, and how she meant to lie abed to-morrow morning for a good long rest; to-morrow being a holiday she passed at home. Also how she had seen a countess and a lord some days before, and how the lord "was much about as tall as Peter;" at which Peter pulled up his collars so high that you couldn't have seen his head if you had been there. All this time the chestnuts and the jug went round and round; and by-and-bye they had a song, about a lost child travelling in the snow, from Tiny Tim, who had a plaintive little voice, and sang it very well indeed.

There was nothing of high mark in this. They were not a handsome family; they were not well dressed; their shoes were far from being water-proof; their clothes were scanty; and Peter might have known, and very likely did, the inside of a pawnbroker's. But, they were happy, grateful, pleased with one another, and contented with the time; and when they faded, and looked happier yet in the bright sprinklings of the Spirit's torch at parting, Scrooge had his eye upon them, and especially on Tiny Tim, until the last.

THE CHRISTMAS CHRONICLES

Nigel Slater

To read **Nigel Slater**, OBE, is to be hungry. You want to pick up
what he's putting down, and eat what he's eating. And not just to
eat: Slater invites you, open-hearted, to enjoy food in all forms, from
newly budding in the damp earth of his famous London garden;
plump in the butcher's window; or cool and smooth in waxed paper
in the immaculate fridge. He has won a frankly outrageous number
of awards and honours for the clean, earthy elegance of his food
writing (which is somehow life writing without ever saying too
much about Slater's private life). His work is a masterclass in how
profoundly we can know a person simply through the way they
think and talk and cook about food. Then again, he described his
extraordinary 2004 memoir *Toast* as 'the most intimate memoir that
any food person has ever written': it describes his 1960s childhood,
grief, sexuality, his complex relationship with his parents, and the
intricate filigree of his relationship to food. Still, though, there is a
precision and a detachment to the intimacy Slater permits us: one
has, always, the sense of being in the cool, firm hands of a practised
pastry-cook. The recipe is the recipe. The food is the point. Deftly
he brings us always back to where he wants us to be, which is to
say, hungry.

There are lads in tights, girls in breeches, elderly men with
pancake make-up, and bare-chested boys in baggy pants. There
are dwarfs and giants, fairies and wizards, a puss in boots and
babes in a wood. There are death threats and dreams, genies in lamps, a
witch, a princess, and pumpkins that turn into stagecoaches. Pantomime
is a gorgeous cacophony of comedy, music, cross-gendering and high
jinks.

As a child I was mesmerised by the slightly sinister, dream-like quality that runs through pantomime. I revelled in being slightly scared while all the time knowing I was in a safe place. The cross-dressing, the psychedelic costumes and the sexual innuendo appealed to a boy sitting in the company of the straightest of parents. The colours, comedy and costumes were more of a draw than the stories, which I always found slightly confusing. Take *Aladdin*. Is it South East Asian, Middle Eastern or East End? Answer, all three.

Most of the political and satirical references were there to amuse the accompanying adults, but not much went over my head. I often found the music terrifying. Especially in *Aladdin*. Rimsky-Korsakov's *Scheherazade* has always sent shivers up my spine. I always went accompanied by adults, Mum and Dad, an aunt or uncle. I adored the way that pantomime, like fairy tales, made me comfortably uncomfortable. It has an effect on the imagination no television or film ever could. Although I have to say the slapstick didn't appeal then, just as it doesn't now. I have never found people falling over terribly funny.

Pantomime has been with us, in various forms, since the sixteenth century. The version familiar to us is influenced by the Italian Commedia dell'Arte, a style of travelling comedy that moved around Italy and France during the sixteenth and seventeenth centuries. Much of the act was improvised, a comedic performance that involved characters, often masked, always in costume, which we would recognise today. The form took hold in Britain to become Harlequinade, with its main characters being a harlequin, a clown and a pair of lovers.

Panto in Britain was originally, as its name suggests, a mime. Silent comedy performed by mostly French actors escaping their own country's clampdown on unlicensed theatres, initially at the Theatre Royal, Drury Lane, and the long-departed Lincoln's Inn Fields Theatre. During the nineteenth century, as stage machinery became more sophisticated, the shows became increasingly spectacular. Trapdoors and trick scenery became an essential part of the story, and the slapstick element took hold. Pantomime developed into a cleverly synchronised tapestry of comedy, song, slapstick, mime and satire loosely based around a well-known fairy story.

The titles are firmly established, though new ones come up all the time. *Aladdin, Cinderella, Dick Whittington, Snow White and the Seven Dwarfs, Puss in Boots, Goldilocks and the Three Bears, Mother Goose* and *Peter Pan* are as popular now as they were a hundred years ago, though each performance will have its own signature. No two versions are alike.

The season for pantomime is short, and tickets sell out like chocolate cake at a village fête. It is now, well before a single mince pie is baked, that you might like to sit down, go online and search what pantos are coming up this year. This may all seem very early, but once word gets round that something is going to be special, seats suddenly disappear.

Tonight, I make a dish of lentils with cream and basil. Essentially a frugal autumn dish, a baked aubergine with a knubby mound of creamed lentils heady with basil.

Aubergine with lentils and basil

serves 4
aubergines – 2 large or 4 small
olive oil – 6 tablespoons
a lemon
onions, medium – 2
garlic – 4 cloves
thyme sprigs – 8
rosemary – 6 sprigs
chestnut mushrooms – 200g
Le Puy or other small lentils – 400g
double cream – 250ml
parsley, chopped – 3 tablespoons
basil – a good handful of leaves
Parmesan, grated – 75g

Halve the aubergines lengthways, then score the cut surfaces in a lattice fashion, slicing deeply into the heart of the flesh but without piercing the skin. Place them skin side down on a baking sheet, trickle generously with some of the olive oil, and season lightly. Halve the lemon and squeeze over the juice. Place under a hot grill, a good way from the heat source, and cook until deep golden-brown. The flesh should be soft and silky.

Peel and roughly chop the onions. Warm the remaining olive oil in a shallow pan, then add the onions, stir, and leave them to cook over a moderate heat. Peel and crush the garlic, then stir into the onions. Pull the leaves from the thyme sprigs. Remove the needles from the rosemary, chop finely, then stir, together with the thyme leaves, into the softening onions.

Quarter the mushrooms, combine with the onions and leave to soften and colour. Season with salt and a little black pepper, then leave to simmer, very gently, over a low heat, partially covered with a lid.

Cook the lentils in a saucepan of boiling water for about fifteen minutes, until tender but with a slight nuttiness to them, adding salt about five minutes from the end of cooking. Drain the lentils, then stir into the onions and mushrooms. Pour in the cream, bring to the boil, then fold in the parsley, torn basil leaves and grated Parmesan and check the seasoning. It might need a little more pepper.

Serve the lentils in shallow bowls or plates, with a halved aubergine on top, or two if they are small.

THE LITTLE LIBRARY CHRISTMAS

Kate Young

In 2015, the *Guardian* sent a tweet asking for opinions on the posthumous publication of a private manuscript by the late Harper Lee. **Kate Young** replied not with an essay, or an article, but simply with a photograph: a perfect plate of fried chicken and rolls, the breakfast made by Calpurnia for Atticus in Lee's *To Kill A Mockingbird*. By the next day, the *Guardian* had asked to publish ten more of Young's literary photographs; six months later, Young had signed a deal to write a cookbook. *The Little Library Cookbook*, its three beautiful sequels and the accompanying blog won prestigious plaudits from the Guild of Food Writers, the World Gourmand Food Writing Awards, and the Fortnum & Mason Awards. This came as something of a surprise to Young, a former biology teacher with a degree in drama, working as a producer at the National Theatre, who considered English to be "her worst school subject". It did not come as a surprise to anyone who had read her beautiful, thoughtful work, which combined a deep love of literature with a rigorous, careful approach to development and to her readers. Like many great food writers before her, Young is also a novelist. Her debut, *Experienced*, is an exuberant, life-affirming queer rom com, and she brings to it all the love, rigour and care that she gave to her cookbooks. And yes: the food in it is delicious. Young divides her time between the Cotswolds and London. ER

There were more dances, and there were forfeits, and more dances, and there was cake, and there was negus, and there was a great piece of Cold Roast, and there was a great piece of Cold Boiled, and there were mince-pies, and plenty of beer.
A Christmas Carol, Charles Dickens

Though I appreciate that they're not always the height of the social calendar, I have a deep affection for office Christmas parties. I know that, for many, they're slightly odd evenings in front of a set menu or supermarket sausage rolls, with an awkward Secret Santa that no one really wants to participate in, and a bunch of colleagues you wouldn't necessarily choose to drink with at 3 p.m. on a Tuesday. But, as with so much at this time of year, leaning in is the key.

I am aware that I may be spoilt by my experience. My first office Christmas party was hosted by my mum; I handed food and drinks around in her physiotherapy practice (where I 'worked' on reception), quietly sampling the Champagne and cheese with my sister, while we pretended to be terribly grown up. The first ones in England happened in theatres, where I loved my colleagues, and where the 11 p.m. karaoke was always startlingly impressive. I'm even more spoilt now that my 'office Christmas party' is just me and my best pal and catering partner Liv (and often Liv's husband Sam) going out for dumplings or steak and a few beers, while very deliberately not discussing the long list of weddings we'll be catering the next year. I realize I have been lucky. But if you're not quite so lucky, don't despair. Even a bad office party is a chance to get to know a colleague who works in another part of the building or, at the very least, an afternoon where no one is emailing you about payroll.

Of course, if the office Christmas party leaves you cold (or, as a freelancer or a student or a retiree or a remote worker, is missing from your calendar), you can always host your own. I often find myself hoping for an opportunity to get a group of my friends together before the year draws to a close, or we all head 'home' for Christmas. A sit-down dinner can feel like too much effort, or require space you simply don't have. But a drinks party that people can drop into, with some good music playing, bowls of your favourite crisps scattered about, and a couple of plates of whatever food you have found time to prepare, is the perfect sort of big group gathering at this time of year.

Champagne cocktails

In Nancy Mitford's *Christmas Pudding*, Paul Fotheringay (masquerading for the season under the name Fisher) suggests some 'economical' Champagne cocktails – the cheapest Champagne, a little brandy, and some sugar – for a party, with the promise that 'people do seem to like them most awfully'. His suggestion is rebuffed by Lady Bobbin, who is convinced that a cocktail habit is a 'pernicious and disgusting' one. I am, unsurprisingly, wholeheartedly on Paul F.'s side.

You can, of course, find delicious crémant, cava and other fizzy wine at a very reasonable price in supermarkets and off-licences, which will be lovely on its own. But if you fancy making an average bottle a little more special, there are plenty of ways to make that happen. And there's a lot of fun to be had in setting up a makeshift bar in a corner somewhere with a couple of options that people can assemble themselves.

Sugar syrup (in advance)
200g/1 cup caster/superfine sugar   100ml/7tbsp water

Dissolve the sugar in the water over a low heat. Allow to cool, bottle, and then store in the fridge.

One for Paul F.
A sugar cube   1tbsp Cognac or other brandy
6 drops Angostura bitters   Fizzy wine

Place the sugar cube in the bottom of a glass, and shake the bitters onto it. Cover with Cognac, and then top up the glass with fizzy wine.

French 75
1tbsp lemon juice   2tbsp gin
1tsp sugar syrup   Fizzy wine

Shake the lemon juice, sugar syrup, and gin together with a couple of ice cubes. Strain into a glass and top up with fizzy wine.

Sparkling sherry

2tbsp sherry	1 Maraschino cherry
1tsp juice from a jar of cherries	Fizzy wine

Mix the sherry and cherry juice together in the bottom of a glass. Drop the cherry in, and top up with fizz.

Liqueur cocktails

Crème de cassis (a kir royale)	Campari (an aperitivo spritz)
Sloe gin (a sloe royale)	Fizzy wine

A tablespoon of spirit/liqueur in the bottom of a nice glass is the simplest way to zhuzh up a lackluster bottle. The two will combine better if you start with the liqueur and then slowly add your fizz.

Fruit cocktails

Fruit juice (pear, orange, peach, apple)	Cordials (elderflower, cranberry)
Soft fruit	Fizzy wine

Add fruit juice to Champagne at a ratio of 1:2 (one part juice, two parts fizz), crush some soft fruit in the glass, or add a tablespoon of cordial to the bottom of a glass before topping it up. An ideal option for brunch/lunch.

*

The tricky thing about Christmas and New Year's Eve is that everything is supposed to be warm and lovely and twinkly. This time of year is *supposed* to be filled with love and joy and kin. The season is so easy to romanticize (you're holding a book focused mainly on just how glorious it can be!), but the inevitable reality is that, often, it is far from perfect.

For so many possible reasons – money, strained relationships, difficult anniversaries, a snap election – this can be a tough time of year.

Though I generally sail through December like the Ghost of Christmas Present, light of spirit and full of love for the season and all that it offers, there have been years where I have struggled. I've spent time trapped under anxiety, triggered by the arrival of the beginning of a new year, and all that I thought I could/should/would have achieved. Despite being lucky in my friendships and my families, I have spent Christmases overwhelmed by loneliness – whether literally alone or in the company of others.

In the face of parties and events, I have plastered a smile on my face that in no way reflected how I was feeling. It is so easy to look at Christmas and imagine that the lights, the relentlessly jolly music, the general cheer, might have a resoundingly positive effect. In reality, these seasonal markers, these constant tiny rituals, can instead serve to remind us of what has been lost. So, if you are approaching Christmas this year with a sense of dread, know that I wish I was there to put a comforting hand on your shoulder. Know too that you are very, very much not alone.

I will almost always turn to time in the kitchen when seeking comfort – I want the reassurance of flour between my fingertips as I make pastry, the smell of a chicken roasting in the oven, the taste of melted butter that's run through a crumpet and down my wrist. But sometimes even making something delicious to eat feels like too much emotional pressure. When it is the shadow of the familiar that causes the ache, time in the kitchen with old favourites only serves to remind me why I am finding things so hard.

I don't know what has the potential to work for you, but I have found the following invaluable to remember in tricky years. If the thought of carrying on as you have in years past is too difficult, take some time to establish new rituals. Visit new places, see new people, watch new films, cook new food. I have found it reassuring to remember that though this is a period of love, joy and kin, it is also a time for rest. It is entirely appropriate to cut corners if you are entertaining; to buy a bunch of reduced price canapés and oven chips on Christmas Eve (either in company or on your own), and spend Christmas watching an array of gloriously terrible films. The joy of some 5,000 years of solstice and, later, Christmas traditions is that there are no rules – you can make the season into anything that will work for you.

In terms of food, stuff that's easy to pick up with one hand is ideal; try to avoid something that's going to fall apart and destroy your carpet the minute someone bites into it. I have yet to make a crisp, fried thing that people haven't adored. Similarly (unsurprisingly) carbs are key – if you're only picking at a handful of things over the course of an evening, you want something that fills you up. I quite like being able to retreat into the kitchen during a party to fuss about a bit and have a breather. If that isn't your vibe, the ginger beer ham and buns, the not-sausage rolls, and the brownies and mince pies can all be prepared and plated when people walk through the door. Alternatively, keep it simple and throw a party like the one Carol and Therese skip in *Carol*: the Kellys' wine and fruitcake party (my dream, quite honestly).

And if in doubt, for the perfect Christmas party recipe, follow Fezziwig's lead in *A Christmas Carol* – plenty of dancing (though only in socked feet in my flat: wooden floors and downstairs neighbours are not a good mix), games, drinks, cake, cold meat, and mince pies.

ZAMI: A NEW SPELLING OF MY NAME

Audre Lorde

'People would say... Audre. What happened to you yesterday?
And I would recite a poem and somewhere in that poem would be
a line or a feeling I would be sharing... I literally communicated
through poetry,' wrote the author, activist (and in her own words)
'Black, lesbian, mother, warrior, poet' **Audre Lorde**. One of the most
extraordinary writers of the twentieth century, it is impossible to
sum up Lorde's impact in a short biography: famed for her fiction,
non-fiction and poetry; respected for her womanist and anti-racist
activism; twice a fellow of the MacDowell Foundation; and the
mother of two children, Lorde manages to tackle the greatest practical
and philosophical issues of our time with lyricism, power and grace.
The extract below is taken from her 1982 'biomythography' *Zami:
A New Spelling of My Name.*

That fall, Muriel and I took a course at the New School in
contemporary American poetry, and I went to therapy. There were
things I did not understand, and things I felt that I did not want
to feel, particularly the blinding headaches that came in waves sometimes.

And I seldom spoke. I wrote and I dreamed, but almost never talked,
except in answer to a direct question, or to give a direction of some sort.
I became more and more aware of this the longer Muriel and I lived
together.

With Rhea, as with most of the other people I knew, my primary
function in conversations was to listen. Most people never get a chance
to talk as much as they want to, and I was an attentive listener, being
really interested in what made other people tick. (Maybe I could squirrel
it off and examine their lives in private and find out something about
myself.)

Muriel and I communicated pretty much by intuition and unfinished sentences. Libraries are supposed to be quiet, so at work I didn't have to talk, except to point out where books were, and tell stories to the children. I was very good at that, and I loved to do it. It felt like reciting the endless poems I used to memorize as a child, and which I would retell to myself and anybody else who would listen. They were my way of talking. To express a feeling, I would recite a poem. When the poems I memorized fell short of the occasion, I started to write my own.

I also wanted to go back to college. The course we were taking at the New School didn't make too much sense to me, and the idea of studying was not a familiar one to me. I had managed high school without it, and nobody had bothered to notice. I entered college believing one learned by osmosis, and by concentrating intently on what everybody said. That had meant survival in my family's house.

When I left college, I said to myself at the time that one year of college was more than most Black women had and so I was already ahead of the game. But when Muriel came to New York, I knew I was not going back to Mexico any time soon, and I wanted a degree. I had had tastes of what job-hunting was like for unskilled Black women. Even though I had a job which I enjoyed, I wanted someday not to have to take orders from everybody else. Most of all, I wanted to be free enough to know and do what I wanted to do. I wanted not to shake when I got angry or cry when I got mad. And the city colleges were still free.

I started therapy on the anniversary of the first day Muriel and I met the year before.

On Thanksgiving Day, we fixed a great feast in celebration and invited Suzy and Sis for dinner. Since even at student rates therapy was a luxury, and we had only one income between us, money became even tighter. The day before Thanksgiving, I took my mail-pouch pocketbook and Muriel put on her loosest fitting jacket, and we went across town to the A&P next to Jim Atkins's, the all-night diner in the Village. We came back with a little capon, two pounds of mushrooms, a box of rice, and asparagus. The asparagus was the hardest of all to get, and some of the tips were broken from being tucked so quickly into Muriel's waistband. But we managed without mishap or detection, and walked home whistling and pleased.

About stealing food from supermarkets—I felt that if we needed it badly enough, we would not get caught. And truth to tell, I stopped doing it when I no longer had to, and I never did get caught.

On our way home we splurged on a pint of cherry-vanilla ice cream for dessert, and Suzy and Sis brought the wine. Muriel made an italian pepper and egg pie, and we had a wonderful feast. I brought out all my Mexican rugs and *rebozos*, and decorated the walls and the chairs and the couch with bright colors. The house looked and smelled holiday happy.

That night, I announced that I had made up my mind to register for college at night in the spring term.

Muriel and I kept Christmas on Christmas Eve, such keeping as we did. We exchanged our presents, grumbled a lot, and prepared to go our separate families' ways the next day. We wrapped their presents, and worried about what we could wear home that would not be too uncomfortable, yet appropriate enough to forestall questions and comments.

On Christmas Day, with many kisses and long goodbyes, Muriel went to Stamford and I went up to the Bronx to my sister Phyllis's home to have dinner with her and Henry and the children, along with my mother and Helen. Phyllis had a family and a real house, not an apartment, so it was tacitly agreed that she keep Christmas. It relieved me of another direct confrontation with my mother's house, and gave me a chance to enjoy my two nieces, whom I loved but did not often see. I made a big project of inviting them down to Seventh Street afterward, but they never came.

Christmas we gave to our families; New Year's we kept for ourselves. They were two separate worlds. My family knew that I had a roommate named Muriel. That was about all. My mother had met Muriel, and as usual, since I had left her house, knew it was wise to make no comment about my personal life. But my mother could make "no comment" more loudly and with more hostility than anyone else I knew. Muriel and I had been to Phyllis's house for dinner once, and whatever Phyllis and Henry thought about our relationship, they kept it to themselves. In general, my family only allowed themselves to know whatever it was they cared to know, and I did not push them as long as they left me alone.

On New Year's Eve, Muriel and I went to a party at Nicky and Joan's house. They lived in a brownstone in the eighties near Broadway. Nicky was a writer who worked on a fashion newspaper and Joan was a secretary at Metropolitan Life. Nicky was tiny and tight; Joan was lean and beautiful, with dark spaniel eyes. Unlike Muriel and I, they looked very proper and elegant in their straight clothes, and for that reason, and because they lived so far uptown, it felt like they lived a far more conventional life than we did. In some ways, this was true, for Nicky in particular. Joan was talking about quitting her job and becoming a bum for a while. I envied her the freedom of choice that allowed her to consider this, knowing she could get another job whenever she wanted one. That was what being white and knowing how to type meant.

This was to be a holiday fete, not simply a wash-your-foot-and-come. I never enjoyed parties much if Muriel and I weren't giving them, although I had started to really enjoy the parties out in Queens that we went to with Vida and Pet and Gerri. Those parties given by Black women were always full of food and dancing and reefer and laughter and high-jinks. Vida with her dramatic voice and sense of the absurd, and Pet with her dancing feet that were never still, made it easy not to be shy, to move with the music and laughter. It was at those parties that I finally learned how to dance.

Joan and Nicky's parties were different. Usually there wasn't much music, and when there was, it was not for dancing. There was always lots of wine around, both red and white, because Nicky and Joan were more Bermuda shorts than dungarees. One of the noticeable differences between the two sets was wine versus hard liquor. But more than one glass of any kind of wine gave me heartburn, and besides it was all too dry for my taste. It was not sophisticated to like sweet wine, and that became another one of my secret vices, like soft ice cream, to be indulged only around tried and true friends.

And there was never enough food. Tonight, for the holidays, a beautifully laid table graced the corner of Nicky and Joan's great, high-ceilinged parlor. Upon an old linen tablecloth that had belonged to Nicky's mother, and bright red poinsettia mats cut from felt, sat little plates of potato chips and pretzels and crackers and cheeses, a bowl of sour cream and onion dip made from Lipton's onion soup mix, and tiny little jars of red caviar with bright green bibs around them. There were saucers of olives and celery and pickles on the edges of the table, and in various corners of the room, baskets of mixed nuts. I kept thinking of the pigs-in-a-blanket and fried chicken wings and potato salad and hot corn bread at Gerri and them's last "do," knowing it wasn't a question of money, because red caviar cost a lot more than chicken wings.

The feeling in the room was subdued. Mostly, women sat around in little groups and talked quietly, the sound of moderation—thick and heavy as smoke in the air. I noticed the absence of laughter only because I always thought parties were supposed to be fun, even though I didn't find them particularly so, never knowing what to say. I busied myself looking through the book-shelves lining the room.

Muriel circulated with ease. She seemed in her element, her soft voice and fall-away chuckle moving from group to group, cigarette and bottle of beer in hand. I studied the books, uncomfortable and acutely aware of being alone. Pat, a friend of Nicky's from the paper, came over and started to talk. I listened appreciatively, greatly relieved.

Muriel and I left shortly after midnight, walking over to the subway on Central Park West arm in arm. It was good to be out in the sharp cold air, even good to be a little tired. We frolicked through the almost empty streets, talking and laughing about nonsensical things, joking about our uptown friends who drank dry wine. Occasional blasts from party horns were still erupting from gaily lit windows, holiday open.

In the freshness and nip of the winter's late night, alone now with Muriel, something powerful and promising inside of me stretched, excited and joyful. I thought of other New Year's Eves that I had spent, alone, or wandering through Times Square. I was very lucky, very blessed.

I squeezed Muriel's hand, and felt her tight squeeze back. I was in love, a new year was beginning, and the shape of the future was a widening star. It was one year to the day that Muriel and I had locked the door of Seventh Street behind Rhea and turned off the fire under the coffee on the stove and laid down together with our hearts against each other. This was our first anniversary.

We went home and ushered it in quite properly, until dawn sang with the rhythms of our bodies, our heat.

Later, we got up, and Muriel cooked a huge pot of hoppin' john, black-eyed peas and rice, which Suzy's friend Lion from Philly had taught her how to do, and of which she was very proud. I laughed to see her strutting around the kitchen rosy-cheeked, waving her wooden spoon aloft in triumph as the food reached exactly the right consistency without becoming mushy.

Evening moved upon us, and as our friends dropped by, we wished each other good times and ate and ate. Some of the women were hung-over, and some were depressed, and some were just plain sleepy from being out all night and thinking of work tomorrow. But we all agreed that Muriel's pot was the best hoppin' john we'd ever tasted, and that it was going to be a super year for us all.

Nicky and Joan were the last to leave. After they had gone, Muriel and I put the dishes and pots to soak in the covered part of the sink, and we climbed back into bed with our notebooks and wrote New Year themes. Muriel chose a subject—A Man from the Land Where Nobody Lives. When we finished, we exchanged our notebooks and read each other's work before moving on to the next theme.

Muriel had written:

The Year 1955

Audi   *Me*
got a new job
started therapy
sent out some poems   NOTHING!
is going back to school

I stared at the notebook page in silence, feeling like cold water had been thrown at me. I reached over and took her hand. It lay cool and still beneath my fingers, without movement. I did not know what to say to Muriel. The idea that anyone could measure herself against me and find that self wanting was truly shocking. The fact that it was my beloved Muriel who was doing it was nothing less than terrifying.

I thought of our life as a mutual exploration, a progress through the strength of our loving. But as I read and re-read the stark outline in her notebook, I realized that Muriel saw that joint becoming in terms of achievements of mine which somehow defined her inabilities. They were not mutual triumphs, the notebook said in inescapable terms, and there was nothing either I or our loving could do to shield her from the implications of that truth, as she saw it.

THE BELL JAR

Sylvia Plath

It is easy to lose **Sylvia Plath**'s life in the shadow of her untimely death. Born in Boston, Massachusetts in 1932, and dying by suicide in the icy London winter of 1963, Sylvia Plath was a poet, novelist, short story writer and enthusiastic cook. She was a Fulbright Scholar, a graduate of Smith College in the US and Cambridge in the UK; and her final poetry collection, *Ariel*, was posthumously awarded the Pulitzer Prize. Her tempestuous marriage to the Poet Laureate Ted Hughes has been much discussed and debated by strangers, but it is safe to say that it was marked with violence, daffodils, writing and passion, and that together they had two children, Nicholas and Frieda. Plath's writing is full of colour, and her life was short but extraordinary.

Arrayed on the *Ladies' Day* banquet table were yellow-green avocado pear halves stuffed with crabmeat and mayonnaise, and platters of rare roast beef and cold chicken, and every so often a cut-glass bowl heaped with black caviar. I hadn't had time to eat any breakfast at the hotel cafeteria that morning, except for a cup of over-stewed coffee so bitter it made my nose curl, and I was starving.

Before I came to New York I'd never eaten out in a proper restaurant. I don't count Howard Johnson's, where I only had French fries and cheeseburgers and vanilla frappes with people like Buddy Willard. I'm not sure why it is, but I love food more than just about anything else. No matter how much I eat, I never put on weight. With one exception I've been the same weight for ten years.

My favourite dishes are full of butter and cheese and sour cream. In New York we had so many free luncheons with people on the magazine and various visiting celebrities I developed the habit of running my eye down those huge, handwritten menus, where a tiny side-dish of peas costs fifty or sixty cents, until I'd picked the richest, most expensive dishes and ordered a string of them.

We were always taken out on expense accounts, so I never felt guilty. I made a point of eating so fast I never kept the other people waiting who generally ordered only chef's salad and grapefruit juice because they were trying to reduce. Almost everybody I met in New York was trying to reduce.

'I want to welcome the prettiest, smartest bunch of young ladies our staff has yet had the good luck to meet,' the plump, bald master-of-ceremonies wheezed into his lapel microphone. 'This banquet is just a small sample of the hospitality our Food Testing Kitchens here on *Ladies' Day* would like to offer in appreciation for your visit.'

A delicate, ladylike spatter of applause, and we all sat down at the enormous linen-draped table.

There were eleven of us girls from the magazine, together with most of our supervising editors, and the whole staff of the *Ladies' Day* Food Testing Kitchens in hygienic white smocks, neat hair-nets and flawless make-up of a uniform peach-pie colour.

There were only eleven of us, because Doreen was missing. They had set her place next to mine for some reason, and the chair stayed empty. I saved her place-card for her – a pocket mirror with 'Doreen' painted along the top of it in lacy script and a wreath of frosted daisies around the edge, framing the silver hole where her face would show.

Doreen was spending the day with Lenny Shepherd. She spent most of her free time with Lenny Shepherd now.

In the hour before our luncheon at *Ladies' Day* – the big women's magazine that features lush double-page spreads of technicolour meals, with a different theme and locale each month – we had been shown around the endless glossy kitchens and seen how difficult it is to photograph apple pie *à la mode* under bright lights because the ice-cream keeps melting and has to be propped up from behind with toothpicks and changed every time it starts looking too soppy.

The sight of all the food stacked in those kitchens made me dizzy. It's not that we hadn't enough to eat at home, it's just that my grandmother always cooked economy joints and economy meat-loafs and had the habit of saying, the minute you lifted the first forkful to your mouth, 'I hope you enjoy that, it cost forty-one cents a pound,' which always made me feel I was somehow eating pennies instead of Sunday roast.

While we were standing up behind our chairs listening to the welcome speech, I had bowed my head and secretly eyed the position of the bowls of caviar. One bowl was set strategically between me and Doreen's empty chair.

I figured the girl across from me couldn't reach it because of the mountainous centrepiece of marzipan fruit, and Betsy, on my right, would be too nice to ask me to share it with her if I just kept it out of the way at my elbow by my bread-and-butter plate. Besides, another bowl of caviar sat a little way to the right of the girl next to Betsy, and she could eat that.

My grandfather and I had a standing joke. He was the head waiter at a country club near my home town, and every Sunday my grandmother drove in to bring him home for his Monday off. My brother and I alternated going with her, and my grandfather always served Sunday supper to my grandmother and whichever of us was along as if we were regular club guests. He loved introducing me to special titbits, and by the age of nine I had developed a passionate taste for cold vichyssoise and caviar and anchovy paste.

The joke was that at my wedding my grandfather would see I had all the caviar I could eat. It was a joke because I never intended to get married, and even if I did, my grandfather couldn't have afforded enough caviar unless he robbed the country club kitchen and carried it off in a suitcase.

Under cover of the clinking of water goblets and silverware and bone china, I paved my plate with chicken slices. Then I covered the chicken slices with caviar thickly as if I were spreading peanut-butter on a piece of bread. Then I picked up the chicken slices in my fingers one by one, rolled them so the caviar wouldn't ooze off and ate them.

I'd discovered, after a lot of extreme apprehension about what spoons to use, that if you do something incorrect at table with a certain arrogance, as if you knew perfectly well you were doing it properly, you can get away with it and nobody will think you are bad-mannered or poorly brought up. They will think you are original and very witty.

I learned this trick the day Jay Cee took me to lunch with a famous poet. He wore a horrible, lumpy, speckled brown tweed jacket and grey pants and a red-and-blue checked open-throated jersey in a very formal restaurant full of fountains and chandeliers, where all the other men were dressed in dark suits and immaculate white shirts.

This poet ate his salad with his fingers, leaf by leaf, while talking to me about the antithesis of nature and art. I couldn't take my eyes off the pale, stubby white fingers travelling back and forth from the poet's salad bowl to the poet's mouth with one dripping lettuce leaf after another. Nobody giggled or whispered rude remarks. The poet made eating salad with your fingers seem to be the only natural and sensible thing to do.

None of our magazine editors or the *Ladies' Day* staff members sat anywhere near me, and Betsy seemed sweet and friendly, she didn't even seem to like caviar, so I grew more and more confident. When I finished my first plate of cold chicken and caviar, I laid out another. Then I tackled the avocado and crabmeat salad.

Avocados are my favourite fruit. Every Sunday my grandfather used to bring me an avocado pear hidden at the bottom of his briefcase under six soiled shirts and the Sunday comics. He taught me how to eat avocados by melting grape jelly and French dressing together in a saucepan and filling the cup of the pear with the garnet sauce. I felt homesick for that sauce. The crabmeat tasted bland in comparison.

'How was the fur show?' I asked Betsy, when I was no longer worried about competition over my caviar. I scraped the last few salty black eggs from the dish with my soup spoon and licked it clean.

'It was wonderful,' Betsy smiled. 'They showed us how to make an all-purpose neckerchief out of mink tails and a gold chain, the sort of chain you can get an exact copy of at Woolworth's for a dollar ninety-eight, and Hilda nipped down to the wholesale fur warehouses right afterwards and bought a bunch of mink tails at a big discount and dropped in at Woolworth's and then stitched the whole thing together coming up on the bus.'

I peered over at Hilda, who sat on the other side of Betsy. Sure enough, she was wearing an expensive-looking scarf of furry tails fastened on one side by a dangling gilt chain.

I never really understood Hilda. She was six feet tall, with huge, slanted, green eyes and thick red lips and a vacant, Slavic expression. She made hats. She was apprenticed to the Fashion Editor, which set her apart from the more literary ones among us like Doreen and Betsy and I myself, who all wrote columns, even if some of them were only about health and beauty. I don't know if Hilda could read, but she made startling hats. She went to a special school for making hats in New York and every day she wore a new hat to work, constructed by her own hands out of bits of straw or fur or ribbon or veiling in subtle, bizarre shades.

'That's amazing,' I said. 'Amazing.' I missed Doreen. She would have murmured some fine, scalding remark about Hilda's miraculous furpiece to cheer me up.

I felt very low. I had been unmasked only that morning by Jay Cee herself, and I felt now that all the uncomfortable suspicions I had about myself were coming true, and I couldn't hide the truth much longer. After nineteen years of running after good marks and prizes and grants of one sort and another, I was letting up, slowing down, dropping clean out of the race.

'Why didn't you come along to the fur show with us?' Betsy asked. I had the impression she was repeating herself, and that she'd asked me the same question a minute ago, only I couldn't have been listening. 'Did you go off with Doreen?'

'No,' I said, 'I wanted to go to the fur show, but Jay Cee called up and made me come into the office.' That wasn't quite true about wanting to go to the show, but I tried to convince myself now that it was true, so I could be really wounded about what Jay Cee had done.

I told Betsy how I had been lying in bed that morning planning to go to the fur show. What I didn't tell her was that Doreen had come into my room earlier and said, 'What do you want to go to that assy show for, Lenny and I are going to Coney Island, so why don't you come along? Lenny can get you a nice fellow, the day's shot to hell anyhow with that luncheon and then the film première in the afternoon, so nobody'll miss us.'

For a minute I was tempted. The show certainly did seem stupid. I have never cared for furs. What I decided to do in the end was to lie in bed as long as I wanted to and then go to Central Park and spend the day lying in the grass, the longest grass I could find in that bald, duck-ponded wilderness.

I told Doreen I would not go to the show or the luncheon or the film première, but that I would not go to Coney Island either, I would stay in bed. After Doreen left, I wondered why I couldn't go the whole way doing what I should any more. This made me sad and tired. Then I wondered why I couldn't go the whole way doing what I shouldn't, the way Doreen did, and this made me even sadder and more tired.

I didn't know what time it was, but I'd heard the girls bustling and calling in the hall and getting ready for the fur show, and then I'd heard the hall go still, and as I lay on my back in bed staring up at the blank, white ceiling the stillness seemed to grow bigger and bigger until I felt my eardrums would burst with it. Then the phone rang.

I stared at the phone for a minute. The receiver shook a bit in its bone-coloured cradle, so I could tell it was really ringing. I thought I might have given my phone number to somebody at a dance or a party and then forgotten clean about it. I lifted the receiver and spoke in a husky, receptive voice.

'Hello?'

'Jay Cee here,' Jay Cee rapped out with brutal promptitude. 'I wondered if you happened to be planning to come into the office today?'

I sank down into the sheets. I couldn't understand why Jay Cee thought I'd be coming into the office. We had these mimeographed schedule cards so we could keep track of all our activities, and we spent a lot of mornings and afternoons away from the office going to affairs in town. Of course, some of the affairs were optional.

There was quite a pause. Then I said meekly, 'I thought I was going to the fur show.' Of course I hadn't thought any such thing, but I couldn't figure out what else to say.

'I told her I thought I was going to the fur show,' I said to Betsy. 'But she told me to come into the office, she wanted to have a little talk with me, and there was some work to do.'

'Oh-oh!' Betsy said sympathetically. She must have seen the tears that plopped down into my dessert dish of meringue and brandy ice-cream, because she pushed over her own untouched dessert and I started absently on that when I'd finished my own. I felt a bit awkward about the tears, but they were real enough. Jay Cee had said some terrible things to me.

When I made my wan entrance into the office at about ten o'clock, Jay Cee stood up and came round her desk to shut the door, and I sat in the swivel chair in front of my typewriter table facing her, and she sat in the swivel chair behind her desk facing me, with the window full of potted plants, shelf after shelf of them, springing up at her back like a tropical garden.

'Doesn't your work interest you, Esther?'

'Oh, it does, it does,' I said. 'It interests me very much.' I felt like yelling the words, as if that might make them more convincing, but I controlled myself.

All my life I'd told myself studying and reading and writing and working like mad was what I wanted to do, and it actually seemed to be true, I did everything well enough and got all A's, and by the time I made it to college nobody could stop me.

I was college correspondent for the town *Gazette* and editor of the literary magazine and secretary of Honour Board, which deals with academic and social offences and punishments – a popular office, and I had a well-known woman poet and professor on the faculty championing me for graduate school at the biggest universities in the east, and promises of full scholarships all the way, and now I was apprenticed to the best editor on any intellectual fashion magazine, and what did I do but balk and balk like a dull cart horse?

'I'm very interested in everything.' The words fell with a hollow flatness on to Jay Cee's desk, like so many wooden nickels.

'I'm glad of that,' Jay Cee said a bit waspishly. 'You can learn a lot in this month on the magazine, you know, if you just roll up your shirt-cuffs. The girl who was here before you didn't bother with any of the fashion show stuff. She went straight from this office on to *Time*.'

'My!' I said, in the same sepulchral tone. 'That was quick!'

'Of course, you have another year at college yet,' Jay Cee went on a little more mildly. 'What do you have in mind after you graduate?'

What I always thought I had in mind was getting some big scholarship to graduate school or a grant to study all over Europe, and then I thought I'd be a professor and write books of poems or write books of poems and be an editor of some sort. Usually I had these plans on the tip of my tongue.

'I don't really know,' I heard myself say. I felt a deep shock, hearing myself say that, because the minute I said it, I knew it was true.

It sounded true, and I recognized it, the way you recognize some nondescript person that's been hanging around your door for ages and then suddenly comes up and introduces himself as your real father and looks exactly like you, so you know he really is your father, and the person you thought all your life was your father is a sham.

'I don't really know.'

'You'll never get anywhere like that.' Jay Cee paused. 'What languages do you have?'

'Oh, I can read a bit of French, I guess, and I've always wanted to learn German.' I'd been telling people I'd always wanted to learn German for about five years.

My mother spoke German during her childhood in America and was stoned for it during the First World War by the children at school. My German-speaking father, dead since I was nine, came from some manic-depressive hamlet in the black heart of Prussia. My younger brother was at that moment on the Experiment in International Living in Berlin and speaking German like a native.

What I didn't say was that each time I picked up a German dictionary or a German book, the very sight of those dense, black, barbed-wire letters made my mind shut like a clam.

'I've always thought I'd like to go into publishing.' I tried to recover a thread that might lead me back to my old, bright salesmanship. 'I guess what I'll do is apply at some publishing house.'

'You ought to read French and German,' Jay Cee said mercilessly, 'and probably several other languages as well, Spanish and Italian – better still, Russian. Hundreds of girls flood into New York every June thinking they'll be editors. You need to offer something more than the run-of-the-mill person. You better learn some languages.'

I hadn't the heart to tell Jay Cee there wasn't one scrap of space on my senior year schedule to learn languages in. I was taking one of those honours programmes that teaches you to think independently, and except for a course in Tolstoy and Dostoevsky and a seminar in advanced poetry-composition, I would spend my whole time writing on some obscure theme in the works of James Joyce. I hadn't picked out my theme yet, because I hadn't got round to reading *Finnegan's Wake*, but my professor was very excited about my thesis and had promised to give me some leads on images about twins.

'I'll see what I can do,' I told Jay Cee. 'I probably might just fit in one of those double-barrelled, accelerated courses in elementary German they've rigged up.' I thought at the time I might actually do this. I had a way of persuading my Class Dean to let me do irregular things. She regarded me as a sort of interesting experiment.

At college I had to take a required course in physics and chemistry. I had already taken a course in botany and done very well. I never answered one test question wrong the whole year, and for a while I toyed with the idea of being a botanist and studying the wild grasses in Africa or the South American rain forests, because you can win big grants to study off-beat things like that in queer areas much more easily than winning grants to study art in Italy or English in England, there's not so much competition.

Botany was fine, because I loved cutting up leaves and putting them under the microscope and drawing diagrams of bread mould and the odd, heart-shaped leaf in the sex cycle of the fern, it seemed so real to me.

The day I went into physics class it was death.

A short dark man with a high, lisping voice, named Mr Manzi, stood in front of the class in a tight blue suit holding a little wooden ball. He put the ball on a steep grooved slide and let it run down to the bottom. Then he started talking about let *a* equal acceleration and let *t* equal time and suddenly he was scribbling letters and numbers and equals signs all over the blackboard and my mind went dead.

I took the physics book back to my dormitory. It was a huge book on porous mimeographed paper – four hundred pages long with no drawings or photographs, only diagrams and formulas – between brick-red cardboard covers. This book was written by Mr Manzi to explain physics to college girls, and if it worked on us he would try to have it published.

Well, I studied those formulas, I went to class and watched balls roll down slides and listened to bells ring and by the end of the semester most of the other girls had failed and I had a straight A. I heard Mr Manzi saying to a bunch of the girls who were complaining that the course was too hard, 'No, it can't be too hard, because one girl got a straight A.' 'Who is it? Tell us,' they said, but he shook his head and didn't say anything and gave me a sweet little conspiring smile.

That's what gave me the idea of escaping the next semester of chemistry. I may have made a straight A in physics, but I was panic-struck. Physics made me sick the whole time I learned it. What I couldn't stand was this shrinking everything into letters and numbers. Instead of leaf shapes and enlarged diagrams of the holes the leaves breathe through and fascinating words like carotene and xanthophyll on the blackboard, there were these hideous, cramped, scorpion-lettered formulas in Mr Manzi's special red chalk.

I knew chemistry would be worse, because I'd seen a big chart of the ninety-odd elements hung up in the chemistry lab, and all the perfectly good words like gold and silver and cobalt and aluminium were shortened to ugly abbreviations with different decimal numbers after them. If I had to strain my brain with any more of that stuff I would go mad. I would fail outright. It was only by a horrible effort of will that I had dragged myself through the first half of the year.

So I went to my Class Dean with a clever plan.

My plan was that I needed the time to take a course in Shakespeare, since I was, after all, an English major. She knew and I knew perfectly well I would get a straight A again in the chemistry course, so what was the point of my taking the exams, why couldn't I just go to the classes and look on and take it all in and forget about marks or credits? It was a case of honour among honourable people, and the content meant more than the form, and marks were really a bit silly anyway, weren't they, when you knew you'd always get an A? My plan was strengthened by the fact that the college had just dropped the second year of required science for the classes after me anyway, so my class was the last to suffer under the old ruling.

Mr Manzi was in perfect agreement with my plan. I think it flattered him that I enjoyed his classes so much I would take them for no materialistic reason like credit and an A, but for the sheer beauty of chemistry itself. I thought it was quite ingenious of me to suggest sitting in on the chemistry course even after I'd changed over to Shakespeare. It was quite an unnecessary gesture and made it seem I simply couldn't bear to give chemistry up.

Of course, I would never have succeeded with this scheme if I hadn't made that A in the first place. And if my Class Dean had known how scared and depressed I was, and how I seriously contemplated desperate remedies such as getting a doctor's certificate that I was unfit to study chemistry, the formulas made me dizzy and so on, I'm sure she wouldn't have listened to me for a minute, but would have made me take the course regardless.

As it happened, the Faculty Board passed my petition, and my Class Dean told me later that several of the professors were touched by it. They took it as a real step in intellectual maturity.

I had to laugh when I thought about the rest of that year. I went to the chemistry class five times a week and didn't miss a single one. Mr Manzi stood at the bottom of the big, rickety old amphitheatre, making blue flames and red flares and clouds of yellow stuff by pouring the contents of one test-tube into another, and I shut his voice out of my ears by pretending it was only a mosquito in the distance and sat back enjoying the bright lights and the coloured fires and wrote page after page of villanelles and sonnets.

Mr Manzi would glance at me now and then and see me writing, and send up a sweet little appreciative smile. I guess he thought I was writing down all those formulas not for exam time, like the other girls, but because his presentation fascinated me so much I couldn't help it.

THE RECIPE CARDS OF SYLVIA PLATH

Can this photograph be food writing? We think so. You have seen cards like this before; if you're a keen cook, you probably own something like it, some scrawled-in notebook or Google doc or Post-its jammed into your collection of recipe books. You figure out what works, and what you like, and then you make a note of it to make it better, different, the exact same next time. You email a friend. You tear a page out of a magazine. You scribble on a supermarket recipe card. You write about food to use it; to soften the space between what is and what will be, between the idea of the thing and the thing itself, to make a template for next time. The job of food writing is to bridge the gap between the real (now) and next time (imaginary); between the here (me) and the there (you). My kitchen is in your hands; and when you write down a note for yourself about a recipe your kitchen lives in that note until the next time you pick it up. This is what food writing is for. This is where food writing really lives: scrawled in the margins of stuck-together pages, pasted into scrapbooks or shuffled into a deck of index cards. Sometimes it's not even written down at all; it's an oral tradition: do it this way, a pinch of that, rice up to the knuckle and water to cover. But it's food writing, all the same. It's the heart of the thing.

And often these texts are ignored. This is, as the Irish poet Doireann Ní Ghríofa would say, a 'female text': the kind of universal text that exists outside the boundaries of what is usually studied or taken seriously as literature. Even when the author of the female text is a great artist. These are the recipe cards of Sylvia Plath, reproduced from the sale of her possessions at Sotheby's in 2019, and by permission of her daughter Frieda. This is Plath's work, too, as much as the poems. These are the things she loved to cook, and she did love to cook. She loved *The Joy of Cooking*. She made tomato soup cake. She was real, and the great poet was a person, and she cooked, and made notes, and wrote it down. And it is hard not to think of these recipe cards as another kind of poem: the art of it, the art of feeding the hungry, of making something where nothing was before.

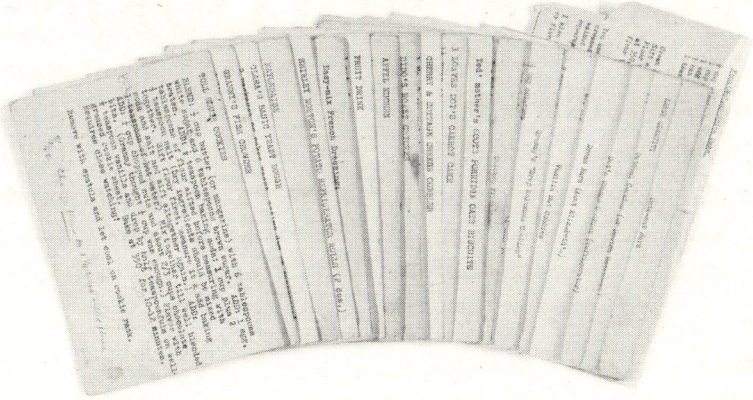

ALONE IN THE KITCHEN WITH AN EGGPLANT *FROM* HOME COOKING

Laurie Colwin

'Even at her most solitary, a cook in her kitchen is surrounded by generations of cooks past,' wrote **Laurie Colwin** in her iconic 1988 memoir *Home Cooking*. A prolific and acclaimed novelist, *Home Cooking* and its sequel, *More Home Cooking*, secured Colwin's place in those kitchens forever. Part memoir, part cookbook, her work is like sitting at the counter of your oldest friend's kitchen while she makes you dinner. So alive is Colwin in her writing that it seems impossible that we don't, and can't, know her personally. She died in 1992, aged just forty-eight, leaving behind her husband Juris; their then-eight-year-old, RF; and a body of beautiful, practical work that sings forever in her absence.

For eight years I lived in a one-room apartment a little larger than the *Columbia Encyclopedia*. It is lucky I never met Wilt Chamberlain because if I had invited him in for coffee he would have been unable to spread his arms in my room, which was roughly seven by twenty.

I had enough space for a twin-sized bed, a very small night table, and a desk. This desk, which I use to this day, was meant for a child of, say, eleven. At the foot of my bed was a low table that would have been a coffee table in a normal apartment. In mine it served as a lamp stand, and beneath it was a basket containing my sheets and towels. Next to a small fireplace, which had an excellent draw, was a wicker armchair and an ungainly wicker footstool which often served as a table of sorts.

Instead of a kitchen, this minute apartment featured a metal counter. Underneath was a refrigerator the size of a child's playhouse. On top was what I called the stove but which was only two electric burners—in short, a hot plate.

Many people found this place charming, at least for five minutes or so. Many thought I must be insane to live in so small a space, but I loved my apartment and found it the coziest place on earth. It was on a small street in Greenwich Village and looked out over a mews of shabby little houses, in the center courtyard of which was a catalpa tree. The ceiling was fairly high—a good thing since a low one would have made my apartment feel like the inside of a box of animal crackers.

My cupboard shelves were so narrow that I had to stand my dinner plates on end. Naturally, there being no kitchen, there was no kitchen sink. I did the dishes in a plastic pan in the bathtub and set the dish drainer over the toilet.

Of course there was no space for anything like a dining room table, something quite unnecessary as there was no dining room. When I was alone I ate at my desk, or on a tray in bed. When company came I opened a folding card table with a cigarette burn in its leatherette top. This object was stored in a slot between my countertop and my extremely small closet. Primitive as my kitchen arrangements were, I had company for dinner fairly often.

I moved in one cool summer day when I was twenty-three. That night I made dinner for two college friends who were known as the Alices since they were both named Alice and were best friends. I remember our meal in detail. A young man had given me a fondue pot as a moving-in present. These implements, whose real function was to sit unused on a top shelf collecting furry coats of dust, were commonly given as wedding and housewarming presents in the sixties and are still available at garage sales of the eighties. They were made of stainless steel and sat on a three-legged base at the bottom of which was a ring, to hold a can of Sterno. Along with the pot came four long-handled forks, two of which I have to this day. (They are extremely useful for spearing string beans and for piercing things that have fallen onto the floor of your oven.) The fellow who gave it to me was fond of a place called Le Chalet Suisse, where I had once enjoyed beef fondue. I felt it would be nice to replicate this dish for my friends.

I served three sauces, two of which I made: one was tomato based and the other was a kind of vinaigrette. The third was béarnaise in a jar from the local delicatessen. I bought sirloin from the butcher and cubed it myself. When my two friends came, I lit the can of Sterno and we waited for the oil to heat.

While we waited we ate up all the bread and butter. One of the Alices began to eat the béarnaise sauce with a spoon. The other Alice suggested we go out for dinner. Once in a while we would dip a steak cube into the oil to see what happened. At first we pulled out oil-covered steak. After a while, the steak turned faintly gray. Finally, I turned one of my burners on high and put the pot on the burner to get it started. Thereafter we watched with interest as our steak cubes sizzled madly and turned into little lumps of rubbery coal. Finally, I sautéed the remaining steak in a frying pan. We dumped the sauces on top and gobbled everything up. Then we went to the local bar for hamburgers and French fries.

It took me a while to get the hang of two burners. Meanwhile, my mother gave me a toaster oven, thinking this would ensure me a proper breakfast. My breakfast, however, was bacon and egg on a buttered roll from an underground cafeteria at the Madison Avenue side of the Lexington Avenue stop of the E train. My toaster oven was put to far more interesting use.

I began with toasted cheese, that staple of starving people who live in garrets. Toasted cheese is still one of my favorite foods and I brought home all sorts of cheese to toast. Then, after six months of the same dinner, I turned to lamb chops. A number of fat fires transpired, none serious enough to call the fire department. I then noticed after a while that my toaster oven was beginning to emit a funny burnt rubber smell when I plugged it in. This, I felt, was not a good sign and so I put it out on the street. With the departure of my toaster oven, I was thrown back, so to speak, on my two burners.

Two-burner cooking is somewhat limiting, although I was constantly reading or being read to about amazing stove-top feats: people who rigged up gizmos on the order of a potato baker and baked bread in it, or a thing that suspended live coals over a pot so the tops of things could be browned, but I was not brave enough to try these innovations.

Instead, I learned how to make soup. I ate countless pots of lentil, white bean and black bean soup. I tried neck bones and ham hocks and veal marrow bones and bacon rinds. I made thousands of omelets and pans of my mother's special tomatoes and eggs. I made stewed chicken and vegetable stew. I made bowls of pickled cabbage—green cabbage, dark sesame oil, salt, ginger and lemon juice. If people came over in the afternoon, I made cucumber sandwiches with anchovy butter.

I would invite a friend or friends for Saturday night. Three people could fit comfortably in my house, but not four, although one famous evening I actually had a tiny dance party in my flat, much to the inconvenience of my downstairs neighbor, a fierce old Belgian who spent the afternoon in the courtyard garden entertaining his lady friends. At night he generally pounded on his ceiling with a broom handle to get me to turn my music down. My upstairs neighbor, on the other hand, was a Muncie, Indiana, Socialist with a limp. I was often madly in love with him, and sometimes he with me, but in between he returned my affections by stomping around his apartment on his gimpy leg—the result of a motorcycle accident—and playing the saxophone out the window.

On Saturday mornings I would walk to the Flavor Cup or Porto Rico Importing coffee store to get my coffee. Often it was freshly roasted and the beans were still warm. Coffee was my nectar and my ambrosia: I was very careful about it. I decanted my beans into glass and kept them in the fridge, and I ground them in little batches in my grinder.

I wandered down Bleecker Street, where there were still a couple of pushcarts left, to buy vegetables and salad greens. I went to the butcher, then bought the newspaper and a couple of magazines. Finally I went home, made a cup of coffee and stretched out on my bed (which, when made and pillowed, doubled as a couch), and I spent the rest of the morning in total indolence before cooking all afternoon.

One Saturday I decided to impress a youth whose mother, a Frenchwoman, had taught him how to cook. A recipe for pot roast with dill presented itself to me and I was not old or wise enough to realize that dill is not something you really want with your pot roast. An older and wiser cook would also have known that a rump steak needs to be baked in the oven for a long time and does not fare well on top of the stove. The result was a tough, gray wedge with the texture of a dense sponge. To pay me back and show off, this person invited me to his gloomy apartment where we ate jellied veal and a strange pallid ring that quivered and glowed with a faintly purplish light. This, he told me, was a cold almond shape.

The greatest meal cooked on those two burners came after a night of monumental sickness. I had gone to a party and disgraced myself. The next morning I woke feeling worse than I had ever felt in my life. After two large glasses of seltzer and lime juice, two aspirins and a morning-long nap, I began to feel better. I spent the afternoon dozing and reading Elizabeth David's *Italian Food*. By early evening I was out of my mind with hunger but feeling too weak to do anything about it. Suddenly, the doorbell rang and there was my friend from work. She brought with her four veal scallops, a little bottle of French olive oil, a bunch of arugula, two pears and a Boursault cheese, and a loaf of bread from Zito's bakery on Bleecker Street. I would have wept tears of gratitude but I was too hungry.

We got out the card table and set it, and washed the arugula in the bathtub. Then we sautéed the veal with a little lemon, mixed the salad dressing and sat down to one of the most delicious meals I have ever had.

Then, having regained my faculties, I felt I ought to invite the couple at whose house I had behaved so badly. They were English. The husband had been my boss. Now they were going back to England and this was my chance to say good-bye.

At the time I had three party dishes: Chicken with sesame seeds and broccoli. Chicken in an orange-flavored cream sauce. Chicken with paprika and brussels sprouts. But the wife, who was not my greatest fan, could not abide chicken and suggested, through her husband, that she would like pasta. Spaghetti alla Carbonara was intimated and I picked right up on it.

Spaghetti is a snap to cook, but it is a lot snappier if you have a kitchen. I of course did not. It is very simple to drain the spaghetti into a colander in your kitchen sink, dump it into a hot dish and sauce it at once. Since I had no kitchen sink, I had to put the colander in my bathtub; my bathroom sink was too small to accommodate it. At this time my bathroom was quite a drafty place, since a few weeks before a part of the ceiling over the bath had fallen into the tub, and now as I took my showers, I could gaze at exposed beams. Therefore the spaghetti, by the time the sauce hit it, had become somewhat gluey. The combination of clammy pasta and cream sauce was not a success. The look on the wife's face said clearly: "You mean you dragged me all the way downtown to sit in an apartment the size of a place mat for *this*?"

When I was alone, I lived on eggplant, the stove top cook's strongest ally. I fried it and stewed it, and ate it crisp and sludgy, hot and cold. It was cheap and filling and was delicious in all manner of strange combinations. If any was left over I ate it cold the next day on bread.

Dinner alone is one of life's pleasures. Certainly cooking for oneself reveals man at his weirdest. People lie when you ask them what they eat when they are alone. A salad, they tell you. But when you persist, they confess to peanut butter and bacon sandwiches deep fried and eaten with hot sauce, or spaghetti with butter and grape jam.

I looked forward to nights alone. I would stop to buy my eggplant and some red peppers. At home I would fling off my coat, switch on the burner under my teakettle, slice up the eggplant, and make myself a cup of coffee. I could do all this without moving a step. When the eggplant was getting crisp, I turned down the fire and added garlic, tamari sauce, lemon juice and some shredded red peppers. While this stewed, I drank my coffee and watched the local news. Then I uncovered the eggplant, cooked it down and ate it at my desk out of an old Meissen dish, with my feet up on my wicker footrest as I watched the national news.

I ate eggplant constantly: with garlic and honey, eggplant with spaghetti, eggplant with fried onions and Chinese plum sauce.

Since many of my friends did not want to share these strange dishes with me, I figured out a dish for company. Fried eggplant rounds made into a kind of sandwich pot cheese, chopped scallions, fermented black beans and muenster cheese. This, with a salad and a loaf of bread, made a meal. Dessert was *always* brought in. Afterwards I collected all the pots and pans and silverware and threw everything into my pan of soapy water in the bathtub and that was my dinner party.

Now I have a kitchen with a four-burner stove, and a real fridge. I have a pantry and a kitchen sink and a dining room table. But when my husband is at a business meeting and my little daughter is asleep, I often find myself alone in the kitchen with an eggplant, a clove of garlic and my old pot without the handle about to make a weird dish of eggplant to eat out of the Meissen soup plate at my desk.

A ROOM OF ONE'S OWN

Virginia Woolf

In 1928, novelist and essayist **Virginia Woolf** delivered two lectures focusing on women and fiction at Cambridge University's women-only colleges (Girton and Newnham). Through them she weaves together historical fact and fiction, introducing women who existed (Austen, Eliot, Rossetti) and those who didn't (Judith, Shakespeare's sister, who meets Nick Greene from Woolf's own *Orlando*). Published as *A Room of One's Own* in 1929, the work concludes that women must have financial independence, and a private space, in order to write well. Woolf's often complex (and sometimes frankly tedious) relationship with class, money and the social order of things is at its clear and generous best here: if women don't have money, they can't write. Without the space in which to make things, nothing can be made.

It is a curious fact that novelists have a way of making us believe that luncheon parties are invariably memorable for something very witty that was said, or for something very wise that was done. But they seldom spare a word for what was eaten. It is part of the novelist's convention not to mention soup and salmon and ducklings, as if soup and salmon and ducklings were of no importance whatsoever, as if nobody ever smoked a cigar or drank a glass of wine. Here, however, I shall take the liberty to defy that convention and to tell you that the lunch on this occasion began with soles, sunk in a deep dish, over which the college cook had spread a counterpane of the whitest cream, save that it was branded here and there with brown spots like the spots on the flanks of a doe. After that came the partridges, but if this suggests a couple of bald, brown birds on a plate you are mistaken. The partridges, many and various, came with all their retinue of sauces and salads, the sharp and the sweet, each in its order; their potatoes, thin as coins but not so hard; their sprouts, foliated as rosebuds but more succulent. And no sooner had the roast and its retinue been done with than the silent serving-man, the Beadle himself perhaps in a milder manifestation, set before us, wreathed in napkins, a confection which rose all sugar from the waves. To call it pudding and so relate it to rice and tapioca would be an insult. Meanwhile the wineglasses had flushed yellow and flushed crimson; had been emptied; had been filled. And thus by degrees was lit, half-way down the spine, which is the seat of the soul, not that hard little electric light which we call brilliance, as it pops in and out upon our lips, but the more profound, subtle and subterranean glow which is the rich yellow flame of rational intercourse. No need to hurry. No need to sparkle. No need to be anybody but oneself. We are all going to heaven and Vandyck is of the company – in other words, how good life seemed, how sweet its rewards, how trivial this grudge or that grievance, how admirable friendship and the society of one's kind, as, lighting a good cigarette, one sunk among the cushions in the window-seat.

If by good luck there had been an ash-tray handy, if one had not knocked the ash out of the window in default, if things had been a little different from what they were, one would not have seen, presumably, a cat without a tail. The sight of that abrupt and truncated animal padding softly across the quadrangle changed by some fluke of the subconscious intelligence the emotional light for me. It was as if someone had let fall a shade. Perhaps the excellent hock was relinquishing its hold. Certainly, as I watched the Manx cat pause in the middle of the lawn as if it too questioned the universe, something seemed lacking, something seemed different. But what was lacking, what was different, I asked myself, listening to the talk? And to answer that question I had to think myself out of the room, back into the past, before the war indeed, and to set before my eyes the model of another luncheon party held in rooms not very far distant from these; but different. Everything was different. Meanwhile the talk went on among the guests, who were many and young, some of this sex, some of that; it went on swimmingly, it went on agreeably, freely, amusingly. And as it went on I set it against the background of that other talk, and as I matched the two together I had no doubt that one was the descendant, the legitimate heir of the other. Nothing was changed; nothing was different save only – here I listened with all my ears not entirely to what was being said, but to the murmur or current behind it. Yes, that was it – the change was there. Before the war at a luncheon party like this people would have said precisely the same things but they would have sounded different, because in those days they were accompanied by a sort of humming noise, not articulate, but musical, exciting, which changed the value of the words themselves. Could one set that humming noise to words? Perhaps with the help of the poets one could. A book lay beside me and, opening it, I turned casually enough to Tennyson. And here I found Tennyson was singing:

> There has fallen a splendid tear
> From the passion-flower at the gate.
> She is coming, my dove, my dear;
> She is coming, my life, my fate;
> The red rose cries, "She is near, she is near";
> And the white rose weeps, "She is late";
> The larkspur listens, "I hear, I hear";
> And the lily whispers, "I wait."

Was that what men hummed at luncheon parties before the war? And the women?

> My heart is like a singing bird
> Whose nest is in a water'd shoot;
> My heart is like an apple tree
> Whose boughs are bent with thick-set fruit;
> My heart is like a rainbow shell
> That paddles in a halcyon sea;
> My heart is gladder than all these
> Because my love is come to me.

Was that what women hummed at luncheon parties before the war?

There was something so ludicrous in thinking of people humming such things even under their breath at luncheon parties before the war that I burst out laughing, and had to explain my laughter by pointing at the Manx cat, who did look a little absurd, poor beast, without a tail, in the middle of the lawn. Was he really born so, or had he lost his tail in an accident? The tailless cat, though some are said to exist in the Isle of Man, is rarer than one thinks. It is a queer animal, quaint rather than beautiful. It is strange what a difference a tail makes – you know the sort of things one says as a lunch party breaks up and people are finding their coats and hats.

This one, thanks to the hospitality of the host, had lasted far into the afternoon. The beautiful October day was fading and the leaves were falling from the trees in the avenue as I walked through it. Gate after gate seemed to close with gentle finality behind me. Innumerable beadles were fitting innumerable keys into well-oiled locks; the treasure-house was being made secure for another night. After the avenue one comes out upon a road – I forget its name – which leads you, if you take the right turning, along to Fernham. But there was plenty of time. Dinner was not till half-past seven. One could almost do without dinner after such a luncheon. It is strange how a scrap of poetry works in the mind and makes the legs move in time to it along the road. Those words–

> *There has fallen a splendid tear*
> *From the passion-flower at the gate.*
> *She is coming, my dove, my dear–*

sang in my blood as I stepped quickly along towards Headingley. And then, switching off into the other measure, I sang, where the waters are churned up by the weir:

> *My heart is like a singing bird*
> *Whose nest is in a water'd shoot;*
> *My heart is like an apple tree...*

What poets, I cried aloud, as one does in the dusk, what poets they were!

In a sort of jealousy, I suppose, for our own age, silly and absurd though these comparisons are, I went on to wonder if honestly one could name two living poets now as great as Tennyson and Christina Rossetti were then. Obviously it is impossible, I thought, looking into those foaming waters, to compare them. The very reason why that poetry excites one to such abandonment, such rapture, is that it celebrates some feeling that one used to have (at luncheon parties before the war perhaps), so that one responds easily, familiarly, without troubling to check the feeling, or to compare it with any that one has now. But the living poets express a feeling that is actually being made and torn out of us at the moment. One does not recognise it in the first place; often for some reason one fears it; one watches it with keenness and compares it jealously and suspiciously with the old feeling that one knew. Hence the difficulty of modern poetry; and it is because of this difficulty that one cannot remember more than two consecutive lines of any good modern poet. For this reason – that my memory failed me – the argument flagged for want of material. But why, I continued, moving on towards Headingley, have we stopped humming under our breath at luncheon parties? Why has Alfred ceased to sing?

She is coming, my dove, my dear.

Why has Christina ceased to respond?

My heart is gladder than all these
Because my love is come to me?

Shall we lay the blame on the war? When the guns fired in August 1914, did the faces of men and women show so plain in each other's eyes that romance was killed? Certainly it was a shock (to women in particular with their illusions about education, and so on) to see the faces of our rulers in the light of the shell-fire. So ugly they looked – German, English, French – so stupid. But lay the blame where one will, on whom one will, the illusion which inspired Tennyson and Christina Rossetti to sing so passionately about the coming of their loves is far rarer now than then. One has only to read, to look, to listen, to remember. But why say "blame"? Why, if it was an illusion, not praise the catastrophe, whatever it was, that destroyed illusion and put truth in its place? For truth... those dots mark the spot where, in search of truth, I missed the turning up to Fernham. Yes indeed, which was truth and which was illusion, I asked myself? What was the truth about these houses, for example, dim and festive now with their red windows in the dusk, but raw and red and squalid, with their sweets and their bootlaces, at nine o'clock in the morning? And the willows and the river and the gardens that run down to the river, vague now with the mist stealing over them, but gold and red in the sunlight – which was the truth, which was the illusion about them? I spare you the twists and turns of my cogitations, for no conclusion was found on the road to Headingley, and I ask you to suppose that I soon found out my mistake about the turning and retraced my steps to Fernham.

As I have said already that it was an October day, I dare not forfeit your respect and imperil the fair name of fiction by changing the season and describing lilacs hanging over garden walls, crocuses, tulips and other flowers of spring. Fiction must stick to facts, and the truer the facts the better the fiction – so we are told. Therefore it was still autumn and the leaves were still yellow and falling, if anything, a little faster than before, because it was now evening (seven twenty-three to be precise) and a breeze (from the south-west to be exact) had risen. But for all that there was something odd at work:

> *My heart is like a singing bird*
> *Whose nest is in a water'd shoot;*
> *My heart is like an apple tree*
> *Whose boughs are bent with thick-set fruit–*

perhaps the words of Christina Rossetti were partly responsible for the folly of the fancy – it was nothing of course but a fancy – that the lilac was shaking its flowers over the garden walls, and the brimstone butterflies were scudding hither and thither, and the dust of the pollen was in the air. A wind blew, from what quarter I know not, but it lifted the half-grown leaves so that there was a flash of silver grey in the air. It was the time between the lights when colours undergo their intensification and purples and golds burn in window-panes like the beat of an excitable heart; when for some reason the beauty of the world revealed and yet soon to perish (here I pushed into the garden, for, unwisely, the door was left open and no beadles seemed about), the beauty of the world which is so soon to perish, has two edges, one of laughter, one of anguish, cutting the heart asunder. The gardens of Fernham lay before me in the spring twilight, wild and open, and in the long grass, sprinkled and carelessly flung, were daffodils and bluebells, not orderly perhaps at the best of times, and now wind-blown and waving as they tugged at their roots. The windows of the building, curved like ships' windows among generous waves of red brick, changed from lemon to silver under the flight of the quick spring clouds. Somebody was in a hammock, somebody, but in this light they were phantoms only, half guessed, half seen, raced across the grass – would no one stop her? – and then on the terrace, as if popping out to breathe the air, to glance at the garden, came a bent figure, formidable yet humble, with her great forehead and her shabby dress – could it be the famous scholar, could it be J – – H – – herself? All was dim, yet intense too, as if the scarf which the dusk had flung over the garden were torn asunder by star or sword – the flash of some terrible reality leaping, as its way is, out of the heart of the spring. For youth ----

Here was my soup. Dinner was being served in the great dining-hall. Far from being spring it was in fact an evening in October. Everybody was assembled in the big dining-room. Dinner was ready. Here was the soup. It was a plain gravy soup. There was nothing to stir the fancy in that. One could have seen through the transparent liquid any pattern that there might have been on the plate itself. But there was no pattern. The plate was plain. Next came beef with its attendant greens and potatoes – a homely trinity, suggesting the rumps of cattle in a muddy market, and sprouts curled and yellowed at the edge, and bargaining and cheapening, and women with string bags on Monday morning. There was no reason to complain of human nature's daily food, seeing that the supply was sufficient and coal-miners doubtless were sitting down to less. Prunes and custard followed. And if anyone complains that prunes, even when mitigated by custard, are an uncharitable vegetable (fruit they are not), stringy as a miser's heart and exuding a fluid such as might run in misers' veins who have denied themselves wine and warmth for eighty years and yet not given to the poor, he should reflect that there are people whose charity embraces even the prune. Biscuits and cheese came next, and here the water-jug was liberally passed round, for it is the nature of biscuits to be dry, and these were biscuits to the core. That was all. The meal was over. Everybody scraped their chairs back; the swing-doors swung violently to and fro; soon the hall was emptied of every sign of food and made ready no doubt for breakfast next morning. Down corridors and up staircases the youth of England went banging and singing. And was it for a guest, a stranger (for I had no more right here in Fernham than in Trinity or Somerville or Girton or Newnham or Christchurch), to say, "The dinner was not good," or to say (we were now, Mary Seton and I, in her sitting-room), "Could we not have dined up here alone?" for if I had said anything of the kind I should have been prying and searching into the secret economies of a house which to the stranger wears so fine a front of gaiety and courage. No, one could say nothing of the sort. Indeed, conversation for a moment flagged. The human frame being what it is, heart, body and brain all mixed together, and not contained in separate compartments as they will be no doubt in another million years, a good dinner is of great importance to good talk. One cannot think well, love well, sleep well, if one has not dined well. The lamp in the spine does not light on beef and prunes. We are all *probably* going to heaven, and Vandyck is, we *hope*, to meet us round the next corner – that is the dubious and qualifying state of mind that beef and prunes at the end of the day's work breed between them. Happily my friend, who taught science, had a cupboard where there was a squat bottle and little glasses – (but there should have been sole and partridge to begin with) – so that we were able to draw up to the fire and repair some of the damages of the day's living. In a minute or so we were slipping freely in and out among all those objects of curiosity and interest which form in the mind in the absence of a particular person, and are naturally to be discussed on coming together again – how somebody has married, another has not; one thinks this, another that; one has improved out of all knowledge, the other most amazingly gone to the bad – with all those speculations upon human nature and the character of the amazing world we live in which spring naturally from such beginnings. While these things were being said, however, I became shamefacedly aware of a current setting in of its own accord and carrying everything forward to an end of its own. One might be talking of Spain or Portugal, of book or racehorse, but the real interest of whatever was said was none of those things, but a scene of masons on a high roof some five centuries ago. Kings and nobles brought treasure in huge sacks and poured it under the earth. This scene was for ever coming alive in my mind and placing itself by another of lean cows and a muddy market and withered greens and the stringy hearts of old men – these two pictures, disjointed and disconnected and nonsensical as they were, were for ever coming together and combating each other and had me entirely at their mercy. The best course, unless the whole talk was to be distorted, was to expose what was in my mind to the air, when with good luck it would fade and crumble like the head of the dead king when they opened the coffin at Windsor. Briefly, then, I told Miss Seton about the masons who had been all those years on the roof of the chapel, and about the kings and queens and nobles bearing sacks of gold and silver on their shoulders, which they shovelled into the earth; and then how the great financial magnates of our own time came and laid cheques and bonds, I suppose, where the others had laid ingots and rough lumps of gold. All that lies beneath the colleges down there, I said; but this college, where we are now sitting, what lies beneath its gallant red brick and the wild unkempt grasses of the garden? What force is behind that plain china off which we dined, and (here it popped out of my mouth before I could stop it) the beef, the custard and the prunes?

Well, said Mary Seton, about the year 1860 – Oh, but you know the story, she said, bored, I suppose, by the recital. And she told me – rooms were hired. Committees met. Envelopes were addressed. Circulars were drawn up. Meetings were held; letters were read out; so-and-so has promised so much; on the contrary, Mr. ----won't give a penny. The *Saturday Review* has been very rude. How can we raise a fund to pay for offices? Shall we hold a bazaar? Can't we find a pretty girl to sit in the front row? Let us look up what John Stuart Mill said on the subject. Can anyone persuade the editor of the ---- to print a letter? Can we get Lady ---- to sign it? Lady ---- is out of town. That was the way it was done, presumably, sixty years ago, and it was a prodigious effort, and a great deal of time was spent on it. And it was only after a long struggle and with the utmost difficulty that they got thirty thousand pounds together. So obviously we cannot have wine and partridges and servants carrying tin dishes on their heads, she said. We cannot have sofas and separate rooms. "The amenities," she said, quoting from some book or other, "will have to wait."

At the thought of all those women working year after year and finding it hard to get two thousand pounds together, and as much as they could do to get thirty thousand pounds, we burst out in scorn at the reprehensible poverty of our sex. What had our mothers been doing then that they had no wealth to leave us? Powdering their noses? Looking in at shop windows? Flaunting in the sun at Monte Carlo? There were some photographs on the mantelpiece. Mary's mother – if that was her picture – may have been a wastrel in her spare time (she had thirteen children by a minister of the church), but if so her gay and dissipated life had left too few traces of its pleasures on her face. She was a homely body; an old lady in a plaid shawl which was fastened by a large cameo; and she sat in a basket-chair, encouraging a spaniel to look at the camera, with the amused, yet strained expression of one who is sure that the dog will move directly the bulb is pressed. Now if she had gone into business; had become a manufacturer of artificial silk or a magnate on the Stock Exchange; if she had left two or three hundred thousand pounds to Fernham, we could have been sitting at our ease to-night and the subject of our talk might have been archaeology, botany, anthropology, physics, the nature of the atom, mathematics, astronomy, relativity, geography. If only Mrs. Seton and her mother and her mother before her had learnt the great art of making money and had left their money, like their fathers and their grandfathers before them, to found fellowships and lectureships and prizes and scholarships appropriated to the use of their own sex, we might have dined very tolerably up here alone off a bird and a bottle of wine; we might have looked forward without undue confidence to a pleasant and honourable lifetime spent in the shelter of one of the liberally endowed professions. We might have been exploring or writing; mooning about the venerable places of the earth; sitting contemplative on the steps of the Parthenon, or going at ten to an office and coming home comfortably at half-past four to write a little poetry. Only, if Mrs. Seton and her like had gone into business at the age of fifteen, there would have been – that was the snag in the argument – no Mary. What, I asked, did Mary think of that? There between the curtains was the October night, calm and lovely, with a star or two caught in the yellowing trees. Was she ready to resign her share of it and her memories (for they had been a happy family, though a large one) of games and quarrels up in Scotland, which she is never tired of praising for the fineness of its air and the quality of its cakes, in order that Fernham might have been endowed with fifty thousand pounds or so by a stroke of the pen? For, to endow a college would necessitate the suppression of families altogether. Making a fortune and bearing thirteen children – no human being could stand it. Consider the facts, we said. First there are nine months before the baby is born. Then the baby is born. Then there are three or four months spent in feeding the baby. After the baby is fed there are certainly five years spent in playing with the baby. You cannot, it seems, let children run about the streets. People who have seen them running wild in Russia say that the sight is not a pleasant one. People say, too, that human nature takes its shape in the years between one and five. If Mrs. Seton, I said, had been making money, what sort of memories would you have had of games and quarrels? What would you have known of Scotland, and its fine air and cakes and all the rest of it? But it is useless to ask these questions, because you would never have come into existence at all. Moreover, it is equally useless to ask what might have happened if Mrs. Seton and her mother and her mother before her had amassed great wealth and laid it under the foundations of college and library, because, in the first place, to earn money was impossible for them, and in the second, had it been possible, the law denied them the right to possess what money they earned. It is only for the last forty-eight years that Mrs. Seton has had a penny of her own. For all the centuries before that it would have been her husband's property – a thought which, perhaps, may have had its share in keeping Mrs. Seton and her mothers off the Stock Exchange. Every penny I earn, they may have said, will be taken from me and disposed of according to my husband's wisdom – perhaps to found a scholarship or to endow a fellowship in Balliol or Kings, so that to earn money, even if I could earn money, is not a matter that interests me very greatly. I had better leave it to my husband.

At any rate, whether or not the blame rested on the old lady who was looking at the spaniel, there could be no doubt that for some reason or other our mothers had mismanaged their affairs very gravely. Not a penny could be spared for "amenities"; for partridges and wine, beadles and turf, books and cigars, libraries and leisure. To raise bare walls out of the bare earth was the utmost they could do.

So we talked standing at the window and looking, as so many thousands look every night, down on the domes and towers of the famous city beneath us. It was very beautiful, very mysterious in the autumn moonlight. The old stone looked very white and venerable. One thought of all the books that were assembled down there; of the pictures of old prelates and worthies hanging in the panelled rooms; of the painted windows that would be throwing strange globes and crescents on the pavement; of the tablets and memorials and inscriptions; of the fountains and the grass; of the quiet rooms looking across the quiet quadrangles. And (pardon me the thought) I thought, too, of the admirable smoke and drink and the deep arm-chairs and the pleasant carpets: of the urbanity, the geniality, the dignity which are the offspring of luxury and privacy and space. Certainly our mothers had not provided us with any thing comparable to all this – our mothers who found it difficult to scrape together thirty thousand pounds, our mothers who bore thirteen children to ministers of religion at St. Andrews.

So I went back to my inn, and as I walked through the dark streets I pondered this and that, as one does at the end of the day's work. I pondered why it was that Mrs. Seton had no money to leave us; and what effect poverty has on the mind; and what effect wealth has on the mind; and I thought of the queer old gentlemen I had seen that morning with tufts of fur upon their shoulders; and I remembered how if one whistled one of them ran; and I thought of the organ booming in the chapel and of the shut doors of the library; and I thought how unpleasant it is to be locked out; and I thought how it is worse perhaps to be locked in; and, thinking of the safety and prosperity of the one sex and of the poverty and insecurity of the other and of the effect of tradition and of the lack of tradition upon the mind of a writer, I thought at last that it was time to roll up the crumpled skin of the day, with its arguments and its impressions and its anger and its laughter, and cast it into the hedge. A thousand stars were flashing across the blue wastes of the sky. One seemed alone with an inscrutable society. All human beings were laid asleep – prone, horizontal, dumb. Nobody seemed stirring in the streets of Oxbridge. Even the door of the hotel sprang open at the touch of an invisible hand – not a boots was sitting up to light me to bed, it was so late.

MARIE

Madeleine Bourdouxhe

Madeleine Bourdouxhe was a Belgian writer who spent her life in both Belgium and in France. Her novel *Marie*, originally titled *À la Recherche de Marie* (an obvious reference to Proust, whom she greatly admired), was published in 1943. She expressed disdain at attempts to suggest it contained elements of autobiography, noting that the only similarity between herself and the central character was that 'we were both married women'. A book at once domestic and existential, concerned with the internal lives of women, it is quoted several times in Simone de Beauvoir's *The Second Sex*.

Faith Evans is an editor, translator, literary agent and founding member of Women in Publishing, and brought Madeleine Bourdouxhe to an English-speaking audience in the late 1980s.

She will be all alone, the whole long evening. Yet she likes solitude, so why is she feeling like this? She will eat in the kitchen, feet on the bar of the stool, knees up to her chin. One plate, and a chunk of bread that she will cut into little pieces with her knife, in the way that she has seen men do on the side of the road. She will make herself some hot coffee, she will read, for a long time, without anything to distract her from her book. She'll spend the entire evening on her own, in a delicious state of solitude.

She looks around her, around Jean and Marie's apartment, letting her gaze wander over the furniture and the belongings. How odd everything seems; has something changed? No, the furniture and belongings have the same familiar, precious look about them, the same halo bestowed upon them by her heart, and her love is exactly as it has always been. Neither the belongings nor the feelings have changed – but they have been confronted.

Resting her hands on her forehead, Marie closes her eyes. How hot it had been! How beautiful the mountain, and the smell of crushed mint beneath their bodies! This desire she felt inside her was so strong, so blissful, so right.

HOW TO EAT A PEACH

Diana Henry

Dubbed 'Jane Grigson's real heir' by the BBC, **Diana Henry** is the Northern Irish author of twelve extraordinary cookbooks, countless articles, and several award-winning and long-running columns. She began writing in 1998 after the birth of her first son, and swiftly became one of the UK's best-loved food writers with her debut, *Crazy Water, Pickled Lemons*. Her global drive to find the best ingredients, techniques and recipes is matched by the care and great beauty of her writing: her books tend to alternate between the intensely practical good sense of books like *Food From Plenty* and the totally transformative, lyrical prose of books like *How to Eat a Peach*. The editors of this anthology are just two of the many emerging food writers Henry has generously encouraged and supported into existence, and without her, the food landscape of the UK would be very different. She lives in London with her sons and travels as much as possible.

Cider and gitanes
Falling in love with France

Dark, flat sheets of cloud hung in the sky above me. By the time I got to Daniel's they belched rain, and I could hear the snarl of thunder. Daniel lived in a poor bit of Bordeaux, in an old apartment with his family, an angry father who swore through every meal, his bird-like grandma, with her floral house-coats and heavily pencilled eyebrows, and his large, silent grandpa who never said anything, except to ask for the salt. I was working as an au pair at a small family-run zoo outside Bordeaux. Daniel was my boyfriend and the zoo-keeper. I often had supper at his place. On this stormy day the film star Romy Schneider had died. Grandma was in tears. In honour of Romy, a bit more money than usual had been spent, there was *oeufs mayo* and leeks vinaigrette, a hunk of beef, pot-roasted with tomatoes and carrots and cut into soft slices, salad and Roquefort. The bathroom in that apartment was housed in a few sheets of corrugated iron and had a rickety door; it was a demarcation rather than a room. The family was not well off, and yet food was always prepared with care. Grandma continued to sob, looking through her Romy Schneider cuttings, and we quietly ate baked pears.

My time in Bordeaux was my second experience of France. The first was an exchange trip, when I was fifteen. The parents in my host family both worked, but every day culminated in a good dinner. The mother would arrive home with fresh pizza dough, ready to be knocked back, finished with a homemade topping and baked; or a friend would turn up for supper with an apricot tart she'd made on her afternoon off. Cooking was even more important when we went for a month to the father's home village (tiny Lamothe-en-Blaisy, though they called it Lamothe-en-Paradis and it was, indeed, paradise). Every day revolved around the preparation of meals. Clothilde, my counterpart, would start thinking about what to cook for lunch as soon as we'd finished breakfast. Would we do brochettes of lamb? What herb would we put in the vinaigrette today? Salad leaves were carefully washed, then swung in a metal basket outside (the drier the leaves, the better the vinaigrette would cling to them). Provisions were delivered in various vans, the cheesemongers and greengrocers negotiating the dirt tracks that wound between the houses. You could smell the mobile *fromagerie* before it had parked. I was astonished that the greengrocer sold summer fruits not in paper bags or punnets, as in Britain, but in palettes. At home my mum counted out strawberries, dividing them equally between me and my siblings; in France there were glistening tarts piled high with raspberries and people bought stone fruits by the tray.

Clothilde and I spent afternoons at her grandma's going through ancient copies of *Elle*, marking up the dishes we wanted to try. Grandma taught me how to make *tarte aux pommes* with a filling of eggs and crème fraîche; Clothilde's brother showed me how to make perfect crêpes. I loved supper at their aunt's house. Meals there always began with crudités and charcuterie. This spread, accompanied by baguette with a crust that shattered when you broke it, seemed the best way to start any meal, and Paris-Brest, which was often purchased, the best way to end it. (My love for that caused shameful transgressions. It was kept in the sideboard, under a cloth, and I would steal slivers between lunch and dinner. When I got caught red-handed, the father smiled, 'C'est bon le gâteau, hé Diana?')

Back at home, my dream of France was nurtured, fed by films – Truffaut, Chabrol and, especially, those of Eric Rohmer (I liked dramas in which nothing happened, except talking and looking and longing) – books and cooking. For years, my notebook of 'dishes to cook' was full of French regional classics, and many of my fantasy meals were served on checked tablecloths with a Jacques Brel soundtrack. In my twenties, I covered almost the entire country with Patricia Wells's *Food Lover's Guide to France* as my companion. I read about places I couldn't afford, or that were so out of the way I would never find them. The book sent me to a farm in Normandy where they made their own cider and served it with platters of ham and eggs, and to a hotel with a cupboard housing fifty kinds of jam. In a small inn on the French-Swiss border – where the air smelt of cool grass – I had a cloud of cheese soufflé and perfectly cooked trout for dinner, then couldn't sleep because of the tinkling of cowbells (I lay in the dark, thinking how wonderful it was not to be able to sleep because of the *sound of cowbells*).

I could have chosen a meal from any bit of France, but the most accessible areas, once I was living in London, were Normandy and Brittany and, later, the coast by La Rochelle. For years, I went to the French seaside at Easter. A trip to Normandy always meant a meal at Les Vapeurs in Trouville, an Art Deco brasserie with paper tablecloths, swift, skinny waiters and teetering towers of *fruits de mer* on avalanches of crushed ice. I couldn't afford the platters then, but I was happy with a pot of mussels cooked in cider, enriched with Normandy cream. Brittany meant buckwheat crepes, more cider and a wilder coastline. It's a place set apart from the rest of France, harsh and no-nonsense, less romantic. Lunch there was oysters and sourdough from a stall on the roadside, supper a roll-your-sleeves-up affair where you tucked into crevettes and crab claws. The salty tang of seaweed and the aroma of caramelized sugar – from mobile *crêperies* – hung in the air.

There was a time when good food meant French food. To me it still does, though now you have to know where to find it. In France, as elsewhere, food has become industrialized. The country has lost its influence, partly because, in the area of haute cuisine, Spain flexed its muscles, then the Nordic countries, though Western chefs still rely on French technique more than any other. My kitchen, like that of many cooks, is now full of Middle Eastern grains and Asian spices. Travel has opened doors. Interest in food has increased, but at the same time we take the old and the familiar for granted; there's a tendency to love the new, whatever is 'now'. Classic French food is both simple and complex. The dishes appear to be easy, but you have to pay attention. Dishes have harmony and what the French call *volupté*, meaning they please the senses. A lot of modern food, in contrast, can be cerebral and austere; the elements sit on the plate but don't come together. A good friend, who is a restaurant critic, often says, 'Whatever happened to deliciousness?' Then we daydream about a perfectly dressed green salad, cassoulet and tarte Tatin.

Even though I'd already learned a lot in our kitchen at home in Northern Ireland, France was the first place that showed me the joy that cooking could bring me, both in the process and in the dishes I could put on the table. It pretty much made me a cook. So France is where we're going first.

Kir Breton

Kirs are usually made with crème de cassis and, traditionally, Bourgogne Aligoté (a white Burgundy), but *kirs Bretons* – and also *kirs Normands* – are made with cider. Just put a drop of crème de cassis in the bottom of each glass and top it up with dry cider… preferably from Brittany or Normandy, obviously.

Leeks with Breton vinaigrette
serves 4

Leeks vinaigrette was one of the dishes that made me fall in love with French food; I ate it on my first trip to France when I went there on an exchange trip. Most people can make leeks vinaigrette without a recipe, but the dressing here, that I tried while on holiday in Brittany, goes beyond the standard and is worth knowing. I usually serve this with the other bits and pieces that make up the French spread they describe (rather modestly) as crudités: radishes, hard-boiled eggs, charcuterie, sometimes other vegetable dishes such as *carrottes rapées* and *lentilles en salade*.

1 scant tablespoon white wine vinegar, or to taste

¼ teaspoon Dijon mustard, or to taste

pinch of ground mixed spice

sea salt flakes and freshly ground black pepper

8 tablespoons extra virgin olive oil

good pinch of caster sugar

1½ tablespoons capers, rinsed and patted dry

½ tablespoon very finely chopped shallot

1 tablespoon finely chopped flat-leaf parsley leaves

½ tablespoon each finely chopped chervil leaves and chives

6 medium leeks

Make the vinaigrette by mixing together the white wine vinegar, Dijon mustard and mixed spice with some salt and pepper in a small bowl.

Whisk in the extra virgin olive oil with a fork. Add the sugar, capers, shallot and herbs and taste for seasoning and balance (you might need a little more vinegar or mustard). It's good to make this about 30 minutes in advance, so that the flavours can meld.

Remove the tough outer leaves from the leeks and discard them. Slice off the tufty bit on the base of each leek, and also the dark green tops. Cut the leeks into 4cm (1½in) lengths. Wash them really well, making sure that you get rid of any grit or soil between the layers. Steam over boiling water – this way the leeks don't become too 'wet' – for 4–6 minutes. They should be completely tender right through (test with the tip of a sharp knife).

As soon as they're done, tip them on to a clean tea towel and gently pat to soak up the excess moisture; the dressing clings to the leeks much better if they're not wet. Immediately put them into a serving bowl and, while they're still hot, dress them with the vinaigrette. Taste to check the seasoning, then serve warm or at room temperature.

Rillettes
makes about 1kg (2lb 4oz)

Home-made rillettes usually taste better than ready-made (at least when you're not in France). They do take time, though not a lot of effort, and this should be an easy meal, so buy the rillettes if you prefer. To render pork fat, cut the fat into cubes, melt it in a heavy-based saucepan over a low heat, then strain the resulting liquid fat through a sieve. This recipe makes more than you need; half the quantity will feed four people and the rest, well sealed with fat, will last for up to four months in the fridge. Halve the quantities if you prefer, but be warned that it's better to make rillettes in large quantities, otherwise it tends to get dry while cooking, so I would recommend making this larger amount.

500g (1lb 2oz) boneless pork shoulder

500g (1lb 2oz) boneless pork belly, rind removed

350g (12oz) rendered pork fat (see recipe introduction), or good-quality bought lard

6 thyme sprigs

3 bay leaves

4 cloves

generous pinch of ground mixed spice

generous grating of nutmeg

plenty of sea salt flakes and freshly ground black pepper

Cut the pork shoulder into strips about 2cm (¾in) across, along the grain of the meat. Cut the belly into slices about 1cm (½in) thick. Put the fat and 100ml (3½fl oz) of water into a broad, heavy-based saucepan and set it over a very low heat. Add all the meat. Tie the thyme, bay leaves and cloves in a square of muslin (or a bit of brand new J-cloth) and add this to the pot. Cook over a very low heat so the liquid just quivers, not bubbles, for about 4 hours. The meat shouldn't brown, just poach, and must always be covered with fat. Make sure it doesn't stick to the pan, and turn it from time to time. It's ready when it is completely tender and feels as if you can gently pull it apart.

Once the meat has cooled a bit, remove the spice and herb bag and shred the meat in the pan, pulling it apart with 2 forks. It should break down into rough, soft strands. Strain the meat through a colander over a bowl and collect the fat. Put the meat into another bowl and add the mixed spice, nutmeg and some salt and pepper; be generous, you need to season well to make good rillettes. Add enough of the fat to make a creamy mixture, and reserve the rest.

Put the mixture into bowls – or pack it into jars with no air pockets, if you want to keep it for longer – cover with greaseproof paper that you've rubbed with pork fat and leave to completely cool; it will firm up a bit. Melt some of the reserved pork fat and pour it over the tops to form a seal. Put the papers back on top and put in the fridge.

The rillettes taste better after a couple of days, though I tend to eat some straight away. If you pack it in jars with no air pockets and cover with 5mm (¼in) of fat, it should last in the fridge for about 4 months. Once you've broken the protective layer of fat, eat within 5 days.

Mouclade
serves 4

Mouclade is eaten in and around La Rochelle, on the west coast of France. There are different versions, but the characteristic ingredient is curry powder.

The dish, when you include saffron as well, has a lovely golden colour.

good pinch of saffron threads
2kg (4lb 8oz) mussels
30g (1oz) unsalted butter
1 small onion, finely chopped
2 garlic cloves, crushed
¾ teaspoon medium curry powder
4 tablespoons brandy
2 teaspoons plain flour
200ml (7fl oz) dry white wine
200ml (7fl oz) double cream
sea salt flakes and freshly ground black pepper
generous handful of flat-leaf parsley leaves, finely chopped

Put the saffron in a cup and add 5 tablespoons of boiling water. Leave to steep for 30 minutes.

Clean the mussels, removing any beards and barnacles (scrape the latter off with a table knife) and washing the shells. Tap each against the sink as you go and discard any that remain open and don't close.

Melt the butter in a pan and gently sauté the onion until soft but not coloured. Add the garlic and curry powder and cook for another 2 minutes to release the curry's fragrance. Add the brandy and let it boil until it has reduced to a couple of tablespoons. Reduce the heat, then stir in the flour, mixing well until everything is smooth. Cook for a minute, then take the pan off the heat and gradually add the saffron and its water, stirring as you do so. Set aside.

Put the wine and the mussels into a large saucepan and cover. Cook over a medium-high heat for about 4 minutes, shaking the pan from time to time, until the mussels have opened. Strain the mussels (use a large colander), collecting their liquor in a bowl underneath. Discard any mussels that haven't opened and put the rest back into the saucepan. Cover to keep warm.

Strain the cooking liquor through a sieve lined with muslin, or a brand new J-cloth (you need to get rid of any sand or grit), and gently reheat the saffron sauce you were making earlier. Gradually add the mussel liquor, stirring as you do so, then bring the sauce to the boil and simmer for about 3 minutes. Add the cream and simmer for a further 4 minutes until it has reduced and the sauce is a little thicker. Taste for seasoning and stir in the parsley.

Put the mussels in a large warmed serving bowl – or keep them in the saucepan in which they were cooked, if you prefer – pour over the sauce and serve immediately.

Crêpes *dentelles* with sautéed apples & caramel
serves 4

The word *dentelles* means 'lace' and refers to the fine, delicate edges of these crêpes. Making them well requires a few tricks, though they're easy to master: quickly tip the pan so that the batter thinly coats the base, pour off the excess every time you add more batter, adjust the heat as necessary, and be careful not to add too much butter. You need a well-seasoned pan that has become non-stick through wear, or a good nonstick pan. The first pancake is always a dud, so don't worry. I was taught to make these by my first French boyfriend. He was called Christophe. I was fifteen. So, for me, this is more than just a recipe.

for the crêpes
125g (4½oz) plain flour
30g (1oz) caster sugar
pinch of sea salt flakes
300ml (½ pint) whole milk
1 egg, plus 1 egg yolk
30g (1oz) unsalted butter, melted,
plus more to cook
crème fraîche, to serve

for the caramel

50g (1¾oz) unsalted butter

125ml (4fl oz) double cream

100g (3½oz) soft light brown sugar

½ teaspoon sea salt flakes

¼ teaspoon vanilla extract

for the apples

2 tart apples, peeled, halved and cored

50g (1¾oz) unsalted butter

1 tablespoon caster sugar

Sift the flour, sugar and salt into a bowl and make a well in the centre. In a jug, beat the milk, egg and egg yolk with 100ml (3½fl oz) of water and gradually whisk this into the well, until smooth. Stir in the melted butter, cover and rest for 1 hour. (Or make this in a blender. Blend for 1 minute, scrape down the sides, then blend for another 5 seconds.)

Meanwhile, to make the caramel, put the butter in a large saucepan (the sauce will bubble a lot and you need room for that) and melt it over a medium heat. Add the cream, sugar and salt and bring to the boil, stirring to help the sugar dissolve. Reduce the heat and simmer for 10 minutes, whisking from time to time. Add the vanilla.

Cut the apples into thin wedges, about 5mm (¼in) at the thickest part, and heat the butter in a frying pan. Don't crowd the pan, or the apples will steam instead of fry. Sauté on both sides until golden (they can still be a little firm in the middle). Sprinkle with the sugar and cook over a medium heat until a little caramelized (about 3 minutes). Lay the apples on a plate in a single layer; if they're on top of each other they continue to cook and can lose their nice sugar-toasted edges.

Melt a very small knob of butter in a well-seasoned or non-stick frying pan and swirl it, just to coat the pan. Ladle in batter – again just enough to thinly coat – quickly swirl it and pour off any excess (these crêpes need to be really thin). Cook over a medium heat until golden underneath, then flip with a palette knife and cook the other side. Add small amounts of butter as you need it, but never too much. If the pan gets too hot and you burn the butter, wipe it out and start again. Keep the pancakes in a pile in a low oven until you've cooked them all.

Serve the pancakes with the apples and caramel – if you've made the sauce in advance, gently reheat it if you like – and crème fraîche.

THE YEAR OF MIRACLES

Ella Risbridger

Writer, anthologizer and editor **Ella Risbridger**'s name is on the cover of this book. But she would be here regardless; after the publication of her genre-defying, bestselling *Midnight Chicken (& other recipes worth living for)*, *The Sunday Times* described her as 'the most talented British debut writer in a generation'. Her follow-up, 2022's *The Year of Miracles (recipes about love + grief + growing things)* was described by Nigel Slater as 'a work of quiet genius', by Nigella Lawson as 'an act of compassion', by Diana Henry as 'a book full of wisdom', and was shortlisted for the 2023 André Simon Food Book Award. Risbridger is also a children's author, columnist, essayist and poetry expert, and a truly perfect host. Her writing is intimate, clever, funny and, above all, generous: she loves people, words, food, nature, and life with joyous, hopeful abandon – her books challenge and invite you to be in love too. She lives in southeast London. KY

Bourride

When I was in my late teens, I lived briefly in a castle.

You can just do this, I thought; *you can just move to France, and live in a castle!*

The food in the castle was terrible, and so I managed sometimes to take the long, slow bus to Aix. I found an English bookshop there; a café that sold cheap coffee; and a restaurant that sold real Provençal food: bread, and butter, and bourride.

Bourride is a sort of half-soup, half-stew thing: rich court-bouillon (fish stock cooked slow with shallots, celery and herbs), transformed with whisked golden aioli into a creamy, garlicky, smoky, saffron-scented broth, thick and rich and shimmering; and within it little slices of potato, poached in the broth until tender, and plump pink prawns, and fat flakes of ivory cod; and the whole thing poured over a chunky, griddled slice of sourdough bread, buttered and charred, so that it soaks up the sweet, smoky oil and rich, buttery cream. More bread to dunk.

I woke up this morning and knew I wanted to make bourride. I woke up this morning with a feeling: a feeling that something had to happen, a feeling like moving to a castle, or a feeling like running away.

So I lived in this castle on a vineyard, miles from anywhere, where I slept in a dirty little attic, and I worked for a family so strange and so old that, even as it was happening, I thought: *someday I'm going to tell this story.* In the end, I ran away from the castle, to live with Nelius in Paris.

I made a life there; and then I met Jim, and moved to East London, and made a life there too; and then I met Jo, and moved to South London, and made a new kind of life again. And now there is Theo, too. Theo who – for now, for a while, forever, who knows? – is here, and alive, and in my life. I prop the phone against the toaster (Georgie's spot) and call him.

'I am sick of living so far away,' he says, by way of hello. 'I'm sick of not being able to see you. I'm sick of the cat not being able to go outside.'

Weetabix wants – desperately wants – to be an outside cat. He pushes his little honey face against the glass of the doors, twines himself out onto the balcony whenever he slips past Theo.

'Look at him,' Theo says, and holds the phone so I can see. Weetabix is chasing a spider; the spider is on the other side of the window. 'He hates this. I hate this.'

'If you hate it,' I say. I stir the soup, decide if I'm brave enough. 'If you hate it, you should move.'

'Move?' he says.

'Near me,' I say. 'Near us. Near me and Jo, so I can walk to you. So you can come for dinner with us. You should move near me.'

'I should move near you,' he says, and then, as if he's just hearing it for the first time, bright as garlic, sweet as oil: '*I should move near you.*'

'If you wanted,' I say, whisking the aioli. People think aioli is going to be difficult, but it doesn't have to be. You just have to be careful, but not cautious. You can't hesitate too much. You just have to do it.

'I think I want,' he says.

'I want, too,' I say; and I am struck again – as always – by the power of saying, out loud, what it is you want; the bright sweet joy when someone answers, and will give it.

For 4
½ white onion + ½ white onion
½ leek + ½ leek
½ fennel bulb + ½ fennel bulb
1 tsp olive oil + 1 tsp olive oil
750ml boiling water
100ml + 100ml white wine
2 fish stock pots
A few sprigs of thyme
115g new potatoes
150g smoked mackerel

150g white fish fillets
120g peeled cooked prawns
Baguette, to serve

For the aioli
3 garlic cloves
3 egg yolks
3 tbsp white wine vinegar
Pinch of salt
250ml olive oil
Lemon juice, to taste

Finely chop one half of the onion, well-rinsed leek and fennel bulb. Most cultures have a three-ingredient base that goes in most things – soffritto, mirepoix, The Holy Trinity – and this might be mine. I am addicted to the bite of fennel, the softness of leek, the sharpness of onion or shallot.

In a heavy saucepan, sauté these three lovely things in a teaspoon of olive oil for 10 minutes. Pour in 750ml of boiling water and 100ml of the white wine, then add the fish stock pots and stir. Thyme in too. This is, basically, an approximation of a court-bouillon, which I know is not the proper way to do things, but I can't get my head around boiling fish heads in a shared flat. So here we are. Let it simmer for perhaps an hour, 90 minutes if you've got it.

For the aioli – it sounds complex but couldn't be easier – grate the garlic into the bowl of a food processor and add the egg yolks, vinegar and salt. With the motor running, gradually drizzle in the olive oil. A little lemon juice, to taste. This is, literally, it: a perfect garlicky mayonnaise that keeps well and can be used for everything you would use mayo for. (We are going to use some of it to thicken the broth, and some of it on bread, for dipping.)

Finely chop the other half of the onion, leek and fennel and sauté them with the other teaspoon of olive oil in a saucepan until soft, about 15 minutes. Add the remaining 100ml of white wine and reduce down by half. This will take about another 15 minutes – and in this time, you should chop the new potatoes into pieces the size of a fingertip.

Strain the fake court-bouillon into a bowl (be careful not to accidentally pour away the precious liquid; you want that!), then pour back into the saucepan. Chuck away the strained-out bits.

Bring your fake court-bouillon to a simmer and add the potatoes. Cook for 5 minutes, then add the fish and prawns and cook for 10 minutes more. Have bowls ready.

Divide the fennel, onion and leek between the two bowls; with a slotted spoon, lift out the fish. Flake the fish (throw away the skin), and divide between bowls. Lift out the potatoes, and divide those between the bowls as well.

A baguette, probably. (Almost certainly a part-bake, given this year.)

Here's the only tricky bit: you need to whisk half of the aioli with all of the broth. The trick to it not splitting is to whisk the broth into the aioli, and not the other way around. So. Put half of the aioli into an empty saucepan (probably the one you sautéed the vegetables in?).

A little at a time, and whisking constantly, add the hot broth. A spoonful of broth; whisk until smooth. Repeat, repeat, repeat.

Pour delicious garlicky broth over fish and potatoes in bowls. Spread remaining aioli on hot baguette. Remember a castle, a long time ago, and a story that got you out of there, and a story that brought you here, and brought you home.

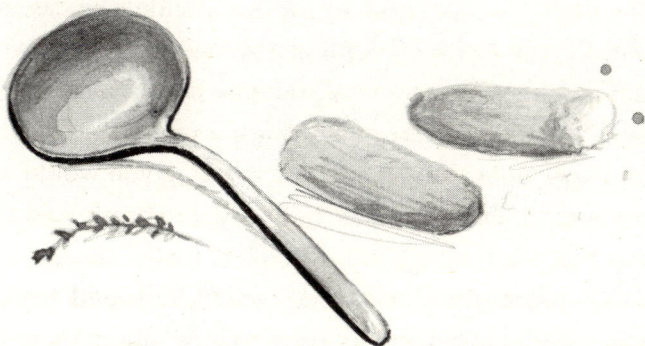

Theo's Chicken

We think the kitten is going to die, and to take our minds off it we are inventing recipes.

The kitten is tiny, the size of two fists plus a tail, and the colour of honey on toast. His name is, of course, Weetabix.

'He's so small,' I say.

'He isn't going to die,' Theo says. We are on the phone again. I am sitting in the doorway of the kitchen; across town he is lying on his bed, the kitten stretched out, trembling, against Theo's heart. He sounds very certain, but I know he can't be. I don't say anything.

'He isn't going to die,' he says again, like he knows.

'You don't know,' I say. 'How do you know that?'

'I do,' he says. 'I just do.'

The kitten's eyes are enormous, but he himself is very small, and he is ill in a way that the vet can't exactly define. It all feels, to me, extremely familiar; and already I feel very afraid that I love the kitten just a little bit too much. He is so small: too small to love, surely.

Don't get attached, I think of Freddy saying; and of Nancy saying *don't fall in love, or anything*, and I worry that it is much too late for all of that. I am attached, terribly attached, both to the kitten and the man who owns the kitten.

'I'm not going to get attached,' I said, out loud. 'I'm not.' I thought of the man standing in my kitchen, leaning against the fridge, looking at the cucumber plants.

I want to know your taste in pepper mills and salad spoons so intimately that I could replace your whole kitchen from a John Lewis catalogue if I had to, he had said. I wanted him to know, too. I wanted him to be part of this kitchen of mine, with everyone else. I wanted him to know things.

After I read the text again, I leant against the fridge and stared at the cucumber plants, as if they would tell me something reassuring; as if they could tell me I'm not falling in love in the kitchen again. 'I'm not,' I said aloud to the triffid cucumber plants. 'I'm not attached, and I'm not in love. Not this time.' The cucumber plants said nothing.

The thing was really, even then, when he sent the text, it was much too late. You can't not get attached; or I can't, anyway. I'm always attached to everything: I live in the centre of a web, like a happy spider, and everything is connected, and everything is attached, and sometimes you just know. I always just know: I have fallen in love a hundred times, and every time I have just known. I would like to be able to tell you that I don't believe in love at first sight. I'd like to be able to tell you that, because love at first sight makes no sense: I can't see any rational reason to believe in meeting someone's eyes and knowing, absolutely, that they are the one.

But here we are: I've never met anybody who mattered in my life without knowing at once.

I met Nancy at a costume party my first year in London; we locked eyes and fell hopelessly in love and knew we were best friends. Danny – a work colleague of Jim, and a stranger to me – turned up an hour early to a dinner party I'd forgotten was happening; we started talking about music and pies and we've been doing that, pretty much, ever since. Rosa offered me a doughnut in a pub; Nora, then three, crawled into my lap at a house party, a bedtime escapee clutching a blankie covered in printed roses. Debo asked me about a (cheerfully gaudy) statuette of Catherine of Aragon in my window; I ran into Nelius's arms outside the Gare du Nord on an unseasonably warm October day; I saw Rachel in a queue and immediately texted a mutual friend to demand we be set up.

I met Jo on a rainy night in Camden a lifetime ago, and I knew I would follow her to the ends of the earth. Her face was painted very white, with cheekbones underlined in grey; and she was wearing a kind of Black Swan costume, and she was standing on a soundstage drinking whiskey and ginger. I made a mental note to order whiskey and ginger, too. Jim called her 'Boss', and she was nice enough to me; and I saw her looking at me to see if I knew what I'd got myself into with this mess of a man. I was afraid of her, and she seemed like somebody from another world, and I thought: *I would follow you to the ends of the earth.*

I am not a person who can decide not to get attached, and stay not attached. Is anyone, really? And so I go back to inventing recipes. I write: *what if we had a chicken with gochujang?* Then I write: *I am out of gochujang. And it will take a couple of days to get here if I order more.*

Miso, Theo says. *Miso and ketchup, mixed. A little brown sugar, a little chilli.*

He says it firmly, like he knows.

And he does. The chicken, when we make it, is perfect – perhaps the best chicken I know now, joint equal with Midnight: sticky and umami and charred and magnificent. It just works, is all I can tell you. It just works, whether it should or it shouldn't. It just does exactly what you want it to do.

It needed sesame oil, and the kitten needed medicine, but he was right about both. It is all all right, in the end, and sometimes nobody dies, and sometimes there's chicken, sticky and rich the night before and cold and tender the next morning. There's always a next morning, and sometimes nobody dies.

One large chicken: for 4 people, for 2 people, for 1 person alone at midnight and in need of bright, deep flavour

2 red onions

1 × 1.6kg chicken

Pinch of salt

1 lemon

For the marinade

50g miso

30g ketchup

2 tsp soft brown sugar *(light or dark!)*

2 tsp chilli oil

1 tbsp sesame oil

2 garlic cloves *(although, this is one of the rare occasions when jarred or paste is absolutely fine, and maybe even better: 2 tsp chopped garlic)*

2 tsp chopped ginger *(ditto)*

Thinly slice the onions into half-moons, and line the roasting tin with them. Set the chicken on top of the onions and sprinkle the skin with a pinch of salt: not too much salt, that's what the miso's for. This is just to dry it out a little, for extra crisp.

Whisk together the marinade ingredients, then slather the marinade generously onto the chicken; get it right into the crevices. You can leave it to marinate for a few hours, if you want, or get straight to it.

Pre-heat the oven to 220°C.

Push the lemon up its little bottom, then slide into the oven and cook for 20 minutes. Turn the heat down to 200°C and cook for a further 50 minutes. It will look burnt. It kind of is. That's the point. (Just trust me.) It will glisten and crackle, all bronze highlights and charcoal shadows, caramel and burn and shine and split.

Serve with...well, look. There are vegetables, there are salads, there are all the trappings of roast chicken – but really what you want here is a big hunk of part-bake baguette and a pickle.

SALT, FAT, ACID, HEAT

Samin Nosrat

Equally passionate about food and words, chef and writer **Samin Nosrat** aims to create work that 'inspires, creates community, and raises cultural, social and environmental awareness'. Born in San Diego to parents who had fled Iran as religious refugees, she studied undergraduate English at Berkeley and trained as a chef in California and in Italy. Nostrat's groundbreaking, multi-award-winning, bestselling debut cookbook *Salt, Fat, Acid, Heat: Mastering the Elements of Good Cooking* was released in 2017, and was selected by the *New Yorker* as one of the ten best cookbooks of the twenty-first century. Drawing on her years as a chef at Chez Panisse, the book is both conversational and deeply, usefully, instructional. It cemented the position that her former boss, chef Alice Waters, had predicted for her: as 'America's next great cooking teacher'. In 2018 she adapted the book as a four-part series with Netflix; the result is a showcase of home cooking, skills passed down through generations, and of the joy of sharing good food. It is a showcase too for Nosrat's generosity and warmth, her insatiable curiosity, and her 'uncommon earnestness on camera'. Nosrat lives in California, surrounded by a multi-generational community of beloved friends.

Crispiest Spatchcocked Chicken
serves 4

Two tricks make this simple recipe the most extraordinary way I know to cook a whole chicken. First, spatchcocking. **Spatchcocking** is the term for removing a bird's backbone and then splaying it so it lies flat, but I like to think of it as a way to increase surface area for browning while decreasing cooking time. (It's also my favourite way to cook Thanksgiving turkey, cutting down cooking time by nearly half!)

The second trick is one I stumbled on by mistake at Eccolo, when one of my cooks seasoned a few chickens and left them uncovered in the walk-in overnight. When I came in the next day, I was annoyed by his negligence. The constantly circulating air of the walk-in—like that of any refrigerator—had dried out the chicken skin, and the birds looked scarily fossilized. But I had no choice, so I cooked them anyway. The dried-out skin cooked up golden and glassy. It was the crispiest roast chicken skin I'd ever seen, even after the bird had rested.

If you don't have a chance to season the chicken and let its skin dry out overnight, season it as early as possible, then pat it dry with a paper towel before you begin to cook it. It'll help achieve a similar effect.

1.8kg whole chicken
Salt
Extra-virgin olive oil

The day before you plan to cook the chicken, spatchcock it (or ask your butcher to help!). Use heavy-duty kitchen shears to snip down along both sides of the spine (the underside of the bird) and remove it. You can start from the tail or neck end, whichever you prefer. Once you've removed the spine, reserve it for stock. Remove the wingtips and reserve them for stock, too.

Lay the chicken on the cutting board, breast side up. Push down on the breastbone until you hear the cartilage pop and the bird lies flat. Generously season the bird with salt on both sides. Place it breast side up into a shallow roasting dish and refrigerate, uncovered, overnight.

Pull the bird out of the fridge an hour before you plan to cook it. Preheat the oven to 220°C, with a rack positioned in the upper third of the oven.

Heat a 25 or 30cm cast iron pan or other ovenproof frying pan over medium-high heat. Add just enough olive oil to coat the bottom of the pan. As soon as the oil shimmers, place the chicken in the pan, breast side down, and brown for 6 to 8 minutes, until golden. It's fine if the bird doesn't lie completely flat as long as the breast is in contact with the pan. Flip the bird over (again, it's fine if it doesn't lie entirely flat) and slide the entire cast iron pan into the oven on the prepared rack. Push the pan all the way to the very back of the oven, with the handle of the pan facing left.

After about 20 minutes, carefully use an oven mitt to rotate the pan 180 degrees so the handle faces right and return it to the very back of the top rack.

Cook until the chicken is brown all over and the juices run clear when you cut between the leg and the thigh, about 45 minutes.

Let rest 10 minutes before carving. Serve warm or at room temperature.

Spicy fried chicken
serves 4 to 6

Gus's in Memphis makes the best fried chicken I've ever tasted. Once, on my way through town, I had lunch there alongside the after-church crowd. Spicy, crisp, and perfectly seasoned, this fried chicken was a revelation. Though I begged the cooks for any hints about how they got the crust so crisp and the chicken so tender, they didn't reveal anything, so I returned home and started to experiment. After cooking a whole lot of fried chicken, I found that cracking a couple of eggs into the buttermilk, as well as double-dredging, resulted in a crust that held up. And while I'm fairly certain the folks at Gus's don't use smoked paprika, I'm now addicted to brushing this sweet-and-smoky spice oil all over the chicken before serving it, so I'm not sure I'll ever be able to do it another way. Unless Gus's finally gives up their recipe.

1.8kg chicken, cut into 10 pieces, or 1.3kg bone-in, skin-on chicken thighs
Salt
2 large eggs
450ml buttermilk
1 tablespoon hot sauce (my favourite is Valentina!)
385g plain flour
1.3 to 1.8 litres grapeseed, peanut, or canola oil for frying, plus 55ml for the spicy oil

2 tablespoons cayenne pepper

1 tablespoon dark brown sugar

½ teaspoon smoked paprika

½ teaspoon toasted cumin, finely ground

1 garlic clove, finely grated or pounded with a pinch of salt

Prep the chicken in advance of cooking. If using a whole chicken, cut it into 10 pieces—follow the instructions on the previous page to get 8 pieces and then add in the wings for a total of 10 pieces. Save the carcass for your next batch of chicken stock. If using thighs, bone them out and cut them in half. Season generously with salt on all sides. I prefer to season chicken the night before, but if you don't have that much time, try to give the salt at least an hour to diffuse throughout the meat before cooking. Refrigerate the chicken if seasoning more than an hour in advance; otherwise, leave it out on the worktop.

Whisk together the eggs, buttermilk, and hot sauce in a large bowl. Set aside. Whisk the flour and 2 generous pinches of salt together in another bowl. Set aside.

Place a wide, deep pan over medium heat. Add oil to a depth of 4cm, and heat to 180°C. Begin dredging the chicken, one or two pieces at a time. First, dredge in flour and shake off the excess, then dip into buttermilk, letting the excess drip back into the bowl, then return to the flour mixture and dredge a final time. Shake off the excess and place on a baking sheet.

Fry chicken in two or three rounds, letting the temperature of the oil drop to and hover around 160°C while the chicken cooks. Use metal tongs to turn the chicken occasionally, until the skin is a deep golden brown, about 12 minutes (closer to 16 minutes for large pieces, and 9 minutes for small pieces). If you are unsure that the meat is cooked through, poke through the crust with a paring knife and peek at the meat. It should be cooked all the way down to the bone, and any juice the meat gives off should run clear. If the meat is still raw or the juice has the slightest hint of pink, return the chicken to the oil and continue cooking until it's done.

Let cool on a wire rack set over a baking sheet.

Combine the cayenne pepper, brown sugar, paprika, cumin, and garlic in a small bowl, and add the 55ml oil. Brush the chicken with the spicy oil and serve immediately.

Variations

- For even more tender meat, marinate the seasoned chicken in the buttermilk overnight.
- To make **Classic Fried Chicken,** omit the hot sauce and spicy oil. Add ½ teaspoon cayenne pepper and 1 teaspoon paprika to flour and prepare as above.
- To make **Indian-Spiced Fried Chicken,** omit the hot sauce and spicy oil. Season the chicken in advance with 4 teaspoons curry powder, 2 teaspoons ground cumin, and ½ teaspoon cayenne pepper in addition to salt. Add 1 tablespoon curry powder and 1 teaspoon paprika to the flour mixture and prepare as above. Make a glaze by heating 300g mango chutney with 3 tablespoons water, ¼ teaspoon cayenne pepper, and a pinch of salt. Brush onto the cooked chicken and serve immediately.

Chicken Confit
serves 4

Take a page out of the French farmwife's handbook and keep confit on hand to save you from dinnertime desperation. Easy enough to make while you watch a movie or do the Sunday crossword, there's no reason not to try this recipe. I make a big batch once or twice each winter. I just stick it in the fridge, where it quickly makes its way to the back of the bottom shelf, a spot I rarely think to look. But I inevitably find it just when I need it most—when an unexpected friend shows up for dinner, or I just can't muster the energy to cook. And, every time, I give silent thanks to that thoughtful, industrious earlier version of myself. You will, too.

If you can't find or make duck fat, pure olive oil will work just fine.

But if you do make the effort to find or render your own duck fat, you'll be rewarded in flavour. (There aren't many other uses for duck fat in the kitchen, but for roasting or frying potatoes, the excess fat from confit is an unforgettable one.) Serve the chicken and potatoes with a pile of rocket or chicories dressed in a bright, honey-mustard vinaigrette and spoonfuls of herb salsa for a welcome acidic contrast.

    4 chicken legs, with thighs attached
    Salt
    Freshly ground black pepper
    4 sprigs fresh thyme
    4 cloves
    2 bay leaves
    3 garlic cloves, halved
    About 900ml duck or chicken fat or olive oil

Prep the chicken a day in advance. Use a sharp knife to slit the skin at the base around each drumstick, just above the ankle joint. Cut all the way around, down to the bone, making sure to sever the tendons. Season with salt and pepper. Layer in a dish with the thyme, cloves, bay leaves, and garlic. Cover and refrigerate overnight.

To prepare, remove the aromatics and lay the legs into a large cast iron casserole or pot in a single layer. If using duck or chicken fat, warm gently in a medium saucepan just until it liquefies. Pour enough fat into the casserole or pot to submerge the meat, and then heat over a medium flame until the first bubbles emerge from the chicken. Reduce the heat so that the fat never surpasses the slightest simmer. Cook until the meat is tender at the bone, about 2 hours.

(Alternatively, cook the whole thing in the oven, at about 95°C. Use the same cues to guide you as in stovetop simmering.)

When the meat is cooked, turn off the heat and let it cool in the fat for a little while. Using metal tongs, carefully remove the chicken from the fat. Grab the bone at the ankle end to avoid tearing the skin.

Let the meat and fat cool, then place the chicken into a glass or ceramic dish, and strain the fat over it, ensuring it's completely submerged. Cover with a lid. Store in the fridge for up to 6 months.

To serve, remove the chicken from the fat, scraping off excess. Heat a cast iron pan over a medium flame, and place chicken, skin-side down, into the pan. As with **Conveyor Belt Chicken**, use the weight of a second, foil-wrapped cast iron pan to help render the fat and crisp the skin. Place the pan on top of the chicken and heat gently to crisp the skin at the same rate the meat reheats. As you start to hear crackles, rather than sizzles, pay closer attention to the meat so it doesn't burn. Once the skin is browned, flip the chicken and continue reheating the leg on the second side without a weight. The whole process will take about 15 minutes.

Serve immediately.

Variations

- For **Duck Confit,** cook 2½ to 3 hours, until the meat is tender and falling off the bone.
- For **Turkey Confit,** increase duck fat to 2 litres and cook 3 to 3½ hours, until the meat is tender and falling off the bone.
- For **Pork Confit,** season 225g pieces of pork shoulder as above and replace the duck fat with lard or olive oil.

AMONG THE BEDOUINS, A KNIFE IS NEVER JUST A KNIFE

Diana Abu-Jaber

'Tell the truth,' the novelist and memoirist **Diana Abu-Jaber** urged new writers in 2005. 'Tell your truth. Be brave. Make writing a regular part of your life, and if you get stuck, cooking is a wonderful method of working through the rough patches.' As advice goes, it's fairly foolproof. Born to a Jordanian father and American mother in Syracuse, New York, Abu-Jaber's work deals with Arab identity, Arab–American identity, family, love, death and food. She works as a professor at Portland State University.

On Nourishment, Betrayal, and Finding Family Histories

It was a familiar homily at our dinner table—the tale of the chicken. Filling our plates, Dad recalled how his mother would place a dish of roasted chicken at the center of the table and watch her nine children fall upon it.

Sometimes the story went that the platter was passed in an orderly fashion, from the eldest at the head, down through the middles, ending with my father and the youngest siblings at the bottom. Other times he described it as a free for all, voices raised, forks and elbows flying.

In either case, Dad generally ended up with a plateful of what he described as "bones and air." But then as he told the story, his eyes would turn narrow and crafty, and he would begin to talk about the secret chicken. Snapping the chicken bones in his hands, he showed my sisters and me the scant but tasty marrow hidden inside. He turned the chicken over and cut out the tender pieces in the back. And he showed us the prize—the meaty, succulent tail. To many Americans, such bits get tossed away carelessly. But to Dad, these morsels had sustained him; me and my siblings needed to be ready for our own journeys.

That's the thing about immigration—you don't stop traveling. It might begin with the thrill of adventure and discovery, but there's also ambivalence and loss—of family, home, and country. Many don't realize that the long and perilous journey doesn't end when you arrive. In many ways that's just the start. As a young father, Dad was already starting to realize this. It didn't matter if his children remained in the land where they were born: they too were going to need signposts and secret cues to guide us on our way. With his stories he gave us the answers to riddles: turn the chicken over, crack its bones open. Tell no one.

But some of this training was more subtle. Dad loved to discourse on the importance of *family*, its unbreakable bonds. But he was also telling another sort of story at the same time—one that I didn't fully grasp at the time. I was the eldest and I knew that siblings could be aggravating. But on a deeper level, they were sacred. I couldn't imagine snatching the food from my sister's mouth. Dad's stories walked a line—extolling the fun and affection of his oversized family; then, casually mentioning the knife fight between himself and a younger brother; or the time his father shot at him for sneaking out to a party, or the time another brother gave away Dad's much-loved dog. *Watch your backs,* he whispered, this world is treacherous and it's hard to know who to trust.

Originally, my grandfather Saleh owned three knives. They had come from my father's father—who'd inherited them from his own father. I didn't know exactly how many generations back they extended—but it was enough to have spiraled into history. Though my father's family now lived in the city, if you looked over their shoulders, you'd see a long line of sheikhs, poets, and Bedouins. Each generation had their trusted tools, secret paths, and shared stories.

One of my jiddo's knives was long, polished silver, studded with precious stones. But after Saleh's death, a village warlord visited my widowed grandmother to pay his respects and to request a keepsake.

I'm not sure why she gave it away. Perhaps my grandmother felt bound to codes of propriety and hospitality. Likely there were unpaid debts. According to Dad, my grandfather was renowned for his ability to enjoy himself. There were many stories involving araq—the potent favorite among Jordanian Bedouins. According to family lore, Jiddo once invited an entire garrison of the British army over for dinner, and they obliged, dressed in full regalia—much to my grandmother's dismay. Whatever the reason, the beautiful, ceremonial knife was given away, leaving two behind.

Knives have a deep and enduring history in the Middle East. Exquisite Egyptian swords and sickles survive from the Bronze Age, and it is still possible to view some of the knives and swords from the prophet Mohamed's personal collection. Bedouins are reputed to carry at least one knife on their person at all times, and this was true for my grandfather as well.

All cultures have their objects of power and desire: from small personal keepsakes to the holy grail to Excalibur. Hitchcock even had a name for it in filmmaking—the Maguffin. The Maguffin is the thing that sets the plot in motion, like the Maltese Falcon—the item that everyone chases, and which may or may not have much value of its own. Among the Bedouins, a knife is never just a knife. It's country, home, and lineage. Worn against the skin, it becomes part of the wearer's DNA, part of their deepest identity.

After his siblings went on to marriage, careers, school, and travel, Dad remained behind to care for his father during his final illness—a brutal task. In gratitude, Jiddo bequeathed his knives to my father. This legacy worked its way into my novel, *Fencing with the King*. In it, the protagonist's brother is haunted by the idea that he has been in some way cheated by their father. In real life, something very similar happened to my father. Perhaps this is inevitable in such a big family—someone always feels cheated because there's never much to go around. This family member, like the character in my book, became obsessed with the knives.

Not long after the death of my jiddo, while my father was out one day, he returned to discover that one of the knives was missing from his room. it was clear that someone had ransacked the place and stolen the large, elegant knife. Dad had felt afraid something like this might happen: he'd taken care to wear the smallest knife as their father had, strapped to his midsection, hidden under his clothes.

The knife Dad kept was worn and humble. To my father the last knife was the most precious of all because it was the daily knife, the one closest to memory. Apparently, this also became clear to the jealous family member. No longer satisfied with the first theft, this person soon began hounding my father, demanding the last knife. This pursuit went on for years, even after Dad moved to the United States, there were calls, telegrams, letters, and visits. It was such a drawn out, monomaniacal campaign that I couldn't even convey it in a way that would seem believable in the novel. I ended up cutting large swathes of the story, editing it down to better fit the larger framework of the tale.

In both real life and the novel, the story of the knife was the story of obsession without reason, the tearing apart of a family in the envious, furious search for *family*—its spirit or essence. This relative was educated, accomplished, celebrated, and far wealthier than my father. Yet somehow none of this was enough. I didn't understand this until I brought it into my novel. As I wrote about this character, I began to grasp the motivations of the actual person—this was an obsession born of deeper insufficiency. In life, as in my novel, the younger son was the favored one. Dad was neither rich or famous, but he had sweetness and an authentic love of the world. This genuine quality couldn't be learned or purchased.

I'd heard the story of the knife many times—how Dad acquired it and managed to hang on to it, but I'd never actually seen the object myself, until one day not long after my fourteenth birthday, Dad abruptly put down his newspaper and said, "Stay there." He brought it downstairs wrapped in a piece of velvet cloth. To be honest, I found the knife a little underwhelming—small and unembellished, with a dull pewter sheath and plain handle. Such is the case with so many items, their beauty or price tag is far outstripped by their symbolic worth. I politely admired it and then Dad put it away.

For years, the phone calls and letters continued between my father and his relative back in Jordan. This person inquired about our health, offered news of the family, and inevitably requested or demanded the knife. This person and their family visited us as well—year after year—returning to the United States, staying at our house, eating dinner with us. We all loved and admired this relation—in truth, they seemed to have everything. But always, Dad said, at some point, his relative would take him aside and ask about the knife.

"What did you say, Dad?" I asked as an adult, years later, incredulous that this had all gone on, quietly, just under our noses.

"That I forgot where it was. Or that I didn't have it, that I'd lost it. Or that someone else had it." He laughed. "I couldn't keep all my stories straight."

"But why didn't you tell us?" I asked. "And why did you let them keep visiting and harassing you like that?"

"Because they're family," he said, as if the answer should have been obvious.

I didn't see the knife again until about ten years ago, after my father died. He didn't leave much behind—just a few small items—and the knife. Mom brought it out, still wrapped in velvet, and said he'd wanted me to have it. My eyes filled. The knife had outlived several generations of owners and thieves, and I'd become the guardian of that legacy. I knew I'd have to write about it someday.

A few years after Dad died, his relative also passed away. I'd thought perhaps they might try to hunt the knife down through me, but now I suspect that the fight had lost its electricity once their adversary had gone. What no one could have predicted was that the knife was almost beside the point.

Not for me though. My interest in knives is essentially academic, but this one is different. It is among my most precious possessions. I love the knife for its protection spell—the way it reminds me of Dad's stories about the treachery of the world and of my own great good luck in having siblings and family that I both love and trust implicitly. I keep it, because like my father, I believe it retains traces of its previous owners—reminding me of the long family line running backward and forward in time, informing my most essential identity. I keep it because we need anchors and totems to hold us in place, secret pathways and instructions to navigate the journeys and riddles of our own lives. We need to know where the extra meat is hidden, how to conjure the necessary charms, where to hide the treasured artifacts.

The knife hums from my father's grip and that of his father before him. It is a stationary point in the world's movements—a name, a home, a bloodline—it's a little information in a land of too much and not enough. It's part of the name of a family.

THE FLAVOUR THESAURUS

Niki Segnit

Niki Segnit's game-changing debut, *The Flavour Thesaurus*, is the kind of book that every serious (and unserious) cook keeps in their kitchen. And if they don't, they should. Combining a passion for flavours with a background in data-driven creative advertising, it is utterly unlike anything else: a guidebook and framework through which to become a better and more independent cook. 'I was running the data,' she told one interviewer in 2019. '[I saw] the patterns.' Segnit's work is all about patterns. Patterns, for instance, that show us the way that one recipe can give you the base for another, as in her sophomore book *Lateral Cooking*; or how the categorization of flavours can crack open a whole new world of experiences, tastes and ideas, as in *The Flavour Thesaurus* and its plant-based sequel. The unlikely combination of almost mathematical precision and frank, funny storytelling is itself classic Segnit: delicious, unexpected, totally new and already familiar all at the same time.

Chicken has a reputation for being bland – the magnolia of foods – and yet standing up to 40 cloves of garlic, or to big flavours like rosemary, thyme and lemon, takes some serious meatiness. The well-exercised joints – legs, thighs – are the tastiest, even more so when cooked skin-on and bone-in. It's the skinless, boneless breast meat, especially from intensively farmed birds, that has earned chicken its pale reputation. It's like a sort of dry tofu for carnivores. The best that can be said of it is that it adds bite to dishes, and doesn't get in the way of more interesting flavours in a sauce – salty, sweet, nutty, fruity, spicy, even fishy.

Chicken & Avocado: Good together, if a little blandly healthy, like those smug couples you see jogging in the park. Give the chicken a smoke and things could start to look up. Or throw them some toasted pine nuts and a handful of raisins, toss through some leaves and dress with something sharp.

Chicken & Bell Pepper: One of the easiest, most foolproof combinations in this book. Deseed 6–8 peppers (red, yellow or orange, not green), chop them into generous chunks and put in a large non-stick saucepan with 8 chicken thighs, skin-on and preferably bone-in too. Leave over a medium heat. Keep an eye on it for the first ten minutes, giving it the odd stir to prevent it sticking. Then all of a sudden the peppers release their juices and you can leave it alone. Put a lid on and cook over a low-medium heat for 30 minutes, or until the pan is half-full of sweet, oily, autumn-coloured stock. It's a bit of a miracle, this – you can hardly believe the rich complexity of the sauce comes from just two ingredients. Season and serve with rice, couscous or French bread, whichever you prefer to mop up with.

Chicken & Caviar: In Sylvia Plath's *The Bell Jar*, Esther Greenwood attends a smart luncheon where she hatches a plan to monopolise an entire bowl of caviar. If, she observes, you carry yourself with a certain arrogance when you do something incorrect at the table, people will think you're original rather than bad-mannered: 'Under cover of the clinking of water goblets and silver – ware and bone china, I paved my plate with chicken slices. Then I covered the chicken slices with caviar thickly as if I were spreading peanut-butter on a piece of bread. Then I picked up the chicken slices in my fingers one by one, rolled them so the caviar wouldn't ooze off and ate them.'

Chicken & Chilli: The Portuguese went to Mozambique and came back with chicken peri peri (or piri piri), a simple dish of flame-grilled chicken marinated in oil, chilli, salt and citrus juice. *Peri peri* is a generic African word for chilli, but usually refers to the hot, simply flavoured bird's eye variety. Having taken to the dish themselves, the Portuguese exported it to their colonies, including Goa, where it's particularly popular. The peri peri diaspora has been accelerated in recent years by the South African chain, Nando's, which, spotting the mass-market appeal of chicken that can make tears run down your cheeks, has opened restaurants in five continents since 1987.

WHAT MRS. FISHER KNOWS ABOUT OLD SOUTHERN COOKING

Abby Fisher

Abby Fisher was a formerly enslaved woman from South Carolina. After moving across the country to California, Fisher earned a living as a pickle manufacturer and published *What Mrs. Fisher Knows About Old Southern Cooking* in 1881. Unable to read or write, she dictated the cookbook to friends. The book was lost following the San Francisco earthquake and fire of 1906, but reemerged at a 1984 Sotheby's auction in New York City. It was reprinted in 1985.

120 Chicken Salad.

Take all the meat from the bones of a boiled chicken and chop it fine in a tray. Save out some of the breast meat so as to lay over the top of the salad when it is made. Chop fine half a bunch of white celery and add to chicken. Season the chicken with pepper and salt, using cayenne pepper to taste. Skim the oil from the boiling chicken to pour over the salad. Milanese sauce for chicken salad: Beat the yelks of three eggs a little, then add one pint of best sweet oil, beating a little sweet oil at a time into the eggs, so as to have it light, until the whole pint is added. Mix a teaspoonful of mustard thoroughly in strong vinegar and put in sauce with cayenne and black pepper to suit the taste. When you put the salad on the platter, pour this sauce all over it and set it in an ice box.

HOW TO EAT

Nigella Lawson

If you are reading this book, you probably need no introduction to **Nigella**. Born in 1960 to the then-Chancellor of the Exchequer and his tea-shop-heiress wife, she studied medieval and modern languages at Oxford before becoming the deputy literary editor of *The Times* aged just twenty-six. On finding the hostess of a dinner party in tears over an unset crème caramel, Lawson was moved to change the world of cooking forever: her ethos of pleasure, beauty and a real joy in food made her first book *How to Eat* an instant classic when it was published in 1998. She has since written thirteen further million-selling cookbooks, accompanying eleven of those with television shows. She remains the nation's Domestic Goddess.

Stock is what you may make out of the bones of your roasted chicken, but mayonnaise, real mayonnaise, is what you might make to eat with the cold, leftover meat. There is one drawback: when you actually make mayonnaise you realise, beyond the point of insistent denial, how much oil goes into it. But since even the best bottled mayonnaise – and I don't mean the one you think I mean, but one manufactured by a company called Cottage Delight – bears little or no relation to real mayonnaise, you may as well know how to make it.

When I was in my teens, I loved Henry James. I read him with uncorrupted pleasure. Then, when I was eighteen or so, and had just started *The Golden Bowl*, someone – older, cleverer, whose opinions were offered gravely – asked me whether I didn't find James very difficult, as she always did. Until then, I had no idea that I might, and I didn't. From that moment, I couldn't read him but self-consciously; from then on, I did find him difficult. I do not wish to insult by the comparison, but I had a similar, Jamesian mayonnaise experience. My mother used to make mayonnaise weekly, twice weekly; we children would help. I had no idea it was meant to be difficult, or that it was thought to be such a nerve-racking ordeal. Then someone asked how I managed to be so breezy about it, how I stopped it from curdling. From then on, I scarcely made a mayonnaise which didn't split. It's not surprising: when confidence is undermined or ruptured, it can be difficult to do the simplest things, or to take any enjoyment even in trying.

I don't deny that mayonnaises can split, but please don't jinx yourself. Anyway, it's not a catastrophe if it does. A small drop of boiling water can fix things, and if it doesn't, you can start again with an egg yolk in a bowl. Beat it and slowly beat in the curdled mess of mayo you were previously working on. Later add more oil and a little lemon juice. You should, this way, end up with the smoothly amalgamated yellow ointment you were after in the first place. I hate to say it, but you may have to do this twice. You may end up with rather more mayonnaise than you need, but getting it right in the end restores your confidence, and this is the important thing.

I make mayonnaise the way my mother did: I warm the eggs in the bowl (as explained more fully later) then beat and add oil just from the bottle, not measuring, until the texture feels right, feels like mayonnaise. I squeeze in lemon juice, also freehand, until the look and taste feel right. If you make a habit of making mayonnaise, you will inevitably come to judge it instinctively too. I don't like too much olive oil in it: if it's too strong it rasps the back of the throat, becomes too invasive. I use a little over two-thirds groundnut oil and a little under one-third olive oil, preferably that lovely mild stuff from Liguria. If you prefer, do use half and half and a mild French olive oil, which is probably more correct, anyway, than the Italian variety.

By habit, and maternal instruction, I always used to use an ordinary whisk. This takes a long time (and I can see why my mother used us, her children, as *commis* chefs). Now I use my KitchenAid (similar to a Kenwood Chef, but American) with the wire whip in place. You can equally well use one of those electric hand-held whisks, which are cheap and useful. Please, whatever you do, don't use a food processor: if you do, your finished product tastes just like the gluey bought stuff. And then, hell, you might as well just go out and buy it.

2 egg yolks (but wait to separate
the eggs, and see below)
225ml groundnut or sunflower oil

75ml extra virgin olive oil
juice of ½ lemon

Put the eggs, in their shells, in a large bowl. Fill it with warm water from the tap and leave for 10 minutes. (This brings eggs and bowl comfortably to room temperature, which will help stop the eggs from curdling, but is optional, as long as you remember to take the eggs out of the fridge well before you need them.) Then remove the eggs, get rid of the water and dry the bowl thoroughly. Wet and then wring out a tea towel and set the bowl on it; this stops it slipping and jumping about on the worksurface.

Separate the eggs. Put aside the whites and freeze them for another use, and let the yolks plop into the dried bowl. Start whisking the yolks with a pinch of salt. After a few minutes very, very gradually and drop by mean drop, add the groundnut oil. You must not rush this. It's easier to let the oil seep in gradually if you pour from a height, holding the measuring jug (or bottle with a spout attached, if you're not actually using measured quantities) well above the bowl. Keep going until you see a thick mayonnaise form, about 2–3 tablespoons' worth, then you can relax and let the oil drip in small glugs. When both oils have been incorporated (first the groundnut, then the olive oil) and you have a thick, smooth, firm mayonnaise, add a few squeezes of lemon juice, whisking all the time. Taste to see if you need to add more. Add salt and pepper as you like; my mother used white pepper, so she didn't end up with black specks.

If you want a sharper more vinegary taste you can add ½–1 teaspoon Dijon mustard to the egg yolks in the beginning. A touch of mustard is fabulous in a sauce verte, or green mayonnaise, which is made by adding 2 tablespoons or so of chopped herbs – sorrel, tarragon, parsley, whatever – and, classically, a handful of spinach, blanched (dunked for a few seconds in boiling water), super-efficiently drained, then minutely chopped into the mayonnaise at the end. I've never actually tried using those frozen spheres of spinach purée, but it occurs to me that you could try one here. Otherwise a little watercress or rocket, chopped with the unblanched herbs, in place of the spinach, is fine. And if you're in the mood, you can add some chopped capers and gherkins (about 2 teaspoons of each) as well. In other words, treat this as what it is in Italian – salsa verde – only hanging in an egg and oil emulsion rather than just bound in the oil; this gives you the go ahead to stir in some minced anchovy if you like too.

I love sauce verte especially with cold pork, but I have to say that every time I eat real mayonnaise, in its bleached-yolk yellow and unmodified state, I am freshly surprised how good it is. And egg mayonnaise – hard-boiled eggs, sliced and masked with light mayonnaise, with or without a criss-crossing of anchovies on top – has to be one of the most fashionably underrated of dishes.

A SMALL BOY AND OTHERS

Henry James

'We must know, as much as possible, in our beautiful art... what we are talking about — & the only way to know it is to have lived & loved & cursed & floundered & enjoyed & suffered —' wrote the novelist **Henry James**, looking over his life. Widely regarded as one of the greatest prose writers in the English language, James was born in New York in 1843, spent much of his life travelling around Europe, and died a British citizen in 1916. Always a little on the outside of every social and cultural group, James' novels are known for an almost detached quality dressed in lavish and impressionist prose. He wrote of himself in his autobiography *A Small Boy And Others* that 'he was to enjoy more than anything the so-far-from-showy practice of wondering and dawdling and gaping', and it is those practices that inform his writing – including the excerpt, from said autobiography, below.

I see a small and compact and ingenuous society, screened in somehow conveniently from north and west, but open wide to the east and comparatively to the south and, though perpetually moving up Broadway, none the less constantly and delightfully walking down it. Broadway was the feature and the artery, the joy and the adventure of one's childhood, and it stretched, and prodigiously, from Union Square to Barnum's great American Museum by the City Hall—or only went further on the Saturday mornings (absurdly and deplorably frequent alas) when we were swept off by a loving aunt, our mother's only sister, then much domesticated with us and to whom the ruthless care had assigned itself from the first, to Wall Street and the torture chamber of Dr. Parkhurst, our tremendously respectable dentist, who was so old and so empurpled and so polite, in his stock and dress-coat and dark and glossy wig, that he had been our mother's and our aunt's haunting fear in *their* youth as well, since, in their quiet Warren Street, not far off, they were, dreadful to think, comparatively under his thumb. He extremely resembles, to my mind's eye, certain figures in Phiz's illustrations to Dickens, and it was clear to us through our long ordeal that our elders must, by some mistaken law of compensation, some refinement of the vindictive, be making us "pay" for what they in like helplessness had suffered from him: as if *we* had done them any harm! Our analysis was muddled, yet in a manner relieving, and for us too there were compensations, which we grudged indeed to allow, but which I could easily, even if shyly, have named. One of these was Godey's Lady's Book, a sallow pile of which (it shows to me for sallow in the warmer and less stony light of the Wall Street of those days and through the smell of ancient anodynes) lay on Joey Bagstock's table for our beguilement while we waited: I was to encounter in Phiz's Dombey and Son that design for our tormentor's type. There is no doubt whatever that I succumbed to the spell of Godey, who, unlike the present essences, was an anodyne before the fact as well as after; since I remember poring, in his pages, over tales of fashionable life in Philadelphia while awaiting my turn in the chair, not less than doing so when my turn was over and to the music of my brother's groans. This must have been at the hours when we were left discreetly to our own fortitude, through our aunt's availing herself of the relative proximity to go and shop at Stewart's and then come back for us; the ladies' great shop, vast, marmorean, plate-glassy and notoriously fatal to the female nerve (we ourselves had wearily trailed through it, hanging on the skirts, very literally, of indecision) which bravely waylaid custom on the Broadway corner of Chambers Street. Wasn't part of the charm of life—since I assume that there *was* such a charm—in its being then (I allude to life itself) so much more down-towny, on the supposition at least that our young gravitation in that sense for most of the larger joys consorted with something of the general habit? The joy that had to be fished out, like Truth, from the very bottom of the well was attendance at Trinity Church, still in that age supereminent, pointedly absolute, the finest feature of the southward scene; to the privilege of which the elder Albany cousins were apt to be treated when they came on to stay with us; an indulgence making their enjoyment of our city as down-towny as possible too, for I seem otherwise to see them but as returning with the familiar Stewart headache from the prolonged strain of selection.

The great reward dispensed to us for our sessions in the house of pain—as to which it became our subsequent theory that we had been regularly dragged there on alternate Saturdays—was our being carried on the return to the house of delight, or to one of them, for there were specifically two, where we partook of ice-cream, deemed sovereign for sore mouths, deemed sovereign in fact, all through our infancy, for everything. Two great establishments for the service of it graced the prospect, one Thompson's and the other Taylor's, the former, I perfectly recall, grave and immemorial, the latter upstart but dazzling, and having together the effect that whichever we went to we wondered if we hadn't better have gone to the other—with that capacity of childhood for making the most of its adventures after a fashion that may look so like making the least. It is in our father's company indeed that, as I press the responsive spring, I see the bedizened saucers heaped up for our fond consumption (they bore the Taylor-title painted in blue and gilded, with the Christian name, as parentally pointed out to us, perverted to "Jhon" for John, whereas the Thompson-name scorned such vulgar and above all such misspelt appeals;) whence I infer that still other occasions for that experience waited on us—as almost any would serve, and a paternal presence so associated with them was not in the least conceivable in the Wall Street *repaire*. That presence is in fact not associated for me, to any effect of distinctness, with the least of our suffered shocks or penalties— though partly doubtless because our acquaintance with such was of the most limited; a conclusion I form even while judging it to have been on the whole sufficient for our virtue. This sounds perhaps as if we had borne ourselves as prodigies or prigs—which was as far as possible from being the case; we were bred in horror of *conscious* propriety, of what my father was fond of calling "flagrant" morality; what I myself at any rate read back into our rare educational ease, for the memory of some sides of which I was ever to be thankful, is, besides the *general* humanisation of our apprehended world and our "social" tone, the unmistakeable appearance that my father was again and again accompanied in public by his small second son: so many young impressions come back to me as gathered at his side and in his personal haunts. Not that he mustn't have offered his firstborn at least equal opportunities; but I make out that he seldom led us forth, such as we were, together, and my brother must have had in *his* turn many a mild adventure of which the secret—I like to put it so—perished with him. He was to remember, as I perceived later on, many things that I didn't, impressions I sometimes wished, as with a retracing jealousy, or at least envy, that I might also have fallen direct heir to; but he professed amazement, and even occasionally impatience, at my reach of reminiscence—liking as he did to brush away old moral scraps in favour of new rather than to hoard and so complacently exhibit them. If in my way I collected the new as well I yet cherished the old; the ragbag of memory hung on its nail in my closet, though I learnt with time to control the habit of bringing it forth. And I say that with a due sense of my doubtless now appearing to empty it into these pages.

I keep picking out at hazard those passages of our earliest age that help to reconstruct for me even by tiny touches the experience of our parents, any shade of which seems somehow to signify. I cherish, to the extent of here reproducing, an old daguerreotype all the circumstances of the taking of which I intensely recall—though as I was lately turned twelve when I figured for it the feat of memory is perhaps not remarkable. It documents for me in so welcome and so definite a manner my father's cultivation of my company. It documents at the same time the absurdest little legend of my small boyhood—the romantic tradition of the value of being taken up from wherever we were staying to the queer empty dusty smelly New York of midsummer: I apply that last term because we always arrived by boat and I have still in my nostril the sense of the *abords* of the hot town, the rank and rubbishy waterside quarters, where big loose cobbles, for the least of all the base items, lay wrenched from their sockets of pungent black mud and where the dependent streets managed by a law of their own to be all corners and the corners to be all groceries; groceries indeed largely of the "green" order, so far as greenness could persist in the torrid air, and that bristled, in glorious defiance of traffic, with the overflow of their wares and implements. Carts and barrows and boxes and baskets, sprawling or stacked, familiarly elbowed in its course the bumping hack (the comprehensive "carriage" of other days, the only vehicle of hire then known to us) while the situation was accepted by the loose citizen in the garb of a freeman save for the brass star on his breast—and the New York garb of the period was, as I remember it, an immense attestation of liberty. Why the throb of romance should have beat time for me to such visions I can scarce explain, or can explain only by the fact that the squalor was a squalor wonderfully mixed and seasoned, and that I should wrong the whole impression if I didn't figure it first and foremost as that of some vast succulent cornucopia. What did the stacked boxes and baskets of our youth represent but the boundless fruitage of that more bucolic age of the American world, and what was after all of so strong an assault as the rankness of such a harvest? Where is that fruitage now, where in particular are the peaches *d'antan*? where the mounds of Isabella grapes and Seckel pears in the sticky sweetness of which our childhood seems to have been steeped? It was surely, save perhaps for oranges, a more informally and familiarly fruit-eating time, and bushels of peaches in particular, peaches big and peaches small, peaches white and peaches yellow, played a part in life from which they have somehow been deposed; every garden, almost every bush and the very boys' pockets grew them; they were "cut up" and eaten with cream at every meal; domestically "brandied" they figured, the rest of the year, scarce less freely—if they were rather a "party dish" it was because they made the party whenever they appeared, and when ice-cream was added, or they were added *to* it, they formed the highest revel we knew. Above all the public heaps of them, the high-piled receptacles at every turn, touched the street as with a sort of southern plenty; the note of the rejected and scattered fragments, the memory of the slippery skins and rinds and kernels with which the old dislocated flags were bestrown, is itself endeared to me and contributes a further pictorial grace. We ate everything in those days by the bushel and the barrel, as from stores that were infinite; we handled watermelons as freely as cocoanuts, and the amount of stomach-ache involved was negligible in the general Eden-like consciousness.

The glow of this consciousness even in so small an organism was part of the charm of these retreats offered me cityward upon our base of provisions; a part of the rest of which, I disengage, was in my fond perception of that almost eccentrically home-loving habit in my father which furnished us with half the household humour of our childhood—besides furnishing *him* with any quantity of extravagant picture of his so prompt pangs of anguish in absence for celebration of his precipitate returns. It was traditional for us later on, and especially on the European scene, that for him to leave us in pursuit of some advantage or convenience, some improvement of our condition, some enlargement of our view, was for him breathlessly to reappear, after the shortest possible interval, with no account at all to give of the benefit aimed at, but instead of this a moving representation, a far richer recital, of his spiritual adventures at the horrid inhuman inns and amid the hard alien races which had stayed his advance. He reacted, he rebounded, in favour of his fireside, from whatever brief explorations or curiosities; these passionate spontaneities were the pulse of his life and quite some of the principal events of ours; and, as he was nothing if not expressive, whatever happened to him for inward intensity happened abundantly to us for pity and terror, as it were, as well as for an ease and a quality of amusement among ourselves that was really always to fail us among others. Comparatively late in life, after his death, I had occasion to visit, in lieu of my brother, then in Europe, an American city in which he had had, since his own father's death, interests that were of importance to us all. On my asking the agent in charge when the owner had last taken personal cognisance of his property that gentleman replied only half to my surprise that he had never in all his years of possession performed such an act. Then it was perhaps that I most took the measure of his fine faith in human confidence as an administrative function. He had to have a *relation*, somehow expressed—and as he was the vividest and happiest of letter-writers it rarely failed of coming; but once it was established it served him, in every case, much better than fussy challenges, which had always the drawback of involving lapses and inattentions in regard to solicitudes more pressing. He incurably took for granted—incurably because whenever he did so the process succeeded; with which association, however, I perhaps overdrench my complacent vision of our summer snatches at town. Through a grave accident in early life country walks on rough roads were, in spite of his great constitutional soundness, tedious and charmless to him; he liked on the other hand the peopled pavement, the thought of which made him restless when away. Hence the fidelities and sociabilities, however superficial, that he couldn't *not* reaffirm—if he could only reaffirm the others, the really intimate and still more communicable, soon enough afterwards.

It was these of the improvised and casual sort that I shared with him thus indelibly; for truly if we took the boat to town to do things I did them quite as much as he, and so that a little boy could scarce have done them more. My part may indeed but have been to surround his part with a thick imaginative aura; but that constituted for me an activity than which I could dream of none braver or wilder. We went to the office of The New York Tribune—my father's relations with that journal were actual and close; and that was a wonderful world indeed, with strange steepnesses and machineries and noises and hurrying bare-armed, bright-eyed men, and amid the agitation clever, easy, kindly, jocular, partly undressed gentlemen (it was always July or August) some of whom I knew at home, taking it all as if it were the most natural place in the world. It was big to me, big to me with the breath of great vague connections, and I supposed the gentlemen very old, though since aware that they must have been, for the connections, remarkably young; and the conversation of one of them, the one I saw oftenest up town, who attained to great local and to considerable national eminence afterwards, and who talked often and thrillingly about the theatres, I retain as many bright fragments of as if I had been another little Boswell. It was as if he had dropped into my mind the germ of certain interests that were long afterwards to flower—as for instance on his announcing the receipt from Paris of news of the appearance at the Théâtre Français of an actress, Madame Judith, who was formidably to compete with her coreligionary Rachel and to endanger that artist's laurels. Why should Madame Judith's name have stuck to me through all the years, since I was never to see her and she is as forgotten as Rachel is remembered? Why should that scrap of gossip have made a date for my consciousness, turning it to the Comédie with an intensity that was long afterwards to culminate? Why was it equally to abide for me that the same gentleman had on one of these occasions mentioned his having just come back from a wonderful city of the West, Chicago, which, though but a year or two old, with plank sidewalks when there were any, and holes and humps where there were none, and shanties where there were not big blocks, and everything where there had yesterday been nothing, had already developed a huge energy and curiosity, and also an appetite for lectures? I became aware of the Comédie, I became aware of Chicago; I also became aware that even the most alluring fiction was not always for little boys to read. It was mentioned at the Tribune office that one of its reporters, Mr. Solon Robinson, had put forth a novel rather oddly entitled "Hot Corn" and more or less having for its subject the career of a little girl who hawked that familiar American luxury in the streets. The volume, I think, was put into my father's hand, and I recall my prompt desire to make acquaintance with it no less than the remark, as promptly addressed to my companion, that the work, however engaging, was not one that should be left accessible to an innocent child. The pang occasioned by this warning has scarcely yet died out for me, nor my sense of my first wonder at the discrimination—so great became from that moment the mystery of the tabooed book, of whatever identity; the question, in my breast, of why, if it was to be so right for others, it was only to be wrong for me. I remember the soreness of the thought that it was I rather who was wrong for the book—which was somehow humiliating: in that amount of discredit one couldn't but be involved. Neither then nor afterwards was the secret of "Hot Corn" revealed to me, and the sense of privation was to be more prolonged, I fear, than the vogue of the tale, which even as a success of scandal couldn't have been great.

ON THE ROAD

Jack Kerouac

Fuelled only by Benzedrine, cigarettes, bowls of pea soup and mugs of coffee, **Jack Kerouac** reputedly wrote the first draft of *On The Road* in twenty days and on a single, taped-together 120-foot sheet of tracing paper. This defining work of the Beat generation describes a Kerouac-esque hero travelling across America, in search of something like God – yet dripping with drugs, jazz and more drugs. In this very short passage from the novel, 'Sal Paradise' eats some peach ice cream.

Meanwhile his young wife prepared a magnificent spread in the big ranch kitchen. She apologized for the peach ice cream: 'It ain't nothin but cream and peaches froze up together.' Of course it was the only real ice cream I ever had in my whole life. She started sparsely and ended up abundantly; as we ate, new things appeared on the table. She was a well-built blonde but like all women who live in the wide spaces she complained a little of the boredom.

FOODISTS

John Bayley

To be described as 'the greatest critic since Coleridge' is one thing; to be described as 'the greatest critic since Coleridge' by one's *wife* quite another. Yet if the wife in question is the astounding novelist Iris Murdoch, it might be worth paying attention. The academic, literary critic and writer **John Bayley** was born in Lahore in 1925, was sent to Eton and hence straight to Oxford, where he remained as inspirational academic and beloved tutor for almost fifty years. In fiction he most loved, he wrote, the 'banality of the here and now'; he believed in the moral value of art, and trusted, always, in the way great literature cracks us open to love.

Food, like sex, is mostly in the head. Or, if that seems exaggerated, what about the thought that thinking about food is the modern growth industry? Restaurants, supermarkets, the media – all encourage display, which like the old underwear advertisements in the tube might seem pornographic if we were not so used to them. The Greens should make us sensitive on this issue, no doubt, as feminists did on the other one. The food in the head industry may be an insult to the Third World, but it also encourages contribution to aid programmes. No longer guilty about sex, we are uneasy about anorexia and bulimia, slimness and fatness, soft foodie dreaming ...

Vice may pay its usual debt to virtue, and yet pomposity on this issue would be out of place. There is still an innocence about greed, particularly when the mouth waters at the thought rather than the thing. A foodie once put a small object into my hand and said with reverence 'bite that'. I bit as directed and received an impression of nothing, no taste, either good or bad. I commented on this. He beamingly agreed. I had missed the point, which was that he had bought this nugget of smoked mushroom in the market at Kiev. He was not unlike the old gardener who waxed eloquent on the virtues of the King Edward potato, adding perfunctorily that it was not 'an eating potato'. Henry James would have seen the point. In 1870 he wrote to his elder brother William from Malvern, England, where the hotel fed him mostly on mutton and potatoes, to say how much he missed 'unlimited tomatoes & beans & peas & squash & turnips & carrots & corn – *I enjoy merely writing the words*'. The words are what counted, and they cheered him. American diners know the same trick, as James Bond observes in the course of one of his adventures. 'Tenderly selected fillets served with dew-fresh ...' and so forth. You can taste that if not the food. It must be added that Henry was suffering from impressively obstinate constipation, brought on as he supposed by the English diet. He reported on it in great detail to William, who was equally copious in sympathy and in remedial measures, while characteristically claiming that he suffered from it just as badly himself, if not worse.

Food may have been mostly on the page for Henry James, though he was a big eater too – three or four 'shirred' eggs each day for breakfast – but his *confrères* across the channel had a much more down-to-earth attitude. For Zola as for Rabelais *alimentation* was for the *ventre*, not the *tête*: the French are foodists rather than foodies. So there is no nonsense at all about this admirable history of the stuff. Yet that is not entirely true, for food in France is a mystique, even in its solidest form; this lends liveliness to a treatise which could be on the heavy side without it. Not that Maguelonne Toussaint-Samat (the name suggests that of her illustrious compatriot of a former era, Anthèlme Brillat-Savarin) is in any sense a plodder – though her table of contents, like that of a good doctoral thesis, takes us methodically through the history of eating and drinking, from the techniques of hunter-gathering to those of stock-breeding and bread-baking, the history of fish and poultry, the arts of distilling and making wine, the lure of sugar, the tradition of fruits, the evolution of vegetables, preserving by heat and by cold. None of this is dull, and it is served up with all the *esprit* of the French intellectual tradition.

The metaphysics of eating are briskly acknowledged at the start. 'At first a purely visceral pleasure, it became an intellectual process when the eyes, which had been laterally placed, moved towards the base of the forehead.' Eyes became bigger than stomachs, at least metaphorically, and with the gourmand came his more refined cousin, the gourmet. After that, as the author shows herself from time to time to be well aware, comes the transformation of foods into words. The novel gets good on this: Post-Modernism in fiction today often takes the form of a commentary on obsession – most lately food obsession as in Jane Barry's *Hungry* and Banana Yoshimoto's *Kitchen*. Jane Austen enjoys mentioning 'fried beef' and refers to green peas – themselves a late arrival and gobbled as a novelty by the Sun King and by Queen Anne on our side of the channel – while Miss Bates and her mother were once baulked of a nice dish of sweet-breads by Mr Woodhouse's fear that they were not quite thoroughly cooked. Food becomes an aspect of Dickensian hyperbole, and a compensatory pleasure of the deserving poor, who can revel occasionally on the fattest of geese and the juiciest of beefsteaks, or carouse on porter and oysters. For Proust it had not only the savour of aestheticism – the Combray asparagus *qui parfumait mon pot de chambre* – but could be a macabre index of the moral life, a domain in which the perfect roast chicken of Françoise is at one with her cruelty to the kitchen-maid. We have heard rather too much of the *boeuf en daube* in *To the Lighthouse*, but it remains a memorable dish, floating with its brown meats and its yellow meats at the solar plexus of the novel, emblem of Mrs Ramsay's martyrdom on the family altar, but also of her detachment, for it is not she but the cook who has taken two days to prepare it in the kitchen.

Hazlitt remarks in an essay that he associates books with what he was eating when he read them: *La Nouvelle Héloise* with *pain au beurre* and a pot of coffee, *Tom Jones* with a roasted partridge. The contents of Rat's picnic basket contains the world of *The Wind in the Willows*; the aroma of a bubble and squeak prepared by the gaoler's daughter cheered up Toad in his prison cell; bacon and broad beans and a macaroni pudding comprised the 'simple but sustaining meal' enjoyed by Mole and Rat and Toad and Badger before setting out to reoccupy Toad Hall. The films? There was that *caneton à la presse* which looked good in Chabrol's film about the man pursuing the motorist who has run over his son; and of course in *Aimez-Vous les Femmes?* an entire girl is served up, looking very dishy among slices of lemon and glazed cucumber. But as the cinema has to put the food in front of you, so to speak, it is really in the same vulgar quandary as the theatre, where cold tea has to be drunk as if it were whisky and soda; or as the TV advertisements, where salmon steak and mixed vegetable must be soused with glycerine to look suitably tempting. Food as an art-form should remain spiritual. Realism never pays.

But to get back to the stuff we actually eat. How many of us who know that milk is pasteurised have also heard of the ingenious Irishman, John Tyndall, who in the 1870s discovered that mother bacteria are destroyed by heating food or milk, but that their offspring survive? These sturdy youngsters have had their powers of resistance much reduced, however, so that they succumb to an ensuing bout of freezing. Tyndallisation, as the experts still call it, subjects the microbes to these alternating and quite mild doses of heat and cold, which wear them down without destroying the flavour and goodness of the nourishment. Or how many of us know that in 1914 the Polish Doctor C. Fink proved that the substance of life exists in the husks of cereals, although he was unable to isolate it chemically? He coined the word vitamin, from *amine*, or bran, though bran has nothing to do with the elements later isolated at Cambridge under the headings ABCD and so forth. Maguelonne Toussaint-Samat dismisses out of hand 'the fashion for vitamin pills, which simply make money for the labs that manufacture them'. What we eat has them all: more of them may do you harm.

Food is a potent source of mythologies, like the pomegranate seeds which Persephone in-advertently ate in gloomy Dis's underworld; having in consequence to spend half the year there and so bringing about the alternation of the seasons. In Greek tradition women had a monopoly of fishing, as water and the sea were the natural feminine element. When the sea-nymph Amphitrite agreed to marry Zeus's younger brother Poseidon this marine matriarchy came to an end. Priests succeeded in depriving women of their fishing rights, and fishing to the Achaeans became a masculine and therefore a noble and dignified occupation. Although the person in *The Waste Land* who is fishing in the dull canal presumably partakes, Tiresias-fashion, of both sexes, how many ladies does one see sitting solitary and meditative by the water's edge, with that slim rod stuck out in front of them?

But when it comes to the preparation of fish dishes French fervour can stretch almost to the mystical. Jules Michelet could scarcely contain his excitement as he contemplated the phenomenon of the herring.

> They live together, hidden in the twilight deeps; they rise together in the spring for their small share of universal happiness, to see the light of day, take their pleasure and die ... they can never be close enough to each other, they swim in dense shoals ... it looks as if a vast island has risen from the seas somewhere between Scotland, Holland and Norway, and a continent is about to emerge ... the sea is solid with herring. Millions of millions of them, billions upon billions. Who would venture to guess the number of those legions?

After this it is something of an anti-climax to enumerate the methods of preparation – the salting, the drying, the discovery that brine, not salt, was the best technique to precede packing in barrels. Wars have been fought for herring, as for cod: 'The Battle of the Herrings', a running fight between English archers and French men-at-arms for possession of a precious convoy, was an important episode in the Hundred Years War. (After all this I would maintain with an almost equal fervour that the only way to eat a kipper is raw, scraping the ambrosial flesh from the oily skin. Cooking a kipper, even for a few minutes, makes it dry and hard.)

The subject of fish seems to produce not only fervour but heavy humour. Anaxagoras, a poet addicted to cookery and a member of Alexander the Great's entourage, used to prepare conger eel stew with such loving care that he was teased by the Macedonian general Antigonus, who demanded what would have become of the *Iliad* if Homer had spent all his time boiling fish. The poet riposted that General Agamemnon would not have done so many great deeds if he had spent the day hanging about the camp kitchens watching poets cook conger eels. At least the ancient Greek military took fish seriously, whereas for Roman grandees it became merely a matter of conspicuous consumption. A large red mullet was auctioned by Tiberius for £4000, but it was all a question of show-business, in the most horrible sense. The unfortunate fish was boiled alive in a crystal pot on the dining table, the water heated very slowly so that guests could admire how its hues changed colour, 'as dusk succeeds sunset'.

After that it is a relief to go back to the Greeks and what sounds the most delicious form of *pasta* ever invented – *artolageion*, or 'bread in the pot'. Pounded lettuce is mixed with wine and fine flour, pounded again with pork lard and pepper, rolled flat and cut in strips and thrown in hot oil. An odd feature of cookery is that the same sort of dish crops up everywhere, and yet is claimed as its own invention by every place that does it. So far from Marco Polo bringing back spaghetti to Italy, it seems the Italians invented it themselves, or perhaps the Swiss did, or the Spanish (*churros* are rather like a sweet and simple form of *artolageion*), or the Koreans, who claim to have handed the secret to the Japanese. Only the English, in their superior way, put in no claims here, though I don't see why they shouldn't make a gesture in the direction of Yorkshire pudding.

Our methodical and encyclopedically learned author, well and even wittily translated by Anthea Bell, lays stress in all her conclusions on the symbolism of food – meat, bread, wine. St Clement of Alexandria observed in an unbuttoned moment that wine is to bread what the contemplative is to the active life. Yet I would suspect that the symbolic resources of food are in the end less memorable than the anecdotal. I shall never forget now when eating asparagus that French ladies in the old days could sometimes tell if a husband was straying in the month of May by taking a discreet sniff at the chamber pot. If she had not fed him asparagus then perhaps some other lady had; for both sexes were convinced that the spruce vegetable possessed infallible aphrodisiac properties. Certainly it is a powerful diuretic, and gives an unmistakable and for many a not disagreeable odour to the urine (Proust's 'parfum'), but no more than any other food or drink can it achieve by its chemistry any sexually stimulating effect. Once again suggestibility is what counts. The ultimate food anecdote is much less piquant, and makes the ancient Romans even more unattractive than one has always known them to be. They invented kissing, or so at least the story goes. And why? So that a husband could tell if his wife had been drinking wine. A casual conjugal *osculum* revealed all; and wine-drinking for women, at least in the stern days of the republic, was a capital offence. Thank goodness society has gone to the dogs since then. Cheers, Madame.

BLACK SEA

Caroline Eden

While primarily based in Edinburgh, **Caroline Eden**'s career has been largely focused on worlds far removed from rainy Britain: as a correspondent for BBC Radio 4, Eden has filed stories from Uzbekistan, Ukraine, Russia, Kyrgyzstan, Kazakhstan, Azerbaijan, Turkey, Haiti and Bangladesh. She is the author of three award-winning books about the food and cultures of (and journeys through) Central Asia: *Samarkand: Recipes and Stories from Central Asia and the Caucasus*; *Black Sea*; and *Red Sands*. A modern-day adventurer, Eden contributes journalism regularly to the *Financial Times*, the *Telegraph*, the *Guardian*, and the *TLS*.

At the foot of Nekrasova Lane in downtown Odessa, a large mansion sits abandoned. Seeds thrown by Black Sea winds have sprouted into spindly trees, their branches reaching awkwardly out of cracks in the crumbling peach-coloured plaster. Paint curls off wooden window ledges, their panes messily boarded up. In 1850, Ukrainian-born Nikolai Gogol, author of *Taras Bulba* and *Dead Souls*, lived here, in what was his uncle's house. Far from the chill damp of Moscow and St Petersburg, Odessa was a sanctuary of sorts, benefiting from a Mediterranean climate come summertime. On the battered facade, a small plaque shows Gogol's heart-shaped face, his eyes cast downwards, his moustache neat.

Odessa was a literary nerve centre for evacuated intellectuals, and for 19th-century Russian writers such as Gogol, and food was a literary vehicle for ambitious themes – satire, catastrophe, ecstasy and doom. To Gogol, the stomach was 'the noblest organ' and his gastric fixation was as apparent in life as on the page. In *Old World Landowners* he pays tribute to Ukrainian pastoral life, detailing harvests. Among the pussy willow and pear trees lay apples drying on rugs, downy-soft animals and carts full of melons. Inside the mottled houses stand decanters of yarrow- and sage-infused vodka and jars of gourds and mushrooms, either pickled with thyme, Turkish-style, or stewed in blackcurrant leaves and nutmeg.

Black Radish and Buttery Dumplings

When not writing about food, Gogol obsessed over his stomach. Famously sickly, he complained that his belly, a place where the devil himself sometimes dwelt, was upside down. And in this large house on Nekrasova Lane, he spent the winter nursing himself and struggling to write the ill-fated second part of Dead Souls, a fantastical phantasmagoric poem-novel about a crooked society. 'Dead Souls are not like pancakes,' he once lamented to another writer, 'they cannot be finished in an instant.'

Failing to complete the full work, Dead Souls later became the most famous book to remain unfinished. Food in the book, often monstrous and queer, is so prevalent that it pretty much forms the main character. Chichikov, the book's protagonist, enjoying a blowout feast with landowner Sobakevich, gorges on 'a sheep's stomach stuffed with buckwheat groats, brains, and trotters' followed by 'cheesecakes, each much bigger than a plate', before finishing up with unusual preserves including 'black radish, cooked in honey'. Elsewhere in the story, even cockroaches appear 'like prunes', and one pie is stuffed with the cheeks and gristle of a 'nine-*pood*' (325-pound) sturgeon.

His stomach was, eventually, to be the death of him. Gripped with religious mania following a pilgrimage to the Holy Land, he sought spiritual guidance from an ultra-orthodox priest who considered writing to be Devil's work. Shortly after, he declared the second volume of *Dead Souls* a flop, burned it at his Moscow house on Nikitsky Boulevard and slipped into a feverish madness. Fostering an acute eating disorder around the time of Maslenitsa (a sun festival heralding the end of winter before Lent when Russians gorge on bliny, butter, eggs and milk), he had doctors administer all manner of alarming treatments. As well as leeches and boiling baths he tried crackpot cures of cherry-laurel water and rhubarb-laced pills. Shortly after, his self-induced 'holy anorexia' killed him.

While the building on Nekrasova Lane deteriorates more with every passing year, a tribute plays out in the rickety café Gogol Mogol across the street. Locals pack the rainbow-coloured benches for salted herring sandwiches and rough Cabernet, ordered from a menu that comes in a hardback book. In the winter the action moves indoors to the antique-filled dining room, thick with the smell of borscht and buttery dumplings.

In These Red-Hot Climates of the East

This louche and cosy café scene is the sort that would have appealed to Anton Chekhov, master of the short story. To him, Odessa meant sun-soaked days and easy living, and in his letters he described one particular routine during the hot summer of 1889. At noon, he would take a young debutante out, dining with her at 'Zembrini's for ice cream'. It was Mark Twain, though, who celebrated Odessa's Italian-style ice cream best. Stepping off the Quaker City, a battleship-converted cruiseliner in 1867, he arrived in Odessa at the end of summer, writing about his journey in *Innocents Abroad*: 'It looked just like an American city; fine broad streets … There was not one thing to remind us we were in Russia.' In holiday spirit, he describes sauntering through the markets and finishing the day's entertainment with a full-on ice-cream debauch. 'We do not get ice-cream everywhere, and so, when we do, we are apt to dissipate to excess. We never cared anything about ice-cream at home, but we look upon it with a sort of idolatry now that it is so scarce in these red-hot climates of the East.'

Twain doesn't say where exactly in Odessa he experienced this feast, but Yiddish author Sholem Aleichem placed his ice-cream-eating characters at the white marble tables of Café Fanconi, Odessa's leading coffeehouse: 'I take my seat at Fanconi's … and ask for iced cream. That's our Odessa custom: you sit down and a waiter in a frock coat asks you to ask for iced cream. Well, you can't be a piker,' is how his character Menakhem-Mendl described the scene.

Odessa was a stopping point for many Europe-trotting writers and intellectuals, and their literature, lives and letters line the walls of the city's Literature Museum, a space as eccentric as its founder, Nikita Brygin, a red-haired former KGB officer who had a passion for books. Walking away from the opera house, down towards the sea, large Hollywood-style pavement stars, carved not with the names of actors but with local-born writers and poets, lead the way. Beside Isaac Babel's star is one of the few females represented, Anna Akhmatova, whom Stalin's culture minister referred to as 'half nun and half whore'. Born just outside Odessa, she is one of the 20th century's greatest poets, her work cruelly banned for decades under the Soviets.

Her majestic poem, 'In the Evening', begins:

There was such inexpressible sorrow
in the music in the garden.
The dish of oysters on ice
smelt fresh and sharp of the sea.

Oysters were also a preoccupation of Odessa's famous temporary resident, Alexander Pushkin, who ate them at a restaurant called Cesar Automne. Despite having an entire museum dedicated to him, as well as multiple city statues and busts, he is represented well within the Literature Museum.

Moving a slumbering red dog aside, I walked into the whitewashed galleries, and through the dead air of an eternal afternoon that lingers in museums such as this. Elena Karakina, noted 'Honoured Worker of Ukrainian Culture' and keeper of the museum for 32 years, guided me, reciting Pushkin in Russian as we went.

But we, we band of callow joysters
Unlike those merchants filled with cares,
Have been expecting only oysters…
From Istanbul, the seaside's wares.

Pushkin spent a year of political exile in Odessa in the 1820s, cavorting with Countess Vorontsova, the wife of the governor, while doodling nudes in the margins of his notebook and rewriting the first chapters of *Eugene Onegin*. To Pushkin, Odessa was multicultural and inspiring. He'd sit with his pipe at a restaurant, swim in the sea or drink Turkish coffee. Distinctive with his long fingernails and mutton-chop sideburns, he would walk with an iron stick made from a gun barrel to dine with Charles Sicard, merchant, former French consul and owner of the Hotel du Nord. Today, that hotel, on Pushkinskaya Street, is the Pushkin Museum, where inside, above polished parquet flooring, his eerie white plaster-cast death mask is fixed to the wall. 'Pushkin's Eugene Onegin was the book to read at school if you were hungry,' Karakina said, looking out from under her bowl-cut hair-do and over her spectacles, her eyes wide. 'Imagine! He writes of roast beef, Strasbourg pies, Limburger cheese and golden pineapple.'

Good Company and Galley Slaves

Karakina knows much of these great writers and literati exiles, of their eating habits and souls. She grimaces as she talks of Gogol's hair falling into a plate of spaghetti and talks of famous newspaper editors eating boiled ham and spaghetti on Odessa's beaches. Becoming ever more lyrical, we end with a vivid description of Jabotinsky's face swimming in watermelon juice. 'I shan't tell you more!' she says, wincing with a girlish laugh.

But it wasn't just Russian writers who lusted after Odessa's literary ambience, prosperity and style. Balzac sends his protagonists to trade there. 'Oh! I will go into business again, I will buy wheat in Odessa … That struck me this morning. There is a fine trade to be done in starch,' he writes in *Father Goriot*. Wheat and bakers made an impression on the British journalist Charles William Shirley Brooks – editor of *Punch* and ardent campaigner for (what was then illegal) human cremation. During his travels to Odessa in 1853, he noted the cornucopia of different loaves that appear like 'manna from heaven', the elegant white loaves that would 'do credit to the fancy baker' and then heavy black bread 'which would seem to require the digestion of an ostrich'. But it is in Odessa's monster market, Privoz, where he is really bowled over. There, he finds succulent 'vegetarian idols' in the form of 'millions of onions, dried beans, mushrooms hanging in mighty ropes, pears of a noble juiciness and a sturdy flavour, purple plums of great size and excellence'. He wonders, as many of us do when we visit markets, who on earth is going to eat it all. 'No population, even one of schoolboys let loose with orders to be moderate, could make a perceptible hole in these mighty stores.'

Another wide-eyed British traveller, John Moore, visiting Odessa in the summer of 1824, watched as Russian families stuffed their carriages to the brim with whatever took their fancy from Odessa's port. In his book, *A Journey from London to Odessa*, he describes the scene as a 'grand mart' with Greeks trading imported 'grapes, perfume, shawls and tobacco from the Levant'; Carrarite Jews dealing in 'the best attar of roses and balm of Mecca', while England sold goods from her colonies, Portugal sent Madeira and port, and Spain 'indigo and drugs'. From Odessa's docks went butter, astrakhan pelts, wax, honey and linseed to Constantinople, taking anything between two and ten days in the summer to get there, depending on the winds. Sometimes Odessa's docks would receive 150 vessels from Constantinople in two days. Any suspicious-looking cargo would be picked over by convicts and galley slaves at quarantine. French and Italian was spoken in 'good company' and Russians drank tea, 'substituting milk for brandy', Moore noted.

Today, Odessa's streets are storytelling writ large, even the most touristy among them. Deribasovskaya, named in honour of De Ribas, is a walkway of kompot cafés and chain stores selling cut-price denim. In the summer, families feast on Napoleon cake and sticky meringues. Among the melée, set back slightly, is a golden chair, positioned on a pedestal. It is a salute to *Twelve Chairs*, the satirical novel by the Odessan Soviet authors Ilf and Petrov, published in 1928. Its main character, Ostap Bender, is an absurd man, someone that Yiddish speakers of Odessa would probably call a *luftmentsh* (a loafer) who claims to be descended from Turkish Janissaries. His task in the story is to find a missing dining room set, including twelve chairs. It is a bizarre tale, yet it has had a surprisingly wide appeal, being transformed into a Syrian TV series, a Mel Brooks film and two Soviet movies. Odessans could not allow themselves to leave this cultural feat unmarked and queues of people wait to pose with the chair.

Odessa has long greased the imagination of writers, and today its literary nature endures. Every shopkeeper in Odessa stands ready with an anecdote or wisecrack and there are endless plaques dedicated to writers. Something of this bookish dynamism lives on in the food, in the markets and in the cafés, connecting memories of its citizens, too. On the way out of the Literature Museum, we stop in front of a cabinet containing Aleksandr Kuprin's work, and it is his fondness for Bessarabian wine and eating fried mackerel on Odessa's Arcadia beach that brings back early memories to Karakina: 'This I remember from my own childhood, we'd catch them with pillowcases, but now mackerel is gone. Maybe it hated Soviet power and swam away.'

Odessan Coleslaw
serves 4

If you love hot radishy flavours try to seek out winter's offering of black radishes. Sometimes spherical, sometimes elongated like daikon, they are soot-black but with a white creamy centre and are bolder than regular radishes. Sobakevich, in Gogol's *Dead Souls*, likes his black radishes doused in honey, and this salad reproduces that sweet bitter flavour mix. Across the Black Sea, in Turkey, radishes are called 'turp' and black ones ('kara turp') are often simply grated and soused in vinegar, olive oil and salt.

For the quick pickled black radishes

200g/7oz black radishes, lightly scrubbed clean

3 tablespoons cider vinegar

2 tablespoons water

1 tablespoon honey

pinch of salt

For the carrots

1 teaspoon caraway seeds

2 tablespoons sunflower oil

1 tablespoon honey

1 garlic clove, crushed

1 teaspoon water

½ teaspoon sea salt

good grind of black pepper

250g/8¾oz carrots, peeled and cut into thick coins

Start with the radishes, cutting them into thick matchsticks, keeping the charcoal-coloured skin on (a mandoline with a julienne blade makes quick work of this). Mix the vinegar, water, honey and salt in a small pan. Stir gently over a low heat until the honey dissolves. Remove from the heat and stir the sliced radishes through. Transfer to a bowl and leave to one side while you prepare the carrots.

Begin by heating a dry frying pan and toasting the caraway seeds for 1–2 minutes until fragrant, then lightly bash them using a pestle and mortar, without crushing them entirely, releasing the scent more. Tip into a large bowl and whisk in the oil, honey (if you measure the oil first, then use the same measuring spoon, without washing it, for the honey, the honey will easily slide off, leaving no sticky residue), garlic, water, salt and pepper, then add your prepared carrots, stir to combine and set aside.

Leave both the radishes and the carrots in their separate bowls for a couple of hours at room temperature to let the flavours develop. Keep any juice created by the carrots and toss in. Serve the pickled radish matchsticks, to taste, on top of the carrots.

If you don't want to use all the radishes at once, place in a sterilised jar and keep in the fridge. They will be good for 3 days or so.

Gogol's Marinated Mushrooms
makes 1 jar

Inspired by the mushrooms described in Gogol's *Old World Landowners*, which are 'Turkish-style', pickled with thyme, these work well on their own, served as an appetiser, or sliced and stirred into stews and salads.

For the marinade

1 teaspoon fennel seeds

1 teaspoon yellow mustard seeds

100ml/1/3 cup plus 1 tablespoon
cider vinegar

150ml/10 tablespoons water

1 bay leaf

1 tablespoon brown sugar

½ teaspoon dried thyme,
or 1 teaspoon fresh leaves

¼ teaspoon salt

1 garlic clove, thinly sliced

5 whole black peppercorns

For the mushrooms

200g/7oz chestnut mushrooms,
cleaned and quartered, stems left on

1 tablespoon sunflower oil

chopped parsley or dill, to garnish
(optional)

salt

Toast the fennel and mustard seeds in a medium pan until they're fragrant
and popping, then remove from the heat. Add the rest of the marinade
ingredients, bring to a boil, remove from the heat and set aside to cool.

Bring a large pan of salted water to the boil and add the mushrooms.
Boil for about 5 minutes until cooked but still firm. Drain and leave to
cool, then mix through the sunflower oil.

Once everything is cool, combine the mushrooms and marinade in a
large bowl and leave overnight. Then pour everything into a sterilised
jar. To serve, drain the mushrooms and serve sprinkled with herbs. They
will keep in the fridge for up to 2 weeks but the oil will solidify, so bring
to room temperature before serving.

Mark Twain's Debauched Ice Cream

makes about 850ml/3½ cups

We don't know what kind of ice cream it was that Mark Twain gorged
on in Odessa, but it would most likely have been something simple but
decadent. This recipe is for a simple no-churn, rich ice cream jazzed
up with a good dash of Caribbean rum. After all, golden-hued 'round-
bellied bottles of Jamaican rum' were regularly smuggled ashore in

Odessa, if we believe what Isaac Babel says.

½ a 397g/14oz can sweetened condensed milk
500ml/generous 2 cups double (heavy) cream
2 teaspoons vanilla extract
4 tablespoons dark rum

Put the condensed milk, cream and vanilla into a large bowl and stir in the rum. Using an electric hand mixer, move around the bowl in a slow clockwise direction until it thickens; this will take around 2 minutes. Using a spatula, scrape into a freezer container, cover with lid or cling film (plastic wrap) and freeze until firm, around 6 hours. Eat within a couple of days, as homemade ice cream doesn't have the longevity of shop-bought stuff.

DEAD SOULS

Nikolai Gogol

Nikolai Gogol's first book, a self-published poetry pamphlet, was so widely derided that he bought back every copy and had them burnt. His career as a lecturer lasted for exactly one lecture, after which he took to 'muttering through his teeth' and 'wrapping his head in a black handkerchief and sitting in silence'. Happily, he found much greater success as a novelist, short story writer and playwright – and never more so than with *Dead Souls*, the novel from which the below extract is taken. Born in what is now Ukraine in 1809, Gogol is regarded as an extraordinary master of the grotesque, the satirical and the unexpected, with an influence on both Russian and realist writing that continues to this day.

Donald Rayfield is an English academic and Emeritus Professor of Russian and Georgian at Queen Mary University of London. He is an author of books on literature, and on Joseph Stalin and his secret police, as well as a translator of poetry and prose.

"Well, my dear, let's go and have dinner," Sobakevich's wife suggested.

"Welcome!" said Sobakevich.

They went over to a table laid with hors d'ouvres, and host and guest each had, as is proper, a glass of vodka. Then they ate as does the whole boundless land of Russia, whether in towns or in villages, a great assortment of salted dishes and other treats. Next they all proceeded to the dining room: in front of them, like a majestic goose, went the lady of the house. The small table was laid for four. The fourth place was very soon occupied by a woman of whom it is hard to say for certain whether she was a lady or an old maid, a relative, a housekeeper, or someone just living in the house: someone of about thirty who wore a colorful headscarf instead of a bonnet. There are people who exist in this world not as objects in themselves but as background dots or spots on an object. They sit in the same place, they hold their head in the same way, they can almost be taken to be part of the furniture, and you would think that no word had ever passed their lips; yet somewhere in the maidservants' quarters or in the pantry they turn out to be quite ooh!-aah!

"The cabbage soup today, my dear, is very good," said Sobakevich, as he took spoonfuls of soup and washed them down by serving himself an enormous portion of what we call *niania* in Russia, made of a sheep's stomach stuffed with buckwheat porridge, brains, and hooves. "A *niania* like this," he continued, turning to Chichikov, "is something you won't get in town, the devil knows what they'll serve you there."

"But they don't dine badly at the governor's," said Chichikov.

"Do you have any idea of the ingredients they use? You'd be put off your food if I told you."

"I don't know what goes on in their kitchens, I can't be the judge of that, but the pork chops and fish stew were excellent."

"That's what you thought. But I know what they buy at the market. That scum of a cook of theirs will buy only what some Frenchman has taught him to: he'll buy a cat, skin it, and serve it up as hare."

"Ugh, what nasty things you say," said Sobakevich's wife.

"I can't help it, my dear, that's what happens there, it's not my fault that they all do things like that. Anything that is good for nothing, what our Akulka throws into the slop bin, if you'll pardon the word, they put into the soup, I mean it, into the soup, that's where it goes."

"You're always telling us things like that when we're eating," Sobakevich's wife again objected.

"Well, my dear,' said Sobakevich, "I'd never do that myself, but I'm telling you to your face that I'm not going to eat disgusting things. You can dip a frog in icing, but I'm not going to put it in my mouth, and I won't touch oysters, either. I know what an oyster looks like. Take some mutton," he continued, turning to Chichikov. "This is side of mutton with buckwheat. It's not one of those fricassees they make in noblemen's kitchens out of mutton after it's been lying about for four days in the market. All these things have been invented by German and French doctors, I'd hang the lot of them. Their idea of a diet is to starve you to death. Those Germans have rickets by nature, and they imagine that they can cope with a Russian stomach! No, they're utterly wrong, it's all lies and nonsense, it's all…' At this point Sobakevich shook his head in real anger. "They talk about enlightenment, enlightenment and that enlightenment is—pooh! I'd use a different word if it weren't indecent to say it at dinner. I do things differently. If you give me pork, put the whole pig on the table; if you give me mutton, bring along the whole sheep; if it's goose, the whole goose. I'd rather eat two courses and eat my fill of them, to my heart's content." Sobakevich's actions confirmed this: he tipped half a side of mutton onto his plate, ate the lot, gnawed and sucked what was left to the last little bone.

"Yes," thought Chichikov, "he's a real trencherman."

"That's not the way I do it," said Sobakevich, wiping his hands with a napkin. "I don't live like that Pliushkin: he has eight hundred souls and he lives and dines worse than my shepherd."

"Who is this Pliushkin?" asked Chichikov.

"A crook," replied Sobakevich. "A more miserly man would be impossible to imagine. Prisoners in shackles live better than he does: he's starved all his people to death."

"Really!" Chichikov responded with great interest. "Are you really saying that his people are dying in large numbers?"

"Dying like flies."

"Like flies, can that be true? And may I ask how far it is from here to his place?

"Three miles away."

"Three miles!" exclaimed Chichikov and even felt his heart racing a little. "And if I drove out of your gates, would that be to the right or the left?"

"I would advise you, in fact, to maintain your ignorance of the way to the dog's door," said Sobakevich. "There are more excuses for visiting a disorderly house than for visiting him."

"No, I had no special reasons for asking. I'm just interested in finding out about all kinds of places," Chichikov countered this objection.

After the side of mutton there were cheesecakes, each one far bigger than a dinner plate, than a turkey the size of a calf, stuffed with all sorts of fine things—eggs, rice, chopped liver, and heaven knows what else—that ended up as a great lump sitting in one's stomach. And so dinner ended, and when they got up from the table, Chichikov felt that he was all of forty pounds heavier. They went to the drawing room, where there was a saucer of jam, which might have been pear, plum, or some soft fruit, but neither host nor guest touched it. The lady of the house left the room to put jam onto other saucers. Taking advantage of her absence, Chichikov turned to Sobakevich, who was reclining in the armchair, making grunting noises after his copious dinner and emitting incomprehensible sounds from his mouth, which every minute he covered with his hand after making the sign of the cross, and said, "There's a little business matter I was meaning to talk to you about."

"Here's another jam," said the lady of the house, coming back with a saucer. "Radish boiled in honey."

"That we'll have later," said Sobakevich. "Off you go to your room, while Pavel and I take off our coats for a little siesta."

Sobakevich's wife began to express her readiness to send for quilts and pillows, but the master of the house said, "It's all right, we'll rest in the armchairs," and she left.

Sobakevich inclined his head very slightly, all the better to attend to the business matter.

SUMMER KITCHENS

Olia Hercules

Olia Hercules, now a prominent anti-war activist, is a London-based chef and food writer. She was born in Kakhovka, Ukraine in 1984, moved to Cyprus in 1996, and took a Masters in Italian from Warwick in the UK. She is the author of four books, among them the award-winning debut *Mamushka*, and most recently *Home Food*. She lives in east London with her husband, the photographer Joe Woodhouse, and their family. A Ukrainian of Russian descent, the 2022 invasion prompted Hercules to turn her skills to activism and fundraising. Her #CookForUkraine campaign, founded with Russian chef Alissa Timoshkina, has raised more than two million pounds for various charities.

On borsch

A whole book could be written on borsch. It is eaten from the formerly Prussian Kaliningrad all the way through the Caucasus and into Iran to the west, south into Central Asia and right across to Sakhalin and Kamchatka to the east. However, I am not afraid to claim borsch here as Ukrainian. It is the Ukrainian traditional dish – a non-blended soup that involves beetroot and as many as seventy other ingredients, depending on region, season, occasion and taste. Apart from its staggering international range and diversity, borsch is also a constantly evolving dish, one that invites curious and creative cooks to experiment, adapt and adjust their recipe. I have heard stories that begin with 'I'm Czech, but my Crimean Jewish grandmother...'; 'Our borsch, made in the Manitoba Mennonite tradition, by way of western Ukraine, is...'; 'My Iranian dad loved this version of my Russian mother's borsch...' The variations are endless.

Borsch wasn't only cooked at home, either. Come the revolution, it was commonly served in Soviet canteens. I love this description from Teffi, a hugely underrated Russian writer who, along with other intellectuals, was forced to flee St Petersburg, via Kyiv and Odesa, for Paris. In *Memories*, written in 1926, she recalls her first impressions of Kyiv: 'Kiev! The station is crammed with people and the whole place smells of borsch. The new arrivals are in the buffet, partaking of the culture of a free country. They slurp away with deep concentration. With their elbows jutting out to either side as if to ward off any encroachment, they seem like eagles hovering over their prey. But how can anyone behave otherwise? ...Your subconscious sticks out your elbows and sends your eyes on stalks. "What if an unfamiliar, vile spoon reaches over my shoulder," it says to itself, "and takes a scoop for the needs of the proletariat?"'

But the ancient precursor of borsch had very little to do with the soup we know today. As far back as 900 AD, at the dawn of Kyivan Rus, early Slavonic people reportedly made it with sour-tasting hogweed. Later on, goosefoot (from the amaranth family), then beet leaves and eventually the root itself began to take centre stage. The origins of the name can be traced back to *buriak*, meaning 'beetroot' in Ukrainian, and etymologically linked to the ancient Slavic *bor* for 'red'. However, there are questions surrounding the issue of colour. In the past, on the territory of present-day Ukraine, borsch would not actually have been red until tomatoes came into play in the mid-1850s. Before that, beetroot borsch would have been seen as 'black', and spring versions that made use of young nettles, sorrel and beet leaves were named 'white', 'yellow' or 'green', depending on the region.

The colour conundrum goes beyond these historical discrepancies. My maternal grandmother, Lyusia, originally from Besarabia, was resolute about the 'correct' colour of borsch. It had to be a deep and dusty rose colour, imparted by the pink flesh of the giant local tomatoes. The beetroot also had to be of a specific variety, something labelled as *borschoviy buriak* at the bazaar. These 'borsch beets' were candy pink and white, similar to the chioggia varieties we sometimes see in shops and markets nowadays. For Lyusia, it came down to aesthetics:

she could not stand the thought of potatoes and other vegetables being stained the same red or, even worse, a purple colour – there had to be a varied colour palette. Of course there was a reason beyond 'eating the rainbow' for her unswerving opinions on borsch. Borsch was best *her way* because it was intrinsic to the environment she lived in: the sandy soil produced paler beets and the local tomatoes grew into juicy, deep pink, gnarled monsters.

Lyusia wouldn't have liked to hear it, but the earliest versions of borsch would have been deep purple, as fermented beetroot *kvas* was – and still is in some places – used to add colour. More importantly, *kvas* serves as a souring agent, and this brings us from colour to flavour. Borsch has developed into a dish with multi-layered, complex flavours: sweet and deeply savoury, often a little hot – but sourness is what defines an excellent borsch today. In the south of Ukraine, this would usually be derived from fresh tomatoes in summer, and in winter from a fermented tomato pulp called *mors*. Closer to the Polish border, fresh or fermented apples would be used to lend acidity, and in central Ukraine, raw sour cherries, unripe apricots, mirabelle plums and green strawberries might have been added in the past. In Romania, Moldova and the neighbouring areas of south-west Ukraine, cornmeal and wheat bran would be mixed with water and sour cherry branches and left to go fizzy, earthy and intensely sour. Of course, borsch-making is not always steeped in tradition, and vinegar and lemon juice as souring agents also figure in modern recipes – even ketchup, a new discovery for those who migrated to the USA, has been adapted with glee.

The stock, more often than not, would once have been vegetarian in farming households, with most of the savoury, 'umami' flavour coming from dried mushrooms, especially in the north and north-west of the country.

When meat was used, pork, beef, rooster and duck were popular choices. Lyusia favoured pork ribs, but my mother liked beef brisket or oxtail – the latter came disconcertingly long, thin and whole, and would fall apart in the tall stockpot after hours of cooking. In the city of Dnipro, I also tried a borsch made using slow-cooked pork preserved for winter (*tushonka*). Using preserved meat in this way made hasty preparation possible when unexpected guests arrived. My mother sometimes used offal, usually chicken hearts and gizzards, to make a quick stock for borsch. In Sumy, north of Poltava, liver is added to the soup.

And, of course, there might be bones – if you are lucky, marrow bones, as in this description from Mikhail Bulgakov's *The Master and Margarita*: 'Nikanor Ivanovich poured himself a tumbler of vodka, drank it, poured another, drank that, scooped three pieces of pickled herring with his fork... and then the doorbell rang. Pelagea Antonovna was just bringing in a steaming soup tureen, one glance at which was enough to reveal that inside the thick, volcanic borsch was hidden the most delicious thing in the world – a marrow bone... His wife ran into the hallway, and Nikanor Ivanovich dragged the bone out of its fiery lake towards him with a ladle. It was quivering and split down the middle.'

By way of contrast, the Russian royal courts of the early nineteenth century served a heightened version: 'Tsar's borsch' might be made from three stocks – veal, morel, goose and prune – with sour cherries used for acidity before tomatoes became de rigueur.

If no other meat was available, there would always be a bit of 'old' salted pork fat in the cellar. Too pungent to be eaten on dark rye bread with shots of vodka, it would be pounded with raw garlic and stirred through the borsch at the very end of cooking. I like to think of it as a Ukrainian fish sauce of sorts. Saying that, in the Kherson region, where I come from, little goby fish used to be butterflied, salted and dried in the sun, then pounded into a rough paste and used in winter to add depth of flavour and extra nutrition to borsch. My grandmother Lyusia would also fry these same fish, which tasted like crayfish, and add them to bowls of borsch just before serving.

Along the Danube River, in Vylkove, Russian Old Believers (who moved there in the early eighteenth century to escape persecution) still cook borsch in the church for the whole of the community. In the past, sturgeon heads and cartilage were included, but today carp more often takes its place. Such borsch is called *nastorchak* – 'the one that sticks out' – presumably referring to the fish heads! And elvers once found their way into borsch in Ukrainian Polisia, a long stretch of woods and marshes in the north of the country, before the eel population became severely depleted.

As for vegetables, *zasmazhka*, a base of slowly fried onion and carrot similar to Italian soffritto, is responsible for bringing sweetness to Ukrainian-style borsch in most regions. Some may also add a little sugar, but my purist family have always relied on gentle frying to coax the natural sugars out of finely diced onion and thinly sliced carrot. Mum never used any extra oil, she would just skim some fat from the surface of whatever meat stock was on the go and slick it into a frying pan. Parsnips would be used in the Vinnytsia region, and earthy celeriac root and turnips might make an appearance in the north. In summer, red peppers are very popular all over Ukraine – in fact, to me, a summer borsch is incomplete without them.

Traditionally, in my home town, smaller varieties of tomatoes would be cut in half, covered with muslin and left to dry, alongside the goby fish, in the blistering sun. These sun-dried tomatoes would then be pounded and added to borsch when fresh ones were out of season. In the Dnipro area, on the border with eastern Ukraine, they traditionally added aubergines to their borsch, which both thickened it and added an extra umami note.

Or the sweetness can come from fruit. In the region of Poltava, prunes and whole pears, slow-dried in wood-fired ovens, are used in poultry and pork borsches. Dried fruit would have originally been added to provide extra nutrients in winter, and this also lent a unique smoky-sweet flavour and a deep 'black' colour to local borsches.

Next let us consider the consistency of borsch. My grandmother Lyusia was a staunch proponent of an intensely thick borsch. She firmly believed that you should be able to stand a spoon upright in the pan, wedged among all the vegetables and red kidney beans. For years I followed her dogma and childishly turned up my nose at borsches that were anything but a semi-stew. Until, that is, a few years ago, when I tried and fell in love with a Christmas borsch influenced by neighbouring Poland – a clear, delicate, crimson consommé with small dumplings called *vushka* ('little ears'), stuffed with wild mushrooms and sauerkraut.

The seasons are responsible for a lot of borsch variations. In spring, heavy tubers might be swapped for young beet tops, sorrel, wild garlic, nettles, soft herbs, spring onions and, more rarely, garden peas, resulting in a much gentler and thinner beast called green borsch, often enriched with a garnish of chopped hard-boiled eggs. Ice-cold, bright-red beetroot broth emerges in the warmer months, perhaps with chopped radishes and cucumbers for crunch, and kefir or buttermilk to add the desired sour note.

Which brings me to the final touches, for a dash of aromatic freshness and even a little heat. Dill and parsley are the most ubiquitous finishing herbs – either fresh or packed with salt into jars to be kept for winter – but in parts of western Ukraine, near the Polish border, there may be speckles of wild thyme and marjoram. A lot of Ukrainians claim not to enjoy spicy food, but chillies will often be added to the stockpot. And in the summer, whole spring onions and raw garlic might be served alongside a bowl of borsch, to be bitten into between spoonfuls.

Soured cream is generally added, either whisked into the whole pot or served on the table, but I tend to leave it out – the creamy sourness is lovely, but I feel it dilutes the flavour. A traditional borsch accompaniment all over Ukraine is *pampushky*: these sweet and savoury fluffy buns, baked side by side or steamed, are covered with a herb and garlic oil called *salamakha* while still hot. But I can never resist a slice or two of traditional crusty, flat, dark rye bread covered in coriander and caraway seeds.

Perhaps the reason borsch has cemented itself as a national treasure in Ukraine is precisely because it is so multi-faceted and readily adaptable. This has enabled it to evolve over the centuries and find avid proponents in every corner of the country and across the globe without losing its essence and its roots. For every Ukrainian, borsch triggers deep memories and feelings of kinship. A delectable meal in itself, a bowl of borsch represents family and sustenance, and connects us to home, wherever we find ourselves.

BE MY GUEST

Priya Basil

London-born, Kenya-raised, Germany-based **Priya Basil** is a writer and political activist. She has published two novels, a novella, two works of narrative non-fiction and numerous essays; her writing has been nominated for the Commonwealth Writers' Prize, the Dylan Thomas Prize and the International IMPAC Dublin Literary Award. Basil's acclaimed *Be My Guest: Reflections on Food*, *Community and the Meaning of Generosity* is a brief but rich conversation about cooking, politics, religion and family. In it, Basil interrogates what it means to be generous and hospitable, and the nature of being a guest, on both a domestic and a global scale. It sits here, at the end of our collection, inviting us to consider the ways in which food and recipes connect us, advocating for the importance, and the great joy, of sitting together around a table.

A recipe is a story that can't be plagiarised. Compare cookbooks by cuisine and you'll find recipes that are almost identical, distinguished by minor variations of ingredient quantity or slight deviations in procedure. Debts are gladly acknowledged, sometimes in the name – 'Julia's Apple Tart' – or in a sub-line – 'Adapted from Yotam Ottolenghi'. Recipes represent one of the easiest, most generous forms of exchange between people and cultures, especially nowadays, with online food blogs abounding and all kinds of once-exotic ingredients available at your local supermarket. Recipes are the original open source, offering building blocks that may be adjusted across time, place and seasons to create infinite dishes. You only need to successfully make a recipe once to feel it is your own. Make it three more times and suddenly it's tradition.

No wonder different societies claim the same food as their definitive, national dish. Hummus in the Middle East may well be the most contested case in point. Fed up of the endless, inconclusive debates about the true origins of this popular chickpea dip, a group of Lebanese hummus-aficionados decided to settle the matter once and for all by setting the record for making the largest tub of hummus ever in the hope that the feat would irrevocably associate hummus with Lebanon above all. The idea of consolidating their ur-hummus credentials by producing such an excess is fitting in the context of the famously profuse Arab hospitality, summed up in the half-joking warning to guests: you'll need to fast for two days before and two days after eating in an Arab household. A year after the Lebanese set their hummus record, the title was taken by a group in Israel who filled a satellite dish with four tonnes of the dip. Months later the Lebanese managed to top that and reclaim the Guinness World Record title. The dispute continues, a mild incarnation of the greater, more intractable regional conflict. I should probably refrain from dipping my finger into such loaded contests about the humble chickpea, but I adore hummus, and my favourite version is one made by a Palestinian friend – without a trace of garlic. And, of course, she is certain hummus was invented in her village.

*

IN THE EXTENDED FAMILY household in Nairobi where Mumji lived with Papaji during the first years of marriage, there was culinary competition of a very different sort. Food was complimented as people never could be. Papaji's family were a reticent bunch. Their approval, if it came at all, took the form of a cheeky pinch or punch. Fortunately, appreciation of edibles did not need to be expressed in words, it could be conveyed in sighs of satisfaction and second helpings and – from the ladies – sidelong requests for recipes. The latter were never obliged: Mumji evolved a repertoire of tactics for rebuffing them. 'Forget the recipe! I'll just make it for you again,' she promised her preferred people, while those she liked less, but dared not risk alienating were told, 'There is no recipe, you just have to watch me make it.' Needless to say, the occasion would never arise. Even in the communal family kitchen she contrived to guard her methods from her in-laws. If she was ever cornered into explaining how to make a dish, she deliberately left out key ingredients or crucial steps. Even – especially – with her own daughter, my mother. Recently Mum asked Mumji to show her how to make gulab jamuns – small, deep-fried balls of milk solids soaked in sugar syrup. 'You can buy the ready mix at the Indian shop,' Mumji said. 'Have you ever done that?' Mum wondered. 'Of course not!' Mumji replied, and changed the subject.

There's someone else in our family who can't share recipes – Mumji's youngest son, an exceptional cook in his own right. The difference is, he'll do his best to tell you, but he's so inventive he can barely keep up with himself. He's one of those people who can rustle up a magical meal from the most mundane ingredients, all without planning ahead or consulting a cookbook. When he founded Foodloom, a catering company he ran with my mother in the early 2000s, they carefully noted details for every signature dish they developed together and still no recipe was ever definitive. However perfect it seemed to us, my uncle had another idea for how it might be improved. I spent periods working for the company while writing my first novel. Whatever job I was assigned, I felt my ultimate duty was simply to eat that exquisite food. I was the kitchen assistant who licks the smidgen of sauce left in the pan, the waitress who gobbles the last samosa on the tray.

Mumji, amazingly, has never even owned a cookbook, which might also account for her caginess about recipes. Alongside her reluctance to share details of her dishes, she is averse to any assistance with making them. Even now, in her late eighties, she doesn't want help in the kitchen. This is not simply down to control-freak tendencies and a fierce habit of independence. It's because she needs to commandeer any praise that the food will elicit. Every compliment and thank you has to be hers. All of it. Every last word, every sigh, every burp. All hers. Only hers. And there's never, ever enough.

'She's an amazing cook,' friends and family say about Mumji, before grudgingly adding, 'but she never shares a recipe.' Perhaps for this reason, Mumji has no really close friends. It's probably also why she finds it hard to ask for recipes. Instead, she eats with sharp attentiveness, turning food over with her fingers, scanning, sniffing and sucking in search of spice traces. Sometimes, she delves deeper with seemingly casual questions: 'Some people put ajwain in everything because it's good for digestion – what do you think?' Afterwards, she'll remark to us how disappointing the dishes were: 'Jassi has no idea about what flavours go together! Who puts sweetcorn with fish?' Or, 'John really fancies himself a chef, but he doesn't have a clue! Did you see the number of cloves in that chicken?' Soon, if not the very next day, the family might be treated to a variation on a dish recently tasted somewhere . . . at Jassi's or John's?

You can feast on Mumji's food, but rarely do you get to do so with her. The first time my husband dined at her table – an invitation that finally came more than a year after we'd met – he followed the example set by the rest of us and filled his plate from the spread laid out for his welcome. But when we started tucking in, he waited. 'What about Mumji?' He pointed to the empty chair. 'She's not coming yet,' I told him. 'Just start,' the others said. Still he hesitated, disabled by a decorum that dictated you don't begin eating until everyone is seated and served. A few minutes later, Mumji entered the dining room bearing a fresh batch of chapatis. Apron sprayed with flour, cheeks red from heat, she went around offering the rotis, but stopped short at the sight of my husband's untouched food. 'Eat!' she ordered. And when he tried to explain she cut him off: 'I'm working hard so you getting everything hot hot hot, and you letting everything go all cold. Eat!' He obeyed and, ever after, reluctantly accepted her peculiar protocol.

Part of Mumji's purpose in serving is to survey how much people are ingesting. She keeps a mental tab on the amount of helpings taken, the bowls of dhal re-filled, the number of rotis eaten. She remembers how much you had last time and is upset if you don't outdo yourself at each subsequent meal. When my brother and cousins were teenagers they could easily consume many rotis apiece. Mumji would gloat and report, as if some world record had been broken: 'He dupped eleven!' There is a special word for it because, of course, nobody just eats her food, they dupp as if it were their last meal on earth.

Dupp, a slangy Punjabi sound, which I like to believe Mumji invented. To dupp is to eat with abandon and to excess. It's a wonderful, reckless activity that often comes with the high price tag of remorse and indigestion. This does not deter dedicated duppers. Nowadays each boy, as Mumji still calls them though all are grown men, might manage six rotis – a healthy appetite by any standards, but Mumji, still nostalgic for the heyday of dupping, continues to roll out dozens of flatbreads. They puff up on her small cast-iron thava to sighs of disappointment and mutterings about how these days everyone is on a diet. She cooks for the moments when someone's appetite will breach the quotidian limits of consumption and she can rejoice.

In contrast – possibly even in reaction – to this, my uncle's philosophy at Foodloom was leave them wanting more. This didn't mean guests were underfed, simply served enough – an aberration in a family for whom eating meant being stuffed, almost suffocating from surfeit.

Descending from such a tribe, it's no surprise that for a long time food for me equalled going overboard: over-buying, over-catering, over-eating. Change came slowly, through a mix of choice and chance. Truth be told, mostly I've been coerced into having less by circumstance – periods of lower income, spells of illness. But that covetous core, *eyes bigger than stomach*, the part of me where greed always trumps need, remains alive and well, and constantly craving.

*

ACKNOWLEDGEMENTS

The editors would like to thank the team at Head of Zeus for commissioning and shaping this project; all the contributors; and in particular those contributors and estates who waived their fee, bent the rules, or otherwise went above and beyond to be part of this book. Thank you for hearing us, for understanding what we have been trying to do, and for making it work.

EXTENDED COPYRIGHT

Publishers, an imprint of Random House, a division of Penguin Random House LLC. All rights reserved;

Tatyana Tolstaya: 'Aspic' published in *Aetherial Worlds*, Daunt Books, 2018, translated by Anya Migdal. Reprinted by permission of Daunt Books Publishing;

Jack Underwood: The poem 'I promise when I lift your egg' from *Happiness*, Faber & Faber Ltd, 2015, copyright © Jack Underwood, 2015. Reprinted by permission of the publisher;

Bryan Washington: from *Memorial*, Atlantic, 2020, copyright © Bryan Washington, 2020. First published in Great Britain by Atlantic Books, an imprint of Atlantic Books Ltd;

Sarah Waters: from *Tipping the Velvet*, Virago, 1998, copyright © Sarah Waters, 1998. Reprinted by permission of the publisher through PLSClear;

Kate Young: from *The Little Library Christmas*, Head of Zeus, part of Bloomsbury Publishing Plc, 2020, copyright © Kate Young, 2020. Reprinted by permission of the publisher;

Michelle Zauner: 'Real Life: Love, Loss and Kimchi' by Michelle Zauner, *Glamour*, 13/07/2016, copyright © Condé Nast.

In some instances we have been unable to trace the owners of copyright material, and we would appreciate any information that would enable us to do so.